THE RULERS
AND THE RULED

political power and impotence
in American communities

THE RULERS
AND THE RULED

political power and impotence
in American communities

ROBERT E. AGGER · *University of Oregon*

DANIEL GOLDRICH · *University of Oregon*

BERT E. SWANSON · *Sarah Lawrence College*

John Wiley & Sons, Inc., New York · London · Sydney

FOREWORD

This book is striking evidence of the fact that political scientists are reawakening to the advantage of studying government at the subnational and particularly the local level. The scientific advantages are obvious enough. Nation states are somewhat limited in number, and are too often constrained by the challenge of participating in a political arena that is relatively dominated by the expectation of violence. The enormous number of local units provides a range of choice that the modern political scientist is learning how to exploit.

That policy advantages can be anticipated is equally apparent. Few questions are more pressing than the readjustment of units of government among themselves, with appropriate regard to the realities of population change, and of different patterns of industrialization and modernization.

By celebrating the renewal of vigor in a vast area of political science I do not want to fall into the trap of exaggerating the separateness of international, national, and subnational phenomena. In the past the development of political science has been held back by an exaggerated sense of the uniqueness of the political process in each territorial arena.

It is, in fact, the dissolution of frames of reference that allowed a sense of separateness to exist that is revivifying research into the political process. What has been happening in American political science is that what were formerly the least well-developed fields have suddenly excelled in formulating and applying theoretical models of the political process. I refer, for example, to world politics. It is redundant to do more than mention the names of Richard Snyder and his colleagues, of Karl Deutsch, or of Morton Kaplan (to go no farther). Although the new models are adapted to the distinctive features of world politics, they are deliberately set within larger frames of theory that refer to the political process as a whole at every level. In the accelerating tempo of political science everyone has been affected, for instance, by David Easton's version of *The Political System,* and other works with a universalizing eye.

If we are to judge by the present book, taken in conjunction with other recent publications, the study of local politics is undergoing the accelerated growth that gives zest and consequence to the study of world politics. Here, too, is the marriage of comprehensive models of the political process with partial models adapted to the distinctive requirements of data gathering and processing in particular arenas.

It is, perhaps, worth emphasizing that this is a genuine marriage and no passing liaison. The categories employed in the present work have acknowledged parents; and with the impetuosity and originality of a new generation, insist upon living their own lives. There is no routine copying or ornamental citation. Rather, there is the healthy self-confidence that comes from sifting the common inheritance for insight and method, and from facing the challenge of describing the actual political process in four communities. Hence there is continuity, the rich continuity that comes when stimulating definitions, hypotheses, and provisional findings of the recent or remote past are reconsidered in the light of experience in field research.

Many of the conceptions laid out here are likely to have a long and respected career among all specialists on government. As the authors recognize time and again, one of the principal difficulties in writing about government is the gap that separates the requirements of ready communication, and the observer's vision of what is communicated about. In order to obtain an audience, it is necessary to employ terms like "democracy" or "autocracy" that are part of the conventional myth of politics. The precut perspectives of elite, midelite, or rank-and-file members of any community coincide only loosely, if at all, with the perspectives of a scientific observer. If he is to obtain even a minimum hearing, an observer must reconcile himself at the start to implying a rough equivalence between a conventional usage and the distinctions that he makes for purposes of inquiry. The scientist's terms are functional; they have references for which he alone must take responsibility. By constructing a loose symbol of equivalence between what conventional audiences expect to hear, and what inquiry has equipped him to say, a political scientist is able to confront conventionally accepted images with functional images that have been tested by research. The result may be to modify conventional perspectives, and ultimately to affect the flow of decision. Often this can be done by providing a renovated symbol, like "guided democracy," that calls attention to selected features of politics and facilitates a series of perspective, communicative, and collaborative changes.

As members of a recognized profession, political scientists do not stand alone, and must take account of conventions that have received varying acceptance among fellow writers and teachers. Scholars pay more heed to professional than to popular usage, since competent colleagues are also engaged in selecting and applying functional categories. In a public order that includes a great deal of freedom of inquiry, no scholar can be coerced to adopt Y's functional distinction as his own. From X's point of view Y's categories are conventions to be studied, explained, and critically evaluated. The same point covers Y's assessment of X. As in every specialized branch of skill and enlightenment activity, it is possible to identify the patterns of acceptance that prevail at a given cross-section in time.

Professors Agger, Goldrich, and Swanson have accomplished a program of research that will contribute to the acceleration of political science as a whole. The four communities can be basing points for further observation designed to exhibit the shifting patterns that condition our capability for facing the future.

HAROLD D. LASSWELL

PREFACE

This is a book about democracy. It is also, and necessarily so, about oligarchy. It is fundamentally an exploration and adventure in political theory in which empirical studies of community politics provide materials for keeping the theory in touch with reality. The four communities selected for our inquiry illuminate, to greater or lesser degrees, national processes and problems of economic growth and instability, of urbanization and rising welfare expectations, of intergroup harmony and discord, as well as the processes and problems of organizing and operating democratic polities. The American community reflects national processes and problems in microcosm; and national processes and problems *are* in many ways the processes and problems of the nation's communities. It is to be hoped that this inquiry into the politics of four communities located in two regions of the United States—the South and the West—will be illuminating and suggestive to the student of national as well as of local politics.

One of our most difficult problems as students of politics was to avoid a personal and professional preoccupation with the fascinating particulars of community politics at the expense of relevant generalizations. It was almost impossible to avoid being entranced by events that actually occurred in the politics of one or more of our four communities. The rise or stirrings of an extreme conservatism—what we call the Radical Right—was witnessed in three of the four cities. The development of what may be one of the dominant political ideologies in the United States—Community Conservation—was seen as a significant factor in the rhythm of political conflict and accord in two of these cities. Programs of urban redevelopment were proposed or initiated in three cities, with strikingly different political outcomes. In the Southern cities, two very different patterns of Negro militancy and revolt were observed. The initiation and pace of school desegregation became political issues of different characters in those two cities. Bitterly resisted annexations of fringe areas had comparable but unexpected consequences of great significance for the politics of two communities; in another, a politically significant battle has raged for years over the principle of private versus municipal ownership in the local economy. Observations of these and other intrinsically interesting matters provided us with the raw material for this book, but any one of them could have served as the subject of a volume. It is to be hoped that those interested in the substance of modern American politics as well as academic theorists will find the following treatment sufficiently concrete and sufficiently abstract for their respective needs.

This book suggests and illustrates an approach to the analysis of political systems through the study of four communities. We have attempted both to build empirically grounded theory and to apply that theory to political events at the community level. The book has been written not only for social scientists but also for currently and potentially active participants in politics—members of the League of Women Voters, precinct workers, PTA members, public-school teachers, city planners—all those who feel a need to participate politically and to be politically aware.

In one sense, the differences among the four research communities are not great, since they are all part of the same country and are subject to the influences of the prevailing system at the national level. But by studying the differences that do exist, we hope to be able to increase our understanding of the way the American and other political systems actually work.

During the late 1940's and early 1950's a variety of forces touching one or another author personally were at work which led to the research for this book. The work of the "Chicago school" of political scientists, for instance, was one of these forces; Frederick L. Schuman's concern for the improvement of the political world through understanding gained from research was a specific example of this. The activity of David B. Truman in the area of public opinion during the early postwar years also had its impact, as did David Riesman's explorations into socio-political psychological problems. The advice and ideas of Vincent Ostrom on how political research should be conducted and his assistance in exploring how theories of decision-making and communications might be applied to community politics were invaluable.

There were probably three major sources that specifically influenced the authors in theory-building and analysis. One was the work of Floyd Hunter, whose *Community Power Structure* was published during the early 1950's. His analysis of Regional City paralleled the work we were doing at that time in Farmdale, although we were to become more consciously concerned with both methodology and comparative design than was Hunter. Hunter's dedication to the advancement of knowledge, his integrity, and his awareness of the necessity for research into the patterns of community politics to improve American democracy challenged many social scientists, including the authors, to continued research investigation.

Shortly after Hunter's book appeared, Robert A. Dahl and Charles E. Lindblom's *Politics, Economics, and Welfare* was published. Its theoretical approach to the conception of the American polity was quite different from Hunter's, in some regards, but it was not specifically about community politics. Dahl later elaborated this approach in *A Preface to Democratic Theory*. His work—especially *Who Governs?*, a study of New Haven politics—together with that of Hunter, with which it conflicts at various key points, has provided a rare but essential element in the development of a disciplined body of knowledge: problems that demand solution by a combination of conceptual analysis, theoretical innovation, and empirical study. Often the problems confronting the political analyst are simply conflicting definitions, trivial arguments about the empirical world, or differences in values. Dahl's work is an unusual example of an intellectually powerful statement of position; it combines a conceptual framework, relevant empirical findings, and an explicit set of values. The critical citation of so much of his work in the pages that follow attests to the provocativeness of his formulations.

Initially, Lasswell and Kaplan's *Power and Society* was considered too conceptually rich and empirically complicated for the limited field research planned. But when we returned to *Power and Society* while working on a revised draft of the present book, we discovered that, although there are important theoretical differences, our work had been brought into close relation with that of Lasswell and Kaplan.

A continual interplay between our empirical findings and theoretical constructs over the past decade resulted, we think, in an integration of various conceptual frameworks which until now have been treated separately, if at all, in studies of community politics. These ranged from relatively abstract, general works on scientific method (of particular importance was Churchman's *Theory of Experimental Inference*), organizational theory and analysis, systems theory, and the so-called decision-making approach, to relatively recent works on concepts such as power and influence. The most serious cost of this endeavor was the increasing distance between our theoretical requirements and the available empirical data. Rather than constrain the analysis to the available data, an effort was made to organize and present what information was collected according to the dictates of the developed theoretical frame.

However, the present book is not mathematical and is subject, therefore, to the disadvantages of what Herbert Simon has called "verbal reasoning." In another connection, Dr. Simon has expressed our feeling about the rigor with which we feel material should be presented to the student early in his study of political systems:

When we have written down, as best we can, the equations of a dynamic system, our troubles have only begun. For now the poverty of mathematics becomes apparent. Of all the possible dynamic systems we might feel impelled to write down to represent particular sets of mechanisms, only a very small proportion have known mathematical solutions. Nonmathematicians can derive no comfort from this fact, however. For if it is impossible to determine mathematically the path of a dynamic system whose differential equations have been written down explicitly, we wonder how verbal reasoning, starting with a vague and indefinite word description of the mechanisms of the system, can reach any answers to this same question. The answer is, of course, that it cannot—except by a legerdemain that consists in introducing a host of implicit and unacknowledged assumptions at each step of the verbal argument. The poverty of mathematics is an honest poverty that does not parade imaginary riches before the world. When we *can* solve a system of differential equations, we receive a precise answer to our questions about the behavior of the system the equations describe. When we cannot solve the system, we can at least be sure which questions we can answer and which we cannot and we are protected from reaching invalid conclusions whose error is concealed by the vagueness of a verbal formulation.*

To the extent C. P. Snow's "two cultures" applies to political inquiry and action, we expect that the effort to be more precise and systematic in political analysis, however inadequately accomplished in this book, will be the way in which the social sciences will serve as a bridge between the physical sciences and humanities. It will do this, we trust, by attracting students with interests in and inclinations toward exploring, dissecting, and controlling physical systems, and

---

* Herbert A. Simon, *Models of Man* (New York: John Wiley & Sons, Inc., 1957).

those with talents directed toward metaphysics and understanding human history, into political analysis. This analysis could lead to an increasingly powerful theory of political systems, with the promise of increasingly enlightened control over the political forces that threaten to increase human degradation and destruction.

Some readers will want to know how we have approached the evaluation and measurement of data. We have not included a discussion of our methods in the body of the book, since the emphasis of the volume is not on methodology, but have presented it instead in an appendix. However, we should like to alert the reader to several methodological considerations to bear in mind as he reads.

First, the time at which random-sample surveys were first made, one of the most important phases of research in each community, was different for the four communities. This mitigated against rigorous comparisons in a number of instances. The first study of Farmdale, Western State, was started in 1952. It was in many respects a pilot study, and our techniques improved as the following studies were made. Almost every improvement in methodology and in the theoretical framework in succeeding studies was accompanied by some loss of comparability. As both the conceptual framework and empirical findings developed, there was always the danger that four distinctive case studies were emerging rather than four comparative ones.

Secondly, the fact that there were only four communities, even though the "cases" were increased by traditional historical methods or by the use of "natural experiments," constitutes a severe limitation on the generalizability of the findings. Conceptual clarification only began when the second case, the community of Oretown, Western State, was put alongside the observations made in Farmdale. So, too, did our understanding begin to increase rapidly as the historical analyses were made in each community. Yet, the paucity of communities encompassed by this study constitutes a methodological constraint of the first order which may be avoided in future comparative studies. A related problem is that the four communities, although they differed in such aspects as size and were located in two regions of the country, were all within the United States. Future community studies that are cross-national in scope are of the highest priority, not only to extend knowledge of political dynamics but also to permit a reevaluation of the sorts of findings and classification schemes presented in this book.

Another kind of shortcoming needs to be noted here. This is the compromise reached in this book between the creation of a jargon and the use of familiar words in unfamiliar ways. The type of regime we call Developed Democracy is a useful case in point. Apart from the conceptually important distinction between types of regimes and types of power structures advanced in this work, one apparent connotation of Developed Democracy is not intended: we do not mean to imply that any one of the regimes classified as a Developed Democracy was fully developed, had reached its limits as a Democracy, or was without the possibility of further improvement. We do not believe that any of the Developed Democracies described herein, or others that may exist in the real world today, approach the ideal. And we do believe that there can be, and that there need to be, major improvements in Developed Democracies. This underlines the fact that we have frequently used a familiar word or a term in this book in a strange or novel way when a newly coined word or term might have obviated possible misunderstandings. What is urgently needed for political research and theory-building is a set of conventionally accepted words, terms, and concepts, as well as sets of conventional operational definitions, to maximize the comparability of inquiry and to avoid unproductive quarrels about the appropriateness of using a particular term or definition. Additional terminology will undoubtedly be both useful and necessary as the science of politics matures, but since no standardized vocabulary exists, the reader should read the theoretical chapters of the book carefully in order to familiarize himself with the authors' definitions.

The question of the identities of the four communities presented an interesting problem. How could we disguise the communities and the political decisions which were made without affecting the validity of the political dynamics we were to portray? Obviously, the communities were given fictitious names. But at the same time we have tried to preserve the economic and social character of each community while modifying its physical and historical description so that it cannot be recognized. Decisions have been camouflaged; they are described in terms that obscure their real identity, but they are, in our judgment and according to our intention, equivalent in substance to the actual decisions made in each community. The categories and subcategories used for the classification of decisions—for example, economic reorganization, civic improvement—are those applicable to the actual decisions. The actions and interactions as well as the perspectives and group identifications of individuals have been described as they were observed in the four research communities, even though precise occupations and other identifying characteristics have been altered. We believe that none of the reports on the variables in which we were interested were affected by these changes that guarantee anonymity to the research communities.

The usual way to read a book is to start at the beginning and to read through to the end. We should like to suggest several procedures for reading this book that will provide the greatest benefit to readers. The professional social scientist may well skim the first three chapters, because he is familiar with many of the concepts discussed; the student will find it profitable to read these theoretical chapters carefully in order to enhance his background. However, the nonacademic reader— the professional or amateur politician, the professional administrator, or the interested citizen and observer—need turn to these chapters only for explanations of unfamiliar words and concepts; he will derive his greatest value from the case studies, which start with Chapter 4. We recommend that the reader approach the book by the course most suited to his background in the social sciences.

A study of this scope has left us indebted to many diverse sources for many kinds of aid. We should like to acknowledge our financial debt to various institutions which, during the last ten years, have contributed funds to help our research: the Kellogg Foundation, the Social Science Research Council, the Center for Advanced Study in the Behavioral Sciences, and the Ford Foundation. Invaluable research time as well as financial assistance was made available by the Institute for Research in Social Science of the University of North Carolina, the Institute for Community Studies and the Office of Scientific and Scholarly Research of the Graduate School of the University of Oregon, the Bureau of Social and Political Research of Michigan State University, and the George M. Schuster Research Fund of Hunter College. These institutions have in no way influenced the results of this study.

While money and time were important to this project, so too was intellectual interchange and assistance from many colleagues in a variety of social science disciplines. Without intentionally neglecting other colleagues to whom we are indebted, we should like to thank David Gold, Frank Pinner, Kurt Back, and David Rogers.

Robert Dubin and James C. Davies read portions of the manuscript at various stages of its development. For their invaluable criticisms we are grateful. Harry Scoble's constructive comments on the entire manuscript went far beyond the call of intellectual duty or friendship. We also owe a debt of gratitude to David Truman for his enthusiastic words at a crucial time.

We are grateful for the time and thought contributed by the many anonymous citizens in the four research communities. The overwhelming cooperation given by people in all walks of life in the course of this study will contribute, we believe, to the increasingly successful future pursuit of political knowledge.

A special word of thanks is due the many graduate students who have contributed to one or another part of the study and to productive interchanges about the subject of the book. They know who they are and what their contributions have meant to us. Our experience with these junior colleagues taught us that their services were not only essential in carrying out the research phases of the project, but that we probably learned as much from them as they did from us in this venture.

To Inez Neigemann, Dorothy Cahill, and Bette Rueping we owe our thanks for their many services as secretaries, record keepers, IBM machine operators, and political researchers.

Molly Agger, Hannah Goldrich, and Jean Swanson all served at least a twofold capacity for the duration of the project. They not only suffered as wives must during such a venture, but they also provided moral support and worked as unpaid or underpaid research assistants.

ROBERT E. AGGER

DANIEL GOLDRICH

BERT E. SWANSON

Eugene, Oregon
March 1964

CONTENTS

1

POLITICS AND THE SCOPE OF GOVERNMENT
IN THE COMMUNITY: conceptual considerations

A political theorist must be concerned with government. Whether he is interested in understanding a whole political system or a specific political process, the basic reference point in his theory-building is a functional-institutional conception. He studies the causes and consequences of the functions of government in people's lives whether he believes that government is best studied in a formalistic, legal orientation, or in a view of man and his world that focuses on the informal and the customary. Politics, in its broadest sense, is that aspect of life in which certain people act to maintain or to shift the patterns of action of government officials. The patterns of politics constitute the political system. The political system is distinct from the social, economic, or religious systems of human groups, at least analytically.[1]

A community is a set of people living in a spatially bounded area that may or may not coincide with a legally bounded jurisdiction of government. Every community has a government. The agencies of that government may be part of the national government, as in unitary, centralized nation-states, or they may constitute municipalities and counties created by state governments, as in federal systems. In either case the community's government can be distinguished from other, nongovernmental agencies and institutions in the community. Modern local governments are open systems; they are affected by what takes place in other systems within the community, by what takes place in other communities, by what takes place in the national and state systems of which they are a part, and by what takes place in foreign countries. However, it is useful to think of them as having functions of their own that affect and are affected by citizens in their own communities.

Local government, as does all government, produces and distributes goods and services. It regulates the production, distribution, and consumption patterns of other institutions in the community. Within limits specified by its parent government, it possesses the ultimate sanction of all minimally effective governments—a monopoly on the right to use physical force to deprive those within its jurisdiction who violate the government's rules and regulations of their life, liberty, or property. Government in four United States cities concerns us here.

This study is primarily concerned with how the people decide to shift or maintain the scope—the ways of functioning—of local government in respect to the economic, social, and welfare systems of communities. It is also meant to provide an understanding of political decisions concerning the organization of government itself: the structure of power and type of regime, and how the rulers relate to each other and to the ruled in making decisions. The relations are of concern both at a moment in time and over a period of time. However, the community's political system includes more than political decisions, its power structure, and its regime. The first three chapters define and explain these and other dimensions of politics that are subsumed under the terms "the polity" or "the political system."

Political history may be viewed as the continuous development of and transformation in the roles and functions of government in man's attempt to control his environment. The roles and functions of government change as changes occur in conditions of life, in the patterns of making a livelihood, living with other people, and sharing in the amenities of civilization. Human society is a set of analytically distinct yet overlapping activities and institutions. Government has authoritative supremacy, a monopoly of legitimate force. Because of this it stands at the pinnacle of economic, social, and other activities and institutions of society. How government operates in relation to these other human activities varies from era to era, from polity to polity, and, over a period of time, within polities. The state of technology, the nongovernmental organization of the processes of production, distribution, and consumption of goods and services, social status, knowledge, and the political doctrines to which people subscribe vary also. Whether and how government overlaps, controls, dominates, or is subordinate to other institutions of society, and also the conditions under which it does so, should not be decided by formal definitions.

This should be investigated by comparative studies of politics such as the present volume.

At both the national and local levels government may be analyzed in terms of its effect upon the economy, social or intergroup relations, and the welfare of its citizens. The history of politics might be viewed as a dynamic movement between opposite poles: an active, interventionist government and a passive, laissez-faire government. For example, the New and Fair Deals expanded the scope of the national government; the Eisenhower administration contracted it; and the direction of the New Frontier is as yet uncertain. To understand these shifts the analyst ordinarily concerns himself with such questions as who controls government, who has most political influence with government officials, and how can the patterns of political power and their changes in the context of national and world economic and military policy conditions be explained.[2] The dynamics of local politics may be investigated similarly.

Of particular interest will be the ebb and flow of political conflict in four communities. Political conflict is sometimes thought to be brought about by aberrant behavior, a symptom that politics is unhealthy. Another view is that political conflict is healthy and inevitable, and produces creative politics. Whichever view one takes, this analysis of the dynamics of political conflict in the four communities will shed light on the nature of politics in the twentieth-century United States.[3]

A cursory study of political history suggests that political conflict is generally most apparent when demands are made for substantial expansion or contraction of the net scope of national or local government. Even when there are no demands for radical shifts in the net scope of government, conflicts may arise over the way government functions within a given domain and to whom it should respond. Although political power for power's sake may be a private motive, these desires are ordinarily presented as being for the improvement of public finance, social justice, or social welfare. Regardless of the way appeals for a redistribution of political power are phrased and of the motives of their makers, they are, in fact, appeals or demands for some sort of shift in the scope of government.

When political issues arise in a polity, the workings of politics become observable. Political conflict, however, may be relatively covert and not apparent to most people. The conflict may be potential rather than actual. Political consensus, agreement that the scope of the local government is appropriate or that a particular trend is desirable, may exist. This consensus may exist for a few interested people while many remain indifferent, or it may extend over a large proportion of the people in the polity. The conditions under which human needs give rise to conflicting political issues are of central interest in our analysis of community politics.

In all four communities conscious and purposeful decision-making regarding the scope of government was observed. Complete political consensus for extended periods of time was absent, but the communities differed in the extent to which there was open political conflict. A fundamental reason for the lack of complete consensus was the diversity of views about utopia in all four communities. Individuals' images of the good community and the good regime, of the proper power structure and the proper role of local government in community affairs, varied. The images of some were determined by immediate needs or problems needing amelioration or solution; others saw the proper scope of government as being a long-range means of achieving the good life in the ideal community. Political ideology was found, somewhat unexpectedly, to be of major importance in the politics of all four communities.

Students of American politics have interpreted the importance of political ideology at the national level in various ways. Some have argued that ideological divisions have come to an end; others have said that these divisions have never been of much consequence in shaping political behavior in the United States. A minority of analysts have seen political ideology as an important factor not only in international politics but also in national and state politics. That political ideology has always had or still does have important effects on American community politics is a proposition that is held by even fewer political analysts.[4]

Political ideology is viewed here as, in brief, a constellation of beliefs and preferences about the nature of the constituent elements in social or community life: Who should rule in the polity? What should the relationship of the government to private institutions be? Where is or should a person be located in the socio-economic-cultural orders of the society and polity? This conception of political ideology, which is discussed more fully later in this chapter, proved useful in understanding the workings of the political systems of the four research communities.

During periods of social, economic, and intellectual change, diverse political interests and divergent ideologies are likely to emerge from what was a more homogeneous set of values. All four communities have experienced currents of change in recent years, particularly since the Second World War. The forces of urbanization and industrialization and the currents and crosscurrents that shaped national politics in the first half of the twentieth century have affected the four communities and the two regions, the West and the South, in which they are located.[5]

The political demands and decisions in the four cities were thus shaped by the larger national and international environment. The general conditions of life throughout the United States at the time of this study resulted in similarities in the potential for political conflict in the four communities. Regional and other special conditions, including the particular historical development of the individual communities, also affected the potential issues. All these conditions that shaped political decision-making can be analyzed in relation to the perspectives and behavior of people in local politics. Thus this analysis is concerned with understanding the conditions—particularly the political conditions—under which potential conflict became actual conflict. It is concerned also with how the variations in the structure and functioning of the four political systems affected the outcomes of political decision-making, whether these outcomes were conflictive or not.

The scope of local government may be considered to affect human values. These values can be grouped under four categories that have psychological as well as social significance. The four categories refer to the institutionalized ways of organizing the production, distribution, and consumption of (1) wealth; (2) civic amenities; (3) social status, respect, affection, or prestige; and (4) governmental rights and obligations of citizenship.

Economic institutions in American communities involve those relationships primarily concerned with the production, distribution, and consumption of goods and services. Social institutions, such as the family, the friendship group, and the voluntary "social" association, more or less specialize in such areas as social status, respect, affection, or prestige. Institutional processes devoted to civic amenities and livability include housekeeping services, so-called public works and services, and preserving public order; planning and guiding development of the uses of land and buildings, including design and aesthetics; recreation, particularly out-of-doors; and health facilities, for example, chlorination and fluoridation of the water supply, and hospitalization. This category of "civic improvement" is a mixture of both public and private goods and services; whereas the areas of economic and social institutions tend to be generally thought of in America as private, even though government itself performs important economic and social functions.[6]

The patterned sets of relationships that constitute the rights and obligations of citizenship are within the institution of government itself. For example, the jurisdiction and boundaries of local government determine who has the right to vote in local elections. Certain groups of citizens, such as Negroes, lower class people of any color, or union officials, may be ineligible, in fact if not in theory, to serve as elected or appointed officials. Citizens serving in government have rights and obligations relative to each other and to citizens at large.

The pattern of these relationships constitutes the organization of the particular institutional area. Local government has direct or indirect effects on other types of institutions at all times. Thus, demands or decisional processes involving shifts in the way government functions in reference to these relationships are classified into four categories: (1) Economic Reorganization, (2) Social Reorganization, (3) Civic Improvement Reorganization, and (4) Governmental Reorganization.

These categories are convenient, heuristic devices used for analytic purposes. Consequently, classifying a political decisional process under these frequently nondiscrete categories is not a simple matter. People have many values; they pursue social, economic, and civic ·livability and citizenship values simultaneously. Thus, the sentiments of those most active in promoting a shift in the functioning of local government are at the focus of attention. Even so, arbitrary classifications are sometimes necessary. For example, a decisional question about annexation of a fringe area may involve other considerations than governmental reorganization. Such a decision might affect levels of services and civic improvements, as well as social and economic relations between urban and rural citizens. A demand for school desegregation may be more a demand for social dignity or respect than for knowledge or income; but it may be both. More will be said about the multiplicity of values when the meaning of political decisions in community life is discussed in Chapter 2.

THE SCOPE OF GOVERNMENT: THE CORE OF POLITICS

It is useful at this point to present in summary form an analogue model of the political process on which the foregoing considerations have been based. This model will be elaborated on throughout the book. A government may be viewed at a moment in time as being more or less involved in people's lives. We may picture two opposite ideal states: one where there is no governmental functioning and one where governmental functioning is ever-present or total. In the one case private institutions meet all citizen needs; in the other a total —totalitarian—government is the sole value-producing, distributing, and consuming institution. The first would best characterize a pre-political society or community; the latter a postpolitical one. Both societies or communities would actually be apolitical. In order to evaluate the analysis that follows, it is essential to understand the rationale for the seeming paradox that these two opposites represent a single condition: the absence of politics.

As we have said, political history may be viewed as a series of large or small movements of government along a continuum of expansion and contraction. Governments may move in one or the other direction or they may alternate, making little net progress in either direction. The extremes of this continuum are situations in which (1) there is no government activity and consequently no governmental intervention in the other institutions of organized life, and (2) government is total. In the second case, government is so pervasive in the organized life of the community that its activities cannot be distinguished from nongovernmental activities. At either extreme, then, it would presumably be impossible, theoretically or empirically, to characterize a functionally distinct government.

There are thus two ways to attain such an apolitical condition. One is to reduce the functions of government; the other is to extend them. The former alternative is preferred by some people who are called reactionaries: they want to return to a previous era or to a state of nature where government is minimal.[7] Most "romantic" philosophical anarchists consider this the preferable path to a society without government. Point A in Figure 1.1 represents this condition as a result of the contraction of the scope of local government.

If life in "nature" is not considered brutish, nasty, and short, if it is considered idyllic instead, the society is pictured as being cohesive and organic, without conflicting social divisions. Philosophical reactionaries may advocate doing away with social antagonisms by returning to the imagined social harmony of earlier epochs.

Other philosophical anarchists prefer the second path: the extension of the scope of government to the point where its functioning cannot be distinguished from "private" sectors of organized life. Points $B-B'$ in Figure 1.1 represent the condition at the end of this path. Marx advocated a political utopia without government, to be achieved through a purposeful, planned extension of government's scope. He believed that the state or government with its monopoly of force would

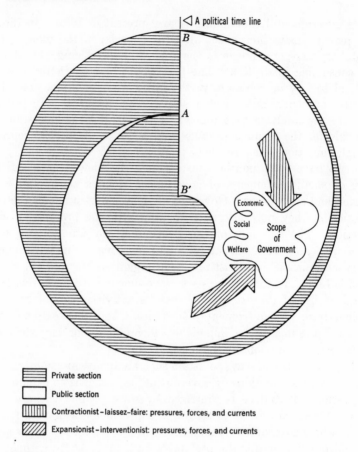

FIGURE 1.1   *Expansion-contraction continuum of the local scope of government.*

"wither away" when the dictatorship of the proletariat was established, rather than at some distant time after the revolution. Some Marxists, particularly Engels, have envisaged the withering away of government as an historical stage that begins after the dictatorship destroys economically based classes which are the reason government exists. Khrushchev blames internal and external capitalist conspiracies for the failure of the Soviet government to begin to wither away. A more paradoxical but intellectually consistent view of Marxist thinking, in some ways more consistent than Engels', would propose that the increasing scope of government is an integral part of the withering-away process, and is in being as soon as, if not before, the revolution. At some undefined point in time, a distinctive or distinguishable government presumably could disappear if it had become inextricably mingled with the day-to-day living patterns of people.

The Marxist philosophical school sees man as historically locked in social conflict. Social antagonisms are expected to increase as history unfolds; it is only after a period of intensive economic, social, and political conflict among classes that the class struggle will end once and for all. The job of preparing for utopian social harmony can then be undertaken by the government of the proletariat. Engels has qualified Marx's view of the beginnings of organized life as being a condition of class struggle: he saw "primaeval communities" to be socially cohesive, cooperative, and harmonious.[8] The suggested model would be closer to Engels' than to Marx's view in that it indicates a return to a hypothetical earlier *agovernmental* condition by the juxtaposition or interpenetration of Points A and $B-B'$ of Figure 1.1.

In order to understand national and international political movements in the nineteenth and twentieth centuries, this belief in the possibility of a withering-away of government by expanding or contracting its net scope is of critical importance. Whether either alternative can be realized is irrelevant for the student of politics. But the existence of these as conceptual possibilities shapes the model of politics for the analyst of community, national, and international politics. Although it would be virtually impossible to reach either extreme, pressures for or actual movements in one direction or the other are possible; these pressures constitute part of the basic forces of politics, local or otherwise, whether or not so intended.

The analogue model of politics may be pictured in the following way. Local government, or any government, is considered to be located in a public space. The boundaries of this public space (curves $A-B$ and $A-B'$ on Figure 1.1) are represented by the extent to which government can actively function in the day-to-day lives of people. The activities of people may be viewed as a community space (the innermost and outermost circles). The private space is represented by the shaded portion of the total community space. In the public space are the currents, forces, or pressures directed toward moving government in the direction of expansion and intervention or that of contraction and laissez-faire, an increase or decrease in the scope of government. Movement in the former direction may result in a greater overlapping of the community space by the public space; movement in the latter direction may result in a relative decrease in the proportion of public to community space. This ratio of public to private space is what we mean by the words "net scope" of government.

The mixed public and private character of activities in which purposeful government regulation is a manifest factor makes any set of curves for such a model of the real world difficult to construct. Further conceptualization and research are needed to make such models more useful and to establish the character of general and particular social-psychological distinctions between governmental and private institutions, as well as the conditions under which such conceptions undergo various kinds of reorganization. It may or may not be that, in social-psychological terms, as government extends its programs into formerly nongovernmental areas and apparently moves toward points *B–B'*, people extend their activities and, hence, community space, so that the ratio of public to private space remains relatively constant.

The action units in this model are people; it is the demands of people that constitute the pressures for a shift in government's scope. It is through the actions of government officials that shifts in local government's scope finally occur. A demand that government act in a particular way may be made by any unit or group of units—any private citizen or government official—in the political system.

Every demand that government act in one way rather than another, or that it function in some way different from the way it has in the past, is a pressure for a shift in government's scope. For example, people may demand a higher level of welfare services. This constitutes a pressure on government to expand. If such demands are made at a time when the level of government services has been declining, it is, nevertheless, a demand for a move back toward the expansionist pole. Suppose a person suggests that his street be paved and the community paves it instead of someone else's. This is not an increase in the net scope of government; the total street paving resources of government are held constant. But for the man whose street is paved, there has seemed to be an increase in government's scope. The scope actually has been balanced by a decrease for those others whose streets were not paved. The petitioner was, in effect, demanding an increased scope of government for himself, but the decisional outcome balanced this demand by reducing someone else's scope of government. Thus, the total or net scope of local government may remain the same, as a result of two, sometimes simultaneous, movements. Such decisional outcomes are regarded as changes in the scope of government wherein there is an *internal* although no *net* shift in scope.

Suppose a question arose as to whether local government ought to build a civic center. Those urging that this be done would be demand-

ing an increased scope of government, whether it was a matter of replacing an existing facility that was in poor condition or in a poor
location, or one of extending government's recreational functions. If
the most appropriate location became a decisional question, the proponents of one or another site would be demanding that government
increase its scope to satisfy *their* needs. In effect, they are saying
that government will be serving them more fully by providing a convenient facility that will enable them to consume a greater amount of
recreational resources than if the facility were located on some other
site. If a proponent of one site asks that a civic center be built or
moved there for aesthetic reasons or because it will take most people,
but not himself, less time to reach the facility, his request is still a
demand for an increased scope of government. Such a person would
be urging government to expand its function to satisfy his aesthetic
or altruistic need, needs as genuine as that for food.

Conflict may be generated by demands for an internal shift of government that would result in the deprivation of other citizens, or by
demands that require a shift in the net scope of government. A demand for school desegregation is a case in point. Opposition to desegregation may be understood as opposition to the increased functioning of government to satisfy a multiplicity of needs of Negroes. Opponents of desegregation might cast the issue in terms of an undesirable
increase in the net scope of government, or as a novel and unwarranted
intervention of government in the social system. But since government has already exercised its authority to decide whose children
should be educated, and how and where, these demands and counter-
demands may be more appropriately viewed as involving a redistribution of government's need-satisfying functions, rather than a change
in the ratio of public to private space. Only when there has been a
change in the ratio of governmental to private satisfaction of human
needs in the community has a net shift in scope occurred. If there
is no such net shift, all other changes in the way government functions
that result in the satisfaction of different needs of different people
constitute internal shifts in the scope of local government.

What of demands to maintain the *status quo* rather than to expand
or reduce the scope of government? Because of *status quo* demands,
political decision-making obviously may result in maintaining rather
than changing the scope of government. Politics was broadly defined
earlier as that aspect of life wherein certain people act to maintain
or to shift what now may be referred to as the scope of government.
If all demands were directed to the maintenance of an extant scope
of government, this would presumably reflect a fundamental con-

sensus. In this unlikely situation, politics would be present but it would be of a very special sort. Even in the absence of political decision-making political demands can be made and political influence successfully exerted to maintain the scope of government. How long such a politics of consensus could endure in a modern, complex community is open to question.

The model of the political process encompasses demands for maintaining a given scope of government even though the demands may be outside a particular decision-making process; this may constitute an effective force for stasis in the body politic. Perhaps no broader definition of politics than that it is the web of political decision-making is required to study the conditions that may result in decisional questions leading to conflict or triggering other decisional processes. However, to understand what conditions produce variations among or within communities in the content of decision-making does require a broader definition. This definition includes action designed to increase or decrease general satisfaction with a current scope of government, even though no shifts in that scope have been or are currently being demanded. It is important that these definitions be clearly understood.

Some analysts of American politics view politics as the resolving of decisional issues or questions; others maintain that it encompasses the conditions that affect the raising of decisional issues and questions. Some analysts have maintained that American politics is characterized by a nearly unitary power structure wherein a relatively few like-minded men rule.[9] Others have countered by attempting to show that in the resolution of decisional controversies, the outcome is a function of compromise by numerous participants.[10] To some, the messages of the mass media and the propaganda of public relations specialists devoted to the glorification of the existing net scope of American government and the American way of life are the central facts of our politics. They presume that the exercise of political influence prevents demands for shifts in the scope of government and the appearance of radical alternatives. To others the influence of the media in particular decisional processes is relatively minor: they believe that the similarity in the various scopes of government that are subject to political decision-making results from the character of modern industrial society and is not due to the manipulation of political consensus by a top power elite.

For example, the "ruling elite model" of American national and community politics offered by such analysts as C. Wright Mills and Floyd Hunter has been criticized by Robert Dahl on the ground that it has not been put to the test of empirical research. Dahl admits that the influence of a ruling elite over ideas, attitudes, and opinions can create "a kind of false consensus" and proposes that this be tested in "a series of concrete cases where key decisions are made." Only in that way, he asserts, can it be determined whether one group initiates and vetoes, while others merely respond to the leaders. However, he does not consider that political influence might be exercised so skillfully by the few that they succeed in averting demands for other scopes of government or in preventing such preferences from being pursued or strengthened to the point of becoming issues in "key decisions."

We would propose studies of influence relations in which it is recognized that the intentions of those attempting to influence others might be to prevent decisional questions from arising or to restrict the domain of decisional choices to a more or less acceptable few. The analyst should recognize that the absence of political decision-making or the existence of a political decision-making process with one particular set of options rather than another might well be the result of political action on the part of a "ruling elite." Since the possibility of such situations may result from a variety of causes, including unintentional political consequences of nonpolitical action, the problem of settling the question empirically is most complex. If we admit the possibility that political demands may be made to maintain a given scope of government and that the demands may not become part of a specific political decision-making process in the usual sense, the relative merits of pyramidal and pluralistic power structures become amenable to empirical tests.[11] Such issues are not likely to be resolved by empirical investigations unless and until a common definition of politics is agreed upon by those in dispute.

In the present study our interest extends to politics in the broad and general sense rather than in the specific, political decision-making one. Exactly what is meant by political decision-making processes is specified in the next chapter. But this is a limited and partial study, because the working definition of politics used in designing these comparative studies has been restricted to a political decision-making context. Actions intended to decrease general satisfaction with a current scope of government were ordinarily embedded in demands for relatively specific shifts in governmental functioning. Such action was accounted for when observations were made of one or another political decision-making process. Action intended to maintain or increase satisfactions with the scope of government, when successful, was not systematically studied because the research focus itself was concentrated upon actions that were part of actual decision-making processes. When the significance of non-decision-making politics was realized, it was too late to extend the research focus appropriately.

In the real world of American community politics, government is far from either apolitical pole. Certain divisions of governmental and private institutional functioning were not at issue in making political decisions that involved questions of government's appropriate functions in a given domain. But in all four research communities there were net and internal shifts in the scope of government as well as conflicts over both. The direction of local government along the expansion-contraction continuum is, in part, the direct or indirect result of men's satisfaction or dissatisfaction with policies made in nongovernmental sectors of society. Systems of decision-making are necessary in the production and distribution of goods and services, status and dignity, and other values. Some men are more powerful decision-makers than others in such systems. Patterns of power relations emerge in private spheres of community life, in the private economic and social institutions. The ultimate sanctions possessed by private—nongovernmental—men of power stop short of force unless public order has broken down. Nevertheless, private men of power may command severe sanctions. For example, an employer can punish or reward by firing or hiring, or by cutting or raising income. Social leaders may use ostracism, rejection, ridicule, or approval to gain or maintain support for their policies. Leaders in different institutional areas may use a variety of sanctions affecting a multiplicity of men's values to enforce policy preferences.

It is when policies backed by such sanctions are considered to be made more appropriately by public government than by private institutions, or vice versa, that shifts in government's net scope may occur. Their direction and character, and whether or not they occur, may hinge on the perspectives of men who have control over governmental decisions. We shall now turn to groups of perspectives on the preferred net scope of government. These perspectives are referred to hereafter as political ideologies.

POLITICAL IDEOLOGIES

Political ideologies are present in national and local politics in the United States. Although they may range from integrated doctrines and eclectic views to inarticulate or even unconscious operating premises, they all affect preferences about the appropriate scope of government. Ideologists range from militant, articulate, doctrinaire proselytizers to passive, inarticulate, apathetic tolerants. Most citizens in the United States probably are closer to the latter pole.

It should be stressed that the components of the ideologies to be described do not always fit together as neatly as the following prototypes suggest; those who subscribe to them are not always conscious, articulate, doctrinaire, or militant in their subscription. Political ideologies are ways of perceiving and reacting to the political system. These perceptions and reactions in turn condition attitudes and behavior toward what the appropriate scope of government ought to be; they may determine, in large degree, a person's political action, or they may have little impact on political behavior, at least under "normal" conditions. They are ways of organizing one's concepts and precepts about politics, and, as is true of any cognitive-perceptual-evaluative structure, they may be shaped by a deeply rooted personality drive or by a surface attitude.

At the outset of this study, we fully expected to find a politics of personal or, at the most, particularistic group interests in the four communities. We did not expect to find an ideological politics, even to the limited extent to which it appeared to exist at the national level. When we perceived the importance of ideology as a factor "ordering" a series of variations in the politics of the four communities—within each community over a period of time and among the four communities at a given time—political ideology became a central analytic concept.[12]

A person may act on the basis of either personal or group interests. This distinction is simply a matter of whether the benefits contemplated are desired for the person himself or for a group of citizens with whom he identifies. The larger category may be a family, a voluntary social or economic association, a racial aggregate, or an occupational category. A group interest, in this sense, may extend to the whole community or nation, to a regional collection of communities or nations, to a worldwide category of people who believe in democracy or in the class struggle, to a particular race, or to mankind as a whole.

Some analysts maintain that those in a particular economic, social, or ethnic category have by definition a group interest. If group interest is not seen in this way, the analytic questions become: to what extent does a potential group interest become an actual group interest, and to what extent do people with a group interest pursue that interest in politics?

In any event, an individual may have either a personal or a group interest, depending upon his psychological identifications and calculations; this interest may be related to and shaped by political ideology or it may have no ideological connection.[13]

By political ideology we mean a system of interrelated ideas about the polity that includes general answers to the following questions:

(1) What sorts of general interests exist in a community, personal or group? If the latter, are the interests community-wide public interests or are they those of less inclusive sectors of the community?

(2) Who ought to make the decisions about the proper scope of government and in whose interests?

(3) What share of available socio-economic and cultural values is a person currently being allocated relative to others in a community?

(4) What role should the government play in allocating values produced in the economy, in the society, and in the governmental institutions themselves?

One may be inclined to view ideology as simply another type of political interest. Ideology, however, is broader and more general than political interest. Unlike mere political interest, it does not refer to the benefits and costs of *particular* policies, although it may refer to those of sets of policies. Furthermore, ideology takes into account the appropriate net scope of government, in general if not in particular. It is useful, therefore, to distinguish between these concepts. We prefer to make the distinction between ideology and interests rather than between ideological and nonideological interests.[14]

Let us suppose that a decisional question has arisen in a community: Should the city government establish municipal parking lots in the downtown business district? Some individuals will have neither personal nor group interests in the matter; others will assess the political question according to their own personal or group interest. One person may decide that such a program would solve his personal parking problems; another may be equally in favor of the plan because he is one of a number of downtown businessmen who will benefit from it. He may then act in favor of that proposal without reference to his political ideology, assuming that he has an ideology or that it is important to him. Suppose, further, that a merchant has an ideology that puts the interests of merchants high on the list of those to be served by the government. If he invoked his ideology in assessing the parking lot proposal, he might find a convergence of his personal or group interest and his ideological doctrine. But if his ideology included the belief that government should not be extended into the economy and he saw municipal parking lots as an undesirable extension of government, his interest and ideology would come into conflict. Many people do not perceive a relationship between their ideology and a particular interest; others may find interests and ideology convergent and reinforcing; for still others the two may be divergent and conflicting.

The decisional preferences of most citizens in the four communities seemed to be more influenced by group and personal interests than by ideology. Some citizens were found to be apolitical—they did not see that local government affected personal or group interests to any great degree in either general or particular decisions. These people tended to be politically nonparticipant. Among those who did participate were people who had neither a nationally nor a community-oriented political ideology but did have personal or group interests; people who had a national ideology which they did not think had local relevance; and people whose political interests were more central and compelling than their ideologies. The proportion of citizens in any of the four communities whose ideologies were of equal or greater importance than their interests was very small. What, then, was the importance of ideology?

First of all, community politics was found to be largely group politics. Relatively enduring groups of people were found to be actively involved in the political decision-making of all four communities. Some of these groups followed or overlapped party or factional lines and some cut across them and were irrelevant to the local parties. They tended to be differentiated along ideological rather than interest lines.

These political groups were of special importance in community politics because they included those who were considered to be the leaders in decision-making by others in the community. The impulse to become a leader and obtain power appeared to be a manifestation of interest in proposed local government programs and of a desire to maintain or impose an ideology on the leaders of the community power structure. The latter desire was most intense in the key members of these political groups.

The key men were important because they had extraordinary political status and influence, at least within their own groups. Very small "inner cliques" were made up of articulate ideologists. These were the active spokesmen for the people who wanted interest-based decisional preferences filtered through the proper ideological sieve. They were the men who in their intimate subgroup operations constituted "a firmly established, authoritative, and continuing organizational center empowered to decide questions of doctrine and discipline." [15] McClosky *et al.* found this to be so, to a greater degree than many analysts suspected, among the leaders of the two major national parties.

In every community some active participants in politics did stand outside the dominant ideologically bounded group or groups; some belonged to more than one of them. Yet much of the variation in the politics of the four communities is understandable only in the light of the variations within the ideological dimension.

Of special concern in this analysis is an examination of the conditions that produce varying degrees of citizen participation and conflict in political decision-making. Most American communities have complex economies and social structures. A potential exists in communities for the politicizing of group interests through existing voluntary associations or through new political organizations. With the organization of political interest groups, a community may experience extreme political group conflict or cooperation. Whether there is conflict or consensus along interest lines, citizen political participation can be either high or low. While these are all logical possibilities, what we actually find is that the informal political organization of ideologically differentiated groups is a necessary although insufficient condition for both extensive citizen participation in politics and intensive conflict in decision-making. Competitive ideological groups give rise to both situations, whereas the competition among groups lacking ideological interests is insufficient to produce "mass" participation of either a cohesive or conflicting character.

Ideologists indoctrinate others with their system of beliefs in order to enlist political participation as a means of achieving their ideological ends. When there is a competition of such political idea systems, each protagonist has to enlist more citizen support than if there were a consensus. Militant ideologists activate interests which become subject to the appeals of the protagonists. Political interests sometimes conflict with the ideological precepts even among the leaders of ideological groups. The extent to which this happens affects the strength of the group in political decision-making. The conditions under which conflict among leaders occurs are also an important subject for political analysis. Ideological groups also differ in the degree to which there is both potential and actual divergence and conflict between ideology and interest in the formation of decisional preferences.

In all four communities ideologists spent some of their time trying to bring together the ideology and the political interests of their members and citizens at large. A lesser degree of doctrinaire orthodoxy within political groups than otherwise might have been the case resulted. Neither this nor the fact that the ideologies had a quality of contingency when used to evaluate decisional options does away with the significance of ideology as an explanatory variable in the analysis that follows.

The five component variables of political ideologies are: (1) conception of the community, (2) preferences as to "who shall rule," (3) the sense of social (socio-economic) class, (4) the sense of cultural class or caste, and (5) attitudes toward the legitimate method of allocating values.

In Figure 1.2, a combination of the first two variables yields 18 possible cells when the conception of the community is treated as a threefold classification, and the answer to "who shall rule?" as a sixfold one. Only seven of these 18 cells were found to have empirical referents in the form of at least one actual political group in the leadership of at least one of the communities. One political group which aspired but failed to attain a leadership position in one community during the postwar period occupies an eighth cell.

The label "conservative" is found in four of these seven cells. Conservative ideologists feel that political leaders should be recruited from among the more affluent citizens. They differ from one another concerning the particular category of affluence from which they feel the political leadership should come—industrialists-financiers, proprietors-professionals, or the propertied generally; they differ also from ideologists—Community Conservationists, Liberals, Radical Leftists, and Supremacists—who consider as qualifying characteristics other dimensions than affluence or property. The Radical Right is treated at this point as a conservative ideology; it will be differentiated from the other ideology in the same cell, labeled Jeffersonian Conservatism, later. The Liberals and the Radical Leftists, as well as businessmen-labor minorities, believe that political leadership should come from the disadvantaged sectors of the community. The Supremacists' requisite condition for leadership is the appropriate race.

Conservatives can also be internally distinguished by their conception of the community. Orthodox Conservatives view their communities as being composed of sections of people having different needs, values, or interests. The leaders should rule in the interests of their sectors and must expect that other sectors will advocate policies that need to be opposed.

Jeffersonian Conservatives, as well as Radical Rightists, view the community as being early Jeffersonian: the community is a collection of individuals and not a set of potentially or actually conflicting interest groups. They distinguish two broad categories of individuals, the propertied and the propertyless, and, like Jefferson, are concerned

Who shall rule?

Conception of community	Industrialists–financiers	Proprietors–professionals	Public officials–administrators	Propertied		Disadvantaged Businessmen	Labor, minorities	Races
				Jeffersonian Conservatives	Radical Rightists			
Individuals								
Interests and interest groups	Orthodox Conservatives	Orthodox Conservatives					Liberals	
Collectivity(ies)	Progressive Conservatives		Community Conservationists				Radical Leftists*	Supremacists

FIGURE 1.2   *Matrix of ideologies: two dimensions.*

*Perforated box indicates that the Radical Leftists did not actually attain political leadership positions in any of the four communities from the end of the Second World War to 1961 even though there was an aspiring group in one community, Metroville, for a short time during those years.

with preserving the particular virtue that belongs to the propertied. They regard the propertyless as being not so much an interest group as a collection of individuals who have been lazy or who lack the personal capabilities that qualify men of property for a ruling voice in community affairs. The Jeffersonian Conservative strongly defends the small rural community, where virtuous men may acquire property and live the good life; the big city is a place where alien philosophies of life and civic corruption deplorably, but inevitably, prevail.

Progressive Conservatives are fundamentally "collectivists" in outlook. They view the community as a collectivity—an organism with a common interest. The welfare of one person depends upon the welfare of others; they recognize that interdependency is the keystone of a naturally ordered community. Since they believe in rule by the industrialists and financiers, they view this rule as necessarily operating in the interest of the collectivity. This political leadership must be benevolent; the attitude of "what's good for the 'X' Corporation is good for the community" indicates an innate complement of self-interest and the common good.

Community Conservationists are also collectivists. They view the community as a complex of mutually interdependent parts where the individual good and the common good are naturally compatible, if not identical. They see the values of community life maximized when political leadership is exercised by men representing the public at large, rather than "special interests." They believe in a "public interest" that may differ from the shortsighted, limited interest of a portion of the community. Elected public officials and appointed professional public administrators must be the guardians, as well as the architects and builders, of this public interest.

Liberals believe that disadvantaged people or those who identify themselves with the disadvantaged should be the political leaders in communities which are complexes of interest groups. Organized labor is one of the major, fundamental interests of Liberalism. In addition, Liberals see racial minorities and even small businessmen as disadvantaged interests. Liberals want public officials to accord the needs of the disadvantaged the highest political status. These needs will be defined by the leaders of the disadvantaged. Community Conservationists want public officials to be accorded the highest political status by all interests, including the disadvantaged.

The Radical Left's ideology advocates rule of the community by those disadvantaged under capitalism. Adherents of that ideology see the community as a collectivity in the Marxist sense and as having a single natural interest in the collective good of the proletariat. This single interest is to be implemented through the political leadership of the intelligentsia. The relatively large, disadvantaged proletariat would rule the community through the very small minority of progressive true believers who may work from the offices they hold in organizations of the disadvantaged, such as labor unions and racial groups.

Finally, the Supremacists believe that race should be the primary criterion for community rule. Race becomes the necessary and sufficient condition for participation as a political leader. Therefore, the appropriate racist sentiment tends to qualify any citizen for a position of political leadership. Supremacists can be either Whites or Negroes.[16]

The third component variable of these political ideologies is the "sense of social class." Social class not only adds depth to the picture of each ideology but also suggests bases for cooperation and conflict among different ideologies and among groups within one ideology. The sense of social class refers to people's self-images with regard to how much social status, respect, and affection they receive from others in the community. These feelings tend to be affected by the occupations people hold, their income or wealth, and their educational attainments. The sense of social class may be based on accurate perceptions of differential social status arising from admission to or exclusion from groups, associations, or organizations, although such admission or exclusion may be based on personal rather than socioeconomic characteristics.[17]

The political ideologies in the matrix in Figures 1.2 and 1.3 were set up to range from very high to low in the measurement of social class, reading from left to right. The Orthodox Conservatives and Progressive Conservatives believe that the industrialists-financiers should rule, because they are the most important, or even superior, men in the community; they deserve their social and political status. The attainment of their high-income-producing occupational positions, whether by birth or through their own efforts, is seen as reason enough for the community to accord them the lion's share of respect or deference. Their wealth alone, apart from their manners or morality, leads naturally to places on boards of directors, or to the organization of country clubs which provide exclusive social settings for the development and maintenance of a sense of high social position.

The Orthodox Conservatives who believe that proprietorial-professional occupations should rule have a sense of high social class, as compared to groups they perceive as their protagonists in the community. They appear not to have quite the same feelings of social

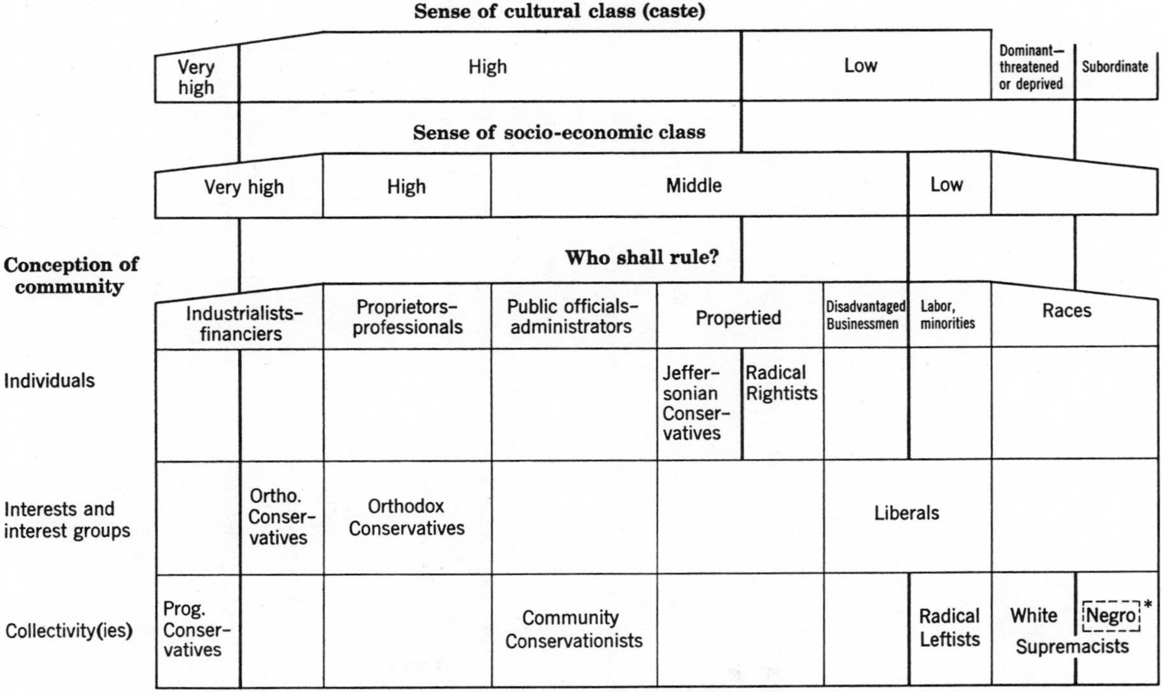

Matrix of ideologies: four dimensions

Sense of cultural class (caste)

	Very high	High	Low	Races
				Dominant— threatened or deprived / Subordinate

Sense of socio-economic class

Who shall rule?

Conception of community	Very high — Industrialists– financiers	High — Proprietors– professionals	High — Public officials– administrators	Middle — Propertied	Low — Disadvantaged Businessmen	Low — Labor, minorities		
Individuals				Jeffersonian Conservatives / Radical Rightists				
Interests and interest groups	Ortho. Conservatives	Orthodox Conservatives			Liberals			Radical Leftists
Collectivity(ies)	Prog. Conservatives	Community Conservationists						White Supremacists / *Negro Supremacists

*The perforated box enclosing Negro Supremacists indicates that there was no political group of this ideology aspiring to community leadership in any of the cities although there were individual Negro Supremacists in both southern cities.

FIGURE 1.3 *Matrix of ideologies: four dimensions.*

superiority as are evidenced by the aforementioned conservative ideologists. The Community Conservationists, the Jeffersonian Conservatives, and the Radical Rightists tend to perceive themselves as properly middle class; this is a matter of some pride and significance to them. Liberals include some people who feel they belong to the middle class and others who feel that they are members of the lower class. Blue-collar and Negro Liberals tend to think that they receive a disproportionately small share of social status. Liberal businessmen and professionals tend to think of themselves as belonging to the middle class. The Radical Leftists have the strongest sense of receiving few social—and economic—gratifications in the community; they feel such gratifications belong to them by right because of the nature of the world and its inevitable historical forces. To Supremacists social class is irrelevant and racial purity is all important.

Another defining characteristic of ideologies is the sense of cultural class, or caste. This refers to the people's self-images and feelings concerning how much status or respect their values, beliefs, opinions, judgments, and ideas receive from others. Sense of cultural class may follow, to a greater or lesser degree, the sense of social class, but there are important differences in the two concepts.

The sense of cultural class may be very general and refer to a host of matters or phenomena: political values, political beliefs, political opinions, political judgments, and ideas about the polity—the political culture—as well as matters of manners, morals, money, and music. Just as we treat theoretically distinct senses of social and economic class as a single dimension, so too do we deal with these various "senses" as a single, composite, general sense of cultural class.[18]

The three sets of political ideologists characterized by a high sense of social class—both kinds of Orthodox Conservatives and the Progressive Conservatives—have a comparably high sense of cultural class (Figure 1.3). The Progressive Conservatives have an extremely high sense of cultural superiority which extends throughout most areas of life. Their sense of cultural class makes them the most aristocratic of any set of Conservatives. When born to the highest social and economic positions, they accept their roles as cultural leaders as a matter of course. They have unquestioned faith that the cultural trends and heritage they oversee are superior to any alternatives. On occasion, they may be influenced by such men of lower cultural class as their professional advisors; but they regard themselves as without peer in the realm of judgment. The two sets of Orthodox Conservatives appear—in our communities at least—less certain that their cultural superiority is infallible, particularly in such peripheral cultural areas as the arts and letters.

Both Community Conservationists and Jeffersonian Conservatives, who identify themselves with the middle social class, have a high sense of cultural class which is comparable to that of the Orthodox Conservatives. Although the Community Conservationists believe their wisdom is superior in civic and political affairs, in some areas they assume that one man's values are as good as another's. For example, Community Conservationists do not see business success as an indication of cultural superiority; they view its attainment as a function of unimportant or chance factors. Their upper-cultural-class feelings derive in part from their awareness that they are currently well informed and highly educated and that they have the most modern, progressive view of what is good for the community. This is in contrast to the old-fashioned, regressive views of most of their articulate opponents, of professional politicians, and, perhaps, of many of the citizens. This sense of high cultural class characterizes Community Conservationists whether they are Harvard intellectuals, city managers or planners, or leaders of the League of Women Voters. Community Conservationists value professionally trained public administrators and stress public planning; they tend to hold in disrepute the professional politician and "dirty politics." They are the most recent of a long line of "reformers," but differ in at least one major aspect: earlier reformers tended to concentrate on eliminating particular evils so that the political system might return to a sort of laissez-faire operation in cooperation with private institutions. The Community Conservationist, in contrast, stresses the need for and the duty of the government to provide long-range planning in the public interest by nonpolitical administrators. There is a socialist-like emphasis on community planning without the socialist objective of increased public ownership of the means of production.[19]

Jeffersonian Conservatives differ sharply from the Radical Rightists in respect to cultural class. The Jeffersonian Conservatives' sense of belonging to the upper cultural class appears to be based in part on their images of themselves as being men of some affluence when compared to the propertyless, and as being believers in eternal verities rather than in the misconceived modern notions of the good life to which eccentrics adhere. In sharp contrast, Radical Rightists sense that they belong to the cultural class which is lowest in regard to community affairs. They feel deprived—not necessarily of social status or access to prestigious social organizations—because they are treated by a frequently subversive community leadership as part of a "lunatic fringe," as people with destructive ideas.

Both Liberals and Radical Leftists have a sense of being members of a low cultural class. The Radical Leftists, much like the Radical Rightists, feel that they are treated unjustly. Moral indignation seems stronger on the part of the Radical Rightists than on that of the Radical Leftists; this may be because the Leftists' belief in historical necessity accords them security, and the Rightists fear that history is constantly moving in the wrong direction. The Radical Leftists resemble in a sense Progressive Conservatives in their elite outlook because the cultural class to which each group feels it belongs is extremely small. Radical Rightists, if elitists, are of a Populist variety. They feel that there are many people in this same low cultural class position who would become associated with the Radical Right if they recognized the truth of the Rightist diagnosis of, and prescription for, the current illness in the body politic.

The Liberals, somewhat split on the basis of their sense of social class—some identify with the middle and some with the lower class— are united in their sense of a common cultural-class plight. They may feel as deprived as either the Radical Right or the Radical Left by the disregard of their cultural standards, but they seem more confident that a change in their relative cultural class position is attainable in the relatively near future.

White and Negro Supremacists may now be treated as separate groups. The White Supremacists see themselves as the racial caste which is currently dominant. However, they feel threatened by an overturn in the "natural order" of caste-control relations. Negro Supremacists feel they are treated as inferior, subordinate people. They feel that their destiny, and that of dark-skinned peoples throughout the world, is to reverse the traditional master-serf relationship.

Two important aspects of political culture are beliefs about the good regime and the good power structure. Of these ten political ideologies—including both types of Orthodox Conservatives and both types of Supremacists—six have as their ideal type of regime a "developed democracy." The various types of regimes and power structures will be defined more fully in Chapter 3. The ideal regime of all the Conservative, the Liberal, and the Community Conservationist ideologies is one wherein the citizens correctly believe that they have full access to the political decision-making process, including the ballot. Radical Rightists feel that an oligarchy is the desirable regime for the foreseeable future. Such a regime exists when some categories of citizens are aware that they do not have access to the political decision-making process. Until utopia is reached, Radical Leftists prefer a situation called "guided democracy." Under this system citizens believe that they have full access to the political decision-making process, but are in error: should certain demands be made for shifts in the scope of government, illegitimate sanctions would be effectively applied to those making the demands. Such a situation prevails where there is a widespread sense of democracy with perhaps some of its forms, but without the necessary conditions to give it substance. Supremacists favor oligarchy for the other race; they vary in their preferences for the good regime for the master race.

All four conservative ideologies prefer a type of power structure wherein power is in the hands of a relatively small proportion of the citizens and the political leadership agrees on one set of values for the general scope of government. Although Jeffersonian Conservatives believe that the relatively large propertied segment should participate in ruling, the actual political leadership will naturally be relatively small in size. Relatively large numbers of shiftless, propertyless people and some misguided people with property are disqualified from sharing in political power and leadership positions because of their attachment to an alternative political ideology. The Orthodox Conservatives think politics is necessary in the competition with other interests for scarce resources; they try to attain or preserve a consensual power structure, in which Orthodox Conservatism is the prevailing political ideology.

The ideal power structure of Community Conservationists, Liberals, and Radical Leftists is more of a mass and less of an elite distribution of political power. The Radical Leftists understand that such a distribution of political power is necessary if they are to move from their present powerless position, in what they consider oligarchies run by and for their enemies, to a position of power in a pseudo-democracy that is guided by them. Community Conservationists prefer to see the masses share in political power through extensive electoral participation in support of the Conservationists and their policies; Liberals envisage the development of a complex of more active political roles for the rank-and-file. Supremacists tend to support a consensual elite power structure as the only safe way of preserving the oligarchy and the dominance of their race.

The fifth factor among political ideologies is a principle of community organization, which, in its most extreme form, may be stated in this way: The good community is a natural product of governmental noninterference with private allocation of social, economic, or other resources according to the individual's ability to compete for them, tempered by mercy and charity. The Radical Rightists adhere to this principle in a most uncompromising fashion. In their political ideology, almost all governmental action is seen as a dangerous violation of this natural law principle. Jeffersonian Conservatives also tend to view the growth of government as unwarranted interference, but they view this somewhat less rigidly.

The major difference between the two is that the Radical Right is restorationist in outlook whereas the outlook of Jeffersonian Conservatives is preservationist. Jeffersonian Conservatism may be strongest in small or rural communities where government is minimal, and the Radical Right tends to be strong in communities where government has grown larger. But Jeffersonian Conservatism places its greatest emphasis on preventing further increases in the net scope of government, whereas the Radical Right stresses the need to decrease the net scope of government. Jeffersonian Conservatives may accept shifts in the functioning of government if the shifts accord with their cultural values, but the Radical Rightist consistently views government as evil. One of the cultural aims of Jeffersonian Conservatism is a community undivided by political controversy. Since the Jeffersonian Conservative has a sense of upper cultural class status and a duty to preserve the community consensus, he is more likely than the Radical Rightist to accept a governmental program if resistance will result in extensive or intensive community conflict. This would be particularly true if the Jeffersonian Conservatives were the political leaders of the polity and able to control administrative decision-making for any governmental program. The Radical Rightist has the hostility that goes with believing oneself treated as a member of an inferior cultural class; he also feels, as a political-cultural value, the need for conflict and extreme forms of political warfare to reestablish the principle of community organization in its pure form and to establish the desired oligarchic type of polity.[20] Both the Radical Right and Jeffersonian Conservatism are hostile to a professional, independent governmental bureaucracy; they see these professionals as men who are, by their very occupations, dedicated to the subversion of this basic principle of community life.

Conservatives other than Jeffersonians tend to have the latter's rhetoric, but differ in their interpretations of what constitutes governmental interference with the private distribution of goods, services, and other values. Alexander Hamilton's advocacy of certain national governmental programs made him no less conservative than Calvin Coolidge's negative sentiments toward government. If governmental programs are seen to serve the interests of the rulers, they may be

thought to strengthen rather than weaken the rule of private allocations of values. The result of this qualification is that Conservatives
have a contingent or dependent outlook toward the appropriate scope
of government.[21] Primary among these contingent factors is whether
or not particular governmental programs hurt or help conservative
socio-economic interests, and the extent to which their adversaries,
the Liberals, are likely to use shifts or expansions in the scope of
government for antibusiness ends. Since these liberal shifts have
been a national trend, the conservative political ideology tends to
be more in favor of the *status quo* and retrenchment than of expansion.[22]

Progressive Conservatives are less opposed to the use of government
where private collectivities are unable or less able to act effectively.
Since they view their rule as benevolent and in the interests of the
entire community, they find it easier than do other conservative groups
to accept government's role as one of the mechanisms for resource
distribution along with the major private corporations and the voluntary civic and social organizations. This is particularly the case when
Progressive Conservatives are in dominant political leadership positions. Thus, they also have a contingent position on the preferred
scope of government. Progressive Conservatives sometimes see such
programs as organized, large-scale charity in everyone's interest, and
government as an efficient welfare-dispensing institution; they may
approve of public welfare programs that are anathema not only to
the Radical Right and Jeffersonian Conservatives but also to Orthodox
Conservatives.

Community Conservationists tend to see government as the most
important institution for producing in the good community values
that are neither produced by private efforts nor actually inspired by
private activities. Community Conservationists do not advocate as
general principles either the circumscription of the private sectors of
the community or a particular scope of government. Their cultural
values are such that the programs of civic improvement and repair
which they favor tend to make them advocates of vigorous, expansionist government. These programs include a stress on the improved
distribution of knowledge through the public schools, cleanliness and
beauty in architecture, planning and guided development of land use
and of the size and character of the community's population, and a
spirit of harmonious cooperation on the part of the citizenry. They
value civic pride, a strong sense of public spirit, and an efficient, cor-
ruption-free, integrated city government. They believe "good government" is possible only where small, inefficient, multiple jurisdictions

do not exist to obstruct nonpartisan, professional public administrators, officials, and civic-minded citizens in their work of building the good community. Since the property tax is still the primary fiscal base of local government, their relative unconcern with the costs and the tax requirements of their programs makes them particularly unacceptable to both Jeffersonian Conservatives and the Radical Rightists. Furthermore, the tax-conscious, property-oriented Rightists are considered members of an extremely inferior cultural class by Community Conservationists. Community Conservationists are not adverse to accepting federal funds for programs of civic improvement. When they do receive such funds they become the mortal enemies of the Radical Rightists who see socialism and the triumph of the Radical Left as the inevitable consequence of the extension of federal funds and planning controls into the local community.

Liberals agree, in general, with the principle that resources should be distributed according to the ability of individuals to compete in the distribution process. They believe that, with the passive or active cooperation of government, the affluent have unfair advantages that only counter-organization of the disadvantaged can overcome. They distrust local government officials whom they do not control for their traditional alliance with the business community; they also look with some hostility on nonbusiness-oriented Community Conservationists and their "modern" conception of good government. Liberals may advocate shifts in local government's scope either internally or in an expansionist direction. They may even advocate contraction in the scope of government if this seems a way to reduce the advantages of the affluent in the competition for scarce resources. Liberals tend to have a very pragmatic approach to the scope of government, particularly at the local level. Although their rhetoric often stresses expansion of local government, their pragmatism and their fear of government when their opponents have power give the Liberals' political ideology the same contingent character as that of the Conservative ideologies.

The Supremacists, both White and Negro, see the appropriate scope of local government in relation to the implementation of their interests in racial supremacy and a rigid caste system. Under some conditions, they see local government as their strongest force against enemies who advocate desegregation, either from without or from within the community. Under other conditions, they try to reduce the scope of local government to repair or prevent breaches in the wall between the races. Their attitude toward the scope of government is variable, therefore, rather than fixed and determinate.

The only political ideology that rejects this principle of community organization completely is that of the Radical Left. To the Leftist, the good community is one wherein government, during the pre-utopian period, distributes resources. Even here there is a quality of contingency about the Radical Leftists' position on the appropriate scope of government. Marxists may work with Liberals or with Conservatives to generate resentment and rebellion among the disadvantaged; the international communist movement often has used this strategy. The flexibility of the Radical Leftists' tactics and strategy, within the framework of fixed long-range goals, lends even to this political ideology a quality of contingency shared by all of the aforementioned political ideologies except that of the Radical Right.

We may return to the earlier point that political ideology may range from a deeply rooted personality trait to a surface attitude. It appears that while any group of ideologists may be deeply committed to ideological precepts, Radical Rightists, Supremacists, and Radical Leftists—the Leftists are currently least important in numbers and political significance in community politics—are people whose ideologies seem to play a more central role in their lives than do the ideologies of other groups. These are "deviant" political ideologies—ideologies subscribed to by relatively few people and in which the preferred type of regime differs markedly from that in most other American political ideologies. Furthermore, Radical Rightists express open hostility to, and engage in open warfare with, the cultural classes they consider their enemies; they use tactics that the latter believe are as radical and as undesirable as are the ends of that ideology. The term "radical" for both left and the right has three connotations. It signifies that these ideologies advocate relatively sharp shifts in the scope of government although such shifts would be in different directions. It also signifies that these ideologies envisage the best political regime as being quite different from the regime desired by other ideologists. Finally, consistent with their preferences for other than developed democratic regimes, the Radical Rightists and Leftists advocate "radical" political tactics such as slander, smears, and secret societies which other ideologists view with disdain.

We purposely refer to government rather than to "local" government in the foregoing section. This suggests what may have been apparent all along: the taxonomy constructed for these political ideologies is relevant for national as well as for local American politics. By a consistent substitution of the word "nation" for the word "community," the Progressive Conservatives have their analogue in the Eisenhower administration and the Community Conservationists in

Kennedy's New Frontier.[23]   These counterparts are not perfect equivalents, of course. Furthermore, some people adhere strongly to one ideology at one level and to another ideology at another.[24] This alone will explain some of the apparent paradoxes of current American politics, both locally and nationally. But our basic point is that political ideology did not disappear at the national level with the end of the Depression or the end of the New or Fair Deal; nor has it been as absent from local politics as many observers seem to think.

Important dimensions of a community's power structure are the extent to which a political leadership is characterized by single or by multiple ideologies and the extent to which there is ideological convergence or divergence. These dimensions will be discussed at greater length in Chapter 3. From the foregoing descriptions, it would seem that some political ideologies diverge substantially from others. If their proponents attained political leadership positions, the extent of the divergence would seem to be clearly established. However, this is problematical; such factors as the strength of the leaders' ideological commitment affect the degree of divergence. This chapter closes with the suggestion that the great ignorance about political ideology in the United States at the community, state, and national levels of government and politics should be reduced by additional research. Except for two follow-up sample surveys in one community, which was revisited several years after the first sample survey for the purpose of testing specific hypotheses, little systematic, comparative information is available on the political ideologies of the citizens at large in our four communities. Even fewer data are available at this time on the genesis and development of ideological orientation.[25] We have included this discussion of ideology in our analysis because we do have some comparative data on its nature and functions, particularly at the political leadership level of the power structure in our four communities, despite the many facets left unexplored.[26]

NOTES

1. The words "polity" and "political system" are used interchangeably in this book. *Polity* refers to a multitude of dimensions that characterize political relations of people in a community and to people viewed as members of a political community. The term *political system* suggests the interrelatedness and interactional character of at least some of these dimensions. Probably the modern classic in the conception, mapping, and discussion of the domain of political analysts is Harold D. Lasswell and Abraham Kaplan, *Power and Society: A Framework for Political Inquiry* (New Haven: Yale University Press, 1950). See also David Truman, "The Impact on Political Science of

the Revolution in the Behavioral Sciences," *Research Frontiers in Politics and Government* (Washington: The Brookings Institution, 1955), pp. 202–231; David Easton, *The Political System* (New York: Alfred A. Knopf, 1953); and William C. Mitchell, *The American Polity* (New York: Free Press of Glencoe, 1962).

2. See Daniel Lerner and H. D. Lasswell, *The Policy Sciences* (Stanford: Stanford University Press, 1951).

3. See Ralf Dahrendorf, *Class and Class Conflict in Industrial Societies* (Stanford: Stanford University Press, 1955). For a critical review of municipal government textbooks, see Lawrence J. R. Herson, "The Lost World of Municipal Government," *The American Political Science Review*, LI (June 1957), pp. 330–346.

4. Among the important exceptions are: Herbert McCloskey, Paul J. Hoffman, and Rosemary O'Hara, "Issue Conflict and Consensus Among Party Leaders and Followers," *The American Political Science Review*, Vol. LIV, No. 2 (June 1960), pp. 406–427; Robert C. Stone, "Power and Values in Transcommunity Relationships," *Current Trends in Comparative Community Studies* ed. by Bert E. Swanson, Public Monograph Series, No. 1 (Kansas City, Mo.: Community Studies, Inc., 1962), pp. 69–80.

5. See Delbert Miller and William Form, *Industry, Labor and Community* (New York: Harper & Bros., 1960), Ch. XIV. For an analysis of the situation of a rural community in the context of these modern currents, see Arthur J. Vidich and Joseph Bensman, *Small Town in Mass Society* (Garden City, New York: Anchor Books, Doubleday & Co., Inc., 1958).

6. For a fairly comprehensive theoretical analysis of five "major systems" in terms of which a community might be analyzed, see Irwin T. Sanders, *The Community* (New York: The Ronald Press Company, 1958).

7. A modern reactionary in this sense is Friedrich A. Hayek; see *The Road to Serfdom* (Chicago: University of Chicago Press, 1944).

8. Engels refers to the "natural simplicity," of such communities; he calls them "wonderful," "natural and spontaneous," and says they produce "splendid men and women." Frederick Engels, *The Origin of the Family, Private Property and the State* (Chicago: Charles H. Kerr & Co., Co-operative, 1902), pp. 117–119.

9. C. Wright Mills, *The Power Elite* (New York: Oxford University Press, 1956); Floyd Hunter, *Community Power Structure* (Chapel Hill: University of North Carolina Press, 1953); Andrew Hacker, "Liberal Democracy and Social Control," *The American Political Science Review*, Vol. LI, No. 4 (December 1957), pp. 1009–1025.

10. Robert Dahl, "A Critique of the Ruling Elite Model," *The American Political Science Review*, Vol. LII, No. 2 (June 1958), pp. 463–469. See also David B. Truman, "The American System in Crisis," *Political Science Quarterly*, Vol. LXXIV, No. 4 (December 1959), pp. 481–497.

11. See Robert A. Dahl, *Who Governs?* (New Haven: Yale University Press, 1961), pp. 468–569. See also two forthcoming studies, Robert Presthus, *Men at the Top: A Study in Community Power* (Oxford, Spring 1964); and Aaron Wildavsky, *Leadership in a Smalltown* (Bedminister Press, 1964).

12. That ideology is relatively unimportant for the citizens at large in the two-party national politics of the United States is documented in Angus Campbell *et al.*, *The American Voter* (New York: John Wiley & Sons, Inc., 1960), pp.

188–215; and in McCloskey *et al., op. cit.,* p. 406. The operational definition of ideologies in these two studies, unlike the present study, refers to policy or decisional preferences and to the traditional liberal-conservative distinctions. See also Philip E. Converse, "The Nature of Belief Systems in Mass Publics," in *Ideology and Discontent,* ed. by David E. Apter and Reinhard Bendix (New York: The Free Press of Glencoe, forthcoming, 1964). In Converse's important analysis, he documents the relatively greater ideological character of "elite" than "mass" American policy perspectives.

Several comments need to be made about such studies. First, in 1959 in selected communities in the West, identical measurements have revealed much stronger correlations between such policy matters as federal-government programs in social-welfare areas and the feeling that big business corporations should not have much to say about how the government is run than those for the Survey Research Center's national sample of 1956. Secondly, in one such study we have found a much greater degree of stability over a four-year period in such policy perspectives on the part of a random sample in one community than Converse has reported for a national sample, and an even greater degree of such stability for such items as attitudes towards a state sales tax. Thirdly, and most importantly, granting the greater ideological character of "elite" than "mass" political thinking in a variety of regards (and in no way do we in the following pages suggest that the masses of a community's citizens are "ideological," although we did not systematically assess the extent to which that may have been true in our communities), our use of the term "ideology" is in various ways quite different from that of the aforementioned studies. See also David W. Minar, "Ideology and Political Behavior," *Midwest Journal of Political Science,* Vol. V, No. 4 (November 1961), pp. 317–331.

13. For a useful conception of political interests, see David B. Truman, *The Governmental Process* (New York: Alfred A. Knopf, 1951) and Harold Lasswell, *Politics: Who Gets What, When, and How* (New York: McGraw-Hill Book Company, Inc., 1936).

14. See Campbell *et al., op. cit.,* p. 192. They define ideology as "primarily political, although the scope of the structure is such that we expect an ideology to encompass content outside the political order as narrowly defined—social and economic relationships, and even matters of religion, education, and the like." See also McCloskey *et al., op. cit.,* p. 427. They properly point out that categorizing parties or politics as "ideological" depends on "how narrowly we define that term."

15. McCloskey *et al., op. cit.*

16. It is common practice to capitalize the word "Negro" and not the word "white." We see no reason for unequal treatment in such a minor but symbolic matter and therefore capitalize both words.

17. For discussions of social class in the United States, see Joseph A. Kahl, *The American Class Structure* (New York: Rinehart, 1957); and W. Lloyd Warner, M. Meeker, and K. Eells, *Social Class in America* (New York: Harper Torchbooks, 1960).

18. The observations and instruments for evaluating and estimating the specific and general senses of cultural class were not precise enough to detect theoretically significant discrepancies between the specific and general sense of cultural class. While the senses of cultural and social class may be highly

correlated under many conditions, we suspect that they diverge significantly in relatively open social class systems. By the use of such terms as "status frustrations" and "the dispossessed," Seymour Martin Lipset and Daniel Bell imply some aspects of what we mean by a sense of cultural class. Once the latter is conceptualized as a distinct analytic variable (of a multidimensional character), it becomes possible to test the degree to which cultural-class position is due to what Lipset and Bell both suggest is the cause of distance and hostility between upper- and lower-cultural-class groups, namely, psychological anxiety or confidence related to position in and understanding of the modern technological, corporate socio-economic structure and international order. We would question a predominant stress on a differential distribution of needs for, and frustrations regarding, social status and would hypothesize more of a socialization in differentiated cultures as a central factor in the motivational complex of forces producing a stratified cultural-class system. Whatever the original cause of different belief systems, their existence provides for the maintenance or the development of cultural-class systems based thereon, related to social class only to the extent that cultural belief systems follow social-class lines. See *The Radical Right*, ed. by Daniel Bell (Garden City, N. Y.: Doubleday & Co., Inc., 1963), especially Chapters 1, 2, 13, and 14.

19. Some of these aspects of Community Conservation are well expressed in Catherine C. Bauer Wurster, "Framework for an Urban Society," in *Goals for Americans, The Report of the President's Commission on National Goals* (New York: A Spectrum Book, Prentice-Hall, Inc., 1960), pp. 223–247.

20. Classifying people as Jeffersonian Conservatives and Radical Rightists, as with the classification of people as ideologists of any other kind, will sometimes result in the problem of marginal or borderline cases. Senator Barry Goldwater may be considered such a case.

21. The late Senator Robert Taft's shift in position from an "anti" to a "pro" stance on such matters as public housing and urban redevelopment illustrates the contingent outlook on the part of Orthodox Conservatives, or, possibly, a movement toward national Progressive Conservatism. For a description of a variant of Orthodox Conservatism at the community level which permits "quasi-public action by private groups for public collective ends" while at the same time maintaining a minimal scope of (public) government, see Stone's description of what he calls "social free enterprise" in *op. cit.*

22. A useful description of Conservative and Liberal ideology, as well as descriptions of the differences in attitudes toward various aspects of the scope of national government by Republican and Democratic party leaders, is to be found in McCloskey *et al., op. cit.* For a discussion of some of the ideological premises of businessmen, see Francis X. Sutton *et al., The American Business Creed* (Cambridge, Massachusetts: Harvard University Press, 1956).

23. That differences between Progressive Conservatives and Community Conservationists, particularly at the national level, may be difficult to discern is evidenced by the fact that many of the objectives mentioned in *Goals for Americans* are held by Eisenhower Republicans and Kennedy Democrats, as well as by Stevenson Liberals.

24. It may be of interest to note at this point that leaders of the three community-oriented Radical Right movements found in our research communities

belonged to and received literature from nationally organized Radical Right groups.

25. James S. Coleman stresses the importance in a large class of conflicts of "a few active oppositionists" who are "sometimes motivated by the hope of power, but often they are ideologically committed to a 'cause.'" *Community Conflict* (Glencoe, Illinois: The Free Press, 1957), p. 8.

26. For a useful discussion on how to study the importance of ideas in political systems, and an explanation of Max Weber's general comparative research design and logic of inquiry, see Talcott Parsons, *Essays in Sociological Theory Pure and Applied* (Glencoe, Illinois: The Free Press, 1949), pp. 151–165.

2

A POLITICAL DECISION-MAKING
MODEL AND KEY CONCEPTS

Whether a person in politics acts in reference to a political ideology or to an interest, as a human being he ordinarily has a variety of values. Political theory ought to take into account the multiple values of men, and also the fact that political action may be directed to satisfy nonpolitical values as well. How can one study politics without including everything as within the analyst's domain? Can we define political power and political decision-making in a way that distinguishes the political from the social or the economic? Can we define concepts in a way that promotes useful political research without taking an excessively narrow, institutional view? The answers to these questions are affirmative because the institutional approach to politics is embedded in a social-psychological approach to political behavior in a way frequently not understood, or misunderstood, by both amateur and professional political analysts.

Even though the dividing line between government and private institutions is sometimes blurred, and joint public and private programs may conceal institutional distinctions, the existence of government as a social-psychological reality governs the direction of our research. People differentiate government from nongovernmental institutions, and this distinction supports the following treatment of political decision-making, community power structures, and types of regimes. Let us turn, therefore, to the individual engaged in political action and to the meaning of political decision-making; both of these concepts derive from our interest in government but encompass private citizens as well as government officials. These concepts indicate that although people's actions may be motivated by many values, it is the analytically and empirically distinguishable motives that permit the development of a distinctly "political" theory.

POLITICAL PRESSURE AND POLITICAL MOTIVATION

Although all acts are stimulated by a multiplicity of needs, which they also affect, they may be differentiated according to the actions of others whom they are intended to influence. If one aspect of every act is the goal of the individual, acts may be distinguished by the end in view, whether it is to affect the actions of government officials —that is, the scope of government—the scope of other institutions, or both. Regardless both of the needs that underlie the actions of people and of their ultimate objectives, acts intended to affect governmental decisions may be classified as political. These acts, however, need not be limited to a single political classification; multiple classifications of acts according to motive reflect the extent to which the political system may overlap social, economic, or other types of systems.

Political action or participation may be considered the evidence of a need for power. The degree to which a person engages in political acts, in contrast to other kinds of action, can constitute a measure of his need for power. This psychological-institutional definition of the need for power, based on the psychological relationship of the individual to the institution of government, does not assume that satisfaction of his need for power is the individual's only goal. Power may be an end in itself, or it may be instrumental to such ends as wealth, prestige, or rectitude. To the individual, the impacts of political acts on other institutions may be even more important than the impact on government.

This view of motivation is analogous to that of the economist who observes action in the marketplace or other economic arenas. The economist assumes that when people act in reference to economic policy, they are motivated by the need to maximize profits. In his analysis he disregards this need except when such action exists. He may regard men not acting in the marketplace either as not needing to maximize profit or as not currently calling this potential need into play. He does not ordinarily ask why people may want to maximize their wealth; nor does he take into account the possibility that action may have other motives than profit-maximization. The economist thus adopts a definition that may appear fictitious. The view of political motivation advanced here is similar.

When political participation is viewed only as a set of actions directed at the scope of government, a person may participate politically without making any perceptible impact on that scope. If a person, by participating in politics, only wants to achieve a sense of power and active participation, he may not care very much what specific impacts, if any, he may have on the scope of government.

What, then, is the place of political participation in politics? Political participation makes up the basic pressures that, in our general model, bear directly upon the scope of government. This definition of political participation delimits this study to a single, general class of acts within the context of the web of government. Other general classes of acts may be distinguished also by the goals of those who act. Economic action is action by means of which the individual intends to influence economic institutions; social action is action by means of which the individual intends to influence social institutions. An individual may believe that any governmental or private institution can satisfy multiple needs and values. If he believes this and if his action is motivated by several values, then he may try to influence several institutions simultaneously and to maximize or satisfy several values. Other individuals may have one institutional domain as the object of their action, whether they are motivated by single or multiple values.

Some citizens may thus act to influence the functioning of government in order to acquire political power as an end in itself; or they may act to acquire wealth either directly from government or indirectly through the impact that government can have on private economic institutions. Either action is political participation and would be whether the targets of the action were members, officials, or leaders of private institutions—the corporation, the union, or the family—or whether they were electors or officials of government. Other citizens may act without having such impacts on the scope of government as one of their goals.

This institutional conception of political acts does not mean that social and economic participation, for example, may not have direct impacts on political participation. The political theorist may want to ask whether variations in the economic or social institutions of a community cause variations in the scope of government. A community's economy may be regulated by local or absentee owners; a social or economic structure may be closed or open. These are variables that refer to complex multidimensional patterns of economic or social participation. But we shall assume that political participation is an ever-present, necessary, intervening variable between such economic or social variables and the scope of government. The scope of government cannot change unless and until one or more persons participate politically, that is, act in political decision-making.

Thus, in order to avoid the impossible task of studying all human action at once, an institutional-psychological conception of politics is adopted. If we were not concerned with understanding the scope of public government, our conception of politics and political participation might follow other than these institutional lines.[1] However, political participation, although necessary, is insufficient to produce the impacts on the scope of government that result from political decisions. To clarify this and to assure that when measurements are made in several communities the focus is on the same sorts of political acts and impacts, the meaning of political decision-making must be clarified. It is necessary to devise a model of decision-making for that portion of the abstract model of the political process (sketched in Chapter 1) that refers to the pressures, forces, and currents affecting the scope of government.

A DECISION-MAKING MODEL

Political decision-making concerns the actions of men in the process of making choices. A process is a series of related events or acts over a period of time. Each act in a decision-making series of acts may itself be a choice or a decision. In order to understand this complex of decisions within decisions, it is useful to conceive of decision-making processes as consisting of six stages and one event: [2]

(1) Policy formulation
(2) Policy deliberation
(3) Organization of political support
(4) Authoritative consideration
Event: Decisional outcome
(5) Promulgation of the decisional outcome
(6) Policy effectuation

The political decision-making process is political only in the sense that those engaged in action at any stage are acting consciously, in some measure, in reference to the scope of government. Any decision-making process, whether intrapersonal or interpersonal, and whether in a family, job, or other institutional setting, may be thought of as involving such stages.

Policy formulation occurs when someone thinks that a problem can be alleviated, solved, or prevented by a shift in the scope of government. The problem—or unsatisfied need—may or may not be perceived by others as a problem or as being appropriate for local government action. Even though there may be widespread satisfaction with many policy areas, the complexities of and the continuous changes in modern life make it likely that problems will arise somewhere to stimulate policy formulation directed toward a shift in the current scope of local government. The formulator, and those participating in any of the stages of political decision-making, may be a private citizen or a government official.

A policy formulation may originate outside the particular polity. For example, as a general policy, municipal ownership of facilities to distribute electric power was first formulated outside one of our communities; a general desegregation policy was first formulated outside another. But whether someone "borrows" a policy formulation from outside the community or whether a policy is of local origin, it must at some time become a preference of a person within the polity in order to become part of a community political decision-making process. A policy preference that is not deliberated once it is formed is a political decision-making process that has been started but is stillborn in the mind of the potential political participant. Policy formulation is a stage that is necessary but not sufficient to sustain the existence of a political decision-making process.

Policy deliberation is the stage following policy formulation. It may take the political-action form of talking, writing, listening, or reading. When a policy formulation—a policy preference for a shift in the net or internal scope of government—is transmitted by one actor to another, and interpersonal deliberation of the policy formulation occurs, a political demand has been made in the polity. It is at this point that the consideration of other policies may generate counter-demands.

Overt action in this context does not necessarily mean publicized action. Indeed, the action may take place behind closed doors, and the most aggressive newspaper reporter or political researcher may never hear of it. What makes research on political relations possible is that, although such actions may be known only to a few people, a sufficient number of those actions may be identified to enable researchers to construct a relatively valid picture of political decision-making processes.

Policy deliberation therefore may be open or secret: it may be restricted to smoke-filled rooms; it may take place at public meetings of the City Council; or it may be a topic of conversation on street corners or in private clubs. As with policy formulation, it is a stage that may be pre-empted either by public officials or by private citizens; or it may be a joint function. Wherever it occurs and whoever participates, this necessary stage is sufficient to allow a political decision-making process to be considered extant.

The decision-making process is considered arrested if a policy proposal is formulated and deliberated but does not advance beyond policy deliberation to the organization-of-political-support stage. Political demands may remain in this stage of decision-making. A decision-making process may be arrested at this point because those who started it believe that organization in behalf of their demands would provoke counterorganization and defeat; or they may even fear severe, illegitimate sanctions if they were to organize. Demands of this sort may be suppressed or repressed as a result of correct or incorrect estimates of others' policy preferences, or of accurate or unwarranted fears that opponents will apply severe, illegitimate sanctions if they push their demands. In any event, political decision-making processes may die in this stage.

Organization of political support refers to such actions as holding and attending meetings to plan political strategy, producing and distributing information, and otherwise mobilizing support for or against demands for shifts in the scope of government. In most communities there are occasions in political life when leaflets are printed, handbills and petitions circulated, mimeograph machines run, and doorbells rung; paid political advertisements are published or broadcast and notices posted. These activities are considered the hallmarks of big-city machine politics. But in the four research communities they all were used to some extent by individuals other than party leaders, precinct committeemen, and their partisan coteries.

The organization of political support does not always require the use of these methods. Necessary political support might be mobilized by a telephone call from a single policy formulator or a few words spoken to one or two officials. On the other hand, a political decision-making process may involve extensive appeals using the highly refined techniques of mass-communications propaganda and public relations.

The decisional process has become a political issue when a demand reaches the stage of organizing political support, and two or more groups oppose each other on an aspect of policy formulation. Issues may be characterized according to the number and the emotional intensity of the individuals who have become actively involved in the issue, the extent to which issues are open or covert, and the extent to which participants view policy questions as involving basic ideological principles.

At times, certain patterns of governmental functioning may become accepted as customary, and demands for change may then take on a moralistic quality. A person's basic political beliefs—the political doctrines or ideology to which he subscribes—his way of life, or his personal integrity may seem to be at stake. It must be remembered that not all political decision-making processes need be issues; the organization of political support may be characterized by consensus rather than conflict. We will examine empirically the role of ideology in the emergence or avoidance of issues in decision-making later in the book.

Authoritative consideration is the next stage of decision-making. A variety of techniques may be used to make decisional choices or to select one of a set of optional courses as the decisional outcome. A demand may be voted upon directly by the citizens; proposed constitutional changes and local charter amendments are decided in this way, as are measures that involve the issuance of special bonds and the levying of special taxes. Other major policy questions also may be decided by citizen votes. The initiative and referendum are two electoral devices designed to give the citizenry a direct method for authoritatively approving or rejecting a policy.

On the other hand, a policy may be selected from several choices by formal or informal balloting in smaller groups of active participants: a city council may vote on a policy proposal without submitting it to the electorate. A small group of private citizens may even make the final decision either by voting down a policy proposal without giving officials the option of voting on it, or by choosing an alternative that is the authoritative decisional outcome, in fact if not in theory. There are occasions when government officials appear to act as independent lawmakers but are really the agents of private citizens.

To control a decision-making process a group of private citizens must control (1) the policy-formulation stage, (2) the policy-deliberation stage, (3) the organizing-political-support stage, or all of these stages. If a policy proposal that is unacceptable to a group of influential private citizens manages to reach officials, the officials may allow these influential private citizens to select the policy and may not exercise their constitutional authority; or the officials may share in the selection of policies with nonofficials. Constitutional, formal authority to choose among several outcomes in decision-making does not mean that the authorities will or can so choose. Even the political status associated with constitutional authority may prove a narrow base for the exercise of political influence, compared to the political status of certain private citizens.

A new policy that effects a shift in the scope of government must be transmitted to an appropriate local government agency for official action, if that shift is to become part of the formal, authoritative code of the polity. If the formulators of a particular policy are themselves government officials, they still must transmit the policy—that is, place the policy on the official agenda for formal consideration—in order for it to become part of the decisions of record, the laws, ordinances, or administrative regulations of government.

But what of a policy proposal that is blocked, vetoed, or otherwise defeated before it is transmitted to governmental authorities? Assume that a private citizen or an official makes a policy suggestion or demand to other private citizens or, informally, to other officials. Then suppose that the proposed policy change is rejected, no action is taken, and the existing rule remains unchanged, either through the action of these private citizens or through informal action by the officials. Although the suggested policy was never transmitted formally to a local agency, political decision-making has occurred: the actual political decision has been to affirm the existing policy. Political decision-making does not mean that existing rules and regulations must be revised or that political decisions may not be made outside the locus of an official government agency.

The objective of demands for shifts in the scope of government may be to see a change in the way government operates without a change in the law or a decision to maintain an existing law. Laws or ordinances, administrative regulations, and judicial decisions, much like constitutions or charters, are often open to a variety of interpretations. Thus, a demand for a shift in the scope of government can be a demand for altered patterns of action by government officials without a formal change in the law or ordinance, administrative regulation, or judicial decision. Inducing government officials to act informally in appropriate ways may be a wiser course of action than attempting to obtain an authoritative modification in the scope of government. Therefore, political decision-making may take place either outside the halls of government or informally within the government, with neither fanfare nor public proclamations.

So far, the word "authoritative" has been used in two distinct but related ways; one is a special case of the other. In Chapter 1 we said that government has "authoritative supremacy, a monopoly of legitimate force." In the phrases *authoritative rule, authoritative code of the polity,* and *constitutional authority,* the word *authoritative* refers to the existence of a governmental policy, that is, of a rule regarding the way men should behave toward each other. The violation of such a policy can be expected to lead to punishments deriving from the monopoly of force possessed by all governments.

In this view, government exists and is "legitimate," even though its citizens despise it, so long as the citizens do not revolt and as long as they expect that force will probably be used to punish violators of policy. If such expectations do not exist, or if the expectations refer not to a legitimate government but to contending groups whose policy views conflict, so that any action might be met by punishment, government has broken down, and anarchy temporarily reigns. Constitutions, written or unwritten, and their subsidiary laws and customs are the plan of government as an institution in which those who govern have effective authority derived from their ability to sanction, using force if necessary. These officials may not express themselves before others do, but theirs is the last voice heard before sanctions are used in the pursuit of social control and public order. By the decision-making stage of *authoritative consideration*—the second sense of the word *authoritative*—we mean the stage of action by the political participants who have the final voice. These participants have the last word in selecting one or another of two or more outcomes as the policy that defines the scope of government for a succeeding time period.

All decision-making processes have *decisional outcomes*. If a particular aspect of the scope of government has been questioned and a decisional process has developed, regardless of the degree of consensus or conflict, the process will influence events thereafter, even though it is no longer extant. A decisional outcome is assessed by comparing the scope of government that existed and was questioned with the scope that exists at the point in time selected for identifying the outcome. This assessment may be done on the basis of a simple scale showing whether there has been change or not, or on the basis of a more complex set of parameters.

A decisional outcome involves purposeful behavior by participants, but does not require particular forms of choice-making. For example, it does not require a formal balloting procedure by either the electorate or their governmental representatives. The "authorities" in the second sense of the term *authoritative* are not necessarily government officials or the electorate acting as officials, as in the case of the "authorities" in the first sense. This is because authoritative consideration in a decision-making process is that stage wherein the participants select one or another of two or more ways in which local government is to function henceforth. Thus, participants in an authoritative consideration stage may be government officials, private citizens, or both. There may be no opportunity for government officials to reject the choice of private citizens of a particular decisional outcome, just as there may be no occasion for any but government officials to participate in selecting one of several outcomes. Private citizens may select an outcome that maintains the scope of government as is, thus obviating any need for a new law or ordinance. But whether a decisional outcome maintains or shifts the scope of government, the question of whether the participants are officials or citizens should be answered by empirical investigation rather than by definition.

An analyst must select a point in time to assess what outcomes have occurred in political decision-making. This point will be discussed further in connection with the concepts of political power and community power structures. The analyst might find that the stage of authoritative consideration has not been reached in one or another decision-making process. Thus, there may be decisional outcomes without authoritative consideration in a decision-making process because demands may not have reached the men who could act to shift the scope of government. When a change in a specific scope of government has become the subject of political demands in a decisional process, the analyst must determine whether the maintenance of the specific scope of government resulted from purposeful resistance by people capable of shifting the scope or from lack of access to people with such capabilities.[3] "Access" refers to the ability to reach the authorities, the men who can choose one or another pattern of local-government functioning as the decisional outcome in a decisional process. If there have been no demands for a shift in the scope of government, there has been no decisional process and, consequently, no authoritative consideration.[4] If demands have resulted in a shift in the scope of government, there has been authoritative consideration, even if a consensus has existed.

An authoritative-consideration stage may exist in a wide range of forms: it may be a distinct stage which succeeds the prior stages and has different participants from those in the prior stages; it may be a stage that partially overlaps earlier stages with some overlapping of personnel; or it may be a stage that is indistinguishable from other stages either temporally or by its participants. Decisional processes range from those with relatively well-developed and distinct stages to those with a single, composite stage that empirically encompasses the four analytic stages. In the decisional process that has a single, composite stage only one set of people—or one person in an instance of complete one-man rule—formulates policy, deliberates, organizes political support, and authoritatively considers the proposed shift in the scope of government at any one time. These participants may decide to adopt or reject a given policy formulation, thereby shifting or maintaining a particular scope of government. In relatively developed and distinct decisional stages, the participants in one stage may or may not be the same as the participants in other stages. Political role specialization may develop in reference to these stages, so that in one community, or in one policy area within a community, some men—"idea men"—specialize in policy formulation, others specialize in deliberative activities, others in the organization of political support, and still others may limit their participation to a final authoritative-consideration stage. Subspecialization in political roles within stages is also possible. For example, some people may specialize in doorbell-ringing and precinct work, others in pamphleteering, and still others in financing during the organization-of-political-support stage.[5] However, political roles in the decisional stages may be more general in other communities or in other decisional processes.

Promulgation of the decisional outcome is also a stage not necessarily reached in a particular decision-making process. If the participants think that an existing policy is the best policy and that it should not be modified, there may be no occasion for an authoritative proclamation of an outcome. If a shift in the scope of government takes place without a formal, public pronouncement, this stage may not be present. But another way of looking at it is that this stage is manifested in the affirmation of an existing policy or in a quiet, covert change of policy. In any event, the present analysis of the decision-making process is most concerned with the four prior stages.

Policy effectuation is the last stage in this model of a political decision-making process. Administrative rather than legislative officials are ordinarily, but not always, the authorities at this stage. The courts may also play important roles in interpreting and shaping a general-policy decision. Private citizens also may join with, or even dominate, public administrators in this stage of political decision-making.

Policy effectuation is included as a stage in the decision-making process not only because a decisional outcome must be applied to be "final" or because its application may substantially change the decisional outcome from what had been intended. It is included primarily because policy effectuation may generate new policy formulations. For example, it may result in reappraisal of the policy, thereby initiating another cycle in the decision-making process. In this sense even policy effectuation is not a final or terminal stage of decision-making.

For a long time the functions of public administrators were regarded by political scientists as distinct from the functions of politicians. Politicians made the general rules in politics, while administrators applied these general rules to specific cases. Recently, the conception of politics and administration as inextricably intertwined has become accepted. In our view a useful distinction ought still to be made between administrative and political decision-making. This distinction does not preclude administrators from active involvement in political decision-making, nor politicians from active participation in administrative decision-making.

Demands that local government shift its scope may be administrative or political. Decisional processes may be similarly categorized. These are terms for polar opposites on a continuum and are therefore matters of degree rather than of kind. An *administrative* demand or decision-making process is regarded by its maker or participants as involving relatively routine implementations of a prior, more generally applicable decision; it implicates relatively minor values of a relatively few people at any one time and has "technical" criteria available to guide the technically trained expert in selecting one or another outcome as *the* decision. A *political* demand or decision-making process is thought to involve either an unusual review of an existing decision or an entirely new decision; it implicates relatively major values of a relatively large number of people and has value judgments or preferences as the major factors in determining selection by "policy-makers" of one or another outcome as *the* decision.[6]

The administrator thus is "in" politics by definition, but whether he is involved in political or administrative decision-making, or both, is an open, empirical question. The politician is also "in" politics, and he may be involved as a participant in the making of administrative as well as political decisions.

The roles played by bureaucrats—"administrators"—in the political system tend to be shaped by the organization of each government and by the constitutional doctrines and practices in each polity. However, a casual examination of political systems at the local-community or nation-state level suggests that official and informal organizations of political systems may diverge as much from one another as do official and informal internal structures of administrative agencies.

Several important consequences follow from these distinctions between administrative and political decisions, based as they are on the psychology of participants. One is that a particular decisional process may be political in one community and administrative in another. Or a decisional process may in time move from the political to the administrative category and back within a single community. Civil servants, bureaucrats, or public administrators may be active participants in political decision-making under some conditions and active participants in administrative decision-making under others.

The existence of administrative decision-making may help to explain the apparent absence of politics in some simple societies. Since administrative decision-making may produce less community conflict than political decision-making, some societies do not permit the development of the latter except under special circumstances; others try to minimize such dangers through institutional arrangements. However, some anthropologists resist viewing government in other than formalistic terms. This may account for Radcliffe-Brown's reluctance to use the term "authority" in describing the polity among the Andaman Islanders. He commented, "Of authority the leading men have little or none, but of influence they have a good deal. Should any one venture to oppose a popular chief he would find the majority of the natives, including many of his friends, siding against him. The words 'chief' and 'authority' seem to imply some sort of organized rule and procedure, and of this there is nothing in Andamans." [7] For example, among the primitive Andaman Islanders the equivalents of governmental positions go to the strongest, most capable hunters. They direct the hunt and decide the day-to-day tactics and strategy for securing food; they thus raise and settle questions about the appropriate scope of government, that is, of how the government—or its equivalent in that society—is to function in meeting needs. Such decisions are matters of active administrative, if not political, decision-making rather than matters that are subject to nonpolitical custom.

Politics in its broadest sense includes both political and administrative decision-making, as well as behavior that is not specifically related to either type of decision-making process. However, some participants may view a particular decisional process as being primarily administrative while others may view the same process as being primarily political. Indexes based not only on the proportions of people viewing a process in one or another way but also on their roles or positions in the political system may have to be developed to account for such complicating, but sometimes analytically useful, complexities.

The stage of policy effectuation may be thought of as an administrative decision-making process that may or may not follow a decisional outcome. The focus of attention in this study is political rather than administrative decision-making. This is not because one sort of decision-making is inherently more "important" than the other: for example, it is possible that small, cumulative shifts in the scope of government through administrative decision-making can contribute more to a change in the scope of government than can political decision-making. Failure to see the administrative and the political as here described until it was too late to make systematic observations of administrative decision-making placed certain problems beyond the domain of this analysis. But the analysis will include administrators insofar as they participate in the making of political decisions.[8]

The decision-making model encompasses intrapersonal decision-making processes, even though the primary concern of the present study is with the interpersonal. When a man—a duly elected head of state or a ruler by act of usurpation—engages in the process of making a political decision by himself, the stages of decision-making either follow one upon the other in sequence in his thought processes or occur simultaneously. A bureaucrat may find himself making administrative decisions as part of his day-to-day activity. He makes demands upon or receives demands from private citizens or his fellow public officials in an administrative decisional process; or he may make demands upon himself as the sole decision-maker. The model is applicable to both individuals and groups.[9]

Summarizing the features of the model of political decision-making, we can say: a decision-making process exists when a political demand is made. A demand is a communicated policy formulation that envisages a shift in the scope of government. The decision-making process may become arrested at this point because those considering the demand are pessimistic about attaining the desired decisional outcome, because they fear the consequences that might ensue if they press their demands, because they are insufficiently motivated, or for other reasons. If counterdemands and counterorganization develop along with political support in behalf of demands, the process has become a political issue.

Decisional outcomes may result from arrested processes, from unopposed demands, from the resolution of a political issue, or as a consequence of effectively opposed and defeated demands which have not become issues. The decisional outcome may or may not be publicly promulgated. A political decision-making process may generate new policy formulations and demands or lead to new policy effectuation—administrative decision-making—that may then generate new political decision-making processes. In order to determine the outcomes of decisional processes, an analyst must specify the point in time at which he is interested in evaluating the outcomes. This will be discussed later, since it is crucial in determining who has had the political power that accrues to those who contribute to decisional outcomes.

Government officials may or may not be the only political actors at any stage of a decision-making process. Theoretically, they may monopolize political action or they may never enter the political scene actively. However, in most American communities they probably do engage in political action and share power with private citizens. But this is something for empirical determination rather than assumption. Since decision-making is not necessarily monopolized by officials, observations must be made to assess the extent to which citizens of a community participate and have power in the making of political decisions.

A SERIES OF KEY CONCEPTS

It is necessary here to define a series of concepts in order to clarify further the foregoing model of political decision-making, and to understand what is meant by community power structure and regime. These two aspects of community political systems are central foci of this study.[10]

DEFINITION 1: *Political participation* is action wherein one goal of the actor is the maintenance of or a shift in the scope of government.

DEFINITION 2: *Political status* is the recognition given by another (others) to a person's presumed preferences concerning the appropriate scope of government.

DEFINITION 3: *Political influence* is the political status accorded the acts of one political participant by another (others).

DEFINITION 4: *Political power* designates the sum of the contributions of political participants to an outcome of a political decision-making process.

DEFINITION 5: A *political role* is a set of acts defining a person's relationships in or to the political processes that determine the scope of government.

DEFINITION 6: A *community power structure* is a representation of selected aspects of political power relations over a specified time period. Alternatively, a community power structure is a representation of selected patterns of the organization that produces the political decisions which determine the scope of government for a specific time period.

6a: Political roles in power structures include those of *political leaders* who have shared in political power by exercising political influence in at least the authoritative-consideration stage of a political decision-making process.

6b: *Authorities* are persons who are expected by others to be political leaders. *Formal* authorities hold governmental office. *Informal* authorities do not have governmental positions.

DEFINITION 7:   A *political regime* is a representation of the rules of political decision-making as understood by the citizens at large and as interpreted by the political leadership. Specifically, a regime refers to expectations about and the probable occurrence of effective illegitimate sanctions of some citizens by others in the event that political demands are pushed to the electoral process if necessary.

Political participation is action intended to affect the attitudes or actions of others in pursuing preferences for a certain scope of government.[11] The participant may be faced with someone who actively resists his demands, and he may take steps to weaken this opposition; or he may try to reinforce or change the disposition of someone who is friendly or receptive; or he may attempt to overcome another's inertia. In all three instances, the political participant intends to have some impact on the political action of another person. He may come face to face with a person he wishes to influence and use words and gestures, or he may remain at a distance and use more impersonal means of communication. He may communicate directly with those whose actions he intends to affect, or he may communicate indirectly through intermediaries. For example, a writer for the mass media or a commentator on television may be participating politically. These are simply special cases of interpersonal political participation.

An election is a special case of political participation, in which government officials are the people who are to be affected immediately and directly. The intended impact of participation on the scope of government may range from a specific shift in a particular program to a general objective, such as having good officials who will produce or preserve good government.

An act of political participation may have a strong or a weak impact on another's political attitudes or actions. Attitude changes may be temporary or enduring; they may lead to changes in overt behavior either immediately or in the long run; or they may have no such effect. To measure political participation, however, we must observe the participant and his acts, regardless of his impacts on others.

Political status may result from political participation, or it may result from nonpolitical acts. A person's political preferences concerning decisional matters may be known or imagined by others, accurately or inaccurately, whether or not he communicates his preferences.

Citizens who do not participate politically may be considered by politicians. The political status accorded them may be governed either by the hope that they will vote—or not vote—or otherwise participate politically in the future, or simply by the feeling that they are members of a community and deserve such political status.[12] Political status may be accorded to people as specific personalities or as anonymous members of such categories as "the citizens" or "the voters." Political status may be positive or negative; the recognition may be respectful or disrespectful.

The meaning of political status may be clarified by considering hypothetical examples of an industrialist and a labor union leader. A leading industrialist may be accorded political status by city councilmen, even though he is not active in politics. Government officials may sense, correctly or incorrectly, that the industrialist might become politically active in opposition to them if they proposed certain policies; for example, if they were to make a factory located in an adjacent suburb subject to municipal taxes by annexing that suburb to the city; if they were to raise property taxes considerably, affecting a plant inside the city; or if they failed to improve a municipal service such as the water supply when such an improvement was thought to be needed by an industry. City councilmen may sincerely respect the industrialist's views, if he has communicated them; or they may respect what they imagine are his views. The industrialist's actions and his economic position may have generated for him, in the minds of others, a political relevance that he neither intended nor perceived.

A labor union leader might also be accorded political status even if he were not participating politically. A desire to integrate him into the "general public" and make him a "responsible" member of the community may lead city officials to consider his known or presumed policy preferences. Or an earlier experience may have taught city councilmen that the labor union leader can get his following to the polls. On the other hand, they may regard his policy views negatively; they may reflect on them and act in opposition to them when making decisions. This is not often a primary consideration, but occasionally such motivation is found.

These illustrations suggest that in order to measure the political status of either a participant or a nonparticipant, we must also observe those who are taking his presumed policy perspectives into account and according him political status. A person's political status may vary not only over a period of time but also according to who acknowledges him.

Political influence focuses on the impacts that political participants have upon the political behavior of others. The actions of influential participants are, at least in part, politically inspired and are taken into account by those who are affected by these actions.

All acts are potential messages from the participant to individuals he wishes to influence, whether or not the participant so intends them, and whether or not the individual correctly receives the message. Significance may be attached to the words, gestures, tone of voice, or style of a participant. These meanings may depend upon who the participant is and what prior relationship individuals have established with him. The significance of an act may also depend on what other acts and messages these other individuals are receiving.

Attaching significance means minimally that an act reaches another who takes it into account. He may interpret the act in a way the participant did not intend, but to some degree, perhaps imperceptibly, his future actions are likely to be affected.[13] Political influence may be exercised directly, in a person-to-person relationship, or indirectly, through intermediaries.

In a receptive relationship, an act or set of acts may increase the likelihood that the individual will act as the participant desires. In a resistance relationship an act may even decrease the likelihood that another will act as the first individual desires. Or an act may even create some likelihood that an individual will act either positively or negatively where he might not have acted at all.

The term "political influence" is limited to acts intended by a political participant to affect someone else's political participation; these acts at least affect the other individual's attitudes, whether in the direction intended by the political participant or not. The participant's impact on the other individual's attitudes may or may not be successful in affecting the latter's overt actions. The impact may be too weak or it may be overcome by other impacts and factors. A single act of a political participant may influence some in one way, others in a different way, and still others not at all. An assessment of political influence requires, then, at least a double referent: the acts of a participant and the impacts of those acts on others.

The study of political influence relations, like individual psychology, needs extensive exploration if a science of political behavior is to be developed. The conditions surrounding the various impacts of political participation, the extent to which the acts of a political participant are accorded political status, and the kinds of political status accorded these acts constitute a virtually unexplored area of systematic political inquiry. The analysis of political decision-making in this book will treat selected aspects of political influence relations as a necessary part of the study of political power, even though much still needs to be learned about political influence *per se*.

Political participation, political status, and political influence relations are represented in Figure 2.1.

In this diagram, *A* is a political participant; *B* is a nonparticipant. *A* is not accorded political status by *C* but is by *D*, *E*, and *F*; *B* is accorded political status by *F* alone. *A* exercises political influence on *D*, *E*, and *F*, directly in the cases of *D* and *E* and indirectly through *E* on *F*, while *A* is attempting, unsuccessfully, to influence *C*.

Political power is an analytic construct referring to the actions of participants that collectively determine a decisional outcome. In any decision-making process, political power may be absent, even though there is political participation and political influence. Political power is accorded only to the contributors to an outcome in a decision-making process, unlike political participation, political status, or political influence, which are concepts that may be applied to people engaged in decisional processes or in quite general political criticisms or approbations. The distinction between decision-making and processes which affect the scope of government less directly can be difficult to discern. But a political decision-making process is not considered extant unless and until demands for some program or more particular shift in the scope of government become the subject of deliberation. Statements of general approval or discontent with a scope of government are *political participation* if they are intended to affect the political attitudes or actions of others, or *political influence* if they

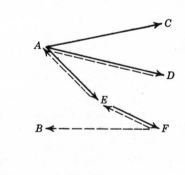

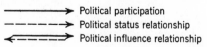

—————▶ Political participation
— — — —▶ Political status relationship
◀— — — —▶ Political influence relationship

FIGURE 2.1

actually result in the intended consequences. In themselves they are not components of a decision-making process nor can they qualify their makers for political power.

When political power exists, it is ordinarily ascribed or accorded to two or more people, unlike political participation, political status, and political influence. Although the latter are relational concepts, they are associated with individuals. Political power almost always belongs to a collectivity, that is, two or more persons, the only possible exception being absolute one-man rule, a situation that even the most totalitarian dictatorships cannot maintain for very long.

A political decisional outcome results from a joint effort in which each participant has a necessary but insufficient impact on others for a decision-making process to proceed through its cycle of stages. The situation resembles the building of a house: a completed house is the result of the joint efforts of architects, carpenters, electricians, and others. Political decision-making is a joint effort which may be marked by cooperation or conflict. Individuals and groups may align themselves against each other. Compromise, or one group's domination by another, may result in a completed house or in a stalemate; either outcome is a function of collective efforts.

The authoritative-consideration stage may vitally affect the contribution of a particular political act to a decisional outcome. When a political decisional outcome is at stake, all prior efforts may be for nothing if those in control of this stage of the process block the decision-making. A participant can exercise political influence when other individuals accord him political status in decision-making, regardless of decisional outcomes. Political power is assigned to participants only in the light of decisional outcomes and contributions thereto.

The owner of a newly built house may have to continue living under his old roof if his architect is dissatisfied with the new house. The city building department may refuse to issue a certificate of occupancy because it considers the new house unsafe or not compliant with the building code. If the decisional outcomes are whether or not the owner moves into his new house, the impact of the architect or city building inspector on the decisional outcome may be greater in this sense than the combined efforts of all the workmen. Similarly, a person may continue to live under an old law or ordinance if his efforts to get a new one are blocked by someone who prefers the existing law and can convert this preference into a decisional outcome.

Another house-building analogy may help to clarify this point, although analogies can be deceptive. Assume that an architect draws the plans for a house, and that workmen follow them closely and the house is built. It may be that, once a house has been built, a city building department feels it has little choice but to issue a certificate of occupancy. One might say, then, that if the decisional outcome is a completely built house with a certificate of occupancy, the architect has had a major role in contributing to the decisional outcome. The decisional outcome results from his plans and directions plus the work of the builder and his men.

The building department also has contributed, even though it may have felt constrained to act in just one way: to issue the certificate of occupancy. One could view the decisional outcome as a foregone conclusion by the time the city building department was faced with the demand for the certificate of occupancy. The issuance of the certificate may be regarded as the authoritative promulgation of an outcome determined by others, if the department had no freedom of action. The probability of an unexpected action may be greatly reduced but there is always some unpredictability where people have a choice. However, it may be best to assume that the building department acted within the authoritative-consideration stage, until the probabilities of such actions have been established empirically.

In reality, city building departments are usually in touch with architects and builders at various times during construction. The city building department, architect, and builder work together in the building process from the time the architect's plans are submitted to the department for a building permit to the final inspection to certify compliance with city ordinances. The decisional outcome is therefore a joint function to which the city officials, the architect, and the builder all contribute.

The next matter for consideration is "Who has power in a political decision-making or building process?" The question is not what effect the actions of participants have on other participants in either a building or decision-making process. The question is what effects the actions of participants have on decisional outcomes. If only two people participate and the actions of one person, as a direct consequence of the actions of another, constitute the decisional outcome, the answers to who has political influence over whom and who has political power are identical. If the actions of one person do not constitute the outcome, or if more than two people are involved, then political influence and political power do not belong solely to one person. The second question as to who has political power is ordinarily and properly asked of sets or groups of three or more people.

As Allen Drury remarks in his political novel, *Advise and Consent:*

In politics and the Senate, he was vividly aware, the shortest distance between two points is very often not a straight line. If you wish A to do something, for instance, you frequently are well advised to go to B, who knows him intimately, or even to C, who is an old pal of B, to start the wheels in motion. The matter of who asks who to do what often assumes a major importance; the whole future of a bill, the whole course of a committee action, the whole completion of a debate, can frequently be changed entirely by the personality of the man who sets it in motion . . .[14] *

In this scheme, if Y ("you") were successful in an effort to get A to act in a particular way, and Y first went to C who then went to B who in turn went to A, six sets of influence relations would exist: Y directly with C and indirectly with B and A; C directly with B and indirectly with A; and B directly with A. There is only one "unit" of political power shared by three or four people, depending on what the decisional outcome is considered to be. If the decisional outcome is A's completed act or the impact of his act—the outcome sought by Y and then C and B—then A is one of the participants and shares power with Y, C, and B. If the decisional outcome is the beginning of initiation of A's action, power would be shared by Y, C, and B only.

Because a number of people are usually involved in the building of houses and the making of decisions about the scope of government, exercising influence in the process does not necessarily lead to an impact on the outcome or end product. If a carpenter constructs part of a house, he may affect the actions of the electricians. In other words, the carpenter has a kind of status with the electrician in the sense that the electrician cannot ignore, and must take into account, the actions of the carpenter. The carpenter may have had no effective impact on the decisional outcome if for some reason the house is not completed, even though he has influenced his coworkers. Political power depends not only on a participant's political influence with other participants, but also on his position in a chain of events culminating in a decisional outcome. If the house is completed—the decisional outcome of interest here—as a result of such joint efforts, we would conclude that all who had a hand in the building process shared political power, even if they had different degrees of political influence and different political roles.

Everyone who exercises political influence to any degree contributes to the decision-making field of forces in a political system. This is implied by the view of political influence as political action which has some impact on another's attitude or action, no matter how imperceptible. An essential task in the study of political decision-making is to locate individuals either inside or outside political decision-making currents.

Using the house-building analogy again, one might ask whether a "sidewalk superintendent" is exercising political influence as he offers free and unsolicited advice to the workmen. If they disregard him, he, of course, has no status with them and consequently no influence. Some sidewalk superintendents may actually have an impact on a building process as a result of their actions. Comments of approval may reinforce the workmen's action; adverse criticism may bring an unnoticed problem to the attention of the workmen, and the sidewalk superintendent might, on occasion, receive the appreciation of the builder or owner.

Suppose that one bystander tells another that the excavation ought to be deeper. The second bystander agrees and joins the first in shouting directions to the foreman and the bulldozer operator. It has already been suggested that if such comments are completely ignored, a person has no influence. But what if such comments have an impact on a fellow spectator? Suppose, further, that their message is received by the foreman who agrees with them but is afraid to modify his action because he fears a superior's reprimand for deviating from the plans. One might say that such sidewalk superintendents are participants who are exercising political influence in the building process, but who lack direct or indirect access to the people who determine outcomes, in this case the foreman's superior.

People may lack access for a variety of reasons, such as fear of the consequences of action, ignorance, or a feeling of inefficacy. People may influence others effectively, but the influence may be dissipated; they may have no effect on decisional outcomes because they do not have access to those involved in the authoritative-consideration stage. Political influence does not necessarily lead to sharing in political power because the influence of some people is more effective in decision-making than that of others, and because even influential people may not have access to the organization of political support or the authoritative-consideration stage of a decision-making process. *A person may lack political power because he fails to acquire influence, because he lacks access, or because he suffers a decisional defeat.*

In this conceptual scheme, every decision-making process has, potentially, one unit of political power to be assigned analytically to the participants who contribute to the outcome in some degree. Accordingly, every participant who has contributed has performed a necessary although ordinarily insufficient task in the production of a decisional outcome. To continue the earlier analogy, if a completed house is taken as the decisional outcome of interest, it would be nonsense to ask whether the architect, the carpenter, or the painter has had more power in contributing to the outcome. The outcome is an indivisible whole; the carpenter's or painter's contribution is as necessary to the finished product as the architect's.[15]

For purposes of analysis, let us assign individuals "some" or "no" share in the unit of political power that accrues to the contributors to a political decisional outcome. If an individual is assigned some share in a unit of power, that share may be regarded as equal to another's share in the same unit. Each power-sharer is assigned the fraction that has a constant numerator of one and the denominator equal to the number of contributors to an outcome. We will not become involved here in the fundamental socio-political problem of allocation of values.[16] This analytic convention permits us to deal with power and its distribution in minimal quantitative terms.[17]

This is not to say that those who share in power may not be further categorized and compared according to the political roles they have performed in the decisional process of interest. *Political roles* are sets of acts defining a person's relationships in or to the political processes that determine the scope of government. Like traditional occupational roles, they may be defined in terms of many perspectives, such as the materials with which individuals work—in the political realm with speeches, paper, pencils, and legwork; in more commonplace occupational realms with nails, sketches, plans, paints, and brushes—the people with whom they interact and the interactional settings—subordinates, superordinates, peers, small groups, masses of people. The basic referent here is an individual's behavior in the process of making decisions. Of special interest in the present study are those who share in power in roles of political leadership. But since role behaviors may be described in numerous ways and relationships in decision-making are complex, a statement of a political role can be only partial, never exhaustive.

The attribution of a share in political power may be accompanied by a description of the decisional outcome, or of the aspects of the scope of government affected by the outcome, in terms of the social-psychological symbols and meanings attached to them by citizens or by the analyst himself. The problems of comparability that are posed when citizens acquire shares in different units of political power—that is, in different decisional processes—are treated more fully in the following chapter. At this point we may say that estimates may be made of the extent to which citizens share in the units of power assigned to a set of decisional outcomes. This is regardless of whether the processes concern specifically identical aspects of the scope of government; regardless of differences in dollar costs or other terms implicated in different outcomes; and regardless of whether one person's share in a unit of political power is $\frac{1}{2}$ while another's is $\frac{1}{10,000}$.[18] Although political decisions are conceived to be commensurable, this does not preclude the categorization and comparisons of people's political power in these and other ways.

It has already been said that while political power is reserved to processes of political decision-making, not all such decisional processes are assigned a unit of political power to be distributed analytically among those who contribute to the outcome. A decision-making process or a house-building process may occur in which, at some point (Time M), a partially finished product may exist, even though it has not yet replaced the earlier one. If the reason for this incomplete accomplishment is effective opposition or resistance by others, it may be concluded that those others share the political power accorded those who have retained the prior policy, or already existing house, as the decisional outcome at Time M.

Suppose, though, that there has not been opposition but simply an inability to reach those people needed to overturn an existing decision. If the possible resistance or inertia of these people were not overcome because they were not reached or contacted, the earlier decision would, in effect, be reaffirmed. This would not be because the others were participating politically—that is, acting uncooperatively by intent —but because those trying to select a new policy did not have access to them. The lack of access does not mean that the inaccessible people have had power; it means that participants exercising influence constitute an insufficient pressure to create a decisional outcome. Hence the question of who shares in political power might be answered "no one." Political power is not invoked by an analyst unless and until a decisional process has proceeded to either a shift in the scope of government or purposeful maintenance of the scope of government despite demands to shift it.

Compromises in political decision-making processes may characterize particular decisional outcomes. Political power is a construct assigned to people on the basis of their impacts on or contributions to outcomes and on the basis of their purposes or intentions. A compromise may mean that those with certain decisional preferences are only partially satisfied. Or it may mean satisfaction of short-term preferences at the expense of long-term preferences. As long as a contributor to a compromise outcome is minimally satisfied with the compromise, he deserves to be accorded a share in the unit of political power.

The analyst must set the point of minimal satisfaction in order to make at least some people eligible for the assignment of the unit of political power. There will be marginal cases, but if a person feels that a compromise is utterly undesirable, it would be contrary to our social-psychological conceptions of political participation and political power to award him a share of the power.[19]

POLITICAL POWER, THE TIME OF OUTCOMES, AND LEADERSHIP

The last point to be made about the model of a decisional process is: since it must be bounded not only spatially but also temporally, the decisional outcome and the authoritative-consideration stage are functions of the analyst's time of observation and measurement. This is a complex, fundamental point, since it may drastically affect the apportionment of political power. An analyst may observe at a moment in time (Time M) a selected set of decision-making processes that had been extant at an earlier specified point of time (Time E) in order to assess the distribution of political power in a community. He may find that some processes have been settled once and for all, that some have been settled temporarily, and that some have not been settled at all and are still at issue. He may find, in other words, that the permanence of the outcomes of decisional processes vary. But assessments of the distributions of political power must be specific with regard to a particular period of time, in this case Time E to M. Because some decisional processes may come into existence during a period of time while others may disappear, the total number of units of political power to be distributed is itself a variable through time. The description of a power structure is a statement of patterns of power relations for a given time period. Both the power relations and description of the structure may shift over time. In other words, the extent to which a power structure is stable or unstable, static or changing, is problematic. This is a matter for systematic inquiry by the analyst interested in the dynamics of power relations.[20]

These conceptions require the analyst to take as decisional outcomes the situation existing at Time M as compared to the originally observed scope of government. If a group of people have been making demands for a shift in the scope of government but have been effectively thwarted by others to Time M, it is those others who share in the unit of political power that the analyst ascribes to the "makers" of this decision. Perhaps the day or week after the analyst made his observations of outcomes, at Time $M + 1$, the active proponents of a shift in the scope of government will overcome the resistance. The decisional outcome thus changes, and the active proponents now share in the political power. But this means a redistribution of political power; it does not mean that the resisters did not deserve to be accorded the political power that the analyst assigned to them as the ones responsible for the decisional outcome of the process during Time E to M.[21]

In this hypothetical example, the analyst must decide when the authoritative consideration stage existed, during Time E to M, in order to identify the political leaders in this process at that time. The political leaders were those who actively resisted the proposed shift in the scope of government immediately prior to Time M; presumably they had some freedom of action to resist or not resist the decisional demands, and shared the political power with any other nonleader participants who may have contributed to the resistance at earlier points in that particular time period.

Political leaders are political participants who have contributed to a decisional outcome and hence are accorded a share in political power, and, moreover, who contributed in at least the authoritative-consideration stage of a decisional process. Thus, the political leadership may also change over time if people are added to the group, if some people are replaced by others, or if the political actions of a personally identical set of political leaders change. A completely new set of political leaders may have emerged during Time M to $M + 1$ with the aforementioned shift in decisional outcome.

Thus the picture of the power structure that emerges from such an analysis is very much affected by the set of decision-making processes selected for assessing the distribution of political power. The identification of political leaders also results from the selection of decisional processes, and the specification of the authoritative-consideration stage is partially a function of the decisional outcomes observed to the time of measurement. Detailed operational definitions and careful analytic procedures are required for comparative studies of power structures across communities for a given time period, or within communities over two or more time periods.

A *community power structure* consists of selected aspects of political power relations over a particular period of time. It refers to the patterns of organization of a community's political decision-making as political power is "produced," "distributed," and "consumed" in the course of shifting or maintaining the scope of government with its associated benefits and costs. This discussion of political decisional outcomes has used the words "product" and "production," as well as the analogy between house construction and the political decision-making process. The implication that political decision-making, like institutions of government and business or specific government bodies and agencies and business firms, is organized to produce outputs—outcomes—was intentional. Since the conceptions of community power structure and regime play such an important part in this study, they now will be explained in greater detail.

NOTES

1. For example, an analyst may see a major national corporation as part of government, even though it does not allocate values in a society with any significant degree of legitimate governmental authority. Political participation then could include actions directed to those quasi-governmental units. Still another view is that all human groups, no matter how small, have governments, at least under some conditions. Political theory ultimately should be extended to all kinds of political systems and subsystems wherever they are located—obviously to the nation-state and to the international arena, but also to the family and friendship group. For an illuminating treatment of families as political systems and the elaboration of a family decision-making model, see Robert S. Cahill, "Television in Family Politics: A Study of the Family as a Political System" (unpublished doctoral dissertation, Department of Political Science, University of Oregon, 1962). A little-appreciated but major issue between students of community power structures is whether research should concentrate on decisions of public government or on decisions of community-wide institutions, including business and industry. See Thomas J. Anton, "Power, Pluralism, and Local Politics," *Administrative Science Quarterly*, Vol. 7, No. 4 (March 1963), pp. 425–457; Letters to the Editor by Robert A. Dahl and Thomas J. Anton, *Administrative Science Quarterly* (forthcoming, December 1963), pp. 250–268 (especially pp. 254–255 and 264–266). While sympathetic to those who urge research on decisions involving "life chances" of people in any institutional arena, our conceptual framework is based on a strategy of first trying to understand the patterns and consequences of decision-making in the social-psychological realm of public government and something of the relationships between that and other community-wide decisional domains. This is not to argue that a strategy of conceptualizing the community power structure relative to a complex of community-wide institutional decision-making structures is either inappropriate or should not be attempted by other analysts as their first step. It is urgently needed.
2. Other stages of decision-making have been proposed by: Edgar Furniss and Richard Snyder, *American Foreign Policy: Formulation, Principles, and Programs* (New York: Rinehart & Company, Inc., 1954), p. 97; and Harold D. Lasswell, *Decision Process: Seven Categories of Functional Analysis* (College Park, Maryland: University of Maryland Press, 1956).

3. Acts intended to influence others by creating or reinforcing satisfaction with an existing scope of government are not treated as demands and, hence, are not by themselves components of decision-making processes. On the other hand, such demands may be seen as part of a special category of "general" decision-making processes.

4. An analyst, alternatively, may maintain that neither political power nor a political decision-making process exists until an authoritative-consideration stage has been reached.

5. There have been few systematic studies of political role specialization. However, Alexander Heard's study, *The Costs of Democracy* (Chapel Hill: The University of North Carolina Press, 1960) discusses the role of solicitors of money in politics; for a study of legislative roles, see John C. Wahlke *et al.*, *The Legislative System* (John Wiley and Sons, Inc.: New York, 1962). See also Lester W. Milbrath and Walter W. Klein, "Personality Correlates of Political Participation," *Acta Sociologica*, Vol. 6, fasc. 1–2 (Copenhagen, 1962), pp. 53–66.

6. Under many conditions of modern political life, the constituent variables may cluster together. The degree to which decisional processes are regarded by participants as (variable 1) routine, as (variable 2) implementations of earlier decisions, as (variable 3) implicating relatively minor values, as (variable 4) directly affecting relatively few people, as (variable 5) subject primarily to technical criteria of choice among alternatives, and as (variable 6) properly "decided" by experts generally may be seen as congruent. However, as one example of another possible pattern, some decisional processes may be regarded as relatively routine but involving major values of many people. It might be fruitful to develop more complex multidimensional schemes for the classification of decisional processes rather than simply viewing them as on a single administrative-political dimension.

7. Anthropologist Radcliffe-Brown commented that "there is no organized government in an Andamanese village." His own description of decision-making there, e.g., directing hunts for food, and the importance of that activity to the marginally subsistent Andaman Islanders would seem to make such decisions of sufficient importance to them to warrant classifying these as among the major political decisions of that society. A. R. Radcliffe-Brown, *The Andaman Islanders* (Cambridge: The University Press, 1933), pp. 44, 47.

8. Since the political decisions in this study were chosen on the basis of how important selected sets of citizens felt them to be, the operational definition of the term "political decision" accorded with these conceptions and thus excluded administrative decisions from those upon which the classification of power structures is based. Among the problems precluded from systematic analysis in this study are those that include relationships between and changes in citizen definitions of political and administrative decision-making as we define them.

9. One man in a policy-formulation stage may make a myriad of decisions in the process of arriving, for example, at a policy demand. Analyses in depth of decision-making processes will arrive ultimately at the molecular, if not the subatomic, level, in contrast to the molar level at which these preliminary analyses of politics must be made. This holds for studies of both the individual's decision-making psychology and the relationships among men in making political decisions.

10. The following concepts and others used in this study are defined operationally in Appendix A. For a useful review of approaches to, and the literature on, the study of community decision-making, see Peter H. Rossi, "Community Decision-Making," in *Approaches to the Study of Politics* (Evanston, Illinois: Northwestern University Press, 1958), pp. 362–382.

11. This definition is commonly accepted, but the element of intention needs to be stressed in order to avoid classifying all human activity as "political," that is, dealing with the scope of government. See Dahl's discussion of "political man," *Who Governs?* (New Haven: Yale University Press, 1961), p. 225.

12. Political status as defined here is similar to what Dahl has called "indirect influence." He suggests that government officials may go to great lengths to adapt their policies to what they correctly or incorrectly believe are the preferences of individuals, constituents, or "the citizens" in general. Dahl, *op. cit.,* pp. 101–102.

13. This conception of political influence accords with Robert Merton's definition of "interpersonal influence," although our conception also encompasses indirect interaction. See "Patterns of Influence," in *Communications Research 1948–1949*, ed. by P. F. Lazarsfeld and F. N. Stanton (New York: Harper & Brothers, 1949), p. 215. It also is consistent with James March's probabilistic notion of influence in his "An Introduction to the Theory and Measurement of Influence," *The American Political Science Review*, Vol. 49 (June 1955), pp. 413–451. What we call political influence Robert A. Dahl terms "power." See his "The Concept of Power," *Behavioral Science*, Vol. 3 (July 1957), pp. 201–215.

14. Allen Drury, *Advise and Consent* (Garden City: Doubleday and Co., 1959), p. 317.

15. The conception of power as distinct from influence has not been formulated precisely this way in the literature. For example, Harold D. Lasswell and Abraham Kaplan's definition of power as one type of influence does not conflict with our definition, but neither does it convey exactly what we mean. They define power as "participation in the making of decisions"; in defining a decision as a policy involving severe sanctions, they say that a decision involves "effective determination of policy" and that participants in decision-making are those "whose acts do in fact matter." They also maintain that "those whose acts are affected also participate in decision-making: by conformity or disregard of the policy they help determine whether it is or is not in fact a decision." We would prefer to view such behavior as ordinarily, but not necessarily, post-outcome behavior, within a stage of policy effectuation or administrative decision-making, or possibly the beginnings of another political decisional process. And since motivation or ends in view are important in our conceptual scheme, the perspectives of "those whose acts are affected" in conforming or disobeying would be important data for us. However, Lasswell and Kaplan's emphasis on decision-making and the more general exercise of power as "affecting *policies* of others than the self" was an important cue for the conceptualization of power as we have defined it. *Power and Society* (New Haven: Yale University Press, 1950), pp. 74–75.

16. This problem, in brief, is that the values created by a collective decisional outcome, whether they are material goods and services, public order and safety, or the perquisites of public office or performance of political roles,

must be distributed according to some set of ethical principles, whether individualistic or egalitarian, according to temporal priority or its opposite, etc.

17. Quantitative analysis of all variables is not necessary in scientific research. In our study we have not attempted to go beyond the crudest approximations of sharing in, or distributions of, political power.

18. Assigning one unit of power to each decisional outcome obviously is not the only way to proceed. The political decisions selected for analysis in the present study are all within a category of decisions perceived to be more important than others to selected sets of citizens. This makes the equal assignment of one unit to each decision not entirely unreasonable.

Although they fail to differentiate power from influence, analysts such as Wolfinger and Dahl stress that there ought to be "power comparability" when assessments are made about the influence of people involved in different "scopes," that is, categories of actions subject to the requirements of the decision or policy in point. In an analysis that is critical of power comparisons, Wolfinger says that the major scope of a school superintendent's power is public education. He says there is no way to compare the impact of two powerful men who are influential in different scopes—for example, in school affairs and in urban renewal. However, if it could be assumed that the two scopes were comparable, the judgment could be that the two men possessed equal power. Even if they were not comparable, a partial ordering might indicate that the men were more powerful than those who had no power in either scope. Since individuals as well as decisions have a multiplicity of values, urban renewal may be conceived as being itself or influencing a program of public education, just as school affairs may be conceived as a component of urban living and renewal. The easy assumption that collections of apparently common choices may be readily identified as scopes, areas, categories, or subjects, and then treated separately, raises as many questions as the assumption that scopes are somehow equivalent. Dahl poses an apparently tougher problem with a question about the comparability of decisions involving making students come to class for an examination on a Friday afternoon and police department enforcement of parking regulations. Yet Dahl himself, in "The Concept of Power," gives the only possible answer to his own question: "The particular definition one chooses will evidently have to emerge from considerations of the substance and objectives of a specific piece of research, and not from general theoretical considerations." Concerning the comparability of decisions on tax legislation in the British House of Commons and in the United States Senate, he says, "Some kinds of comparisons will seem more artificial than others. But these are criteria derived from theoretical and empirical considerations, independent of the fundamental meaning of the term 'power.'"

Besides that comparability of the political decisions selected for study herein because of their perceived general importance, they are treated as commensurable because the scope of government is considered to be a set of actions or functions that consists of multiple subsets of overlapping and interpenetrating actions. The emphasis herein is not on distinctions between subsets, or "subscopes," but on their similarities, although we are aware of the risks of robbing the inquiry of much of its potential richness and producing results of limited theoretical significance. These criticisms have been levied by Robert A. Dahl against Floyd Hunter's study of Regional City.

We submit that it is better research strategy to run such risks than to encounter their opposites, that is, producing through research overwhelming amounts of detail based on differentiations that mitigate against generalization and theory-building. See Robert A. Dahl, "The Concept of Power," *op. cit.,* p. 206.

19. Although the present study had little occasion to make precise assessments of such satisfactions, there were instances of power not being accorded to a political participant—among the potential political leaders, for example—because the "minimal satisfaction" criterion was not met. Typically, there were instances of respondents' reporting being "dissatisfied" with a particular decisional outcome, whether or not the outcome represented a compromise. It would seem that simple satisfaction-dissatisfaction scales could be developed for this purpose. Or, an analyst might want to assign power in such a way as to ignore this matter of satisfaction; intention and impact of action relative to decisional outcomes might provide a satisfactory operational definition.

20. Those who use a power-attribution or reputational method and those who use analyses of decision-making to establish the dimensions and outline of a community power structure recognize, at least abstractly, that distributions of power are inherently changeable over time; but most of their analyses of power-structure changes have tended to be historical rather than "experimental," that is, analyses of what happened in the recent past rather than what happens after an initial empirical investigation is completed. Assuming the validity of reports that certain citizens are powerful "today" or were powerful yesterday, last week, or last month, whether the evidence has been derived from focused interviews and continuing observations of a current period of decision-making or not, the further assumption that those citizens will be able to retain their relative power positions tomorrow or thereafter may be reasonable. But one of the important tasks of research is to test this assumption, how long and the degree to which it may be the case and the conditions under which it may not be the case. For an historical analysis of decisions that did identify a general change in the pattern of decision-making, in an aspect of the power structure, see Roscoe C. Martin, Frank J. Munger, *et al., Decisions in Syracuse* (Bloomington: Indiana University Press, 1961), especially p. 306.

21. Richard C. Snyder, H. W. Bruck, and Burton Sapin are properly concerned with the time element and the specificity of objectives in delineating decisional units. However, it is not clear whether they take a different position from most analysts in regarding decisional outcomes as events that occur only at particular moments in time, events that the analyst may have to wait for, rather than assuming, as we do here, that outcomes must be specified by an analyst at a point in time selected by him, and may sometimes change at successive points in time. See their *Decision-Making as an Approach to the Study of International Politics* (Princeton: Foreign Policy Analysis Series No. 3, 1954).

3

COMMUNITY POWER
STRUCTURES AND REGIMES

In this chapter, we shall elaborate upon the meanings of community power structure and regime and develop typologies of each. We also shall discuss various classificatory considerations because of their theoretical importance. Our ultimate aim is to label the four communities of this study according to their power structures and regimes as of Time E to M, the period that ended when the full-scale sample surveys were first conducted in each city; and as of the other time periods from the end of the Second World War to 1961.

A community power structure's major activities as it functions as an organization are making political decisions that determine the scope of government. Members of this organization include all citizens in the community, even though some may be permanently or temporarily inactive. On occasion the organization may be dormant and political decision-making momentarily absent. Actually, the substance of the organization consists of the day-to-day political relations of the people who compose it. The community power structure represents power relations that have produced the past interactions, interrelations, and the functions of the parts and of the whole.

A *structural* picture is like a snapshot portraying relationships as they existed at the moment the shutter was tripped; a *functional* picture resembles a movie made over a period of time. Actually, the snapshot or structural picture is meaningful only if something is known about the previous action of the elements in the picture. A snapshot of an automobile engine would be meaningless unless one possessed information about the functioning of the engine and its component parts. A snapshot of the human circulatory system would be meaningless without knowledge of the direction of blood flow or the interaction of the heart muscles in the functioning of that system; at least, it would have a very different meaning without such knowledge.

Therefore, a community power structure represents, in a static fashion, some of the many patterns of earlier dynamic power relations between people.[1] Patterns are sets or sequences of events which may be described in a variety of ways by an analyst. A particular pattern may or may not have a high probability of repetition in succeeding time periods. From moment to moment within time periods, events have patterns that range from random to nonrandom. At any particular moment possible patterns might include a small or a large proportion of events. There is no one "real" pattern. The number of possible patterns is bounded only by the imagination of the analyst. They must ultimately be assessed in terms of asserted theoretical utility—that is, the types of patterns to be described and compared must be justified or criticized on the basis of their presumed usefulness for maximizing understanding of phenomena, whether these phenomena relate to the world of political power or to subatomic relations.

The term "organization" as it is used here is intended to denote repetitiveness and relative stability in the patterns of power relations over a period of time. This is not to suggest that a particular degree of repetitiveness or a particular level of stability is the norm in making political decisions. However, the word "organization" is used to indicate that ordinarily there were some nonrandom relationships in political decision-making. If all aspects of political power relations were random and unpredictable, the power structure would be completely disorganized. This would amount to anarchy, a situation that is theoretically conceivable but extraordinary in the real world. Generally, random patterns exist within nonrandom patterns of a community's power structure.

Political leaders are analogous to the managers in a business organization. The managers of the firm are the men who contribute to manufacturing a product by exercising influence in the stages of production where important choices exist that shape the character of the final product. Thus, an economic production process may be thought of as a set of decision-making processes: one process may relate to the initiation of production, including product specifications; another may be the process of deciding upon the rules for accepting or rejecting an output as a satisfactorily completed, marketable product. Men may specialize in managerial roles, or their managerial facility may be restricted to one or another process. Some may serve in general managerial capacities in the organization.

A group of political leaders or political managers may have a few or many rivals. Managerial rivals could be either new aspirants seeking to enter the ranks of the political leaders for the first time or a group of rivals whom the present managers have replaced. It also is possible that political leaders are the sole possessors of political power because they are the only people who can influence decision-making. In business terms, they may be a group of self-employed people without any employees. Or, to continue the business analogy, they may be heads of a large organization, overwhelmingly outnumbered by the nonmanagerial staff. In such processes as contributing to the quality of a product, the authoritative-consideration stage could extend over the whole production process, thereby distributing managerial roles throughout the firm, from titled executives, through designers, to workers on the assembly line. This could also be the case with community power structures.

A community's political decision-making organization may have a nonmanagerial working force as do most business organizations. The formal organizational chart and the formal lines of authority cannot be taken at face value in analyses of the way a business organization functions. Nor can the formal constitution of the community be taken as an accurate representation of the community's power structure. It may be assumed that constitutions are less a series of "must" —obligatory—statements than a series of "may" or "ought"—permissive or hortatory—statements. Constitutions do require government officials to make the formal authoritative promulgations, to serve as the organization's spokesmen, under specified conditions. But constitutions do not require government officials to be the leaders in political decision-making. When decisions are made, whether or not they require authoritative promulgation to the citizens at large, the extent to which private citizens or government officials are the exclusive or contributory political leaders is a matter for empirical inquiry.

The community power structure also encompasses less inclusive political organizations. Some of these are formally organized in such a way that their charters stipulate their concern with the scope of government. Others are in fact political groups which are organized manifestly for economic, social, or civic purposes, but are used with some frequency by a proportion of their membership for political purposes.[2] Thus, there are groups of political leaders in the formal and informal subsidiary political organizations within the encompassing community political organization. These lesser political leaders are the members of each organization who have managerial roles in determining decisional outcomes of their own organization. Thus, individuals who are leaders of subsidiary political organizations or groups within the community are not always leaders of the community power structure. It cannot be assumed that the community's formal constitution designates the offices to be held by the political leaders of the polity. It is not necessarily valid to conclude that the most powerful people in a component political organization are also among the most powerful political leaders of the larger, encompassing organization. But political leaders of the community power structure actually may be political leaders of the less inclusive, subsidiary political organizations. These are empirical questions whose answers may be shaped by the formal constitutional system but which are decided by *real politik*.

The active members of the community power structure may or may not be aware of the existence and nature of the structure as an analytic conception. Awareness of organizational dimensions is generally clearer within families or firms than in community power structures; such factors as relatively small size and the explicit specification of central tasks in corporate charters, employment and marriage contracts, contribute to awareness. Families and firms may have more initial consensus on their primary tasks than the community power structure. Consensus, however, is a matter of degree. Members of large business organizations that have extensive division of labor may not agree on the purposes and scope of the organization. Consensus in the family can be disrupted by a variety of factors, and it is not unknown for family members to grow so distant from each other that only an analyst sees how the members function as an organization. It is also possible that a community power structure is ruled by a few men—a company town, for example—whose images of political purposes are as self-conscious and as much in consensus as those of some families or firms. This also is an empirical matter. Although these analogies must not be pushed too far, many of the processes in firms and families that need to be explained are similar to processes that need explaining when the power structure in a community is viewed in comparable organizational terms. Theory-building in regard to community political systems as well as so-called administrative behavior would profit, we suspect, from a frame of reference that views all human groups as organizations as well as from the perspective that all organizations have political systems of one kind or another.

FOUR TYPES OF POWER STRUCTURES

The conception of a community power structure as a functioning organization has led to a typology of power structures based on two variables: the extent to which political power is distributed broadly or narrowly over the citizenry, and the extent to which the ideology of the political leadership is convergent and compatible or divergent and conflicting.[3] By dichotomizing each variable, four types of power structure are delineated.

The typology indicates that if only one political leadership group shared a single ideology, the power structure would be consensual, whether mass or elite.[4] There may be two or more political leadership groups, whose ideologies could be either compatible or conflicting. An example of a condition of compatible ideologies would be two sets of political leaders representing different socio-economic interests but agreeing on a compromise-bargaining-trading perspective; an example of a conflicting-ideology condition would be two sets of political leaders who had such firm emotional commitments to an overall program for the scope of government relating to all areas of life that the loss of a single decisional battle or the prospect of compromise would be almost intolerable.[5] These conditions are based on the findings in the four communities, findings we would expect in communities throughout the United States. But if communities in nations marked by more violent ideological conflict were compared with these American communities, the American communities might all have to be classified as consensual in character rather than competitive.

This simple typology of power structures raises several points. As one example, the competitive-consensual dimension is based upon the

Political leadership's ideology	Distribution of political power among citizens	
	Broad	Narrow
Convergent	Consensual Mass	Consensual Elite
Divergent	Competitive Mass	Competitive Elite

FIGURE 3.1 *Types of power structures.*

state of ideology in the groups that have attained positions of political leadership in a power structure. However, two Consensual Elite structures may differ in the extent to which there are groups of people aspiring to enter the leadership. One may face no outside challenge; another may have to face a group that has been actively aspiring to take over leadership without success. Such differences are noted if they occur.

As another example of a point suggested by this typology, the broad-narrow power dimension raises the question of the extent of overlap between the leadership and the rank and file. As has already been indicated, political leaders may comprise a small proportion of or be the entire working force in a community power structure. Power structures that are classified as mass in character might still have a minority of citizens sharing in power, although the minority would be larger than that of elite power structures. This also is an empirical question. Nor does this typology as it stands provide for classifying power structures according to the extent to which there are decisional conflicts with "winners" and "losers." A politics of personal or group interests theoretically may produce as intense a conflict as that of competing ideologies. Interest groups may be competing politically at the same time that ideological consensus exists at the leadership level of the power structure. Political participation may be high and political power broadly distributed whether there is a single ideology or convergent ideologies represented at the leadership level of the power structure. This is one reason for positing the possibility of a Consensual Mass power structure.[6]

The criteria used to classify a community power structure should be made explicit. For example, the problem of estimating and comparing distribution of political power among citizens in such a way that a community power structure can be classified as mass or elite depends directly upon the decisional processes selected for making the estimates. If one decision that has brought shares in political power to many citizens is overlooked, the distribution of power may be underestimated. We made our assessments from those decisions that a widely representative panel of officials of the communities' formally organized voluntary associations regarded as very important. These decisions will obviously differ from community to community in number and character. The specific political decisions that have emerged in each community and the sense of importance they evoke from the citizens are both relevant to the classification of power structure types. With the exceptions of school desegregation and school consolidation, decisions that were concerned with the functioning of the public schools were excluded from consideration, because we purposely phrased questions to elicit responses about decisions involving municipal government.[7] Otherwise the decisions in each community come from a variety of scope areas and are classified under one or more of the general categories of local government decisions: economic, social, governmental reorganization, or civic improvement. To classify power structures by type we must compare the distribution of power among citizens in each set of selected decisional processes that took place in a specific time period. The assessment of broad or narrow distribution of power is not specific to subdomains or subsets of decisions.[8]

The distribution of political power may vary from decisional process to decisional process within a community during a given time period. We classified a community power structure as mass to the extent that the distribution of power was broader in one or more decisional processes of the selected set than it was for any of the processes in another community.[9] In those communities classified as having mass power structures, there were ordinarily narrow or elite distributions of political power in most decisional processes. But the central interest here is in the gross differences in patterns of such distribution from community to community.

As with the other classificatory variables to be discussed, the categories used to define the power structure emerged from an interplay of theoretical interests and the actual comparisons of the four communities. The degree of ideological convergence or divergence of leadership and the degree to which power is distributed broadly or narrowly among the citizens are relative matters that depend on the comparison of real situations, rather than upon an arbitrary yardstick.[10] If communities vary slightly on either count the use of different classificatory terms could lead a reader to focus on insignificant differences. Generally, however, the differences observed are sufficiently large to obviate this danger. For example, if we compared one of the four research communities to a power structure in still another community, our Competitive Mass power structures might be classified as Consensual Elite structures, thereby eliminating this basis of comparison among the original four. Rather than use categories with values fixed in an *a priori* fashion that would have masked important differences between and among the four research communities, we decided to use relative standards in classifying power structures.

The typology of power structures touches upon several issues which are current among students of community politics. A portion of the literature on community power structures suggests that in many American communities the norm is the power structure that we call Consensual Mass. Some studies have reported that political-interest-group competition stimulated political participation—that is, of a substantial minority of citizens. Interest-group competition also is supposed to result in a dilution of ideological perspectives and frequent compromises, as well as in victories and defeats for the constituent groups among the political leaders. The extent to which and the conditions under which a Consensual Mass power structure exists or emerges is one of the important empirical questions in this study.

Other analysts report that they have found what we would call Consensual Elite power structures: one interest group rules and very few citizens participate in the making of the most important political decisions. Consensual Elite power structures have been called "power elite" or "ruling elite" systems; Consensual Mass power structures have been termed "pluralistic" systems. Obviously what is found depends on the operational definitions, the classificatory procedures, and the categories used. Those who have discovered pluralistic systems have charged that research that has found power elite structures is in the nature of a self-fulfilling prophecy.[11] The difficulties result, they say, from having observed only the reputedly powerful in action, without even having attempted to reconstruct carefully the political decision-making process in which the "elite" presumably have acquired their power. Also, the political activities of the citizens at large are not systematically observed. However, the "pluralists" are equally open to criticism. They have neither examined the ideology of the leadership nor used comparative studies to actually assess the relative degree of "massness" or "eliteness" in the distribution of political power. Thus, nobody as yet has explored the real world of American community politics to see the extent to which the four power structure types that we have outlined have empirical counterparts.[12]

The number of political leaders who are government officials is also an issue among students of community politics. Pluralists take the position, specifically or implicitly, that there are more government officials than private citizens among political leaders, and that government officials tend to be the key political leaders, particularly if they are elected rather than appointed. Major decisional options are not shaped by an influential ruling elite so much as they are by "technical" factors which, assuming there is a desire for "functional rationality," would lead rational men to similar choice situations or decisional outcomes, regardless of socio-economic class or official position. Those who have found a "power elite" take the opposite point of view. They argue that government officials are "second level" or "secondary" leaders; that government officials act as agents or servants of the "top" leaders, who may play their leadership roles from behind the scenes. The response to the pluralist rationality position might well be that it stresses technical constraints on human values and choices unnecessarily; that it may not be valid for all decisions; and that it takes too much for granted.[13]

This controversy rests partially upon an unstated difference of opinion regarding how political status is distributed. The pluralists argue that elective officials accord political status to the eligible electorate—what has been termed "indirect influence"—because they need to cater to voter preferences; this distribution of political status makes a "power elite" or Consensual Elite power structure suspect. This would not affect our classification of power structures even if empirical findings affirmed such patterns. Power structures, as we use the concept, specify the relations of people as political decisions are made and units of political power, rather than political status, are produced and distributed.

The distribution of political status also might provide insight into the dynamics of political systems; it could be built into a typology of power structures and used to distinguish particular types of power structures from one another. Thus, even a Consensual Elite power structure could exist in a "polyarchy," the term given by Dahl and Lindblom to polities characterized by government officials' according citizens a relatively high degree of political status.[14]

One other disagreement between pluralists and power elite proponents needs to be noted. Pluralists have characterized the power elite view as one that assumes the political primacy or exclusiveness of the upper class: the key political leaders have or attain similar social and/or economic class backgrounds and serve relatively narrow class interests in their decision-making. Government officials presumably also represent the interests of such an "elite." Pluralists argue—on the basis both of faith and of what they have reportedly found in some communities—that diverse socio-economic, ethnic, and racial groups are represented in the political decision-making of American community power structures, and that government officials represent the general and/or diverse special interests but not such a class interest. Some pluralists go on to argue that even when the socio-economic class positions of decision-makers are similar, the political interests of members of the same class tend to be different.[15] We will examine the extent to which various socio-economic classes are represented, and how, in political decision-making as the power structures are studied.

The theory-builder is constantly faced with the question of which dimensions he should combine with others to produce typologies, and which dimensions might be related to one or another classificatory type. In studying the power structures of community political systems, we have decided to restrict the major power-structure typology to two dimensions, in the interest of simplicity of presentation and because we have so few research communities. We shall be dealing unsystematically with other dimensions as we study these simple types of power structures and their changes over time. We shall now try to clarify the general power structure model, of which we have four types, by examining in abstract terms the place of elections in this analytic scheme.

POWER STRUCTURES: ELECTIONS

According to our conception of political leadership, the voters in the majority could be regarded as among the political leaders of the power structure. Citizens' votes on measures, when special elections are held, usually occur immediately prior to the decisional outcome. They result in the selection of one of the choices—usually two—on the ballot: approval of a demand for change in the scope of government, or rejection of that demand and a decision to maintain a particular scope of government. There is always an election—that is, making a choice between or among two or more outcomes—in the authoritative-consideration stage of the making of any political decision. When the choice is to be made by those citizens eligible to participate in municipal elections, a special case of such choice-making exists.

Decisional processes involving a citizen ballot are composed of at least two processes, each of which has an authoritative-consideration stage: one is the process of choosing outcomes for the ballot; the second is the selection of one outcome by the citizens as voters. The attempts that are made, between the time the measure is selected to be put on a ballot and election day, to persuade a citizen to vote for or against a ballot measure may be considered a third process. Thus, there are at least two or three sets of political leaders instead of one. We shall identify and analyze the behavior of only those political leaders in each community's power structure who are influential enough to be included in at least the authoritative-consideration stage preceding election day. This analytic decision rests on a differentiation of political-leader roles: citizens who are political leaders because they vote on election day are distinguished from citizens who are active political leaders. This distinction is made on the basis of the difference in their relationship to the political process that determines the scope of government.[16]

Determining whether the distribution of political power among the citizens is broad or narrow encompasses the contributions that citizens may make to decisional outcomes as participants in formal community-wide elections. Special attention is paid to how many citizens participate in selecting outcomes in formal elections open to all eligible citizens. Informal quasi-elections in which substantial segments of the citizens or the community at large may express a decisional preference without entering a voting booth are considered as well. Because we do not have systematic data on the voting behavior of citizens in every decisional process that involved informal or formal citizen elections, we constructed an index of political participation based on actions other than actually casting ballots. Our index of political influence is, in turn, based on this political-participation index. Since political participation includes discussion, attending meetings, and taking more active parts in decision-making, the index, when considered along with what took place in the authoritative-consideration stages, produces a fairly accurate picture of the distribution of power up to, but not including, election day.

Instances of high citizen turnouts in voting for special measures were not observed when pre-electoral measurements indicated that the distribution of political power was narrow or elite. But high citizen turnouts sometimes did occur in elections of government officials when the distribution of political power was otherwise narrow. In this theoretical scheme we distinguish between elections for government officials and elections on measures. The choice of candidates in an election may range from men who apparently will have little effect on the scope of government to those who will make great changes. Candidates may run on platforms that promise major shifts in the scope of government if they are elected, or platforms that promise no shifts at all. Even when one candidate is explicit the position and preferences of other candidates may be impossible to discern. Moreover, campaign platform promises may bear little resemblance to the actual scope of government after the election. Regardless of whether candidates do or do not take a position on the appropriate scope of government, elections of officials are regarded here as events that in themselves do not change or maintain scopes of government, but that can affect the probabilities that postelection political decision-making processes will affect those scopes.[17] The question of whether community power structures are mass or elite does not refer to the distributions of what we might call the electoral power accorded the contributors to the selection and election of candidates for office.[18] The broad or narrow distribution of such electoral power among the citizens will be especially noted.[19]

POWER STRUCTURES: TIME, CHANGE, AND INSTABILITY

Types of power structures are inferred from political decisions that may change over periods of time; therefore the types of power structures also may change over periods of time within communities. The importance of time and the *changeability* and *instability* of community power structures may be illustrated if we imagine a power structure that is static.

One property or characteristic of political power as an analytic construct is that it may emerge and then disappear; it may be absent or pervasive in the polity, regardless of how widely or narrowly it is shared; it generally fluctuates between these two extremes. The second characteristic of political power is that it can be distributed unequally among citizens and, in fact, usually is, regardless of whether the society is simple or complex. This means that political power may be redistributed among citizens over time.

Political power has the additional characteristic of being discrete analytic units specifically bounded in time and space. As we have already indicated, units of political power are assigned to those political participants who contribute to decisional outcomes; the outcomes as well as the identities of the participants must be established relative to a specific point in time. At a subsequent moment of time, an entirely new unit of power may be assigned. This means that at Time M a decisional outcome may be "negative" because of successful resistance by political participants; at Time $M + 1$, a day or a year later, the outcome of a continuing issue may be "positive." This may result, for example, from a shift in position by one or more of the participants. Whatever the reasons for the change in outcomes, one decisional outcome may exist at Time M, with one unit of power assigned to the contributors to that outcome; and at Time $M + 1$, an opposite outcome may have occurred, with another unit of power assigned to a different set of contributors. When an outcome and its contributors are identical from one time to another, new units of power are assigned, even though the decisional question or issue remains the same.

There are two unlikely sets of conditions under which a static power structure might exist: if no political decisions have been made during two consecutive time periods, or if political decision-making has not proceeded to a point where the analyst can say that political power exists. In such situations the power structure might be regarded as nonexistent and, hence, static. The more numerous or longer the time periods, the less likely it is that such conditions would hold. If all the outcomes of decisional processes involving power maintain rather than shift the scope of government through two consecutive time periods, and if the same people participate in decision-making, the power structure might be considered perfectly stable, although it is changing by definition. Invariant relationships and constant patterns exist, even though changes are occurring as time passes, in the analytic units of power assigned in the two periods, if in no other respect. Power structures tend to change over a period of time under the following conditions: as new decisional processes are born; as existing decisional processes end in shifts in the scope of government; as people cease to participate and as others begin to participate; as the participants acquire or lose power; as participants change their decisional preferences; and under combinations of these or other conditions.

The power-structure dimension that concerns the ideology of the political leadership also is potentially changeable; like the distribution of power, it is a variable. Assuming the proportion of citizens sharing in political power to be relatively constant, a single vote can rearrange the political leadership and change the community's power structure from competitive to consensual or vice-versa. For example, if a seven-man city council has two groups contending for political leadership positions and four of the men consistently vote together to defeat the other three, a power structure might be considered consensual. If, however, one of the four begins to vote periodically with the minority of three, the power structure becomes competitive.

Another important consideration is that an individual's political ideology may change. There may be no change in the proportion of citizens participating and the same people may be sharing in political power over a period of time; but if the ideological orientations of the political leaders shift and produce a greater degree of ideological divergence or convergence, or if aspiring political leaders emerge and succeed or disappear, the power structure may change.

Political change is the norm for power structures; political stasis for any appreciable length of time is an extremely unusual occurrence. It would be unlikely for a contemporary community in the United

States to have a power structure that does not change over a period of time in any of the ways mentioned. The rate of such change may vary considerably, however, from polity to polity, or from time to time in one polity. The variation in the amount of power—number of units—and the redistribution of power may differ considerably over time, as may the frequency with which decisional outcomes shift the scope of government, the number of changes in personnel that take place, or the degree of change in the ideological orientations of the political leadership. Such differences are of interest in this study.

In this scheme, political instability and political change are conceptually different. Power structures whose rates of change are relatively steady may be regarded as extremely stable. For example, suppose that over a series of consecutive time periods, the proportion of people who share in political power in a community increases at a constant rate. Suppose, further, that the factors responsible for this steady increase are known, and that through measurement of these trends we can predict that the proportion should continue to increase in the next time period. This community has a more stable power structure, even if it changes in type from elite to mass, than that of another community with a more fluctuating, less predictable distribution of power.[20]

If the probabilities of changes in power structures were changing rapidly, rates of political change might increase or decrease. However, the level of political stability would need to be ascertained rather than assumed in any case. A power structure that has been relatively static may suddenly begin to change rapidly. But whether the power structure has become more or less stable or remains equally stable depends on the probability of further changes in succeeding time periods. The rate of change may be relatively high; it may be low; it may be moderate; or it may fluctuate rather than settle into one pattern. Instability of and change in types of power structures are of interest here, as are instability and change in another aspect of political systems—their regimes—to which we now turn our attention.

FOUR TYPES OF REGIMES

By "regime" we do not mean the structure of political power but rather the "rules of the game" in political decision-making as political leaders and other citizens in a polity conform to and interpret them.[21] Polities have both power structures and regimes; the term *democracy* is applied to regimes.[22] By themselves, the four types of power structure reveal nothing about the state of democracy in the community. Theorists or philosophers of democracy do not insist that a single or convergent set of ideologies among political leaders is incompatible with democracy, nor that a broad distribution of political power is a necessary component of democracy.[23] In fact, a high level of satisfaction with life in a community and a low level of unsatisfied needs might be expected to produce or reinforce a Consensual Elite type of power structure in a democracy.[24]

The writings of political philosophers offer two variables for defining the extent to which a polity's regime, regardless of its type of power structure, is democratic. The first is a sense of electoral potency. This exists where citizens believe that they can attempt to obtain authorities responsive to their decisional preferences through elections without suffering illegitimate sanctions. As Harold D. Lasswell has said, people in a democratic government "must be free of intimidation. Moreover, they must have confidence in their capacity to exert effective control over decisions, whether or not they vote on any given occasion."[25] The second variable is the probability that citizens' efforts to shift or maintain the scope of government will be blocked by the use of illegitimate sanctions.[26] The four types of regimes that result from dichotomizing each variable are presented in Figure 3.2.

One of the two variables defining regimes refers to elections rather than other forms of political participation. The constitutional guarantees of freedom of speech, right of assembly, and right of petition may be considered analogous to stages of decision-making: policy deliberation, organization of political support, and authoritative consideration. If citizens are deprived of any one of these rights—the right to become involved in any one of these stages—democracy be-

	Probability of illegitimate sanctions blocking efforts to shift the scope of government	
Sense of electoral potency	Low	High
High	Developed Democracy	Guided Democracy
Low	Underdeveloped Democracy	Oligarchy

FIGURE 3.2   *Types of regimes.*

comes an empty symbol in reference to the political decision-making process.[27]   Although these rights and stages are necessary for a full-blown democratic political process, they are not sufficient to guarantee it.   The right to petition or to organize political support behind decisional preferences may be useless if the electoral process is controlled by and restricted to a small set of inaccessible people.   The formal structure of democracy may exist without the core electoral process; in some nation-states, the electoral process only masks tightly controlled policy-deliberation, organization-of-political-support, and authoritative-consideration stages.[28]   It is assumed that the sense of *electoral* potency will be low if citizens do not feel that they can freely and effectively speak, assemble, or petition.[29]

An optimistic feeling about the right to use elections in order to express preferences is a necessary but insufficient element in a fully developed democracy: the optimism may be unjustified.   It is possible that if such optimism were to lead citizens into attempting to use elections or other methods to affect the scope of government, they would be countered by illegitimate sanctions which would render their expectations invalid.   Thus, it is only when electoral potency is realistically considered high, when there is a low probability of illegitimate sanctions' being used effectively to block efforts to shift the scope of government, that the regime is classified as a Developed Democracy.   "Sense of electoral potency," then, refers to the expectations that citizens can use elections to obtain authorities responsive to their decisional preferences regarding the appropriate scope of government.   It does not mean that they must feel sanguine about their prospects of electoral victory; only that this political channel is available.

If the sense of electoral potency is high but mistaken, the regime is labeled a Guided Democracy.[30]   Oligarchy is the absence of either of these attributes of a democracy.[31]   An Underdeveloped Democracy is a regime in which the electorate's sense of electoral potency is lower than it realistically should be: the probability that illegitimate sanctions will be used effectively is low.   The term "democracy" is thus reserved for regimes in which at least one of the two attributes of democracy is present.

It would be unrealistic and utopian to suggest that in real world politics men can interact and not sanction one another.   An aspect of political maturity, as of human maturity, is the realization that it is not always possible to please everyone; loss of status or prestige is to be expected at some times in a political career.   Social ostracism or economic boycotts, when applied for the first time in a polity, may effectively deactivate those who are making certain demands.   Paradoxically, the more such sanctions are used, the more they may become both expected and accepted. Thus, they can lose their illegitimate character and their effectiveness. Changes may occur in the effectiveness and illegitimate character of sanctions as alternative social group satisfactions develop and alternative economic opportunities emerge from shifts in the local economy.[32] An analyst must keep these possibilities in mind when classifying regimes by type and assessing changes in regimes. Regardless of the difficulties introduced by the notion of "illegitimate" sanctions, our position in this study is that it is possible, useful, and, indeed, necessary to the scientific analysis of "democracy" to specify the importance of such sanctions in classifying regimes.

For our purposes we regard such sanctions as loss of employment opportunities in the private sectors of the economy and extreme social ostracism as among the major illegitimate political sanctions. However, we might also include the right to a job in the government itself, particularly in the established civil service. Ordinarily, civil servants are not as free to become involved in political activities as are private citizens. Because there may be some question about this matter, we shall assume in this study that loss of government jobs, failure to be promoted or receive salary increases that are normally expected in the bureaucracy, or failure to obtain expected positions as a consequence of political activity are legitimate sanctions. This assumption might be thought incompatible with the classificatory prerequisites we have set up for a Developed Democracy. We do not think that any regime in the present study would need to be reclassified even if the operational definition of illegitimate sanctions were broadened in this particular regard. It should be stressed again that the effectiveness of illegitimate sanctions needs to be assessed for the purposes of classifying regimes.

The conception of illegitimate sanctions in the present context has a broad two-fold referent. On the one hand, they refer to a set of procedures wherein otherwise legitimate sanctions, including incarceration, capital punishment, fines, or restrictions on economic activities are regarded as illegitimate because of their use in an arbitrary, capricious, personalized, unpredictable, unequal, or unfairly discriminatory manner. In other words, the way they are used violates accepted norms of legal and judicial procedures. They apply legitimately to an act already declared unlawful by the constitutional authorities, but their application may not meet norms of due process. In Lasswell and Kaplan's terms, democracy implies a juridical rule, a "government of laws, not of men" in this sort of procedural sense.[33] In its second sense, the conception of illegitimate sanctions refers to relatively severe deprivations, excluding relatively minor withdrawals or withholding, of affection, respect, or money that are considered to be wrong when used for the purpose of preventing or punishing peaceful, politically motivated behavior. Although, normally, government officials are the potential violators of legal and judicial procedures, private citizens with either the knowing assistance or the unwitting cooperation of police, judges, or other government officials may be responsible for illegitimate sanctions in either sense.

Because of what historical analyses indicate to be the development of substantially juridical regimes—in the first, procedural sense of illegitimate sanctions—in all four of our research communities following the Second World War, the major concern herein is with assessing expectations of illegitimate sanctions in the second sense. Negro citizens, particularly in one of the Southern cities, feared that police and judicial procedures would be used in a discriminatory manner, violative of the equal-protection-of-law aspect of due process. However, the most likely sources of illegitimate sanctions were groups of private citizens, particularly those with relatively large amounts of economic, social, and political power. We look to the political leaderships, whether consisting of government officials, private citizens, or both, in estimating, at various points in time, the likelihood of the use of illegitimate sanctions, primarily in the second sense.

The *potential sanctioners* are those men whose leadership positions in a particular time period, Time E to M, enable them to block political demands by applying illegitimate sanctions. Those who are *potentially sanctionable* are the people who prior to Time M have been deliberating political demands which they intend to continue to make after Time M, and for which they might organize political support. Prior to Time M, these demands may have been pushed beyond the policy deliberation stage, or they may have been suppressed or repressed because of fear of the use of sanctions, legitimate or illegitimate. They are, in other words, men with unsatisfied political demands.

The *permeability* of the power structure is another way of viewing the "probability" dimension of a regime: permeability varies with the probability that certain political demands can be pushed to the electoral process, if need be, without having illegitimate sanctions applied to those who make the demands. Lasswell and Kaplan define the "permeability of a group" as the "ease with which a person can become a participant." They use the term again when discussing impartiality of rules, or what we have called the probability dimension of regimes. However, their conception of a juridical rule seems to be broader, encompassing particular power-structure patterns also. It implies a separation of powers. In contrast, our analytic objectives are to assess the relationship between Developed Democracy and other kinds of regimes on the one hand, and such patterns of political decision-making—that is, certain aspects of power structures—on the other.

Our definition of permeability does not mean that a permeable set of power strata will necessarily be permeated, and thereby altered, in a subsequent period of time.[34] Neither does it mean that certain political demands will be pushed to the electoral stage; nor that if so pushed, the demands would constitute the decisional outcomes, for they might be defeated by political opponents. Proponents may refrain from pushing their demands because they do not feel that the demands are sufficiently appealing to others, or because they believe the power structure to be impermeable, even if such is not the case.

An Underdeveloped Democracy exists when citizens who have political demands to make feel impotent because they erroneously expect that illegitimate sanctions will be used against them. A sense of electoral impotence may lead to a self-fulfilling expectation: a citizen who fears sanctions may not make his demands because of that fear; one who does not fear sanctions may make the sanctions ineffective by disregarding them. The mistaken belief that illegitimate sanctions will be used may result from the use of such sanctions in the past, and the failure of the potentially sanctionable to recognize a subsequent decrease in the disposition to use them. Or this mistaken belief may be rooted in a myth from the past maintained as an operative belief in the present.

In a Guided Democracy, as in an Oligarchy, illegitimate sanctions may or may not be actually invoked. Occasions for their application may not occur in either regime. Such sanctions accomplish their purpose through deactivating citizens who are making demands that are opposed by political leaders. Deactivation occurs not only when the consequences of continued participation are understood but also when a participant's energies are effectively redirected toward other ends. If a person begins to lose customers as a result of a politically inspired boycott, he may direct all of his efforts to his business and leave politics alone—at least for the while. He may even be unaware that the loss of customers is due to a politically inspired boycott. He may maintain his faith in democracy by treating this illegitimate sanction as an idiosyncratic event that will not be repeated. Guided Democracies may or may not be more stable than Oligarchies, in which the actual rules of the game are understood by the potentially sanctionable.[35] In Oligarchies illegitimate sanctions may accomplish their purpose to greater degree by discouraging "undesirable" citizen political activity than by deactivating the desperate or the martyr.

Deviation from a Developed Democracy on either dimension of regimes constitutes a departure from the hitherto unmentioned principle "majority rules." Polities are Developed Democracies to the extent that an electoral outcome is determined by counting each citizen's ballot as equal to every other citizen's ballot, with the victory going to the man with the greatest number of votes—a majority or a plurality—and to the extent that citizens understand, correctly, that they may cast ballots without suffering illegitimate sanctions. The typology of regimes discussed here emphasizes the rights of minorities or powerless majorities to become the ruling majority; it stresses the fact that the spirit or intent of the democratic rule for weighing and counting votes can be violated in fact as well as through law. But since the compound democratic rules of one citizen, one vote, and victory to the man who gets more votes tend to be universal in modern cultures, this does not pose special classificatory problems, and certainly not in American communities. Infringement of these rules because of the use of an open rather than a secret ballot would be taken into account when one assessed the condition of the two defining variables of regimes.[36] There is a special difficulty, however, if in some political systems such rules are not part of the political culture.

Because of the general theoretical significance of this problem, there follows an attempt to clarify it, even though the problems involved in classifying regimes and extending typologies for future studies will be discussed later. Suppose that the votes cast by a particular segment of citizens, such as the community elders, members of a particular clan or party, or those in a certain socio-economic position, are weighed more heavily than those cast by the vast majority of citizens. This deprives many citizens of the right to have their votes carry as much weight as those their fellow citizens carry; it also deprives them of the right to have electoral outcomes determined by a "fair count" of the votes cast. This, then, is as much an illegitimate sanction as taking away a citizen's liberty or property or depriving him of his social relations because he made a political demand, nominated a candidate, or voted for the "wrong" man. But suppose that "majority rule" was not regarded as a right by anyone in a polity. Suppose that such weighted voting was accepted as right and proper and regarded as the fair count. In very simple societies such situations are probably common. In the more complex nation-states of today, including the so-called "people's democracies," the trend seems to be for greater acceptance of equal-count–majority electoral rules. In those nation-states deviations from Developed Democracy more commonly come from violations of the rights of access: certain segments of citizens are prevented from participating in elections.

Two feasible classificatory options are present in considering regimes that do not adhere to democratic electoral rules or that use some method, accepted by citizens as right and proper, other than elections in selecting political leaders—such as the principle of divine right in absolute monarchies. One is to develop two (or more) typologies of regimes for the different constitutional arrangements. If this is done, the further option exists of labeling regimes in such a way that one kind of "democracy" can be distinguished from another when they are compared with other sorts of regimes; such terms as "people's democracies" and "Western democracies" represent this conceptual option. Unnecessary and even harmful confusions and misunderstandings may result, however, when a quite common, traditional term is used in referring to new types of regimes for propaganda purposes; such is the case with the Communist use of the term "democracy." On the other hand, it may be equally awkward for political theorists to use new words for regimes that have in common with the condition of Developed Democracy the two defining variables used here, but have different methods of counting and weighing ballots.

The other basic classificatory option, and the one preferred here, particularly for cross-national studies, is to have a single classificatory typology, but with more subcategories and dimensions. In order to utilize this option we have adopted a yardstick that accords with the traditional Western conception, with the values of the authors, and with what we think is the trend throughout the world in the status of these electoral rules. This assumes that when we speak of a sense of electoral potency—citizens' expectations that they can use elections to obtain their decisional preferences without suffering illegitimate sanctions—we imply that elections, by definition, include these rules of electoral counting and weighing. It also assumes that in nations or communities where citizens do not make use of such electoral rules, and do not value the rules, it is likely that illegitimate sanctions would be used to block citizen efforts to affect the scope of government. If it were to be useful to differentiate among those regimes classified as Oligarchies under some conditions, that would, in effect, introduce a new crosscutting typology that would distinguish Oligarchies within which citizens did not consider such electoral rules to be a proper part of the basic political rights from those in which citizens did consider the rules an aspect of the good polity.

RELATIONSHIPS OF REGIMES TO POWER STRUCTURES

A Developed Democracy theoretically may have any type of power structure; similarly, an oligarchic regime theoretically may have at least three, if not all four, types of power structure. Ordinarily, Oligarchies are thought of as regimes in which citizens justifiably feel that they are impotent as an electorate, and as power structures with a single, united political leadership sharing but one ideology, in which relatively few citizens share in political power. This is a Consensual Elite structure in the terms of our typology. However, a similar regime–power-structure combination where the leadership has become divided ideologically into two competing groups—a Competitive Elite structure—also is possible. It is even possible to conceive of an oligarchic regime to which citizens have become so accustomed that relatively large numbers of citizens contribute to decisional outcomes in one way or another—a Consensual Mass structure. An oligarchic regime with a Competitive Mass power structure is most difficult to imagine. Yet it is conceivable that two or more otherwise ideologically antagonistic leadership groups can agree upon who should not share in power.

Underdeveloped Democracies are theoretically and logically possible but, empirically, they may not exist as types of regimes. Similarly, although we can conceive of an Oligarchy with a Competitive Mass power structure, a regime and power-structure combination of that type may not exist in the real world. Theoretically, every one of the four types of regimes may exist with any one of the four types of power structures. The combinations and recombinations found in the four research communities over time are of central interest in the following chapters.

Actually, it is inaccurate to suggest that the writings of democratic theorists nowhere require that political power in a Democracy be distributed broadly.[37] Because of their current prominence and appropriateness to this study, we shall re-examine the views of those modern democratic theorists referred to earlier as pluralists.[38] Although each pluralist has his own views, and ambiguity exists at a variety of crucial points, the following presentation of the pluralist position in regard to the interlocking character of a democratic regime and type of power structure seems to be an accurate summary of major tenets that they share.

As one pluralist puts it:

A pair of competing party hierarchies, a polyarchal political structure in which many minorities participate, a pattern of interest groups and pressure politics appear as the most effective ways in which modern democracies can operate.[39]

It would appear that in the pluralist view, regimes, or constitutional-legal orders, have primarily one dimension: a rule of law or the absence of illegitimate sanctions at one pole and rule by arbitrary fiat or the prevalence of illegitimate sanctions at the other. Types of power structures in American communities also are differentiated on the basis of one dimension: the degree to which citizens acquire political power when they oppose a political leadership, either through direct participation in decision-making or by using the ballot to replace an unresponsive set of officials. The term "democracy" is usually applied to those power structures that are inclined toward the appropriate pole on this dimension, the implicit assumption being that such democratic power structures have the appropriately "democratic" rules of law.[40] Oligarchies are power structures in which the ruling minority is entrenched; this minority does not lose in decision-making conflicts. Oligarchies also are assumed to be regimes that rule by the threat or use of illegitimate sanctions, rather than by law.

Pluralists assume that few American communities are Oligarchies. The only community that has been described as an Oligarchy was New Haven, Connecticut, before the middle of the nineteenth century.[41] Yet pluralists seem to distinguish Democracies according to the degree to which they have institutionalized democratic processes or the extent to which they have become what might be called (in a different sense than we define this term) "Developed" Democracies.

They assume that in Democracies, whether developed or underdeveloped, some citizens whose political interests differ to some extent will periodically make conflicting political demands. In more developed Democracies, competitive and complementary political interests are organized. Men who want to be elected to governmental positions because of personal or group interests tend to organize in parties. Usually, parties stand for somewhat different political programs. Since parties periodically must gain electoral support from the citizens at large, these programs must appeal to a relatively wide variety of political interests, thereby diluting what otherwise might tend to be an ideological politics. To gain and maintain elective office, officials must compromise conflicting demands; but they are likely to suffer decisional defeats periodically during their tenure in office or even be turned out of office on occasion, as minorities whose demands they could not meet rally to their electoral opponents.

A Developed Democracy in the pluralistic sense is more likely to exist, they suggest, in a large metropolis than in a small city or suburb. It is in the large, complex city that a heterogeneous citizenry is to be found; this citizenry is differentiated along social, economic, ethnic, and racial lines which become group interests and lead to, or facilitate, the formation of political interest groups. It is in the large metropolis that electoral competition is likely to develop. The pluralists expect to find in large cities the power structure that we call a Consensual Mass power structure. This, as we have mentioned, would have relatively broad distributions of power in elections and periodically in nonelectoral decision-making; and competitive parties and political interest groups would share pluralistically in the political power that accrues to those who, on occasion, successfully oppose the group in power or force the latter to compromise.

In the small city, according to the pluralists, the rule of law can be more easily undermined, so that an oligarchic regime and a Consensual Elite power structure might exist, representing a dominant interest.[42] Illegitimate social and economic sanctions are more likely to be used effectively in the "extended family" type of community, where political difference is seen by the father-leaders of the community as political deviance that threatens the whole group. Even if democracy exists in a small community, the power structure may be of the type that inhibits the expression of divergent political interests and that does not encourage the organization of opposition groups. Thus, there may be little overt opposition to the decisional preferences of the political leadership, which may itself not bother to run for elective office; electoral competition, which allows alternative programs to be offered to the voters, also may be absent. In our terminology, such polities would have democratic regimes, but such power structures would be Consensual Elite.[43]

Comparable situations presumably existed in the patrician communities of yesterday; perhaps they still exist in an occasional larger, but still homogeneous, simple city of today. The modern, metropolitan suburb is today's counterpart of yesterday's small city which had comparably "underdeveloped" democratic politics.[44]

The present study is specifically interested in exploring the nexus assumed by the pluralists to be increasingly the norm in American communities: a democratic regime and Consensual Mass power structure. Because the present typology of regimes is based on two major dimensions, the connections presumed by pluralists between Developed

Democracies and Consensual Mass power structures are of special interest. At the same time, we also shall explore the pluralist image of deviation from the norm: the existence of Oligarchy and a Consensual Elite power structure in small towns. One of our communities is very small; a second is much smaller than the third and fourth. Although a study of four communities can do very little in the way of assessing norms or typical patterns in the country as a whole, it is hoped that the findings will illuminate what are sometimes the hopes and values—rather than the empirical findings—of those democratic theorists who are committed to pluralism as the most desirable kind of political system for communities and nation-states.

THE POLYARCHAL DEMOCRACY

At this point, we must clarify the differences in orientation between the present study of democracy and the studies of pluralists. Important differences between their approach and ours may be misunderstood because of the many similarities in theoretical interests. We shall use the work of Robert Dahl, one of the most influential of that "school," to illustrate the difference in orientation.[45]

In constructing a theory of democracy, Dahl starts by treating

as a single class of phenomena all those nation states and social organizations that are commonly called democratic by political scientists, and by examining the members of this class to discover, first, the distinguishing characteristics they have in common, and, second, the necessary and sufficient conditions for social organizations possessing these characteristics.[46]

In dealing with all so-called Democracies as actual Democracies, Dahl and other pluralists run the risk of assuming that a characteristic common to all Democracies is not shared by other political systems that are commonly thought to be Oligarchies or dictatorships or to belong to a class of non-Democracies. Secondly, by putting all so-called Democracies in a single class or category at the outset he creates a risk that those political systems or their subsystems—for example, communities within nation-states—will be thought to resemble each other more than they resemble purported non-Democracies. This may lead to a situation in which the degree to which they are Democracies will be assumed without the necessary empirical study.

These considerations introduce the need for a comparison of those systems that political theorists have classified as Democracies and those that have been called non-Democracies. It is useful to identify the similarities and differences between two such categories in order to derive and clarify criteria for classifying political systems, empirically and systematically, as Democracies or non-Democracies. When these criteria have been established from the interplay of theoretical preferences and observations, they should be applied to determine the validity of the less systematic and more intuitive labeling that has already taken place. Then they can be used to classify polities that have not yet been labeled.

That pluralists sometimes do not systematize their criteria in this way can be illustrated by Dahl's discussion of Soviet and "Western" citizens.[47] Assuming that at least some Soviet citizens would prefer to vote against the ruling slate for a rival slate, they are said to be situated in a nondemocratic regime because a vote against the ruling slate carries with it "living death in a concentration camp." In contrast, any American citizen "who perceives a set of alternatives, at least one of which he regards as preferable to any of the alternatives presently scheduled, can insert his preferred alternative(s) among those scheduled for voting," presumably without running such risks. The scheduling of such alternatives is regarded as one of the most important conditions of the type of Democracy, termed "polyarchal" which describes the "normal American political process."

For the moment we can assume that in Dahl's view the probability that illegitimate sanctions will be applied is one of the criteria that differentiate Democracies and Oligarchies. He admits that no polity, including the United States, approaches the ideal; but he disposes of the problem that he notes is posed by the present situation of American Communists and by American Negroes "in the past" by defining American "Polyarchal" Democracy in a way that obscures the implied differences between the conditions of Soviet and American citizens.

Dahl defines the normal American political process, a Polyarchal Democracy, as "a political system in which all active and legitimate groups in the population can make themselves heard at some crucial stage in the process of decision." [48]   Admitting that if a group is inactive it cannot be heard, Dahl maintains that there are still possibilities for that group to be represented in decision-making. Active members may "include among their own goals the protection or advancement of inactive members"; active members may "expect that presently inactive members may become active in the future."[49] Thus, by the operation of what is termed "indirect influence" or, in our terms, the politically active according a positive political status to the inactive, the inactive may still get a hearing.

The inactivity of a group may be determined by "free choice, violence, intimidation, or law."[50]   In the United States, Negroes in the past were, and Communists today are, presumably inactive not entirely out of free choice.   Assuming that both legal prohibitions and informal intimidation operate to produce the inactivity, it is asserted that "Communists are not now a legitimate group."   Their political activity is not "accepted as right and proper by a preponderant portion of the active."   This does not violate democratic norms, it is contended, because such norms only hold for those groups considered "legitimate"; even intimidated and outlawed groups such as Communists may become active by using or threatening "violence" or, in undefined ways, by "motivating the ingroups to incorporate the outgroup" and thus restore the legitimacy of the latter.   Unfortunately, the same case may be made for the outgroups in the Soviet Union.[51]

What appeared to be a distinction between democracy and nondemocracy, based on the probability of whether the political leadership will use illegitimate sanctions or not, thus disappears.   What was an attempt to argue that in a Democracy there is no real danger of tyranny by majorities over minorities is disposed of by asserting that if the political activity of a minority is regarded as wrong and improper by a preponderant majority of the politically active, the minority does not possess minority rights in a Democracy.

One of Dahl's key points is that in order to survive, such systems require an "underlying consensus on policy . . . among a predominant portion of the politically active members."   Thus, although a minority rules in both a democracy and a dictatorship, "the characteristics of polyarchy greatly extend the number, size, and diversity of the minorities whose preferences will influence the outcome of governmental decisions."   Dahl's argument that in polyarchal democracies "minorities" rule, even though these active groups must agree on some basic policy preferences, converts the problem of comparing polities on a democratic-dictatorial basis into an empirical question.   He is aware of this when he recognizes that in some countries without a democratic electoral process the pre-electoral stage of decision-making could be more democratic than that of the proverbial democracies, although he rejects the possibility on his assessment of the evidence.[52]

We are not suggesting that no important differences exist between the regimes in the United States and the Soviet Union.   Compared to regimes in many other countries, all four of the present research communities are probably Developed Democracies, even though they seem to have very different types of regimes when compared only to one another.   What needs to be understood is that if the dimensions used to classify regimes—such as whether citizen expectations that illegitimate sanctions will be used if they participate politically are valid or not—are assessed on the basis of the popular belief that a country or community is democratic or otherwise, empirical study becomes superfluous. If such dimensions are used initially to discriminate between types of regimes, but then regimes are classified in terms of power structures, it is impossible to empirically examine presumed relationships between regimes and power structures.[53]

Clearly, political status as it is accorded by political leaders— particularly elected officials—to active or inactive citizens is a most important variable in Dahl's conception of Polyarchal Democracy. A competitive electoral process in so-called Democracies and its absence in so-called Oligarchies or dictatorships makes such regime variables as the permeability or probability dimension seem relatively unimportant when Dahl discusses types of political systems. Nor should the end result of competition in polyarchy be minimized. According to Dahl, "continuous political competition among individuals, parties, or both" makes for the responsiveness of governmental leaders to nonleaders in such a way that "the distinction between democracy and dictatorship still makes sense." [54]

His basic argument that Democracies are polities wherein active legitimate groups can make themselves "heard effectively at some crucial stage of decision" seems to rest on two lines of reasoning. First, even superficial observation suggests that in the United States "decisions are made by endless bargaining; perhaps in no other national political system in the world is bargaining so basic a component of the political process." [55] Secondly, the fact that there has been only one instance in which a minority felt itself so unheard and so disregarded by a majority—or by an authoritative minority—that it revolted leads to the assumption that, normally, minorities with intense feelings are heard. By "heard" Dahl means that "one or more officials are not only ready to listen to the noise, but expect to suffer in some significant way if they do not placate the group, its leaders, or its most vociferous members." [56] Thus, small groups are steadily "appeased." But at this point in Dahl's argument there is an important ambiguity. While Dahl states that a group may be satisfied by "expression of the appropriate emotions," his main argument seems to be that over a period of time it is probable that a group will receive some positive satisfactions through compromises and bargains over decisional outcomes. Such groups thus share in political power (our definition) and "minorities rule." If minorities do not exercise political influence effectively and acquire power by so doing, according to Dahl, they at least are accorded sufficient political status to prevent revolutions stemming from the disregard of their intense preferences by the majority.

The absence of revolution and the stability of the political system are high values to pluralist and to many nonpluralist democratic theorists, as well as to theorists of "dictatorship by the proletariat." They certainly are evidence that groups not heard do not revolt; but they are by no means evidence that groups necessarily are heard, in the sense apparently intended. Groups not only may be deactivated by illegitimate sanctions but they also may remain frustrated politically for very long periods of time. Groups that are so frustrated may even become apolitical; their intense preferences may become less intense as apathy sets in.[57] Although many pluralists, Dahl included, seem to take the position that minorities have a "right," natural or otherwise, to have their decisional preferences satisfied in a Developed Democracy, we do not assume this in our theoretical framework.[58] In the present study the degree to which minorities are heard, whether through the exercise of political influence or because of political status, is a political-system variable and needs to be investigated, even for Developed Democracies.[59] The absence of revolution does not indicate that broad policy consensus underlies minor differences in decisional preferences only in Polyarchal Democracies, in view of the absence of revolt in the Soviet Union. Not all minorities who feel deprived of their "natural rights" can or want to revolt. The possibility that, even in the absence of revolution, restricted or extensive policy consensus may exist should be explored in community studies in the United States, and is to some extent in this book.

That groups are not heard directly, even in United States communities, may be inferred from various reports by journalists and social scientists. These journalists and social scientists have described some cities as "ruled by a small, entrenched economic-political oligarchy, which played rough with its foes and often winked at the trespasses and errors of its friends." [60] In this Texas city, now famous as the home of Billie Sol Estes, a person was reportedly fired from his job for his active opposition to the political leadership, while another was reportedly threatened that "the city administration [would] crack down on him on a flimsy ordinance-violation charge" unless he switched his advertising from an anti- to a pro-city-administration newspaper. In a California city in which one might not expect to find what some would dismiss as "Texas politics," a businessman reported that if he were quoted as saying anything against the man referred to by the writer as the community's "benevolent tyrant," he would probably lose his job the next day.[61] The Lynds reported in

1937 that in the midwestern city they call Middletown, there was probably some measure of truth in a businessman's statement: "If you don't join up with the inner ring, you can't work with them and you can't work against them, and you won't get the credit to run your business if they are not for you." [62]   That "inner ring" did not refer to machine politicians, but to a family prominent in Middletown's business and social affairs.   The Department of Justice in 1960 asked a federal court to grant an injunction against acts of "economic reprisal" by landowners, merchants, and bankers in one county of a Southern state against Negroes who had registered and voted in the November 1960 election.   Among the acts intended to "threaten, intimidate, and coerce" Negro residents were:

> Termination of leases or sharecrop arrangements; termination of employment of Negroes; refusals to sell necessities to them, even for cash; refusals to extend credit or lend them money; refusals to renew insurance policies; and circulating lists of Negro registrants to help merchants penalize them.

That such groups as American Negroes—and to some extent their primary antagonists, White Supremacists—still may not be "heard," even indirectly, is attested by the fact that in some communities they have resorted to civil disobedience, if not to revolution.[63]   On occasion, groups may use abnormal channels of political participation, such as the sit-in, strike, and mass demonstration, to indicate that they feel they are not being heard adequately.   Nor are these the only indications of a sense of low political status.   Regardless of the trend wherein formerly outlawed groups have become more legitimized, communities in the United States may still differ considerably in the extent to which such groups are accorded political status and their political preferences taken into account, whether they are active or inactive.

Some of the central features of Polyarchal Democracy will be explored in this study.   Classifying regimes with the fourfold typology which we have presented permits assessment rather than assumption of the degree to which groups are treated as legitimate.   Of the many groups that could have been considered, the following were given special attention in the four cities: industrialists, merchants, blue-collar workers, city and suburban-fringe dwellers, ideological groups, and, in the two Southern cities, racial groups.   Variations in political activity and in the extent to which groups considered legitimate were "heard" in their community politics are also of interest.[64]

Unfortunately, measurements of "indirect influence," or the political status accorded to inactive citizens by political leaders when the latter made decisions, were inadequate to assess directly the extent to which the four communities were such Polyarchies. Since all four communities have institutionalized election processes, we cannot compare those that do and those that do not have the ballot. However, because whether a community does or does not have regular elections for officials is naturally constant, other variables that pluralists treat as characteristics or determinants of Polyarchal Democracy may be better assessed. These other variables include party and electoral competition, the position of elected officials—particularly the mayor—in the political leadership, and the relative importance of officials' political ideologies and their need to be reelected.

The model of Polyarchal Democracy assumes that it will be most highly developed when there is party and electoral competition to nominate and elect officials as the key political leaders. The interest of these officials presumably will be to maintain citizen support at the ballot box rather than to pursue an ideology; they will base decisions on a sensitivity to the interests of potential political groups and will strive for the satisfaction of active political groups. Since the research communities vary on these characteristics, we have the opportunity to explore these features of the pluralist Polyarchal Democracy further.

SOME CLASSIFICATORY CONSIDERATIONS: REGIMES

The assessment of the "probability" dimensions poses such special problems as how to classify sanctions as legitimate or illegitimate. Within the United States there is some degree of consensus on what constitute legitimate or illegitimate sanctions. In this cultural context, the major types of illegitimate sanctions are loss of job or economic advancement and extreme social ostracism, involving expulsion from formal or informal social organizations, because of "undesirable" political participation. In cross-cultural studies, illegitimate sanctions might be restricted to loss of life and imprisonment. As we have already indicated, this would probably result in the classification of most American communities as Developed Democracies. In other cross-cultural studies, putting pins into dolls might function as the psycho-political equivalent of causing someone to lose his job and would have to be treated as a comparable illegitimate sanction.

The effectiveness of illegitimate sanctions must be assessed in the context of existing conditions. By "the context of existing conditions" we mean that a particular action, such as a boycott, loss of a job, or social ostracism, may not be an effective sanction if the sanctioned person has alternative sources of economic or social gratification. These acts may occur under various types of conditions and may vary in the extent to which they effectively block political participation. This also means that changing conditions may make an effective illegitimate sanction ineffective, and vice versa.

It is necessary to study prior time periods in order to assess the "probability" dimension, that is, what is likely to happen in a future time period. The state of the "probability" dimension can be assumed not to have changed if there is evidence that an effort to shift the scope of government has been blocked recently by the use of illegitimate sanctions, if the sanctioners are still able and disposed to act in the same way, and if the situation of the potentially sanctionable citizens has not changed. Given such conditions, the situation at Time M, the time of measurement, is projected and presumed to hold for the next period of time, Time M to $M + 1$. On the other hand, illegitimate sanctions may never have been used; they may never have occurred, or only in the distant past. The crucial consideration in such cases is the disposition of potential sanctioners in the event of certain political demands. The validity of these estimates depends upon the ability to assess correctly the relationships between attitudes and actions, not only of the potential sanctioner but also of the potentially sanctionable. Therefore, the ultimate validity of classifying regimes on this basis depends on further developments in attitude research and the work of social psychologists. However, the uncertainties of knowledge in this area should not delay classifications such as the one under consideration, since they are essential to explorations of political democracy. Such classificatory efforts may even add to our knowledge of the relationship of attitudes to overt actions in politics.

Can regimes be compared and classified if, in a set of decisional questions selected for classifying purposes, one or more of the questions is of concern to people in one polity but of no concern to those in another polity? By "no concern" we mean that people never have had occasion to think or to formulate policy preferences about a question, or that they are indifferent to the matter. How can the potentially sanctionable be identified if a demand has never been deliberated?

One approach to the problem is to examine the perspectives of the people interested in the decisional question in the polity or polities in which it exists. From these perspectives it may be possible to identify the people in another polity who would be the potentially sanctionable, and then to classify regimes on the basis of the same kinds of potential political demands. However, we have rejected this approach in favor of one that classifies regimes on the basis of political demands that are extant in each polity, although these may vary by number and kind from polity to polity. A similar approach was taken in classifying power structures by type.

In this connection let us consider a decisional preference for Negroes to serve as city councilmen. Suppose that in one city Negroes were already serving in such positions and that this regime was classified as a Developed Democracy on the basis of a selected list of ten decisional questions. In a second city, Negroes wanted to run for election to the city council, but were afraid to do so. The second regime might be classified either as an Oligarchy or as an Underdeveloped Democracy, depending on the assessed state of its probability or permeability dimension. Suppose that in a third polity, there are no Negro citizens and, therefore, no decisional preferences with regard to their serving as councilmen; but on the basis of the remaining extant decisional questions, say six in number, suppose that the third regime was classified as a Developed Democracy.

The type of regime is based on estimates of an existing situation; therefore, both the first and the third regimes would be classified as Developed Democracies, even if the reason that there were no Negroes in the third city was that a planned exclusion policy existed, formulated by the city fathers, real estate groups, and neighborhood associations. In this hypothetical illustration, the potential sanctioners could be identified, but no one would be potentially sanctionable. If Negroes managed to move into the third city during Time M to $M + 1$, it would be necessary to determine whether the city could still be classified as a Developed Democracy for that next period.

The first and third polities in this illustration were Developed Democracies which differed in both number and kind of decisional questions. Such differences could affect the comparative levels of political conflict and the stability of both the power structures and regimes of the polities; and in addition made it "easier" for the third city to become or remain a Developed Democracy than for the first city to do so.

The set of decisional processes selected as the basis for classifying regimes by type includes those that have become subjects of policy deliberation, at least of informal political discussion, in any of the four cities. It is ordinarily larger than that selected for classifying power structures, since it may include processes that have been repressed or tabled during a policy-deliberation stage, before reaching the point where political power can properly be assigned by the

analyst. Although such processes are not included among those selected to classify power structures, they may differentiate one type
of regime from another. Election and nomination decisions are considered but not actually used in classifying power structures. Since
they are significant in the conception of regime, however, they are included in the sets of decisional processes used to classify regimes.

In selecting decisional questions in order to determine types of
regimes, policy formulations not being deliberated were excluded from
consideration. This was done on the assumption that the four communities were sufficiently "democratic" to allow for at least covert
deliberation of intensely held political preferences. This, in turn,
assumed that two or more persons with an intense preference wanted
to deliberate it, and that people with such a preference had been able
to find others who shared that preference so that they could at least
discuss it.

Such conditions might not have existed. There is, therefore, the
possibility that there may be serious repression of decisional preferences in at least one of the four research communities, so that classifying any of them as a Developed Democracy, for example, may distort
reality. If decisional preferences for the establishment of a socialist
city government were being repressed by some citizens because of the
fear of illegitimate sanctions, but the proponents of the preference
were unable to locate one another, so that a demand as we define it
was not in being, a regime might still have been classified as a
Developed Democracy. To the extent that people develop decisional
preferences but do not let them be known for fear of being sanctioned
illegitimately, the likelihood of even covert, informal deliberation may
be reduced. A regime thus could be classified as a Developed Democracy when there were instances of severe repression of demands due
to fears of illegitimate sanctions, either because classifications are relative to situations in other selected communities where there may be
fewer such instances, or because the operational definitions used herein
were insufficiently rigorous.[65]

The estimate of permeability of the power structure is affected by
assumptions about the form of political action in which the potential
participants may engage. Theoretically, the effectiveness of sanctions is partly a function of the number of people participating, because this affects the alternative resources available to any one participant. The effectiveness of sanctions is also partly a function of
the characteristics and relationships among these potentially sanctionable people. The effect of a given sanction may vary with the character of the political roles played by the potential participants, and with

the connections and interrelationships such roles would have with each other.

The probable tactics of the potentially sanctionable thus need to be examined, as do the images held by the potential sanctioners of the tactics likely to be adopted by their opponents. These images may affect the disposition of the potential sanctioners to use illegitimate sanctions. Estimating the "probability" dimension is quite complicated because, at this stage, it involves speculation for which only further research and theoretical development can provide a firmer foundation.

We can improve the accuracy of regime classifications to the extent that we can accurately predict structuring or restructuring of the political leadership from one time period to another. Permeability may be estimated as low for either of two reasons: an existing political leadership may already be disposed and able to prevent the potentially sanctionable from attaining entry to the political leadership through illegitimate sanctions, or, in the event of further political pressure by the sanctionable, new political leaders who will block demands by the use of such illegitimate sanctions may join or replace the present political leadership.

On the other hand, the probability that illegitimate sanctions would block future political demands may be low, either because the present political leadership will not or cannot effectively use illegitimate sanctions, or because existing political leaders will be supplemented or replaced by another set of leaders in Time M to $M + 1$. To estimate permeability, then, the analyst must take into account both the probable reactions of present political leadership to a set of political demands and the probable reactions of other potential sanctioners—politicized people not yet possessing leader roles.

Time and Changes of Regimes

It should be clear by now that a regime's classification may change over time. Changes may occur either through shifts in the sense of electoral potency or through shifts in the permeability dimension. People may become more or less sanguine about the meaning or significance of the electoral process; such changes in expectations may result from shifts in their own political demands or roles, because they see shifts in the behavior of others, or because of personal cognitive reordering. A polity's regime may change, theoretically, whether or not people enter or leave the polity from time to time, a process that occurs inevitably in all communities.

The potentially sanctionable in one period may be cynical about their rights to use the electoral process in support of their political demands. In another period they may cease making these demands—they may change their decisional preferences or they may leave the community. In any event, the level of electoral expectations in the polity may rise drastically from one time period to the next. In another case, the potentially sanctionable may find that acting upon political demands no longer occasions the severe deprivations it has occasioned in the past. It is theoretically possible that even people with the most cynical or pessimistic outlooks may still be driven by inner compulsions or by a perspective such as "nothing to lose but our chains" to engage in political behavior calling forth severe sanctions. Alternatively, people with sanguine electoral expectations may find that potential sanctioners have changed their decisional preferences, their behavior, or both, so that particular political demands which did not meet with severe, illegitimate sanctions in the past now do. The result might be a decline in the sense of electoral potency.

It may occur to a potentially sanctionable person, without any substantial changes in his decisional preferences or behavior, that he has already been suppressed for political reasons. There may be a sudden, sharp drop in his previously high level of electoral optimism. He may have known that he was being boycotted but have been unsure or mistaken about the reasons. He may suddenly perceive the political motivation underlying the boycott. Therefore, a Guided Democracy may change to an Oligarchy in the next period, as a result of insight which leads to an increase in expectations of severe illegitimate sanctions.[66]

The state or condition of the sense of electoral potency may change over time, as may the permeability of the power structure. As decisions are made to shift or maintain the scope of government, political demands may be born or become intensified, disappear or become weaker. Those who are potentially sanctionable and those who are potential sanctioners may change over time. Even if no shifts in the identity of these two sets of politicized people occur, the means by which the potential sanctioners may exercise illegitimate sanctions may increase or decrease. The propensity to use such sanctions may also change.

Finally, interaction between the two classificatory variables may account for changes in types of regimes. Changes in the sense of electoral potency may lead to changes in the degree of permeability of the power structure, and vice versa.

Studies of political change should explore these interrelationships in order to be able to specify the conditions under which particular regime types are stable or unstable. Theoretically, the disjunction between the two classificatory dimensions in both Guided and Underdeveloped Democracies makes both types of polities less stable than Developed Democracies or Oligarchies; however, such unstable situations can continue for an indefinite period. The present study only begins to analyze political change and instability in regimes and power structures.

Another classificatory problem related to political change is whether a single polity may be classified as having two or more types of regimes. Such a question would arise if different relationships existed among the classificatory variables for different decisional preferences or processes within a polity. It may be that when such a question arises as how much police and fire protection is to be provided by the city government, the regime is a Developed Democracy; but when it is proposed that labor union leaders serve on the city council the regime becomes an Oligarchy. Our first classificatory preference or rule is to classify regimes on the basis of any deviation from the condition of Developed Democracy in the selected set of decisional processes and preferences. A second classificatory rule is to call a regime that deviates from this condition an Oligarchy, the category furthest from Developed Democracy, if that represents one of the choices revealed by analysis. This leaves unresolved the problem of classifying regimes that are either Underdeveloped or Guided Democracies, if a regime is found to be of such a mixed type.

An analyst might find in one polity a set of citizens with a low sense of electoral potency who would not, or could not, be effectively and illegitimately sanctioned and a set of citizens who are not aware of the actual disposition and ability of political leaders to sanction them illegitimately should they organize in behalf of their political demands. Although we were not faced with that problem, a multiple classification is possible in such situations. As theory is elaborated, our classificatory rules might well be superseded by others that provide for multiple classifications as the norm rather than the exception.

More Complex Regime Typologies for Future Studies

This examination of classificatory problems will conclude with suggestions for modifications that should be considered in future studies of regimes, particularly those of the Developed Democracy and Oligarchy types.

There are several ways of classifying types of Oligarchies which we shall mention. It has already been suggested that if it is probable that political participation within a polity will be met by the use of such illegitimate sanctions as death or imprisonment, the particular lines drawn for this study between an Oligarchy and other types of regimes may need to be redrawn. We shall elaborate on another way of distinguishing Oligarchies.

The traditional civil liberties are analogous to the stages of our decision-making model: free speech, free assembly, and the freedom to petition correspond in some ways to policy deliberation, organization of political support, and authoritative consideration. Free elections are the "last chance" to change the authorities who determine decisional outcomes and the scope of government. Freedom of thought is the basis of all civil liberties; policy formulation is basic to all decision-making processes. The more totalitarian the regime, the harder the rulers try to eliminate institutional mechanisms that produce uncontrolled political actions that take these forms or correspond to these stages. While control of any stage renders all prior stages futile, it is dangerous for rulers to permit any one of the stages to exist.

There seems to be a natural order of difficulty in suppressing these basic political liberties or in eliminating institutional mechanisms that facilitate uncontrolled expression of political behavior. Formal elections open to all adult citizens are the simplest to eliminate. Petitions, appeals, and demands made directly to the political leaders are fairly easily restricted to politically "eligible" segments of the citizenry. If necessary, ancestries can be checked, ghettos established, and yellow stars sewn on the garments of the ineligible. But the right to assemble is more difficult to control. Assembly does not need to take place in a public forum nor does it need to be formally organized. Political parties may be eliminated, but clandestine organizations dedicated to opposition or overthrow of the regime require more alert internal-security forces.[67]

The formally organized opposition groups may be prevented more easily than may small informal groups which covertly deliberate policies and the possibilities of action. The most totalitarian rulers will not even stop here but will try to prevent the thinking that results in subversive policy formulations, to propagandize the younger generation and control dissident elements in the older. The family may find itself in a setting where no one may speak without fear that his mate or his child will serve as an informer. The difficulty in controlling the policy-formulation stage is attested by the tenacity of the family as an important unit of social organization in all regimes, and by the magnitude of efforts by totalitarian regimes to control it.

The primary purpose here is to indicate how the classification of Oligarchy might be extended in cross-national, comparative research to differentiate more or less totalitarian Oligarchies. Although none of the research communities is a totalitarian regime, the foregoing remarks can be illustrated by the following example. One Southern city appeared to be an Oligarchy through the 1930's. Just before and during the Second World War, the Negro subcommunity was allowed to organize political support through such organizations as the local chapter of the National Association for the Advancement of Colored People (NAACP) in order to request that White government officials shift the scope of government in various ways. Prior to that time such organizational activity and such petitioning probably would have provoked the same reaction as did efforts by Negroes to nominate candidates both before and during the war: effective, illegitimate sanctions. The difference in the degree of oligarchic control from the thirties to the forties was significant, although the immediate postwar situation still warranted the Oligarchy classification for this regime.

The typology of regimes also may be elaborated and extended for Developed Democracies, as for Oligarchies. In some communities, regimes may be classified as Developed Democracies which have a highly effective propaganda system, controlled by a consensual political leadership and devoted to developing or maintaining citizen support for that leadership. In others, a Developed Democracy may be due more to political education and to a nonmanipulative political-socialization and information process. There are human limitations to the communication of information; selectivity in the transmission of messages is required by the nature of man. However, one may still distinguish among communication processes by determining the degree to which communicators intend to deceive others. Political propaganda, or what could be called political manipulation, is knowingly communicating false information intended to influence political behavior. Political education is communicating presumably true information for the same purpose. Both the political propagandist and the political educator, either of whom may be a father, a teacher, or a politician, use techniques of communication that in one sense deserve the label "brainwashing." But the propagandist communicates "facts" that he may believe false or irrelevant, whereas the educator communicates facts that he considers to be both true and relevant; if they are not, the educator tags them with appropriate warning signs.[68]

In Developed Democracies, as well as in other regimes, political values are inculcated in the young through what have been called political-socialization processes. Regimes of the same type, such as Developed Democracies, may be differentiated according to the degree to which communication from adults to children and from politicized adults to apolitical adults is propaganda or education. Estimates of the effects of intended deceit and the extent to which political manipulation is deliberate are also relevant to a classification of Developed Democracies or other types of regimes by such a dimension as political manipulation.

Somewhat paradoxically, it is possible that the more frequently people act manipulatively, the less likely they are to be successful, so long as there is some variety in the messages sent and received. A relationship is frequently assumed to exist between a competitive power structure and Developed Democracy. This relationship, which will be explored in the present study, may be due in part to the variety of political mesages communicated by competitors when it exists. Even the theorists of democracy who postulate this apparently logical relationship may admit that competition and variety of political groups and messages may vary within or among Developed Democracies. It is expedient, therefore, to elaborate subtypes of Developed Democracies.

Another dimension that might be introduced into the typology of regimes is citizen apathy. Two regimes, equally deserving to be classified as Developed Democracies, may differ considerably in the degree to which their citizens are indifferent to politics. Moreover, it is possible that Developed Democracies with mass power structures may differ sharply in the degree to which the citizens not sharing in political power are politically interested or apathetic. Even if the sense of electoral potency is high, and there is little fear of illegitimate sanctions, there may be variations among communities with Developed Democracies in citizen fear of legitimate sanctions, pessimism about the prospects of winning in an admittedly fair political fight, or cynicism about the responsiveness of officials in office or of those who might replace them. Apathy itself can be conceived as a multidimensional variable which necessitates further classifications, not only of Developed Democratic regimes, but also of all four types of regimes identified by the elementary fourfold classification used in this study. The reader should appreciate by now the limited scope of our inquiry, as well as the unlimited fund of knowledge awaiting the further development of such political typologies and of research utilizing them.

It would be unfortunate if the word "Developed" as it modifies

"Democracy" is misunderstood. It is not only intended to denote a state of affairs in a political system as compared to a particular set of other political systems, however far from an ideal state of affairs that might be. It is also restricted to the two specified dimensions. It does not extend to those mentioned above or to others that could be identified as classificatory variables. Elaborating the earlier statement that minorities do not have a right to have their decisional preferences satisfied in a Developed Democracy may help to clarify the conceptual alternatives underlying the terminological option that we adopted.

It is quite possible that a system of segregation by race or socioeconomic class, whether maintained by law directly or indirectly, produces political conditions that constitute deviations from what we have termed Developed Democracy. On the other hand, it is conceivable that under some conditions, if not under most modern American conditions, communities with such segregation systems can have at the same time a relatively high sense of electoral potency among both segregators and segregated and a low probability that illegitimate sanctions would be used effectively by the former against the latter. Even with civil rights, a minority may be unable to convince the majority that government should do away with segregation. This is imaginable, however unlikely, if there were a very strong commitment to democratic rules of the game and a faith by the segregated that over the long run they would convince a sufficient number of segregators of the errors of their ways and that segregation would then be abolished by a majority. Since other kinds of reactions than these can easily be visualized, one might find few if any cases in the real world, but it would be useful to examine communities empirically in that connection. Given such special circumstances of the American Negro as his violent enslavement, the obliteration of any political heritage other than his new one in the New World, and his attainment of a nonslave status through the deeds of men who then preached inevitable progress by hard and good work and through faith in a just God and a fundamentally benevolent, manipulatable political order, it is not entirely surprising that in one of our two Southern cities such dynamics seemed to have produced prior to the time of field work just those kinds of reactions—to the point of that regime's deserving the classification Developed Democracy when compared to the other three regimes.

A system of segregation may take its political toll in other ways than by generating or reinforcing fears of illegitimate sanctions, producing a condition of low resistance to such sanctions and a disposition by segregators to exercise them to maintain political, racial, and/or socio-economic dominance. Assuming that such are not the consequences in a particular community of a system of sharp segregation, and theoretically they may well be the consequences, there are still other important political implications of systems of segregation that bear on the concept of Developed Democracy. One might conceive of democracy as a political system that ensures not only permeability of the political leadership of the power structure in the sense of minimizing the role of illegitimate sanctions but also *maximum accessibility to top power positions*. This does not mean that democracy in that sense would require actual penetration by masses of people of the political leadership; a power structure in a democracy might still be a consensual or competitive, mass or elite type.

Some citizens' channels of access may be closed by the political actions of other citizens that, by definition, intentionally—as at least one end in view—are directed to that end. Besides such illegitimate sanctions that impair freedom of speech, assembly, petition, and electoral participation, there are a variety of extrapolitical conditions that can have the same effects. Such conditions are different in kind from illegitimate sanctions, in the sense that they can apply constantly to some categories of citizens in such a way as to make them relatively disadvantaged in exercising their political rights or in using the channels of political access to the political leadership, which rights and channels they may enjoy on an apparently equal basis with all citizens. Illegitimate sanctions, on the other hand, involve an actual or threatened or feared differential allocation of resources consequent upon someone's engaging in political activity permitted others in the polity.

In what ways does a system of segregation constitute ordinarily a set of constant political liabilities for the segregated? Assume for the moment that the segregated are not disqualified politically by formal or informal laws, such as the White primary, "grandfather" clauses, poll taxes, etc. Residential segregation makes it more difficult for the segregated, for example, to engage in personal political dialogues with the segregators. This constitutes a political impediment for minority points of view to become majority opinions over time. This is analogous to the political implications of socio-economic structures. The more sharply structured and differentiated are classes, the more likely it is that those at the bottom suffer the political disadvantages encountered by the poor—a fact of political life that has resulted in the unequal distribution of the political liabilities as well as the relative economic costs of the poll tax. Not all prisoners, whether physically in jail or in such socio-psychological prisons as ghettos, lose their civil rights, but their opportunities to participate politically in the larger community are less than perfect.

As segregation in school and society impairs personality development among its victims, their political personality may also be impaired. That is, segregation may result in the failure to develop political interest, competence, and a sense of political responsibility. The resulting political apathy means that the segregated may formulate no demands for a shift in the scope of government, and hence the regime can be, "by default," a Developed Democracy. This would be the case because, as we define it, regime type depends upon citizens' formulating demands.

If widespread political discourse and equal opportunity to obtain political influence and power are dimensions to be built into a typology of regimes, the more segregated communities are less likely to be Developed Democracies, even if the sense of electoral potency and the permeability of the power structure were both high relative to illegitimate sanctions.

The conceptual alternative adopted here was to reserve the term Developed Democracy to the more restricted sense. This means that such types of regimes are probably far from ideal not only relative to the two defining dimensions, and in the degree of citizen apathy, cynicism, or manipulation found therein, but also in terms of the distribution of such political disadvantages or liabilities as those associated with systems of segregation. By adopting that terminological convention self-consciously, and by pointing to such other options, we hope to reduce the ambiguities that ordinarily creep into discussions of democracy. By restricting the meaning of the term Developed Democracy to its narrow sense we also hope to underline the need for additional modifying adjectives or alternative terms in thinking about such other dimensions of democracy as the patterns of political liabilities or disadvantages present in such regimes. Such classificatory labels as Equalitarian and Nonequalitarian Developed Democracies might be in order to enrich our vocabularies so that we could consider intelligently the riches to be mined from the various ways of conceiving political regimes. We would also hope that our use of the more restricted conception of political democracy would result in a greater realization that men may have other than political needs and values, e.g., for social or personal dignity, which may not automatically be realized by the improvement of Developed Democracy in the United States or by its establishment abroad, since in its narrow sense it could exist alongside racial, socio-economic, or cultural segregation. It is useful to be aware of the limitations of such regime constructs as they are used conventionally, but also of the possibility of elaborating and extending them to encompass specifically dimensions that are at issue in an ambiguous way and that need to be intentionally built into, or cast out of, political system concepts.

Our analysis is limited to a two-dimensional typology of political regimes, not only because the number of our communities is so limited, but also because very little attention has been given by political theorists to conceptualizing rigorously, defining operationally, and measuring such dimensions as the distributions of enduring political liabilities in communities. In developing ideal typologies of political regimes based on such additional dimensions, it is important not only to think abstractly about such matters as relative political disadvantages over time in obtaining access to others in the community, but also to think about such matters in light of patterns of socioeconomic, demographic, technological, and other factors that may themselves change over time. The development of suburban living patterns marked by occupational and racial homogeneity may have implications for patterns of political liabilities which need to be thought about more intensely. Not only may new measurements need to be taken periodically, since patterns of political liabilities may gradually change, but ideal types of political regimes may need to be reconsidered and new typologies developed, particularly toward the Developed Democracy part of a regime taxonomy. In any event, we can do no more than point out the delimitations of our own study and trust that it will result in more serious efforts to pursue some of the directions pointed to here.

THE ANALYTIC APPROACH

These preliminary theoretical chapters may be concluded with a short summary statement of the overall orientation and design of the analysis that follows. A community's political system is conceived as a congeries of patterns, analytically distinguishable from one another on the basis of a variety of theoretical perspectives. This analysis is concerned with the interrelationships between and among several selected kinds of possible patterns derived from these perspectives. There are seven primary perspectives for viewing a community as a polity: (1) the patterns of decisional preferences; (2) the patterns of political participation; (3) the patterns of political-influence relations; (4) the patterns of power relations that constitute the community's power structure; (5) the patterns that constitute the formal institutions of local government; (6) the patterns of decisional outcomes produced by the power structure; and (7) the type of regime.

These patterns may be so congruent that from specification of one pattern, specifications of others may be inferred with relative accuracy. For example, if a particular distribution of decisional preferences is reflected in a particular distribution of political demands and associated political acts that constitute political participation, in such a way that the former may be inferred from the latter, these two patterns would be said to fit perfectly. If all political participants shared in political power during a particular period, that is, if there were complete accord in decisional preferences and each participant contributed something to a decisional outcome, identification of the powerful people in the polity would also be identification of the political participants. A different but equally perfect fit would be congruence in the patterns of participation and power wherein the analyst could not attribute political power to the participants during a particular period because decisional processes had not reached the point at which political power could be assigned.

If specifying the patterns of political influence revealed the patterns of political power, there would be a perfect fit between the two. But it is possible that those people having a comparable degree or type of political influence occupy dissimilar positions in the power structure. There may be discrepancies between the political influence and political power of citizens that vary among communities and, over time, within communities. Hypothetically, there also may be a perfect fit if, when Developed Democracy exists, the community proves to have a council-manager form of government; or if, when the council-manager form of government is found, the community's power structure is discovered to be Consensual Elite in type. If net increases in the scope of local government occur only when the community has a political leadership in its power structure that has a heterogeneous social-class background, the association between these two patterns would be perfect. If the fit in all these types of patterns were perfect, the description of the type of polity would also permit the analyst to reproduce at least some portions of the other patterns. Patterns could be integrated and the number of perspectives reduced. The unlikelihood of this occurrence, and the fact that over a period of time there may be changes in the degree and character of the association between these patterns, provide both the opportunity and the challenge to develop a political theory that explains the interrelationships among the patterns. To the extent that such interrelationships can be understood, knowledge of community political systems is generated.

In this study, we are trying to assess the extent to which cause-and-effect relationships exist among these patterns. At the outset, however, the analysis takes the form of pattern-fitting. The first form of the analysis is substantially static, in the sense of comparing associations among the patterns found in the four communities in selected time periods. Observation and measurement of selected aspects of the seven patterns are made initially at Time M for a period of one to two years prior—Time E to M—in all four communities. Alternative logical possibilities exist concerning the direction of relationships and sequences of events. Which patterns are partial causes or partial consequences of which other patterns? When observations are made of analytically distinguishable but simultaneously occurring events, as is the case here, it is very difficult, and frequently impossible, to separate the true logical alternatives of cause and effect from the false. The same may be said for analyzing in this static fashion the relationships between ecological variables—such as size, growth rates, and regional location—and socio-economic-system variables on the one hand, and the seven political-system variables on the other. Perhaps because political theory is less developed than economic or social theory, it is frequently assumed that the direction of the cause-and-effect sequence flows from the latter to the former. An assumption that political decisions or the community power structure can affect the community's economic or social system, its size, and even the cultural significance of such invariant factors as its regional location would seem to warrant investigation.

Observations were extended backward and forward in time in order to be able to make more valid interpretations of cause-and-effect relationships and to understand changes in the relationships among the seven types of patterns and between these and selected demographic, socio-economic variables. The historical analysis was carried back to the year 1946 in each community, and current political history was studied up to 1961. This resulted in a total of sixty time periods for the four communities. The investigation after Time M was conducted in the spirit, if not with the best methods, of a natural or quasi-experimental study.[69] We could then undertake a dynamic analysis in which the values of some of the major variables could be plotted from one time period to another, and hypotheses specifying directions of cause-and-effect relationships could be tested.

The dynamic analysis is limited by the following factors. Because these were not true experimental situations, the analysis of change was restricted by the natural occurrence of events. Generally, no experimental control of who was exposed—and when—to experimental stimuli was possible. However, a degree of such control was possible for the periods following Time M regarding the scheduling of observations and measurements. For the periods prior to Time M, even this natural-experimental kind of control was not possible. Moreover, the further one goes back in time in historical reconstruction, the more difficult it is to make valid and reliable measurements, or, in some instances, to make any measurements at all.[1a] Not only were there such serious limitations in observing events in the relatively distant past as imperfect or missing records and problems of recall, but also there were limitations on data-collection imposed by the scarcity of research resources. The lack of funds likewise imposed limitations on the collection of data in the "natural-experimental" period immediately following Time M, as well as in the subsequent time periods. Finally, limitations of time and space prevent the testing or presentation of the results of a multitude of hypotheses derived from or relevant to the developing theory, even though the data were collected and are adequate for that purpose.

Research teams were in the field in full strength during the period immediately following Time M, but in later periods there was a greater reliance on informants, third-hand reports, and newspaper accounts. The questionable validity of some of these data and the need to test certain key hypotheses led to an additional field study in one of the Western cities. This included another sample survey and a panel study involving reinterviews with a subsample of the respondents. Rather than restrict the report to an analysis of these "hard" data collected by rigorous methods and our best possible research design, reports are made on findings of theoretical significance, regardless of the uncertain validity of some of them. We now shall turn to the four communities and the two regions in which they are located.

NOTES

1. The distinction we make between structure and function is not the same as the distinctions suggested by such analysts as Talcott Parsons or A. R. Radcliffe-Brown (see Radcliffe-Brown's *Structure and Function in Primitive Society,* Glencoe, Illinois: The Free Press, 1959, p. 179). When we use the term "function" in connection with the relationship between one structure and another, or between substructures or subsystems of the polity, it is ordinarily to be interpreted simply in a cause-and-effect frame of reference.
2. Scott Greer and Peter Orleans refer to the network of voluntary formal associations in a community as the "parapolitical structure." See their "Mass Society and Parapolitical Structure," *American Sociological Review,* Vol. 27,

No. 5 (October 1962), pp. 634–646. Their parapolitical structure encompasses our subsidiary political organizations and other associations as well, but both concepts assume that constitutional or formal purposes of associations should not determine classification as political or not.

3. The analyst must decide which of the many aspects or dimensions of political-power relations merits investigation first. Additional subcategories of these two variables, as well as additional dimensions, may be introduced to produce a more complex set of power-structure types. We constructed the present typology by adapting and reducing much more complex, multidimensional schemes to the limited number of communities and measured variables available in this study.

4. The terms "mass" and "elite" are used in a somewhat special sense to refer to the extent to which proportions of the citizens share in political power, that is, purposefully contribute in various ways to decisional outcomes. They do not refer to comparisons of the size of political leaderships, although it may be that elite distributions of power are associated with relatively small political leaderships—"elite" in a more traditional sense. Nor do these terms as used here have any connotation of permanence or long duration.

5. We might point out here that the measurement of the relative degree of convergence or divergence of the political leadership's ideology rests on operations designed to establish the degree to which the opposition, if there is more than one political leadership group, is viewed as a power-monopolizing, mortal enemy which threatens the community's way of life or as a power-sharing opponent whose political success, while undesirable, will not injure the community irreparably.

6. A Consensual Mass power structure might exist even if there were no political-interest-group conflict within the framework of a single ideology, if some citizens feel strongly that their civic duty is to participate. It is important to understand, however, that in the absence of ideological conflict among the political leaders, the power structure is classified as consensual no matter how conflicting the interest-group politics may be.

7. For every question about participation in local government and community affairs, a corresponding question was asked about participation in school affairs. However, the data derived from the latter questions have not been included.

8. As a result, we do not distinguish between and among common power structures even though they may differ in regard to the kinds of decisional categories under which citizens may have acquired their power.

9. Future studies may classify types of power structures further by distributions of power by category or scope areas; they may use multiple classifications according to the distributions of power by particular decisions, or averages or other summary statistics.

10. It should be stressed that the classification "mass" does not necessarily mean a majority—50 per cent or more—of the adults or of the eligible participant citizens. Cf. Robert A. Dahl, "The Analysis of Influence in Local Communities," in *Social Science and Community Action,* ed. by Charles R. Adrian (East Lansing, Michigan: by the Board of Trustees, 1960), p. 28; and Herbert McClosky, "Ideology and Consensus in American Politics" (unpublished paper delivered at the 1962 Annual Meeting of the American Political

Science Association). McClosky defined "consensus" as a state of agreement equaling or exceeding 75 per cent, recognizing the arbitrariness of setting a specific figure for a continuous variable. Such specifications are in order when a sufficient number of readings have been taken on such variables as the distribution of power to ensure having cases on both sides of the specified figure, or when it is unimportant for a particular analysis that comparisons be made on the particular variable.

11. See Raymond E. Wolfinger, "Reputation and Reality in the Study of Community Power," *American Sociological Review,* Vol. 25 (October 1960), pp. 636–644.

12. Delbert C. Miller presents five types of community power structures based on dimensions that may characterize the political leadership in his "Democracy and Decision-Making in the Community Power Structure," in *Power and Democracy in America,* ed. by William V. D'Antonio and Howard J. Ehrlich (Notre Dame, Indiana: University of Notre Dame Press, 1961), pp. 25–71. See also the three types and one sub-type in Peter H. Rossi, "Theory and Method in the Study of Power in the Local Community" (unpublished paper delivered at the 1960 Annual Meeting of the American Sociological Association).

13. See Floyd Hunter, *Community Power Structure* (Chapel Hill: University of North Carolina Press, 1953); C. Wright Mills' *The Power Elite* presents a comparable picture of government officials as second-level men in the national power structure. For an opposing view see Daniel Bell, "The Power Elite Reconsidered," *The American Journal of Sociology,* Vol. LXIV, No. 3 (November 1958), pp. 238–250. Bell, for example, takes for granted the "national interest" and "national survival." *Ibid.,* p. 250.

14. Robert A. Dahl and Charles E. Lindblom, *Politics, Economics, and Welfare* (New York: Harper and Brothers, 1953). See also Robert A. Dahl, *A Preface to Democratic Theory* (Chicago: The University of Chicago Press, 1956) for an elaboration of the meaning of "polyarchy."

15. See Wolfinger, "Reputation and Reality . . . ," *loc. cit.*

16. Voters are not usually considered part of the political leadership, even though the decisional choices made by citizens as voters are, in a fundamental sense, acts of leaders. A community is committing itself to a policy whether a citizen's actual contribution is 1/2,000 (if there are 2,000 voters on a winning side) in a community-wide election or ⅙ (if there are six men contributing jointly to the selection of an outcome) in a nonelectoral, authoritative-consideration stage. One reason we do not ordinarily describe voters as political leaders is that often a smaller proportion of them than of political "leaders" participate in the stages prior to the voting itself, or in the decisional processes that may precede elections.

17. We maintain that under a variety of conditions the probabilities vary that policy- or decision-making outcomes in interelection periods are affected by the outcomes of elections for men. For comparable conceptual distinctions between elections for men and those for measures, see Robert A. Dahl, *A Preface to Democratic Theory,* pp. 71, 73, and 124–132, and Delbert C. Miller, "Democracy and Decision-Making in the Community Power Structure," *op. cit.,* p. 113, who differ dramatically, though, in their respective views about the character of the modal connection between electoral and interelection decisions in American communities.

18. An analyst may prefer to treat the selection and election of candidates as decisional processes under the government-reorganization category. This was impossible in the present analysis because not enough appropriate data were available.

19. There appeared to be narrower distributions of power in "nominations decisions" when the community power structure was elite than when it was mass. High voter turnouts could and sometimes did occur even when the nominations were controlled by a few citizens, and even when candidates were unopposed in an election.

20. A sudden change in the power structure from one period to another theoretically could have taken place, even though it seemed highly improbable. Or an error might have occurred in the calculation of the probability. Or, again, the probability might have changed with dramatic rapidity. As theory based on improved research develops, even rapid, revolutionary change may become more predictable. See James C. Davies, "Towards a Theory of Revolution," *American Sociological Review,* Vol. 27, No. 1 (February 1962), pp. 5–19.

21. This conception is more specific and narrower than, but congruent with, David Easton's definition of a regime in "An Approach to the Analysis of Political Systems," *World Politics,* Vol. IX, Number 3 (April 1957), p. 392. See also Lasswell and Kaplan's use of the term "regime" in *Power and Society* (New Haven: Yale University Press, 1950), pp. 130–131, wherein they seem to refer primarily to the sense-of-electoral-potency variable. Our usage of regime is not the customary one, which refers only to the governors rather than to both the governors and the governed.

22. Space limitations preclude a comprehensive analysis of the various meanings that "democracy" has been assigned in the past. The rationale for restricting the term "democracy" to regimes, as defined, will be discussed.

23. This statement holds for both political power and political influence, as defined, subject to the qualifications introduced below.

24. This proposition, of course, is testable. In the process of operationally defining such terms as "level of satisfaction with life in a community," some definitions may yield different empirical findings. It is so frequently taken for granted that Consensual Elite power structures are "undemocratic" that the reader needs to be specially sensitized to differences between power structures and regimes.

The notion that there may be a relationship between dissatisfaction and political participation—apart, for the moment, from political influence or power—depends on one's conceptions of the "political." James Reichley, for example, makes a powerful case for the existence of a political instinct by broadly defining politics as "the participation of human beings in the activities of conserving, distributing and improving the values that are created by a civilized community." He then points to low participation of groups in "real politics," that is, in more narrowly defined, institutional terms. See his *The Art of Government* (New York: The Fund for the Republic, 1959), pp. 124–125. Robert A. Dahl's conception of *Homo civicus,* of man as "not, by nature, a political animal," rests on his conception of the "political" in the latter, restricted, institutional sense. See his *Who Governs?* (New Haven: Yale University Press, 1961), pp. 223–226. Much of the argument over the degree to which man is a political animal could be resolved if common conceptions of the political were adopted, although which conception is most useful for what purpose still might be disputed.

25. We might have referred to this variable as the sense of freedom from intimidation, rather than calling it, as we do, the sense of electoral potency. See Harold D. Lasswell, *The Analysis of Political Behaviour* (New York: Oxford University Press, 1949), p. 8.
26. This is analogous to aspects of what Lasswell and Kaplan term "the rule"; *op. cit.*, pp. 208–214.
27. Mass turnout at the polls is a well-known phenomenon in totalitarian countries but at variance with traditional conceptions of the democratic process, assuming that citizens have pre-electoral rights.
28. One of the inescapable dilemmas of the proponent of democracy is that none of the conditions discussed here are completely attainable, since there are equally valued practices which exist at the same time. For example, if the protection of human rights results in incarceration in penal or rehabilitation institutions, there is an inescapable interference with the offender's freedom of action to engage in political discussion or efforts to organize political support.

    This is not to argue against utopian thinking, since history attests to the periodic realization of what had been assumed to be unrealizable goals. In the present illustration, to the extent that crime can be reduced in a society, lessening the degree or extent of incarceration, political freedom can be increased. The substantial reduction or even elimination of crime and of such other conditions as segregation, which impair the health of a body politic, are worthy of being included as elements in programs to improve political systems. Classificatory problems, however, result from setting the standards for a Developed Democracy too high. Therefore, we do not mean to suggest that for regimes to be classified as Developed Democracies their pre-electoral stages have to be completely "uncontrolled."
29. This is a working assumption, which should be investigated in a cross-cultural study of politics where political cultures differ in the values placed on such stages.
30. Argentina might be considered an example of a Guided Democracy when Peronistas were allowed officially to run for office in 1962, following which the Frondizi administration was overthrown by the military. Both before and after that period Argentina had a more oligarchic character. The sense of electoral potency apparently was high when the ban against Peronistas was lifted; at the same time, the military was prepared to use illegitimate sanctions to prevent the shifts in the scope of government expected if those elected took office.
31. This restricted usage of the term "Oligarchy" to denote a type of regime is not common. "Oligarchy" usually refers to what we would call a type of power structure, in which political power is restricted to a small set of citizens. See Lasswell and Kaplan, *Power and Society*, p. 218; see also Robert A. Dahl, "The Analysis of Influence in Local Communities," *op. cit.*, p. 28.
32. The strength, flexibility, and continued growth, as well as some of the less ideal aspects, of the American constitutional system stem from the fact that the Bill of Rights does not to any great extent specify illegitimate deprivations, but broadly states that citizens may not be deprived of certain rights.

The general principle thus permits judicial interpretation according to the particular impacts and consequences of acts under various conditions; these acts may vary in the extent to which they effectively hinder political participation under different conditions.

The judiciary has frequently had the task of making periodic reassessments of what sets of acts may constitute illegitimate sanctions, as in the case of minority political, religious, racial, and cultural (including gangster) groups. When progress towards a continued expansion of protected political liberty has been delayed for long periods through legislative inaction or deadlock, the judiciary may find itself burdened by its legislative functions. Such is the case in the current Negro Revolt, resulting in increasing demands for legislative and possibly constitutional revision directed toward specification of what kinds of acts are illegitimate when applied to thwart demands by Negroes for shifts in the scope of local and state governments. See John P. Roche, "The Curbing of the Militant Majority," *The Reporter*, July 18, 1963, pp. 34–38.

33. We use Lasswell and Kaplan's statement that "a plurality of power centers is more important in this regard than formal limitations of authority," that is, to make a rule juridical, as a hypothesis, rather than an assumption. We prefer not to assume that a single political leadership group or "center of power" automatically leads to a condition that prevents "effective challenge of decisions" in Lasswell and Kaplan's sense. See Lasswell and Kaplan, *op. cit.*, pp. 31–35 and 232–234.

34. In discussing democracy, Lasswell and Kaplan stress an equalitarian rule which comprises *access* to power. *Ibid.*, p. 236.

35. The four types of regimes posited here are consistent with Lasswell and Kaplan's conception of the problematic character of what they term regimes and rules when they say, for example, that "the polity may be characterized as having a republican regime and an oligarchic or even autocratic rule." *Ibid.*, p. 220.

36. Equal weight per voter is characteristic #2 in Dahl and Lindblom's definition of polyarchy, *op. cit.*, p. 277.

37. Lasswell and Kaplan, for example, although it involves an important empirical generalization on their part, define democracy as a rule under which power is widely distributed; in a republic the weight of power is distributed throughout the domain; in an oligarchy power is in the hands of a group of rulers (*op. cit.*, pp. 218–220). They further define a democracy as a juridical commonwealth, that is, a rule which is impartial and under which opportunities exist for the effective challenge of decisions. They then assert that a plurality of power centers is important in maintaining a juridical rule (pp. 232–235). The result is a conception of democracy that stresses both equality of access to power and its wide distribution. Our definition of democracy is restricted to the matter of access. Their proposition that "a democratic regime is a necessary condition for democratic rule" means that Underdeveloped Democracy, in our terms, would not exist in the real world. *Ibid.*, p. 237.

38. A recent criticism of pluralists and of power elitists that implies a commitment to a widespread sharing of political power as a fundamental component of democracy is to be found in Peter Bachrach, "Elite Consensus and Democracy," *The Journal of Politics*, Vol. 24, No. 3 (August 1962), pp. 439–452.

39. Robert C. Wood, *Suburbia: Its People and Their Politics* (Boston: Houghton Mifflin Company, 1959), p. 282.

40. Although characteristics #1 and #6 of polyarchy as defined by Dahl and Lindblom do refer to severe penalties for political action (*Politics, Economics, and Welfare,* pp. 277–278), Robert Dahl's later distinction between oligarchies and democracies is based on this power-structure dimension. See his "The Analysis of Influence in Local Communities," *op. cit.,* pp. 27–28. However, Dahl does describe New Haven in regime terms: as having relatively honest voting counts (with occasional manipulation of the small number of absentee votes), elections "free from violence and, for all practical purposes, free from fraud," as having a "political stratum" committed to an axiom that prizes legality and constitutionality ("although a certain amount of legal chicanery is tolerable"), and "violence is not and seems never to have been a weapon of importance to New Haven's rulers." *Who Governs?,* pp. 3–4, 94, and 311. That other American communities might differ in these regards is noted by the comment that New Haven is not and has not "fallen at any time into the kind of semi-dictatorship occasionally found in other American communities." *Ibid.,* p. 311.

41. Robert A. Dahl, *Who Governs?,* pp. 11–24. Dahl's classification of New Haven as an Oligarchy prior to about 1840 apparently was not based on regime type. The classification seems to rest on the evidence that the political leadership was a single, unified group committed to a single ideology, with common upper-class backgrounds and interests, in whose hands rested top political, economic, and social power. This group had almost invariable success at the polls, the implication being that not only did other citizens fail to oppose them successfully but they also failed to make opposing political demands during that period. Thus the term Oligarchy seems to have been based on power structure assessments.

42. The dangers to the rule of law in small towns as a consequence of the operations of a spirit of fraternity are discussed by Robert C. Wood, *op. cit.,* pp. 276–280. Since the pluralists have not explored comparatively the distribution of political power among the citizens, we do not mean to imply that they have specifically indicated that a mass type of power structure is the norm in large American cities. Minority political participation has increasingly been recognized by all schools of thought as the norm in American community politics. Yet the dominant connotation seems to be that there is a wider distribution of political power over the citizens in larger than in smaller cities, in cities with a competitive party politics than in cities with one party dominance, etc. Although the extent of ideological divergence in the political leadership has rarely been studied in a conscious, systematic, comparative manner, the implication is clear that most pluralists do not think that ideology is a major variable at all. It is safer to conclude that they posit Consensual-power-structure situations as the norm, but we think that it is a fair statement that they also perceive relatively mass distributions of power as the other power-structure-dimension norm.

43. Springdale, as described by Arthur J. Vidich and Joseph Bensman, is in many ways of this character. See *Small Town in Mass Society* (New York: A Doubleday Anchor Book, 1958).

44. See Robert C. Wood, *op. cit.*

45. Dahl's major works in this connection include, with Charles A. Lindblom, *Politics, Economics, and Welfare*, his *A Preface to Democratic Theory*, and his *Who Governs?*

46. Robert A. Dahl, *A Preface to Democratic Theory*, p. 63. Copyright 1956 by the University of Chicago.

47. *Ibid.*, pp. 69–70.

48. *Ibid.*, p. 137.

49. *Ibid.*, p. 138, fn. 15.

50. *Ibid.*, p. 138.

51. This is not to argue that the regimes in the United States and in the Soviet Union are equally democratic; rather it means that limiting the conception of democracy to "active and legitimate" groups begs rather than answers the question about the differences between such regimes.

52. Dahl, *op. cit.*, pp. 66–67, fn. 2, and 132–133.

53. The authors feel that it is useful, for a variety of reasons, to distinguish between regimes and power structures until co-variations between and among them have been established empirically. We would call Dahl and Lindblom's characteristics #3 and #5 in their definition of polyarchy power-structure dimensions, and the other four characteristics regime dimensions. See *Politics, Economics, and Welfare*, p. 278.

54. Robert A. Dahl, *A Preface to Democratic Theory*, p. 132. There is an important ambiguity in this stress on competition, given the stress on an underlying consensus on policy and an implied dislike of ideological competition on the part of pluralists generally.

55. *Ibid.*, p. 150.

56. *Ibid.*, p. 145.

57. Robert C. Wood cites difficulties in maintaining competition and controversy in small towns as one of the reasons that democracy—as he and other pluralists define it—is difficult to develop or maintain there. See Wood, *op. cit.*

58. By limiting the term "democracy" to regimes, as defined, our theoretical framework in effect sets less stringent criteria for a Developed Democracy than do such analysts as Lasswell and Kaplan and Dahl and Lindblom.

59. Although this is a difficult research problem, it is not the same as that raised by a number of political theorists when they talk of "individuality," "freedom," or "autonomy" as corollaries of democracy. Robert C. Wood, for example, in talking about the "quest for freedom," suggests that an important ingredient of democracy is the ability of men to expand the number of alternative choices, to express and articulate individuality, and to engage in what might be called autonomous political action. Such political creativity or invention may be related to, but is something conceptually separate from, the matter of groups being "heard" or not in the formulation and communication of demands. These creative political acts should be explored to establish what kinds of political and nonpolitical individuality, freedom, or autonomy are possible or are effected by different kinds of political regimes. To do this necessitates the creation of models of the individual participant as a potentially creative political person, but little has been done toward this end. A promising line of inquiry is the conceptualization of various politically relevant psychological traits of individuals, such as political efficacy, cynicism, alienation, authoritarianism, and the measurement thereof, with studies of the relationship between the frequency of such types of people or attributes and types of political systems. Perhaps it might be assumed that certain

kinds of people (e.g., the highly inefficacious, etc.) are unlikely to engage in political creativity; but to assume that those more likely to create will do so under any political conditions is a matter that needs careful investigation. The often implicit assumption that democracies breed political creativity while nondemocracies breed political conformity would profit from such inquiry.

60. Fletcher Knebel, "The Predicament of Pecos, Texas," *Look Magazine,* July 31, 1962, pp. 76–78.

61. *Time Magazine,* November 17, 1961, pp. 40–41.

62. R. S. and H. M. Lynd, *Middletown in Transition* (New York: Harcourt, Brace and Company, 1937), p. 79.

63. For a description of illegitimate sanctions allegedly in use in Mississippi not so long ago, see Barbara Carter, "The Fifteenth Amendment Comes to Mississippi," *The Reporter,* January 17, 1963, pp. 20–24. Nor do we need to dwell on the murder of Medgar Evers and other Negro leaders and even Negro children.

64. Because of the limits of the methods used, our concern is restricted to general assessments of the extent to which political demands were extant that had not been met to at least some degree in decisional outcomes at particular points in time.

65. To include any policy formulated but not deliberated in any polity creates the more serious risk of setting impossibly ideal standards for the existence of Developed Democracies. Such ideal standards are necessary and desirable goals to improve democracy, but they must not preclude analytic distinctions that may usefully be made among nonideal polities. Thus, if a Developed Democracy were, by definition, a regime in which no citizen hesitated to make any political demand, regardless of the fundamental change involved, there would be no regime deserving the classification of Developed Democracy or even of Guided Democracy. This would render the classification scheme useless for purposes of comparative analysis. Similarly, if the probability had to be zero that such a demand would be blocked by illegitimate sanctions in order for the regime to be on the low side of the probability dimension, there would be no Developed or Underdeveloped Democracies. This would impede any further exploration of those gaps that exist between classified Developed Democracies and ideal models of Developed Democracy.

66. Too little is known about individual psychology to assume that changes in environment are necessary to insight, although a continuing condition or situation over time might be treated as a change in the environment from the point of view of an individual. Obviously, such a change might result from events in the environment rather than intraindividual insight.

67. The program of political suppression by White citizens in South Africa is but one of numerous efforts to control and eliminate political assembly by the opposition. That program provides that individuals can be forbidden to participate in public political activities, can be confined to a particular area, and even that they can be confined to their own homes for a period of years.

68. This distinction between propaganda, or manipulation, and education is congruent with some but not all definitions of those concepts.

69. Perhaps the best work on the feasibility and usefulness of quasi-experimental designs for political and social science investigations is that of Donald T.

Campbell, Department of Psychology, Northwestern University. See Campbell and Julian C. Stanley, "Experimental Designs for Research on Teaching," in *Handbook of Research on Teaching,* ed. N. L. Gage (Chicago: Rand McNally, 1963). See also Morris Janowitz's appeal for an experimental approach to the study of community political systems in his "Community Power and 'Policy Science' Research," *Public Opinion Quarterly,* Vol. XXVI (Fall 1962), pp. 398–410.

70. Arthur Schlesinger, Jr., in an address to the 1962 annual meeting of the American Historical Association, was reported as shuddering a little when he thought how confidently he had analyzed decisions of the Jackson and Roosevelt Administrations. He was quoted as saying, "The sad fact is that, in many cases, the basic evidence for the historian's reconstruction of the really hard cases does not exist—and the evidence that does exist is often incomplete, misleading, or erroneous." New York Times, Western Edition, December 31, 1962, p. 7, col. 1. Schlesinger's comments apply with full force to the present study. Nevertheless, the historical analysis is an important part of this work. Even the analytic assessments derived from historical research on the early post-Second World War periods, where problems of validity and reliability were greater than for the immediate past (the year prior to Time *M*, the point of initial, intensive field research), are included herein.

4

TWO REGIONS AND FOUR COMMUNITIES:
social, economic, and governmental structures

The political analyst who compares the politics of two or more communities within a country should tell the reader something of their socio-economic and governmental structures, the general community environment, and the character of the regions in which they are located. This is especially the case when two of the four research communities are in one region of the United States, the West, and the other two are in another, the South. It is generally assumed that regional differences play a significant part in the structure and functioning of community politics. The differences and similarities between the two regions and among the four communities should be described.

THE TWO REGIONS

Western State is divided into several major physical areas. The two cities selected for study are located in a mining area that contains much of the state's population. This area is dominated by a valley with a very large metropolis at one end. Stretching east and west through the valley is a population belt, linked to the metropolis by a major U. S. highway, a railroad line, and a navigable river. It is a valley of mines, farms, towns, and small cities.

The two communities of Farmdale and Oretown are located at the eastern end of the valley, about 35 miles apart, and 250 miles east of the metropolis. Farmdale lies close to a mountain range in the level agricultural area of the valley. Oretown is near the foothills of this range, where the major mineral deposits are found. The city is built on an overflow or flood plain of a river system, and occasionally the river floods the surrounding area.

The region's population increased much more rapidly from 1930 to 1950 than did that of the nation as a whole during the same period. The per capita income of the region surpassed the national average in the late 1930's and remained high until the mid-1950's. Most of this growth was the result of expanded industrial activity during and after the Second World War. The increase in industrial activity and population caused a correspondingly rapid increase in urbanization. Besides the increase in size of such Western cities as Los Angeles, San Francisco, Seattle, Portland, and Denver, hamlets and villages became towns, and towns became cities. By 1950, Farmdale was a large town, or very small city, with over 1,500 population; Oretown was a small to medium-size city of about 15,000 inhabitants.

The economic structure of Western State had shifted a little from mining industries, which prior to the 1920's accounted for the big share of the area's employment. The shift was toward the manufacturing, trade, transportation, and service industries. However, the state's economy was still relatively immature and lagged behind the rest of the country in the development of manufacturing.

The section of Western State in which Farmdale and Oretown are located had two primary sources of income: mining and agriculture. Industry was heavily concentrated in the extraction and primary processing of minerals and agricultural resources. Further processing took place in centers located nearer the nation's large markets. This section of the state suffered an immediate disadvantage and a serious long-run danger in the exchange of raw materials for finished goods. The section was particularly vulnerable to the business cycle of its underdeveloped and not very diversified economy. The long-run danger was the possible depletion of the economy's material base.

Western State was searching for a means of sustaining its level of economic activity and promoting future economic growth. Different approaches to the problem were advocated by those who urged further diversification within the mining industry and by those who sought economic diversification through new types of industry. Any program for the economic future of the state had to take into account the resources of the region. It was generally recognized that the area suffered because it depended on costly transportation to get its products to distant markets. However, state government officials tended to be optimistic about the future prospects for industrial development of the state. This feeling was based partly on wishful thinking, partly on satisfaction with the postwar prosperity, and partly on the feeling that living and recreational resources associated in people's minds with "the West" would guarantee future growth and prosperity.

Although the rate of population growth decreased drastically in the 1950's, immigrants still were coming to Western State from other sections of the country. They included older people looking for a pleasant environment in which to spend their retirement and younger people moving west from all sections of the country in search of economic opportunities. However, when the migration of settlers into the section of the state where Farmdale and Oretown are located decreased, old-timers seemed happy that the area would not suffer the fate of a growth rate similar to that of Los Angeles. The image of subdivisions and industry dotting the scenic landscape, plus the problems associated with urban life, were not viewed with great favor. Indeed, it appeared to many as if current problems required resolution before inviting new ones.

In some respects Southern State resembles Western State and in some respects it differs sharply. There are three major sections in the state: a flat agricultural area that is "typically Southern"; a mountainous tourist-trade area; and the primarily industrial-manufacturing sector. Petropolis and Metroville are in the primarily industrial-manufacturing area, a center of urban growth in Southern State. The plantation system had been developed in the agricultural area with large farms, tenant farmers, and sharecroppers. The biracial plantation culture sharply distinguishes the South from the West. Negroes traditionally serve as the labor force in these farming operations, and racial segregation is most complete in areas of greatest Negro density, the so-called Black Belt.

Metroville and Petropolis are cities with populations of 90,000 to 100,000. Metroville is about 100 miles to the east of Petropolis. Although the state's population more than doubled from 1900 to 1950, the rate of growth in recent years has been far behind that of Western State. Emigration has exceeded immigration by a substantial margin. Whites have been leaving the state at a faster rate than they have been moving in and Negroes emigrate at a particularly rapid rate.

Although emigration among Negroes has been related partially to their restricted opportunities to enjoy the good life, emigration by both Whites and Negroes also is related to the economic problems of the region and of the state. Even though the region has undergone industrial development over the years, particularly the growth of manufacturing, it has remained basically agricultural, as has Southern State.

Compared to the nation, both region and state have a disproportionate number of people engaged in farming, a large number of unskilled workers, and a small number of skilled, professional, technical,
and managerial people in industry. This occupational and income distribution is partly a result of the concentration of Southern State's
manufacturing in low-wage- and low-value-producing industries. For
example, average weekly earnings in all manufacturing employment
in Southern State were about 50 per cent lower than in the nation during the 1950's. Southern State not only shared the economic problems
of the South; it also found itself falling behind other Southern states
in economic progress.

As in Western State, leading government officials of Southern State
stressed the need for continued industrialization to solve basic problems. This industrialization, which would have provided further
impetus to urban growth, also would have required people to continue
to leave the farms for industry and thus alleviate a basic economic
problem of farming: too many small, marginal farms. There was
more sense of urgency underlying industrial promotion in Southern
State than in Western State. But the Northern industries most interested in moving were firms trying to escape unions and high wages,
the sort of industry least likely to alleviate problems of low income,
underemployment, and excessive numbers of full-time or part-time
farmers.

The plight of the Negro marginal farmer who moved into segregated
cities compounded the state's economic difficulties. It was difficult
for Negroes to find jobs outside of the Negro subcommunities in the
cities, and those available were ordinarily the lowest paying. This was
the case in both Petropolis and Metroville at the time of the study.
The result was an urban situation in which large numbers of citizens
with very low incomes burdened the entire community. "Under-
consumption" in the economy was paralleled by "overconsumption"
of city services; Negroes had to have a certain level of city services
even if they did not have the means to pay for them. This gave to
even the small cities of Southern State some of the problems of the
giant metropolises of the North that have relatively large Negro subcommunities.

Economic opportunities were even more sharply limited for the city
Negro in Southern State; social segregation practices in education, in
restaurants, and in recreational and transportation facilities were
traditionally stricter there and added to the social tensions in intergroup relations found, to some degree, in every urban center in the
United States. Interdependence and interconnections among members

of a city inevitably create problems as well as benefits. The need to increase wealth, to enhance the prospect of city living, to attain greater security and dignity, and to allocate these values between socially and psychologically distinct subcommunities created distinctive economic and social problems of community life in Southern State. It is difficult, if not impossible, to assess such community divisions based on color and racial lines, with their associated emotional intensities and psychological consequences, as comparable to some relatively mild community divisions in racially homogeneous Farmdale and Oretown. Yet it is unwarranted to assume that some degree of segregation and social distance based on occupational or social class distinctions, neighborhood residence, ethnic origins, or length of residence are not part and parcel of universal tendencies, with potentially similar impacts on community politics. The logic of our comparative study is, in fact, to assess the underlying similarities of apparently distinctive community characteristics.

We turn now to a more detailed description of the four communities.

THE FOUR COMMUNITIES

Farmdale, Western State, U.S.A.

Farmdale is one of the smallest incorporated cities in Fir County, Western State. It had a population of less than 2,000 in 1950.[1] In the prior two decades Farmdale experienced considerable growth, but the rate of increase lagged far behind that of other cities in the immediate area. While Fir County experienced an increase in population of more than 75 per cent from 1940 to 1950, Farmdale increased by only 25 per cent.

Gradual growth has characterized the town since its settlement after the Civil War. The economic base has been a diversified type of agriculture in the surrounding area that supports the retail trading establishments in town. Over the years a few small industries that became an important source of employment for the local people were added. ' In more recent years the developing tourist industry has helped to support a number of motels, cafes, and service stations. Agricultural activities in the region expanded at a comparatively slow rate during the 1940's, while the wartime demand for minerals was reflected in the population boom in those cities whose economies were more directly geared to large-scale mineral processing. The increasing utilization of available farmlands accounted for Farmdale's growing reputation as an agricultural center; but the absence of large industrial installations was reflected in the failure of the town to keep pace with urban growth in the surrounding area.

Two population processes were occurring simultaneously during the 1940's and 1950's. Large numbers of young people who had been born and brought up in Farmdale were moving away to seek opportunities elsewhere. At the same time, newcomers were moving in, particularly young adults, who represented a small part of the great wave of regional immigration. Many of these newcomers were small business-men who came to the community hoping to share in the general economic expansion of the area. However, the rate of turnover of small businessmen in the town was extremely high during the 1950's. The local economy was not expansive during the postwar years.

Besides the deficiency in local business opportunities, two other economic problems began to develop; one was related to the economy of the community, and the other to the economy of the immediate region. The first of these was the defection of local shoppers to the larger, more modern, and more attractive markets of nearby Big City. The second was the fact that the instability in the national market of the area's major industry created unemployment, even in Farmdale. Although it was not primarily a manufacturing town, the community's few industrial units, one of which was of medium size, were components of the area's major unstable industry. Perhaps of even greater consequence than local unemployment was the related decrease in consumer spending in the stores of Farmdale. By the early 1950's economic dislocation resulting from these conditions, although not critical, had become serious enough for some members of the community to consider ways in which the situation might be im-proved. Some thought was given to encouraging new industries to come to traditionally rural-oriented Farmdale.

The working force of Farmdale and its environs had the following characteristics: about 20 per cent of the working force were farmers; about 30 per cent were engaged in white-collar occupations, with proprietors the largest subcategory; there were few professional men and technically trained people and very few clerical and sales per-sonnel, since the typical business establishment in Farmdale was owner-operated. The rest of the working force, about half of the employed, were blue-collar workers.

The residents of Farmdale expressed a very high regard for their town. Many reasons were offered in support of this opinion. Farm-dale has a beautiful setting; it is situated amid highly productive farm-lands. Winters are mild and the humidity is very low during the dry summer months. Recreational opportunities are plentiful and available to everyone. The desirable aspects of urban life are available in nearby Big City or in the major metropolis 250 miles away, but the strains of urban living and the unattractive environmental features of bigger cities are absent from Farmdale. There are no ugly industrial stretches, no smog or noxious fumes, no extensive slums, and no major traffic problems.

Antagonisms arising from interracial, interreligious, and labor-management relations virtually did not exist at the time of the study because of the lack of racial or religious minorities or large factories. The town originally was settled by German farmers whose descendants constituted a majority of the community. One occasionally heard that the Germans were a closed group or that they "ran the town," but the little feeling of this sort that did exist was not of the type to divide a community along rigid lines. The number of newcomers in the community was another source of potential conflict. But these immigrants had come fairly equally from the different sections of the United States, so no one sectional group posed a distinct threat to the old-timers. There was an occasional expression of concern over the number of "Arkies" and "Okies" streaming into the region, and an occasional derogatory remark about "a poor White Southerner," but there were few people from those sections of the country in Farmdale. Thus, the community seemed to enjoy harmonious intergroup relations that were personally satisfying to many of its inhabitants. The visitor found an air of friendliness on the main streets. When a man in overalls entered the bank to deposit a check, he frequently spent a few moments in friendly conversation with the manager. To this extent at least, there was an equalitarian and intimate atmosphere about the town.

At the time of the study the physical appearance of Farmdale revealed an absence of extremes in the style of life of most of its inhabitants. Although the better and the poorer sections of town were roughly delineated by the railroad tracks, few homes were in a state of drastic deterioration. Most of the houses were comfortable and well kept. Homes on newer residential streets were conservative in style and size. The absence of any large yards or estates suggested that, at least in these respects, social class differences were not great. Even the new areas just outside the city limits, where some of the wealthier people lived, were not very different in appearance from the more typical middle-class areas in town. The south part of the city "across the tracks" had older, less valuable homes and fewer paved streets and sidewalks than other sections of Farmdale.

In 1950, 75 per cent of the residents owned or were buying their own homes. In this predominantly agricultural area, most farmers also owned their own farms. Migrant laborers were used to harvest crops, but remained in the community for only a short period each year. Data on family incomes confirm this impression of an essentially middle-class community. In the 1952 sample survey of the people, only one person, of 260 interviewed, reported an income of $25,000 or more per year, and less than 5 per cent made over $10,000 a year. Almost half the families had annual incomes between $4,000 and $10,000. More than 90 per cent of the adults over the age of 25 had at least 7 years of schooling; about 15 per cent had some college education.

According to the sample survey of 1952, slightly more than half the adult residents of the city and the surrounding fringe area had moved to Farmdale since 1941. This was a smaller ratio of newcomers to old-timers than in Oretown, but a much larger ratio than in either Southern city. The Census of 1950 revealed that Farmdale had a higher percentage of older people—55 to 64 years of age and over 65 years of age—and a smaller proportion of young adults—in the 15–24 and 25–34 age brackets—than any of the other three cities, presumably because of the migration of younger people who were leaving to seek their fortunes elsewhere.

There was a fairly simple but widespread network of voluntary associations in Farmdale. Slightly less than 10 per cent of the adult population were members of labor unions, although about one-third of the entire blue-collar working class was unionized. More than half these memberships were in the local unions of neighboring towns. The business community had neither a chamber of commerce nor a merchants association, but the various service clubs performed some of the functions of such organizations on a small, sporadic scale. The Republican party was minimally organized in this community, and the Democratic registration exceeded the Republican, although there was no local Democratic party organization. This may have been a factor in the consistent electoral triumphs of the Republican minority in elections for county, state, and national representatives. One of the county's state representatives was a Republican resident of Farmdale.

Slightly more than half the adult citizens of Farmdale belonged to one or more formally organized voluntary associations. This includes voluntary groups associated with churches but does not include labor unions and churches. More than half the adult members of labor unions were integrated into the community through one or more nonlabor-union formal organization; but the union was the only membership in a formally organized voluntary association in the community for somewhat less than half of them. While Americans are often considered a nation of joiners, the contention that practically every citizen belongs to at least one formally organized voluntary association is far from correct. National studies of memberships suggest that the proportion of adult nonjoiners may be over 50 per cent, with sharp variations in that figure from community to community and within communities, by such factors as position in the socio-economic structure, race, and religion.[2]

Farmdale had, at that time, a relatively simple local governmental structure. A mayor was elected on a nonpartisan ballot for a two-year term; he voted in case of a tie within the city council and appointed the council committees and certain officials upon the advice and consent of the council. The city was divided into six wards; the six members of the council were elected on a ward basis and served six-year terms.

There was no city manager. An appointed city recorder served as the chief administrative officer. He kept the records and served as the finance officer; he was *the* clerical staff and the part-time judge of the recorder's (municipal) court. A fire chief organized a volunteer fire department; a police chief was in charge of a small force. In addition, an engineer supervised the municipal sewage-disposal plant, and a single officer supervised street, sidewalk, and road improvements. With the small number of persons involved and the minimal level of city functioning, considerable cooperation, mutual aid, and informality in the handling of municipal business existed.

The sewage-disposal plant was the major modern addition that had been made by municipal government. The city's water supply was drawn from several deep wells, and a private electric-utility company supplied street lighting. There was no municipal recreation program, but city officials helped maintain certain parklands donated for such purposes by private associations. Building inspections were conducted by a committee of councilmen. The planning commission was one of the two agencies of local government staffed by appointed officials. The other agency was the important lay budget committee, which had the task of deciding the level of local government expenditures. Local government in Farmdale also had no health or welfare functions or programs; the Fir County government administered programs of public welfare for all the citizens of the county, including those of Farmdale and Oretown.

The public school system in the Farmdale area was operated through an independent school district which levied its own property taxes. The school levies were considerably larger than the levies of the city government. The tax rate of the municipality of Farmdale was lower than that of Oretown or other communities of larger size.

Oretown, Western State, U.S.A.

Oretown and its fringe areas form the industrial component of a metropolitan area, the city having 15,000 inhabitants. It is located close to Big City, a much larger community. Oretown grew during the 1940's from a town slightly larger than Farmdale to its present size. This boomtown growth occurred through a great expansion of war-related manufacturing industry during the Second World War. Although a number of smaller firms failed, conversion to peacetime production was generally successful, so that a town that was once small—one major mining company and retail trading establishments —became an industrial city of moderate size and continual growth.

The population explosion produced a virtually new community. According to data derived from the sample survey of 1953, only 1 per cent of the adult residents had been born in Oretown. The newcomers were highly mobile young adults. This is illustrated by the fact that 60 per cent of the adult population had lived in two or more cities during the 7 years following the Second World War. By 1953 only 25 per cent of the entire population of Oretown had resided there for a period of 10 years or more.

Oretown had several distinct residential areas. The more well-to-do businessmen had their homes on the outskirts of town, while a new housing development attracted the younger professionals and businessmen. Many of the old-timers who worked as blue-collar employees in Oretown's oldest industrial concern were concentrated in another section of the city. Annexations following the Second World War incorporated a large number of middle-income, skilled and semi-skilled workers who were newcomers to Oretown. There was a rapidly growing fringe area. Part of the area where many of the newcomer blue-collar workers lived had low housing standards and major sewer, drainage, and street problems.

Since its founding in the late 1800's, the mining industry has played a prominent part in the economy and affairs of Oretown, whose history was that of a one-industry, "company town." At the turn of the century, the Johnson Company, which employed some 250 workers, moved into Oretown from another region. It maintained the largest payroll in the community, and its officials took a leading part in the life of the community.

The Second World War changed the economic and social life of Oretown in basic ways. Many new plants moved into the area; these were mainly absentee owned. Their management took little interest in community planning and development, though some junior executives took part in civic affairs. The top executives preferred to reside and assume civic roles in larger and more cosmopolitan Big City.

Oretown, as an industrial city, was different from the semirural, retail trading economy of Farmdale. Less than 1 per cent of Oretown's working force was engaged in agriculture. Blue-collar workers comprised almost 70 per cent of the employed, as compared with 50 per cent in Farmdale. There were four times as many machine operators as in Farmdale. There were also twice as many in service, clerical, and sales positions in Oretown as there were in Farmdale. Personal incomes were comparable in these two Western communities, although slightly larger in Oretown. The educational level of the two populations was also comparable, with a slightly larger proportion of poorly educated in Oretown than in Farmdale.

The ratio of young adults and children to the rest of the population was greater in Oretown than in Farmdale. Whereas about half the population of Farmdale had moved there during and after the Second World War, more than three-quarters of the population of Oretown were recent arrivals.

Like Farmdale, Oretown's population was heavily White native-born American of Protestant belief, though there was a Catholic church and parochial school. The factories were almost completely unionized: 25 per cent of the adult population belonged to a labor union; about 60 per cent of the entire blue-collar working class were union members. The network of formally organized voluntary associations was more elaborate than Farmdale's, although a smaller proportion of citizens were members. Businessmen had an active Chamber of Commerce in addition to many other civic and service clubs. Both the Republican and Democratic parties had local organizations; registered Democrats outnumbered Republicans, but competition in county, state, and national elections was intense. Half the citizens of Oretown belonged to no formal organization; of the remainder, almost one-fifth belonged only to a local labor union. In contrast to Farmdale, where a majority of labor-union members belonged to at least one other community organization, more than two-thirds of the union members in Oretown belonged only to a labor union.

While new industry brought prosperity, the increased population created problems. The influx of people complicated service and house-keeping functions of local government. An expanded school system was necessary to accommodate the children of the young, newcomer families. Basic services had to be extended to newly developed sections of town. New demands were made for expanded recreation facilities. City planning and zoning were introduced to control the growth of the city.

Oretown was a community of single-family housing, with few rental units. However, mixed industrial and residential areas appeared with the wartime and postwar building boom. These housing developments, located on the edge of town, were poorly constructed, and frequently met only the minimal F.H.A. standards; but these were comparable neither to big city slums nor to the sort of marginal, makeshift housing provided elsewhere for migrant workers. Nevertheless, there was increasing concern for the future of property values and aesthetic standards. Suggestions were made to develop city planning, zoning, ·and annexation.

Flood control became more imperative as the periodic overflow from nearby rivers threatened many new residences. Medical reports from various governmental agencies ascertained that the health of hundreds of families was endangered by unsanitary conditions resulting from inadequate drainage and sewage disposal in the heavily settled area directly north of the city. Oretown's largest factory was located in this area. The company disagreed with these medical reports and opposed annexation because it already had its own large-scale sewage-disposal system which it considered adequate. It could see no advantage and considerable expense in such a measure.

In the immediate postwar years, as the community began to resolve some of its many problems, concern was expressed more and more often about the future of the local economy. The major industry was declining after the period of wartime prosperity. Small firms began to close or to sell out to larger competitors. People wondered whether Oretown dared to rely much longer on a single industry.

Various proposals were offered. One was that Oretown ought to consolidate with nearby Big City, thus becoming part of a more economically diversified and secure community. Big City had manufacturing plants, a college, active wholesale and retail trade, and a generally more diversified economy. The property values and assessed valuations of Big City were higher than those of Oretown. Over the years Big City had served as a model for Oretown's citizens. While Big City's image was sometimes regarded favorably by the citizens of Oretown, as in the case of its very successful, municipally owned power company, more often community jealousy and fears of domination evoked unfavorable sentiments toward Big City. These feelings were compounded by the resentment of a workingman's town toward a predominantly white-collar community. The negative feelings seemed to be more widespread than the positive ones among the citizens of Oretown, so that the proposed merger of the two cities received little favorable consideration.

Another suggested solution was that Oretown try to acquire new factories from another industry, thus diversifying its economy. The city offers advantages for certain types of industry: available industrial sites are located near good rail and highway facilities and can be served by cheap electric power. The municipal utility used its low electric rates to attract a small chemical plant, which consumed enough electricity to make the low electric-power rate a major factor in its decision to relocate. But other such firms did not follow, since they were being established increasingly in the Midwest, where lower transportation costs have tended to undercut the traditional hydro-electric-power advantages of the West.

Oretown's younger migrants had moved there for economic opportunity. During the immediate postwar years labor-management negotiations became tougher. The Korean War brought an upsurge of prosperity, but by the end of 1953 labor and management were girding for battle and there was the possibility of major strikes in the months immediately ahead. During its era as a one-company town and also during the prosperous years of the Second World War, Oretown had not known serious labor-management conflict. Even though people still felt that neither side would intentionally disrupt harmonious relations between industrial executives and the heads of the two major labor unions, there was an uneasiness about the economic future. These factors, along with the trend toward consolidation in industry, the disappearance of many small mining firms, periodic short-term unemployment, and job instability, contributed to the concern about the local economy on the part of the blue-collar workers of Oretown. By 1953, the local economy was the focus of attention of Oretown's citizens.

Merchants shared the concern of their counterparts in Farmdale during these periods of unemployment. Their proximity to Big City made them even more upset about competition from that city's larger retail-trading establishments. In addition, the merchants of Oretown saw that industrial unrest and strikes might severely disrupt sales to their blue-collar customers. They also saw sharper competition between the business establishments of Main Street and the new business section in a recently annexed part of town. Although the municipal utility, a unit of local government, had been of major assistance in attracting the new chemical company, there were relatively few who urged that local government try to ameliorate their community's immediate economic problems.

Oretown had a council-manager government. The city-manager form was introduced immediately after the Second World War, over substantial minority opposition. The mayor, elected for four years, had the authority to appoint city council committees, prepare a "state of the city" message, and appoint, with council approval, members of the city planning commission, the library board, and special study groups. He, like the mayor of Farmdale, could vote only if the council was evenly divided. The six members of the city council were elected by wards on a nonpartisan basis for four-year terms. The city's charter provided for the initiative, referendum, and recall. In Oretown these devices of "direct democracy" were used frequently in a local politics marked by frequent "mass" interventions in the operation of local government.

The city's full-time appointive officials included a recorder—the chief financial officer—a police chief, a fire chief, a city engineer, and a part-time city attorney. These men were all appointed by the city manager. There was also a municipal judge.

Oretown had a fragmented local government, with autonomous law-making and supervisory boards for the municipal utility, the school system, and the park-and-recreation district. The members of each independent board were elected in separate elections. The municipal utility had an elected board and a full-time superintendent who supervised the publicly owned electric utility which was established by popular vote in 1949. The city's water system was owned and operated by the private company that operates the competing electric utility. The private company competed with the municipal utility throughout the city, which was only a fraction of the area in which the private company sold electricity. The municipal utility operated only within the city limits. It was a nonprofit organization, operating on revenue bonds authorized by the electorate; these bonds were to be repaid from revenues derived from the sale of electricity. The electricity rates of the private and municipal power companies were identical and low, compared to rates elsewhere in the private company's marketing area.

The five-man, elected school board operated a large consolidated district which encompassed the rural-urban fringe of Oretown. There was a heavy emphasis on athletics in the schools; consequently, the sporting events and athletic contests held in the high school's large stadium attracted heavy community attendance and attention.

The special, independent park-and-recreation district was one of the first of its kind in the region. Its area of jurisdiction included the city and rural-urban fringe areas. The park board, like the municipal utility and school boards, had five members, elected at large. A park director supervised an extensive network of parks, swimming pools, and recreational facilities. The district retained its own legal counsel.

Each unit of local government, except for the municipal utility, had the legal authority to levy its own tax on the real property in its jurisdiction. In addition, each unit could request permission from the electorate to sell bonds in order to raise capital equipment funds. The bonds could be repaid or retired and the interest paid annually from additional property-tax levies. All four units had been authorized by their electorates to issue special bonds. Residents of the city proper paid property taxes to three units of local government: the municipality, the park district, and the school district. Residents in the fringe area paid property taxes to the school and park districts. In addition to these local taxes there were, of course, taxes levied by the county government. The school tax rate was about three and one-half times that of the municipality; the municipality tax rate was, in turn, about four times that of the park district. The municipal utility paid the city government and the school district an annual sum in lieu of local taxes; this was approximately equal to the amount that would have been due if the municipal utility were privately owned and subject to taxation.

These brief sketches describe the two Western communities in the early 1950's, at the beginning of our field research. Comparable descriptions follow of Petropolis and Metroville, the two Southern communities, as of 1958, when field research was begun there.

Petropolis, Southern State, U.S.A.

Petropolis was a small village in an agricultural area until the late 1800's. As in Metroville, the capital accumulated in the first and still dominant industry was used to start other industrial operations by the early 1900's. Petropolis, like Metroville, grew about 25 per cent in population during the 1940's; this is about the same rate as that of Farmdale. During the 1950's, the rate of increase dropped rapidly, until, by 1957, the city and the suburban population virtually stopped growing.   Petropolis had a population of about 100,000, of which approximately one-third was Negro.

Compared to either Western community, Petropolis had an immobile population.   More than one-third of the adult citizens were born there.   About 80 per cent of both races had lived in the community more than ten years.   Newcomers to Petropolis were traditionally drawn from rural areas, but in recent years there had been more highly educated business, managerial, and professional immigrants from other urban areas.   Population growth due to rural migration dwindled in Petropolis County as economic conditions grew more favorable in other nearby cities.

Petropolis, like Metroville and other cities of Southern State, is a city of two subcommunities, one White and one Negro.   But unlike that of Metroville, the Negro subcommunity of Petropolis had a small, extremely wealthy set of people whose income was derived from the ownership and control of loan companies and investment houses, specializing in the sale of stocks and bonds.   The firms were managed and staffed by Petropolis Negroes.

Even this small upper class in the Petropolis Negro subcommunity had to face the problems of a segregated society.   There were segre-. gated Negro residential sections and very little social desegregation even for the wealthy, highly educated Negro community leaders. There was no public school desegregation by 1958, although a few Negro children had for several years been enrolled in a parochial school; a few others attended a predominantly White, very exclusive private school.   Occasional social and professional contacts occurred between a few Negroes, mostly educators, and a few White faculty members from a nearby state university.   There were economic and political contacts between the organized Negro community leadership, the economically dominant Negro businessmen, and some White business, civic, and political leaders.   However, the great majority of the Negro citizens in Petropolis were of lower-class status.   Almost all of their social contacts were with members of their own race.

The economy of the Negro subcommunity in Petropolis, while providing well-paid jobs for a few, did not solve the occupational and income problems confronting the average Negro.   Negroes had either to hold jobs that directly serviced the Negro community, or to work in industry owned and managed by Whites.   Industry generally adhered to the unwritten Southern racial rule: Negroes shall not be in charge of Whites, nor shall they work side by side with them.   A few small plants owned by Whites employed only Negroes.   Menial, low-paying domestic service, or unskilled, custodian-janitorial types of jobs were traditionally held by Negroes. In the major industries the most unskilled jobs were reserved for Negro workers.

The difference in the economic situation of Whites and Negroes in Petropolis was reflected in the following comparisons. Three times as many Whites as Negroes held professional, technical, managerial, official, or proprietorial positions. There were five times as many Whites with clerical and sales jobs. More than 85 per cent of the employed Negroes had blue-collar jobs, as compared to less than 50 per cent of the employed Whites. Even within the blue-collar occupations there were major differences. Almost ten times as many Negroes as Whites were employed in unskilled, common labor. Twice as many Whites held skilled-worker or foreman positions; three times as many Negroes were service workers. Almost one-fifth of the employed Negroes worked as domestic servants or in other private-household jobs; these were almost exclusively Negro occupations. An average of about 20 per cent of the Negro labor force was unemployed during the middle 1950's, compared to less than 5 per cent of the Whites. More than 50 per cent of the Negro families had an annual income of less than $2,000 per year; more than 75 per cent had an annual income of less than $3,000 per year. The comparable figures for Whites were about 40 per cent and 60 per cent. It will be recalled that only about one-third of the Oretown families had an annual income of less than $3,000 per year. The differences in income between these Southern and Western cities was very large; the Petropolis Negroes as a whole were at the bottom of the income scale.

About 7 per cent more of Oretown's working force was in manufacturing jobs. These jobs paid more than manufacturing jobs in Petropolis. On the other hand, one-third more of Oretown's labor force worked at blue-collar jobs than did the White labor force in Petropolis; there were more than seven times as many men in common laboring jobs in Oretown as there were in the White subcommunity of Petropolis. Incomes were simply much lower for Whites holding comparable jobs in Petropolis than they were in Oretown.

The Negroes of Petropolis had less education than the Whites; more than half the adult Negroes had less than a seventh-grade education. About 10 per cent had at least some college education. In fact, the proportion of college-educated Negroes in Petropolis was not much below the proportion of the college-educated in either Western community. The White subcommunity of Petropolis was far better educated than the Negro, but there were more White citizens who were either very poorly educated or very highly educated than in either of the Western cities. About twice as many Whites in Petropolis as in the Western cities had less than a seventh-grade education; but about twice as many had gone to college as in Farmdale or Oretown.

In the economy of Petropolis there were a small number of absentee-owned corporations in one industry; each of these employed several thousand workers. The corporations in a second industry were of medium size; other industries were represented by smaller firms. There was a network of financial institutions owned by Whites in Petropolis. Automation was well under way in both major industries, creating an ever-greater surplus of labor, both Negro and White.

Petropolis suffered from two disadvantages that Metroville did not share: it was located at a greater distance from good railroad transportation and from major interstate highways and also was farther away from the heaviest concentrations of the state's urban population. New industry from the North tended to settle in the part of the state near Metroville, rather than in or around Petropolis.

Another disadvantage concerning attraction of new business and industry was heavy unionization. Local proponents of economic growth asserted that many Northern firms who might consider moving to the state were avoiding unions and consequently passed over Petropolis as a possible location. About 10 per cent of the Whites and a smaller percentage of Negroes were members of unions in Petropolis. Compared to many other cities of Southern State, including Metroville, this percentage was high. Somewhat more than one-third of all working-class Whites were unionized, compared to about one-third in Farmdal and three-fifths in Oretown. The Negro working class was proportionately twice as large, but the proportion of union members was much lower—about 6 per cent. Workers in the largest plants and industries were organized in Petropolis, and there was a strong central labor council.

Petropolis was a Democratic electoral and organizational stronghold in Democratic Southern State. The unions, White and Negro, were well represented among the officials of the local Democratic party. A small proportion of Negroes joined the local Republican party and constituted about half of the active Republican party workers.

The proportion of White citizens of Petropolis who belonged to formally organized voluntary associations was about the same as that in Oretown: half the adults in each city belonged to one or more voluntary associations. Oretown was the more unionized city, and the proportion of Oretown's citizens who belonged to only a labor union and to no other voluntary association was considerably larger than that proportion in Petropolis. The White labor unionists in Petropolis formed a much more distinct "subculture," however, in that they were more isolated from their community's civic-associational life than were labor union members in Oretown. A much greater proportion of the small union membership in Petropolis belonged to no other voluntary association.

Members of the Negro subcommunity of Petropolis were "joiners." Their membership rate was higher than that of either the Petropolis Whites or the citizens of Farmdale. Aside from church affiliation, almost two-thirds of the Negroes in Petropolis belonged to one or more formal organizations. Nearly 20 per cent of the adult Negroes of Petropolis belonged to the National Association for the Advancement of Colored People. Unlike the White unionists of Petropolis, the Negro union members tended to be members of other Negro organizations as well. They were as "integrated" in this way into their subcommunity as union members of Farmdale were integrated into the larger community there.

Petropolis had its segregated residential areas. The Negro section was a slumlike ghetto of great population density, poorly paved streets, and few trees. The homes, single- or two-family structures, frequently had three, four, and sometimes more families living in them. The entire area was in disrepair. The Negro business district was located in the residential area, along with a large complex of ugly industrial buildings. The wealthier Negro families of Petropolis lived near the Negro college; this was a neighborhood of much pleasanter physical appearance. A number of White residential areas were also suffering from urban blight.

Petropolis had only one small residential section inhabited by the affluent. The White citizens who lived in this area had expensive homes on large, heavily wooded lots. The area adjoined the downtown central business district and contained no vacant land for additional houses. A substantial number of Petropolis' White industrial executives and business leaders lived in Chestnut Hills, an exclusive suburb outside the city limits. Here the atmosphere of exclusion was enhanced by the very palatial homes around the rolling hills and greens of a country club.

The White families most closely associated with the early industrial development of Petropolis were the Bacon and Leek families. These two sets of kinfolk were known for their local charitable works and involvement in community affairs. One branch lived inside the city; many of their wealthy White associates lived in Chestnut Hills. The civic leaders living in the city seemed to have an interest in its quality, character, and physical future which those who resided outside the city lacked. It was the city group who seemed most concerned with the hodgepodge of neighborhoods, the areas of mixed land use, and the extensive slums inside the city.

The council-manager form of government had long been established in Petropolis. The mayor was elected for a two-year term, and had more authority than the mayor of Oretown. He not only presided at council meetings and appointed council committees, but he also could vote on all questions coming before the council and appoint members of the city's public-housing commission and various advisory boards and agencies.

The council consisted of 14 members, elected at large for four-year terms. A minority were nominated by the citizens at large, and a majority were nominated on the basis of wards. The voters could recall any elected official. All city officials were elected on a nonpartisan ballot, although in this traditionally Democratic city candidates were ordinarily Democrats. The Negro subcommunity's strength was such that they could nominate from one ward and elect one Negro councilman, which they had done for several years. They accomplished this through disciplined bloc voting with voting support from a White minority.

A municipal planning commission was created during the Second World War. The city council passed a modern zoning ordinance in the early 1950's for the commission to supervise, assisted by the city department of planning. This ordinance considerably changed zone classifications, reduced areas reserved for commercial use, required that buildings be set back farther from the street, and provided for the inclusion of off-street parking for new buildings. At the same time, the city also established a special commission to hear appeals and grant relief from these more restrictive provisions of the zoning ordinance. The postwar effort to make professional planning and guided development more effective was weakened through exceptions granted by the special commission.

Unlike Oretown, most governmental activities in Petropolis were found within the single structure of city government or in conjunction with the county. The city operated its own public-housing agency, water and sewer systems, and park and recreation programs. It had its own school board. The health and library authorities were joint city-county agencies. Members of the public-housing agency were appointed by the mayor. The agency constructed, owned, and operated, with the assistance of federal funds, two low-rent housing projects—one for Negroes and one for Whites—which consisted of over 500 dwelling units. A municipal-recreation citizens' commission, appointed by the mayor, advised the head of the park and recreation department at City Hall. The city government also maintained two cemeteries, one for White and one for Negro citizens.

Petropolis, with nearly 75 per cent of the population of the county, had its own school system; the city council appointed the school board. However, responsibilities for education were shared with the state and county. The city's school budget had to be approved by the elected officials of the county government. Of the total school budget, the state contributed over 50 per cent, the county approximately 20 per cent, and the city about 25 per cent. The city's share came from a property tax levy approved by the voters; it was primarily intended to pay for additional teachers and higher teacher salaries in the city than in the county schools. The county had a major role in school finances and operated the schools in the city's fringe area. The state had an even more important fiscal role in the city's schools, as well as the major role in setting the curriculum. The city itself had the option of maintaining segregation or changing to desegregated schools. This local option was provided by a state law enacted after the Supreme Court's decision of 1954. The city school board, by the spring of 1958, had decided to maintain segregation. The county school board made the same decision for its school system.

Petropolis had an annual municipal budget of several million dollars. The county government was well known to the citizens of Petropolis, because it was located in the city, contributed financially to city schools, and joined the city government in extensive health and welfare functions. The city and county jointly had a large, active health department which provided many services, particularly for the poorer citizens. There was also a joint city-county library system which maintained separate library facilities for Negroes and Whites in Petropolis. The county also provided separate public hospitals in the city, for Negroes and for Whites. The airport was a joint governmental venture. County government was more active in meeting the needs of city dwellers in both Petropolis and Metroville in comparison with the two cities of Western State.

Whether the activity was a municipal government, a county government, or a joint function, the biracial subcommunity tradition was recognized and reinforced. This was done through the use of police power to enforce private patterns of segregation in public institutions. Negro and White children were educated in separate schools. Adults of both races were given vocational training in isolation from one another. Negroes and Whites were born apart in separate hospitals, read and played apart in separate libraries and parks, and lived with members of their own race, even in public housing. Death was segregated: Negroes and Whites were buried in different cemeteries, where equal facilities were maintained, even if they were not in the hospitals, schools, libraries, and housing.

Metroville, Southern State, U.S.A.

Metroville was a city slightly larger in population and area than Petropolis. Its Negro population was proportionately larger than that of Petropolis. There were other differences between the two cities which we will mention, but there was an overall similarity between them.

Both cities developed from smaller agricultural communities around the turn of the century when major units of comparable manufacturing industries located near them. Smaller units of a second manufacturing industry then came to both cities. In recent years, Petropolis had developed into more of a financial center than Metroville. A third major industry located near Metroville after the Second World War, when a very large manufacturing corporation established a regional operation. Compared to other communities of Southern State, both cities were manufacturing centers; a slightly larger proportion of Metroville's working force was employed in manufacturing.

Neither city had the large apartment houses of the big industrial cities of the North; neither did they witness the disappearance of a distinctly rural, agricultural countryside. Although smokestacks abound, when the two cities are compared to New York, Pittsburgh, or Detroit, they appear to be overgrown villages. However, they both would give a visitor from Oretown or Farmdale a feeling of great density and size. The distinctive areas of Negro housing and businesses would be familiar to visitors from any major industrial city or region in the United States.

There had been a steady population growth in Metroville which, in recent years, was faster than the growth rate of Petropolis. An important factor in the influx had been the deteriorating economic situation of rural residents. The typical small farmer had found it more difficult to survive the exigencies of unpredictable weather, complicated technological developments, the rising costs of farm operations and consumer goods, and the decreasing or fluctuating prices of farm products. The typically large size of farm families meant that at least some of the children of a farmer were increasingly disposed to look to the city for a livelihood. Negroes from rural areas throughout the South constituted one of the major categories of people moving to Metroville. Since most were poorly educated, they had to look for unskilled work in the city's large factories. This was also true of Whites.

Even though newcomers had continued to move to Metroville over the years, there was a much larger proportion of natives than in either Western community at the time of the study. More than one-third of the White adults were born in Metroville. Only about one-quarter of the Negro citizens were born there, compared to about one-third of the Negro citizens of Petropolis. About one-third of Metroville's White citizens had arrived since the Second World War; only one-fifth of Petropolis's White citizens came during this period. There were proportionately fewer Negro newcomers in both Southern cities. The major influx of Negroes took place in the 1930's and in the early war years. Since then it appears that many Negroes have used both Metroville and Petropolis as "way stations" on their route north to find economic opportunities that were lacking in both Southern cities.

Metroville was a community of even greater physical contrasts than Petropolis. Negro slum areas in Metroville appeared to be more extensive and less livable than those in Petropolis. The area of better Negro residential housing was more restricted. Incomes of Negroes were lower. There were more very affluent White citizens, proportionately and numerically. The White millionaires of Metroville resided inside the city, on large estates or in reconstructed mansions. This internal contrast in the physical appearance of Metroville extended to the central business districts of the White and Negro subcommunities. The central shopping area of Metroville was more stylish and less dilapidated than that of Petropolis.

Apart from the greater proportion of Negroes employed in manufacturing in Metroville and the greater proportion of Negroes employed in loan companies and investment houses in Petropolis, the occupational structures of the two Negro subcommunities were almost identical, as were the occupational structures of the two White working forces. The greater proportion of Negroes in manufacturing in Metroville was reflected in the proportions of Negroes who operated machines: one-third in Metroville and one-quarter in Petropolis. Otherwise, the Whites of Metroville had the managerial, professional, clerical, sales, and comparable white-collar jobs; the Negroes were relegated the blue-collar jobs, particularly domestic service and unskilled occupations.

In both cities, the proportion of domestic servants, service workers, and unskilled laborers in the Negro labor force approached 50 per cent. This was about seven times the proportion of Whites in each city employed in comparable positions. The rate of unemployment among

Whites in Metroville, over the past few years, had been about half that of those in Petropolis. Incomes of White citizens in the two communities have reflected this. Only about 25 per cent of the White families of Metroville had annual incomes of less than $2,000, and 50 per cent had less than $3,000; about 40 per cent had less than $2,000 and 60 per cent less than $3,000 in Petropolis; about one-third of the families in the two Western cities had incomes of less than $3,000 per year. In Metroville 60 per cent more Whites had incomes of over $10,000 per year than in Petropolis.

The relative situation of Negro families in the two Southern cities was less clear. Although the rate of reported unemployment among Negroes in Metroville was about half the rate of Negro unemployment in Petropolis, average family incomes were somewhat lower in Metroville. This may have resulted from greater union organization among Negroes in Petropolis, which would mean higher wages but increasing unemployment as industry declined. Approximately 35 per cent of the White working class of Petropolis was organized; only 12 per cent was organized in Metroville. Excluding domestic servants, about 15 per cent of the Negro working force of Petropolis was organized; only 5 per cent was organized in Metroville. The wages of the average White worker in the nonunion factory of Metroville were as high as, if not higher than, the wages of the union worker in Petropolis. This was not true for Negroes. Management had a consciously paternalistic attitude towards the White worker in Metroville, based on a wage level that was competitive with that of comparable union labor, and designed in part to keep unions out of the major industries. This policy did not extend to the unskilled Negro worker.

There had been some improvement in the economic situation of Negro citizens of Metroville during the past decade. Although increasing numbers of both Negro and White workers made living wages, it was obvious that very large proportions of both racial groups—particularly Negroes—still had submarginal and marginal incomes. The basic change was in the occupational structure of the Negro labor force; but this did not mean an immediate or even a long-term increase in incomes. For example, the proportion of Negroes operating machines had increased, while the proportion working as domestic servants had decreased. The relatively prosperous manufacturing sector of the Metroville economy employed Negroes on the assembly line in plants where the supervisory staff was White. There was even a token, experimental effort at desegregation in one of the few large, new, absentee-owned plants. This took the form of hiring both a few highly trained Negroes to work with White fellow technicians and a small number of Negro workers for the assembly line itself.

Still, Metroville Negroes had a great distance to go to attain even the limited employment that skilled Negro workers had in Petropolis. Moreover, these changes in the economic role of Negroes in Metroville did not noticeably affect the social separation of the two subcommunities. The associational life of Negroes and Whites was still completely separate. Negro businessmen had their own organizations, and the relatively few highly educated Negroes met together in fraternities and sororities. These were social centers which served as channels for numerous welfare and civic-service activities, directed by the Negro "elite" for the less fortunate members of the subcommunity.

One of the striking contrasts in the economies of the two cities was the degree of union organization in their manufacturing industries. The major industry in Metroville was nonunion; as we have mentioned, that of Petropolis was fully organized. There also was a greater degree of union organization in Petropolis's second major industry. Only in the third largest industry of Metroville, established after the Second World War, was there appreciable labor-union organization.

Another contrast was the degree of local versus absentee ownership of the major industrial corporations. In Metroville the families who started the major industries and major banking institution still lived in the city, managed these large industrial enterprises, and retained control through ownership of the largest blocks of voting stock. The Leek and Bacon families of Petropolis were active in the city's earliest industrialization, and at the time of the study were among the city's leading financiers. But most of the families of Petropolis who had been the owners and managers of the largest firms left the city when they sold their interests to outsiders in the 1930's and early 1940's. The largest companies were controlled by nonresident executives. In Metroville the pattern of local family entrepreneurship was maintained.

Some of the "first" families of Petropolis had become rather distant legends; those of Metroville, although legendary, were very visible. Their community activities included the private construction of numerous public works that served as memorials and testaments to their continued interest in the city of their birth. Before the Second World War, the first families of Metroville lived in almost feudal isolation on large estates outside the city. Company houses, company stores, and community hospitals were provided for the sustenance of the industrial working class, but this was the extent of their sense of *noblesse oblige* until the postwar years.

Since that time, the civic leadership has re-entered the city physically through annexation and psychologically through their various private programs devoted to the public welfare. In addition, expanded programs of local welfare were endorsed to provide for the indigent of both races. Public housing programs were introduced to replace the old-fashioned company housing. Segregation was maintained, but Harmony House was established. This was an organization of White and Negro civic leaders whose purpose was to ameliorate the condition of the Negro subcommunity. After the legislature of Southern State provided for the possibility of local public school desegregation, the initiation of token desegregation in the city's schools was considered. Metroville's elite desired to be leaders of a city nationally known as the cosmopolitan center of culture in the state.

There was a great gulf between the Negro and White subcommunities and between the upper-status Whites and the White citizens of lower social status in Metroville. The Democratic party was one possible organizational vehicle for connecting more closely the two parts of the White subcommunity as well as the two racial subcommunities. However, few of the White civic leaders were personally active in the local party politics; many identified themselves as Independents and others as Republicans in national politics. Fewer Negroes were active as precinct workers than in Petropolis. Neither White union officials nor many members of the blue-collar segment of the White subcommunity were active in local Democratic politics. The local Democratic party organization was actually staffed by highly educated, middle- or upper-middle-class White citizens and a few Negroes of comparable position in the socio-economic structure of the Negro subcommunity.

Although the educational levels of White and Negro citizens of Metroville were practically identical to the educational levels of their counterparts in Petropolis, the pattern of participation in the voluntary associational life was very different. Church-going was a pervasive norm in both subcommunities of Metroville. Otherwise, Metroville Whites and Negroes were similar in their nonparticipation in voluntary associations. Approximately two-thirds of the adults in each of Metroville's subcommunities belonged to no formally organized association except a church; in comparison, about half the White citizens and one-third of the Negro citizens of Petropolis, half Oretown's citizens, and about two-fifths of the citizens of Farmdale belonged to no formally organized association.

The small fraction of White union members in Metroville were even more isolated from the community's other voluntary associations than White union members in Petropolis. On the other hand, the smaller segment of Negro union members were invariably members of one or more voluntary associations in the Negro subcommunity of Metroville. This resembled, in a more extreme fashion, the pattern found in Petropolis, where Negro labor-union members, much more than White union members, belonged to another association in their racial subcommunity.

The local governmental structure of Metroville was a city manager system, with an elected, "weak" mayor and a ten-man city council. As in Oretown, the mayor voted only in the case of a tie in the council. He and the councilmen were elected for two-year terms, the latter on a ward basis. Metroville had partisan local elections, unlike the other three cities. The ward lines were drawn to ensure the election of one Negro to the city council. The overwhelming Democratic registration traditionally ensured an elected officialdom of Democrats in Metroville.

There were many more appointive boards and commissions in Metroville than in any of the other three cities. The mayor not only appointed the council committees; he also nominated and appointed, sometimes by himself and sometimes with the approval of the council, the members of these numerous boards and commissions. Many of these were token appointments, but others were to important policy posts. Among the more important agencies were the city school board, the public housing agency, the recreation board, the hospital commission, the urban renewal agency, and the municipal liquor commission. Many, but not all, of the paid positions in city government were filled by the city manager under the rules, regulations, and general supervision of a civil service commission.

The city manager was the chief administrative officer for a city, with a multimillion-dollar budget and well over 1,000 city employees. The budget and the number of city employees were both approximately twice the size of those of Petropolis. This did not include the many employees of the city school system which, as in Petropolis, was supervised by the appointed city school board but financed, in large measure, by the state and county governments.[3]

One of the reasons, apart from larger population and areal jurisdiction, for the larger payroll and expenditures in Metroville than in Petropolis was the operation of municipal hospitals, segregated institutions for Negroes and Whites. In Petropolis the hospitals were under the control and jurisdiction of the county government, but in Metroville they were part of the municipal government.

Besides providing hospital facilities, the municipal government under the aegis of its public housing agency operated large, segregated public-housing complexes. One out of every twelve Negro families inside the city limits lived in such a unit. The number provided for Negro families was several times that for Whites. In both housing and medical care, the Negro subcommunity of Metroville relied much more on the municipal government than did the Negroes of Petropolis. As in Petropolis, municipal recreational facilities, libraries, and cemeteries were segregated.

The county government was headed by an elective five-man commission. Its primary functions were to provide schools for the non-urban areas, administer various welfare programs, and build highways. It participated with the city in a joint planning agency whose jurisdiction extended into the fringe area around the city. Traditionally, the county government attempted to minimize its scope relative both to programs and to the property-tax rate. There was still a tax-rate differential between county and city, but it was much less than it had been prior to the Second World War. The county government, over the past decade, contributed larger proportions of tax funds to municipal programs available to the residents of the entire county.

The county's participation with the city in various joint programs, its extensive welfare activities apart from the municipal hospital facilities, its extensive property holdings just outside the city, and the county government's physical location in the city of Metroville all have contributed to its prominence as a local governmental unit for residents inside of the city limits. It is the primary governmental unit for residents in the urban fringe area. Recent annexations, and local-government consideration of future annexations, impressed many suburban and fringe-dwelling residents with the fact that their citizen obligations and benefits were related to the county rather than to the municipal government. Whereas the White fringe-dwellers and the rural inhabitants of the area around Metroville ordinarily looked to the county government as "their" government, Negro citizens, inside or outside the city limits, regarded the municipal government as their representative—at least to some degree. They had direct representation in city government through a Negro councilman who also served on the city school board, but they had no such minority-group representation on the elective county commission nor prospects of acquiring it in the near future.

Having sketched briefly some of the major aspects of the social, economic, and governmental structure of the two Southern and two Western communities, we shall describe their recent political histories in Chapter 5. These histories extend from the Second World War until the municipal election in each city that marks the beginning of the time period during which we conducted our more systematic and intensive examination of each community's politics.

NOTES

1. The four communities are described as of the last municipal election prior to the time the major field work started in each—1950 for Farmdale, 1952 for Oretown, and 1957 for Petropolis and Metroville. These descriptions are based in large part on Census data, random-sample surveys of the adult populations in each community, and material from each community's newspaper.
2. See Charles R. Wright and Herbert H. Hyman, "Voluntary Association Memberships," *American Sociological Review*, Vol. 23, No. 3 (June 1958), pp. 284–294, and the references cited therein. See also Basil G. Zimmer and Amos H. Hawley, "The Significance of Membership in Associations," *The American Journal of Sociology*, Vol. LXV, No. 2 (September 1959), pp. 196–201.
3. Although the number of part-time employees—which fluctuates during any year—made it difficult to estimate, the proportion of full-time, paid local-government employees—except school employees—was approximately 0.4 in Farmdale, 0.6 in Oretown, 1.0 in Petropolis, and 1.5 in Metroville to every 100 citizens living inside the city limits.

5

POLITICAL HISTORY: *1946 to Time E*

We will now review, in narrative form, the political history of the four polities from the end of the Second World War to Time *E*, the beginning of the period with which the systematic field research is concerned. The limitations of space prevent a more complete account of what happened before the periods of field research. But an effort will be made to touch upon some of the main shifts in the scope of government, the origin of new, important demands, and some of the relationships among political groups involved in political decision-making during the earlier periods. The power structures and regimes in the four communities in these time periods will be classified by type in Chapter 11.

FARMDALE

Farmdale has been described as a little town whose residents were generally satisfied with its semirural, stable character. But pressures related to demographic and economic trends in the immediate region began to impinge increasingly on the political system of the community after the Second World War. The growth of population since the early 1940's increased the demand for city services. Competition for customers from the attractive shopping centers of Big City was beginning to threaten local merchants. The gradual decline in economic opportunities for the youth of the community was also becoming a concern. The economic problems caused by the short term instability of the local mining industry led some citizens to begin to think about appropriate solutions. During the war years, these situations had received relatively little notice, but with the end of hostilities, attention naturally began to shift from the global scene back to the community.

The Community Conservation Administration

The cessation of war gave the editor of the local paper, George Norris, the opportunity to turn his attention to the many problems of local government which had been postponed or allowed to drift during the war. He placed before the community a series of proposals concerning such matters as parking regulations on the main street, the need for a sewage disposal plant, a zoning plan, additional recreation facilities, and a chamber of commerce to induce industry to Farmdale. "A community never stands still," he said. "It either grows or it dies."

He first asked the city officials, a group of small merchants with rural backgrounds, to facilitate shopper parking in the business district. The council concurred, but not before an extensive campaign was conducted by the Men's Club. This club was dominated by Jeffersonian Conservative businessmen and farmers who campaigned to combine the city ordinance with an appeal to the residents of Farmdale not to park in the area. This illustrated their concern that private effort be used to resolve community problems. At the same time the council agreed to furnish water for residential purposes to the growing number of fringe area residents requesting it.

The council also took the initiative and created a veterans' employment committee to assist returning veterans in finding jobs in Farmdale. The members were three Conservatives: "Judge" Catis and his two nephews, School Board member Don May and his brother, Bill May. They viewed this venture as only a temporary, *ad hoc* arrangement, rather than a permanent expansion in the scope of government.

Several citizens, encouraged by the receptivity of the council to change and the supporting voice of Norris, formed a Farmdale Advancement club. This club became the nucleus of a Community Conservation group which had some Liberal adherents. Its major aim was to improve economic conditions in the community. The first project on the agenda of the club, and one of the primary reasons for its creation, was the public power proposal being deliberated in the area. The club supported the creation of a People's Utility District (P.U.D.), to include the rural sections of the county as well as Farmdale. Prior to the war, there had been several unsuccessful moves to establish a countywide P.U.D. Big City had had a municipal power system for some 20 years, and Oretown had been waging a long battle to create its own municipal utility. The members of the Advancement club felt that a P.U.D. could provide lower rates, better service, and more power by taking advantage of the federal government power program in the region. The proposed P.U.D. would encourage the location of new industry in the area and would bring electricity to farms. The ensuing campaign by the Conservatives included charges of "socialist scheming" as well as charges that the advocates of P.U.D. did not pay taxes. The Conservative campaign was led by Kenneth King, the new publisher of the Farmdale weekly paper. The Advancement club mobilized a coalition of small businessmen who urged the industrialization of Farmdale and farmers who shouted the Populist battle cry against the Wall Street millionaires. The citizens of Farmdale voted to remain with "free enterprise and the American way of life" by a margin of six to five, in a large turnout at the polls.

The Conservative victory was followed by the election as mayor of Norris, who had just retired as publisher of the local paper, and three like-minded councilmen. This strengthened the Community Conservationists, even though the defeat of the P.U.D. had weakened Liberal elements. In addition, Norris had the support of John Anderson, farmer-businessman, who had been a leader in the P.U.D. movement.

The first proposal of the new administration was to provide a sewage disposal plant. The state government had been gradually pressuring the cities along rivers and streams to construct disposal plants to reduce the pollution problem. Farmdale was located in an area of poor drainage, and was subject to seasonal flooding. A big flood had recently inundated much of the community, and its aftereffects illustrated the need for a disposal plant. The Norris administration saw no alternative and advocated a large plant which not only would meet present needs but also would allow for normal population expansion and any new industry that might locate in Farmdale. To accomplish this, the city applied for federal funds, available on a grant-in-aid basis.

While the sewage-plant application was pending, the Community Conservationist administration moved along three fronts. First, it sought to enlarge the water system to help attract new industry; the proposed system was to be five times as large as the system in existence. Second, it established a citizens' committee to study and discuss the need for a coordinated recreation program, which would include such new facilities as a swimming pool. Third, it asked the voters to approve charter revisions. The major change was the creation of wards whereby four out of the six councilmen would be elected to rep-

resent the different parts of the city. Little concrete action was taken
to enlarge the water and park systems. The informal political process
of Farmdale was slow moving, and efforts to reach consensus were unsuccessful. The Conservatives opposed the tax increase that would
follow the adoption of the proposals. Community Conservationists
were unprepared to force the issue at the time but continued to discuss
the need. The revision of the charter had little opposition and was
passed at a special election with a low voter turnout.

The Community Conservationists felt most strongly about the
sewage disposal plant. They saw no reason not to share in the federal
funds available, even though it would mean an added burden on the
city treasury. The Conservatives were vigorously opposed in view of
the probability of increased taxes, the prospect of federal government
intervention in local projects, and the relationship between the proposal and future industrial expansion of the community, which they
felt to be most undesirable. Councilman Anderson, a well-informed
advocate of the project, found himself involved in a bitter and often
personally vituperative campaign. The Community Conservationists
prevailed: two-thirds of a large turnout of voters supported this increase in the scope of government. This victory led the Community
Conservationists to follow with a proposal to annex a large development on the outskirts of town. Again, the voters approved in a heavy
turnout, by a margin of four to one.

The Community Conservationist victories were sufficiently costly to
the Conservatives to increase their frustration. The Conservatives began gradually to make themselves more visible in the civic and
fraternal organizations of the community, while the Community Conservationists began to fight among themselves. Councilman Anderson
suddenly challenged the leadership of Norris in the 1948 mayoralty
race. His motivation was more personal than ideological. The two
agreed about most policy matters, but Anderson considered Norris
too old and inflexible for the aggressive leadership needed to confront
the growing influence of Conservatism. Not only did Anderson lose
the vigorous campaign, but Conservatives replaced Community Conservationists on the council.

The Conservative Resurgence

The Conservatives, who now dominated the council, could delay or
destroy the Community Conservationist hope to industrialize the
community. For example, they refused to lease a site of municipally
owned land to an industrial prospect, to provide it tax relief, or to

guarantee such city services as water, sewer, and other utilities. Nevertheless, a company did locate on the outskirts of town, because of ready access to railroad and highways and the availability of labor and large tracts of land for the plant. The Conservatives could not prevent this move. But the Community Conservationists had had their day. They had lost several authoritative positions and had to rely on the Mayor, who was a retired old man, unable to mobilize widespread Community Conservationist sentiments. Thus the group was fragmented and without adequate means of communicating their policy objectives. Even "their" local newspaper had been sold to a man generally sympathetic to Conservatism.

From 1948 to 1950 the Conservatives gained political influence by organizing informally through a "poker club," which met regularly and included the inner-core Conservative leaders. Their strategy was to work quietly and inconspicuously through their communication links with the Main Street businessmen and certain prosperous farmers. This strategy became apparent when they conducted a secret mayoralty write-in campaign for Bill May against Mayor Norris in the election of 1950. This surprise tactic resulted in the election of May by a two-to-one margin in a heavy turnout. In his first public speech, May clarified the broad outline of the Conservative policy he would follow when he emphasized that he would work to consolidate the gains already made by the city rather than introduce any new policies.

ORETOWN

The political events in Oretown from the close of the Second World War to Time E (1952) were an extension of a long history of political turmoil. The problems arising from the phenomenal wartime and postwar growth of the community impinged on the lives of most residents. Political controversy associated with these problems abounded. In 1952, and in the preceding decades, controversy in Oretown was so intense as to appear at times almost catastrophic for the political system. The political process was threatened by paralysis, not because of dedication to the *status quo* but because of disagreement over basic political values.

The Conservative Administration

During the war, the proprietors along Main Street had become prominent in community affairs. They replaced the leaders of the major mining company, who were busily engaged in economic competition with the operators of new and large absentee-owned mines which had located on the outskirts of Oretown during the wartime boom. The small Main Street businessmen, Conservative in orientation, held uneasy sway over a political system prone to explosive expressions of dissatisfaction. They soon learned that holding official positions in local government did not give them much authority with the citizens. In fact, their economic position as retailers made them much more sensitive to the possibility of economic sanctions than those who controlled the one industry in town and, thereby, the economic life blood of the community.

Uneasy in office, the Conservative leaders dealt with the demands for increased services in three ways. First, they decided that the solution to the problem was to improve the physical plant of the community. They considered the role of local government to be the traditional one of taking care of streets, sidewalks, and sewers, and providing police and fire protection. If pressed, they would include parks, a city garbage dump, and possibly a municipal water system in their program. They proposed improvements for the former during their short tenure in office. In the attempt to avoid the appearance of making arbitrary decisions, they held no less than 15 special elections to gain approval for their programs during their four-year "domination" of city government. Generally they prevailed, for participation in these decisional processes was low and the voters were in a mood to support needed improvements.

The second method used by the Conservatives to deal with costly civic improvement proposals was to advance governmental reorganization. They advocated the adoption of the council-manager form of government, which would include a city engineer to oversee the design of new sewer lines, manage the details of street repairs, and provide service to the downtown business district. However, the citizens wanted physical facilities and not administrators. A one-mill levy for the salary of the city-manager was attached to the ballot proposal to change the structure of government, and it was voted down. Six months later, after the organization of a "good government" drive, the Conservatives finally won voter support for a city manager. They then asked and received voter approval to build a new city hall to house the expanding government.

An additional move for governmental reorganization was the establishment of a recreation district. This district comprised an area several times the size of the city and included the rural-urban industrial fringe. Actually, this proposal had been advocated by the industrialists themselves prior to the war. They had agreed that their employees needed recreation and had gone to the state legislature for authority to create a special district for this purpose. The war prevented the implementation of this scheme, and it was left to postwar leaders to begin operation with a board of directors dominated by Conservatives and a small budget. The creation of this district met the Conservatives' ideal of "nonpolitical" local government. It also provided the basis for Oretown's claim to its rural-urban fringe as part of the community and forestalled any encroachment by the neighboring city.

The third method of the Conservative administration, not unrelated to the second, was the enlargement of the political system through annexation. Since additional revenue was required to meet the cost of the new programs, they eyed the assessed valuation of property in the growing fringe area; this property would double the current valuation of the community. Secondly, they saw no reason why industry, much of which was located in the fringe area, should remain free from sharing the cost of programs designed to meet the problems for which industry itself had in part been responsible through the influx of new workers. Finally, they saw annexation as a means of adding prestige to Oretown by making it one of the larger cities in the state. Little did they realize that the assimilation of the newcomers, about equal in number to those presently living in Oretown, might create political problems because of their class characteristics, their relative unconcern for the town's past tradition, and their aggressive demands for even more innovation on the part of local government.

These Orthodox Conservatives were ideologically ill-prepared to meet a final but crucial problem: the need for improved utility services. Since 1930, the private company that provided both water and electric service had been under attack by proponents of a municipal utility. In fact, this issue had effectively divided the community into two hostile camps. Industrialists defended the private utility because of a mutually advantageous relationship based on harnessing part of the mining operation to the generation of electricity. In the prewar contests, these industrialists threatened that they would have to suspend operation or reduce the number of workers if the private power company were replaced by a city-owned utility. The downtown businessmen also opposed the "socialization" of the utility service, although they were not in an economic position to threaten voters in the postwar period. Instead, they appointed a study committee to examine the feasibility of solving the water problem, which they felt to be a more traditional and acceptable function of local government.

This approach did not satisfy the advocates of a municipal power system. Their champion, businessman Calvin Lovegren, challenged the "weary antediluvians who have controlled the city." Lovegren was not pioneering in a new venture. The advent of the New Deal federal power program had stimulated an already active public power movement, which had been successful in Big City, where lower rates and better service were available. He and other businessmen could no longer tolerate insufficient service because their businesses suffered. They had had to bring water by the barrel from outside the city and to have a lantern ready when the regular power outages occurred during late afternoon. In fact, at one point, the power company, plagued by as many as 13 outages a day, advanced the scheme that citizens on alternate sides of the street should cook their meals at designated hours in the evening to prevent further outages. The housewives of the community were furious and many joined Lovegren in his battle. He also won the support of labor unions, whose members objected to the periodic closing of the mines for lack of electric power. Democrats who saw an opportunity to advance their policy preference for public power and to gain an authoritative position in Oretown's nonpartisan but Republican-dominated government also supported Lovegren.

The Conservatives insisted that the need to improve the water supply should have priority. They stood on the principle of private enterprise. Furthermore, they did not take Lovegren, "a chronic critic," seriously, remembering his ineffectiveness on the power question during Chamber of Commerce meetings.

The incumbent Mayor refused to stand again for election against Lovegren in what promised to be a heated campaign. Meanwhile, a staunch Conservative agreed to have his name entered but would not campaign, since he believed that a man should be sought for political office and that the man should not seek the office.

The Liberal Administration

The election of Calvin Lovegren as Mayor in 1948 was generally understood to be a mandate by the voters of Oretown for City Hall to adopt an aggressive approach to the solution of the problems created by the rapid growth of the community. Lovegren advocated and had campaigned vigorously on a program of creating a municipal utility to serve the power and water needs of the expanding residential population, and continued industrial development and future urban growth. He saw this as the "life blood" of Oretown's industrial future, and in his campaign he deplored the inadequate and costly services rendered by the private utility. He also vigorously advocated improved street, sewer, and drainage facilities.

Lovegren entered office with a big broom to clean out what he considered the inefficiency, lack of initiative, and conservatism of city government. He started by replacing two high-level administrators. It was evident that he had little sympathy for the city-manager form of government which had just been established, or for the notion of a "weak" mayor which it seemed to imply. Lovegren was supported in this attack by newly elected Councilman Longacre, who had developed the Longacre area, which had just been annexed to Oretown. This development included a shopping center which competed with the downtown businessmen. The councilman labored and lobbied for immediate public improvements for this area. The shake-up at City Hall was motivated partly by a desire to redistribute city services in this way. Lovegren and Longacre were willing to play "ward politics" and to build a political organization based mainly on labor and the Democratic party to compete with the Conservatives.

The change at City Hall was met by a variety of responses throughout the community. The city employees were, on the whole, uncooperative. For example, when Lovegren forced the City Manager to fire a department head, the whole department resigned in protest. The Conservatives formed a "good government" committee to protect the Manager and other city employees. The local newspaper publisher, a leader of the Conservatives, characterized Lovegren as a troublemaker who was too controversial to run the town well.

While public controversy echoed about him, Lovegren managed to bring about a major shift in the scope of government. He met with federal officials and retained a technical staff and an attorney to draw up the necessary plans. Four months after assuming office, he surprised everyone when he announced a plan to establish a municipal power system designed to give better service at lower rates and to enhance the industrial potential of the local economic base through diversification. The surprise maneuver caught his opponents off guard, for they had expected him to fight the battle of "good government." But for Lovegren, the power issue was the big issue. He attacked the power company, in the manner of Western agrarian Populists, as greedy Eastern financiers milking Oretown for every last nickel. On the other hand, the power company supporters denounced Lovegren's proposal as a sinister plot of CIO socialists and Democratic carpetbaggers who had recently descended on the community from "abroad." The Conservatives on Main Street maintained silence, for they felt they could ill afford to alienate either side in the tightly drawn contest.

Instead they openly fought those trying to abolish the city-manager form of government. The only recommendation expressed by the local editor, who had been a defender of the private utility since 1935, was his plea that if Lovegren prevailed, he should not create a duplicate power system but instead buy out the private power company.

The voters agreed with Lovegren on the big issue by a 54 to 46 per cent margin. The newly annexed Longacre precinct voted two to one for the proposal. At the same time a bare majority of the voters supported the Conservatives on the proposal to abolish the office of city manager, thereby retaining it.

Lovegren plunged headlong into preparing for either the purchase of the private power company's properties or the construction of a new, competitive system. He delivered an ultimatum to the company either to come to terms within 60 days or he would begin construction of the new system. He frankly preferred a new system, believing that the facilities of the power company were totally inadequate. Lovegren was also suspicious of the sincerity of the power company in any negotiation. The company had no intention of quietly fading away and fought vigorously to delay the mayor's program.

Negotiations between the city and the company failed. This gave Lovegren the opportunity to proceed with his plans for an entirely new system which would compete with the private company. The Conservatives, through a Reform City Government Committee, struck back at Lovegren by petitioning for his recall. They charged him with rushing the community into the power business without reasonable negotiation and fair play. They accused him of secrecy in the conduct of city business and of by-passing the services of both the City Attorney and the City Manager. They criticized him for building the first installations of the city power system in the Longacre section as a gesture to Councilman Longacre. The state public utility commission, under a Republican administration, was induced to allow the private utility to reduce its rates to compete with the municipal rate.

On the eve of the recall election, Lovegren again changed tactics. Faced with opposition to his priority program, he switched to an attack on the operation of city government. He asked for the resignation of the City Manager because he had not rid the city of "incompetent employees," as well as for other reasons.

Lovegren successfully withstood the attempted recall: the vote against the recall was four to three, with a heavy voter turnout. However, he was immediately faced with wholesale resignations among city employees, including most of the high-level administrators who supported the City Manager. The entire police force quit, as did two councilmen.

In many ways the result of the recall election was a hollow victory for Lovegren. He had served only 16 months, and the remainder of his term was to be marked by Conservatives taking the initiative and effectively overshadowing the Mayor. They proposed and successfully campaigned to create an agency, independent of the Mayor, to operate the public utility. The voters supported this move to separate politics—City Hall—from the business of government. At the same time, the Conservatives, in full control of the independent school district, consolidated Oretown schools with small rural districts in a fringe area that included most of the big industrial firms. They also pressed for a large park-and-recreation bond issue. And even though they controlled this independent unit of local government, it took three consecutive elections for the voters to approve their plans. Clearly, neither the Liberals nor the Conservatives captured the loyalties of the voters during the Lovegren administration.

The Conservatives, well represented in social and civic organizations, used the Chamber of Commerce to compete with City Hall. Through this channel they developed four programs which paved the way for the moderate administration that would effectively challenge Lovegren. The leaders of the Chamber of Commerce first proposed that a state highway improvement and relocation project by-pass the heavily congested downtown shopping center. This would stimulate business by providing more parking facilities and at the same time would reduce traffic congestion. They persuaded the state highway department to back them up and forced the city to acquiesce. As a result a group of Liberal small businessmen close to Lovegren resigned from the Chamber of Commerce, and Councilman Longacre blocked the by-pass of his business district.

The second program was for a community hospital to be financed with voluntary subscriptions, but no federal funds. This would prevent the "socialized" city hospital rumored to be a Lovegren proposal. The Conservatives were keenly aware of the need for medical facilities. They also believed that a community hospital would encourage professional people to come to Oretown. Citizens of Oretown had been smarting under the criticism of the Big City press, which emphasized the problems, the controversy, and the "lunch bucket" character of Oretown. The community had a long-standing inferiority complex as a "wet" town, a place without "culture," a place where political squabbles prevented the resolution of such problems as open sewers, dirty drinking water, power outages, and bad streets. In fact, few of the industrialists and civic leaders actually lived in Oretown. The leading civic leader could not run as the Conservative candidate for mayor because he lived outside the city limits. The hospital drive failed because there were few large contributions from industrialists who were accustomed to using the physicians and hospital in Big City. Lovegren played no role in this decisional process, and the citizens seemed to be confused about the division of opinion between the merchants and industrialists on the matter.

The Chamber of Commerce then turned to an industrial promotion program in cooperation with the newly formed Oretown Municipal Utility (OMU). The superintendent, chairman of the industrial development committee of the Chamber of Commerce, sponsored a drive to encourage diversification of the community's industrial base. OMU had low-cost power to offer which presumably would attract new industry to Oretown. As an administrator, the superintendent's objective was not to become identified as either a Conservative or a Liberal, since he needed customers to insure operating efficiency. His public announcement of the addition of 100 men to the industrial payroll did not hurt his cause in the competitive battle with the private company for residential customers.

The fourth program of the Conservatives, a five-year tax levy to minimize the effect of future defeats of city budgets, was successful. It was accomplished while Mayor Lovegren was on an extended vacation. The Conservatives also returned to their advocacy of a sewage disposal plant. Both of these measures were the special projects of a young councilman, Michael French, who was to lead the move toward moderation and the eventual defeat of the controversial Lovegren.

The Election of a Community Conservationist Administration

The next major event to gain the attention of the voters of Oretown was the election for mayor in the fall of 1952. Calvin Lovegren chose to run again. His principal opponent was City Councilman Michael French, a young attorney. French had lived in the community only a few years. In that period he had taken part in a number of community welfare activities, and he belonged to civic and fraternal associations. Apart from more personal and occupational advancement motives, French decided to run because he thought Oretown needed a new kind of mayor. He believed that Lovegren was too doctrinaire, dogmatic, and disputatious. Among his active supporters were Lovegren's predecessor as mayor, a former councilman who had resigned in protest against Lovegren, and the former city attorney. The manager of the private power company, other Conservative leaders, and many of the more affluent citizens and businessmen of the community were also in French's camp.

French also was encouraged in his candidacy by Ben Kelly, a young Main Street businessman. Kelly organized the French campaign so successfully that he became known as the leader of the "Kelly machine," a bipartisan political group composed of young professionals and Main Street businessmen committed to better local government. It became the nucleus of a Community Conservationist leadership group headed by Mayor French. Although the group was primarily Republican in national elections, French, a Democrat, worked closely with organized labor and the local Democratic party organization during his campaign for mayor and thereafter in order to attain objectives which he thought would be advantageous to the whole community.

There was a third candidate in the mayoralty race, a merchant from the Longacre district. He had been persuaded to run by friends in labor, business, and city government circles. His campaign managers were Donald Scott, a leading advocate of municipal power, and Councilman John Longacre, both friends of Lovegren. The merchant's entrance into the race was alleged to have been instigated by Lovegren in a last-minute effort to pull votes away from French.

Lovegren campaigned vigorously on his record of establishing the Oretown Municipal Utility and managing to make municipal improvements with a low tax millage. French concentrated on making his name familiar to the voters by means of radio and newspapers. He made public appearances whenever and wherever people would listen to him. His campaign stressed "good" and "competent" government. French identified himself as a Democrat and a supporter of OMU. By 1952, Oretown had a predominantly Democratic registration. French's support of OMU was sincere, but it also was calculated to weaken Lovegren's claim to be the only Liberal candidate who would and could protect the utility. Despite French's public stand in support of municipal power, the private power company officials continued to support him, convinced that any candidate was better than Lovegren.

In this three-way race, the voters had to choose between the controversial incumbent Mayor Lovegren, young Councilman French, and the Longacre businessman. All three men proclaimed their faith in the municipal utility; they all had some ties with organized labor; and they all were supported, in part, by some segments of the business community. The election of November 1952, resulted in a victory for French. Community Conservation was established as the dominant ideology at City Hall. Lovegren ran last in this three-way race. The voters chose the most moderate of the three candidates to serve as Oretown's Mayor for the next four years. Whether this signified the end of ideological conflict in Oretown's politics or not will be discussed later.

PETROPOLIS

At the end of the war Petropolis was in a state of some deterioration. Both the Depression and the war had been hard on local governmental facilities and services, and also had affected the community's financial capacity. But citizens perceived two additional problems. First, the economy of Petropolis had begun to decline, and the community began to fall behind the economic and industrial growth of its neighbor cities. Although Petropolis was an industrial city characterized by absentee ownership, it found itself unable to sustain the postwar industrial boom. This was attributed, in part, to the city's high degree of unionization, relatively rare in Southern State, which discouraged industrial prospects. The second problem was the Whites' relationship to the Negro subcommunity. Petropolis' Negroes were comparatively well organized, highly educated, wealthy, and politically active, and they had effective leadership in this city of traditional segregation. The resolution of any community problems involved race relations and the position of the unions.

Political power before, during, and just after the war resided largely in the hands of the Bacon and Leek families, their relatives, friends, and business associates. Three generations of Bacons and Leeks lived in Petropolis, and intermarriages between the two families were common. One of the very elderly Leeks still kept an eye on his business domain. His earlier liberalism, evident in his civic endeavors and in such activities as trying to ease the financial situation of the small farmers, was tempered by a growing conservatism: he was becoming increasingly willing to accept the *status quo* in Petropolis; even if he was not satisfied, he at least was averse to change. Proposals for improvements, whether to introduce county planning and zoning or to fluoridate the city's water supply, met with his forceful and usually successful opposition. Younger members of the family seemed to prefer progress to stability. They advocated the revitalization of the economy through attraction of new industry, improvement of the appearance of the city, and the gradual recognition of the aspirations of the Negro subcommunity and its leadership.

The Conservative Administration

From the end of the Second World War to 1947, the *status quo*-oriented Bacons and Leeks prevailed in local politics. They were quite Conservative in their outlook. The Conservative forces resisted city expansion, industrial growth, labor in politics or economic bargaining, and any relaxation of racial barriers. They attempted to stress the importance of the housekeeping functions of local government and to make a series of minor civic improvements. They satisfied a Negro demand for the acquisition of a particular building for recreational purposes, but they refused to appoint a Negro to the school board, and otherwise ignored demands by Negro leaders for equality in educational facilities and instruction. When a minor city administrator suggested that it was necessary for big industries to add sanitation and pollution-prevention facilities to their plants, the Conservatives strongly opposed the idea, stating that such an increase in expenses would force the companies to relocate in other communities.

Sensing the rising recognition of the need for new industry, the Conservatives and some nonallied businessmen set up a private fund drive to use in industrial promotion. These funds were to be supplemented by municipal money. Industrialists opposed to new industry successfully argued that such use of tax revenue was illegal.

By the election of 1947, it was apparent that Negroes were being frustrated by the *status quo,* and that they were beginning to register and vote in increasing numbers. The Conservatives also sensed a general impatience over the conditions of street, school, and recreational facilities. This campaign proceeded consensually, and the election resulted in the issuance of civic improvement bonds.

Relatively unresponsive to the Negroes, the Conservatives soon ran afoul of a large sector of the White subcommunity: the blue-collar workers. The city employees, with the backing of the city's industrial unions, had organized a union. The Conservative city administration refused to recognize it and later refused demands for a dues check-off arrangement. The ensuing controversy was intense and seemed to infuse the blue-collar workers with a renewed sense of militant solidarity. They rejected offers of third parties to mediate the dispute, claiming that, indeed, there was no possibility of compromise.

In the midst of this, a demand arose to increase sharply the amount of money given to public education in the community. Organized labor immediately supported it; the Conservatives opposed it on the grounds that current resources were adequate, and that higher taxes would drive industry from the city. But the bond issue was authorized by a wide margin in a special election.

The rising sense of efficacy of formerly marginal, potential political interest groups became more apparent. It was a time of ferment in Petropolis. Respected Negro leaders felt constrained to speak out against overly militant efforts to achieve equality. Underneath the surface, labor leaders seemed to be "hatching" something. Radical stimuli from national politics intruded also, as the Progressive Party began its ultimately unsuccessful campaign to mobilize the "underdogs." This aided the liberal, as opposed to radical, Negro and union leadership. These liberals claimed that their people required substantial policy gains or else they would opt for extremism. Unlikely as the latter alternative might have been, the Conservative leaders were so remote from the rank-and-file worker or Negro that the threats seemed great. The administration extended recognition to the city employees' union and met some of its demands.

At this juncture, a new, aspiring leadership group, which had a Liberal ideology, clearly emerged. Goaded particularly by the local congressmen's zealous support of the newly enacted Taft-Hartley law, the labor leadership had joined forces behind a dissident businessman to take control of the local Democratic party organization. Although the new group failed to wield the influence it desired in party politics at the state level, it successfully unseated the congressman it considered opposed to its interests, and thus provided the group with an early victory of some magnitude. This dramatically illustrated to the restless Negro leadership the potential value of a political coalition with the emerging local labor-Liberal political organization.

The new party leader was John Jay, a young man who had once thought to acquire a position of leadership in local affairs through earnest participation in civic activities, within the regular limits informally established by the Conservative "city fathers." After putting in his time as an apprentice, he had found that seniority was really the key to top positions within that group. Impatiently, he turned his ambition and considerable talent elsewhere. His frustration coincided with the activation of organized labor in politics which led to the formation of the Liberal political group. The head of the local labor council, Fred Ames, became the second-in-command of Jay's Democratic party executive committee. Since he was aware that the Negroes were ripe for political mobilization, Jay assayed the possibility of a broader coalition which had few precedents in the South: the Negro citizen and the White blue-collar worker.

Petropolis' Negroes years before had organized an informal group called PESNEG (Petropolis Society for Negro Education and Growth). Its leadership had been recruited largely from officials of the locally owned Negro businesses. Organized during the Depression, the primary goals of PESNEG were the welfare of the Negro community, equality between Negroes and Whites, and the ultimate elimination of segregation in various areas of social, economic, and political life. At first, PESNEG had functioned as a kind of mutual aid and protection society for the member Negro leaders. It helped generate for its members social status as well as power within the Negro community, which gave them some status in the eyes of White leaders. It served to keep militancy under control within the Negro community and thus protected the economic positions of its wealthiest and most influential members. It supported Negro education by campaigns to obtain private donations from wealthy Whites for the Negro technical institute in Petropolis.

For many years, the organization's *modus operandi* was not so much collective action as individual, person-to-person, Negro-White relations. This form of cross-racial contact produced dividends for the Negro business leaders. However, by the late 1930's PESNEG had made a discernible shift toward organized, if gentle, political action. This shift in tactics was due to several factors: PESNEG had assumed much of the character of a government for the Negro community, even though it lacked such official authority as police power, power to tax, and power to spend tax monies. The wealthy few in the Negro business community believed in the racial philosophy attributed to Booker T. Washington. In essence, the credo professed that hard work, thrift, and the other elements of the Protestant Ethic would achieve for Negroes what it had for the Christian White society. Rather than demand that Whites accord wealth or respect to Negroes, Negroes would earn both for themselves by pursuing the virtuous life, an increasingly dubious proposition.

While wealth had accrued to a small number of Negro entrepreneurs, little respect was accorded them by Whites during the Depression decade. When the cream of Negro society held formal dances in a municipal building, both the ladies' and men's restrooms were locked to keep them for Whites only. When lower-class Negro violence threatened persons or property of the Negro upper-class, police protection was hard to find. When streets in the Negro sections needed paving, it was discovered that tax funds were committed almost wholly to White sections of the city.

The logic inherent in the idea that political action was the best way to further policy goals became compelling as younger, highly educated Negro leaders began to make their voices heard both inside and outside PESNEG. These young men were less patient than the Negro socio-economic "elite." They had not experienced personally the satisfactions to be gained from individual White contacts which the latter had.

Negroes comprised almost 40 per cent of Petropolis' population in the immediate postwar years, but they represented only a tiny fraction of the registered electorate. A primary problem for PESNEG was the registration and organization of Negro voters. While this was a task of great magnitude, particularly in regard to the large number of illiterate or semiliterate low-income people, prospects were not entirely bleak. The Negro business group was joined by educators and professionals to constitute a small but significant spearhead for voter activation. An influential Negro newspaper, the *Negro News*, was published weekly by William Steer, an active member of PESNEG and a leading member of the Petropolis chapter of the National Association for the Advancement of Colored People. Although this paper did not reach everyone in the Negro subcommunity, it provided a channel for communication to a wide range of potential voters.

Since the Negro subcommunity was a smaller and, in many ways, simpler society than its White counterpart in Petropolis, it relied more on informal, person-to-person communications in political, civic, and social matters than did the White subcommunity. Thus the church congregation, the kinship group, and the neighborhood grapevine were available to PESNEG, even if radio broadcasts or the daily newspaper columns were not. Such primary face-to-face contacts can be very effective in exercising political influence—possibly more so than the printed political advertisement, the mailed leaflet, or the radio or television speech.

However, PESNEG's leaders realized the need for an organization, a network of professionals to work between them and the potential voters. In Petropolis few people believed that one, two, or even a dozen election campaigns by amateurs would determine the final outcome of the demands in the PESNEG platform. But the Democratic party, led by John Jay, seemed to provide a useful and professional organization base.

For at least some Negroes, participation in the Democratic party meant part-time paid employment as party workers and, as a result of such party work, prestige within the Negro community. Some Negro party workers were drawn into contact with White politicians; by working with Whites on common tasks, they developed a cross-racial dignity difficult to acquire for almost all Negroes except members of the financial elite.

The Community Conservationist Administration

As the mayoralty election of 1949 neared, the Conservatives began to deliberate the possibility of slum clearance and redevelopment, in an attempt to avoid the loss of further authoritative positions of leadership to the Liberals, who were beginning to make demands for such municipal programs. But the question of low-cost housing became involved. Conservatives took a position of strong opposition to public housing, particularly if it were to be financed by the federal government. This became the primary issue of the campaign.

John Jay decided to support the nomination of a young professional man who had been a war hero. Although Jay's position was much more liberal than that of his candidate, the young man was a Community Conservationist of sufficiently progressive orientation to be acceptable to both Jay and his White labor and Negro associates. Jay's candidate took the position that a federal housing program should be sought unless local private means soon were found to solve the problem. His opponent represented a general Conservative antipathy to federal intervention in local affairs. The intense campaign further activated the formerly politically inert union and Negro rank and file, and Jay's man won, five to three, carrying the Negro districts by an enormous margin.

Under the new administration, policy changes were not long in coming. Negroes made a formal demand for the appointment of Negro election officials in predominantly Negro districts. The demand was met. The city council appointed a committee to investigate the manner in which Petropolis might avail itself of assistance through the new federal public housing act. Finally, the local government agreed to the city employees' demand for a union dues check-off system. On other matters Negro demands were rejected, especially those directed to the Conservative-dominated school board.

In 1951 the Jay machine was also successful. The Mayor did not seek reelection, since he had received a higher-level political appointment. John Jay worked for the election of Ed Plunkett, a local merchant with Community Conservationist views. Jay thought Plunkett could unite the left and the center, the Liberals and the Community Conservationists. Plunkett's opponent was an ultraconservative businessman. After a bitter contest Plunkett was elected by a narrow margin. Paid political advertisements served notice to the reading public that the race issue had entered local government elections in no uncertain terms.

This expanded Liberal-Community Conservationist coalition had its most striking postwar success in the municipal elections of 1953, when a Negro was elected to the city council. Frank Eldon, a business leader, received virtually the entire vote in the predominantly Negro precincts. This was sufficient to overcome a heavy adverse vote in the all-White precincts, where three-fourths of the voters chose his opponent. Four of the other five PESNEG-endorsed candidates were elected. The Mayor, Ed Plunkett, was unopposed for reelection. The PESNEG leaders felt that Mayor Plunkett was a man with genuine understanding of the problems and aspirations of minorities, since he himself belonged to a minority religious sect in Petropolis, which was almost entirely a city of two major Protestant denominations. Although he had lived in Petropolis for 20 years, some people still regarded him as a newcomer and not truly a loyal Petropolis citizen. Even though he was selected "Man of the Year" by the combined service clubs during the Second World War as a result of his civic service, and even though he was elected president of the Downtown Business Association, he was still considered a newcomer by some White civic leaders. Plunkett's political career shows a striking parallel to that of John Jay insofar as their early civic activities and later rejection by the Conservative leaders are concerned.

Mayor Plunkett had been induced to run for mayor in 1951 not by John Jay but by some of his fellow merchants. But when PESNEG and the Jay machine enthusiastically supported his candidacy, many White supporters dropped away. Once he was in office, his "ineligibility" for membership in Chestnut Hill Country Club, where many of the wealthier White civic leaders discussed community affairs and local political matters, made it difficult for him to organize support for his policy program. In spite of this difficulty Plunkett, as mayor, impressed many people as being exceptionally able, judicious, and fair to all groups, without committing himself to the interests of only one, whether the Negro subcommunity or his fellow merchants. Conservatives who had considered running against Mayor Plunkett in 1953 felt that he was too popular to defeat but that he could and would be stopped by a Conservative city council. In this they were mistaken to a considerable degree.

By 1953, PESNEG's political power in the Negro community was firmly established. It advanced steadily toward its basic goals. A public low-rent housing project was opened to its first occupants early that year. Several hundred units were planned, of which a majority were to be built for Negro occupancy and 40 per cent for White. This program was established by the city government with federal funds. John Jay was a prime mover in this program, and a close associate of his became a member of the local public housing agency.

Additional jobs in city government were given to Negroes. Not only were some employed on street and sidewalk repair crews, but Negroes were also hired in such higher-status positions as policemen, the traditional first rung in local government employment for such minorities as the Irish immigrants in New York and Boston.

Negroes were not particularly successful in obtaining better employment in the large manufacturing firms of Petropolis. Greater progress might have been made in this area if their political allies, the White labor-union people, had worked more actively for desegregation in the factories. Those White union officials who were sympathetic because of moral, ideological, or political interest were faced with a rank and file who not only were concerned with job competition but also held deep-seated anti-Negro feelings. And a number of the White labor-union officials were not receptive to a change in the traditional pattern of employment. This cleavage placed a strain on the Negro-White labor coalition and became an even more serious obstacle after the Supreme Court's school desegregation decision of 1954.

This period also was marked by changes in the planning and guided-development functions of the city government. Mayor Plunkett advocated and received regulatory powers over the building of new residential subdivisions. The zoning ordinance was substantially revised to take account of postwar growth and present land-use trends. Over some resistance, a greater degree of authority was secured for an expanded city department of planning. This function of local government was becoming more important to Mayor Plunkett and his close associates as the key to the solution and prevention of community problems.

The 1954 election witnessed an unprecedented set of events for Negroes in local politics: George France, the Negro president of the Southern Loan Company, entered the race for county commissioner. His decision to seek county office, even though his chances for electoral victory were less than in the urban electorate where Negro voting strength was concentrated, reflected the Negro leadership's growing confidence in their political strength. France represented the dominant segment of PESNEG leadership, which was gradualist. The gradualists believed that desegregation was inevitable; that more could be gained by not provoking active White opposition; and that well-meaning White leaders would be able to accomplish more if precipitous actions were avoided by PESNEG. They feared a prosegregation reaction that could encumber the freedom of action of the sincere White leaders. Although they did not advocate a "do-nothing" program, they chose to proceed very cautiously, by means of local political action. Since their efforts at political action were increasingly successful, even though economic and social walls between the races remained substantially unbreached, their policy of caution seemed to them to be justified.

France's nomination to county office marked the beginning of severe strain on the Negro-White labor coalition. This cleavage was reflected in the opposition of a few White labor-union officials to the priority assigned by the Jay machine to France's campaign. The dissidents preferred a strategy of trying to capture a larger number of county government posts instead of concentrating on the election of George France.

In the first primary, France received a plurality insufficient to prevent a run-off primary, even though the two predominantly Negro precincts gave 98 per cent of their votes to France. White labor leaders who had argued against concentrating all their efforts on one race said "never again" when, in the run-off, France was defeated by his White opponent.

Racial considerations were minimal in the municipal elections of 1955. In contrast to the elections of 1953 and 1951, there was less racial division in the vote for councilmen. PESNEG endorsed five councilmen, all of whom won a majority in the predominantly White precincts. The absence of much White opposition to the PESNEG-endorsed candidates largely resulted from the latter's endorsement of candidates adjudged most capable, regardless of their attitudes toward desegregation.

Mayor Ed Plunkett ran unopposed, as he had in the previous election. Racial harmony in this election was also due in some measure to Eben Bacon Jr.'s candidacy for the city council. Coming from Petropolis's first family, he had the support of the more conservative White groups as well as of the Negro leadership who were aware of his liberal attitudes on racial matters. Less than 25 per cent of those registered went to the polls in 1955, an unusually low turnout. This drop-off was greater for Whites than Negroes, indicating the greater importance of electoral success to Negroes than Whites at that time.

The period between the Supreme Court's decision and the fall of 1956 was one of watchful waiting on the part of PESNEG in regard to school desegregation. A special commission had been appointed by the Governor to make a study of the situation and to recommend a state plan on school desegregation. PESNEG's leaders felt cautiously optimistic. Although the Court's decision was clearly unpopular, the primary reaction to it by the Governor and the officials of the state was that Southern State was law abiding and that massive resistance was to be avoided. A pupil-assignment law already had been passed by the legislature. This seemed to offer a basis for limited compliance while delaying widespread desegregation.

Although the "go fast" faction in PESNEG continually sought a more widespread compliance, most Negro leaders felt that the larger cities of the state, including Petropolis, were soon likely to make a substantial start toward desegregation in the schools. Total desegregation could be accomplished only gradually, since residential segregation still existed. With the prospect that individual localities would have some freedom of choice concerning school desegregation, these Negro leaders felt that it was important for the entire PESNEG leadership to support an atmosphere in Petropolis favorable to desegregation. This required caution in matters such as initiating lawsuits to force admission to schools. It also required greatly increased efforts to gain political power in the community.

In the fall of 1956, the state government's locally oriented plan for meeting the requirements of the desegregation decision was promulgated. Political success at the local level became even more urgent. Since local boards of education could call an election to close the public schools, the admission-policy sentiment of Petropolis board members was critically important. The Petropolis City Council was empowered to appoint members of the city school board, a fact which made control of local government directly and immediately relevant to the school desegregation policy. An organized minority of the registered voters legally could also force an election, regardless of school board policy. Thus it was equally important not to stimulate counteraction and counterorganization by prosegregation citizen groups, as PESNEG's leadership strengthened its political forces.

However, during the time the overall state approach to the Supreme Court decision was being developed, prosegregation forces were beginning to organize in Petropolis. A group led by two young attorneys formed the Petropolis Committee on Race Relations (PECORR). This was a variation on the recently formed White Citizens Councils of Southern State and of other states in the South. PECORR also had a very small membership. Few of the White civic leaders with like sentiments belonged to it, possibly because it seemed too closely akin to the low-status Ku Klux Klan to merit their active support. At first PECORR was simply a group in which like-minded people could communicate with each other, rather than a political organization with a specific program of action and policy goals.

By 1956 the increasing strength of the Conservatives was even more significant for community politics, since they had remained a fragmented group after their series of defeats by the Liberal-Community Conservationist coalition. Many Conservatives lived in the exclusive Chestnut Hills suburban area, and the Chestnut Hills Country Club became a natural meeting place for discussions of political policy and strategy. Differing as they did on many specific policies, their common political conservatism was defined by a firm belief in a low tax rate and restricted powers of local, state, and national government. They were particularly concerned that local government stay out of the domain of social relations, and they were strongly indignant about "dirty politics," as symbolized by the Jay machine.

Conservatism in Petropolis was weakened by diverse internal interests. Those in favor of bringing in new industry were opposed by those who wanted to maintain a surplus, inexpensive labor supply; those who endorsed features of "good government" which were costly or involved vigorous local planning were opposed by those who objected to local government expenditures or all public planning at any level of government. Perhaps the major drawbacks to political action were that so many members were unwilling to run for office themselves, to work actively in the dominant Democratic party, or to try to attract younger political aspirants to their ranks.

The revitalization of Conservatism thus stopped short of an actively organized local movement. However, in 1956, it coincided with a major split in the White labor wing of the Jay machine and a move by PECORR to take over the local Democratic party organization. A major controversy developed over both the local and state tickets; antimachine and antiPESNEG sentiments drove the opening wedge in the hitherto unified White labor front. With PECORR activists in the vanguard, John Jay's ten-year rule as Democratic chief came under sharp attack. He was retained as party chairman by a very narrow margin.

While these political events were unfolding in Petropolis, the attention of some White leaders was turning to another area of community life. This concerned the community's present economic state and prospects for future urban growth and economic development. State leaders had approached the basic problem of the state's underbalanced and relatively static economy by developing programs to attract new industry to the state; a department of the state government was entrusted with this task. Funds were appropriated to provide risk capital for small industry and business. Plans were made to cut corporation taxes, assertedly to compete with neighboring low-business-tax states.

An important feature of this state program was the "Laboratory Locus," publicized as a locale of great natural advantage for certain types of industry. This area of the state included Petropolis and its neighboring cities, each of which had a major university or technical institute. The idea was that businesses and industries in need of research personnel and facilities would find them already available in the physical science, engineering, and medical laboratories of these institutions. The research and development activities of electronics and engineering industries in Los Angeles, near Stanford University on the San Francisco Bay Peninsula, and near MIT in Cambridge, Massachusetts, served as models for the concept of the Laboratory Locus. A large industrial tract near Petropolis was donated by a wealthy industrialist to an intercity organization formed to help make this concept a reality.

A number of Petropolis business and civic leaders also formed a local organization to promote new payrolls specifically for that city and for the future Laboratory Locus area. A Committee on Industrial Development was formed; members were drawn from the most important businesses and banks, and included some Negro leaders, representatives of labor, and local officials from the largest industries. Both the city and county governments annually contributed money to the new organization, which hired a full-time executive secretary.

The active direction of this organization became centered in a handful of men, mainly Community Conservationist leaders, who worked closely with the executive secretary. A complementary organization was formed to purchase industrial sites and to otherwise facilitate the movement of new industry to Petropolis. A companion investment company was organized so that citizens might participate in developing the industrial tracts for the anticipated new industries. The Committee on Industrial Development was able to acquire, through subscription from local businessmen, capital and a few hundred acres of land for housing prospective manufacturers.

A number of serious problems were encountered by the Committee. First, Petropolis was at more of a disadvantage than other cities in the region with regard to such industrial-location factors as proximity to raw materials, extent of labor-union organization, and size of market. Then the committee discovered that property owners had begun to price land out of the market when they heard the committee was looking for good industrial sites. An even greater obstacle was the inactivity of most of the committee members, due partly to lack of interest, but due also, in some cases, to basic opposition to the program.

Certain members of the Chamber of Commerce, which had been relatively inactive in industrial promotion, resented what they considered to be a usurpation of their function. Some members of the Downtown Business Association foresaw undesirable competition from the new retail establishments that would spring up in an industrializing, expanding city. Finally, some of the largest locally owned manufacturing companies were expected to oppose either an increase in labor costs, due to a greater demand for labor, or increased taxation to pay for services for an expanded population or to subsidize new industry.

The Committee on Industrial Development had an important stake in harmonious intergroup relations in Petropolis; this stake included both labor-management and race relations. The executive secretary of the Committee felt that at least 50 per cent of the firms throughout the country who were relocating were trying to avoid unions. Strikes in Petropolis might discourage those firms from relocating there. Racial strife might have a comparable effect!

Both organized labor and the Negro community were vitally interested in the success of the Committee. Labor was looking for more and better jobs. However, although organized labor expressed every intention of cooperating in the drive for new industry, its members helped to organize a picket line in a neighboring city when a large nonunion firm moved there. Those in Petropolis who were concerned most about attracting new business and industry deeply resented this incident, which emphasized the divisions of interest of the different groups involved in the alliance seeking new industry.

All the Negro members of the Committee were officials of the Negro investment and brokerage institutions and leaders of PESNEG. They presumably had a great stake in helping to bring new industry to Petropolis, because economic opportunities were more limited for Negroes than for Whites. However, the interest alignment was not that simple.

Some of these Negro leaders were more wary than others of actively supporting any shift in the race-relations pattern that might threaten to disrupt their business relations. Possible repercussions from job desegregation were unpredictable. Other leading members of PESNEG felt that the advent of new desegregated industry would do little to change the immediate situation of Negroes, since few Negroes were qualified to take other than unskilled jobs. They believed that an improved educational system—particularly technical education—was the key to mass Negro economic improvement. Some other leaders of PESNEG doubted that a major desegregated industry would be interested in locating in Petropolis, or that such industry would be allowed by the economically dominant White firms to move there. Even certain White members of the Committee on Industrial Development believed the rumors that an unidentified White industrialist member of the Committee was contacting prospective firms in order to discourage their coming to Petropolis so that he could maintain a supply of cheap labor.

Among the most active directors of the Committee were Mayor Plunkett and members of the Bacon and Leek families. Free space was given to the executive secretary of the Committee in one of their office buildings. John Leek traveled about the country interviewing industrial prospects. He offered funds, if needed, to help pay the moving expenses of desirable companies. These members, together with a handful of business associates, were convinced that Petropolis was at the crossroads: it would either expand or die. They envisaged a dynamic, growing city with an enriched cultural, social, and economic life. They felt that a necessary condition for, and consequence of, such community dynamism was a shift in the strictly segregated society toward a more open, flexible biracial pattern.

While the industrial development program was being worked out at the state level in 1956–1957, and while the Petropolis Committee was wooing prospective industries, opposition to the Liberal Negro-White coalition erupted again into open conflict. In the municipal elections of 1957, Mayor Plunkett was faced with the biggest fight of his political life. Plunkett's opponent, Ralph Todd, had been elected to the city council some years earlier with the endorsement of PESNEG. Todd, a respected businessman, was active in welfare work in Petropolis. He was a quiet, self-made man whose opinions, when offered, were accorded great deference. As a strict Conservative, he favored minimum governmental activity and expenditures, believing that private action—for example, his own voluntary work in the welfare field—was an appropriate and sufficient means of solving most problems.

Initially Todd's campaign was based on his personal qualifications and his low-tax philosophy of government. But the campaign soon became hostile and race baiting. Mayor Plunkett was pictured as the candidate of PESNEG and the Negro subcommunity. A weekly "hate sheet," published by a PECORR adherent who was devoted to the cause of strict segregation, tried to stir up emotion and further racial hatred in an effort to defeat Mayor Plunkett. It placed the mayoralty contest in an anti-Negro, anti-religious-minority frame. Just before the election, posters appeared all over town. These urged people to vote, and only incidentally suggested a vote for Todd. The idea was that if the ordinarily apathetic lower-class Whites could be stirred up, their prosegregation sentiments would almost automatically lead them to vote for Todd. Mayor Plunkett, the younger Bacons and Leeks, and their partisans were surprised to learn how many of their presumed "friends" turned to Todd. Some expressed embarrassment at the mud-slinging, racist campaign; others seemed to indicate by their silence that, while overdone, the basic charges nevertheless were well founded.

In a massive turnout on election day, Mayor Plunkett won by less than one per cent. All the other PESNEG-endorsed candidates were elected to the council, including one Negro, Dan Standish, a PESNEG leader and wealthy financier. Following its usual practice, PESNEG did not endorse only pro-Negro candidates; in one notable instance they supported a White civic leader who was openly opposed to school desegregation. The patterns of politics that followed upon the election (Time *E*) will be discussed later (see Chapter 6).

METROVILLE

The key political leaders of Metroville since the 1920's had been a small group of economically dominant White citizens—the owners and managers of the largest corporations and a handful of others. These people had a tradition of active involvement in civic affairs and of making substantial donations to public health and welfare, recreation, and cultural activities. This group was of critical importance in determining whether or not there would be an eventual reorganization of the two racial subcommunities into a single polity and economy—if not into a single social system. Steps had been taken in this direction, and visible progress had been made since the immediate postwar years toward producing community harmony. This group was instrumental in establishing Harmony House, a social agency seeking improved economic conditions and opportunities for Negroes. Members of the group also promoted programs of public housing for poor Whites and Negroes. They supported an active city planning department, introduced the city-manager form of government, and supported public hospitals, a large-scale recreational program, and extensive cultural activities.

During the Second World War, Metroville underwent the equivalent of a decade, perhaps even a generation or more, of urbanization and industrialization. This happened at a time when those who normally wielded political influence were preoccupied with matters other than community control. Immediately following the war, the normal system of political decision-making in Metroville was threatened with far-reaching and even violent transformation. The political process in Metroville remained, in some measure, a reaction to that threat.

Metroville emerged from the war as a decaying, unattractive community compared to Petropolis, Oretown, and Farmdale. Many houses in the slum areas had only community faucets in the back lots. Rats were not restricted to the worst slums. The downtown streets were narrow, off-street parking facilities were inadequate, and severe traffic congestion resulted. During the Depression and the Second World War, city and county taxes had been very low; consequently, there was a deterioration of public facilities. The racially separate school system was operating with subsistence budgets. Public libraries, both White and Negro, were virtually nonfunctioning. The city's water supply was so outmoded that disastrous water shortages threatened the inhabitants. The sewage disposal plant contaminated nearby streams. Municipal health facilities had declined to the extent that they became a serious political issue in the postwar period. In summary, Metroville appeared on the verge of physical collapse.

At the end of the war, the city itself was tightly knit physically, spiritually, and politically. Physically, all economic activity—banks, stores, shops, warehouses, and even industries—was packed into the central core. The city sat by idly while the bulk of the residential growth developed in the rural-urban fringe. No annexations of these new residential clusters had occurred for decades, so that the residents worked in the city and used city services without contributing to their support. In fact, the county and the city leaders placed the heaviest financial responsibility on the city taxpayers. For example, Metroville's taxpayers paid a combined city-county tax that was over four times the amount paid by the county taxpayers.

Political leadership resided with a small group of local industrialists who ruled with benevolent paternalism. The community in the immediate postwar years was described elsewhere as "the city of the very rich with no middle class" and an "overgrown village." The contemporary industrialists, descendants of the founders of the industrial complex, had a strong religious heritage. The community had been settled by a religious sect which preferred to withdraw from the influences of the outside world. They believed that religion was best expressed through hard work and the doing of good deeds. The close ties and common outlook of the civic leaders were embedded in a common industrial and religious network and a web of kinship connections.

There was much articulate dissatisfaction with the situation of the community at the end of the war. The business leaders were dissatisfied generally with the operation of local government. Citizens were annoyed with traffic congestion, poor schools, and antiquated Blue Laws, which were so strictly enforced that on Sunday it was impossible to see a movie or ball game, much less buy a soft drink. The Negro subcommunity was increasingly unhappy with its lot, which, in general, was equal to that of the lowest stratum of poor, illiterate White citizens.

Most of these dissatisfactions were gradually resolved or "managed" in the next few years, but race and labor relations erupted into open conflict. A wave of support suddenly developed within the Negro subcommunity for a militant, left-wing union that toward the end of the war tried to organize the major industry in the city on a biracial basis. Despite vigorous opposition by Metroville's industrialists, who until that time had not been seriously threatened by union activity, the union organizers called a major and prolonged walkout. Negroes predominated on the picket lines, a phenomenon of protest unheard of in Metroville. Plans were prepared for a White labor-Negro coalition to run candidates for municipal offices. At the height of the turmoil, a race riot was narrowly averted; this demoralized the militant Negro leadership. The final blow for the participating Negroes (as well as for many prounion White workers) was to read in an article in a major Metroville magazine that a number of the union's local White leaders were political "radicals." The strike was broken; the industry remained unorganized.

The White leaders of the community learned a lesson from the abortive "revolt." They turned the focus of attention away from industry and proposed an agenda of civic improvement—but not before another nerve center was challenged: the public morals protected by the community's Blue Laws. They reluctantly gave in to widespread, popular demands to change them.

The movement for civic improvement was guided by a Committee for Better Government whose ideology was Conservative but of a progressive type. The Committee, organized on a nonprofit, "nonpolitical" basis, was devoted to the maintenance and improvement of good government in the city and county. The membership comprised mainly industrial, business, religious, and civic leaders. There were only two Negroes and no representative of labor on this very

large committee. In a talk before a prestigious civic club, Gerald
Smith, Sr., founder and president, stressed the first specific objective
of the Committee: a balanced budget on a "pay-as-you-go" basis for
local government. This meant higher local taxes to end the practice
of refunding bonds, and consolidations of overlapping city-county
functions to achieve efficiency.

To accomplish its objectives, the Committee and other groups, organizations, and foundations dominated by these top industrialists and
financiers brought in experts to make a series of studies and reports
on what should be done to give Metroville a good government and the
community a progressive atmosphere. In the period from the Second
World War until 1957, Time *E*, such studies had been made on city-
county financial relations, school consolidation, community development—including the promulgation of a master plan for future land-use
patterns in the city—race relations, agricultural problems, water, hospital care, recreation, health, education, and welfare.

The first move of civic leaders was to reorganize the structure of
local government: the system of a part-time mayor and city council
was replaced by the city-manager form of government. This followed
closely their pattern of using experts to bring about more efficient
operations and greater order in local governmental affairs. Then they
adopted a "pay-as-you-go" financial plan of taxation that drastically
increased the tax rate for county residents and raised city taxes to a
lesser degree. The tax increases and a series of sales of self-liquidat-
ing bonds was an unprecedented program for raising capital in Metroville. Millions of dollars were invested in the school systems. The
water system was rebuilt and the sewage disposal plant replaced.
A planning commission was created to enforce a master plan of
"orderly" land uses.

Although local government was being professionalized, rejuvenated,
and refurbished, its net scope was expanded somewhat less than has
been implied. The top civic leaders stepped up individual, voluntary
efforts to improve the community. These men, known for their past
philanthropy, had given the community parks and major cultural and
recreational facilities. After the war they decided to mix private
philanthropy of gigantic proportions with public capital funds. In
the period from the end of the Second World War to Time *E*, millions
of dollars had been raised in this manner. A large proportion of this
money was contributed to such projects as a convention hall, a series
of separate parks for White and Negro citizens, a community center,
a home for the aged, a library, an athletic field, and other public

facilities. The most ambitious program was the multimillion-dollar creation of a new campus for the White college in Metroville.

As one can surmise, sharp tax increases and such civic improvement projects as had been approved by the well-to-do resolved few of the pressing problems of the White working class and Negroes of all social classes. The effort at unionization and local political action had failed. The Negroes had no basis upon which to form a biracial coalition such as that which emerged in Petropolis during the same period. However, the mayoralty primary of 1949 presented an opportunity for these subordinate groups to express dissatisfaction. A perennial candidate for public office, G. A. Peterson, developed a new campaign stance with a vigorous attack on the traditional community leadership, the "vested interests." He appealed to Whites and Negroes of the working class, and to the people in the recently annexed areas. The new city residents had had their property taxes more than doubled already, and the new civic improvement program promised a nearly sixfold total tax increase within a very few years. The candidate promised to give every taxpayer true value on his tax dollar; he attacked in vitriolic terms the traditional rule by the few, appealing to the average citizen to join in a democratic crusade. The community leaders fought back through their representatives in city government and by backing the incumbent Mayor's campaign. When Peterson won by a very small margin in the primary, his enemies considered supporting the Republican candidate in the general election. However, they decided that this would be too dangerous a tactic in Democratic Southern State, would threaten their continued control of the useful Democratic party, and would be an extreme provocation to Peterson. They decided to announce their formal support of Peterson in the general election. He was elected Mayor of Democratic Metroville with relative ease.

The rhetoric of the new Mayor allowed the "downtrodden" to believe that they now had a political warrior who would challenge the "ruling elite," and for a brief period after his election he did so. But even though the Negro community and the low-income groups in the poorer White neighborhoods had provided the Mayor's most important electoral support, they were an unstable power base with which to maintain authority if he came into conflict with the community leaders. Thus, once elected, he cast around for possible links with the White leaders whom he had so harshly attacked. He soon found William Polk, leading industrialist and a chief executive of the industry in which labor unrest had occurred, to serve as his political adviser.

This bond insured Peterson's political future and it provided the traditional White community leaders a politician who could stand as a representative of the "masses," Negro and White.

It was to be expected, then, that Mayor Peterson would continue with the civic improvement program which the leaders had launched earlier. He left all efforts for economic reorganization and industrial development to the White economic community leaders. The city administration vigorously tackled the problem of traffic congestion: it banned on-street parking in the downtown section, installed parking meters to control "dead storage" parking, constructed a large number of off-street parking areas, instituted a one-way-street system, and planned and constructed a series of expressways, bypasses, and parkways. Despite objections from merchants and the other property owners who were affected adversely, these programs moved ahead without interruption.

The new administration, aware of the interests of its principal supporters, acted on five major proposals. Three of these—city-owned liquor stores, urban redevelopment, and public housing—involved increasing the scope of local government. Public housing, to be built with federal funds, was applauded by the Negro subcommunity, even though it was to be segregated. The remaining two proposals, rehabilitating the city mental hospital system and increasing recreation facilities, involved improvement of existing city programs. These were temporarily under study by citizen committees—of top leaders of the White subcommunity—and expert commissions, as had been the procedure in the past. Decisions on the mental hospital's problem and recreation facilities were not finally made until during Time E to M, 1957–1958, and will be discussed further in Chapter 6.

Peterson, perceiving the enthusiasm in the city for exercising the "local option" of establishing municipal liquor stores, led the battle of the "wets." A countywide referendum was held on the question. This was defeated through the strong moral suasion of the religious leaders. The vote in the city was much more favorable. The Mayor then appealed to the county commissioners to allow the city to hold a referendum; this appeal was granted over the vigorous opposition of the church officials. When the matter was again put to the voters, they approved.

Peterson then attacked the problem of the slums of Metroville. These were inhabited by his chief electoral supporters: Negroes and lower-class Whites. An earlier report by a planning consultant had pointed out that residential housing was in great need of governmental action to eliminate the high proportion of substandard dwelling units.

Cognizant of the newly passed federal housing act of 1949, the Mayor applied to Washington for assistance for a public housing program. Unfortunately, Southern State had not provided legislation to enable localities to engage in public housing activities. Temporary failure here encouraged him to focus on urban redevelopment. After detailed study he was able to convince the civic leaders that it would be in the interests of themselves and the community to redevelop portions of Metroville. These leaders prevailed on the state legislatures to provide statutory authority for the city to proceed with an urban-redevelopment program. In the meantime, authority had been granted by the state for the proposed public-housing projects. Within a few years these projects housed a small but significant number of Negro families, as well as a number of low-income Whites.

Mayor Peterson maintained the electoral loyalties of large but marginal segments of Metroville through the electoral campaigns of 1951, 1953, and 1955. To do this he had granted a series of minor concessions to demands from the Negro subcommunity for such things as unskilled jobs with the city; he had held out the promise of school desegregation and additional public housing; and he had spoken out on occasion for the rights of the working man. White municipal employees constituted another electoral bloc in support of his administration. Many middle- and upper-class White citizens were impressed with his programs to improve and develop housekeeping services, his programs of civic and cultural improvement, his increasing stress on efficiency in local government through annexations of fringe areas, and his increasing attention to urban renewal and redevelopment. Although there had been opposition to him in the previous elections, by 1957 it appeared that he could no longer maintain his favorable political position without a fight.

The common views of Mayor Peterson and the Progressive Conservative leaders, which, in effect, regulated and limited the political activity of the Negroes, were not generally known in Metroville. As a result of the widely known fact that a large proportion of the Negroes voted consistently for Peterson, in what amounted to the hated "bloc vote," and as a result of increasing fears on the part of White segregationists of what Peterson's administration might do in the way of desegregating the public schools, a considerable anti-Negro, anti-Peterson vote appeared in the 1957 election. This vote was largely unorganized, perhaps because the dominant Democratic party was controlled by the Progressive Conservative leaders who by now had accepted Peterson, even if many still regarded him with disdain. It was reflected in a heavy outpouring of support for Peterson's Republican opponent in the general election, who, realizing that he lacked the support of the community leadership, was surprised at his own "good showing," and found little apparent reason to explain it. This, too, suggested the unorganized nature of the anti-Peterson vote. The activation of the "anti's" seemed to be due, in part, to the continuously rising tax rate associated with the civic improvements desired by the leadership and implemented through the city administration.

By Time E, the existence of widespread opposition signified a developing problem for the Mayor. As the cost and scope of civic improvements expanded past the point where even the wealthiest, most community-minded of Metroville's first families could contribute all the necessary funds, the burden of progress would continue to shift more heavily to the individual taxpayer. The taxpayer, however, had not been educated to accept this, accustomed as he was to community benefits by donation. Furthermore, Negro leaders, though still behind Peterson, were beginning to demand a sharper break with the past in the relations between races. The relationship between the developing issues of race relations and the expensive civic improvements seemed to be the key to whether or not the Progressive Conservatives could maintain their monopoly of manifest political leadership positions and Mayor Peterson his position as head of the city government.

SUMMARY

The Second World War was a period of great significance, both for the United States as a nation in the world community and for the cities and towns within the nation. Twentieth-century processes of urban growth and industrial development were accelerated during these years, creating especially severe problems for the inhabitants of more densely populated communities. Urban services which had existed before the war and which had originally been designed for smaller populations, could not accommodate the conglomerations of city and urban fringe dwellers which existed at the end of the war. Nor were the city dwellers willing to accept the lower level of living to which many of the urban newcomers had been accustomed in their former rural residential locations. At the same time, life in the city or the suburb created discomforts and problems that the farmer had not known. Although city life was not completely different from life in the romanticized, idealized countryside, on the farm the owner or tenant did not find himself prohibited from building an outhouse if sewer lines or septic tank were not available. Neither did the rural resident have to cope with such problems as the dangers of heavy traffic to his child, or the construction of a factory next to his home.

This period witnessed not only the "revolution of rising expectations" among peoples in underdeveloped countries throughout the world, but also significant increases in the expectations of an abundant life and a higher level of amenities on the part of citizens of the United States. During the war and the immediate postwar period in this country, the breakdown of insular localism within the nation-state was hastened through a standardized system of communications, extralocal organizations and associations, and modern systems of transportation. Preferences and proposals about the kinds of civic improvements possible and the manner in which they might be brought about rapidly crossed community, state, and regional lines. This "nationalization" of values, expectations, and preferences was reflected in sets of relatively common demands in our four communities for shifts in the scope of local government. These demands were modified in some degree by the individual characteristics of each community.

Population increases and expanded "gross community products" immediately after the war were relevant conditions of political decision-making in Oretown and Petropolis. Decisions regarding the scope of local government in civic improvement revolved around the question of whether the net scope should be returned to prewar levels or increased slightly. They also revolved around the question of whether or not local government should be reorganized so that it might more effectively create and operate civic-improvement programs. Major net increases beyond prewar levels in the scope of local government were advocated in underdeveloped, semirural Farmdale and quasi-feudalistic Metroville in order to provide civic improvements. Whatever variations there were in the scope of local government in the four cities by 1946, similar sorts of demands were made and, to some degree, satisfied in all four communities. This resulted in expanded or new local government programs of civic improvement. Thus the modern problems of urban life were met to varying degrees in these communities by postwar shifts in the scope of local government.

In Farmdale, these efforts were successfully sustained until 1948, when a *status quo*-orientated Conservative group first slowed further expansion and then succeeded in taking complete control of City Hall through the election of one of their own men as Mayor. The new programs stopped far short of the aspirations of some citizens, particularly those who considered an expanded program of municipal improvements necessary to attract new industry to stimulate the increasingly stagnant local economy.

In Oretown, the civic-improvement programs were carried out by the Conservatives of Main Street until 1948. Then, a Liberal group embarked on a conflict-generating expansion of local government: the establishment of a municipal electric utility. The election of 1952 marked a return to moderation in City Hall with the election of a Community Conservationist Mayor who was devoted to the community-planning and guided-development functions of local government.

In Petropolis, expanded programs of civic improvement were begun by the Conservative leaders, who dominated community leadership positions until 1949. The Liberals then gained power through successful electoral efforts to install a more congenial city administration in office. In succeeding years, a more active city government and coalition of Community Conservationist and Liberal leaders pushed for various net increases and internal shifts in the functioning of local government. This culminated in a major effort to reverse the increasing deterioration of the local economy, particularly in its industrial sector.

Metroville was the scene of an explosive but momentary surge of radicalism, designed to transform an almost feudal regime which had allowed the city to be treated as a small-village appendage of the county and county government. This movement was quickly replaced by a Progressive Conservative regime dedicated to the task of raising the growing city from its neglected small-village status to the forefront of progressive postwar communities.

All four cities witnessed successful governmental reorganizations. Oretown and Metroville adopted the city-manager form of government to improve the administrative efficiency of City Hall. The only community without a city manager by Time E (1950) was Farmdale. In that community the major energies directed to local-government reorganization had been devoted, successfully, to the task of consolidating the fragmented, independent public-school systems of the city and surrounding areas.

Oretown saw the creation of a new unit of local government: a special district designed to satisfy the recreational needs of city and fringe-area residents. A municipal utility also was set up under the control of an independent unit of local government. This independent unit resulted from the presumption that citizens would receive the best service if the utility were operated by a professional public administration which was free from the impediments of local politics. Concern with the common problems of their suburban and city populations led to annexations of fringe areas in all four cities. A major effort was made in Metroville to develop formal and informal working arrangements between the county and city governments through joint boards so that local government could function on a broader metropolitan basis.

By the end of the Second World War, the traditional subordination in community life of such social groups as blue-collar workers and Negroes was even less acceptable to some citizens than was the increasingly inadequate functioning of local government in providing housekeeping services for more people with higher expectations about their standard of living. The New Deal policies of recognizing unions and advocating more racial equality became, during the fight against fascism, statements of democratic principle which some could not shed as easily as rifles and uniforms when the war was over. In Farmdale, substantial citizens dreaded the possibility that militant unions might develop in the community. It was feared that younger veterans and "radical" union leaders together would irresponsibly bring about increased costs in municipal government and property taxes. Such fears were alleviated only when veterans were successfully integrated into the local economy. This was the result of the active assistance of a special committee of leading citizens, and the failure of "boomer" businessmen to attract any significant amount of large-scale industry and union labor to the community. In Oretown, unions and a large blue-collar working force had come to the community during the Second World War. Liberals, led by Mayor Lovegren, were successful in rallying support from organized labor partially through an attack on what was termed Wall Street's control of the profit-hungry private utility. But primarily they gained support because the working men identified themselves as newcomers who needed city services rather than as a deprived, downtrodden socio-economic class. The widespread distribution of residential mortgages in Oretown and the tradition of relatively secure unionism may have mitigated against the development of working class demands for both social and political status; such demands are associated with a feeling of being discounted or even degraded by local government officials who are the agents of the affluent. Mayor Lovegren could not have been mistaken for such an agent.

Demands for political status and feelings of being politically deprived seemed to be much more widespread in Petropolis and Metroville, among both Whites in the blue-collar working force and Negroes of all occupational statuses. In both cities, the end of the Second World War brought with it an increase in the militancy of White labor and the Negro subcommunities. This militancy was expressed in demands for informal local governmental reorganization which would provide access to officials by union members and Negroes as a regular, informal practice, rather than as a formal but seldom exercised right. It was manifested in the unsuccessful effort to form a racially integrated union in Metroville to secure its position in the local economy and, simultaneously, to push demands for representation in City Hall and in the local Democratic party. After this union movement was aborted, socio-political discontent led to Mayor Peterson's short-lived representation of labor and the Negro subcommunity. His local governmental reorganization substantially reduced the degree of access which labor and Negroes had obtained temporarily. The gerrymandering of Negro voters into one ward ensured that, for the foreseeable future, Negroes would have one seat, but no more, on the city council.

In Metroville Negroes were accorded a measure of social status without any substantial change in the pattern of local government functioning through the establishment of a Harmony House, the termination of selected segregation practices, the appointment of one Negro to the city school board, and the possibility of token public-school desegregation after the state had adopted permissive policies for minimal community compliance with the Supreme Court ruling. The exclusion of Negroes from the paternalistic, politically influential group of the Progressive Conservative leaders, except in subservient roles, preserved the sense of general political impotence of many leaders of the Negro subcommunity. The demoralization of the White labor movement continued.

The postwar political history of Petropolis stands in sharp contrast to that of Metroville. The outcomes of comparable racial and class demands for political access and reorganization differed. In these years, the political organization of the Negro community was strengthened; White labor was formally organized for political action; a coalition of these two groups captured the local Democratic party; and access to City Hall was extended through the electoral success of their endorsed candidates.

The Liberal Negro-White labor coalition represented the numerically dominant wing of a larger political coalition. Mayor Plunkett and members of Petropolis's leading families were, like Mayor French's new administration in Oretown, the proponents of progress through moderation and consensus. The moderate Community Conservation orientation of these men made their alliance with Liberals uneasy and something less than perfectly stable. Community Conservatives desired better city government; they wanted a scope of government that was effectively responsive to the new and ever-changing needs of the community as a whole through the development of planning for public purposes; and, in particular, they were trying to strengthen the declining economy. These desires led them to work with Conservative industrialists, financiers, and merchants, who were mistrusted and disliked by the leading White and Negro Liberals.

However, the political strength of Conservatives and of White Supremacists in Petropolis was such that it could thwart significant rapprochements between the rank-and-file citizens of the two racial subcommunities. Public school desegregation had not yet occurred, and, in contrast to Metroville, there was little reason to be optimistic that it would be initiated in the fall of 1957. Community Conservationists strongly felt the need to reorganize the bifurcated social structure of Petropolis and to distribute both employment and economic advancement opportunities, as well as social status, more equally to the citizens of both races and all social classes. These needs cemented their coalition with the Liberal leadership. At the same time they led to increased hostility on the part of their White Supremacist opponents. As Mayor Plunkett entered his fourth term in office, he continued to walk a tightrope. Whatever moves he made in the direction of improving race relations reinforced his political bonds with the Liberal leadership and with his rank-and-file Negro supporters. Such bonds weakened his attraction for the White Supremacists in the ranks of organized labor. A wedge had been driven directly into the Liberal coalition itself over the issue of whether or not a Negro should have run the more difficult race for county commissioner in 1954. What would happen to the uneasy balance of political forces in Petropolis from the time of Mayor Plunkett's reelection to the time of the next municipal elections, two years hence, was hard to foresee.

It is clear that politics played an important part in all of these cities during the postwar periods.. The pressing problems of life in the modern community were not completely solved in any of the communities, even though some of the problems ceased to be subjects of political decision-making. But such problems do not always disappear, even if they cease to be involved in politics. Human flexibility and adjustability cannot be underestimated, and even problems that are very severe can be tolerated for unbelievably long periods of time. The open character of these American communities—that is, their location in a national and federal system in which individuals and messages from other communities and other political levels cross their boundaries—makes it likely that some problems that are tolerated will eventually become sufficiently intolerable that they will again be subject to the operation of politics. Problems grow in severity and new problems occur.   We are interested in the similarities and differences in the patterns of politics in these four communities as they concern efforts to prevent, ameliorate, or solve problems.   The political histories of the four communities since the Second World War suggest that there were indeed similarities and differences in their politics that were not simply a function of "objective" factors such as size and regional location.

Before analyzing these patterns and classifying the four communities by type of power structure during the postwar period, we shall examine more intensively the workings of their political systems during the next time period of interest.   We first shall examine the political decisions made in each community in the period we designate as Time E to M.

6

POLITICAL DECISION-MAKING
PROCESSES: *Time E to M*

In this chapter we shall examine the demands for shifts in the scope of each community's government—that is, the subjects of political decision-making processes that existed at some time during or throughout the one- to two-year periods following the municipal elections designated as Time E. Only demands for general policy changes, nonroutine changes in the scope of government that participants considered to have a relatively direct impact on important needs of a large number of citizens, are included. Such demands seek new *de facto* or authoritatively proclaimed outcomes to expand, to contract, or to shift the scope of local government internally. Thus, political participants envision a new pattern of local governmental activity or functioning that would satisfy the needs of some of the citizens.

Time M is the time at which the samples of respondents in each community were first interviewed. Besides describing the general political demands in each polity during Time E to M, we also must examine the outcomes of each set of demands made by Time M. We shall note the outcomes of decisional processes because differences in patterns of decisional outcomes are one of the political-system variables in which we are interested. Furthermore, the decisional outcomes of these processes must be known or adjudged at Time M in order to assess the distribution of political power in each community from Time E to M. It will be recalled that political power is the unit attached to outcomes of political decision-making processes and assigned to the politically participant contributors to decisional outcomes.[1]

TABLE 6-1

Farmdale, Time *E* to *M* (1950–1952)

I. Economic Reorganization		II. Civic Improvement				III. Social Reorganization	IV. Governmental Reorganization
A. Economic Base	B. Stimulation of Business	A. Housekeeping Services	B. Community Planning and Guided Development	C. Recreation	D. Health		
1. Attract new industry	5. Relax enforcement of traffic and parking regulations	7. Improve street and sidewalk paving and repairs "across tracks"	11. Approve proposed state highway bypass	12. Establish municipal swimming pool			14. Annex fringe residential areas
2. Extend city services to proposed plywood plant	6. Establish municipal ownership of, and improve, street lighting, particularly for the central business district	8. Expand general street and sidewalk paving and repairs		13. Establish municipal park-and-recreation program			
3. Establish chamber of commerce		9. Establish municipal garbage-collection service					
4. Establish public electric power system		10. Expand and improve water supply					

TABLE 6-1 (Continued)

Oretown, Time *E* to *M* (1952–1954)

I. Economic Reorganization		II. Civic Improvement				III. Social Reorganization	IV. Governmental Reorganization
A. Economic Base	B. Stimulation of Business	A. Housekeeping Services	B. Community Planning and Guided Development	C. Recreation	D. Health		
1. Eliminate the private utility*	5. Establish municipal parking lot in the central business district	6. Establish modern sewage disposal plant			7. Establish municipal hospital*		8. Annex fringe residential and established industry area
2. Eliminate the municipal utility*							
3. Cease industry-attraction efforts							
4. Revive industry-attraction efforts							

* Designates authoritative consideration by an informal quasi-election.

TABLE 6-1 (Continued)

Petropolis, Time *E* to *M* (1957–1958)

I. Economic Reorganization		II. Civic Improvement				III. Social Reorganization	IV. Governmental Reorganization
A. Economic Base	B. Stimulation of Business	A. Housekeeping Services	B. Community Planning and Guided Development	C. Recreation	D. Health		
1. Cease industry-attraction efforts	4. Reestablish two-way traffic and on-street parking in the central business district		6. Construct centralized governmental center		9. Fluoridate the water supply	10. Begin desegregation in public schools	16. Annex area of established industry
2. Apply to state for establishment of technical training center*	5. Permit shopping-center construction in residential zone		7. Conduct comprehensive community planning and improvements study			11. Permit efforts to desegregate eating facilities without arrest	17. Consolidate city and county schools
3. Provide water outside city to industrial park			8. Initiate planning phase of urban-renewal program in Negro slum area			12. Create biracial municipal race-relations commission	18. Annex fringe residential area
						13. Initiate improvement of race-relations program by new municipal commission	
						14. Block reelection of top officials of local Democratic party*	
						15. Elect extreme segregationists to top offices in local Democratic party*	

* Designates authoritative consideration by an informal quasi-election.

TABLE 6-1 (Continued)

Metroville, Time E to M (1957–1958)

I. Economic Reorganization		II. Civic Improvement				III. Social Reorganization	IV. Governmental Reorganization
A. Economic Base	B. Stimulation of Business	A. Housekeeping Services	B. Community Planning and Guided Development	C. Recreation	D. Health		
1. Establish county industrial park	6. Initiate program of central business district redevelopment	10. Make major capital improvement in water system †	13. Request state authority for countywide zoning	18. Build municipal swimming pools	20. Expand White mental hospital	21. Begin desegregation in public schools	22. Consolidate city and county schools
2. Initiate industry-attraction efforts	7. Relax enforcement of traffic and parking ordinances	11. Make major capital improvement in sewer system †	14. Extend zoning further from city limits	19. Expand park-and-recreation facilities			23. Annex fringe residential areas
3. Apply to state for establishment of technical training center	8. Rezone residential area to business classification	12. Improve streets and build expressways †	15. Build additional public housing units for Negroes				
4. Build a new regional airport	9. Permit shopping center construction in fringe area		16. Initiate planning phase of urban-renewal program in Negro slum area				
5. Make major capital improvements in airport			17. Increase authority of City Council relative to planning commission in rezoning				

† Designates authoritative consideration by a municipal election.

To review the theoretical framework briefly, decision-making processes exist if demands are being deliberated, that is, if political preferences have passed beyond policy formulation into a policy-deliberation stage and thus have become political demands. Pressures on the functioning or scope of government are assumed to be extant if political demands exist. These pressures may remain or subside even if no decisional outcome is reached by a selected point in time. For example, political demands may cease to be deliberated because their makers consciously decide to stop demanding or unconsciously "sublimate" their desires. Such subsidence of political pressures may result from internal, intra-individual shifts in values or perceived needs, or from a fear of legitimate or illegitimate sanctions, or both. The sets of political decision-making processes listed and described here include only those that have reached the authoritative-consideration stage by Time M; therefore, they qualify those who participate in them for some share of the ascribable units of political power.

Political decisional processes that have become arrested or fixated in the policy deliberation stage, and those that have subsided without the invocation of political power, are excluded from consideration at this time. These are treated in a later chapter, when particular attention is paid to the sense of electoral potency in the body politic of each community as a possible explanation for such arrested political decision-making processes. Any instances of the use of illegitimate sanctions in the political decision-making processes to be described here will be taken into account when we classify the regimes in Chapter 11.

In the minds of both participant and nonparticipant citizens, decisional processes may involve multiple values and affect several areas of life. For some participants political demands may represent narrowly defined, institutionally related preferences; for others, political demands may stand for broadly defined, cross-institutional preferences. Although a certain amount of classificatory arbitrariness is inescapable, one important analytic operation is classifying to the best of the analyst's ability political decisional processes on the basis of the question or questions the active participants indicate are at issue regarding the future functioning of local government. The meanings that citizens attach to political preferences, demands, and outcomes— and the compatibilty or conflict of such definitions—shape basic patterns of politics.

The political decision-making processes were classified under one or more of the following: Economic Reorganization, Civic Improvement, Governmental Reorganization, Social Reorganization, and various subcategories. When a decisional process is listed more than once because of multiple perspectives of particular participants or different perspectives of different participants, it is described under its first classification and then noted under another category. Table 6-1 contains a list of the political demands and their outcomes by Time M; each decision is classified under only one category to afford the reader a simple summary of the sets of political decisions extant in each community during Time E to M.[2]

ECONOMIC REORGANIZATION IN FARMDALE

Economic Base

With the election of Mayor May in 1950, postwar public agitation for economic and industrial development and urban growth rapidly subsided. A few citizens who saw a more active government policy to attract industry to Farmdale as appropriate, useful, and the only way to solve personal economic problems continued to deliberate the

TABLE 6-2 Political Decision-Making Processes in Farmdale: Time *E* to *M*

Economic Reorganization

A. Economic Base	(Outcome)	B. Stimulation of Business	(Outcome)
1. Attract new industry	–	5. Relax enforcement of traffic and parking regulations	+
2. Extend city services to proposed plywood plant	–	6. Establish municipal ownership of, and improve, street lighting, particularly for the central business district	–
3. Establish chamber of commerce	–		
4. Establish public electric power system	–		
⎡10. Expand and improve water⎤ ⎣ supply (II) ⎦	–(+)	⎡ 7. Improve street and sidewalk⎤ ⎢ paving and repairs "across⎥ ⎣ tracks" (II) ⎦	–
		⎡11. Approve proposed state high-⎤ ⎣ way bypass (II) ⎦	+
Outcome Totals (Multiple Listing)	4 – 1 – (+)		2 – 2 +
Outcome Totals (Single Listing)	3 –		1 – 1 +

KEY: – Unsuccessful or defeated political demands
    + Successful political demands
    –(+) Minor compromise or substantially unsuccessful political demands

NOTE: The brackets around certain decisional processes indicate that they are also classified under another major category or subcategory. The Arabic numeral corresponds to the number assigned to the decisional process in Table 6-1, wherein there was a single listing of decisional processes. The Roman numerals designate the other major categories under which the bracketed decisional processes are classified.

problem. The resulting demands proposed to the political and civic leadership were for a specific program of active recruitment of new industry by government officials through organized promotional activities. However, the demands were met by absolute resistance on the part of the government officials and other civic leaders, so that no political power accrued to their makers.[3]

A plywood plant expressed on its own initiative some interest in locating in Farmdale. The question of whether the city government would extend its services to the prospective industry was raised. Although a few citizens emphatically favored such extension because of the benefits it would bring to the community, the decision of the city government was against it, unlike a comparable decision to locate a metallurgical plant in Oretown.

This decision was followed by a specific policy suggestion on the part of several citizens: the city government should facilitate the attraction of new industry to Farmdale by supporting and working with a proposed chamber of commerce, which could be established to take on the active promotional job that neither the small city government nor the voluntary civic organizations were staffed to do. The decisional outcome was that the suggestion was not accepted and the scope of government was not shifted in this way.

The earlier minority preference for a municipal utility seemed, by Time E, to have become a vague, nonpolitical formulation; it appeared to be a question of individual preferences for having electricity bills reduced without reducing consumption of electric power. In a few cases, these preferences became political demands for the establishment of a local public power system; these demands were purposefully ignored by Mayor May's city administration, which wanted a privately owned power system.

Political demands involving the city's water supply continued to be made in this period. Occasionally someone demanded that the City Council arrange for additional municipal wells or a more modern system of water supply to provide a sufficient amount of water for the needs of new industry. A few housewives, and a few businessmen also, expressed demands for improvement in the municipal water works. For example, appliance dealers felt that the sediment and gravel in the city well water made the use of washing machines, and washing in general, very difficult. Other citizens were concerned with the potential water shortage during the dry summer months unless the city acquired greater water supply reserves.

Newspaper editorials urged people, particularly the women of Farmdale who had to do the family washing, to let it be known that they were in favor of expanding the city's water supply and improving the water system. The publisher of the paper preferred this shift in the scope of government because he strongly felt that Farmdale should try to attract additional business and industry. His efforts, and presumably those of his female readers who exercised political influence with and through their husbands and other male associates, resulted in a minor political victory, but his major objective was not accomplished.

The City Council did decide on a minimal expansion in the water supply by increasing the number of wells. This satisfied most of the active proponents of this shift in the scope of government, whose primary aim was civic improvement. At the same time, those who feared the gravitational pull that the provision of an assured, large supply of inexpensive water might have on prospective new industrial plants and factories were not dissatisfied. The proponents of new industry felt that the slightly expanded water supply was as likely to meet the industrial needs of heavy consumers of water as a tiny morsel of food was to satisfy the needs of a ravenous lion. As one citizen put it, Farmdale was in a situation comparable to that of a person trying to lure a hungry animal into a trap with a handful of bird-seed when thousands of other people were baiting their traps with large, luscious steaks and roasts.

Stimulation of Business

Demands that the local government participate more actively in stimulating the existing private business, particularly the mercantile sectors of the economy, continued to be made periodically, without much more success. A demand that overtime parking and minor traffic violations in the central business district be treated leniently in order to encourage people to shop in Farmdale was successful. The City Council and the Mayor issued an order to that effect to the police department. A few merchants also demanded that the city government assume responsibility for installing more extensive street lighting for the central business district. This was a service that the private utility provided the municipality. These demands were effectively resisted and defeated.

There were two other segments of the business community adversely affected during this period by political decisions concerning the relationship of the local government to the local economy and questions of civic improvement. The stores, motels, and business establishments located along the major highway that bisected the town were dependent, in part, on the tourist trade. Their owners were not consulted when the city fathers approved a state highway commission proposal for a new freeway to bypass Farmdale. This decision was made quietly and informally by the City Council in meetings with a few other political leaders of Farmdale. Those adversely affected were unaware at the time of the initiation of field research that this decision had been reached several months earlier.

The few merchants on Main Street who were located in the poorer section of the city, across the railroad tracks, had been demanding periodically that street paving and sidewalk maintenance be improved for their area instead of for other areas of the city. Their demands were made to and through a city councilman whose residence and business were located in this "underdeveloped" section of the city. He added his voice to that of his constituents, but their demands were not satisfied by the City Council. The policy of applying most of the sparse local government housekeeping resources to the more established segment of the business district and to the better residential neighborhoods of Farmdale was periodically reaffirmed by decisions that denied the petitions of residents of the poorer part of town.

ECONOMIC REORGANIZATION IN ORETOWN

Economic Base

Decisional battles over public versus private power continued, and became even more intense after the establishment of the municipal

TABLE 6-3   Political Decision-Making Processes in Oretown: Time *E* to *M*

Economic Reorganization

A. Economic Base	(Outcome)	B. Stimulation of Business	(Outcome)
1. Eliminate the private utility *	−	5. Establish municipal parking lot in	
2. Eliminate the municipal utility *	−	the central business district	+
3. Cease industry-attraction efforts	−		
4. Revive industry attraction efforts	−		
Outcome Totals (Multiple Listing)	4−		1+
Outcome Totals (Single Listing)	4−		1+

KEY: −   Unsuccessful or defeated political demands
+   Successful or victorious political demands
*   Authoritative consideration by an informal quasi-election

NOTE: The Arabic numeral corresponds to the number assigned to the decisional process in Table 6-1, wherein there was a single listing of decisional processes.

utility in Oretown several years prior to 1952, Time E. These controversies still were not finally resolved in early 1954, Time M. They were open political issues involving opposing demands for net increases and decreases in the scope of local government. For our analytic purposes, the condition of the scope of government at Time M determines the outcome, even though no final settlement was reached by that time. One decisional process involved demands that the municipal utility become the only utility in Oretown; this would expand the scope of government even further. The second process involved demands that the municipal utility be abolished; this would reduce the scope of government to what it had been before 1948. Both of these decisional processes were viewed by at least some of the protagonists as crucial in determining the character and quality of the community's economy in the future.

Those who advocated the further net increase in the scope of government engaged in a variety of tactics to accomplish their objectives, including economic warfare. Sustained efforts were made to capture the customers of the private utility for OMU (the municipal utility). Representatives of OMU established customer contacts in order to retain or gain customer loyalty; electricity users were offered additional services ranging from repairs on their electric appliances to help in moving household furniture. These were like the free dishes or glasses or automobile lubrications offered gasoline purchasers in a price war among service station operators. Some customers switched back and forth from one utility to the other when both utilities began to offer these inducements. Some businessmen could not decide which side they were on or wanted to remain neutral in this battle for survival; they took their residential service from one utility and their business service from the other. Many consumers of electricity signed up or stayed with one or the other utility, or switched from one to the other, for "fringe benefits"; others took the opportunity to participate politically in order to help determine the decisional outcome according to their preferences. Not all of the active participants were ideologically motivated, but some certainly were.

Some of the active proponents of the single municipal utility brought pressure to bear on the state public utility commission. This tactic failed when the commission refused to change its earlier ruling that the private utility company could charge lower rates in Oretown than in the rest of its service area in order to compete with OMU. Some of the active supporters of OMU tried to get the city government to proceed with an offer to purchase the assets of the private utility. They hoped to end the decisional issue in this way. However, they were not successful.

The proponents of the decrease in the scope of government were comparably active and equally unsuccessful in this period of controversy. In their pursuit of customers, "dossiers" were prepared and kept up-to-date on the citizens of Oretown. Each customer's file contained such information as occupation, size of family, and length of residence, as well as information on club and organization memberships, political and religious affiliations and attitudes, and even matters of morals. If a known partisan of OMU were arrested on a charge of driving an automobile while under the influence of liquor in a city two thousand miles away, the temperance people of Oretown could be notified immediately in an effort to undermine attachments to OMU and to attract the "drys" among OMU's customers to the private utility.

These economic efforts to win political victory were sufficient to reduce the number of customers and the sale of electricity to far below the estimates made by an engineering consulting firm before OMU was established. But these reductions were insufficient either to cause the economic collapse of OMU or to cause the officials of OMU to sue for peace. Nor were any of the more manifestly political tactics any more successful in gaining for the partisans of the private utility a favorable resolution of the decisional issue.

The conceptual options open to the political analyst in specifying decisional processes and outcomes, and their different consequences for assessing who has had how much political power, can be illustrated clearly here. One option is to regard the foregoing conflict as one decisional process, the outcome of which was equally frustrating and undesirable to both sets of protagonists. Three decisional outcomes might have been possible: first, to eliminate the private utility and expand the net scope of government; second, to eliminate the municipal utility and contract the net scope of government; and third, to retain the two-company competitive situation. Since the third was the actual outcome at Time M, the active participants who may have had political influence but who preferred either the first or the second outcome would not be accorded any share in the political power assigned to the victors. It so happened that a few of the active participants preferred the third decisional outcome. Of these, some wanted the "fringe benefits" to be continued; others thought competition the ideal American economic situation; still others believed that if either one of the utilities became an actual instead of a theoretically "natural" monopoly, electricity rates were bound to rise. It was probable that electricity rates would rise if the private utility were the victor;

but it also was feared that, in the long run, it would happen even if the municipal utility were the lone survivor.

Another conceptual option is to consider this struggle as two separate decisional processes with two analytically distinct outcomes. Instead of treating the two sets of opposite demands as a single decisional process, one set might be treated as one decisional process and the second set as another. In the case of demands to eliminate the private utility, the alternative outcomes would be to eliminate it or not. Demands for elimination of the municipal utility also had two possible outcomes. Two units of political power would thus exist: those who successfully resisted the elimination of the private utility would share in the unit of accrued political power; those with the opposite preference also would share in the political power that accrued to those who effectively thwarted efforts to kill the municipal utility.

The option of two processes with two outcomes is considered more desirable in this analysis. It seems to accord more with political reality, intuitively if in no other way. The failure of either "side" to gain their major decisional objectives did not preclude them from intending to thwart—effectively, as it turned out—the efforts of the other. In both cases, failure was partly a result of purposeful counter-pressures, political action to resist the pressures being exerted by opponents for a shift in the scope of government. It seems more appropriate in such situations to recognize the effectiveness of these counterpressures by attributing political power to each set of protagonists. The few who preferred the *status quo* and helped to defeat both sets of demands for a shift in the net scope of government would be credited with more political power than their pro-municipal-and pro-private-utility fellows. They share in the power accruing to the victors in two decisional processes, rather than one.

During Time *E* to *M* one set of demands was focused on the activities of local government regarding the reorganization of the economic base and the economic development of Oretown. These demands came from citizens who opposed government action to guarantee employment opportunities. They demanded that local government officials cease their industry-hunting activities. The demands were discounted by those who took credit for bringing the new metallurgical plant to Oretown prior to Time *E*. However, the scope of government was contracted, although advocates of the contraction had little to do with it.

Those in the municipal utility who had participated actively in bringing the large metallurgical company to Oretown, and government and political figures who had worked with them in this effort, shifted their attention to other matters during Time E to M. They began to concentrate on putting the municipal utility on its feet; on making public power the only electric power available in the city; and on making the municipal utility strong enough to survive the increasingly severe competition from the private utility. During Time E to M, a major effort was made to improve the various programs of city government through improved administration. The French administration and other political leaders gradually had come to think that attracting new industry was within the province of administrators and a matter of administrative decision-making. For example, they believed that new industry was necessary, since selling more electricity in large loads to new plants would contribute to the more efficient operation of the municipal utility; they were incidentally trying to create new job opportunities for working people. New-industry hunting slowly ceased to be a decision-making issue as administrators turned their attention to what they considered more urgent matters of administrative and political decision-making. Thus, the ultimate contraction in the scope of government was not accomplished by those who urged the contraction as a political objective. These people suffered a decisional defeat. The contraction resulted from shifts, by local government officials and their associates, of their own patterns of activities in the context of other motivations rather than from intentional activity to accomplish this political objective. Thus, the resulting political power accrued to those who resisted the demands, even though those who made the demands eventually got their way.

Before Time M, as local government ceased its industry-attracting efforts, a few demands were made that local government continue such efforts. These demands were resisted, not because they were considered to involve undesirable decisional preferences, but because officials claimed more pressing duties. For example, countering or conquering the private utility had a higher priority. As the battle between the two utility companies and their respective supporters unfolded with a new fury, these political demands subsided. The situation was similar to that which existed when demands were made that local government divest itself of a function considered by some to be within the legitimate authority of such private organizations as the Chamber of Commerce and the private utility.

Private utility companies traditionally have been active in inducing and helping new industry to locate within their service areas. However, representatives of the private utility in Oretown ignored demands that they continue or expand their industry-attracting activities. Some citizens most bitterly opposed to municipal electric power made serious efforts to discourage prospective industry from settling in Oretown by informing an occasional prospect that he would not want to come to a "socialist community." Further demands that new industry be encouraged came to be directed to the municipal utility as a naturally interested party. These also were unsuccessful.

Stimulation of Business

During Mayor Lovegren's four-year administration prior to the 1952 local election of Mayor French, public-works programs such as and expanded street-paving program, partly financed from city tax money, and the installation of storm drains and sewers represented significant net expansions in the scope of government resulting from the outcomes of conflicting decisional issues. After the 1952 municipal election, these civic-improvement programs were continued. When they eventually were modified, it was through routine, administrative decision-making processes. Mayor French made a major effort to consolidate the local government's gains through increasing the efficiency of governmental activities in these areas. For the most part, this was a consensual consolidation with general citizen satisfaction. The local government tax rate was reduced early in Mayor French's administration without sacrificing the level or quality of services.

Two of Mayor Lovegren's closest associates were still on the City Council. They were among the few who were dissatisfied with these developments because of the meaning and the implications to them of "efficiency." They felt that efficient administration meant the preservation or improvement of the developed residential and downtown central business district. They feared that such efficiencies would take place at the expense of their own, more recently annexed and relatively underdeveloped, Longacre section of town. They disliked the reduction in the tax rate because it promised to strengthen the general public's support of their opponents in the city administration. Their dissatisfaction with the French administration's definition of "good government" resulted in major decisional controversies involving an attempt to recall the two councilmen. However, this did not occur until 1955, after Time *M*, and will be discussed in a later chapter.

The basic underlying economic implications of public-works programs came to the fore in the minds of the opponents of the French administration. Their frustration and hostility became greater than ever when the French administration organized political support behind a policy proposal for the city government to expand its scope by establishing municipally owned parking lots. The principle of municipal versus private ownership did not become the issue. The first municipal parking lot to provide additional off-street parking was proposed for Main Street and not for the Longacre shopping area, which had ample parking facilities. The decisional alternatives were whether the facilities would be built or not, not whether it was to be located in one or the other section of town.

Opponents of the municipal lot argued that it was an unfair gift from the city government and the taxpayers to the downtown merchants; its proponents countered that it was a housekeeping service of local government that would improve and benefit the whole community. The convenience for all citizens shopping downtown, the alleviation of traffic congestion, and the need to improve Oretown's image in order to compete with its Big City neighbor as a matter of civic pride were invoked to counter the charges of special privilege for the few at the expense of the average citizen. A majority of the City Council and the Mayor gained their decisional objective once again when the first city-owned parking lot in the downtown area was built.

ECONOMIC REORGANIZATION IN PETROPOLIS

Economic Base

The city government of Petropolis continued to participate actively in trying to attract new industry to the city during Time E to M. Its major efforts in this area were directed to and through the Committee on Industrial Development. Besides city contributions to the annual budget of that organization, Mayor Plunkett was one of the four or five most active leaders of the Committee. He, members of the Bacon and Leek families, the full-time executive director, and one or two other civic leaders met regularly to formulate policy for the group, to develop programs, and to plan strategy and tactics to attract new industry.

A few leading industrialists remained opposed to new industry because of the possibility that there would be increased competition for available labor and higher labor costs. A few others, particularly people connected with the city's university, were opposed to major new industry because they foresaw a major increase in population that would decrease the amenities of living in Petropolis. Some of these opponents of new industry unsuccessfully demanded that the

TABLE 6-4   Political Decision-Making Processes in Petropolis: Time *E* to *M*

Economic Reorganization

A. Economic Base	(Outcome)	B. Stimulation of Business	(Outcome)
1. Cease industry-attraction efforts	−	4. Reestablish two-way traffic and on-street parking in the central business district	+
2. Apply to state for establishment of technical training center *	+		
3. Provide water outside city to industrial park	+	5. Permit shopping center construction in residential zone	+
⎡16. Annex area of established industry (IV)⎤	−		
Outcome Totals (Multiple Listing)	2 − 2+		2+
Outcome Totals (Single Listing)	1 − 2+		2+

KEY: −   Unsuccessful or defeated political demands
       +   Successful or victorious political demands
       *   Authoritative consideration by an informal quasi-election

NOTE: The brackets around certain decisional processes indicate that they are also classified under another major category or subcategory. The Arabic numeral corresponds to the number assigned to the decisional process in Table 6-1, wherein there was a single listing of decisional processes. The Roman numerals designate the other major categories under which the bracketed decisional processes are classified.

city government withdraw from the Committee on Industrial Development.

Early in 1958, the local government was given another opportunity to extend its activities in the economic development of the city. Due in no small measure to the efforts of Eben Bacon, Jr., an appropriation was authorized by the state legislature to provide for a series of technical training centers in a limited number of cities throughout the state. These were to serve those areas where there was the greatest need for post-high-school vocational programs for city residents and people from the surrounding rural areas. Members of the city government of Petropolis worked actively to demonstrate to the state government both the need for such a center in their city and the willingness of the city school system to cooperate in developing the program, since the centers were to be part of the school systems. Although many of the opponents of new industry opposed the application because of their expectation that this would be an inducement for industry to come to Petropolis, some industrialists supported it because they foresaw desirable shifts of the costs of employee training from themselves to a broader tax-paying group.

Competition was keen among the cities of the state for these training centers, since the state had not appropriated sufficient funds for every city that wanted one to have one. The city government decided to try to get a training center for Petropolis. The next decisional question was whether the city government should spend sufficient money to construct a building to house the training center. While the state would pay for instructional staff and equipment, the city had the responsibility of housing the center. This became a conflicting political decision-making process during the summer of 1958—after Time M— and will be treated in a later chapter.

Another demand for a shift in the scope of the city government toward more active involvement in developing the economy of Petropolis was made when the Locus Laboratory requested that the city extend its water system to guarantee the large industrial site a sufficient supply of water for prospective industries. This became a controversial matter because some people felt that this would ultimately be unfair to the taxpayers of Petropolis: the limited supply of water for the community's needs would have to be expanded at some future date, and even though prospective customers would pay for the water that they used, such a shift in the scope of Petropolis' government was opposed because it seemed to some that one of the other cities in the Locus Laboratory area ought to provide the water and take the risks of having to develop new sources of water supply sooner than planned. Others felt that the city of Petropolis should not continue to expand its economic development activities, particularly for an area outside of the city; still others were primarily opposed to an expansion of the community's and the area's industrial base and felt that this was a demand that they could oppose openly, whereas the presumably popular Committee on Industrial Development and the industrial training center could not be as effectively resisted by forthright open opposition. After extensive consideration by the city council, the city government decided to agree to supply the water to the Locus Laboratory.

Of most serious concern to those government officials and private citizens who desired a more active city government were the interrelated matters of the city's tax base and its annexation program. These individuals wanted civic improvements to improve livability in the city, and to make the city more attractive to newcomers, particularly new corporations with new payrolls. However, the large sums of potential property-tax monies that could assist materially in paying for large-scale, costly city improvements were not available because the large industrial properties lay outside the city limits. In fact, these multimillion-dollar properties had been deliberately left unincorporated, under the county government's jurisdiction, when adjacent land had been annexed to the city of Petropolis.

Demands for annexation of this land had not by Time M overcome the anxiety—shared even by some of the proponents of this governmental reorganization—that the corporations involved might retaliate in ways that would injure the economy of the city and the revenue position of the city government more than the additional property valuation would benefit the city. Most of those who had such fears recognized that these absentee-owned companies probably would not pick up and move their large manufacturing operations from Petropolis because of the tremendous cost in vacated plant and equipment. However, Petropolis was likely to lose the benefit of future expansions in these industries to other cities if the proposed annexation took place. Most of those in the Plunkett administration, including the Mayor himself, resisted the pro-annexation demands; they expected that extensive political conflict and turmoil would be the minimal result of annexation, and that this would be an additional obstacle to efforts to improve the city and stimulate and develop its economy. Thus, those citizens making the demand for the annexation had been defeated by Time M.

Stimulation of Business

During this period, demands were made that the city government take an increasingly active role in stimulating business in Petropolis' existing private economy. It seemed to Mayor Plunkett that the key to Petropolis' future as one of the state's leading cities was the rejuvenation and revitalization of the central business district. Prior to Time E, a decision had been reached for the city government to make a sustained effort to ring the downtown area with a series of city-owned and -operated off-street parking structures. One such parking structure had been built and a second was being planned. During Mayor Plunkett's second term in office, a master thoroughfare plan had been developed by traffic consultants. The implementation of various aspects of this general plan became a series of political decision-making processes during Time E to M.

The Mayor and a city council committee developed specific plans to relieve traffic congestion and to improve shopping conditions in the center of the downtown business district. On their recommendation, the police department made one of the busiest downtown streets a one-way thoroughfare and banned parking on this street. Shortly after this change in policy, a large number of merchants petitioned the city council to reverse this formerly administrative, but by then political, decision. Although the Mayor and others strenuously resisted this demand, the council was sharply divided and the petitioning merchants were successful. Their major argument was that they should not be asked to bear the cost of trying to improve the entire downtown area; their businesses suffered because their customers had no convenient parking space. The major counterargument was that the citizens should be able to drive through the center of the city without hindrance.

Those who urged farsighted, long-range planning to guide the city's development and redevelopment and to maintain, conserve, and improve the city soon met another decisional defeat. Mayor Plunkett and some of his close associates felt that city officials should insist on conformity to zoning ordinances for the good of the whole community. A large shopping center was proposed for a residential neighborhood, which would require an exception to the zoning ordinance if a building permit were to be issued by the city's building department. In accord with the advice of the city planning commission no building permit was issued. Representatives of the shopping center appealed to the city council to reverse the building department's ruling and thus instituted a political decision-making process. Those who urged that no such exceptions to the zoning ordinance be made were defeated in the city council. The victors included those who felt that government should not restrict the right to use one's property freely, and those who felt that, in this instance, the right to build a shopping center took precedence over the rights of individuals in the neighborhood who wanted to prevent a land use that might be detrimental to their own properties. Mayor Plunkett and his close associates felt that this shift in the internal scope of local government was a serious setback to their program of nonpolitical administrative decision-making in the important municipal functions of community planning and guided development.

ECONOMIC REORGANIZATION IN METROVILLE

Economic Base

During this period, political demands also were being made in Metroville for local government to take a more active role in developing the industrial base and stimulating the existing businesses in the local economy. People who demanded that the city government work to

TABLE 6-5   Political Decision-Making Processes in Metroville: Time *E* to M

Economic Reorganization

A. Economic Base	(Outcome)	B. Stimulation of Business	(Outcome)
1. Establish county industrial park	+	6. Initiate program of central bus-	
2. Initiate industry-attraction efforts	−	iness district redevelopment	−
3. Apply to state for establishment of		7. Relax enforcement of traffic	
technical training center	+	and parking ordinances	−
4. Build a new regional airport	−	8. Rezone residential area to busi-	
5. Make major capital improvements		ness classification	+
in airport	−	9. Permit shopping center con-	
		struction in fringe area	+(−)
		⌈16. Initiate planning phase of ur-	
		ban renewal program in Ne-	
		⌊ gro slum area (II)	+
		⌈14. Extend zoning further from	
		⌊ city limits (II)	−
		⌈17. Increase authority of City	
		Council relative to planning	
		⌊ commission in rezoning (II)	−
Outcome Totals (Multiple Listing) 3−			4−
2+			2+
			1+(−)
Outcome Totals (Single Listing) 3−			2−
2+			1+
			1+(−)

KEY: −   Unsuccessful or defeated political demands
           +   Successful or victorious political demands
       +(−)   Major compromise or substantially successful political demands

NOTE: The brackets around certain decisional processes indicate that they are also classified under another major category or subcategory. The Arabic numeral corresponds to the number assigned to the decisional process in Table 6-1, wherein there was a single listing of decisional processes. The Roman numerals designate the other major categories under which the bracketed decisional processes are classified.

get new industry were defeated in their decision-making efforts: they were not successful in persuading Mayor Peterson's administration to take action, since the latter felt that the economic base of the city was not at all within its area of responsibility or authoritative jurisdiction. The organized efforts that were made to attract new industry to the city were undertaken by a few interested people working to activate the Chamber of Commerce in pursuit of this goal.

Efforts to interest the county government in becoming active in attracting new industry were more successful. County officials overcame opposition within their own ranks and began to move ahead with the development of an industrial park on county land for several reasons: revenues therefrom would reduce the costs of county government; an industrial park would be a progressive civic improvement; and the land was considered an excellent site for the expansion of existing industries in Metroville. Thus, some movement in the direction of more and diversified industry for Metroville was commencing, even though the municipal government had nothing to do with the decision.

As in Petropolis during period E to M, demands were made that Metroville try to procure one of the industrial training centers that were to be equipped by the state government and operated with state funds. However, in Metroville the effort was directed to and through the county as well as the city government. In this, as in other decisional processes, more attention seemed to be paid to the county government in political decision-making than in the other three communities of our study.

The county commissioners were receptive to the idea that they provide funds for the construction of a facility that would meet the needs of business and industry for better trained, more skilled workers. However, they did not act quickly enough to marshal the facts that persuaded state officials to award such facilities to Petropolis and other communities in Southern State by Time M.

Two decisional processes, involving the major airport serving Metroville and the county, extended past Time E into the period of our concern. In both instances, proponents of the measures considered rural conservatism to be responsible for their defeat. Business, industry, and private citizens depended upon roads and planes for transportation, since there was only intermittent train service in the area. During this period, demands arose—as they had periodically before Time E—for the construction of one modern airport, capable of handling jet aircraft. The airport would serve Metroville, its neighboring cities, and the numerous rural counties in that area of the state. Some of these cities already had constructed a single airport to serve their joint needs, and Metroville had an airport under the jurisdiction of a county administrative commission. This county commission and the county commissioners would not listen to the demands of a few Metroville businessmen for the revival of talks with the neighboring cities regarding a new joint airport for the several urban centers and their surrounding rural areas.

When a second set of demands was made for additional expenditures to modernize and improve the existing airport, the county government resisted. They maintained that most county residents were not interested in improved air travel, and that there were many costly governmental services and facilities of higher priority being planned. After Time M, these demands were to increase in intensity, but, in the meantime, those who had resisted them acquired political power in this decisional process. The two sets of airport demands were framed as measures designed to strengthen the business and industrial base of the community in the air age, and as housekeeping services of responsible local authorities. Although proponents expected the benefits to exceed the costs, these perspectives did not prevail.

Stimulation of Business

Occasionally, sporadic efforts were made to activate the city government to try to stimulate retail trade in Metroville. A few citizens began to demand that the city planners initiate a program to redevelop and improve the central business district; this would improve the economic prospects of retail businesses in particular. These demands were turned down by the chief local government officials, who maintained that such improvement was up to the individual merchants and private organizations such as the Chamber of Commerce. The Chamber of Commerce did begin to become involved in the program with the assistance of the city planners; however, the latter were not acting in their official, governmental capacities.

Most civic leaders and government officials took the attitude that the merchants should solve their own problems. During Time E to M, some of the merchants demanded that one-way streets be made two-way streets and that on-street parking be permitted for customer convenience and improved retail sales. These demands were rejected because they were considered to violate a sensible general policy. Companion suggestions that the police enforce the overtime parking ordinances less rigorously also were turned down. General policies in regard to these matters had been adopted earlier by men convinced that these policies were in the interests of the community as a whole. Officials to whom these demands were made did not consider the policies to be currently in need of amendment or review. For the most part, those urging these changes in governmental policy—that is, in the functioning of local government—viewed their decisional demands as of general importance, to be decided on nonadministrative grounds. But the Mayor, the City Manager, and the others in the city administration to whom demands were addressed considered the demands specific petitions for relief of individual problems, to be appropriately decided by technical considerations. Because of the perspectives of those seeking changes, this analysis treats such demands as political rather than as administrative decision-making, even though one set of political leaders selected outcomes on the basis of "administrative" criteria during Time E to M.

Two specific rezoning requests moved from the administrative- to the political-decision-making-process category in this period. Both decisional outcomes were setbacks for those who believed that the professional planner's image of the good city should determine the overall land-use patterns of development; but at the same time these outcomes were not victories for those who felt that local government's functions of planning and guided development should be curtailed or contracted. They were victories for those who felt that such administrative decision-making could help increase livability if carried out in a flexible fashion, subsidiary to the interests of the business sector of the community.

One request made to the planning commission was that a residential area be rezoned to become a business area. A civic leader had offered to sell a residential property to one of the community's largest firms for the construction of an office building. The professional planners and certain lay members of the planning commission had serious reservations about the wisdom of rezoning an entire area on the basis of a single request. Although they also thought that residents in the area might object, they went ahead and complied with the rezoning request. After this decisional outcome had been authoritatively promulgated, some of the area's residents did object informally, but it was too late.

The proposed office building site was a small parcel of land, owned by one individual, in a very large undeveloped tract. The owner hoped that the proposed development would stimulate the economic development of all the land in this area. This argument was presented to the planning commission. Those on the planning commission who had misgivings about the demand felt that open opposition to the request was not worth the risk of endangering important civic-leader support for increasingly active municipal planning in Metroville.

In the second decision-making process involving rezoning, the city council upheld a recommendation by the planning commission that a requested zoning exception for a suburban shopping center be rejected; this administrative decision-making process became a political decision-making process subsequent to that outcome, after Time E. The reason for the planning commission's recommendation was that they felt that orderly, rational development precluded the construction of shopping centers on arbitrarily chosen sites outside of the downtown business district. There already was a shopping center close to the newly proposed one, and both were within the zoning jurisdiction of the city government. A number of residents of the area also had petitioned against the requested exception and the city council quickly satisfied the objecting petitioners.

After the city council turned down the request for the exception to the zoning ordinance, the shopping center entrepreneurs returned to the planning commission and tried to persuade them to change their decision. By Time *M*, the planning commission had been induced to grant the request. The commission also recommended to the city council that the proposed site of the shopping center development be substantially reduced, but this was a minor compromise that satisfied few of the planners. The city followed the suggestions.

Opposition to the zoning-exception request by downtown businessmen had been expected by some of the members of the planning commission and the city council. Additional suburban shopping centers threatened the economic position of the central business district. However, the expected pressures did not develop. Nor did the residents of the area continue to petition against the proposed shopping center in this second round of the decision-making process. The planning commission and city council did not believe that the residents of the area had changed their feelings of opposition; but since there were no new formal petitions, they discounted such sentiments and heeded instead the open pressures applied by those planning to develop the shopping center. According to members of the planning commission, the representatives of the shopping center had not hurt their cause when they enlisted the cooperation of a very prominent civic leader in the reconsideration of their request.

During Time *E* to *M*, planning was started for an urban-renewal program for the section of the city with the heaviest concentration of Negroes. An urban-renewal grant was secured from the federal government to survey and make plans for redeveloping this large slum area. A special urban-renewal commission, established by the local government just prior to Time *E*, surveyed the area and planned the redevelopment. A few civic leaders opposed this move; some thought the expenditure was unnecessary and others felt that the costs of such urban redevelopment should be paid by Metroville, without federal government participation. However, an urban-renewal planning project was begun for a tract of several hundred acres. Several thousand Negro and a few White families lived in this tract, on narrow and unimproved streets. Intermixed with the several hundred acres of residential housing, which, for the most part, was substandard, were commercial and industrial lands.

Before the decision to apply for a planning grant was finally reached, a certain amount of potential opposition was averted, and some of the initial opposition in the White subcommunity was eliminated. The active proponents of urban renewal among the government officials and civic leaders sketched some of the economic factors underlying their decisional preference. After renewal many more acres of the area would be zoned for industrial and commercial uses. Sites for the expansion of some of the city's industries would be available in a good location. The acreage devoted to residential uses would be reduced substantially, as would the number of families in this congested area. Streets would be fewer in number but widened for modern traffic conditions, and a proposed expressway would pass through this area. It was estimated that local tax revenues would increase several hundred per cent; at the same time, substandard dwelling units would be eliminated. Even the feelings of some extremely Conservative ideologists who stood strongly for states' rights were reduced in intensity. In the course of deciding whether or not to attempt to secure a federal preliminary-planning grant, it was estimated that the city's share in this multimillion-dollar project would be less than one-fifth of its total cost.

A minority opposition was defeated when the decisional outcome to go ahead with the application for federal funds was reached. This minority had emerged for several reasons: federal monies were involved in the project; large amounts of rental property in the area were owned by relatively few people, who were realizing large returns on their slum-housing investments (less than 10 per cent of the several thousand dwelling units were owned by their occupants); and additional public-housing units seemed in the offing. Some of the Negro leaders of Metroville were assured that additional public housing would be provided for the Negro families dispossessed from the area who could not find equally low-cost housing. This ensured support, or at least no active opposition, from a considerable segment of the Negro subcommunity's leadership. The continued implementation of this decisional outcome seemed to be assured. Urban renewal would eliminate an unsightly, undesirable sector and thus provide a substantial civic improvement through an inexpensive, cooperative municipal-federal planning and development activity; and there were benefits to be gained through the impact of urban renewal on the manufacturing segment of the business community. However, when public housing for those to be dispossessed became an actual problem after the planning program was started, fuel was added to the decisional controversy that was to develop after Time M.

Finally, decisional processes existed concerning city-county relations regarding community planning and guided development by local government, as well as questions of government stimulation of business. Some years prior to Time E, a joint city-county planning commission had been established. The state legislature had given the City Council the power to zone for a limited distance beyond the city limits; the county commissioners eventually were authorized to extend this zoning to an area in the county even further from the city limits, but this was not done until after Time E. A zoning ordinance had been passed, and the city-county planning commission was to administer this ordinance in its limited jurisdiction in the fringe area and in the city. The city council also had adopted a rule that, in cases involving property inside the city limits, the planning commission's recommendations could be disregarded if 75 per cent of the city council voted to do so.

During Time E to M, a few citizens demanded that the county commissioners extend zoning to the authorized limits. These demands were defeated. Also during this time, serious efforts were made by a few city property owners to weaken the planning commission by reducing the proportion of affirmative votes necessary to overrule the planning commission on zoning and rezoning decisions to a simple majority of the city council. The supporters of the planning and zoning functions frustrated these efforts when the city council formally retained their self-limiting 75 per cent majority rule.

Civic leaders and firms that owned very large amounts of land seemed generally satisfied with an administrative decision-making process in community planning and guided development that they considered to be properly responsive to their needs. However, there seemed to be increasing resistance and resentment by other property owners and developers to the extension of the jurisdiction of the planning commission to a larger metropolitan area, and even to the current scope of this local governmental function. As the city's population continued to increase and suburban areas developed, property values also continued to rise, particularly on land that could be developed or redeveloped for commercial and business purposes and for housing subdivisions accessible to shopping centers. As property exchanges increased, some of those who were affected began to view zoning regulations that thwarted profit-making and profit-taking as increasingly onerous and unnecessary restrictions on legitimate economic activities.

The city's large annexation of fringe areas just prior to Time E also had created resentment. Several thousand citizens had become subject to city taxes without their approval. Whether the economically frustrated property owners and developers could or would effectively employ their growing disenchantment with the roles of Mayor Peterson, the city manager, and other public administrators was a question of increasing concern to the Peterson administration by Time M.

CIVIC IMPROVEMENT IN FARMDALE

Housekeeping Services

In the minds of active participants, three of the decisional processes regarding housekeeping services also were economic-reorganization processes and have already been discussed. They were the demands for a publicly owned electricity-distribution system, expansion and improvement of the municipal water supply, and improvement and repair of streets and sidewalks in the poorer part of the business and residential sections of town. Except for a compromise on the water system, which satisfied the proponents of civic improvements but did not satisfy those who wanted this shift in scope to attract new industry to Farmdale, the decisional outcomes were negative. Those who wanted to increase the scope of the city government's programs by providing new housekeeping services or expanding current ones suffered two additional decisional defeats during Time E to M.

Demands were made by a few individuals from every section of town to expand the general street paving and street repair program throughout the community. These demands for a general shift in the scope of government were resisted and defeated, as were demands that the city take over the garbage-collection firm. In Farmdale as in Oretown, garbage collection continued to be a community function carried out by private firms operating under regulatory franchises from the city government.

Community Planning and Guided Development

The few men responsible for approving the state plan to bypass Farmdale felt that this was a key decision in preserving the small, good community through proper long-range planning and guided development. Those who preferred the possibility of guided growth—not a boomtown industrial and population explosion—had seen vacant land within the city substantially disappear by Time E. The only immediate possibility of more efficient and beneficial planning and development was an expansion of the city limits through annexation of fringe areas. Annexation was not a focus of demands by the pro-

TABLE 6-6 Political Decision-Making Processes in Farmdale: Time E to M

Civic Improvement

	A. Housekeeping Services	(Outcome)	B. Community Planning and Guided Development	(Outcome)	C. Recreation	(Outcome)	D. Health	(Outcome)
7. Improve street and sidewalk paving and repairs "across tracks"		—						
8. Expand general street and sidewalk paving and repairs		—						
9. Establish municipal garbage-collection service		—						
10. Expand and improve water supply		—(+)						
4. Establish public electric power system		—						
11. Approve proposed state-highway by-pass				+				
[14. Annex fringe residential areas (IV)]				—				
12. Establish municipal swimming pool						—		
13. Establish municipal park-and-recreation program						—(+)		
Outcome Totals (Multiple Listing)		4— 1—(+)		1— 1+		1— 1—(+)		
Outcome Totals (Single Listing)		4— 1—(+)		1+		1— 1—(+)		

KEY: — Unsuccessful or defeated political demands
 + Successful or victorious political demands
 —(+) Minor compromise or substantially unsuccessful political demands

NOTE: The brackets around certain decisional processes indicate that they are also classified under another major category or subcategory. The Arabic numeral corresponds to the number assigned to the decisional process in Table 6-1, wherein there was a single listing of decisional processes. The Roman numerals designate the other major categories under which the bracketed decisional processes are classified.

ponents of new industry; they felt that city services could easily be extended to new plants in the fringe if it became necessary.

A few city-dwellers saw annexation of some residential fringe areas as a wise local governmental reorganization and as useful to the institutionalization of a rational program of community planning and guided development. A very few residents of the fringe areas of Farmdale also made demands for annexation to the city. Demands for annexation from suburbanites were few. Perhaps this was partly because the school district provided educational facilities and services for both the city and fringe areas, the fire district and volunteer fire department serviced the outlying areas as well as the city, police protection was provided by the county sheriff's office, and welfare programs were primarily county-government functions. Relatively few services were provided by Farmdale's municipal government to city-dwellers that were not provided by the county government to residents in the fringe area. However, problems with septic tanks and wells, and the costly fees charged by the city for sewage- or water-line extension beyond the city limits resulted in an occasional but unsuccessful demand for a change in the city's anti-annexation policy.

Recreation

There were two decisional processes in this period regarding recreational improvements. One civic leader advocated a community swimming pool as a needed civic improvement. The outcome of his demand was negative. A merchant demanded the establishment of a city-government recreation program to satisfy some of the recreational needs of children and adults. In particular, he urged the city council to assist in providing facilities for a semiprofessional baseball team; baseball was the one nonpublic-school spectator sport available to adults in Farmdale. The outcome of his demands also was negative.

The decision not to expand the scope of government in this way was followed by efforts on the part of some of the political leaders to help provide facilities for the ball team through private donations and efforts. Organized support behind demands for a government-financed recreation program for children was anticipated and forestalled by a decision to establish a youth organization under the direction of the two-man police department and with voluntary adult participation in the program. No city funds were allocated directly for this function; it did, however, constitute a minor shift in the scope of government insofar as it involved a little time expended by the police force in the form of a semiofficial police athletic league. This satisfied none of the handful of highly active proponents of a municipal recreational program.

CIVIC IMPROVEMENT IN ORETOWN

Housekeeping Services

Former Mayor Lovegren's forces suffered several decisional defeats during the first 18 months of his successor's administration. They were unable to block the municipal parking lot for their central-business-district competitors. Housekeeping services were expanded in spite of their efforts. A sewage-disposal plant was constructed for Oretown; they had opposed it, because they felt that other local governmental expenditures were of higher priority, that it was an unnecessary expense, and that it was action typical of such bureaucrats as the city manager and his fellow public administrators, who used the notion of the general health and welfare to justify the imposition of their personal values on a powerless citizenry. Although prior to Time E citizens had voted in favor of a bond issue to build a sewage-disposal plant, its opponents continued their efforts to prevent its construction. These efforts were to no avail; the plant was finally built, by Time M.

Community Planning and Guided Development

Both the Lovegren-Longacre group and the French administration were defeated in their common but uncoordinated effort to eliminate the private utility as a competitor of the municipal utility. Both groups shared in the political power accruing to the successful defenders of the municipal utility during Time E to M. These active participants in this decisional process had strikingly different community-planning and guided-development perspectives. The Lovegren-Longacre group supported the municipal utility in order to redeem their rule and repudiate the notion that professional public administrators and a vigorous administrative decision-making process constituted the best local government. Mayor French's forces saw the same decisional outcomes as necessary steps in resolving community conflict, which would permit the effective development of the administrative-political "good government" movement, disliked by their predecessors in City Hall.

TABLE 6-7 Political Decision-Making Processes in Oretown: Time E to M

Civic Improvement

A. Housekeeping Services	(Outcome)	B. Community Planning and Guided Development	(Outcome)	C. Recreation	(Outcome)	D. Health	(Outcome)
6. Establish modern sewage disposal plant *	+	1. Eliminate the private utility * (I)	–			7. Establish municipal hospital	–
5. Establish municipal parking lot in the central business district (I)	+	2. Eliminate the municipal utility * (I)	–				
		7. Establish municipal hospital * (II-D)	–				
		8. Annex fringe residential and established industry area (IV)	–				
Outcome Totals (Multiple Listing)	2+		4–				1–
Outcome Totals (Single Listing)	1+		–0–				1–

KEY: – Unsuccessful or defeated political demands
      + Successful or victorious political demands
      * Authoritative consideration by an informal quasi-election

NOTE: The brackets around certain decisional processes indicate that they are also classified under another major category or subcategory. The Arabic numeral corresponds to the number assigned to the decisional process in Table 6-1, wherein there was a single listing of decisional processes. The Roman numerals designate the other major categories under which the bracketed decisional processes are classified.

This period of continued political conflict witnessed one relatively consensual decisional process: the improvement of community health facilities. This brought political foes together for almost the first time in four years. The decisional outcome was *not* to build a municipally owned hospital, but to erect a hospital run by a voluntary board of private citizens in the community. In contrast to the earlier abortive efforts by Conservatives, the new plan for a community hospital was to utilize federal funds in constructing and equipping it. During the 1952 campaign, Mayor French had stated forcefully that he would work for a municipal hospital if a community hospital were not forthcoming through voluntary civic efforts. A few people preferred to see the scope of government expanded by the creation of a municipal hospital and refused to contribute to or cooperate in the new-community-hospital drive. Most civic, governmental, and political leaders —Mayor French, his council opponents from Longacre, officials of the private utility and OMU, and officials of management and labor from the industrial plants—were involved in active fund-raising roles. A group of women even prepared weekly breakfasts to assist in raising funds. The citizen money-raisers were welded into a cohesive group, which by Time *M* was well on its way to making the proposed community hospital a reality.

A number of those who were collecting and contributing the money for the hospital were not acting politically. Others purposely did or did not participate in the hospital drive with the conscious objective of resisting or bringing about a proposed shift in the scope of government. Those who did want to shift or maintain the scope of government were indeed participating in political decision-making, and were among the winners or losers, depending on their decisional preferences. Most of these political participants shared in the political power earned by the victors.

Even Mayor French deserves to be accorded some share of the political power; his operative, immediate preference was to have a community hospital erected through voluntary efforts. The possibility of a municipally owned hospital, second in his order of preference, was used to influence certain uncooperative citizens who otherwise might have resisted or failed to contribute their support to a community hospital. In fact, Mayor French joined some of his political opponents in active leadership roles in defeating his own proposal of a municipally owned hospital. He knew, however, that if they suffered a decisional defeat here or were unable to reach their present objective, he and they would be on opposite sides in the next political decision-making process which would then be triggered off. We shall consider whether or not this cooperative effort altered the character of political conflict in Oretown, as some had intended, in a later chapter. Mayor French also intended the effort to demonstrate what community spirit could accomplish when organized behind planning and development goals that were in the common community interest. The hospital question was the one process classified under the Health subcategory of Civic Improvement political decisions made in Oretown during Time E to M (Table 6-7).

A new decisional process was initiated when, both inside and outside the city, people began to recognize the need for solving safety and health problems in one of the fringe areas. One of the largest industrial employers in the community was located in that area. The managers of this firm did not participate very much in civic and local-government affairs, to the periodic chagrin of city officials, including Mayor French. The firm had its own water supply, sewage facilities, and police and fire protection, and had little involvement with Oretown. Its mining operations added to the growing problem of water pollution, but there were few visible evidences of positive direct contributions to municipal life by this company.

After the Second World War, workers from the company and other newcomers built houses in this unincorporated area, contributing to health and sanitation problems. The area consisted of low-lying land, subject to intermittent flooding from nearby rivers. The water table was so high that many septic tanks could not be operated safely. Sewage was discharged into open ditches, which drained into the river that served as the major water supply for Oretown. Infectious disease rates assertedly were much higher in this area than in Oretown, while Oretown had higher rates than did Big City, only a few miles upstream.

The efforts by some of the residents in this outlying area to incorporate as a small independent city failed. The large mining company was opposed to any plan that meant paying taxes to both city and county governments. Demands then were made that the area become a part of Oretown. Mayor French and others in his administration looked with favor upon this proposed governmental reorganization. However, opposition was widespread and developed from several different directions at once.

Many of the small property owners and homeowners were opposed to the idea of becoming taxpaying citizens of the city, as was the area's industrial firm. Mayor French's political opponents in the Longacre section, which had been annexed to Oretown several years earlier, were opposed to further annexations for fear that sewer, drainage, and other improvements in newly annexed areas would divert city funds from improving their own section of town. They also believed that the proposed annexation would increase local taxes to pay for what appeared to be extremely costly solutions to the sanitation and housekeeping-service problems of the area. The private utility also opposed the annexation, because it would permit the municipal utility to extend its service into an area that was then exclusively served by the private utility; the municipal utility was restricted to serving areas within the city limits, but annexation would bring this fringe area within the city limits.

Although this annexation remained the subject of decisional processes, the outcome at Time M was that this area would not be annexed. By Time M, the annexation issue had not been pushed to a vote of the citizens of that area and the city, a procedure required by state law for municipal annexations. Even though this proposed reorganization of local government was defeated by the apparent strength of the opponents at a pre-electoral stage, the French administration felt bound not to consider the matter a closed issue. They believed that the increased tax base that would result from bringing one of the community's largest employers into the city was essential to the future civic improvement and progress of the city. Annexation of this densely populated, problem-ridden area also would permit an intelligent areawide approach to community planning and guided development. This high-priority political objective was frustrated, at least for the moment, by the negative outcome of the annexation decision-making process.

CIVIC IMPROVEMENT IN PETROPOLIS

Housekeeping Services: Community Planning and Guided Development

In Petropolis during Time E to M, proponents of major civic improvements met with six defeats and two victories in eight political decision-making processes. The reestablishment of two-way traffic and on-street parking on a major thoroughfare in the central business district meant the triumph of business stimulation over improved housekeeping services. However, it was a setback to those who felt that citizens should submit to the informed, expert, administrative decisions of professional technicians. The city council's reversal of the planning commission's decision to permit a shopping center to be built in an area zoned for residential land uses was considered a comparable setback.

TABLE 6-8　Political Decision-Making Processes in Petropolis: Time E to M

Civic Improvement

A. Housekeeping Services	(Outcome)	B. Community Planning and Guided Development	(Outcome)	C. Recreation	(Outcome)	D. Health	(Outcome)
4. Reestablish two-way traffic and on-street parking in the central business district (I)	+	6. Construct centralized governmental center	−			9. Fluoridate the water supply	−
6. Construct centralized governmental center (II-B)	−	7. Conduct comprehensive community planning and improvements study	+				
		8. Initiate planning phase of urban-renewal program in Negro slum area	−				
		4. Reestablish two-way traffic and on-street parking in the central business district (I)	+				
		5. Permit shopping center construction in residential zone (I)	+				
		17. Consolidate city and county schools (IV)	−				
		18. Annex fringe residential area (IV)	+				
Outcome Totals (Multiple Listing)	1+ 1−		3− 4+				1−
Outcome Totals (Single Listing)	-0-		2− 1+				1−

KEY:　−　Unsuccessful or defeated political demands　　+　Successful or victorious political demands

NOTE: The brackets around certain decisional processes indicate that they are also classified under another major category or subcategory. The Arabic numeral corresponds to the number assigned to the decisional process in Table 6-1, wherein there was a single listing of decisional processes. The Roman numerals

In an effort to begin physical redevelopment of the congested, unsightly core of the city, it was suggested that a governmental center be developed where the widespread city, county, state, and federal government operations might be brought together in an adjacent, natural grouping of new structures. This was intended to be a housekeeping service to aid citizens and officials who might have dealings with two or more government agencies; moreover, it was felt that the arrangement might help stimulate and facilitate intergovernmental cooperation and coordination in productive municipal planning and development, which were vital to the future of the city.

In order to consolidate public buildings, a major expenditure was necessary to acquire already built-up blocks in the city, since open land or undeveloped lots had disappeared long before. Prior to Time *E*, the voters had approved a bond issue for the building of a city athletic stadium. It was generally felt that attempts to extend the scope of government further in recreational or cultural areas would doom the government-center idea. The city government employed special planning consultants who recommended a development which included neither a civic auditorium nor other "cultural" facilities; this was because the government feared that the voters would resist the whole project if such expenditures were included. By Time *M*, the plan for a government center had met with such active opposition, in spite of such compromises, that its proponents did not try to get it approved at that time. This was the third civic-improvement defeat for the Plunkett administration.

There were continued efforts to make the city government a more active and effective participant in solving problems of the city, and a leader in formulating and administering programs to restore Petropolis to a state of civic health. Under the direction of the Plunkett administration, a special study was made of priority civic improvements in land-use patterns and the role of city planning in making those improvements. The decision to do the study was a political decision of the Mayor, some of the administrative people in City Hall, and a few of their associates in the civic leadership. It had certain attributes of an administrative decision. However, those who made the decision publicly announced that the study was intended to affect the entire citizenry of Petropolis—or at least this was their hope. It was viewed by these active participants not solely, or even primarily, as a study of how the city might most efficiently arrive at already preferred or predetermined goals; instead, it was considered to be a study that would help formulate, clarify, shape, and influence civic goals, values, and needs. This was one of the two decisional victories in the area of civic improvement for the proponents of a more vigorous planning and development function for city government. While it was something of a "paper" victory, there was hope—and fear by opponents of this objective—that it would contribute to the success of subsequent decision-making by proponents of municipal planning and development.

One of the policy formulations on which the study group agreed and which it included in its report dealt with the possibility of an urban-renewal program for the largest, predominantly Negro, slum section of Petropolis. When the city government's planners and officials developed a preliminary urban-renewal plan, this demand, stated as a possibility in the report, set off another political decision-making process. The estimated net cost of the renewal and redevelopment plan was almost two million dollars. Under the federal urban-renewal program, if the city proceeded with its application for federal funds and such funds were approved by the Housing and Home Finance Agency in Washington, D. C., the city government would pay one-third and the federal government two-thirds of the net cost. The city manager was one of the first to announce his opposition to this extension of government activity; he maintained that such a program was not necessary. Others opposed the demand for urban renewal, on the grounds that such a cost to the city was unwarranted and that the use of federal funds was undesirable.

While Mayor Plunkett and White and Negro members of his political coalition previously had been charged with being extreme radicals because of their attitudes and actions in regard to race relations, this was the first time in several years that the charge of "socialism" had been leveled at a city administration for a non-race-relations policy preference. The urban-renewal program was related to the situation of the Negro subcommunity in Petropolis, but the active opponents of urban renewal, who were primarily White citizens, seemed to be most upset because of ideological considerations not specifically connected with White Supremacy. They believed that urban renewal violated individual property and political rights as well as local and states' rights. This program meant "federal dictation" by "bureaucrats, politicians, liberals, and socialists" in Washington and their counterparts in the local community. Even the earlier decision to participate in the federal public-housing program had not seemed to evoke so serious an ideological response in the community. By the time the survey research was conducted, the advocates of urban renewal for Petropolis had not broken the roadblocks mustered by the anti-urban-renewal forces.

School consolidation was the fifth decisional defeat for those trying to bring about or to speed shifts in local government's civic-improvement programs and activities. Several years earlier a special citizens' committee had conducted a study and had recommended that city and county schools be combined under a single governmental unit. Resistance had been very strong, so the matter had been dropped. During Time *E* to *M*, demands for this public-school consolidation were revived by those who felt that efficient good government required that the jurisdictions be merged into a single governmental-administrative unit, capable of planning and guiding the development and improvement of public schools. This proposed governmental reorganization to provide equal educational opportunities to the citizens of the whole area was considered a necessary forerunner to the development of consolidated countywide local governmental institutions, through the merging of city and county government. It was to parallel efforts to make the city's still segregated public schools for Negroes "equal" to those for Whites. Hearings were held, but by Time *M* it had not been decided to consolidate the schools. County government officials formed the center of open resistance.

During Time *E* to *M*, local government was reorganized through annexation of a large residential fringe area to the city. This was the second success for those advocating shifts in the scope of local government to improve the amenities of urban life. Access to city housekeeping services was a factor in the preference of many residents of this area for the annexation. However, the annexation resulted in a greater number of public charges that City Hall was dominated by a power-hungry political group, dedicated to extending their dominance over an ever-widening area and increasingly large numbers of citizens. Although individuals dedicated to the improvement of community planning and guided development were satisfied to some extent by this annexation, at the same time they feared that further improvements in these functions might be threatened by such reactions.

Health

A sixth defeat took place when a set of demands for a civic improvement regarding community health was made and blocked during this period. These demands were for fluoridation of the city's water supply. When the demands reached the stage of formal, authoritative consideration by government officials, opponents charged that fluoridation was a most serious violation of individual freedom, that putting such materials in drinking water was a most heinous crime which only a despotic government would contemplate. Realizing the emotional nature of the controversy, city councilmen, a majority of whom personally favored fluoridation, conducted a straw vote of the citizens. When a majority of those casting ballots indicated opposition to the fluoridation proposal, the council tabled it. This action constituted a decisional defeat for its active proponents.

CIVIC IMPROVEMENT IN METROVILLE

Housekeeping Services

In Metroville during Time E to M, the pattern of outcomes of political decision-making processes in regard to housekeeping services was different, to some extent, from the pattern in Petropolis. Those who desired to improve the municipal housekeeping services for the citizens of Metroville met with two defeats and three successes in the five decisional processes in the housekeeping services subcategory. The two defeats came in the decisions involving the improvement of air transportation facilities and services that already have been described.

The street-improvement program was developed in the mid-1950's around a system of expressways and then linked with the new federal interstate-highway program. Additional funds were needed for parts of the city's street-construction and -improvement program. A large bond issue, based on the general street-development plans adopted before Time E, was submitted to the voters in 1958, just before Time M; a small fraction of the registered voters approved it by a narrow margin. In the same election, bond issues for expansion and modernization of the city's water supply and sewer system also were approved, but by wider margins. These bonds were to be paid off by fees charged to water consumers and users of the sewage system. These three efforts to maintain or improve the quality of the housekeeping services of local government were successful, even though there was individual, unorganized citizen opposition to the programs.

Community Planning and Guided Development

Of the eight decisional processes in Metroville during Time E to M, in which at least some of the active participants favored the strengthening of professional community planning and guided development, only one resulted in an outcome which these participants con-

TABLE 6-9 Political Decision-Making Processes in Metroville: Time E to M

Civic Improvement

A. Housekeeping Services	(Outcome)	B. Community Planning and Guided Development	(Outcome)	C. Recreation	(Outcome)	D. Health	(Outcome)
10. Make major capital improvement in water system *	+	13. Request state authority for county-wide zoning	−	18. Build municipal swimming pools	−	20. Expand White mental hospital	−
11. Make major capital improvement in sewer system *	+	14. Extend zoning further from city limits	−	19. Expand park-and-recreation facilities	−		
12. Improve streets and build expressways *	+	15. Build additional public-housing units for Negroes	−				
[4. Build a new regional airport (I)	−	16. Initiate planning phase of urban-renewal program in Negro slum area	+				
[5. Make major capital improvements in airport (I)	−	17. Increase authority of city council relative to planning commission in re-zoning	−				
		[6. Initiate program of central business district re-development (I)	−				
		[8. Rezone residential area to business classification (I)	+				
		[9. Permit shopping-center construction in fringe area (I)	+(−)				
Outcome Totals (Multiple Listing)	2− 3+		5− 2+ 1+(−)		2−		1−
Outcome Totals (Single Listing)	3+		4− 1+		2−		1−

KEY: − Unsuccessful or defeated political demands   +(−) Major compromise or substantially successful political demands
+ Successful or victorious political demands   * Designates authoritative consideration by a municipal election

NOTE: The brackets around certain decisional processes indicate that they are also classified under another major category or subcategory. The Arabic numeral corresponds to the number assigned to the decisional process in Table 6-1, wherein there was a single listing of decisional processes. The Roman numerals designate the other major categories under which the bracketed decisional processes are classified.

sidered a positive accomplishment. One other outcome was thought to be a successful resistance to an attempt to cripple this function of municipal government.

The failures included the unsuccessful attempt to involve the city government in a program of redevelopment for the central business district and the rezoning of a residential area to a business classification upon the request of a civic leader interested in developing his property there for commercial purposes. Another failure occurred when the city permitted the construction of a shopping center in the adjacent fringe area. Resistance to demands that zoning regulations be extended still further from the city constituted an additional defeat for the pro-planning people. Demands that city government formally request the state legislature to authorize zoning for the entire county also were resisted effectively by Time *M*. Successful opposition to efforts to weaken community planning and guided development, in the interest of stimulating economic enterprise, was the outcome of the abortive attempt to increase the authority of the city council at the expense of the planning commission in considering requests for rezoning.

The one positive accomplishment perceived was the initiation of the planning phase of an urban-renewal program for the redevelopment of a large Negro slum. Expansion of the public-housing program itself remained a decisional process during Time *E* to *M*. An earlier plan for several hundred public-housing units for Negroes had been blocked in the courts and was still in litigation. The local public-housing commission, its legal staff, and the city attorney still were trying to get a favorable decision by appealing to higher courts. Even though articulate opposition to this additional program of public housing seemed to be increasing, efforts to get it approved and underway continued. A lower court had ruled that the planned public-housing units technically violated the city's zoning ordinance. With the strength of the court decision behind them, the opponents of public housing had successfully defeated this shift in the scope of government by Time *M*. This was a setback for those who had hoped to use the expanded public housing for Negroes, and the promise it provided for continued slum clearance, to build public support in both the Negro and White subcommunities for more active municipal planning and development.

The proponents of a strengthened and expanded municipal operation in community planning and guided development, through professional administrators and planners, accepted their decisional defeats gracefully; they feared that otherwise they might stimulate the opposition and weaken or destroy the current activities of local government in this area. This was in contrast to the situation in Petropolis, where activists with these same perspectives continued to press for their decisional objectives at the cost of continued or even increased political conflict over the extant issues. Such persistence was present in three other political decision-making processes in Metroville: two that are listed under the recreation subcategory and one under the health subcategories.

Recreation

There were practically no swimming facilities in Metroville besides those at the country clubs, to which few people had access. In the extreme summer heat and humidity the lack of swimming facilities became more and more depressing to some people. Every day the nation's mass media told of the joys of swimming in pools that were within the price range of the average citizen. Few residents of Metroville were "average" in this Madison Avenue sense, and few could afford such a facility. However, the municipal swimming pools in a neighboring city made it apparent that they could be provided by city government. Municipal swimming pools became the subject of demands for a shift in the scope of government.

The second set of demands was for neighborhood parks and recreation areas, particularly in the poorer sections of town, where park facilities were not adequate. The large city parks did not meet the needs of many children and parents, since recreation areas were not always within easy walking distance of their homes.

These two sets of demands were integrated in a single proposal by the city recreation commission. The proposal asked the city council for a public vote on a bond issue to provide both segregated swimming and wading pools and funds for the acquisition of park sites, particularly for small neighborhood parks. A tax levy to help finance the operation of this expanded program also was to be presented to the voters. Shortly after Time E, the city council approved the plan; the bonds were to cost several million dollars.

It was customary that a wealthy person, family, or local foundation make a major contribution to the fiscal or site requirements of large-scale recreational facilities. This was rejected at the outset as an alternative to a bond issue. No one in the civic leadership came forth as the enthusiastic sponsor, the "angel," for either the swimming pools or the neighborhood parks. The idea of swimming pools did not capture the interest or arouse the excitement of those with great resources, as had medical facilities, a community center, a college, and even an arena for sporting events. Neither were small neighborhood parks of sufficient concern to any of the potential donors who earlier had given very large parks to the city.

The newspaper, noted for its active interest in such civic improvements as expanded recreational facilities, urged editorially a pay-as-you-go plan for acquiring park sites; they suggested that the money should be part of the annual budget, as a substitute for the bond issue. Members of the recreation commission and others felt that presently available land either would be gone or would be too costly by the time such a plan for acquiring sites was put to such use; they continued to push for passage of the bond issue. The civic leaders were divided on the merits of and the need for voting on the bond issue. Even some of those in favor of expanded recreational facilities feared that a defeat at the polls might trigger off a series of defeats for other important civic improvements. The few active opponents of the measure urged its defeat on the grounds that integrated swimming pools were most undesirable. They maintained that even if they were established as segregated facilities, litigation to desegregate the pools could be expected, and that also was undesirable.

The Chamber of Commerce then strongly urged a postponement of the bond election because there were civic improvements other than recreational facilities requiring bond issues. By a close vote in the City Council, the proposed cost was cut drastically through the elimination of the proposed swimming and wading pools. This occurred only after several White civic leaders pointedly stressed the recent demands by Negroes in one neighboring city to integrate separate White and Negro swimming pools which had served as models for the advocates of municipal pools in Metroville. Such segregationist sentiments were repeatedly expressed by White citizens in meetings that the city recreation commission held with various civic groups to discuss the proposed programs.

The opponents were more active in their opposition than were the proponents in their support of the proposal. Leaders of the Negro community felt that recreational facilities were terribly inadequate in their neighborhoods and informally organized strong electoral support for the bond-issue and tax-levy measures. Their demands were defeated by an overwhelming majority in the same special election that approved money measures for streets, sewers, and water improvements. Although the Negro ward from which the one Negro councilman was elected voted overwhelmingly for the recreational measures, the total vote, which was not a large one, was equally overwhelming against them.

Health

An issue which had a much greater spectator interest than recreation arose at about the same time in regard to the improvement of the city's mental hospitals—one for Negroes and the other for Whites. Although by the summer of 1958, Time M, the great interest of White citizens apparently was not due, to any great degree, to racial considerations, conflict involving race was present and affected the decisional outcome. Racial considerations were to become open and decisive factors by the time the citizens were brought into the decisional process in the fall of 1958, after Time M.

To understand the hospital issue as it developed, one must understand the race-relations situation in Metroville during 1957–1958. We shall examine, therefore, the decisional process in regard to desegregation of the public schools in order to clarify racial attitudes.

By state law, school districts could, if they desired, provide for desegregation. In the fall of 1957, shortly after Time E, the announcement was made that Metroville would be one of the few cities in the state to admit a selected number of Negro students to formerly all-White schools.

This decisional outcome emerged from the activities of a small group of the most important White political leaders in Metroville. Constitutional lawyers among the civic leaders' legal counselors and representatives in the state legislature made it quite clear that, if Southern State did not desegregate some of its schools, the Supreme Court might overrule the state plan to minimize desegregation as an evasion of their compliance edict. The postwar racial and industrial conflict was pointed out to remind people of the difficulties that Metroville might suffer if the improved, and evidently harmonious, race-relations situation were to be disturbed by an unnecessarily rigid segregation policy. Perhaps the most forceful argument used to induce the few strong segregationists in the civic leadership to go along with the local desegregation decisional option was that token desegregation in a city of segregated residential areas made it unnecessary to fear widespread desegregation in the public schools.

Leaders of the Negro subcommunity were kept informed, but they did not participate actively in this decision-making process. In general, they looked with satisfaction upon this decision of the White civic and political leaders. The Negro leadership, for the most part, accepted the political "realities" that shaped the decisional process and outcome. However, individual Negro spokesmen still felt sharp frustration because more widespread desegregation was not provided for immediately. In order to make the decisional outcome embody actual school desegregation, a number of Negro leaders worked with some Negro parents to submit applications for admission of Negro pupils to White public schools for the fall of 1957, and they discouraged others. This administrative selection procedure was an integral part of the policy adopted in the decision to initiate token desegregation in Metroville. These applications were regarded by those engaged in preparing them as private demands. The decisions were to be administrative, that is, each case would presumably be decided on the basis of such technical criteria as the relative distance of the Negro and White schools from the applicant's home. Several Negro children were finally granted permission by the school authorities to attend two formerly all-White high schools. With none of the sorts of incidents that marked the initiation of desegregation in a neighboring city in Southern State, in communities in Tennessee, and in Little Rock, Arkansas, the citizens of Metroville witnessed the beginnings of desegregation with the seating of these few Negro youngsters in otherwise entirely White classrooms in the city schools for Whites.

Later in 1957 and during 1958, many Negro leaders began to be concerned about what might happen in the fall of 1958 when Negro students applied for admission to White schools closer to their homes, particularly since even federal troops in Little Rock had failed to weaken Faubus and his fellows in their determination to resist the Supreme Court's decision. In the winter of 1957, an organization of White segregationists was belatedly formed in Metroville. Their avowed purpose was to resist further desegregation in the public schools.

The White citizens who were disturbed by this limited desegregation seemed to be on the verge of explosive action. For several years, they had had no opportunity to act openly on the basis of their feelings of racial supremacy, since harmonious race relations, at the expense of some relaxation in segregation barriers, was clearly the general policy being pursued by an apparently unified White political and civic leadership. The newspaper had attempted to communicate this perspective to all of the citizens who were not otherwise informed through their formal associational and organizational channels of communication with the civic leadership. Violation of this general policy was thought to be something that would bring severe sanctions, both legitimate and illegitimate, to bear on violators, whether they were Whites who wanted to repair the breaches in the walls of segregation, or Negroes who wanted these walls to fall all at once. In a later chapter, we shall examine the transformation from administrative to political decision-making in regard to admission of Negro pupils to White schools as this general race-relations policy continued to suffer further setbacks in the fall of 1958, after Time *M*.

It was in this setting that the decision-making process regarding the city mental hospitals unfolded. Several years earlier, a special consultant, employed by the municipal mental hospital commission, had recommended the modernization of the Negro hospital, the improvement of the White hospital, and a general expansion of facilities, since there was a shortage of hospital beds. There had been periodic demands for hospital improvement for a number of years. Both hospitals had been donated to the city by leading families of Metroville. Shortly after the Second World War, a wealthy patron of community improvements had offered land, without charge, for the construction of a new White hospital. Citizens had approved a multimillion-dollar bond issue for building a new hospital on that site; but even though the city's leading families donated over a million dollars, the Korean War's impact on the costs of construction made these funds insufficient. Instead of building a new hospital, the money was used to improve the existing hospitals.

Shortly after Time *E*, a special study committee of leading citizens recommended the construction of a small, open-ward, "minimum security" branch hospital for Whites on a new site and that the present city hospitals be retained and improved. The Negro hospital was not in need as much of expansion as of renovation. The site that had been offered previously was no longer available, but the acquisition of another small site for the branch hospital was not regarded as particularly difficult. The decisional outcome about hospital improvements and expansion seemed to have been reached. Six months later, however, the special citizens' committee reversed itself and suggsted that an entirely new White hospital be built on a new site; that the present White hospital become the Negro hospital; and that the present Negro hospital be abandoned. The new White hospital was to be several times the size of the proposed branch hospital in bed capacity and was to be located on a much larger site. The new plan was estimated to cost more than twice as much as the previous plan. The new plan was approved by both the Mayor and the official municipal hospital commission. It then was recommended to the county commissioners as something they should put to a county-wide vote of the citizens.

The civic leaders on the special citizens' committee originally had been split into three camps in their decisional preferences. Those who had urged the expansion of the White municipal mental hospital on its present site had compromised with the advocates of an entirely new White city hospital in agreeing to build a branch hospital, which had been the first preference of some of the committee members. At the insistence of two members, who changed their minds about compromising, the plan was changed again; all but one member of the committee finally agreed to go along with the latest plan. The outcome was a defeat for this adamant supporter of the proposal to expand the White hospital on its present site. But those who joined in adopting the final plan did not yet share in the political power accruing to those responsible for expansion of the White hospital, since that expansion had not been accomplished by Time M due to the intra-group conflict.

The issue, as it had developed in the special citizens' committee, was between the advocates of minimizing costs and those who felt that a new site for the White hospital was imperative because of its present location in an increasingly "undesirable" location. By "undesirable" they meant that the formerly all-White neighborhood in which the White hospital was located was changing to a predominantly Negro neighborhood. All of the members recognized that the still salvageable Negro hospital could not be sold for a great deal of money. To one group, this was a material factor, while to the second, it was not as important as the race factor.

The civic leader who had led the committee to reverse itself was a die-hard segregationist. He had gone along, although not happily, with the other White civic leaders in their post-1946 efforts to improve race relations. It seemed to him that desegregation of the public schools was a most unwise decision, no matter how much control was exercised over its rate. Few citizens, White or Negro, knew at the time that the race-relations factor had become so involved in this decisional process. Among these few, however, were a number of the Negro leaders who were very sensitive to race-relations considerations in local political decision-making.

Thus, the decision was consistent with the first preference of the relatively few White Supremacist civic leaders. The adjustments in race relations, carefully worked out over the past decade, were threatened by the increased tension that began to spread from certain Negro leaders to others in the Negro subcommunity. In contrast, most of Metroville's White citizens were uninformed and unaware of the racial factors that were shaping the thinking of those responsible for the decisional outcome.[4] But the next decisional process regarding the allocation of costs and benefits threatened to make the entire citizenry aware of the racial connotations and to lead to an open decisional struggle between Negroes and Whites.

The Mayor met strong resistance when he approached the county commissioners and urged them to hold a bond election so that the citizens of the county could pay a share of the costs for the construction of the new White hospital and the renovation of the older White asylum to serve Negro citizens. The county commissioners referred the matter to a subcommittee for study of the financial implications of the plan. One of the county commissioners was the sole dissenting member of the special citizens' committee. His violent opposition to the latest plan had been ignored by the other decision-makers. By Time M, whether citizens of the county would be asked to authorize the necessary construction funds or not was still in question.

Other unresolved questions were whether or not the Negro subcommunity would support the plan, in view of its racial overtones; and whether the poorer White citizens would vote their racial sentiments or their pocketbooks when and if they were informed of the racial rationale for the new plan. The newspaper had fully reported the decisional process as it had unfolded, but had not specified the racial factors involved. The paper's editorial policy-makers still were uncertain, by Time M, whether to support or to oppose the latest plan; this reflected the uncertainty and divided opinion within the traditionally consensual White leadership of Metroville.

Thus, Metroville's ordinarily efficient political decision-making process broke down over the recreation and the hospital-expansion issues. The public dispute over recreation reached the city council before a close vote eliminated the municipal swimming-pool facilities. The election on the recreation bond issue and special tax levy divided the electorate along sharp racial lines because of effective informal organization in the Negro subcommunity, an atypical phenomenon in balloting on special measures in Metroville. These questions, together with the hospital-expansion issue, led to conflict within the ranks of an ordinarily consolidated White civic leadership during the authoritative-consideration stages of decision-making. In the hospital-expansion issue, this division, although not its basis, came to be known publicly, with great spectator interest in the issue within the White subcommunity, and increasing personal importance of the issue to at least the portion of the Negro leadership cognizant of its racial connotations.

GOVERNMENTAL REORGANIZATION IN FARMDALE AND ORETOWN

We have already mentioned the defeat of the demands for further annexations in Farmdale. This outcome was dictated by the preferences of the governmental and political leadership, which favored a

TABLE 6-10   Political Decision-Making Processes: Time *E* to *M*

Government Reorganization

Farmdale	(Outcome)	Oretown	(Outcome)
14. Annex fringe residential areas	–	8. Annex fringe residential and established industry area	–
Outcome Totals (Multiple Listing)	1 –		1 –
Outcome Totals (Single Listing)	1 –		1 –

KEY: –   Unsuccessful or defeated political demands
        +   Successful or victorious political demands

general policy of planning for the development of Farmdale as a small, quasi-rural, retail trading community without the influx of new industry or new population.

Annexation of a problem-ridden area of industrial and residential land use was blocked in Oretown for somewhat different reasons. Fringe-dwellers strongly opposed annexation. The disposition of governmental officials to annex this area with its high-valuation industrial property was offset by their fear of increasing the sharp political conflicts in the community. They also felt that the annexation might be postponed until a more efficient and effective administrative decision-making process was established within the present city limits.

GOVERNMENTAL REORGANIZATION IN PETROPOLIS

In Petropolis, ten decisional processes seemed to some of their active participants to have direct implications for the organization or reorganization of local government. The desired extension of the city's limits and jurisdiction over the unincorporated industrial area was defeated because of widespread fears of undesirable consequences for the community's industrial base from retaliation by the industrial annexees. Since merchants had organized successfully to overrule the parking and traffic plan developed by administrative officials, and since the construction of a shopping center had been permitted in a residential area in spite of the advice of professional planners, the Plunkett administration began to fear that a local governmental reorganization was informally, but effectively, underway. Such reorganization might give those with special interests, such as merchants and real estate developers, effective political power in decisions that were within the jurisdiction of public administrators.

A preference for consolidating local government and enlarging the jurisdiction of its institutions to allow them more effective, metropolitan-wide community-planning and guided-development functions was frustrated by the decisional outcome to resist the merger of the city and county school systems. However, the preference was satisfied partially by the annexation of a large residential fringe area, even though this annexation seemed to add to the hostility toward the public administrators and the increasingly professional administrative decision-making in City Hall. Those who had been unsuccessful in resisting the annexation charged that the city manager and the city planners, in violation of the sentiments of the citizens, had dictated an enlargement of the city against the will of the people.

TABLE 6-11   Political Decision-Making Processes in Petropolis: Time *E* to *M*

Government Reorganization

	(Outcome)
16. Annex area of established industry	−
17. Consolidate city and county schools	−
18. Annex fringe residential area	+
[4. Reestablish two-way traffic and on-street parking in the central business district (I)]	+
[5. Permit shopping center construction in residential zone (I)]	+
[9. Fluoridate the water supply (II)]	−
[12. Create biracial municipal race relations commission (III)]	+
[13. Initiation of improvement of race relations program by new municipal commission (III)]	−
[14. Block reelection of top officials of local Democratic party * (III)]	+
[15. Elect extreme segregationists to top offices in local Democratic party * (III)]	−
Outcome Totals (Multiple Listing)	5 − 5 +
Outcome Totals (Single Listing)	2 − 1 +

KEY: −   Unsuccessful or defeated political demands
       +   Successful or victorious political demands
       *   Authoritative consideration by an informal quasi-election

NOTE: The brackets around certain decisional processes indicate that they are also classified under another major category or subcategory. The Arabic numeral corresponds to the number assigned to the decisional process in Table 6-1, wherein there was a single listing of decisional processes. The Roman numerals designate the other major categories under which the bracketed decisional processes are classified.

The question of who should rule, the citizens at large or local government officials, was present in both of the foregoing decisional processes and came to the fore in the decisional question of whether or not the city's water supply should be fluoridated. The opponents of fluoridation, who finally were successful in this process, charged that this would endanger the water supply, and that it would be a violation of individual liberty. To many of the active proponents as well as to some opponents of fluoridation, the real issue was whether the people or their elected representatives should make this decision. The city council's use of an informal, postcard ballot was regarded by both friends and foes of fluoridation as a victory for those who were demanding a major reorganization of local government in the direction of "direct democracy."

Although these were not manifestly race-related decisions, the most articulate spokesmen of "the people" in opposition to the "bureaucratic usurpation of power" were leaders of such organizations as PECORR, an organization unalterably opposed to any suggestion of desegregation. These efforts to reorganize the local government were used as evidence that the Plunkett administration and its friends were conspiring not only to "mongrelize the White race" but also to take away all decision-making rights from the citizens.

We have listed four other political decision-making processes under both the social-reorganization and governmental-reorganization categories. Active participants viewed these processes not only as demands for providing greater or lesser social status to both Negro and White citizens, through shifts in or maintenance of the scope of local government, but also as demands for greater or lesser opportunities for members of racial categories to participate in the governmental process in the community. To understand these decisional processes, we shall review the situation of the Negro subcommunity in relation to the functioning of local government in Petropolis up to Time *E*.

Demands that the Negro sections of Petropolis receive a larger share of the civic improvements provided by local government had met with a fair degree of success by the mid-1950's, but demands for improvements in the sections of the city where the wealthier Negroes lived were more successful than those in the major Negro slum section. These included such civic improvements as parks, schools, street paving, street lighting, and police protection. Even public housing had been provided for a tiny fraction of low- but comparatively steady-income Negro families through the establishment of a local government public-housing authority which participated in the federal public-housing program. Negro citizens demanded, individually or collectively, through PESNEG or through informal neighborhood associations, additional shares of the local government's resources that were being devoted to public works, public health, and public safety. For the most part, these demands were viewed by those making them and by governmental officials, particularly the city manager and his administrative staff, as right and proper. However, they were to be decided on the basis of technical and administrative, rather than value-preference, political criteria. Responsive administrative decision-making, a good deal of which had favorable outcomes for individual Negro petitioners, became a major mechanism, during this period, in ordering political relationships between the White and Negro portions of the community.

Before the 1930's and the rise of PESNEG, such administrative decision-making apparently had occurred less frequently. The proportion of negative outcomes for the Negroes making the demands had been higher. During the 1930's and the first part of the 1940's, as Negroes began to view such demands as political demands, the decisional outcomes became more variable. Starting with the election of Mayor Plunkett's predecessor, and continuing through Mayor Plunkett's administration, came the period of revitalized, more change-oriented administrative decision-making; the city government became more responsive to the needs and demands of at least the more upper-class segments of the Negro subcommunity.

However, even with successful Negro political organization during the period prior to Time E, and the 1957 reelection of a city administration generally sympathetic to the aspirations of Negroes, segregation was retained in the provision and use of various city services and facilities; there was effective resistance to the lowering of the substantial color barriers in the private economy and in the community's social structure, especially in regard to employment and housing opportunities. Besides the one Negro city councilman and the one Negro member of the city school board, the major channel for the non-electoral participation of Negroes in city government decision-making was through their organized channels in the local Democratic party which had direct and indirect connections with City Hall.

In an effort both to improve the social, economic, and civic relations between the two racial subcommunities and to give additional direct governmental representation to leaders of the Negro subcommunity, Mayor Plunkett and some of his close associates created a city commission, to which civic leaders of both races were appointed. The commission was to survey and make recommendations about various aspects of racial accommodation and conflict in regard to public and private institutions and behavior. The members of the commission represented all points of view regarding desegregation, except the view that complete desegregation ought to be instituted immediately.

This decision to extend local government into official, institution-alized consideration of and communication with both subcommunities about race-relations conditions, and possibly to formulate policies in regard to improving race relations, was a significant victory for those who had pressed for this shift. The next decisional demand, however, resulted in a defeat for the same people: when the new municipal race-relations commission appeared before the city school board to request information about the board's possible plans to initiate desegregation, the board refused to discuss the matter with the commission. Those favoring strict segregation policies and those opposed to the city government's activities in the race-relations area began to exert pressure for the new commission to end its efforts to improve race relations. As a result, several of the more White Supremacy-minded members of the commission resigned. The political power that had accrued to those who had participated and successfully exercised some political influence in the decision to establish this biracial commission was thus countered quickly by their opponents' success in thwarting the commission. The ultimate success of the commission as a functioning organization was in question when the race-relations aspects of Petropolis party politics made front-page headlines.

After the narrow defeat of Mayor Plunkett's opponent in the mayoralty contest of 1957, the next electoral opportunity to reduce the potential political influence and power of politicians who represented Negro groups and organized labor in City Hall and to curtail the political deference or status presumably accorded Negroes and organized labor by the city government, came almost a year later, in 1958. Although this decisional process was not open to all of the citizens of Petropolis, the election by the local Democratic precinct workers and other party officials of a new chairman and executive secretary afforded the occasion for this demand to be pushed by its proponents. The leaders of PECORR organized opposition and John Jay and Fred Ames lost their positions as official heads of the local Democratic party.

To win this victory, segregationists had to activate and work with White citizens who were much more moderate in their race-relations sentiments. These citizens appeared to have been persuaded by the argument that City Hall and the Democratic party needed to be rescued from a political machine and "spoils" politics. In their eyes, Jay was an unscrupulous, unprincipled politician, Ames was an irresponsible labor-union agitator, and some of their Negro associates were power-hungry ward heelers, interested only in their personal welfare or, at most, in the welfare of a racial minority. They cared nothing for the public interest or the public welfare of the whole community of Petropolis.

When the entrenched leadership of the Democratic party had been turned out, the next decisional question became the selection of a new chairman and secretary. The moral indignation of the moderate allies of PECORR subsided. A number of these moderates became even more indignant at the demand that the new chairman represent an equally extremist point of view, that of the rabid White Supremacists, who seemed to be unrepresentative of the large majority of the "responsible" civic leaders of Petropolis. These moderates were effective in electing as the new chairman and executive secretary two men who did not represent the extreme segregationist point of view.

Therefore, by Time M, there seemed to be no substantial net shift in Negro citizens' access to local government, although the loss of the top posts in the local Democratic party may not have been compensated fully by the new biracial local government commission. In any event, the situation was such that it could be predicted fairly safely that political decision-making concerning access to local government by members of both racial subcommunities would continue after Time M.

GOVERNMENTAL REORGANIZATION IN METROVILLE

In Metroville during Time E to M, three of the political decision-making processes involved important governmental reorganization. However, none of the processes were concerned with the question of opportunities for members of one or the other racial subcommunity to participate politically in the local governmental process. More than in any other community, the appropriate division of the citizenry into city-dwellers or county-dwellers, subject to the jurisdiction of particular institutions of local government, was in question. As in Petropolis, the question of who should rule, the people or their governmental officials, began to be a most serious consideration in political decision-making.

Two questions involving the schools were current in this period. They were part of one decision-making process: whether or not to consolidate city and county functions. A combined city and county school bond issue for the construction of a series of new schools and additional rooms in existing school buildings and a proposed increase

TABLE 6-12   Political Decision-Making Processes in Metroville: Time *E* to *M*

Government Reorganization

	(Outcome)
22. Consolidate city and county schools	—
23. Annex fringe residential areas	—
[17. Increase authority of City Council relative to planning commission in rezoning (II)]	—
Outcome Totals (Multiple Listing)	3 —
Outcome Totals (Single Listing)	2 —

KEY: —   Unsuccessful or defeated political demands
        +   Successful or victorious political demands

NOTE: The brackets around certain decisional processes indicate that they are also classified under another major category or subcategory. The Arabic numeral corresponds to the number assigned to the decisional process in Table 6-1, wherein there was a single listing of decisional processes. The Roman numerals designate the other major categories under which the bracketed decisional processes are classified.

in the school tax of residents of the county living outside of Metroville was presented to the voters. Part of the tax increase was to be used to supplement teachers' salaries in the county school system to raise them to the same level as salaries already paid by the city school system to its teachers. The proposed increase in school taxes was defeated, but the bond issue for the school building program was approved.

These electoral outcomes were defeats for activists who had worked for the tax increase and against the bond issue. The managers of the newspaper also had advised the voters, through editorials, to defeat the bond issue and increase the taxes. At least some of these defeated activists who urged a "no" vote on the bond issue and a "yes" vote on the tax increase did so because of their position on school consolidation. Most proponents of consolidating the city and county schools into one school system felt that equalization of city and county teachers' salaries would make the consolidation easier to accomplish. They also felt that a long-range building program, such as the one envisaged by the proponents of the bond issue, might greatly delay consolidation. However, most of the active "friends of the schools," who, in fact, also were sympathetic to school consolidation, could not be persuaded to delay the school building program. Many other voters obviously either were opposed to or simply unaware of this relatively sophisticated strategy by the proponents of school consolidation.

Demands that the elected city councilmen retrieve some of the authority that had been transferred to the city planning commission were, in part, demands for a greater role in decision-making for government officials, and a lesser role for certain private citizens. As we have indicated, these defeated demands were an expression of preference that elected representatives, instead of technicians such as city planners, engage in community-planning and guided-development functions. But they were also, in part, an indication that there was resentment against the political roles played by the city planning commission, theoretically a nonpartisan, politically disinterested body, who were perceived by some to be serving the interests of the very few. Some of those making these demands preferred a local government reorganization in which citizens of even modest or low social and economic status could veto, through elections, undesirable actions of the formal *or informal* authorities engaged in deciding questions of municipal planning and development.

In another political decision-making process, involving the proposed annexation of an additional fringe area, some of the active participants felt that this proposed reorganization of the jurisdictions of the city and county governments also raised questions about whether government officials or private citizens should make such decisions. The large annexation before Time *E* seemed to have whetted the appetites of certain members of the Chamber of Commerce for increasing the population of the city by moving the city limits farther out from the city center. For the most part, these were the people most interested in attracting new industry. Atlanta, a major southern metropolis, became a model for these "expansionists" of how large Metroville might become if properly guided.

By Time *M*, additional annexation had been resisted successfully because of a somewhat unexpected alignment of forces. Political leaders in the county resisted further annexations because of what they asserted was the rural desire for independence. Inside the city, many of those who had worked for the last major annexation opposed the additional one because they felt it was premature. They joined those who opposed any departure from the traditional boundary divisions for which plans had not been carefully worked out to accommodate additional numbers of city residents. This required planning and zoning studies, cost-benefit analyses, plans for public-works programs, and assessing the implications of additional annexations for school consolidation.

During and after the previous annexation, those concerned with community growth perspectives—including the Mayor—had felt that rather strong resentment had been created against the city government by citizens in the annexed area who had not wanted to become city taxpayers. Unless the new annexation were carefully planned, it might provide those who were already hostile to City Hall with an issue for creating additional mistrust and hostility. Some individuals also feared that the proposed annexation might create additional hostilities between City Hall and the county government at a time when the former wanted the latter's cooperation in supporting the proposed new White hospital on a countywide tax basis.

SOCIAL REORGANIZATION IN THE SOUTHERN CITIES

Petropolis

In Petropolis, there were seven decisional processes that significantly involved local government's impact on the future distributions of social status between the two racial subcommunities. In the two pairs of decisional processes, one concerned with establishing a new biracial city government commission and the other with the leadership positions in the local Democratic party organization, there were opposite decisional outcomes. In addition, the decisional process in which the initiation of an urban-renewal program for the large Negro slum area was blocked constituted a defeat for those who hoped such a program would enable local government to assist in the generation of additional social status for a segment of the Negro subcommunity. Some of the proponents of urban renewal—both Negro and White—had hoped that the elimination of slum life and improved housing and neighborhood conditions would result in lower crime and vice rates in the Negro subcommunity, and ultimately would ease social and racial hostilities on the part of Whites who were upset by social conditions in the Negro slums.

Demands for desegregation were resisted successfully beyond the opening of the school year in the fall of 1957, and up to Time M in 1958. While a few members of the Negro subcommunity demanded immediate and complete desegregation, most of the Negro leadership, while preferring this, demanded only that desegregation begin, however limited and partial it was at the outset. Some of Petropolis' political and civil leaders, including Mayor Plunkett, also took this latter position. Before Time M the city school board voted, by a

TABLE 6-13   Political Decision-Making Processes in Petropolis: Time *E* to M

Social Reorganization

	(Outcome)
10. Begin desegregation in public schools	—
11. Permit efforts to desegregate eating facilities without arrest	—
12. Create biracial municipal race-relations commission	+
13. Initiate improvement of race-relations program by new municipal commission	—
14. Block reelection of top officials of local Democratic party *	+
15. Elect extreme segregationists to top offices in local Democratic party *	—
[8. Initiate planning phase of urban renewal program in Negro slum area (II)]	—
Outcome Totals (Multiple Listing)	5 —
	2 +
Outcome Totals (Single Listing)	4 —
	2 +

KEY: — Unsuccessful or defeated political demands
　　　 + Successful or victorious political demands
　　　 * Authoritative consideration by an informal, quasi-election

NOTE: The brackets around certain decisional processes indicate that they are also classified under another major category or subcategory. The Arabic numeral corresponds to the number assigned to the decisional process in Table 6-1, wherein there was a single listing of decisional processes. The Roman numerals designate the other major categories under which the bracketed decisional processes are classified.

majority of one, to retain the completely segregated school system. Desegregation demands thus were defeated in this period, as they had been previously.

Two Negro families in Petropolis initiated a lawsuit to protest the state's provision for local option in regard to desegregation. But this did not seem to lessen the resistance of those among the city's White leadership who ideologically opposed any desegregation, no matter how moderate. These opponents of even token desegregation did not like the fact that Negroes had initiated the legal action, but they, too, were in favor of doing away with the local option. Their attitude, of course, was based on motives different from those of the Negro petitioners: they wanted state laws prohibiting any degree of desegregation in any community. This lawsuit, as well as the continued demands made by "moderate" Negro leaders, appeared to weaken the resistance of some White civic leaders who until then had felt the time had not yet arrived to make such a decision. These men began to feel that unless desegregation was started, the invalidation of the state's position permitting token desegregation might result in the development of a situation similar to that in Little Rock: local violence, federal troops, and the kind of community image that would keep new business and industry away. Although the decision to maintain segregation in the city's public schools had not been reversed by Time M, such feelings and fears became even stronger with the unfolding of the next decisional process.

Segregation of citizens in such activities as pursuit and consumption of food, shelter, and knowledge was deeply rooted in Petropolis because of both custom and governmental authority, by informal citizen behavior and the formal monopoly of physical force possessed by government. If demands arose for changes in customary segregation practices, and if these demands were backed by organized, militant action designed to crack the walls of segregation, the critical question would be the local government's interpretation of its police power. This could become a vital element in the continuation or discontinuation of segregation, as was the case in Little Rock, in Albany, Georgia, in Birmingham, and in other cities of the South. In Petropolis, a small group of Negroes demanded that the city government change its policy toward segregation in eating facilities. This group of youthful Negroes, with their minister, walked into the "Whites only" section of a candy store and requested service. When they refused to leave, the owner had them arrested for trespassing. Their demand that the city government not arrest them, that the city authorities service their needs instead of the needs of those citizens who wanted segregation, was defeated. Their conviction in a municipal court was later upheld by a higher state court.

This defeated demand was one of the incidents antecedent to the lunch-counter and restaurant sit-ins by Negroes in many parts of the South. While this occurred three years before the series of sit-ins throughout the South, it may not have gone unnoticed by the group of students who eventually triggered off the wave of later sit-ins. Actually, although the Negroes who participated in this process failed to attain their primary objective—eating with Whites in a restaurant —they did accomplish a secondary objective—they were arrested. After Time M, demonstrators who engaged in certain antisegregation activities in Petropolis purposefully were not arrested. This resulted in a frustration of both their primary and secondary political goals. Since the demonstrators viewed getting arrested as the invocation of administrative decision-making in relation to political decision-making goals, the arrest was an administrative decision-making victory, even though the outcome of demands for a shift in the scope of local government in the political decision-making process was unsuccessful.[5]

Metroville

Six political decision-making processes in Metroville were classified as social-reorganization processes; five of these already have been mentioned under other categories, since there were multiple perspectives involved. These five processes all constituted defeats for those who were demanding shifts or the maintenance of the scope of local government that would satisfy the need of Negroes for additional social respect or status; they constituted victories for those who sought to retain the traditional, dominant social position of Whites.

These decisions included the outcomes of the two recreational processes: one satisfied White Supremacy sentiments by eliminating any present provision for integrated swimming- and wading-pool facilities;

TABLE 6-14   Political Decision-Making Processes in Metroville: Time *E* to *M*

Social Reorganization

	(Outcome)
21. Begin desegregation in public schools	+
[15. Build additional public housing units for Negroes (II)]	—
[18. Build municipal swimming pools (II)]	—
[19. Expand park and recreation facilities † (II)]	—
[20. Expand White mental hospital (II)]	—
[22. Consolidate city and county schools (IV)]	—
Outcome Totals (Multiple Listing)	5 —
	1+
Outcome Totals (Single Listing)	1+

KEY: —   Unsuccessful or defeated political demands
        +   Successful or victorious political demands
        †   Authoritative consideration by a municipal election

NOTE: The brackets around certain decisional processes indicate that they are also classified under another major category or subcategory. The Arabic numeral corresponds to the number assigned to the decisional process in Table 6-1, wherein there was a single listing of decisional processes. The Roman numerals designate the other major categories under which the bracketed decisional processes are classified.

the other was the defeat of proposed park improvements, particularly for areas of heaviest Negro concentration. Another decisional outcome, in large measure due to racist sentiments, was the postponement of the proposed expansion of the White mental hospital; still another was the failure of the school-consolidation measures, urged by some Negro leaders as a way of desegregating the public schools in the county, since token desegregation had begun in the city schools. Another effort by the White political leadership to extend an additional degree of social status to the Negro subcommunity was frustrated when the opposition was able to obtain judicial hearings in its efforts to block an extension of the municipal public-housing program for Negro citizens. The initiation of an urban-renewal program for the Negro slum area was not, in the view of the active White proponents of this program, particularly significant to the distribution of social status between Negroes and Whites.

Token desegregation was initiated through a process of political decision-making in which a small number of leading White citizens participated actively. In Metroville during this period, the one major shift in the functioning of local government was this limited desegregation in the public schools, which minimally redistributed social status and dignity.

SUMMARY

Some of the differences we have described in the patterns of the political decisions during Time E to M in each community may be summarized briefly. With minor exceptions, the demands of individuals in Farmdale who wanted a more active municipal government to strengthen the industrial base, to stimulate business, to improve amenities in civic life, and to extend the benefits of the city's government to suburbanites were defeated by advocates of the *status quo*. In Oretown during Time E to M, the French administration engaged in consolidating, rationalizing, and preparing for new shifts in the scope of local government in order to improve the city and to make government better and more efficient through reorganizations. In contrast, Mayor May's administration during the same period in Farmdale was working to prevent future shifts in the scope of local government. Although the political decisions made in this period in Oretown generally had outcomes similar to those in Farmdale, three decisions were indicative of differences in the politics of these communities during Time E to M.

The decisional preferences of Oretown's downtown merchants were satisfied by a major shift in the scope of local government which provided a municipal parking lot in the central business district. A modern sewage-disposal plant resulted from another decisional process; this represented a defeat for the advocates of minimal housekeeping services. The negative outcome of demands for a municipal hospital was a comparable shift from the *status quo,* since it was a victory for those demanding the creation of a quasi-public community hospital.

Two of these three decisions were characterized by intense group conflict in Oretown, as were both decisions concerning the municipal and private electric utilities. In sharp contrast, Farmdale's political decisions were made quietly, without a great deal of public conflict. In Oretown, formally organized associations of merchants participated actively in decision-making, as did labor unions; but in Farmdale, only informal associations of merchants existed; organized labor, as such, was not active in the political decision-making of this period. Relatively few political decisions were made in Oretown during this period. Whether this was due to group conflict that channeled citizen attention and energies away from potential decisional matters, or the French administration's efforts to avoid further political conflict, or to other factors, is not known.

Similar contrasts were to be found between Metroville and Petropolis. In fact, there are striking similarities in the patterns of political decision-making of little Farmdale of Western State and much larger Metroville of Southern State; equally strong resemblances can be recognized between Oretown and Petropolis. In Metroville, as in Farmdale, organized labor was not actively involved in political decision-making during Time *E* to *M*. The interests of individual merchants were advanced in certain political decisions, but in the two decisions concerning proposed shifts in the role of local government to stimulate retail trade in Metroville, the outcomes were negative. In Petropolis, as in Oretown, organized labor was active in political decision-making; in both cities, organizations of merchants were active, successful participants in decisions about stimulating the major mercantile sectors of the local economy.

In both Oretown and Petropolis, city administrations were actively concerned with the health of the mercantile sectors of their cities, even though both had higher-priority concerns. In Oretown, Mayor French pushed for the municipal parking lots because it represented a convenience for all the citizens, rather than because it was in the economic interests of the downtown merchants. In Petropolis, Mayor Plunkett's major concern was trying to improve the community through the planning and development functions of local government and through industrial development and diversification; his administration unsuccessfully opposed the preferences of the merchants that were in the direct interests of the merchants. Compared to Mayor May's "no growth" city administration in Farmdale and to Mayor Peterson's administration in Metroville which invariably placed priority on the decisional preferences of the major industries, the local governments of Oretown and Petropolis were very sympathetic to the political interests of their merchants during this period.

Another difference between Petropolis and Metroville was that Negroes contributed to decisional outcomes in the former, but not in the latter. Negroes were successful in almost half of the political decisions wherein their relative social status was at stake in Petropolis during this period. Even though public schools were not desegregated, they acquired political power by participating effectively in two decisional processes. In Metroville, Negroes benefited from the decision to initiate token desegregation but did not acquire political power; they also were frustrated by the outcomes of five other decisions in the same period. Many of Metroville's political leaders still were trying to advance their community "to the forefront of progressive postwar communities." However, demands by Negroes that municipal government help them acquire increased status relative to White citizens, or appeals by Whites for shifts in the scope of local government that would result in such gains for Negroes were rejected because they were considered "too drastic" by some of the White political leaders. This attitude contributed to decisional defeats for White citizens who had been trying to improve the recreational, educational, and hospital facilities during Time E to M.

There follows a series of questions about the differences between these two sets of communities. These differences include the degree to which organized labor was active in decision-making as a political interest group, the degree to which the self-conceived political interests of merchants were advanced by decisional outcomes, and the degree to which Negroes in the Southern communities successfully contributed to decisional outcomes during this period of interest. The answers to these questions—which will be given in the following four chapters—are not intended to explain the original reasons for the differences, but they will describe the differences in greater depth. We shall attempt to explain some of these differences when hypotheses involving periods before and after Time E to M are tested in the last chapter of this book.

To what extent were the following a reflection of differences in political interests: the apparent lack of participation in decision-making by organized labor in Farmdale and Metroville and the powerlessness of merchants in Farmdale and of both merchants and Negroes in Metroville, when compared to their visibility and power in Oretown and Petropolis? Or were the political interests of these groups comparable? Was the need to participate or have power weaker in Farmdale and Metroville than in Oretown and Petropolis? If the latter alternative is the case, did the political leaders of Farmdale and Metroville take the political interests of such groups of citizens into account—that is, accord them positive political status—more than in Oretown and Petropolis? To what extent was the political support organized behind the demands of merchants in Farmdale, and both merchants and Negroes in Metroville, less adequate than in Oretown and Petropolis? Were illegitimate sanctions being used against, or feared by, labor, merchants, or Negroes in Farmdale and Metroville more than in Oretown and Petropolis? If so, was this associated with a greater repression of or more poorly organized support for political demands in Farmdale and Metroville than in Oretown and Petropolis? Was there, in other words, a difference in types of regimes between Farmdale and Metroville on the one hand, and Oretown and Petropolis on the other? Was the difference in the character of decision-making conflict associated with a difference in regimes?

The questions of immediate concern in the next chapter are these: Was the noticeable difference in the pattern of decision-making conflicts, between Farmdale and Metroville on the one hand, and Oretown and Petropolis on the other, associated with differences in the distributions of citizen political participation and influence? Specifically, were the apparently more restricted, less open decision-making conflicts in Farmdale and Metroville associated with less extensive citizen participation and narrower distributions of citizen political influence than in Oretown and Petropolis? Or were the citizens of all four communities similar in the extent to which they participated and attempted to exercise influence in politics? Were the aforementioned differences in decision-making conflict restricted to a very few protagonists?

Was the apparently greater representation of relatively disadvantaged groups in political decision-making in Oretown and Petropolis restricted to their spokesmen or leaders? Or did it extend to the rank-and-file members of those sectors of the community? Specifically, were diverse socio-economic and racial categories of citizens proportionately represented at the upper levels of the political-influence structure in Oretown and Petropolis? Was there a proportionate underrepresentation of disadvantaged groups in Farmdale and Metroville?

In Metroville, Petropolis, and Oretown there was some citizen resentment over certain political decisions; was this directed toward more developed and possibly less accessible and less responsive bureaucracies and elected administrations than in Farmdale? Therefore, might we not find in Farmdale, with its minimal government, a "town meeting" type of political process where the *status quo* decisions were made with public approval and extensive participation by citizens of all socio-economic statuses? Was Metroville's politics more similar to Oretown's and Petropolis', rather than Farmdale's, than we supposed on the basis of the foregoing report of decisional questions and outcomes? We shall begin to answer these questions with information collected from random samples of the citizens in each community at Time M about their political behavior and other characteristics during Time E to M.

NOTES

1. Whether a decisional outcome represents a shift in or the maintenance of the scope of local government depends upon the form in which the demands were made and in which the process was described. Special care needs to be taken in interpreting the notations for successful ($+$) or unsuccessful ($-$) outcomes, particularly when processes are multiple-listed under two or more classificatory categories.
2. See Linton C. Freeman and others, *Local Community Leadership* (Syracuse: Syracuse University Press, 1960), pp. 7–14, for a listing of the issues in the Syracuse metropolitan area during 1955–1960, and the criteria used to select those decisions. See also the list selected for study in Robert A. Dahl, *Who Governs?* (New Haven: Yale University Press, 1961), pp. 332–334.
3. This is the first of nine political decision-making processes listed under the Economic Reorganization category in Table 6-2. The decisional processes are discussed in the four cities in the order in which they are listed in that and the following tables, which is on a multiple-listing basis.
4. There was no relationship, for example, between segregationist sentiments and preferences for a new White hospital, a branch hospital, or expansion of the present White hospital on its present site as measured in interviews with a random sample of White adults in Metroville at Time M.
5. In a peculiar but real sense, these Negroes could not at this time fail to acquire a share in power given their preferences in favor of any of the possible decisional outcomes. Knowing that success is inevitable may produce political action that would not be taken if the situation and alternatives are conceived differently, as involving risks of losing. "The Lord is with me," or comparable sentiments of a martyr, means that even death or incarceration may be sufficiently satisfying outcomes to warrant an analyst assigning to the martyr some share in the unit of power attaching to an outcome.

7

CITIZEN POLITICAL-INFLUENCE
STRUCTURES: *Time E to M*

Electing officials is not direct participation in making decisions about the scope of government. However, municipal elections of men to office may have direct consequences for the political decision-making processes following the election, since it is probable that whoever is elected will influence the occurrence of various future political acts that constitute political pressures on the scope of local government. The probability varies according to who is elected to office. Conceptually, elections of officials do not in and by themselves constitute the selection of particular policies to be followed in the future functioning of government. The selection of candidates and their election to office may mean, in some cases, a high probability that certain decisions affecting the scope of government will be made; but other nominations of and balloting for potential office-holders may have only remote significance for the political decisions that follow. Elections range from relatively clear-cut, informal consideration of alternative policies to an issueless choice among personalities.[1] With this in mind, we turn now to the municipal elections held in each city immediately prior to the point in time designated Time *E*.

MUNICIPAL ELECTIONS: TIME *E*

To review briefly, municipal elections were legally nonpartisan in Farmdale, Oretown, and Petropolis.[2] There were no primaries in either Farmdale or Oretown, but a nonpartisan primary was held in

Petropolis, followed immediately by the general election. Party primaries were held in Metroville a short time before the general election. In both cities of Western State, elections for local officials were held in November, the time of elections for congressional, and every four years for Presidential, candidates. In both cities of Southern State, the primaries and elections for mayor and councilmen were scheduled in the spring of odd years when no other state or national elections were held. This difference must be kept in mind when comparing turnout figures.

Farmdale: November 1950

The ordinary procedure for nominating candidates in Farmdale was for a small number of citizens to sign a petition placing the candidate's name on the ballot. This had been done in 1950 by friends of Mayor George Norris. Although the organization of Community Conservationists had broken up when Anderson had opposed Norris unsuccessfully in the mayoralty election two years earlier, few Community Conservationists expected anything out of the ordinary to prevent Norris' reelection in 1950. No effort was made to replace Conservative city councilmen, so that in the 1950 municipal election two Conservative candidates ran unopposed for the two council posts to be filled.

In a campaign launched just before the election, the friends of Bill May organized an extraordinary and effective write-in campaign for him. The election of May as Mayor marked the beginning of a Jeffersonian Conservative administration. Besides those active in buttonholing and telephoning citizens to write in May's name, few citizens appreciated the *status quo* platform to which May and his friends were dedicated. Citizens were urged to write in his name on the grounds that he was younger, better informed, and even more virtuous and respected than Norris. For the citizens at large, this was an election for personalities rather than policies. Approximately 80 per cent of the registered voters cast ballots in that municipal election. This followed the turnout pattern that had been usual in Farmdale since the Second World War, both for men and for measures. A few special elections had been held on such measures as whether or not to establish a public electric utility in the Farmdale area; whether or not to approve bonds for the sewage-disposal plant; and whether or not to annex a particular fringe area. A comparable proportion of registered voters turned out to vote on these measures.

Oretown: November 1952

In Oretown in 1952, 80 per cent of the registered voters cast ballots in the three-way race for mayor and to fill three council posts, two of which were contested. Decisional preferences of the candidates as well as personal attributes were more clearly at issue than in Farmdale in 1950.

Mayor Lovegren had taken a no-compromise, pro-municipal-electric-power position; Councilman French had indicated a position of greater compromise, although he did not want the private utility to continue to compete with OMU. The third candidate served the function of drawing votes away from Lovegren on the basis of personality differences. The decisional question involving the sewage-disposal plant also became an electoral issue: Lovegren was against it and French for it. Citizens were told that a vote for French was a vote for a community hospital, a new downtown parking lot, and, if necessary, continued community growth through annexations. Lovegren's campaign did not mention a community hospital; he maintained that he was against the expenditure of tax monies to aid the downtown merchants by providing them with public parking facilities; he was for saving money through the elimination of wasteful programs and jobs at City Hall; he also was opposed to expansion through annexation, because of the cost. The election of Mayor French did not mean that the citizens were giving him a mandate on any or all of the above policies; but the contest was far more than a matter of personalities, at least in terms of the voluminous campaign oratory emanating from these two sides in the three-way contest.

The high turnout was consistent with the previous pattern in municipal elections. In fact, Oretown had the most developed electoral process of any of the communities prior to Time E, both in frequency of special elections and in a consistently high degree of turnout. The initiative and referendum were both frequently used, allowing direct, popular expression of preferences on decisional matters. The recall also was common in this city of "direct democracy." [3] Even before the Second World War, the recall had become a traditional type of formal electoral participation. There were over a dozen special elections from the end of 1944 to the end of 1948; citizens voted on almost as many measures from 1948 to 1952. The hard-fought mayoralty election in 1952 was in Oretown's tradition of extensive citizen participation in elections.

Metroville: Spring 1957

The 1957 election in Metroville was parallel to the 1950 election in Farmdale. There was a comparable absence of specific policy issues, despite a mayoralty contest. On the other hand, a general decisional question existed in the contest, and the turnout, though not high compared to our other cities, was higher than usual for Metroville. About 15 per cent of the eligible voters turned out for the Democratic primary to nominate Mayor Peterson by a substantial margin over his opponent, an attorney on the city council. In the general election, the Republican candidate received a vote unprecedented for a Republican: almost half the votes cast by about 20 per cent of the city's eligible voters. Ordinarily, even in contested primaries and elections, less than 20 per cent of those who were registered voted; this was a greater percentage than ordinarily voted in special elections. Turnouts were approximately the same for White and Negro registered voters.

The major theme of the 1957 mayorality election was that the particular candidate and his party could do a better job of giving the citizens good government than could the opposition. In this city of overwhelming Democratic registration, the Republican candidate could not stress party as much as Mayor Peterson could. The role of the local government in the social structure—particularly in Negro-White relations—was the major implicit issue. The Mayor's public image was that of friend of the Negroes and the working man. However, the race-class divisions were less a matter of campaign statement than gossip and innuendo. The Republican candidate and the local Republican organization wanted to capture Negro support, as did the national Republican party in its revitalized efforts to crack the solid South. The Republicans in Metroville dared not risk disillusioning potential Republican Negro voters who may have been disenchanted by the White Southerner's influence in the national Democratic party. On the other hand, it could not afford to lose potential White votes with a campaign directed to Peterson's Negro supporters. Therefore, the race issue became muted, although it sharply affected the balloting. In the all-Negro precincts, Mayor Peterson won by votes of 10, 30, 60, and 100 to 1.

Thus, in Metroville, even in the hotly contested mayoralty election of 1957, the unusually high turnout was considerably lower than that for the uncontested mayoralty election in Farmdale. The Farmdale election, however, had been held at the time of state and congressional elections, so that these turnouts cannot be compared strictly; the more appropriate comparison of turnout is in the two Southern cities.

Petropolis: Spring 1957

In Petropolis about one-third of those registered voted in the 1957 general election for mayor and councilmen. The mayoralty race was decided by a handful of votes; but the overt racial issue contributed to the largest turnout since the openly race-related election of 1951, when slightly more than 50 per cent of those registered cast ballots. More Negroes voted than Whites, as had become the traditional pattern in Petropolis since the development of an efficient political organization in the Negro subcommunity. Only in 1955, when the mayor's post was uncontested, did turnout in Petropolis decline to the low turnout typical of Metroville's municipal elections.

In Petropolis as in Oretown, issues were sharply drawn in the mayoralty contest at Time E. Unlike Metroville, here race relations became open issues. Besides endorsing Mayor Plunkett's reelection, PESNEG also endorsed a slate of candidates for the City Council. According to an editorial in the major daily newspaper, the basic racial issue was

. . . whether one segment of the Negro community will maintain its control of the government of Petropolis . . . whether the so-called labor-Negro bullet votes will still be able to select or reject at will the city's mayor and the councilmen or will the white citizens regain their dominance over civic life.

In the race issue, Mayor Plunkett was represented as an advocate of public school desegregation—token desegregation had not yet occurred—and as an advocate of relaxation of racial barriers in local government employment and even in various social situations. All of these assertions were based on his actual decisional preferences, although his opponents cast them in extreme terms. Hostile propaganda posed Plunkett's reelection as the continuation of Negro representation in City Hall, to the exclusion of Whites. Plunkett focused his campaign on the problems of reviving a declining local economy. His opponent stressed economy in local government and the need to resist further tax increases; he met his supporters at least part-way in their image of him as defender of an unyielding White Supremacy policy. A spokesman of PECORR added to the public's interest in this election by running on an anti-Plunkett administration platform for city council; he was unsuccessful. Mayor Plunkett was reelected by a small margin.

Turnout and Registration Compared

Voter turnout at Time E was equally high in Farmdale and Oretown; both turnouts were higher than in Petropolis, which had a higher voter-turnout rate than Metroville. This followed the pattern that had been established during the postwar period. The municipal elections in the Southern communities relied on their own pulling power, whereas in the Western cities voters had the attraction of state and congressional contests; in Oretown the citizens had the added attraction at the polls of the Eisenhower-Stevenson competition in 1952. However, these factors obviously were not responsible for the relatively greater turnout in Petropolis than in Metroville. A slightly greater number of Negro citizens in Petropolis turned out to vote than of their fellow Whites; in Metroville there was no such difference. The overall difference between Petropolis and Metroville in citizen participation in these municipal elections cannot be appreciated until registration figures are taken into account.

On the basis of the best estimates that could be made from official registration figures, population estimates, and the sample surveys, the proportion of eligible citizens registered to vote was similar—approximately 75 to 85 per cent—in Farmdale, Oretown, and Petropolis. The proportion of registered White citizens of Metroville was lower, and the proportion of Metroville's registered Negro citizens was even lower —less than 50 per cent. The latter difference means that, even though the proportions of registered White and Negro citizens turning out to

Turnout (as a proportion of registered voters)	Registration		
	High (75% or more)	Medium (50 to 75%)	Low (less than 50%)
High (60% or more)	Farmdale Oretown		
(20% to 60%)	Petropolis: White and Negro		
Low (less than 20%)		Metroville: White	Metroville: Negro

FIGURE 7.1   *Registration and turnout in municipal elections: Time E.*

vote in Metroville was similar, the White citizens as a whole had a voting advantage based on both their larger proportion in the population and their greater registration. Therefore, by Time *E*, citizen participation in municipal elections for office-holders was extensive in Farmdale and Oretown, less extensive in Petropolis, and restricted in Metroville, particularly for the Negro subcommunity.

The assumption that the municipal elections in Farmdale and Metroville at Time *E* were regarded by citizens as relatively issueless when compared to the elections at Time *E* in Oretown and Petropolis was based on inspections of press reports, campaign literature, and reports from informants. If we can assume further that, ordinarily, elections of candidates with conflicting platforms result in more postelection discussion of policy than do elections of candidates on personality, the sample surveys provide indirect evidence that those elections were, in fact, issueless. This evidence is based on reported rate of discussion of "local government or community matters during the past year with friends" and the rate of voting regularity in local elections reported by the respondents in the sample surveys.

Only in Farmdale and in the White subcommunity of Metroville did larger proportions of the respondents state that they voted at least "sometimes" than had reported they engaged in such discussion with friends even "once in a while." For the other samples, more discussion was reported than voting. This supports the impression that in Farmdale and in the White subcommunity of Metroville proportionately more people were voting in the absence of concrete policy concerns than in the other communities; Negroes of Metroville voted and discussed issues less than the citizens of any other community or subcommunity. Because of the differences in registration and turnout between Farmdale and Metroville at Time *E*, we shall examine further the questions of whether citizens of Metroville were more satisfied with the current scope of local government or apathetic toward it, and whether they felt electorally impotent or not because of fear of illegitimate sanctions. We shall try to determine whether or not it was considerations such as these that led to the lower electoral participation in Metroville than in Farmdale. We also shall be concerned with why the citizens in Farmdale and Metroville seemed to vote as a ritual and to take little interest in issues and choosing among several preferences about the scope of government, and whether or not this attitude was carried over to political decision-making during Time *E* to *M*. This possibility was suggested by the differences in the intensity of group conflict among the active protagonists in these two sets of communities, as was noted in the previous chapter's description of political decision-making during that period.

CITIZEN PARTICIPATION: TALKING, MEETING, AND ACTIVIST ROLES

Respondents were asked in each sample survey how often they discussed local government and community policy matters with friends, civic leaders, and local officials; if they attended meetings at which policy matters were major subjects of consideration; and whether they had taken "a more active part" regarding any local government or community issue. Responses to these items are presented in Table 7-1. The samples in both Petropolis and Metroville were classified by race. The data in this chapter, for the most part, are presented separately for the White and Negro respondents of each Southern city because of the possible political differences between these racially distinct subcommunities.

A consistent pattern is discernible in these data: citizens of Farmdale and Metroville ranked lowest on every one of the participation questions. The one exception was that White citizens in Metroville reported a higher rate of at least occasional discussion with government officials than Negro citizens of Petropolis. Otherwise Oretown and the two subcommunities of Petropolis ranked first, second, or third on every item.

A political-participation index was developed by assigning composite scores to the communities and subcommunities on the basis of their rankings on each of these five participation items. For example, the sample that had the highest proportion of respondents reporting at least occasional political discussion with friends was assigned one

TABLE 7-1   Proportion of Sample Engaging in Political Participation

	Community Sample					
	Petropolis				Metroville	
Political Participation Item	Oretown (N = 742) %	White (N = 353) %	Negro (N = 237) %	Farmdale (N = 255) %	White (N = 295) %	Negro (N = 228) %
Discuss with friends at least occasionally	81	68	65	56	58	55
Discuss with civic leaders at least occasionally	32	34	38	18	27	25
Discuss with local officials at least occasionally	21	27	16	15	20	12
Have attended one or more meetings	13	11	18	7	3	4
Have taken a more active part	12	11	15	5	5	4

TABLE 7-2   Rank-Ordering and Scores on Political-
Participation Index

Sample	Rank-Order	Total Scores
Oretown	1.5	10
Petropolis Negroes	1.5	10
Petropolis Whites	3.0	11
Metroville Whites	4.0	22
Farmdale	5.0	24
Metroville Negroes	6.0	28

point; the sample with the lowest proportion was assigned six points.

The resulting order indicates that Oretown and the Negro subcommunity in Petropolis were tied for the first rank as the most active samples; then followed the White subcommunity of Petropolis, the White subcommunity of Metroville, Farmdale, and the Negro subcommunity of Metroville, in that order.[4] The difference in scores between the first three, Oretown and both subcommunities of Petropolis, and the second three, Farmdale and both subcommunities of Metroville, was considerably larger than the comparable difference within each set. Thus citizen participation was relatively high in Oretown and Petropolis and relatively low in Farmdale and Metroville.

Citizen Participation as Electors in Decision-Making

By the use of the ballot in special elections, citizens may vote in roles comparable to their roles as electors of officials. The high frequency of special elections held in Oretown prior to Time *E*, including recall, initiative, and referenda elections, has been noted. Was the difference in the rate of citizen participation between Oretown and Petropolis on the one hand, and Farmdale and Metroville on the other, paralleled by differences in the degree to which citizens voted in the making of political decisions during Time *E* to *M*?

None of the fourteen decisional processes in Farmdale during Time *E* to *M* resulted in the formulation of ballot options for the electorate. The electorate in Metroville had such opportunities most frequently, although relatively few citizens took advantage of them: only about 10 per cent of the registered voters participated in the elections. Specific electoral issues in Metroville were whether or not to approve bonds and a special tax for recreation, for schools—as a prerequisite to consolidation of the city and county schools—and the water, streets, and sewage systems. The results of the school measures were a defeat for proponents of school consolidation; the recreation measures were voted down; the water, sewage, and street bonds were approved.

In Oretown no formal election was held for any of the eight decisional processes, but there were three informal or "quasi-elections." That is, authoritative consideration of decisional options was open to a sizable segment of the population; an outcome was determined by the frequency with which substantially similar actions were performed in behalf of an option; each action was given about the same weight as every other action.[5] Oretown's quasi-elections occurred in three decisional processes: one involved the establishment of a community hospital and two involved the municipal-private utility issue.

The outcome of the hospital process depended on raising sufficient funds to establish a private community hospital rather than a municipally owned hospital. The fund-raising was organized so that citizens received personal appeals to contribute whatever they could afford. A substantial portion of them contributed, thereby engaging in this quasi-electoral political role.

The selection of one of the two competing utilities, the choice to remain a customer of one or to switch to the other, was open to most citizens in Oretown. To the extent that these actions had a political motive—a motive related to the preferred scope of government —the personal choice constituted political participation in a quasi-electoral role. People could "vote" in these "elections" throughout Time E to M. People shared in political power by contributing to each outcome, since the two utilities' gains and losses of customers determined outcomes. Apparently many citizens shared these units of political power, since they felt themselves to be participating politically as well as making an economic decision in their choice of utilities.

In Petropolis, there were no formal elections in which the citizens participated in the authoritative-consideration stage of decisional processes; but, as in Oretown, citizens played quasi-electoral roles. In one case all citizens could participate, and in the three others a significant portion of them could do so.

A decisional process concerning fluoridation of city water was settled by an informal, postcard vote: citizens were asked by the local officials to send in a postcard indicating their preferences; many citizens responded. The city council adopted a rule that they would accept the majority preference. In this way fluoridation was defeated. In a decisional process about whether or not to apply to the state government for a technical training center, the decisional outcome rested on the businessmen of Petropolis. The active proponents of such a center ruled that they would submit an application only if they received completed questionnaires from a specified, substantial proportion of the businessmen who had been requested to give information on their needs for skilled workers. Whether the businessman returned the questionnaire, or did not return it because he was opposed to the training center, he was playing a quasi-electoral role in the decisional process. More than the specified number of questionnaires finally were returned. Other such decisional processes were two Democratic party elections for officials, open to relatively large numbers of citizens. Forces on all sides made major efforts to recruit inactive Democrats to participate in the balloting that determined these two decisional outcomes. Thus, the absence of formal elections in the eighteen decisional processes in Petropolis is somewhat misleading in light of these four quasi-electoral processes.

From the foregoing analysis we find that the formal and quasi-electoral process in the authoritative consideration of decisional processes was used least often in Farmdale. Comparatively extensive quasi-electoral citizen voting was found in both Oretown and Petropolis. Metroville had a greater proportion of formal elections than any other community, but only a small proportion of citizens voted in any of these.

SUMMARY: THE ASSOCIATION BETWEEN DECISION-MAKING CONFLICTS AND CITIZEN POLITICAL PARTICIPATION

We now may answer, in part, one of the questions raised in the summary of Chapter 6. The apparently more restricted, less open decision-making conflicts in Farmdale and Metroville were associated, with some exceptions, with less extensive citizen participation. Perhaps the most important exception was the high citizen turnout in the municipal election at Time E in Farmdale; but even that election was issueless compared to the decisional positions of candidates in both Oretown and Petropolis at Time E. (Although the turnout in Farmdale may have been ritualistic, its possible significance in promoting future political instability, change, and conflict will be examined later in this analysis.)

The greater frequency with which local referenda were held in Metroville than in Farmdale during Time E to M also will be referred to later in the analysis. This was another exception, even though the extent of such participation was less than it had been for quasi-electoral participation in decision-making in Oretown and Petropolis during the same period. The controversial ballot measures concerning recreation and school consolidation may have signified a change in Metroville's usually covert decision-making conflicts. However, we must leave this consideration until the pre- and post-Time E to M periods are analyzed in a later chapter.

The citizens of Oretown and Petropolis ranked higher on every one of five political-participation items than the citizens of Farmdale and Metroville, with one exception. The exception was that Petropolis' otherwise highly participant Negro citizens discussed political matters with government officials less often than did White citizens of Metroville. The scores and position of the communities on a composite participation index clearly indicated more extensive citizen participation in Oretown and Petropolis than in Farmdale and Metroville.

We turn now to an examination of the distributions of political influence in the four communities. This will enable us to answer the second part of the aforementioned question: whether or not the differences in the pattern of decision-making conflicts between Farmdale and Metroville, on the one hand, and Oretown and Petropolis, on the other, resulted from differences in the distributions of citizen political influence between these sets of communities. We also will begin to answer the other questions posed at the end of Chapter 6: whether or not the greater representation of relatively disadvantaged groups in political decision-making in Oretown and Petropolis extended through the body politic to the citizens at large, or whether little Farmdale stood alone or with Oretown and Petropolis in the extent to which citizens of all social ranks participated in political decision-making during Time E to M.

POLITICAL-INFLUENCE STRUCTURES

Political-influence structures were constructed to range the citizens in each community sample from low to high according to the scores they received on an index of political influence. This index or structure was based on two probabilistic assumptions: first, if more people participate politically, they are more likely to exercise political influence; second, if political participants act in settings wherein other political participants are present, they are more likely to exercise political influence than political participants who act outside of such settings. The index of political-influence position was constructed, therefore, from composite measures of political participation and memberships in what we call subsidiary political organizations, voluntary associations in the community—including labor unions, but excluding self-identification as members of political parties—in which a specified proportion of the members themselves were active political participants in community affairs. Garden clubs, the PTA, and chambers of commerce are examples of such subsidiary political organizations.

Since the index of political influence largely depends on the distribution of political participation, it is not surprising to find, when the differences we have reported are considered, that the broadest distribution of political influence was in Oretown and Petropolis, and the narrowest in Farmdale and Metroville.

The index of political influence was so constructed that the completely nonparticipant, the "zeros," were in the lowest stratum, even though a few of these in each community were members of subsidiary political organizations. Those in the next stratum, with scores of one point, participated in one of the five specified ways but were not members of any subsidiary political organization. The participation of most of these consisted of discussing political affairs—for the most part occasionally—with friends.

Those in the two top strata, the "twos" and "threes," were political participants who belonged to subsidiary political organizations. Consideration of subsidiary political organizations changes the comparative citizen political participation picture to some extent. The high proportion of completely nonparticipant citizens in Farmdale and Metroville remains stable, but the proportion of Farmdale's citizens who are at the upper end of the political-influence structure is similar to the proportions in Oretown and particularly in Petropolis. A

TABLE 7-3 Political-Influence Structures

Political-Influence Score	Community or Subcommunity					
	Farm-dale	Ore-town	Petropolis		Metroville	
			White	Negro	White	Negro
(High)						
3	10%	14%	11%	14%	2%	1%
2	20	29	22	16	2	5
1	28	39	39	36	57	50
0	42	18	29	34	39	44
(Low)						
Totals %	100%	100%	101%	100%	100%	100%
N	(254)	(738)	(354)	(237)	(295)	(222)

comparison of citizen memberships in subsidiary political organizations indicates that Farmdale had almost as high a proportion as Oretown, and higher than any other community or subcommunity. For example, 15 per cent of the Farmdale sample belonged to two or more such organizations; only 3 per cent of Metroville's Negro sample belonged to two or more, and only 1 per cent of its White sample. There are two reasons for this: first, in Farmdale more citizens belonged to the voluntary-association network, which was more extensive than in any other city; and, second, there was a greater tendency for active political participants to be members of voluntary associations in Farmdale than in the other communities. Without attempting to answer the question at this point, we may note here that this may indicate that the *status quo* decisions made in Farmdale during Time E to M had the active approval of a greater segment of the city's population than, for example, in Metroville, given the scarcity of influentials there; this possibility was pointed out in the previous chapter. It would depend, in part, on the "representativeness" of this active influential segment of the citizenry.

ACTIVE INFLUENTIALS IN THE POLITICAL-INFLUENCE SUPERSTRUCTURE

Political Representation of Socio-Economic Categories

Many normative questions traditionally are discussed in relation to representativeness. Regardless of how one conceives of the structure of a political system, there are basic controversies about the appropriately "democratic" system of representation. This is a subject of concern not only to adherents of democracy; the writings of fascists and syndicalists, as well as Communist theorists, demonstrate a universal concern with representation.

Near the root of diverse value positions on the proper scheme of representation are assumptions about the schemes existing in American and foreign communities, and about the nature of current trends.[6] An empirical exploration of these assumptions and some of the related propositions would seem to be valuable for proponents of diverse value positions. We shall attempt to clarify some of the leading assumptions about political representation as it purportedly exists in the United States in order to make the purpose of the following analysis more lucid.

The first point we shall examine maintains that hierarchical political and socio-economic class structures are related closely. Regardless of how the strata or "classes" are defined in both structures, some observers see a decided overlapping, particularly at the top: those who are most powerful and those in the top economic and social position purportedly are often the same people.[7] Proponents of this view frequently adhere to the propositions that socio-economic position determines or radically shapes political interests, and that the political interests of the affluent ordinarily are served to a much greater degree than the interests of the impoverished or disadvantaged, because of the assumed overlap between high socio-economic and political positions. Men of wealth and power may control even elected officials on matters of real importance, because such officials either act as their agents through political influence or political status relationships or share their interests.

Although studies in the United States have demonstrated a relatively strong correlation between socio-economic position and political participation, some analysts reject this point of view. They interpret differential participation along socio-economic class lines as a reflection of different degrees of interest in politics.[8] Apathy due to inadequate education about politics is decried; but this does not mean that the upper strata will necessarily take advantage of the lower.[9] They argue that similar positions in socio-economic structures conceal divergent and often conflicting socio-economic interests. The interests of the absentee industrialist presumably are different from those of the Main Street merchant in the typical American city. Occupational groups of comparable social rank frequently have divergent interests; an interest-group politics, based on a multiplicity of interests which extend beyond the occupational, ensures discrepancies between the socio-economic and political structures. They argue further that since the socio-economic-political-structure relationship is not perfect, the nonaffluent, through a minority of their own people at the top of the political power structure, frequently prevent the political advancement of interests of the affluent men of power. Ordinarily, those of low social rank have enough power to counter the demands of those of higher social rank through organizations such as labor unions, through coalitions of disadvantaged groups, and through positive assistance from government, even in spite of active opposition by "vested" interests.

Proponents of this view represent the "pluralist" school of thought. They may stress the multiple, overlapping political-interest-group memberships that presumably create channels of connection, cooperation, and common political interests between people of lower and upper socio-economic status. Some stress the compatible proposition that the conflicting character of organizations to which people of similar socio-economic class belong creates intraclass political-interest conflicts. Basic to the pluralist position is the belief that, since elected officials need to be reelected by voters from all levels of the socio-economic structure, they will be inclined to resist demands from an "elite" that conflict with interests of those of lower status.[10]

If the top of the political structure numerically overrepresents upper-class people—some would argue that it is the middle classes of moderate interests who are most overrepresented—it also may be argued that people of upper-class backgrounds may represent the interests of the relatively underprivileged, the "common man." A Franklin Delano Roosevelt, a G. Mennen Williams, and even a Nelson Rockefeller may seem to be extreme examples, but they actually are sometimes viewed as evidence of a widespread practice of the wealthy and powerful representing marginal group interests. This would constitute a rejection of the proposition in the first view that socio-economic position determines or radically shapes political interests.

Both of the aforementioned viewpoints and their more complex and sophisticated variations would benefit from an empirical exploration of the actual state of representation. We shall do this by investigating the extent to which citizens of upper-class status are numerically overrepresented at the upper reaches of political-influence structures; the extent to which such overrepresentation, if it does exist, varies from community to community; and the extent to which numerical representation—that is, proportional, under-, and overrepresentation —affects the interests of particular socio-economic and racial groups in political decision-making, either personally or through people of different social backgrounds. In this last instance, we shall examine efforts to influence and the power accruing to those who effectively do influence outcomes; however, the investigation of this will not be completed until a later chapter, in which we describe the types of power structures in each community during Time E to M, since we are still dealing with political-influence relations and not with assessments of power, that is, effective influence in decision-making. Nor will the second item be covered completely in this section, since it must include the descriptions of the political leadership, the roles of elected officials, and the ideological perspectives of the leadership in each community.

Although we expect that in all four of our communities there was an overrepresentation of upper-class people at the top of the political-influence structure, we also expect to find variations in the degree of overrepresentation.[11] As Sidney Verba has said,

Comparative studies would greatly increase the precision of our explanations of political behavior. . . . . If, however, we could find different relationships between income and political activity in different societies, we might begin to isolate those variables in the political and social structure that intervene between class and political behavior.[12]

Verba points to Angus Campbell's and Stein Rokkan's findings that in Norway the relationship ordinarily found in the United States between occupation and participation in politics is reversed: workers and farmers are the most active and white-collar workers the least active. The opposite relationship almost invariably is found in American politics. We intend to use the four communities as Verba's "different societies"—the intercommunity variations, if any, in the degree of relationship between educational level, income, and occupation, on the one hand, and position in the political-influence structure on the other—to inquire more deeply into the dynamics of interaction between the socio-economic and political structures.

Before we test such hypotheses, one additional—and often overlooked—mode of analysis should be mentioned. When comparative research is being done, the question of political representation, as we use the term, needs to be approached in two distinct ways. In a single "case study" of a political system, one can compare the proportions of particular socio-economic categories in the highest strata of a political-influence structure with their proportions among the citizenry as a whole in order to estimate numerical representation. But when one is dealing with two or more political systems, one also must determine whether or not particular socio-economic categories are comparatively equally represented in the highest strata of their political-influence structures. One does not compare the citizens only within their own polities; one compares, besides, the citizens of one polity with the citizens of another. This additional mode of analysis is particularly appropriate if the socio-economic composition of the communities varies.[13]

We may best clarify this point with a hypothetical illustration. Suppose that in one community, 90 per cent of the working force had blue-collar jobs; in a second, an equally high percentage had white-collar occupations. Let us further suppose that *within* the first community, blue-collar workers were underrepresented in the top stratum of the political-influence structure: only 80 per cent of those who were politically influential were blue-collar workers. In the second community, one could conceivably find an overrepresentation of blue-collar workers: 20 per cent were influential in politics, compared to a 10 per cent proportion of the entire citizenry.

Even though in this illustration the blue-collar workers are under-represented in the political-influence superstructure in the first community, compared to their proportion in that body politic, four out of five of them are among the most influential citizens, compared to only one out of five in the second community although there blue-collar workers are overrepresented. It would seem that in order to understand differences between these two political systems and the political roles of blue- and white-collar people, the most important datum is the comparative, cross-community difference in proportion of labor and white-collar representation in the political-influence superstructures, rather than internal, within-the-community data on the political-structure representation of different socio-economic categories. The knowledge that in one community a particular socio-economic category tends to be overrepresented at the top of the political influence structure compared to the same category in another community indicates important aspects of the character and functioning of political systems. In addition the knowledge that such socio-economic categories in one community constitute greater or lesser proportions of the top political stratum than in other communities provides even more information about the functioning of political systems.[14]

Testing Two Numerical-Representation Hypotheses

We call those citizens in the top stratum of the political-influence structure in each community the *active influentials*. They received scores of three points on the index of political influence. These three political-influence points were based on their reports that during the previous year they had discussed local politics at least occasionally with friends—most of the active influentials, it so happened, also reported such discussions with local government officials, civic leaders, or both—and that they had attended a meeting at which a community policy matter was a major subject of discussion, that they had taken an activist role in one or more local issue, or both. In addition, they reported that they belonged to at least one organization in the community that the subsequent analysis revealed to be a subsidiary political organization, since at least 10 per cent of its members were in the particular random sample credited with three or four of a possible four points on an index of political participation. Thus, the active influentials not only were active political participants, but they also were members of subsidiary political organizations. Theoretically, their political participation was more likely to be politically influential than the participation of those outside such political organizations. We shall test the hypotheses about numerical representation of socio-economic categories in the political-influence superstructure by examining such representation at the active-influential level of the political-influence structure.

If the structure of political influence follows socio-economic lines in the four communities, those of high socio-economic status would be overrepresented, relative to their proportions in each community, among the active influentials. To put this in the form of two hypotheses:

Hypothesis 1: Upper class socio-economic characteristics are proportionately represented—that is, not proportionately overrepresented—among active influentials in these communities.

Hypothesis 2: The degree to which upper-class characteristics are overrepresented among active influentials will not vary from community to community.

If Hypothesis 1 is rejected, there is evidence for the overlapping of the socio-economic and political-influence structures (but not for the proposition that communities overlap in their socio-economic and political-*power* structures). If Hypothesis 2 is rejected, the different degrees of overlapping between the socio-economic and political-influence structures need explanation. We expect Hypothesis 1 to be rejected; but if it is not, Hypothesis 2 becomes irrelevant and the proposition that the political interests of the advantaged are ordinarily advanced to a much greater degree than the interests of the disadvantaged, because of the assumed overlap between high socio-economic and political positions, would have to be reformulated or rejected. We expect Hypothesis 2 to be rejected also, thereby requiring at least modification of such notions. A more specific, directional form of the second hypothesis, which we expect to be unable to reject, is as follows:

Hypothesis 2A: Citizens of upper-class socio-economic status were numerically better represented among the active influentials of Farmdale and Metroville than among the active influentials of Oretown and Petropolis, although they were slightly but visibly overrepresented in the latter cities.

According to the findings presented in Table 7-4, Hypothesis 1 can be rejected for three of the four communities, but not for Oretown. In Oretown the highly educated, middle- and upper-income groups were overrepresented slightly in the ranks of the active influentials, but so were blue-collar workers. In Farmdale, there was a greater

TABLE 7-4 Percentage Deviations of Selected Characteristics of Active Influentials from Community Samples

Characteristic— Deviation from Sample	Farmdale (N = 25)	Oretown (N = 102)	Petropolis Whites (N = 37)	Petropolis Negroes (N = 33)	Metroville Whites (N = 5)	Metroville Negroes (N = 2)
Occupation						
Managerial-						
Professional-						
Proprietorial	+16	−1	+22	+22	+26	+44
Blue Collar	+5	+5	−15	−13	−34	−3
Housewives	−19	−10	−6	−10	−14	−15
Farmers	+10	—	—	—	—	—
Income						
Over $10,000	+3	+3	+18	+11	+51	0
$4,000–$9,000	+8	+9	+12	+24	−23	+85
Under $4,000	−11	−12	−30	−25	−28	−85
Education						
College	+28	+10	+25	+30	+76	+39
Two to four years high school	−13	−5	−5	+8	−43	+24
Less than two years high school	−15	−5	−20	−38	−33	−63

overrepresentation of the highly educated and much more overrepresentation of business executives and proprietors. This brings us to Hypothesis 2, which, as expected, also can be rejected. The more advantaged segments of Farmdale were better represented at the active-influential level of the political influence structure than in Oretown; but this was even more the case with Petropolis and Metroville.

Among Metroville's White active influentials, blue-collar workers were most underrepresented. The small managerial sector of Metroville's Negro subcommunity was represented by one of the two active influentials; the very large segment of low income and poorly educated people were not represented at all at that political-influence structure level. The managerial, professional, and proprietorial sectors of Petropolis' White and Negro subcommunities were overrepresented; blue-collar workers were more underrepresented than in Farmdale. The lowest income groups were as underrepresented as they were among Metroville's high-income White active influentials. The poorly educated also were underrepresented more than their counterparts in either Western city, particularly among Petropolis' Negro active influentials.

To summarize, the middle and upper classes generally were overrepresented and the lower classes underrepresented among active influentials. The differences in representation were most sharply defined in the Southern cities, particularly Metroville, and least sharply defined in Oretown. Therefore, Hypothesis 2*A* must be partially rejected because of the exception to the expected socio-economic–active-influential relationship in Oretown, and because there was a stronger overrepresentation among active influentials of the advantaged in both racial subcommunities of Petropolis than in Farmdale.

The Negro subcommunity itself may be viewed as a disadvantaged subcommunity, compared to its White counterparts in the two Southern cities. Assuming that each city had a single political-influence structure, the findings reported in Table 7-3 indicate that Negro citizens were represented proportionately at the active-influential level of their political-influence structures. In fact, they were overrepresented slightly in Petropolis, and the difference in Metroville, where there were relatively few active influentials, was negligible.

We should note in passing that in every community and subcommunity, housewives, another traditionally if not legally disadvantaged group in politics, were underrepresented among the active influentials; but the degree of underrepresentation was not as great as it was for the lowest-income category in five of the six samples. Actually, women in every sample were even more underrepresented among active influentials than housewives. It was the working women, particularly those in clerical and other white-collar positions, who were the most underrepresented of the female occupational categories in every one of the political-influence superstructures.[15] We also should note that in Farmdale, the only community with as much as 10 per cent of the working force in farming occupations, farmers were overrepresented among the active influentials. In fact, they had twice the representation at the active-influential level that they would have had if they had been represented according to their proportion in the community—that is, 20 to 10 per cent.

We now shall turn to the second method of examining and comparing the socio-economic characteristics of these sets of active influentials. The difference in the two modes of analysis can be illustrated easily by two examples. Housewives were as underrepresented among active influentials in the Negro subcommunity of Petropolis and Metroville as they were in the White subcommunity of those cities (Table 7-4). However, the proportion of Negro women who were housewives was about half of the comparable proportion among White women because so many Negro women worked, particularly as domestic servants. Therefore, housewives comprised less than 10 per cent of the entire active influential strata in the Negro political-influence structures of Petropolis and Metroville, compared to one-third and one-fifth of the active influentials in the White subcommunities (Table 7-5).

Blue-collar workers were underrepresented about equally in the Negro and White political-influence superstructures of Petropolis, relative to their proportions in their respective subcommunities (Table 7-4); but, because a much larger proportion of citizens were blue-collar workers in the Negro subcommunity than in the White subcommunity, the Negro active influentials were much more a blue-collar group than the White active influentials. It already has been noted that there was a stronger overrepresentation of the advantaged

TABLE 7-5   Distributions of Selected Characteristics of the Six Sets of Active Influentials *

| | | | Community or Subcommunity | | | |
| | | | Petropolis | | Metroville | |
Characteristic	Farmdale (N = 25)	Oretown (N = 102)	Whites (N = 38)	Negroes (N = 33)	Whites (N = 5)	Negroes (N = 2)
Education						
College	44%	23%	58%	42%	100%	50%
Two to four years high school	28%	42%	29%	34%	0	50%
Less than two years high school	28%	35%	13%	24%	0	0
Income						
Over $10,000	8%	7%	32%	13%	60%	0
Under $4,000	44%	31%	3%	38%	0	0
Occupation						
Managerial-Professional-Proprietorial	28%	10%	42%	30%	40%	50%
Blue Collar	32%	46%	13%	48%	0	50%
Housewives	24%	29%	32%	9%	20%	0
Farmers	20%	—	—	—	—	—
Age						
Over 55 years	28%	22%	16%	24%	20%	0
Under 35 years	44%	25%	32%	42%	20%	0
Length of Residence						
Less than 10 yrs.	46%	67%	18%	22%	20%	0
Party Identification						
Democratic	40%	55%	58%	71%	0	100%
Republican	56%	36%	13%	6%	40%	0
Independent	4%	7%	26%	16%	60%	0
None	0	2%	3%	6%	0	0

* In a few cases respondents did not provide the information requested, so that the percentages may be calculated on slightly different numbers of active influentials than their numbers (in parentheses) in the samples.

among the active influentials of Petropolis, including the Negro subcommunity, than in Farmdale. This second mode of analysis indicates that among Petropolis' Negro active influentials were proportionately more blue-collar workers than among Farmdale's active influentials, thereby qualifying or modifying the implications of the earlier comparison.

When the socio-economic characteristics of the six sets of active influentials are compared, we find that Metroville's White active influentials were the most "upper class." There was no blue-collar or low-income representation at all; and all five of Metroville's White active influentials in this sample were college-educated people. The two Negro active influentials of Metroville had moderate incomes; one was college-educated, the other had finished high school; one was engaged in a prestigious occupation, the other was a blue-collar worker. Compared to the Negro subcommunity as a whole, these Negro active influentials were relatively upper class; but compared to the White active influentials of Metroville, they were of considerably lower social rank.

Petropolis' White active influentials clearly were next to Metroville's White active influentials in terms of social-class characteristics. Those in Petropolis differed from those in Metroville in that there was some blue-collar-worker representation; their wealth and formal education were more modest, but they were a more upper-class set of people than those in any other sample's category of active influentials. The Negro active influentials of Petropolis resembled their Negro counterparts in Metroville and the active influentials of Oretown in that there was a heavy blue-collar representation in their ranks. On the other hand, the ratio of blue-collar to managerial-professional-proprietorial people resembled the ratio in Farmdale. In fact, the income and educational characteristics of Petropolis' Negro active influentials was similar, in general, to those of the active influentials in Farmdale. Both were of considerably lower socio-economic rank than the White active influentials of Petropolis, who in turn, as we have noted, were of lower rank than the White active influentials of Metroville. Oretown's active influentials were the most working class in character; they had relatively moderate or low educational levels, and moderate or low incomes. The ratios of blue-collar to top business and professional occupations among active influentials ranged downwards from 4.6:1 in Oretown to 1.8:1 in Petropolis' Negro subcommunity, 1.6:1 in Farmdale, and 1:1 in Metroville's Negro subcommunity, and reversed to a 1:3.2 ratio in Petropolis' White subcommunity, and finally to the completely nonblue-collar White active influentials of Metroville.

Several other characteristics of active influentials were of some theoretical significance to the functioning and stability of these political systems.[16] The active influentials in every sample were predominantly middle-aged, except in Farmdale and Petropolis' Negro subcommunity (Table 7-5). In these two samples, the younger adults, people under 35 years of age, were the largest single category, although in both samples there were more middle-aged and older active influentials. In both Farmdale and Oretown, the majority of the adult citizens had moved there during and after the boom years of the Second World War. Although these "newcomers" were underrepresented numerically among the active influentials, the proportion of newcomers among the active influentials in both Farmdale and Oretown was much higher than in any other community. Two-thirds of the active influentials of Oretown and almost half of those in Farmdale were newcomers. Only in the Negro subcommunity of Petropolis were newcomers overrepresented, compared to the citizens at large in that subcommunity; but the proportion of newcomers to oldtimers there was about one to four, comparable to the ratio among the White active influentials of both Petropolis and Metroville. The Negro active influentials of Petropolis were much younger and more of a newcomer category than were the Negro active influentials of Metroville; the latter were middle-aged "old-timers."

The party identification of the active influentials also varied in an interesting way (Table 7-5). The proportions of self-identified Democrats, Republicans, and Independents were similar for the citizens at large in the two pairs of communities; for the two slightly Democratic Western cities and for the two predominantly Democratic cities in one-party Southern State. But the Democrats were underrepresented and in the minority of active influentials in Farmdale, whereas they were proportionately represented and in the majority in Oretown. In both Negro subcommunities, Democrats predominated among the active influentials; a very large proportion of Negro citizens in Metroville had no partisan identifications—even "independent" —and were not represented at the active influential level. The two active influentials were both Democrats. In the White subcommunity of Petropolis, a majority of the active influentials were Democrats; there were a few Republicans and a substantial number of Independents. In equally Democratic Metroville there were no Democrats, a large number—in fact, a majority—of Independents, and a sizable minority, 40 per cent, of Republicans. We shall examine the place of local party organizations in the structures of political influence and political power later. For the moment we shall treat partisanship as a factor that may have shaped political interests and political decision-making, particularly among the active influentials in the political-influence structure, from Time E to M.

A Partial but Insufficient Explanation

It is tempting to construct from the foregoing findings an explanation for the differences in the patterns of decision-making representation, conflict, and outcomes between Oretown and Petropolis on the one hand, and Farmdale and Metroville on the other. Such an explanation might be based on the degree to which the socio-economic and political-influence structures of these communities overlap; the degree to which the socio-economic composition of their political-influence structures varies because of differences in overlap and differences in their socio-economic structures, or both. The explanation would be parsimonious, assuming that variations in political decision-making result substantially from political interests which, in turn, result from socio-economic position.

Critical portions of both the viewpoints we have mentioned about the extent to which the political is a function of the socio-economic would be incorporated. Those of the first viewpoint would be correct insofar as some communities resembled what they regard as *the* pattern in American communities: political decision-making is done quietly by and in the interests of the socio-economic "dominants" in the community. Those of the second viewpoint would be correct insofar as some other communities had more substantial minorities of disadvantaged groups personally represented in the political-influence superstructure with enough power to veto and occasionally thwart the demands of the advantaged and, at times, advance the political interests of the disadvantaged in conflicting political decision-making. The latter's more complex arguments, that those of high socio-economic positions have divergent political interests or that some represent the political interests of disadvantaged groups, would not have to be considered.

Such an explanation would not be concerned with what caused variations in the degree to which particular socio-economic categories were represented in the political-influence superstructures. It would take such variations for granted and attempt to explain, thereby, variations in political decision-making patterns. It might start by pointing to Oretown and Metroville as communities which had active influentials at the opposite ends of a socio-economic scale; even the Negro active influentials of Metroville were of higher economic class status than the active influentials of Oretown. This contrast is compatible with the contrast between the open, intense conflict in political decision-making during Time E to M in Oretown and the more restricted, less open decision-making conflicts in Metroville. In Oretown the disadvantaged groups were personally represented in decision-making; in Metroville such disadvantaged groups as White labor and Negroes either were frustrated by decisional outcomes or were inactive. The failure of downtown merchants to gain favorable decisional outcomes in Metroville, in contrast to the success of their Oretown counterparts, also is understandable, since there was a greater proportion of such merchants among Oretown's active influentials. Actually, none of Metroville's active influentials—not even the husbands of the two White housewives or the Negro active influentials— had a proprietorial occupation; they were all industrial executives, financiers, or professional men.

The major difficulties with such an interpretation come from findings on the socio-economic characteristics of Farmdale's and Petropolis' active influentials. Farmdale resembled Metroville in some aspects of political decision-making during Time E to M; Petropolis resembled Oretown. Yet the socio-economic composition of Farmdale's active influentials resembled that of Petropolis' Negro subcommunity and Oretown more than it did that of Metroville. Petropolis' White active influentials resembled the White active influentials in Metroville more than they did those of Oretown.

The explanation could be advanced that Petropolis' Negro active influentials played the same sorts of conflict-producing roles in decision-making that labor-union officials and activists among blue-collar workers in the active-influential category played in Oretown's politics. The Negro active influentials in Petropolis not only were substantially blue-collar workers, but they also had low incomes and were a relatively young group of people. Such characteristics, along with the marginal racial status of the Negro active influentials, may have produced the same sorts of militancy that were found in Oretown among both organized labor and marginal merchants from the Longacre business district.

In Farmdale, so this explanation might continue, the more advantaged businessmen were low-income proprietors who feared the competition that might come with new industry and community growth and who actively approved and contributed to the *status quo* outcome of the decisions made during Time E to M. That such a large proportion of the active influentials there were young blue-collar workers is more difficult to reconcile with organized labor's apparent lack of participation in political decision-making during that period. This apparent anomaly might be explained partially by the fact that more than half of the blue-collar workers who lived in Farmdale held jobs in cities other than Farmdale. This was not the case in other cities. Farmdale served as an outlet for their personal participation in community political affairs, but—and this was actually the case—they did not actively participate as representatives of organized labor.[17]

In small Farmdale an atmosphere of conformity may have stifled "natural" political interests of groups such as organized labor, so that these interests were not expressed through self-identified representatives of labor as a political interest group. Furthermore, the heterogeneous socio-economic backgrounds of the active influentials may have operated in a town-meeting type of decision-making, so that the comparatively large proportion of Farmdale's citizens who were at the bottom of the political-influence structure felt that their political interests were being looked after by their active influential friends and neighbors. This possibility was suggested in the preceding chapter.

The trouble with the foregoing explanation is that it is no longer as simple as it purports to be. Moreover, it conflicts with certain other crucial empirical findings. *Post facto* explanations are suspect both because they develop rationales for unexpected findings that remain untested by further research and because data to test assumptions that may underly such rationales sometimes disconfirm them. Let us explore such explanatory difficulties as they relate to our four communities.

As we already have indicated, many of Farmdale's blue-collar workers were employed and belonged to organized labor in other cities. We also found that a city councilman actually served as the spokesman for generally lower-class people from the "wrong" side of the tracks. But further analysis suggests that one of the crucial assumptions that "explains" the unexpected relationship between the socio-economic characteristics of active influentials and the patterns of decision-making in Farmdale is not valid. This assumption was that the active influentials, or a major segment of them, were participating *en masse* in making political decisions during Time E to M. Analysis of what policy matters the active influentials reported discussing and in what matters they took an active part reveals that the assumption is wrong in two respects. First of all, a much smaller proportion of active influentials in Farmdale than in any other community reported that they had actively participated in or discussed any of the political decisional processes extant during Time E to M. Instead, with few notable exceptions, they reported that they were concerned with the scope of local government in "general terms"—gossip about their local officials, or "inside dope" on personalities. Thus the assumption is erroneous that decisional outcomes emerged as a result of the participation in decision-making of a broadly representative set of active influentials. Second, the policy matters that were reported as subjects of discussion or more active efforts by the active influentials were generally matters of specific improvements, of an administrative rather than a political character.

Such housekeeping-service improvements as the paving of a particular street constituted the major subjects of political concern on the part of the active influentials. Some of the active influentials living on particular streets reported signing joint petitions with neighbors to obtain street improvements, but few participated in demands for expanding the general street and sidewalk paving and repair program, which were the subject of political decision-making during Time E to M. Such demands for improvements indicated dissatisfaction with particular aspects of the current scope of local government, although ordinarily they were not demands for general program changes to increase that scope. Certainly most of Farmdale's active influentials did not concur in the negative outcome of that decisional process, as the town-meeting image might suggest. The minority of active influentials who did concur, and how they concurred, will be discussed later.

The reason we have advanced to explain why Petropolis, whose affluent White active influentials resembled their affluent fellow Whites in Metroville more than they did the active influentials of Oretown, was more like Oretown than Metroville in having a conflict-ridden politics cannot be accepted without question. It has been suggested that the disadvantaged Negro active influentials, of whom a large proportion were blue-collar workers, generated conflict as did the less advantaged among Oretown's active influentials. Petropolis had a conflicting racial politics during Time E to M. However, the racial issues did not find Whites on one side and Negroes on the other; nor were the conflicts only racial in character. The blue-collar Negroes were not the spearhead of the militant Negro political force, even though they were important to that force. White organized labor was prominently aligned with the Negro political grouping. If Oretown's, or even Farmdale's, proportion of blue-collar workers among active influentials is taken as a standard, White blue-collar workers clearly are represented less well among White active influentials in Petropolis than their prominence and contributions to a conflicting political process might have suggested.

There are other reasons that this explanation fails. The description of Farmdale's blue-collar workers, in which we say that they did not act politically *as* blue-collar workers or as representatives of organized labor but as citizens of the community, departs from the postulated simple socio-economic, political-interest–political-action relationships. Introducing the small size of Farmdale as a factor to explain the absence of upsetting, anti-*status quo* political interests among active influentials of heterogeneous socio-economic characteristics is a comparable deviation from the argument. Apart from the empirical finding that open political conflict in decision-making also was absent in Metroville, the largest of the four communities, such factors as city size introduce dimensions that the presumably parsimonious, simple explanation would not need if it were valid as is.

Reasoning such as the following, however correct it may be, also goes beyond the bounds of the simple explanation. It might be supposed that Negroes were more satisfied politically in Metroville than in Petropolis. This might have resulted, for example, from the decision to initiate school desegregation in Metroville. The presumed greater satisfaction in Metroville's Negro subcommunity then might have led to less political participation and, hence, to less open political decision-making conflict in Metroville than in Petropolis. The implicit assumption that the subordinate Negro subcommunities shared common political interests would be consistent with the simple explanation. However, the assumed differences in the satisfaction of such interests which might have led to differences in conflict-producing political demands are a more complex proposition; therefore, the explanation that similarities and differences in the socio-economic and racial composition of political superstructures produce similarities and differences in patterns of political decision-making is too simple.

The simple explanation that political interests result from the socio-economic positions of active influentials and that variations in the former result from variations in the latter from community to community is partially true, but it is inadequate. Its inadequacy leads us to the next question: whether or not particular socio-economic and racial categories did have comparable political interests from community to community, and whether or not such political interests were represented by active influentials who were members of other categories.[18] We shall begin to answer that question in the next section by describing specific interests or perspectives of the several sets of active influentials. The interests or perspectives of active influentials some-times are different from those of citizens who are lower in the struc-tures of political influence, and, more importantly, they sometimes differ from community to community.

Perspectives of Active Influentials

Although data on the decisional perspectives and political interests of the active influentials are neither comprehensive nor rigorously comparative from city to city, there is some value in trying to describe and compare such orientations as much as is possible.

Farmdale

The matters of special interest in Farmdale include the extent to which the active influentials, particularly the merchants and blue-collar workers, indicated political interest in economic reorganization. If such interests existed, were they consistent with decisions during Time *E* to *M* to resist more active governmental intervention in the local economy? Were the political interests of active influentials in accord with the outcomes by Time *M* that decided that local govern-ment would not initiate or expand civic improvement programs, ex-cept in two minor matters, in Farmdale?

If we assume that political interests exist to the extent that in-dividuals consider the maintenance of, or shifts in, the scope of local government sufficiently relevant to their welfare that they discuss it with family, friends, government officials, or civic leaders, the re-sponses to what local government or community matters the active influentials reported discussing in such settings answer these ques-tions. In the matter of civic improvement, we find that almost 85 per cent of the active influentials in Farmdale reported that they had discussed one or another item of civic improvement in one or more of these settings. Even 15 per cent of the citizens in the intermediate strata of the political influence structure—between the active influen-tials and the completely nonparticipant "zeros"—reported that they discussed such matters. The bulk of the civic improvement items were in the housekeeping-service subcategory. More than half the active influentials expressed either a general dissatisfaction with the condi-tion of their streets, roads, sewers, or other public works or a specific complaint about a particular street, road, or sewer condition. It would seem reasonable to assume that such complaints indicated po-litical interests that constituted predispositions in favor of some action by the local government to improve housekeeping services, rather than positive satisfaction with such aspects of the scope of local government.

Although such general or particular political interests, with a few exceptions, did not become concrete policy formulations and political demands in political decision-making processes, the political interests of Farmdale's active influentials were not unanimously consistent with the patterns of the civic-improvement political decisions during Time E to M. Four of the twenty-five active influentials in the sample apparently did have *status quo* political interests. Two were proprietors, one was a farmer, and one was an attorney. All four were affluent and sanguine about their own economic prospects. They were active participants in political decision-making in opposition to the one active influential who demanded a reallocation of local-government resources to improve streets and sidewalks in the poorer section of town, one of the political decision-making processes taking place during Time E to M. The one active influential who took an active part in trying to get the municipal water supply expanded was outnumbered by these same four active influentials.

Although none of the citizens in the sample below the active-influential level reported discussing matters of community planning and guided development, four active influentials had discussed the need to improve such local-government functions. For example, one active influential was concerned with whether or not the nearby river was being polluted by the major mining operation in Farmdale. The four active influentials with *status quo* political interests were opposed to adjusting the current scope of local government in this matter. When these men were informed of the decision of a few civic leaders to approve the state plan to build a new highway bypassing Farmdale, a decision that was revealed in confidence to only a few of Farmdale's citizens, they approved wholeheartedly.

The most active proponent of the establishment of a municipal park-and-recreation program happened to be included in the random sample and was one of the active influentials. His decisional preferences accorded with those of two other active influentials who apparently considered Farmdale's recreational opportunities inadequate; however, they did not participate in bringing pressure to bear behind this political demand. This illustrates the existence of prorecreational political interests among the active influentials, rather than political interests that consensually were opposed to shifts in this aspect of local government's functioning.

That there was a division of political interests on this matter, as on matters of civic improvement, is attested by the opposition of the same four affluent active influentials. The complete absence of discussion and apparent lack of political interest among citizens below the level of the active influential is evidence not that the two negative outcomes in political decision-making resulted from the preferences of the citizens at large, but rather of their disinterest. At the active-influential level some political interests clearly were frustrated; those of others were satisfied.

On the question of the active influentials' political interests in their local government's role in the local economy, we find that, with but two exceptions, apparently none of the active influentials—marginal or more affluent merchants, miners or other manual workers, farmers or housewives—had any political preferences. Certainly some of the active influentials had economic or business problems; but they did not see that these had political relevance. Apparently they saw these interests as private economic interests rather than as personal or group political interests.

The exceptions were important in this connection. One active influential had taken an active part in defeating demands that, with or without the assistance of local government, a chamber of commerce be established to facilitate the attraction of new industry to Farmdale. This man was a merchant and one of the four pro-*status quo* active influentials. He reported that he had discussed the need to improve "the publicity of the city"—the public image of the city as a good place to shop—and thereby stimulate retail trade without changing the scope of either local government or the private-association network in the community. The other exception was an active influential who participated unsuccessfully in decision-making to provide additional street lighting for the central business district. He also was a merchant, but his political interests obviously diverged from those of the other merchant. Neither of them was able to say that his position reflected the current political interests of the mercantile sector, as far as we can determine from the analysis of the content of political discussion.

If the active influentials had discussed the local tax rate extensively, a case might be made that the pattern of *status quo* decisional outcomes reflected a taxpayer interest in keeping the costs of local government at a minimum. A sizable number of citizens lower in the political-influence structure, 15 per cent in fact, did report that they had discussed the local tax situation. However, only one of the twenty-five active influentials in this sample reported that local taxes were a significant subject of discussion. If those interested in keeping taxes minimal were pleased by the outcomes of the decisions made in Farmdale during Time E to M, it apparently was not because they were represented by a sizable segment of active influentials who were similarly concerned with the tax level. It also might be supposed that the substantial minority of farmers among Farmdale's active influentials—that is, 20 per cent—had opposed municipal programs of civic improvement and industrial expansion which they considered unnecessarily costly and, in fact, unnecessary. However, except for the one *status quo* farmer, none of the active-influential farmers assumed such a position in his reported discussions. In fact, the others reportedly had discussed the need for improved housekeeping services and miscellaneous rural improvements.

To summarize, the minority of active influentials opposed to civic-improvement shifts in the scope of local government saw their interests prevail in political decision-making, over and against a more substantial number of active influentials whose political interests seemed to predispose them favorably toward such civic-improvement programs.[19] A comparable minority of *status quo* active influentials successfully pursued policies designed to resist shifts in the role of local government in the economic life of the community, not over the opposition of other political interests, but rather in the face of apparent disinterest in such matters on the part of most active influentials. Apparently neither business nor organized labor were interested in such matters. This political disinterest, the nonparticipation of many of the pro-civic improvement active influentials in the political decision-making processes whose outcomes favored anti-civic improvement interests, the roles of the four *status quo* active influentials in political decision-making, and the general pattern of hold-the-line decisional outcomes in Farmdale during Time E to M will be explored further when the organization of the political superstructure is analyzed more fully.

Oretown

The respondents in Oretown were not asked what matters they had been discussing, as were the respondents in Farmdale. Instead, the political interests and perspectives of Oretown's citizens and, therefore, of the active influentials, were inferred from responses to a series of attitudinal questions about various aspects of their community—for example, electric-power and light services, and street construction and maintenance—and about various aspects of their political system, such as the responsiveness of their city officials. Their attitudes also were inferred from questions about their behavior in making such political decisions as the one concerning the community hospital and in regard to such matters as whether they were customers of the private or municipal electric-power company.

Turning to political interests in regard to economic reorganization, we may ask if active influentials, or particular socio-economic categories of active influentials, were more pessimistic about economic or employment opportunities than the citizens at large or particular socio-economic categories of citizens. Although this would not be, for example, evidence of political interests in favor of local-government efforts to attract industry to Oretown, it can be assumed that such interests would be less likely if citizens were content with the present economic situation. If working-class citizens with low incomes were dissatisfied with the economic opportunities, would this be reflected in the perspectives of their counterparts at the active-influential level? If the answers are affirmative in both cases, did organized labor, in all strata of the political-influence structure, resent the fact that the French administration did less and less to bring new industry to Oretown as Time M approached? This is a rhetorical question, since the answers to the prior questions were not affirmative.

We found that only a handful—3 per cent—of citizens and of the active influentials rated economic opportunity as "poor." Fewer than one in five citizens and an identical proportion of active influentials assessed economic opportunity as either "not very good" or "poor." There was no correlation at all between level of income or occupation and evaluation of the condition of the local economy. Apparently neither the active influential members of organized labor nor the merchants of Main Street or the Longacre district represented political interests that demanded local-government action to improve poor economic conditions. Nor was political interest for or against municipal electric power organized along such socio-economic-group lines at the active-influential level.

The active influentials were relatively more pro-municipal power than were the citizens as a whole, assuming that taking one's service from one or the other utility was an index of such attitudes: half the active influentials, but only one-third of the citizens at large, were customers of the municipal utility. However, there was absolutely no relationship between occupation of the active influentials and the company from which they took their electric service. What had seemed to be, during the Lovegren administration, a fight between public and private power, the major protagonists being organized labor and merchants from Longacre on one side and merchants from Main Street and the industrialists on the other, had become by Time *M* a more complex socio-economic political-interest alignment. The stalemate in political decision-making in this controversy can be explained partly by this balance of municipal- and private-power sentiments among the active influentials; but it also resulted from satisfaction with the improved service and low rates that emerged from the "unnatural" competition between these natural monopolies.

A cleavage of interests still existed between the blue- and white-collar citizens: blue-collar workers demonstrated greater dissatisfaction with street construction and maintenance than did white-collar workers, as did blue-collar active influentials. This dissatisfaction obviously was related to the residential areas in which blue-collar workers lived: the newer areas of town and the fringe areas, where there were few or minimal municipal services. Former Mayor Lovegren, his associates in the labor movement, and his political allies in Longacre—the most recently annexed area wherein such facilities as streets, sidewalks, and street lights were less adequate than in the sections of town where the more affluent business and professional men lived—continued to deal with such inadequacies as socio-economic interest-group demands. They represented themselves as the spokesmen for organized labor and the "common man," hoping to capitalize on the feelings of mistrust between labor, on the one hand, and management and the more affluent downtown merchants, on the other.[20] Mayor French's administration was trying to develop programs for the "whole community" and not for particular sections of town or socio-economic categories; he had to contend not only with the distrust of some of those downtown merchants and the industrial executives who disliked his earlier policies, which they labeled anti-industrialist, anti-private power, and New Dealish, but also with the suspicions of blue-collar workers that their political interests were endangered by his opposition to the Lovegren political forces.

Such political perspectives were observed in response to items intended to measure political cynicism, trust, and distance of citizens from their local-government officials. The respondents in every sample, except for Farmdale, were asked if they felt that their city officials were responsive "pretty much" to the wishes of "the citizens" or of "the more influential people," or if they "do not pay much attention to what the people want but tend to do what they themselves think best." Selection of either of the latter choices was treated as evidence of political cynicism; selection of the first item, "the citizens," was treated as an indication of political trust. Respondents who could not answer the question because they did not know were classified as politically distant.

The active influentials as a category were much less distant from city officials than were the citizens lower in the political-influence structure. About one out of twenty active influentials, compared to one out of five citizens of lower political-influence rank, were politically distant. The active influentials also were considerably more cynical about politics than were the citizens of lower political-influence rank. However, when the white-collar active influentials were compared to the blue-collar active influentials, we found that blue-collar active influentials were both slightly more cynical and considerably more distant. The French administration's efforts to develop community harmony and political consensus on the basis of common interests—"the public interest"—had not eliminated political suspicion and mistrust; this particularly was true of the working-class citizens of the community, but it also was true of some businessmen. These perspectives constituted at least predispositions to assess political interests as distinct and "uncommon."

When those same data are analyzed further, we find that active-influential blue-collar workers indeed were concentrated in the fringe areas adjacent to, but outside of, the city. The blue-collar workers inside the city were less distant from, but more cynical about, their city officials than were the blue-collar workers in the fringe areas. Opposition by fringe-area residents to annexation already had been a factor in the political decision of the city officials not to annex a large problem-ridden area. We shall have occasion in a later chapter to describe something of the political interests and increasing cynicism among fringe-area residents, of varying occupations and social levels, as city officials renewed their efforts to annex an additional area to the city several years after Time M.

Petropolis and Metroville

Information on the political perspectives of the active influentials in the two Southern cities and their subcommunities is more adequate than it was for Oretown; but certain information about Petropolis' Negro subcommunity is lacking. Respondents in the several samples at Time M were asked what they considered to be "the most important issues, problems, or projects facing [their community] at the present time"; they also were given forced-choice attitudinal questions about selected political matters.

We first shall use an optimist-pessimist ratio in describing and comparing attitudes toward economic conditions in Petropolis and Metroville. Optimists were those who evaluated economic opportunity in their community as "very good"; pessimists were those who rated it as "not very good." The ratio of optimists to pessimists among the White active influentials of Petropolis was 1:2; among Negro active influentials it was 1:6. Both of the Negro active influentials of Metroville were pessimists; the White active influentials were neither pessimists nor optimists; they apparently were "satisfied," since they rated economic opportunity as "good." Compared to Oretown's active influentials, among whom optimists outnumbered pessimists by a 2:1 ratio, the active influentials in Petropolis evaluated their local economies much more pessimistically. If such pessimism were conducive to the development of political interests that supported shifts in the scope of local government to improve economic conditions, these findings would help to account not only for the apparently consensual transition in Oretown from political to administrative decision-making in regard to industry-acquiring activities of the city government, but also for the almost entirely consistent set of decisional outcomes in Petropolis which satisfied political interests that were in favor of local government's efforts to improve the economic base and to stimulate, or not interfere with, retail business in the city.

The difference in the degree to which the White active influentials of Petropolis and Metroville were optimistic about their local economies is empirically associated with the fact that merchants were not represented personally at that level in Metroville, and so heavily in Petropolis. Data were lacking for comparison of the political interests of merchants among the active influentials of Farmdale and Oretown; but the absence of merchants among the White active influentials of Metroville, compared to the small but proportional representation in Petropolis' active influentials, conceivably might have contributed to one of the differences, during Time E to M, in the patterns of political decision-making in the two communities. This possibility rests on the assumption that merchants, in general, would tend to have stronger political interests in increasing or maintaining local government's role in stimulating the local economy than would industrial executives. Industrialists might tend to oppose the attraction of new industry because of expectations that this would create unnecessary and undesirable competition for labor. Such an assumption also underlies an explanation that the demands made by individual White merchants in Metroville for shifts in the scope of local government to revitalize the local economy were frustrated to a greater degree than in Petropolis because there was more personal representation by merchants at the active-influential level in Petropolis than in Metroville.

Fortunately, we may investigate rather than assume that merchants, but not industrialists, had political interests such as the following: stimulation by local government of business, through such policies as central-business-district redevelopment; relaxation of parking restrictions and traffic regulations; and attraction of new industrial payrolls. One possibility to be examined is that these interests actually were represented by the White active-influential merchants of Petropolis and not, for example, by the industrialists among the White active influentials of either city. If, however, we find that the industrialists of Petropolis had been equally concerned with and in favor of such policies, then the crucial question would not be why the White merchants of Metroville were underrepresented among the active influentials, but rather, why the White active-influential industrialists had different political interests in the two Southern cities.

Whatever the findings, reported below, on these possibilities, the question still remains of why the economically pessimistic Negro active influentials of Metroville did not join the Whites interested in initiating industrial-attraction activities by the city government as their racial counterparts had done in Petropolis. Still other questions bearing on a presumed relationship between socio-economic position and political interest are whether or not the difference in economic perspectives of White active influentials in the two Southern cities reflected a difference in the comparable evaluations of the local economy by those citizens lower in their respective political-influence structures; and whether or not the political interests of the political-influence super- and substructures within each community and subcommunity were complementary, if not identical, or divergent. It is to these questions and assumptions that we now turn.

If a pessimistic evaluation of the local economy leads to the development of political interests favorable to local-government action to assist in the reorganization of that economy, the assumption we first mentioned must be questioned. Pessimism among the White active influentials of Petropolis was not restricted to the merchants but also was evident among the industrialists in that category. Thus, if the mercantile sectors of the White subcommunities of both Southern cities had political interests favoring a net increase in the scope of local government in economic reorganization—for example, parking-violation enforcement—the political interests of the White merchants of Metroville could have been represented by nonmerchant active influentials, as the nonmerchants among Petropolis' White active influentials presumably were representing the political interests of merchants as well as their own in that city.

That the White active influentials of Petropolis, *regardless of socio-economic position,* had political interests more favorable to an expanding role of local government in the economy than did the White active influentials of Metroville is attested to by the following findings: 97 per cent of the White active influentials of Petropolis approved, while 53 per cent "strongly" approved, of the Locus Laboratory, the large regional industrial park intended to strengthen the industrial base of Petropolis and neighboring cities. Only 60 per cent of Metroville's White active influentials approved of a proposal for a similar facility for their area, and of these only 20 per cent expressed strong approval. In response to a question about their attitudes towards "spending some local tax money to attract new industry to this area," 95 per cent of Petropolis' White active influentials approved—22 per cent "strongly"—compared to but 60 per cent of Metroville's White active influentials, none of whom "strongly" approved.

The active influentials of both communities were asked specifically how active they had been in efforts to attract new industry to their respective cities; 35 per cent of Petropolis' White active influentials reported discussing the matter and trying to influence others to support industrial promotion; 11 per cent were even more active "in seeking to affect the outcome." Only one of the five White active influentials of Metroville reported a similar level of conversational concern, and he restricted his efforts to discussion. These respondents also were asked what they considered to be "the most important issues, problems or projects facing [their community] at the present time." Among Petropolis' White active influentials, race relations was the most frequently mentioned item; the depressed economy, particularly the need for new industry, was second in frequency. Economic conditions were mentioned by about one-fourth of the White active influentials in Petropolis but not by any of the White active influentials of Metroville. Once again there were no differences between the merchants and other occupational categories of White active influentials in Petropolis in these regards.

Thus a key question appears to be why Petropolis' White active influentials of diverse occupations had a set of economic and political interests in regard to the need for economic stimulation that differed considerably from those of the White active influentials of Metroville. An examination of the association between the economic and political perspectives of active influentials and citizens lower in the political-influence structures in the two White subcommunities will begin to answer this question. In Oretown there were two optimists to every pessimist among both the active influentials and those in the political-influence substructures. The economic pessimism of Petropolis' White active influentials also was reflected in the substructures, where the ratio of optimists to pessimists was 1:2. The absence of pessimists among Metroville's White active influentials was not due to an "under-representation" of the pessimistic White citizenry, as might have been expected. Although incomes of White citizens of Metroville were generally below those of the citizens of Oretown, the optimist-to-pessimist ratio of 3:1 was higher than in Oretown. There were fewer optimists and also fewer pessimists in the Metroville White subcommunity than in Oretown, but more citizens were "satisfied" in the Southern than in the Western city.

When we classified citizens according to income level, we found that at every one of six income-level categories, except for those few making more than \$10,000 per year, there was a consistent difference: Petropolis' White citizens were proportionately more pessimistic than Oretown's citizens; Oretown's citizens, in turn, were more pessimistic than Metroville's White citizens. Thus the difference in the degree of economic pessimism between the two sets of Southern White active influentials is paralleled by a difference in economic pessimism of those lower in the two structures of political influence. Therefore, the possibility that the affluent White active influentials of Metroville were keeping the political lid on a substructure of economically pessimistic citizens with different political interests must be discounted.

We also examined the political interests of the White-citizen substructures in the two Southern cities in regard to economic reorganization matters. The White citizens of Petropolis, both active influentials and those lower in the political influence structure, indicated more concern for, more active involvement in, and greater approval of efforts to improve local economic conditions than did their counterparts in Metroville. It is interesting to note that both within and among the four Southern subcommunities, the more pessimistic people were in their evaluation of economic conditions, the more frequently they mentioned economic conditions in response to the question concerning "the most important issues, problems, or projects" in their cities. For example, the ratios of optimists to pessimists decreased among the citizens at large from 3:1 in the White subcommunity of Metroville to 1:2 in both Metroville's Negro subcommunity and Petropolis' White subcommunity, and to about 1:8 in the Negro subcommunity of Petropolis; at the same time, the proportions of respondents mentioning economic conditions as among the most important matters rose from 4 per cent to 22, 25, and 53 per cent in these four samples, respectively.

Before turning to the Negro subcommunities, we shall examine the perspectives of the White active influentials in regard to several other subjects of political decision-making. When asked specifically about a municipally sponsored program of redevelopment downtown, even though it was not a subject of decision-making in Petropolis during Time *E* to *M*, the White active influentials and citizens of lower political-influence rank were overwhelmingly in favor of the idea. In Metroville, where it had been unsuccessful by Time *M*, the citizens still favored it, although there was more opposition. The White active influentials were split, however, with a substantial minority—40 per cent—opposed. If it can be assumed that merchants of Metroville favored this policy formulation, as a substantial majority of merchants in that sample clearly did, then the absence of merchants among Metroville's White active influentials may have worked against the political interests of this sector of the community.[21]

On other matters of community planning and development—redevelopment of the central business district is classified under this category—we find that the attitudes and concerns of the White active influentials and of those lower in the political-influence structure of Petropolis were comparable. In Metroville, on the other hand, the White active influentials differed considerably from the White citizens of lower political-influence rank in this regard. In general, the White citizens were unconcerned with such matters of community planning and development as zoning regulations, extending the city limits through annexations, and other matters classified under governmental reorganization, such as city and county school consolidation. Such items were mentioned by Metroville's active influentials as important community issues, problems, or projects only slightly less often than race relations, their primary concern. For example, they were much more in favor of school consolidation and metropolitan growth and consolidation than were the citizens in the political-influence substructure.

Still another point of contrast between Metroville's active influentials and those in the political influence substructure was in their attitude toward hospital improvement. The mental-hospital decision was of far greater spectator interest to the White citizens in the political substructure than it was to the White active influentials. It had been reported from day to day in the newspaper without any mention of the race-related considerations that had created such difficulties for the small group of men engaged in its authoritative consideration.

There was no relationship between attitudes toward Negroes and preferences regarding decisional outcomes among either the small set of White active influentials or the much larger number of White citizens of lower political-influence rank. Among the three outcomes seriously considered, one involved a White Supremacy attitude—building an entirely new White hospital in a non-Negro area; the other two were primarily economic cost-benefit choices—expanding the White hospital on its present site, or building new branch hospitals as needed to increase bed capacity. The preferences of the White active influentials and the White citizens of lower political-influence rank were not appreciably different, since each choice was favored by a comparable proportion of each category. However, there was a major difference in the degree to which it constituted a political interest or concern. For White citizens of moderate, low, or no political influence the hospital matter followed race relations as one of the most important current issues, problems, or projects in Metroville; almost half the White citizens below the active-influential class mentioned this item. Only one of the five White active influentials mentioned the mental-hospital problem in response to the same question. Their attention was apparently focused upon race relations and efforts to increase the size of Metroville.

Metroville's active influentials differed to some degree from the White rank-and-file citizens in yet another attitude: active influentials were divided on matters such as public housing, whereas the White rank-and-file citizens overwhelmingly approved. The one mention of public housing as one of the most important community problems was by a White active influential in Metroville, a realtor-builder, who volunteered the opinion that the public-housing problem was a blot on the community and should be eliminated. Another opponent of public housing among these White active influentials expressed his opposition to the idea of downtown redevelopment on the grounds that he was opposed to any program that might involve federal funds. In contrast, more of Petropolis' active influentials agreed with the pro-public-housing sentiment of the White citizens at large than in Metroville. Although a minority of the White active influentials were opposed to public housing, the successful opposition to the related matter of urban renewal apparently was not a victory for a majority in either the political-influence superstructure or substructure in Petropolis' White subcommunity.

We now shall turn to the perspectives and interests of the Negro active influentials and rank-and-file Negro citizens in the two Southern subcommunities. We have already mentioned that Petropolis' Negro citizens were more pessimistic in their evaluation of their local economy than any of the other subcommunity samples—the optimist-to-pessimist ratio was 1:8. Metroville's Negro citizens, unlike their White fellow citizens, were as pessimistic as the White citizens of Petropolis—both had 1:2 optimist-pessimist ratios, compared to a 2:1 optimist-pessimist ratio among Metroville's White citizens. We have also indicated that economic conditions, which almost none of the White citizens in Metroville mentioned as being among the most important issues, problems, or projects facing their community, were mentioned by over one-fifth of Metroville's Negro citizens in this connection; this is almost as frequently as they were mentioned by White citizens of Petropolis. The Negro active influentials of Petropolis were as pessimistic in their evaluations and even more prone to mention economic conditions as an important issue, problem, or project than the Negro citizens of lower political-influence rank. Although both Negro active influentials of Metroville were pessimistic, neither mentioned economic considerations.

It would seem that in the Negro subcommunity, at all levels of the political-influence structure, there were political interests that would have been sympathetic to local government's pursuit of policies of redevelopment of the local economy in Metroville. In view of such political interests, it would seem that Negro active influentials and the rank and file would have constituted at least a potential political interest group that could work either by themselves or with the minority of White citizens in favor of appropriate political decisions to shift the scope of local government in this direction. In Petropolis, the Negro subcommunity—particularly the active influentials—were active indeed in political decision-making in regard to economic reorganization during Time *E* to *M*. In Metroville, however, there was no comparable participation by Negroes in political decision-making during that period.

We may begin to understand this apparent anomaly through a more detailed examination of the perspectives about the economic condition of these respondents. Analyzing the particular aspects of the economic conditions mentioned as among the most important issues, problems, or projects facing their community, we find that Metroville's Negroes most frequently mentioned "unemployment." [22] None of the Negro respondents in Metroville, active influentials or otherwise, mentioned the need for new industry in connection with their need for employment. Over half the White and about 10 per cent of the Negro respondents in Petropolis specifically mentioned the need for new industry in response to the same question. Two-thirds of the responses of Petropolis Negroes in this "economic conditions" category had to do with better jobs, job advancement, and less discrimination against Negroes in employment. Among Negro active influentials in Petropolis, the need for new industry loomed even larger as a specific concern. Neither of the Negro active influentials of Metroville mentioned any economic condition in this connection.

It would seem that the availability of jobs was central in the economic perspectives of Metroville's Negro subcommunity; this need is regarded as relating specifically to a need for new industry among Petropolis' Negro citizens, who also were concerned with racial equality and "desegregation" of existing job opportunities. The economic concerns of White citizens in Petropolis were associated even more closely with the need to attract new industry to the community; in Metroville's White subcommunity, there was apparently little concern with particular features of local economic conditions.

The differences in the economic concerns of Negroes in Metroville and Petropolis suggests the inadequacy of the thesis that "objective" economic conditions determine economic as well as political interests and perspectives. In an earlier chapter, we reported that the rate of unemployment was much higher among Negroes in Metroville than among Negroes in Petropolis: but it is in Petropolis, rather than in Metroville, that we find the need expressed for new industry to create new jobs for the un- and underemployed. Even though incomes were slightly higher in Metroville than in Petropolis, the much greater degree of concern about equality of opportunity in the Negro subcommunity in the latter is surprising. It seems clear that the consideration of the problems of the local economies was shaped in such a way as to cause a specific policy, the attraction of new industry, to be prominent in the minds of Negroes and Whites in Petropolis, but not in Metroville. The persons who were responsible for this shaping and how they went about it are among the subjects of consideration in the following chapters. However, we cannot assume, in the light of these findings, that the political interests of comparably marginal groups of Negroes were the same from community to community.

At this point it would seem appropriate to amend an earlier inference. It now seems fair to say that the Negroes of Metroville seemed to have had economic worries that were prepolitical, compared to their fellows in Petropolis. If, as among Metroville Negroes, the problem had been seen only as unemployment, solutions might have been, and in fact were, looked for within the framework of the existing economy, which was organized and subject to private decisions made by private owners and managers. If, as among Petropolis Negroes, the problems had been seen as the need to create new jobs by attracting new industry and to relax communitywide and government-enforced or accepted policies of racial discrimination in private industry, solutions might have been—and in fact were—looked for in shifts in the policies of local government. One way of putting this is to say that the Negroes of Metroville had *potential* political interests not shared by Whites because they were much more dissatisfied about economic conditions than were the Whites. The Negroes and Whites of Petropolis had *actual* political interests, compared to the potential political interests of the Negroes of Metroville, in regard to such decisional questions as the role of local government in industrial promotion and in the creation of municipal fair-employment-practice policies.[23] Petropolis' Negro citizens were involved in the political decision-making processes, during Time E to M, concerning the creation and initiation of a program by the new biracial municipal race-relations commission; they also were involved in such decisional processes as the two elections of the top officials in the Democratic party. As we shall indicate in a later chapter, the difference in the degree to which both political interests and political interest groups were actual or potential in the Negro subcommunities of Petropolis and Metroville seems to have been interrelated.

One of the consequences, or at least corollaries, of such differences in political interests seems to have been a differential degree of Negro participation in political decision-making processes in the two cities, as well as a differential degree of political conflict. That such participation differential did exist specifically in connection with decisions about economic reorganization, as well as generally in political decision-making, is born out by the following findings. Neither of the two Negro active influentials and only 7 per cent of the citizens in the political substructure of Metroville's Negro subcommunity reported that they had urged others in conversation or sought more actively to help attract new industry to that city; 35 per cent of Petropolis' Negro active influentials and 21 per cent of citizens of lower political-influence rank participated in these ways. With the exception of the one White active influential in Metroville who reported being active, the comparable figures for the White active influentials and those of lower political influence rank were similar to those figures for their companion Negro categories. Therefore, both Negro and White citizens of Petropolis were involved more actively in the politics of economic reorganization than were either the economically concerned Negro or the economically more satisfied White citizens of Metroville.

The active involvement by Negro civic leaders in the efforts of the biracial Committee on Industrial Development to attract new industry served as a focal point for attacks on new industry by a small minority of White opponents. Although they were unsuccessful, industrialists who opposed industrial promotion efforts because they feared that it would make "cheap labor" more expensive used the active Negro support of such efforts to generate the opposition of anti-Negro White Supremacists to the whole idea of "pro-Negro" Northern industrialists and "foreign, radical labor-union organizers" coming to Petropolis. The Negro association with White organized labor, particularly in their support of the latter's aversion to nonunion firms in and around Petropolis but also as a consequence of the political-bloc character of the association, gave to White Supremacists a reason and a weapon for engaging in the sharp political conflict that was more apparent in Petropolis than in Metroville during Time E to M. The popular establishment of a state-supported technical training center, favored even by some of the industrialists opposed to new industry for Petropolis as useful in training their own employees, also created conflict centering on the political interests pursued by Negroes in creating a nonsegregated training center. This was to become one of the central political issues in Petropolis after Time M. But even by Time M, the Negro subcommunity's active interests in political decision-making regarding reorganization of the local economy—particularly because these interests were pursued personally by the relatively large segments of both Negro and White active influentials—seemed to have contributed to widespread community political conflict in other decisional processes as well. These patterns stand in sharp contrast to the situation in Metroville, where Negro and White subcommunities were differentiated by their levels of economic pessimism and concern but resembled each other in their inactivity and the associated absence of Negro-White political conflict in regard to economic reorganization and related political decisions.

Although Metroville's White citizens had been concerned about the mental-hospital question, the Negro subcommunity, including the two Negro active influentials, were not concerned with this matter. The question presented to the public was framed in terms of how best to expand the White hospital; therefore, it is understandable that only 1 per cent of the Negro respondents, compared to one-third of the White respondents in Metroville, mentioned the hospital decision as among the most important issues, problems, or projects facing their community.

Of far greater concern to Negro citizens at all levels of the political influence structure were housing conditions: the need for more public and better private housing, and the need for slum clearance. These aspects of community planning and development were mentioned by one out of every four Negro citizens and by one of the two Negro active influentials of Metroville. It was of little or no concern to the White citizens at large or to the White active influentials who were more concerned with housekeeping services or such items of community planning and development as zoning regulations and annexations.

A comparable division of interests between Whites and Negroes existed in Petropolis. About half the Negro active influentials and one-third of the Negro citizens of lower political-influence rank mentioned housing and slums as among the most important community concerns; their White counterparts expressed almost no concern with such matters. Once again, however, we found that in Metroville such matters as additional public housing were within the decision-making domain of Whites rather than Negroes.

In Petropolis Negro citizens were active in support of the controversial urban-renewal proposal, which included slum clearance in a predominantly Negro area of the city and additional public housing for Negroes, although they had not been successful by Time *M*. Metroville's urban-renewal proposal also was intended to eliminate and redevelop a Negro slum area. But the proposal was advanced only incidentally in the interests of Negro housing and living conditions and primarily in the interests of industries needing room for expansion. More to the point is that in Petropolis the urban-renewal proposal was developed and pursued by a combination of Negro and White participants; in Metroville, following the general pattern, the decision was made "by Whites only." Opposition by a few White citizens to federal intervention in the local community was handled quietly and covertly in Metroville; in Petropolis opposition from Whites with similar perspectives became, typically, more open and pregnant with the possibility that racial conflict might burst forth.

The possibility already has been suggested that the noninvolvement in political decision-making by Negroes in Metroville may have been related to their greater satisfaction with their condition than Negroes in Petropolis. That this is an inadequate explanation is suggested by the aforementioned findings that, while lacking actual *political* interests in economic improvement, Metroville's Negro citizens were considerably dissatisfied with their economic and employment status, as well as with their housing conditions. Race relations was the subject reported most frequently among the most important community issues, problems, or projects in three of the Southern subcommunities. It ranked second to economic conditions for Petropolis' Negro citizens, but was mentioned by a greater proportion of that sample than of any of the other samples. If the salience of something viewed as an important community concern is an index of a potential or actual political interest, then these findings suggest that the Negroes of Metroville shared an interest in race relations with those in the other three subcommunities. These data contravene the thesis that noninvolvement in political decision-making by Negroes in Metroville resulted from satisfaction with their lot and the feeling that race relations were of no interest to them.[24]

We now may examine more directly the possibility that the decision to initiate public school desegregation in Metroville, but not in Petropolis, by Time M had resulted at least in a greater degree of optimism about race relations in Metroville's than in Petropolis' Negro subcommunity. Using an optimism-pessimism ratio similar to that used for assessing perspectives about economic conditions, we find that Petropolis' Negro citizens had the lowest ratio of optimists to pessimists of any sample in the ratings of their city's "race relations." Their ratio of optimists to pessimists was 1:4; in the Metroville Negro subcommunity it was 1:2; and it was 1:2 in the two White subcommunities.

However, these ratios are somewhat misleading. Although a larger proportion of Metroville's Negroes than of any other sample were optimists—they rated race relations as "very good"—a larger proportion than in either White sample also were pessimists who rated race relations as "not very good." This proportion was almost as large as it was among Petropolis' pessimistic Negro citizens. The higher the respondents were in the political-influence structures in both Metroville's and Petropolis' Negro subcommunities, the higher the proportion of pessimists. At the active-influential level the cross-community difference disappears; none of the Negro active influentials in either city were optimistic about the condition of race relations. Thus the initiation of school desegregation in Metroville did not eliminate a negative evaluation of race relations on the part of a sizable segment of Negro citizens, particularly among the important Negro active influentials and those of lower, but still relatively high, political-influence rank.

It is conceivable that the reaction by White citizens to public-school desegregation increased anti-Negro sentiments in Metroville, especially among the White active influentials. This might explain the series of defeats suffered by the White proponents of increasing accommodation to the presumed political interests of Metroville's Negro citizens for such things as extending desegregation to the county schools through consolidation and not depriving Negroes of social status and dignity by moving the White hospital from the increasingly Negro to an all-White neighborhood. Another possibility is that school desegregation in Metroville testified to the more tolerant attitudes of Whites toward Negroes—at least among White active influentials—in Metroville than in Petropolis. Of course, it might be that White Supremacy sentiments were comparable in the White political-influence structures of these two cities in Southern State and that the differences in the political involvement by Negroes and in the outcomes of decisions concerning matters of social reorganization were due to other factors.

Sentiments of racial superiority were, in fact, comparably widespread among the White citizens of both communities. All four samples were asked whether or not they viewed members of the other race as inferior, equal, or superior "by nature" in regard to the characteristics of intelligence, morality, responsibility, and ambition.[25] The proportions of the White samples selecting the "Negroes are inferior" response on these items range from 62 to 72 per cent in Petropolis and from 61 to 72 per cent in Metroville.[26] The proportions of each of these samples that selected the "Negroes are the same" response range from 11 to 20 per cent in Petropolis, and from 14 to 21 per cent in Metroville. The remaining respondents could not or would not answer; a very few, by error or otherwise, indicated that Whites were inferior to Negroes. Small but discernible minorities of Negroes expressed sentiments of racial superiority in response to these questions. For example, 13 per cent of Petropolis' and 15 per cent of Metroville's Negro citizens said that Negroes were superior to Whites in intelligence.[27]

However, there was a striking difference in the racial perspectives of the White active influentials in the two cities. Although 78 per cent of Petropolis' White active influentials held racist sentiments— they indicated a feeling that Negroes were inferior in intelligence to Whites—compared to 62 per cent of the White citizens of lower political-influence rank, only 20 per cent of the White active influentials of Metroville held comparable racist sentiments, compared to 62 per cent of the White citizens of lower political-influence rank.

This difference extends to attitudes toward various school-desegregation policies. The respondents were asked about their attitudes toward policies of passing a Constitutional amendment to deprive the United States Supreme Court of its power to order desegregation; of the state government's withholding funds from school districts that desegregate; of closing the public schools in the event of desegregation; and of using force, if necessary, to prevent public school desegregation.[28] The findings, summarized in Table 7-6, indicate that the pro-

TABLE 7-6   Attitudes towards Public-School-Desegregation Policies by Whites in Petropolis and Metroville

	Community Sample	
Attitudes toward Desegregation Policies	Petropolis Whites	Metroville Whites
Amend Constitution		
Approve	62%	48%
Undecided	17	28
Disapprove	21	24
Totals %	100%	100%
N	358	305
Withhold state funds		
Approve	35%	34%
Undecided	20	21
Disapprove	45	45
Totals %	100%	100%
N	355	304
Close schools		
Approve	34%	30%
Undecided	14	20
Disapprove	52	50
Totals %	100%	100%
N	354	311
Use force, if necessary		
Approve	13%	11%
Undecided	8	9
Disapprove	79	80
Totals %	100%	100%
N	356	306

portion of citizens in these White samples who disapproved of the Supremacist plan increased steadily in both cities from amending the Constitution through withholding state funds and closing the schools to using force. The only major attitudinal difference between the White citizens of the two Southern cities was found in regard to amending the Constitution: a larger proportion of the White citizens of Petropolis than of those of Metroville favored the proposal. The initiation of school desegregation in Metroville may have increased uncertainties about the wisdom of a move against the Supreme Court; but it apparently neither increased nor decreased prejudice on the part of White citizens, assuming that the pre-school-desegregation racial attitudes of White citizens in both cities were pretty much the same.

In regard to the other, more immediate, policy possibilities, supremacist preferences were outnumbered by nonsupremacist preferences. The extremist proponents of force were outnumbered by those among the White citizens who disapproved of its use by about 7:1 in Metroville and 6:1 in Petropolis. Although the extremist position apparently was not dominant in either Southern city by Time M, it cannot be assumed that it was not advocated by significant numbers. For example, 15 per cent of Petropolis' White citizens "strongly" approved of closing the schools in the event of desegregation; an equal percentage "strongly" disapproved. Even in Metroville, with its initial, peaceful experience with school desegregation, the comparable proportion was 11 per cent.

As with sentiments of racial superiority, White active influentials represented the conflicting policy attitudes of the White citizens at large in Petropolis; in contrast, the White active influentials underrepresented the White Supremacist policy perspectives of the White citizens of Metroville. For example, among the White active influentials of Petropolis, a distinct minority preferred the use of force, if necessary, to prevent public school desegregation in that city; among the White active influentials of Metroville there were no advocates of violence. Twelve per cent of the White citizens of Metroville "strongly" disapproved of closing their schools, but 60 per cent of the White active influentials took the same position with equal intensity. Thus Metroville's active influentials were atypically accommodating in their racial policy perspectives, compared to the White active influentials of Petropolis, who resembled the more racist White citizens of both cities.

Another index which combines a measure of racial sentiment and political action in school desegregation may provide an overview of these patterns of accommodation in race relations in the two cities.

This index of accommodation-racism was developed on the basis of responses to questions about the superiority, inferiority, or equality of the other race and about the respondents' concern with the matter of public-school desegregation prior to Time M, the time of the interviews, but following the initiation of desegregation in Metroville. *Active racists* are those who felt that members of the other race were inferior in intelligence and who reported that they had at least discussed the matter of public-school desegregation with friends and acquaintances. *Active accommodators* are those who felt no such sense of racial superiority in regard to intelligence and were comparably participant in the school-desegregation matter. Those who indicated that they had been inactive were classified as *potential racists* and *potential accommodators* on the basis of their sense of racial superiority or equality in regard to intelligence.

From the findings presented in Table 7-7, it can be appreciated that Petropolis' White active influentials not only were slightly more racist than the White citizens of lower political-influence rank, but also were more actively so. In Metroville, the White active influentials were much more actively accommodating than their White fellows lower in the political-influence structure. The difference between the White active influentials in the two cities in this regard is dramatic. The political pressures in Petropolis, particularly at the active-in-

TABLE 7-7 Proportions of Active and Potential Racists and Accommodators among Whites and Negroes in Petropolis and Metroville

	Community Sample							
	Petropolis				Metroville			
	Whites		Negroes		Whites		Negroes	
Proportions of Racists-Accommodators	A.I.	Be-low A.I.	A.I.	Be-low A.I.	A.I.	Be-low A.I.	A.I.	Be-low A.I.
Active Racists	68%	57%	10%	9%	20%	57%	100%	9%
Active Accommodators	16	17	87	55	60	22	0	52
Potential Racists	10	17	0	4	0	19	0	8
Potential Accommodators	6	9	3	32	20	3	0	31
Totals %	100%	100%	100%	100%	100%	101%	100%	100%
N *	31	263	30	158	5	237	2	187

Key: A.I. = Active Influentials

  Below A.I. = Lower Political Influence Rank than Active Influential

  * The N's are exclusive of the relatively large numbers of respondents in each category who could not answer the question about intelligence of the other race.

fluential level, pitted a substantial majority of active racists against the minority of active accommodators in the matter of public school desegregation. This White minority, together with the consensual Negro active influentials, constituted a small majority of members of the political-influence superstructure in favor of at least some such shifts in the scope of local government. These findings contributed to a better understanding of the mixed pattern of success of efforts to reallocate benefits between the two racially distinct subcommunities through political decision-making in Petropolis during Time E to M. However, political decisions, including the question of public-school desegregation, were not settled by majority vote, so that at best our understanding at this point is incomplete.

If all political decisions actually reflected the majority point of view at the active-influential level of the political-influence structure, or even the "public opinion" of the citizens assumed to be equal in political influence, we still would have the problem of understanding the decision to initiate public-school desegregation in Metroville, since during the same period other decisions were unfavorable to the accommodation point of view. Nor do the foregoing findings of a greater degree of active accommodation and generally less-anti-Negro attitudes on the part of Metroville's White active influentials account for the defeat of the White citizens there in a series of decisional questions that invoked racial considerations during Time E to M. Nor, as another example of a problem to be explored in succeeding chapters, do these findings account for the decisional victories achieved by those in favor of local government action to maintain and increase social status for Negro citizens of Petropolis. Achieving those decisional successes during Time E to M resulted, in part, from the cooperation between Negroes and Whites, particularly White members of organized labor. However, the survey findings indicate that members of organized labor among the White active influentials in Petropolis actually were as racist in perspective and behavior on these same measures as their counterparts of higher socio-economic status. In terms of relative numbers alone, the political perspectives and behavior of these White active influentials do not account for the political strength and decisional victories of those in the White subcommunity who favored increasing accommodation between the two races in Petropolis during Time E to M, although they contribute to our understanding of the strength of the forces resisting shifts in the scope of local government toward social reorganization of this two-subcommunity city.

The reader by now may have wondered how much the White active influentials of these two cities differed in their race-relations perspectives as a result of differences in such socio-economic characteristics as educational level. In many Southern communities the more highly educated are less racist than those of lower educational levels.[29] We have already noted that Metroville's White active influentials were much more uniformly a highly educated set of people than their fellows in Petropolis (Table 7-5). In both of our White samples, racism related directly to the level of education. Respondents with less than high school educations had racist or supremacist views of Negroes and positions on desegregation policy proportionately three, four, and even six times as frequently as their college-educated brethren in both Metroville and Petropolis. And the highly educated Whites who had acquired positions of active influence in the political-influence structure of Petropolis shared the racial norms of the highly educated of that city. In Metroville those among the highly educated who had acquired similarly high political-influence positions were far less racist than other highly educated citizens. Therefore, in addition to the differences in racial attitudes and action of those in the political superstructure and substructure of Metroville that may have been due to differences in educational level, the White citizens who became active influentials in Metroville had or developed politically more accommodating racial views than their equally well-educated fellows lower in the political-influence structure there.

Regardless of their more accommodating perspectives, the White active influentials of Metroville did not associate politically with Negro citizens as much as did their counterparts in Petropolis. One of the sample survey findings supports this assessment, initially based on the historical reconstruction of political decision-making during Time *E* to *M*. When asked, the White active influentials of Metroville reported, to a man, that they had "occasional" associations with Negroes, but that they did not associate with Negroes "frequently." In contrast, one-third of the White active influentials of Petropolis reported associating with Negroes "rarely or never," but 30 per cent reported "frequent" associations with Negroes in their polity. It would seem that Metroville's White active influentials were generally more sympathetic to the interests of, but personally some distant from, the Negro subcommunity than those in Petropolis. In the latter city, the White active influentials were predominantly hostile—a minority was sympathetic—to the interests of the Negro subcommunity; some were at a great distance from, but others were close to, Negroes as political friends or foes.

In passing, we should note that small minorities of Negroes in the political-influence substructures also were classified as active racists (Table 7-7), as were a comparably small proportion of Negro active influentials in Petropolis. And both of Metroville's Negro active influentials received the same classification on the basis of images of Negroes as "superior" to Whites in intelligence. Although it seems likely that views of the other race as inferior or of one's own race as superior would constitute a predisposition to adopt a Supremacist ideology on the part of the currently advantaged or superordinate group—that is, White citizens—the same assumption might not hold for members of the subordinate group. We suspect that the so-called Negro active racists, although disposed to take pro-Negro or anti-White postures on policy and decisional matters when such perspectives were invoked, were expressing less an inclination to become "supreme" or pursue a Supremacist ideology than indignation over a socio-political situation that violated fundamental premises about human equality. In other words, given appropriate and comparable conditions, we suspect that proportionately fewer Negroes classified as active racists would have pursued a Negro Supremacist policy than Whites who were so classified.

On the basis of this index we also find that in Petropolis the Negro active influentials were as accommodating as were Negroes of lower political-influence rank; but the former were much more active in this regard than the latter. Neither of the two Negro active influentials of Metroville were active accommodators. The difference in the degree to which pressure for continued change in the relative positions of Negro and White citizens emanated from the two political-influence superstructures in these Negro subcommunities is again underlined by these findings.

POLITICAL TRUST, CYNICISM, AND DISTANCE IN THE SOUTHERN CITIES

The Negro citizens of Petropolis were the most politically cynical about their city officials of any of the samples, including the city and fringe samples of Oretown. They were more cynical than were the White fringe-dwellers of Petropolis, who were somewhat more cynical than the White city-dwellers of that city. Political distance was less for the White suburbanites of Petropolis than for the suburbanites of Oretown; but the former were somewhat more distant than their city-dwelling White fellows. The usual pattern of fringe inhabitants' being more distant from city officials than residents of the city itself was not the case in Metroville. There, the White city-dwellers not only were no closer to their city officials on this measure, but they also were much more cynical about them than were the White fringe-dwellers. Metroville's Negro subcommunity was almost as cynical as the Petropolis Negro subcommunity, so that Mayor Peterson's administration had to face an even more cynical set of city inhabitants than did Mayor French in Oretown. Mayor Plunkett in Petropolis had to contend with a cynical Negro subcommunity, but the White inhabitants of the city were relatively more trusting.

The Negro subcommunities within the cities of Petropolis and Metroville were as distant from their county officials as were the city- and fringe-dwelling inhabitants of Oretown. The White citizens of both Southern communities were much closer to their county officials, particularly in Metroville. In Metroville, the fringe-dwellers were more trusting of county than of city officials. This seems to reflect the greater political relevance for city affairs of the county governments in Southern State—both Southern cities being county seats—and it also seems to reflect, as we have already indicated in discussing political decision-making during Time E to M, that county government was more implicated in decisional questions in Metroville and Petropolis than in either Western city. Yet these findings suggest a racial division in orientations toward the county governments in both Southern cities. They also suggest that in the analysis that remains to be made special attention should be paid to the political relationships between the city administration and the county, especially in Metroville, in regard to such matters as future growth of the metropolitan area through annexation.

Something of the existing political cleavage between the city and county governments in Metroville is evident in the findings about political cynicism on the part of active influentials. Although they were considerably less distant from their city and county officials than the rank-and-file citizens, each set of active influentials manifested patterns of political cynicism and trust comparable to those lower in their respective political influence structures. The one exception was the White active influentials of Metroville, who evidenced a relatively high degree of political cynicism about their local government officials, matched by a comparable cynicism about the county officials. Mayor Peterson's city administration was faced not only with a relatively cynical set of White and Negro rank-and-file citizens, but also with relatively cynical active influentials in both subcommunities.

SUMMARY

The foregoing analysis was intended primarily as a comparative description of various aspects of political behavior in the four communities. Based for the most part on interview materials collected at Time M concerning political participation, political influence, and political perspectives extant or presumedly operative during Time E to M in each community, these findings provided a way of fitting certain noticeable patterns in political decision-making during that period to patterns of participation, influence, and perspectives. A clearer picture of community similarities and differences in patterns of politics has emerged; but certain apparent anomalies or incongruities from community to community also have been noted. It is premature to attempt to explain why, for example, there was apparently such widespread concern with economic conditions and appropriate political interests in Petropolis, but little concern in either Metroville or Farmdale. Nor is it obvious why the active participation in Petropolis', but not in Metroville's, decision-making by White organized labor and Negro political forces during Time E to M was not manifested in accommodation sentiments by union members among the White active influentials there. Of interest also is the difference discovered between the accommodating White active influentials of Metroville and the racism of their counterparts in Petropolis, the reasons for the difference, and why the consequences for political decision-making varied. The explanation that is needed for these and other somewhat unexpected differences is more complex than that socio-economic position leads to socio-economic interests which produce particular political interests which are then reflected in political decision-making. For example, the extent to which such groups as organized labor in Farmdale and Metroville were less visible in political decision-making than their counterparts in Oretown and Petropolis during Time E to M was derived from an historical reconstruction of those decisional processes based on newspaper accounts, interviews with people mentioned therein or other likely participants, and a chain referral process wherein some participants referred the interviewers to other participants. Organized-labor and Negro prominence in Petropolis, in contrast to their "invisibility" in Metroville, also was observed through these historical methods. The use of sample surveys provided a way to investigate a cross-section of each community and subcommunity in regard to such things as their positions in their political-influence structures and their political perspectives. The fact that White organized labor was represented by a small but primarily racist set of active influentials in Petropolis means that its decision-making visibility and positions may have resulted from vocal representation by a few labor-union officials of more accommodating perspectives who did not happen to be selected for inclusion in the randomly drawn, fractional sample. These possibilities will be discussed later.

In any event, the preceding analysis suggests that there were indeed differences in the political interests of comparable socio-economic categories from community to community; this question was posed for further investigation in the summary of the preceding chapter. Nor were such differences explicable solely in terms of differences in the degree to which the political leaderships accorded such groups of citizens positive political status in terms of the latter's presumed political interests, a matter that will be explored more fully. An explanation for some of the observed differences between socio-economic position and political interests, and between political interests and participation in decision-making, will be offered in a later chapter.

The next two chapters are intended to continue the descriptive analysis as preliminary to, but leading toward, such an explanation, and toward a model connecting political influence, interest groups, and perspectives—interests and more general attitudes. Repeated references have been made to the active influentials as being at the top of the political-influence structure, that is, as constituting the political superstructure. Aside from the fact that the sampling procedures used mean that only a fraction—hopefully, a representative fraction—of the active influentials have been subject to descriptive analysis, this useful working conception now needs to be revised according to the theoretical frame of reference set forth in the first three chapters.

In the following chapters we shall turn our attention to the political leaderships of each community's political structure. These leaderships will be treated as the political superstructures of which only a portion of the active influentials are members. It has already been pointed out that in Farmdale only a small proportion of the active influentials attempted to exercise political influence in making political decisions during Time E to M. However, even attempts to affect decisional outcomes do not necessarily mean that participants share in the political power attributed to the contributors to decisional outcomes. The concept of political leadership, as we use it, refers to individuals who, there is reason to believe, deserve to be accorded a share in political power, and they have earned that share in at least the authoritative-consideration stage of one or more political decision-making processes. Thus, we now turn our attention to the political leaderships, the political superstructures, of the several community political-*power* structures. Two different operational definitions will be described as they have been used to identify political leaders. A comparative description also will be presented of some characteristics of the leaders, of their organization at that level of their power structures and between that level and the political power substructures, and something of their ideologies and perspectives as these were observed at Time M.

NOTES

1. For an interesting discussion that summarizes some of the empirical findings on the relation between national elections and policy preferences, see V. O. Key, *Public Opinion and American Democracy* (New York: Alfred A. Knopf, 1961), Chapter 18, pp. 459-480.

2. The recent literature on nonpartisan municipal elections is surveyed in Charles Press, *Main Street Politics* (East Lansing, Michigan: By the Board of Trustees, Michigan State University, 1962), pp. 65-75. See also Eugene C. Lee, *The Politics of Nonpartisanship* (Berkeley: University of California Press, 1960).

3. See W. B. Munro (ed.), *The Initiative, Referendum and Recall* (New York: The Macmillan Co., 1913).

4. Robert A. Dahl found that in New Haven, Negro citizens who were registered voters participated in local politics more than did White citizens. See his *Who Governs?* (New Haven: Yale University Press, 1961), pp. 293-296.

5. "Open to a sizable segment of the citizens" means that the expectation was relatively widespread that many citizens could vote at relatively low costs, even though not constitutionally specified. The exercise of the voting option might require an expenditure, as in voting on the establishment of a hospital through donations, but even in voting for local officials one might lose some income for the time it takes to go to the polls. These are considered minor, normal costs of access to elections in democratic regimes, although under some conditions the costs might be so large as to make an electoral process inaccessible to many eligible voters and, hence, undemocratic.

6. There is increasing consensus among both critics and defenders of the current American system of political representation that, apart from such questions as numerical representations of urban and rural citizens, the formal and informal governmental authorities come disproportionately from the more advantaged sectors of society. Defenders tend to stress the commitment of this advantaged "political stratum" to democratic norms, rules of the game, or, in our terms, regimes. See V. O. Key, "Public Opinion and the Decay of Democracy," *Virginia Quarterly Review*, Vol. 37, No. 4 (Autumn 1961), pp. 481-494; Andrew Hacker, "Liberal Democracy and Social Control," *The American Political Arena*, ed. by Joseph R. Fiszman (Boston: Little, Brown and Co., 1962), pp. 91-105; and Herbert McClosky's "Ideology and Consensus in American Politics" (unpublished paper delivered at the 1962 Annual Meeting of the American Political Science Association).

7. This view is essentially that of C. Wright Mills and Floyd Hunter.

8. It is conceived as related to a host of other variables as well, many of which are correlated with interest and socio-economic position, including leisure

time available, sense of political confidence or efficacy, feelings of civic duty, etc. See Robert E. Lane, *Political Life* (Glencoe, Illinois: The Free Press, 1959), Chapter 16, pp. 220–234; and Robert A. Dahl, *op. cit.,* pp. 282–301.

9. For example, Robert A. Dahl maintains that the political stratum does not constitute a homogeneous class with well-defined class interests. *Ibid.,* p. 91. Nelson Polsby agrees with this viewpoint in "How to Study Community Power: The Pluralist Alternative," *The Journal of Politics,* Vol. 22 (August 1960), pp. 474–484.

10. Included in our category of "pluralists" are two influential political scientists who have posited this in their analysis of the American political system. See Pendleton Herring, *The Politics of Democracy* (New York: Rinehart & Co., Inc., 1940); and E. E. Schattschneider, *Party Government* (Rinehart & Co., New York, 1942).

11. A report that describes the occupational composition of "top" and "key" influentials in eleven cities, including one English and two Mexican cities, is to be found in William V. D'Antonio and others, "Institutional and Occupational Representations in Eleven Community Influence Systems," *American Sociological Review,* Vol. 26 (June 1961), pp. 440–446. Peter H. Rossi, in reviewing various community studies, finds that business and professional persons play more than their proportional part in the affairs of the local community. He also points to the role of government officials, labor unions, and voluntary associations as playing greater or lesser roles from community to community. See his "Theory and Method in the Study of Power in the Local Community" (unpublished paper delivered to the annual meeting of the American Sociological Association, New York, 1960).

12. Sidney Verba, "Political Behavior and Politics," *World Politics,* Vol. XII, No. 2 (January 1960), p. 288.

13. It is equally appropriate when socio-economic structures are similar, but under that condition the calculation of the representativeness of political-influence strata based on intracommunity comparisons automatically gives a picture of the cross-community differences or similarities of influence-strata composition. Political sociologists have tended to use the intracommunity basis, because of their interest in the shaping of the political structure by the socio-economic. Political scientists have tended to stress cross-community comparisons because of their interest in the political effects, given socio-economic compositions, of political strata. The aforementioned study by D'Antonio and those of other sociologists used both modes of analysis in an exploratory fashion.

14. If socio-economic characteristics of politically influential people shape decision-making, the political system may have consequences for the socio-economic systems of communities. An example might be a town with little industry, few blue-collar workers, and a set of white-collar political decision-makers who pursue policies of keeping out new industry and additional blue-collar workers, thereby maintaining the current patterns of representation of blue-collar workers and proportions of blue- to white-collar workers in the political superstructure. The importance of zoning and planning regulations in shaping the character of communities is stressed by Gladys M. Kammerer and others, *City Managers in Politics* (University of Florida Monographs, Social Sciences, No. 13, Winter 1962), pp. 76 ff.

15. It would seem that the popular picture of the sad plight of the American housewife deserves reassessment. The picture of housewives' having little opportunity to participate in local politics would need to be refined in terms of socio-economic status.

16. Such factors as age and length of residence bear on theoretical notions that political conflict is related to the strength or weakness of citizen ties to moderating institutions in the community. Young newcomers of relatively low social standing, for example, may be less likely than older, long-term residents of higher social standing to be integrated in moderating social institutions and may evidence a less restrained style of political behavior. See James Coleman, *Community Conflict* (Glencoe, Illinois: The Free Press, 1957). For an analysis in a set of Florida communities of the importance of newcomers of a type different from the old-timer residents to interest conflict and to effects on the tenure of city managers, see Gladys M. Kammerer and others, *op. cit.*

17. Arthur J. Vidich and· Joseph Bensman sketch a similar picture of the industrial worker in their rural community. See their *Small Town in Mass Society* (Garden City, New York: A Doubleday Anchor Book, 1958), pp. 94–96. Other studies have pointed to a stronger sense of being a member of a union or of the working class on the part of unionists or blue-collar industrial workers.

18. Peter H. Rossi makes the point that even when a political party representing lower status and class groups has candidates running for public office, the candidates of such parties are probably not themselves lower status or class. "Theory and Method in the Study of Power in the Local Community," *op. cit.* For an important study of group perspectives in one city, see Morris Janowitz, Deil Wright, and William Delany, *Public Administration and the Public—Perspectives Towards Government in a Metropolitan Community* (Bureau of Government, Institute of Public Administration, University of Michigan, No. 36, 1958).

19. For a description of comparable interests "unrepresented" in political decision-making in another small community, see Arthur J. Vidich and Joseph Bensman, *op. cit.*, pp. 124–126.

20. Although far from being an isolated, homogeneous subculture, organized labor in Oretown appeared to be receptive to some degree to appeals to them as an underdog group deprived of their fair share of city services—partially because they tended to live in the same areas of the town. See Daniel Katz and Samuel J. Eldersveld, "The Impact of Local Party Activity Upon the Electorate," *Public Opinion Quarterly*, Vol. 25 (Spring 1961), pp. 1–24. See also Robert H. Salisbury, "St. Louis Politics: Relationships among Interests, Parties, and Government Structure," *Western Political Quarterly*, **XIII** (June 1960), pp. 498–507.

21. The interest of downtown merchants, among others, in saving the downtown area is described by Norton Long, "Decisions in Metropolitan Areas," in *The Polity*, ed. by Charles Press (Chicago: Rand McNally & Company, 1962), pp. 156–164.

22. Economic conditions were mentioned by only 4 per cent of the respondents in the White random sample in Metroville, who mentioned race relations, the hospital matter, housekeeping services, and school consolidation, in that

order of frequency, as the most important issues, problems, or projects facing their community.

23. This is a somewhat different use of the terms "potential" and "actual" interests from David Truman's usage in connection with interest groups. A potential political interest group differs from an actual political interest group in regard to differences in the degree to which people are interacting on the basis of some current political attitude. See his *The Governmental Process* (New York: Alfred A. Knopf, 1951). As used here, the term potential political interest refers not to the possession of a political attitude that could serve as the basis of political-interest-group formation and interaction, but to the possession by individual members of a category of a sense of dissatisfaction that could serve as the basis for the formation of political attitudes and groups.

24. Negro citizens in Petropolis named the following items, in descending order of frequency, as the most important community issues, problems, or projects: race relations, economic conditions, housekeeping services tied with housing. The comparable ordering for the Negro citizens of Metroville was: race relations tied with housing, followed by economic conditions and then by housekeeping service. A major difference between the two subcommunities, apart from the relative stress on housekeeping services by Petropolis Negroes and the differences in the kinds of economic problems mentioned, was that the proportion of respondents mentioning nothing at all was twice as high in Metroville as in Petropolis among Negro respondents. Inability to respond to this question may be interpreted as a form of political "satisfaction," but such satisfaction may not be due to a positive evaluation of living conditions but to apathy, a sense of resignation, passivity, or psychological withdrawal. The data reveal rather striking differences in these patterns of political perceptions or cognitions which are frequently overlooked when generalizations are made about "the" Negro's interests or concerns, regardless of possible cross-community differences.

25. These questions were constructed by Melvin J. Tumin, *Desegregation: Resistance and Readiness* (Princeton, N. J.: Princeton University Press, 1958), Appendix C, pp. 227–228.

26. Compare these findings with those of Tumin's among White citizens of Greensboro, North Carolina prior to any school desegregation in that city. *Ibid.*, p. 228.

27. Some, but not all, of these responses may have been due to misunderstanding of the questions, coding errors, etc.

28. The questions were constructed by Melvin J. Tumin, *op. cit.*, pp. 236–237. See also *op. cit.*, p. 45.

29. *Ibid.*, pp. 83–104. See also Norman I. Lustig, "The Relationships Between Demographic Characteristics and Pro-Integration Vote of White Precincts in a Metropolitan Southern County," *Social Forces*, Vol. 40, No. 3 (March 1962), pp. 205–208.

8

THE POLITICAL LEADERSHIPS

Political leaderships consist, at any moment, of those people who have acquired power during the immediately preceding time period through effectively exercising political influence in the authoritative-consideration stage of one or more decision-making processes. From the dynamic functioning of men in the process of making political decisions—that is, in their political-power relations—the political analyst must make and order his observations to construct the static, structural representation known as the community power structure. A set of political decision-making processes has been selected and described for Time E to M in each community (see Chapter 6). For each process the analytic judgment was made that a unit of political power could be attributed to those who had contributed to the outcome by Time M. An historical reconstruction of every one of the selected political decision-making processes was then used to assess when and where the authoritative-consideration stage occurred, prior to each decisional outcome. The method for doing this began with the examination of a set of people in each community who were reputedly powerful. They became "expert witnesses" who testified to their own actions and the actions of others in the selected decision-making processes. These interview data were supplemented by data derived from analysis of newspapers and other documentary materials such as the minutes of local government agencies, diaries, and personal memoranda.

MANIFEST AND LATENT LEADERS

The selection of reputedly powerful people was begun through officers of a representative sample of the subsidiary political and non-political organizations and associations in each community. These officers were asked to designate or nominate those whom they considered the most important people in political decision-making in the community. It was assumed that these nominations reflected personal assessments of what had happened prior to Time M, the point at which the nominators were interviewed. Whether or not those whom the nominators believed powerful in the past actually were powerful after that period was treated in this study as a hypothesis to be examined and tested after Time M.

The nominations were not accepted as necessarily valid assessments of the political power, political influence, or political-leadership positions of the nominees. The candidates were classified either as active influentials or as people of lesser degrees of political influence through methods similar to those used to classify people in the random samples. Then they were classified according to whether or not they had participated politically in one or more of the political decision-making processes during Time E to M. They were classified further on the basis of whether or not their decisional preferences when participating were satisfied by the decisional outcome at Time M. Finally, those nominees who were thought to have shared in the political power accruing to the contributors to a decisional outcome during this time period were then classified as probable political leaders or not on the basis of whether or not the historical reconstruction of these decision-making processes revealed that they had participated in the authoritative-consideration stage, if not in other stages, of one or more decisional processes. If so, a nominee met the operational definition of political leader in a community's power structure.

The political leaders identified by these procedures were classified as Manifest Political Leaders, here referred to as Manifest Leaders.[1] The word "manifest" is used to mean obvious or evident; the Manifest Leaders were those whom presumably well-informed officials of the community's voluntary organizations considered to be the most obvious leaders. Potential Manifest Leaders had to have been nominated by a minimal number of our informants. Even though, as it turned out, an overwhelming proportion of those nominated with the specified degree of frequency met the additional criteria set forth above for Manifest Leaders, those finally identified as such constitute only a fraction of the political leadership of each community's power structure.

It became clear as the political decision-making processes were reconstructed that other people also deserved to be classified as political leaders. Some of these had been nominated as important people in decision-making, but not frequently enough to be placed on the initial list of potential Manifest Leaders. These people were less "manifestly" powerful than others, but many of them were still part of the political leadership. However, others who received no mention at all by the nominating officers also met the criteria set forth above for classification as political leaders. These relatively unobtrusive people are the Latent Political Leaders, here referred to as Latent Leaders.

There has been a major controversy in the literature of community politics concerning the validity of identifying members of a political superstructure from the judgments of informants, of presumably knowledgeable citizens of a community.[2] To the extent that the critics of such methods do not distinguish political influence from political power, their own methods are ambiguous. They do not seem to recognize the possibility that political influence may be exerted in a way that might affect political preferences, the likelihood of policy formulations and demands, and hence, the occurrence or non-occurrence of political decision-making itself. They are thus open to criticism, since they advocate the identification of the political leadership only by observations of action in extant political decision-making. These critics of so-called reputational methods imply that there is no certainty, nor even a high probability, that people attributed political power by their fellow citizens actually are powerful in decision-making; they also question whether or not these are the only, or even the most, powerful people in decision-making. Identifying Latent Leaders as we do here, as well as checking on the decision-making behavior of the Manifest Leaders, is a more valid means of mapping the political leadership than is possible through the use of only an attributed-power measure. This method also reduces the length to which the inference about the probable impacts in decision-making of the reputedly powerful must be stretched, even though in itself it does not solve the problem of not recognizing those who play important pre-decision-making political roles.

Latent Leaders have been identified in two ways: samples of the Latent Leaders were culled from the subsamples of active influentials in each community by ascertaining through the interviews whether or not active influentials had participated in one or more of the decision-making processes occurring during Time E to M and, if so, whether or not their decisional preferences seemed to accord with the relevant decisional outcomes. Because it was impossible, with the resources available, to ascertain whether or not these random-sample respondents had participated in the authoritative-consideration stages of the decision-making processes, a third criterion, weaker than the one used for Manifest Leaders, was introduced: the classification as Latent Leaders of only those active influentials who appeared to have been relatively satisfied participants in one or more decision-making processes and who reported discussing local government or community matters with local government or civic leaders at least sometimes.

A second method of identifying Latent Leaders was to use the historical reconstruction of the decisional processes to see whether the formally elected and appointed authorities had participated in authoritative-consideration stages. For this classificatory purpose, it was not necessary for the local-government officials to have participated in *formal* authoritative-consideration stages. It was sufficient that they had been active participants in such a stage of decision-making, whether or not they were acting in official capacities and whether the setting was governmental or private in character.

THE LATENT LEADERSHIPS: COMPARATIVE SIZES

In all four communities, the elected municipal officials were actual political leaders. In Oretown and Petropolis the officials were political leaders in proportionately more decision-making processes than the officials in Farmdale and Metroville; but our intention here is to classify leaders on the basis of minimal sharing in political power in the authoritative-consideration stage, that is, on the basis of leadership roles in at least one political decision. For example, in Farmdale the City Council and the Mayor authoritatively considered only one set of decisional demands, just prior to Time M, so that every member of the City Council deserved to be classified as political leaders. This was the decisional question about annexing an additional fringe area. Although the general antiannexation policy had been set and affirmed prior to Time E, in a private group setting, the City Council reassessed the policy and arrived at the negative outcome during Time E to M. Some of the elected officials also participated in the other extant political decisions as private citizens who were political leaders. The further question about the extent to which elected and appointed officials were Manifest and Latent Leaders shall be considered shortly.

Turning now to the Latent Leaders from each sample of active influentials, the findings are as follows. Only four of the twenty-five active influentials in the sample in Farmdale were classified as Latent Leaders. These were the four men we have mentioned who had strong *status quo* political interests. This represents 1.6 per cent of the total sample. However, three of these four Latent Leaders were also among the Manifest Leaders of Farmdale. Therefore, excluding these three political leaders, the proportion of Latent Leaders in the Farmdale sample is only about 0.5 per cent. In Oretown, nineteen of the 102 active influentials turned out to be Latent Leaders—2.6 per cent of the total sample.

Seven of the thirty-eight White active influentials of Petropolis were classified as Latent Leaders, or 2 per cent of that sample. For the Petropolis Negro respondents a somewhat different operational definition of Latent Leader had to be used, since the data on participation in decision-making were not comparable to the data collected in the other sample surveys. In that sample, the criterion that the participation in decision-making and the preferences of Latent Leaders should be consistent with decisional outcomes was replaced by a requirement that active influentials classified as Latent Leaders must have reported that they had worked in the key Negro subcommunity political organization, PESNEG, on an "important community problem, policy matter, or issue." Using that operational definition, ten of the thirty-three Negro active influentials there, or 4.2 per cent of the total sample, were classified as Latent Leaders. In Metroville, three of the five White, and one of the two Negro, active influentials were classified as Latent Leaders, or 1 per cent of the White sample and 0.5 per cent of the Negro sample.

Although these sample findings are subject to the possibility of sampling errors, the actual numbers of Latent Leaders in every community and subcommunity, except in little Farmdale, appear to have ranged from several dozen to more than 200 people. This finding is to some degree a by-product of the operational definitions we have used. If a stronger definition of Latent Leader had been adopted, fewer Latent Leaders would have been found in each sample and the estimate of their numbers in each community would have been smaller.[3] However, it is our feeling, on the basis of the historical reconstruction of the decisional processes during Time E to M, that this picture of the breadth of these political leaderships, particularly of their latent portions, agrees more with political reality than the picture of a very small number of men monopolizing political-leadership positions.

In the small community of Farmdale, our findings suggest that the political leadership was relatively well known; there were few people playing political-leadership roles who escaped the attention of the informed portion of the citizenry, our informants, who are officers in the voluntary associations of the city. This observation also is partly a by-product of the methods used to identify the Manifest Leaders. If a much larger number of informants had been asked to identify a sufficiently large number of men whom they considered to be powerful, the overlap of Manifest and Latent Leaders would have been greater in all cities. Since the number of informants and the number of nominations were limited, it is not surprising that so few of the Latent Leaders were named sufficiently frequently to be classified as Manifest Leaders in the larger communities. For example, in Farmdale the high sampling rate made it much more likely that the randomly se-lected sample included Manifest Leaders by chance than in the larger communities where sampling rates were lower.

No matter how arbitrary the operational definition of Latent Lead-ers had to be, and regardless of city size, the *proportion* of citizens in the Latent Leaderships was higher in Oretown and Petropolis than in Farmdale and Metroville. Since we had no data from other studies to compare with our cross-community percentage differences, and because of the sampling-error problem, it is difficult to assess the significance of the differences we have found.[4] However, it is worth noting that there is a pattern in the differences discovered to this point between the two sets of communities. There was more extensive citizen political participation in Oretown and Petropolis than in Farm-dale and Metroville. There was a comparable difference in the dis-tributions of political influence positions. If the relatively small proportion of Latent Leaders in Farmdale is assumed to be valid, the relatively large percentage of active influentials there assumes a different significance than it otherwise might. To the aforementioned differences, then, we can now add that there was a wider distribution of latent-political-leadership positions in the bodies politic of Oretown and Petropolis than in those of Farmdale and Metroville.

We shall analyze further the positions of these sets of Latent Lead-ers in their political superstructures and comment upon the signifi-cance of this difference in the sizes of the Latent Leaderships later in this study when we have described the organization of each political leadership. This description will be based upon, and will follow, the description of the manifest portions of each political leadership. We shall turn now to the Manifest Leaders in each community.

THE MANIFEST LEADERSHIPS

Numbers of Manifest Leaders

Variations in randomly selected samples represent, within limits, variations in the several universes from which they were drawn. Our samples of the citizens in these communities and subcommunities may be used to compare proportions of Latent, but not Manifest, Leaders. Regardless of differences in city size, the differences in proportions of active influentials or Latent Leaders in the samples can be assumed to reflect differences in such proportions of citizens in the several communities, except for possible questions about the representativeness of the samples and sampling errors. No such assumption can be made about the irrelevance of such matters as city size in estimating and comparing the sizes of Manifest Leaderships from community to community.

The initial distinction between the Manifest and Latent Leaders is a difference in reputation, renown, or visibility to presumably informed citizens. Our informants were members of the associational officialdom of the community. A reputational method is an effort to identify every member of a universe rather than to obtain a sample. Since consensus of judgments—that is, the frequency with which particular people are named by informants—constitutes the initial procedure for including or excluding citizens from a hopefully complete enumeration of the most renowned Manifest Political Leaders, it may or may not be true that there should be a large number of nominators for a large city and a small number for a small city in order to obtain comparably renowned names. The method we used was to have similar numbers of informants in the several cities, with an identical number of nominations required for a person to be classified initially as a potential Manifest Leader. Apart from the identical operations we have described that were used to cull the probable Manifest Leaders from others named with the specified frequency by the informants, the nonequivalence of the panels of informants may be responsible for the fact that the number of those designated as Manifest Leaders differed from community to community. We cannot be certain that our panels of informants were equally successful in identifying "equally visible" potential Manifest Leaders.

The characteristics and behavior, although not the number or size, of these sets of Manifest Leaders can and will be compared from community to community, since there is something of value that can be learned from describing and comparing the reputedly most powerful individuals in the political power structure, even though the less noticeable members may not all be included in each set. Moreover, information on the samples of Latent Leaders and those in the infrastructure will be used to supplement the information derived from studying these sets of Manifest Leaders.

The numbers of people classified as Manifest Leaders on the basis of the aforementioned operational definitions were: 14 in Farmdale, 38 in Oretown, 41 and 20 in the White and Negro subcommunities of Petropolis, and 22 and 19 in the White and Negro subcommunities of Metroville.

A special problem arose in connection with the identification of Manifest Leaders in the two Southern cities. Reflecting something of the bicommunity character of their societies, Negro informants differed from White informants in their nominations of the most important decision-makers in their cities. Since our theoretical framework is such that each city conceptually had a single political power structure, whether or not that structure reflected racial or other boundaries or cleavages between segments of each citizenry, the place of the two racial categories of Manifest Leaders in the political-leadership level or in the substructure of each city's power structure is of central interest in the following analysis. In other words, the extent to which Negro political leaders were integrated into the single political leadership of the power structure is of critical concern. We are interested in both the extent to which divisions existed within the Manifest Leaderships along racial lines, and the extent to which differences existed between Petropolis and Metroville in how many Negroes who were manifestly political leaders in their own subcommunities also were political leaders in decision-making affecting the entire community.

White and Negro Manifest Leaders nominated by associational officials of their own race are described separately at the outset for clarity. Another reason for this is the assumption that nominators will give more thought to and be most aware of the identity of the prominent political leaders of their own subcommunity. This initially separate treatment of White and Negro Manifest Leaders poses a special classificatory problem: to anticipate an important conclusion, the additional operations performed to determine whether or not the nominees exercised political influence effectively in an authoritative-consideration stage or one or more decision-making processes revealed that the Negro nominees in Petropolis, but not in Metroville, probably were powerful political leaders in the community as a whole, who should be classified as Manifest Leaders of the community power structure. This also was the case with the White citizens most frequently nominated as potential political leaders. To the extent that Metroville's Negro Manifest Leaders were in fact such, most played their leadership roles in pre-electoral, post-alternative-policy-formulation stages of formal voting, unlike their racial fellows in Petropolis.

Rather than resort to an additional classificatory label such as Negro Civic Leaders for the potential Negro Manifest Leaders of Metroville, since they clearly deserve to be thought of as civic leaders in their own subcommunity, we shall refer to them as Negro Leaders; Negro Latent Leaders will be referred to as such. The reader should remember that in Metroville there was a substantial deviation between nominations and the application of the additional criteria to establish whether or not individuals who were nominated actually were political leaders in the total community.

Except for the Negroes nominated as potential Manifest Leaders in Metroville, 96 per cent of the individuals who were nominated in the other communities and subcommunities—133 of 138—met the additional criteria for Manifest Leaders. If such a reputational method was so accurate in identifying members of political leaderships, assuming that the additional operations provided valid evidence of political leadership, criticisms of such methods are undeserved. However, we can overlook neither the exception, Metroville's Negro subcommunity, nor the fact that such a method does not include the less visible portions of the political leaderships—that is, the Latent Leaderships—except, perhaps, in the very smallest communities. With these considerations in mind, we turn now to the task of describing the Manifest Leaderships in the research communities.

Characteristics of Manifest Leaders

In general, fewer women were Manifest Leaders than were active influentials (Table 8-1). The one minor exception is found in the Metroville Negro subcommunity. The Manifest Leaders of Farmdale and of Metroville's White subcommunity and the Negro Leaders of Petropolis were entirely male. Whatever their political significance, if any, these findings indicate that the four research communities were typical of many other American communities and of the nation in the underrepresentation of women in the most prominent portions of their political leaderships.

The six sets of Manifest Leaders were predominantly of upper socio-economic status. Except for Oretown, the active influentials

TABLE 8-1   Distributions of Selected Characteristics of the Six Sets of Manifest

Community or

Characteristic Proportion	Farmdale		Oretown	
	M.L. (N = 14)	A.I. (N = 25)	M.L. (N = 38)	A.I. (N = 102)
Sex				
Male	100%	68%	92%	59%
Education				
College	86%	44%	79%	23%
Less than two years high school	0	28%	3%	35%
Income				
Over $10,000	50%	8%	50%	7%
Under $4,000	7%	44%	13%	31%
Occupation				
Managerial-Professional-Proprietorial	79%	28%	95%	10%
Blue-collar	0	32%	0	46%
Housewives	0	24%	5%	29%
Farmers	21%	20%	—	—
Age				
Over 55 years	28%	28%	26%	22%
Under 35 years	7%	44%	24%	25%
Length of Residence				
Less than 10 years	7%	46%	42%	67%
Party Identification				
Democratic	0	40%	29%	55%
Republican	72%	56%	68%	36%
Independent	28%	4%	3%	7%
None	0	0	0	2%

Key: M.L. = Manifest Leaders
      A.I. = Active Influentials
      *   = This is the man who was the editor of the local labor-union newspaper.
      †   = Comparable data unavailable.

overrepresented the more advantaged, more affluent sectors of their communities or subcommunities. The Manifest Leaderships, including that of Oretown, were uniformly more advantaged and affluent than their active-influential counterparts.

Young male adults were almost as rare in the Manifest Leaderships as were women of any age. Only in Oretown were men of less than 35 years of age more or less proportionately represented in the Manifest Leadership—that is, relative to their proportion of the adult citizenry—as was the case with that community's active influentials. The active influentials in the Petropolis Negro subcommunity were disproportionately young; but the Negro Leaders consisted exclusively

Leaders and Active Influentials

Subcommunity

	Petropolis				Metroville			
	Whites		Negroes		Whites		Negroes	
	M.L. (N = 39)	A.I. (N = 38)	M.L. (N = 20)	A.I. (N = 33)	M.L. (N = 22)	A.I. (N = 5)	M.L. (N = 19)	A.I. (N = 2)
	95%	51%	100%	58%	100%	60%	89%	100%
	89%	58%	100%	42%	100%	100%	100%	50%
	0	13%	0	24%	0	0	0	0
	78%	32%	60%	13%	100%	60%	†	0
	3%	3%	0	38%	0	0	†	0
	95%	42%	100%	30%	100%	40%	100%	50%
	3% *	13%	0	48%	0	0	0	50%
	3%	32%	0	9%	0	20%	0	0
	—	—	—	—	—	—	—	—
	48%	16%	55%	24%	41%	20%	21%	0
	6%	32%	0	42%	0	20%	0	0
	6%	18%	10%	22%	18%	20%	5%	0
	55%	58%	45%	71%	27%	0	63%	100%
	3%	13%	20%	6%	18%	40%	5%	0
	42%	26%	35%	16%	55%	60%	32%	0
	0	3%	0	6%	0	0	0	0

of middle-aged or older men. The largest proportions of Manifest Leaders over the age of 55 years were found in the two Petropolis subcommunities and in the Metroville White subcommunity. The Metroville Negro Leadership had the smallest proportion of older men among its Manifest Leadership. Like the active influentials there, the Negro Leadership was overwhelmingly middle-aged.

The Manifest Leaderships also underrepresented the newcomer segments of their respective populations. Oretown had the largest proportion of Manifest Leaders who had lived in the community for less than 10 years; but even there the masses of newcomers to the city were substantially underrepresented among the Manifest Leaders. The newcomers were most underrepresented among the Manifest

Leaders of Farmdale, where newcomers constituted a large proportion of the community's population. The active influentials in the Petropolis Negro subcommunity had overrepresented both younger people and newcomers; but the Negro Leaders of Petropolis underrepresented newcomers as well as young adults.

It is worth noting certain differences between the active influentials and Manifest Leaders in some of these cities. Farmdale's youthful, newcomer active influentials of relatively heterogeneous socio-economic backgrounds, a substantial minority of whom identified themselves with the Democratic party, had a contrasting set of the most prominent political leaders. The Manifest Leaders there were, for the most part, more affluent, older men who had arrived in the community before the Second World War and who were entirely Republican or Independent in party identification. Oretown's Manifest Leaders were a much more white-collar, affluent, well-educated set of people than were the active influentials there. Old-timers were more numerous, as were Republicans, among the Manifest Leaders than among the active influentials of Oretown. The significance of these discrepancies between the characteristics of Oretown's Manifest Leaders and those of its active influentials will be evaluated after we describe the characteristics of groups of Manifest Leaders in the next chapter.

Among the White and Negro Manifest Leaders of Petropolis, older, upper-middle- and upper-class, old-timer residents were more overrepresented than they were among the active influentials of either subcommunity. The heavy blue-collar and young-adult representation among Petropolis' Negro active influentials was completely absent from the Negro Leadership there and was almost completely absent from the White Manifest Leadership of that city. There was a larger minority of Republicans in the ranks of the Negro Leaders than in the ranks of the Negro active influentials in Petropolis.

Among Metroville's entirely upper-class White Manifest Leaders, there was not even a minority of young adults, as there had been among the White active influentials. Although there was a minority of Democrats in their ranks, the White Manifest Leaders of Metroville were predominantly Independent in their party affiliations and less Democratic than any of the other Southern Manifest Leaderships. The Negro Leaders of Metroville were also a more upper-class grouping than the Negro active influentials of that subcommunity; but their class positions were far lower than those of their White counterparts, as we shall see shortly.

To return to the uniformly high socio-economic positions of every Manifest Leadership, we may profitably focus upon occupations. In none of the Manifest Leaderships were either blue-collar workers as such or white-collar clerical workers represented. Only in the White Manifest Leadership of Petropolis was there a labor-union leader and he was the editor of the locally published labor-union newspaper. In this respect they were all elite groups compared to the citizens at large of their respective communities. But this general uniformity obscures major differences in the occupational structures of the four leaderships (Table 8-2).

TABLE 8-2 Occupations of Manifest Leaders

	Farmdale		Oretown		Petropolis				Metroville			
					Whites		Negroes		Whites		Negroes	
	No.	%	No.	%	No.	%	No.	%	No.	%	No.	%
Industrial Executives												
Senior officers	1		4		7		0		12		0	
Junior executives	0		1		0		0		2		0	
Subtotals	1	7	5	13	7	18	0	0	14	64	0	0
Bankers-Financiers												
Senior officers	0	0	3	8	8	21	6	30	4	18	1	5
Proprietors												
Retail	5		10		6		1		0		3	
Wholesale	0		0		3		0		0		0	
Services												
Insurance and/or real estate	1		2		2		0		0		2	
Miscellaneous	1		0		1		0		0		0	
Funeral director	1		1		0		1		0		1	
Media *	1		1		2		1		0		0	
Subtotals	9	64	14	37	14	36	3	15	0	0	6	32
Farmers	3	21	0	0	0	0	0	0	0	0	0	0
Housewives	0	0	2	5	1	3	0	0	0	0	0	0
Professionals												
Public administrators	0		3		2		0		0		1	
Educators	1		2		3		3		1		4	
Attorneys	0		5		2		3		3		1	
Ministers	0		3		1		4		0		4	
Others	0		1		1		1		0		2	
Subtotals	1	7	14	37	9	23	11	55	4	18	12	63
Totals	14	99%	38	100%	39	101%	20	100%	22	100%	19	100%

* The publishers of the weekly newspaper in Farmdale and the biweekly in Oretown, the editor of the local labor-union newspaper in Petropolis, and the publisher of the Negro newspaper in Petropolis are all classified in the media subcategory of proprietors. The publisher of the large-circulation daily newspaper in Petropolis is classified as a senior industrial executive while the editor and special feature writer of the equally large Metroville daily newspaper are classified as junior executives in the industrial executive category. The large size and assets of the latter warrant their being treated as industrial corporations.

The business and professional people who were the Manifest Leaders of Metroville were primarily the top executives—owners and managers—of the city glass and metal-processing industries, the financiers of their mammoth banking enterprise, and officials in their owned and controlled enterprises, including the city's newspaper combine, the city's exclusive college-preparatory school, and the city's major prestige law firm. The lowest-status occupations held by Manifest Leaders there included the president of the aforementioned "prep" school, the editor of the paper, and a columnist who wrote about local affairs. The latter two men were classified as junior executives.

In Metroville, the percentage of White Manifest Leaders who were either industrial executives or financiers was 82 per cent. In the Petropolis White Manifest Leadership, the comparable figure was 39 per cent; in Oretown it was 21 per cent; and in Farmdale it was 7 per cent. In Petropolis, two of the seven industrial executives among the White Manifest Leaders worked for absentee-owned firms, compared to only one of twelve senior industrial executives in the Manifest Leadership of the White subcommunity of Metroville. However, the substantially greater proportion of absentee-owned industry in Petropolis was not adequately reflected by this difference. The largest absentee-owned manufacturing firm in Metroville was represented by the industrialist we have mentioned; but one of the two chemical firms which had the largest number of employees in Petropolis and was also absentee-owned was not personally represented in the Manifest Leadership.

Oretown was like Petropolis in respect to the political representation of absentee-owned industries in the persons of Manifest Leaders. Although the largest employer, an absentee-owned manufacturing firm, was represented by three of the five industrialists among the Manifest Leaders, the numerous other absentee-owned manufacturing firms were not represented at all. In Farmdale, there were no major absentee-owned industries; the one industrialist in the Manifest Leadership was the owner of the single medium-size mining company.

Metroville's Manifest Leadership consisted primarily of an elite of industrialists and financiers; proprietors were not among them. Proprietors constituted slightly more than one-third of the White Manifest Leaders of Petropolis and the Manifest Leaders of Oretown. Retail merchants predominated in this category in Oretown, but there was more diversity in Petropolis. Retail merchants, in fact, constituted 27 per cent of all the Manifest Leaders of Oretown but only 15 per cent of the White Manifest Leaders of Petropolis. Farmdale had the

Manifest Leadership with the greatest proportion of shopkeepers and small businessmen: 64 per cent.

In Farmdale there was one occupational category that was unrepresented among the Manifest Leaders of any other city: three of the fourteen Manifest Leaders were farmers. Only one lived inside the city; he drove back and forth between his home and farm. The 21 per cent of the Manifest Leaders who were farmers was representative of the proportion of farmers in the rural fringe area around Farmdale; but less than 1 per cent of the residents of the city itself were engaged in farming.

The last general occupational category of the Manifest Leaders is professional people. There was a wide variation in the proportions of professionals among the Manifest Leaders of our four communities. They ranged from 7 per cent in Farmdale to 23 per cent in the White subcommunity of Petropolis, 18 per cent in the White subcommunity of Metroville, and 37 per cent in Oretown. There were additional variations in the professional subcategories.

There are five subcategories of professionals: public administrators or career civil servants, educators, lawyers, ministers, and miscellaneous others. In Metroville three of the White Manifest Leaders, 14 per cent, were attorneys at law, two of whom were senior partners in the prestigious corporate law firm that handled much of the legal work of the major glass industry. The third was a respected municipal judge. In Petropolis there were two lawyers among the White Manifest Leaders, neither of whom represented a prestigious law firm: one was a woman in independent practice; the other worked for the state in the Petropolis area. Oretown was the city with the most lawyers in the Manifest Leadership. These men constituted almost half the practicing attorneys in the community at that time. In Farmdale there were no attorneys among the Manifest Leaders; but the one Latent Leader among the active influentials was the leading lawyer in town and the legal advisor to the municipal government.

There was one educator among Metroville's 22 White Manifest Leaders: the president of the exclusive prep school for White children. In Petropolis the two educators among the White Manifest Leaders included the president of a White college and a professor on the faculty of that college. The educators among the Manifest Leaders in the two Western communities included the superintendents of their respective school districts and, in Oretown, one of the assistant superintendents. In neither Southern city was the public school system directly represented at the Manifest Leader level. However, the retired county school superintendent in Petropolis was a White Manifest Leader.

There were no public administrators among Metroville's White Manifest Leaders. There were two in Petropolis: the city manager and the county manager. Farmdale and the county in which it is located did not have a manager form of government. In Oretown the city manager was not in the Manifest Leadership. However, there were three public-administrator Manifest Leaders, in addition to the school superintendent: the director of the recreation district; the head of the county planning department, who did the professional planning in Oretown by contractual arrangement; and an appraiser for the county government.

The ministry was represented by three ministers in the Manifest Leadership of Oretown and by one minister in the Manifest Leadership of the White subcommunity of Petropolis.

A summary picture of the occupational characteristics of each of these four Manifest Leaderships is as follows. Farmdale's Manifest Leadership consisted of small businessmen, particularly retail merchants, and men engaged in moderately large farming operations. In Oretown the Manifest Leadership was predominantly a leadership of businessmen, professional men, particularly lawyers, and a few industrial executives. Petropolis' White Manifest Leaders were a more heterogeneous collection: financiers, industrial executives who were primarily from the locally owned paper firms, businessmen from relatively large units of the various sectors of the local economy, and professional people. In Metroville, the White Manifest Leaders were predominantly chief executives of the largest home-owned glass-manufacturing firms; there also was a minority of bankers and attorneys.

In both Negro subcommunities, ministers and educators abounded among the two Negro Leaderships, which were predominantly professional. While most other Negro Leaders of Metroville were small businessmen, a striking minority of those in Petropolis were financiers from the major Negro-owned loan companies and investment houses.

Among the Negro Manifest Leaders in Petropolis was the well-known publisher-editor of the widely read Negro newspaper in Petropolis; there was no Negro paper in Metroville. Both Negro Leaderships were extremely well educated. Seventy-nine per cent of the Negro Leaders of Metroville and 65 per cent of the Negro Leaders of Petropolis had some graduate or professional training beyond college. Only 45 and 31 per cent of their Manifest Leader counterparts in their respective White subcommunities had comparably high educational levels. Although the Negro Leadership of Metroville was more highly educated, the number of financiers among the Negro Leaders of Petropolis was one reason that the latter had considerably larger incomes than the former. The Negro Leaders of Metroville, like the active influentials in that subcommunity, were atypically upper class. However, even apart from considerations of caste, they were far below the elite socio-economic positions of the White Manifest Leaders of Metroville in occupational positions and income levels. The Negro Leaders of Petropolis were a more upper-class grouping than the Negro active influentials in that subcommunity, who were in turn more upper class than the Negro citizenry. Strictly in terms of their socio-economic positions, they were closer to the rank of the White Manifest Leaders of Petropolis than were the Negro Leaders of Metroville to the White Manifest Leaders of that city.

We already have noted that, among the professionals in the White Manifest Leaderships, there were three public administrators in Petropolis and two public administrators in Oretown. Among those in the White Manifest Leaderships of Metroville and of Farmdale there were none. There was one public administrator in the Negro Leadership of Metroville, the superintendent of a municipal park for Negroes, and none among the Negro Leaders of Petropolis.

We now will describe the elective and appointive positions in local government held by the Manifest Leaders of these four cities. The extent to which Manifest Leaders were career civil servants only begins to tell the story of the extent to which the Manifest Leaders overlap the formal governmental authorities in their communities.

Formal Authority of the Manifest Leaders

Neither the Mayor nor any of the eight elected city councilmen belonged to the White Manifest Leadership of Metroville. However, 45 per cent of the latter did hold appointive positions on the boards, committees, and commissions of the city government: the city's advisory budget committee, the hospital commission, the recreation commission, the urban-renewal board, the public-housing commission, and the library board. None of the members of the city school board were Manifest Leaders, nor was the city manager; but the city attorney, also the legal advisor to the city school board, was one of the Manifest Leaders. An elected county commissioner, an appointive member of the joint city-county planning commission, and an elected state senator also were White Manifest Leaders of Metroville.

Twenty-three per cent of the White Manifest Leaders in Petropolis held elective posts in the city and county governments. These included the Mayor, six of the twelve city councilmen, and two of the five county commissioners. In addition, the aforementioned city and county managers were among the White Manifest Leadership. Other White Manifest Leaders were on the lay budget committees; one was an appointive member of the city school board; two were appointive members of the city's public-housing authority; and others served as formal authorities on additional appointive boards and commissions of local government. Finally, a state senator, a state representative, a member of the state highway commission, and the attorney who worked for the state were among the White Manifest Leadership of Petropolis.

The Negro Leaders of Metroville had a greater number of men in their ranks with *appointive* positions on the various municipal commissions and boards than did the Negro Leaders of Petropolis: 47 per cent of the former held appointments to one or more local government body, as compared to 25 per cent of the latter. The Negro city councilman in each city belonged to the Negro Leadership. In Metroville, one Negro Leader was the administrator of a municipal park for Negroes; another worked part-time in the city attorney's office; and a third was principal of an all-Negro public school in the city. None of the Negro Leaders of Petropolis were on the city payroll.

The Mayor of Oretown and one of the six city councilmen were in the Manifest Leadership of that city. The independent municipal utility's elected board was represented by one Manifest Leader and the independent park district was similarly represented by two elective members of its board. The other elective formal authority among the Manifest Leaders of Oretown was a member of the board of education of the independent school district.

In addition to these elected local-government authorities among Oretown's Manifest Leaders, there were the aforementioned public administrators: the school superintendent and his assistant; the superintendent of the park district; the head of the county planning department, from whom Oretown's city government received its technical city planning services; and a county property assessor. In addition to these five full-time civil servants, the Manifest Leaders included the attorneys for the city government, for the municipal utility, and for the park district's board; one lawyer held the latter two posts. The funeral director among the Manifest Leaders was also the county bailiff. Excluding the Manifest Leaders who held positions of formal authority in local government by virtue of appointment to lay boards and commissions, we find that one-third of Oretown's Manifest Leaders either held elective office or worked as paid full-time or part-time administrative officials in local governmental positions.

The Manifest Leadership of Farmdale contained the highest proportion of elected authorities of any of the four cities: 50 per cent of the Manifest Leaders held elective posts, four in the city government —including the Mayor—and three on the independent school board. In addition, the school superintendent was a full-time public administrator; another Manifest Leader was an elected representative to the state legislature.

Excluding state offices, the proportions of elected local officials in the several Manifest Leaderships ranged from a high of 50 per cent in Farmdale, through 23 per cent in the White subcommunity of Petropolis and 16 per cent in Oretown, to 5 per cent in the two Negro Leaderships and in the White Manifest Leadership of Metroville. The greatest overlapping of Manifest Leaders and administrative officials of local government was found in Oretown and in the Negro subcommunity of Metroville; there was little or no such overlap for the other Manifest Leaderships. The proportions of Manifest Leaders on the city payroll in full- or part-time administrative positions ranged from a high of 18 per cent in Oretown through 16 per cent in the Negro subcommunity of Metroville, 7 per cent in Farmdale—one man, the school superintendent—and 5 per cent in the two Southern White subcommunities to zero in the Petropolis Negro subcommunity. The proportions of elected officeholders and people working full time or part time on the payroll of one or another agency of local or county government in these Manifest Leaderships ranged from 57 per cent in Farmdale through 34 per cent in Oretown, 28 per cent in the White subcommunity of Petropolis, 21 per cent in the Negro subcommunity of Metroville, and 9 per cent in the White subcommunity of Metroville to 5 per cent in the Negro subcommunity of Petropolis.

The nexus between the Manifest Leaderships and local government was, in numerical terms, a strong elective-office overlap in Farmdale, moderate electoral and administrative overlapping in Oretown, a moderate administrative overlapping in the Metroville Negro subcommunity, and little overlap at all in the White subcommunities of Metroville or Petropolis. However, the estimated administrative overlap was based not on numbers of municipal employees, but on the character of the two positions held by the public administrators in the White Manifest Leadership, the city and county managers, making for a strong overlap in the White Leadership of Petropolis.

A Summary Note on the Characteristics of Manifest Leaders as Categories

Additional consideration will be given to these socio-economic, partisan, and formal governmental positions of the Manifest Leaderships as soon as the political group structure among the Manifest Leaders, hitherto treated simply as categories, has been described. At this point we shall summarize briefly the foregoing findings. Congruent with the so-called power-elite point of view, all of these prominent portions of each community power structure's political leaderships are of considerably higher socio-economic standing than the citizens at large.

However, there were differences from one Manifest Leadership to another in the degree to which members were of superior socio-economic rank which cannot be explained in terms of differences in the socio-economic structures of their communities. For example, the management of the largest absentee-owned industrial firms were adequately represented personally among the Manifest Leaders of Farmdale and Metroville but were not represented to the same extent in Oretown and Petropolis. Moreover, there were variations in the degree to which less affluent segments of the citizenries, such as blue-collar workers, were represented in the less visible portions of each political leadership and in the top ranks of the political substructures, that is, among the Latent Leaders and active influentials. Furthermore, these findings do not explain why, for example, organized labor, which was personally unrepresented among Oretown's Manifest Leaders and minimally among Petropolis' White Manifest Leaders, was so active and to some degree successful in political decision-making in those two communities—but neither in Farmdale nor in Metroville—during Time E to M.

The differential degree of overlap between the Manifest Leaders and the local governmental officialdom from community to community is relevant to both the pluralist and the power-elite points of view about the political importance of elected and appointed government officials. If a simple pluralist line of reasoning were adopted, one might have expected to find that the relatively extensive participation and conflict in political decision-making in Oretown and Petropolis were associated with the greatest degree of overlap between their most prominent political figures and their top officials. Instead we found the greatest degree of such overlap in Farmdale and the least overlap in the Negro subcommunity of Petropolis. Or, if the proportion of elected officials among the most renowned political leaders is taken as the measure of relative political importance of formal authorities and private citizens of top economic power, proponents of a power-elite point of view might have expected the comparatively covert, quiet, and restricted decision-making in Farmdale and Metroville to be associated with little or no overlap between the formal authorities and the Manifest Leaderships there, in contrast to a greater degree of overlap in the more conflicting, mass-participation politics of their sister cities. But this was apparently the case only in Metroville, not in Farmdale. If some community power structures are dominated by "power elites," if they have political leaderships composed of men in top socio-economic positions, and if this arrangement accounts for such differences in the patterns of political decision-making as have already been noted in Farmdale and Metroville on the one hand and Oretown and Petropolis on the other, then these findings suggest that elected officials may have different positions in at least the manifest portions of such political superstructures. These "ifs," as well as a fuller description of the place in each political leadership of elected officials, are treated specifically in the description and analysis that follows.

MANIFEST LEADERSHIP CLIQUES

The Manifest Political Leaderships so far have been treated as categories or sets of unrelated individuals. By the use of informants and sociometric techniques it was possible to determine something of the group structure and interrelations within the Manifest Leadership of each community. In each city the informants were asked whether or not there were influential men who were known to differ strongly with each other, either in general or in specific instances, in regard to the best policies of local government. The informants then were asked which, if any, of these nominees they felt were "leaders of the people or groups who felt as they did about the best policies of local government." This procedure resulted in the identification of *inner cliques* of reputedly antagonistic political groups.[5]

Three rival cliques were identified in this manner in Oretown and two in the White Manifest Leadership in Petropolis. Only two people in the Manifest Leadership of Farmdale and one person among the White Manifest Leaders of Metroville were reputedly dissidents or policy deviants in regard to particular aspects of local government's scope. However, they did not appear to be leaders of rival groups. Neither rival cliques nor dissident individuals were identified by this method in either Negro subcommunity in the Southern cities. The judgments of the Manifest Leaders themselves as to the most influential among them were used to identify three-person inner cliques of the presumably single political groups in Farmdale, both subcommunities of Metroville, and the Negro subcommunity of Petropolis.[6] Only in Oretown was a clique named whose members were not in the Manifest Leader category.

There were, then, three cliques of political leaders identified by this procedure in Oretown: two cliques of four men each and one of three men. Four- and five-person cliques were identified in the White subcommunity of Petropolis. Some of the informants suggested that the five-person clique might really be two cliques consisting of two and three people each. One three-person clique was identified in Farmdale, one in each subcommunity of Metroville, and one in the Petropolis Negro subcommunity. In addition, one Manifest Leader in Oretown and one in the White subcommunity of Petropolis were included in the set of analytic operations to be described below, because informants judged that, although these men were not in any one clique, they were very influential. Their views reputedly were sought and respected by "all sides" in their communities.

The Manifest Leaders had all been asked:

Which of the people on this list do you generally or have you worked with closely on community projects or policies?

and

. . . which ones would you say have views which are most similar to yours about the needs, policies, and future of (this city)?

The next set of analytic operations consisted of tabulating and mapping responses to these questions by members of the aforementioned inner cliques, the dissidents, and the uncommitted in regard to one another. Fellow clique members proved to be among those named by members of each clique in response to both questions. The members of the single inner clique in Farmdale and in the Metroville White subcommunity did not name the dissident in each Manifest Leadership in response to these questions. Neither in Oretown nor in the Petropolis White subcommunity did inner-clique members name members of the presumably rival inner cliques as men of similar views with whom they had worked closely on community projects or policies. The men "above" cliques in these two Manifest Leaderships were chosen by one or more members of the rival cliques. These procedures validated, in part, the judgments of our informants.

A series of questions addressed to each Negro Leader was used to identify the clique structure in the two Negro Leaderships. The responses to these questions did not indicate the existence of rival groups in either Negro Leadership. Although there were still some differences among individual Negro Leaders in regard to the preferred pace and strategy of political efforts to accomplish desegregation, formerly distinctive "go slow" moderates and more radical "go fast" leadership groups, such as those in Petropolis' PESNEG before 1953, had disappeared as distinguishable leadership cliques by 1958. In both Negro Leaderships, the three men most frequently nominated by the Negro Leaders themselves as among the most influential men in general and in regard to local governmental, party, or school matters were classified as the inner cliques in these one-group Negro Leaderships.

The aforementioned inner cliques and uncommitted individuals are identified in Figure 8.1 by classificatory labels to be discussed below, by name, and by occupation.

The next step was to tabulate and map inner-clique members' responses to the same questions, according to which of the remaining Manifest Leaders in each city worked closely with members of each clique and had "similar views." In Oretown and in the White subcommunity of Petropolis, some of the remaining Manifest Leaders were attached, by this procedure, to one or another rival inner clique. Some of them were found to be "uncommitted" in that they were not named by a member of any inner clique, or they were named by members of two or more cliques; in either event, they themselves named either no inner-clique member or named members of two rival cliques. In Farmdale, all but two of the Manifest Leaders were named by one or more of the three members of the inner cliques as men they worked closely with on community projects and with whom they shared views about the needs, policies, and future of the community. These exceptions were the two men identified by the informants as dissidents. In Metroville, eighteen of the other nineteen White Manifest Leaders either were identified by one or more of the inner-clique trio as men of similar views or said, themselves, that the inner clique's policy views accorded with their own views. The one exception was the person named by the informants as a policy deviant. However, he identified other non-inner-clique Manifest Leaders as men of similar views and was identified similarly by a number of them.

Before analyzing the policy perspectives and decisional preferences of the larger Manifest Political Leadership groups, we shall describe briefly the political ideology of the inner cliques and some of the

Farmdale
Jeffersonian Conservative Inner Clique
  Mayor Bill May—farmer
  Don May—farmer
  "Judge" Catis—retail merchant
Dissidents
  Councilman Cox—retail merchant
  Kenneth King—publisher

Oretown
Inner Cliques
  Orthodox Conservatives
    Robert Hill—retail merchant
    William Tuesday—retail merchant
    Alvin Tuesday—retail merchant
    Hans Restow—retail merchant

  Community Conservationists
    Mayor Michael French—lawyer
    James Watt—industrial executive
      (jr.)
    Ted Ford—public administrator
    Ben Kelly—retail merchant

  Liberals *
    Calvin Lovegren—retail merchant
    John Longacre—real estate
      developer
    Donald Scott—labor-union official
Uncommitted
  Wilbur Rake—lawyer

Petropolis
Whites
Inner Cliques
  Orthodox Conservatives
    Ralph Todd—industrial executive
    Edward Star—banker
    Lawrence Phelps—banker
    Martin Astir—industrial executive,
      banker

  Community Conservationists
    Mayor Plunkett—retail merchant
    Eben Bacon, Jr.—broker
    Mrs. Ann Burgett—housewife

  Liberals
    John Jay—real estate salesman
    Fred Ames—labor-union official,
      editor

Uncommitted
  John Leek—industrial executive

Negroes
Liberal Inner Clique
  Councilman Standish—investment
    counsellor
  Frank Eldon—broker
  Lou Griffin—investment counsellor

Metroville
Whites
Progressive Conservative Inner Clique
  William Polk—industrial executive
  Harold Allen, Sr.—industrial execu-
    tive
  Samuel Trump, II—industrial execu-
    tive

Dissident
  Williston Russell, III—lawyer

Negroes
Progressive Conservative Inner Clique
  Councilman Vida—minister
  Reverend Meeter—minister
  Samuel Best—educator

* These three men were a Latent Leader clique.

FIGURE 8.1 *Inner cliques, dissidents, and uncommitted at the political-leadership level.*

characteristics of the clique members. The content of their political ideologies was derived from open-ended interviews, published statements, and correspondence that was made available; it provided the descriptive name for the larger leadership groups in which they were central figures.

POLITICAL IDEOLOGIES OF THE CLIQUES

Four Conservative Cliques

"Jeffersonian Conservative" describes the ideology of the three-man inner clique in Farmdale. The men who were nominated most frequently by their Manifest Leader peers as most influential in the community included Mayor May, who was a farmer; his brother, who served on the school board and also was a farmer; and the Mayor's uncle, who was serving in the state legislature. All three were Taft Republicans. Thus, two of the three farmers among the Manifest Leaders were in the inner clique. They were both wealthy, and their uncle, a Main Street merchant, was even wealthier.

They all firmly believed in the Jeffersonian utopia, as they understood it. If other citizens wanted to enjoy the relatively high, although unpretentious, levels of living attained by these three and their poor immigrant fathers, they should work hard in order to reap the rewards that come to the industrious.

They regarded problems of modern life as those of the lazy, impatient person who looked to the city for the more immediate rewards of a superficial sort; for what could a city offer except the misery Jefferson described in the urban centers of the Eighteenth Century? Civic virtue was an impossibility in the modern city, as life in the not-so-distant city of Oretown would show the naive. They viewed political controversy and bitter community conflict, pitting neighbor against neighbor, as the inevitable outcomes of the metropolitan life that corrupted the civic virtues of rural America.[7]

Civic virtue was considered the summation of the virtue of the citizenry as individuals. One could not live a self-reliant life as an individual except on a farm or in a small community in a farming area. A rapidly growing or big city was both consequence and cause of the moral degeneration of Americans. Those who wanted something for nothing looked to government at all levels to provide what the frontiersman and individual farmer provided for himself. Voluntary mutual aid and assistance became impossible when, instead of property-owning people reciprocally helping each other, large numbers of people had nothing to contribute to the common effort. It was natural, but undesirable, that those with nothing turned to government to get something from their more affluent, virtuous neighbors.

Private charity increasingly was being replaced by governmental doles which stimulated the breakdown of the good community. This breakdown also was quickened by the immoral and unscrupulous but quick-minded and energetic few who gained power and prestige from entering politics and speeding up the processes that make a large city infamous. Others, less energetic but equally adverse to hard work, became public bureaucrats and administrators, adding impossible burdens to the already overladen backs of the minority of industrious, moral property-owners.

The cities of the East offered the clearest examples of the evils associated with urban growth. There the greed of anti-Jeffersonian industrialists was equaled only by the un-American philosophy of Southern European and Russian aliens who came to work in the factories and mines. These were prototypes of what needed to be rejected by the children of frontiersmen and of industrious immigrants from England and Northern Europe living in such American Western communities as Farmdale.

The most immediate danger to the integrity of the community came not from the poor or the politically power-hungry, but from well-meaning, misguided citizens who advocated new or expanded public programs requiring local government expansion. Such people failed to understand that once the local government began to increase its scope, a chain reaction would be begun, making an Oretown of Farmdale. They also misunderstood the nature of community improvement, which was, in the eyes of this Jeffersonian Conservative clique, a matter for personal or group efforts by private citizens working voluntarily together.

The serious charge of community disloyalty could be leveled at those whose personal interests put them on the side of shifts in the functioning of local government that not only would lead to dangerous net expansions in the scope of government in the future, but also would immediately set Farmdale on the road to urban growth. Such growth would destroy forever a good community in a region and in a country where bigness and density were increasingly the twin social evils that make individual civic rectitude impossible.

The two farmers in the inner clique, as well as the third Jeffersonian Conservative clique member, believed that the emphasis should be placed on preserving the relatively virgin small community in an increasingly despoiled larger society. The third member of the clique was in a business—selling and buying mortgages—that not only was symbolic of the modern, mobile urbanized society, but that also could profit from an increased population in Farmdale. Yet growth in population would not necessarily mean that he would receive more fees from mortgage transactions; nor did growth in the industrial base necessarily mean lower property taxes for any of the inner clique. A rapidly expanding population might bring new mortgage companies to the community, with the end result being less, rather than more, business for Judge Catis' firm. With new industry might come disproportionate increases in the cost and tax level of municipal government to combat such social phenomena as crime and delinquency which could be expected to arrive with the industrial working force. Factory workers would be younger people with large families, and the propertied would be expected to contribute their share of increased school costs for educating the children of such newcomers. It also would cost quite a bit of money to convert the volunteer fire department to a full-time, paid operation. The net result would be higher taxes. These three men used exactly these arguments in opposing new industry for Farmdale and in opposing those sets of demands for shifts in the scope of local government believed to lead to undesired city growth.

Although they were affluent, the inner-clique trio in Farmdale considered themselves typically middle class, socially and culturally. Although they were sophisticated about state, regional, and national political affairs, well read, and members of extracommunity organizations, they took pride in their informal dress, in the "commonness" of their recreational and social pursuits, and in their disdain for pretentious forms of "cultural" activities. They were proud of being men of the people. They strongly believed that sound citizens of some property had to safeguard the collective interest in a small community by serving in local government. They felt that the community had nearly come to ruin in the postwar period because its leadership was overly responsive to citizen demands, such as the desire for a new, expensive sewage-disposal plant. They felt that this violated the sacred property-tax structure, and that it had to be avoided in the future by means of a conservative fiscal policy and constant watchfulness.[8]

There were conservative inner cliques in both Oretown and Petropolis, but they differed from the Jeffersonian Conservatives of Farmdale as well as from each other in some aspects of their political ideologies. The Oretown and Petropolis cliques were Orthodox Conservatives. The four men of the inner clique in Oretown were all relatively well-to-do, hard-working retail merchants. Two were brothers who owned an appliance store, one owned a furniture store, and one owned the largest restaurant in Oretown. The four were close friends, and their business establishments were near each other on Main Street. Like their conservative-clique counterparts in Farmdale, all four were Taft Republicans; but unlike the Jeffersonian Conservatives in the smaller community, they could not and did not believe in or advocate the preservation of the very small, nonindustrialized community: by 1953, Oretown already had passed through its population explosion, and it always had been a one-company, industrial town. Nor did the Orthodox Conservative inner clique of Oretown adhere to an ideology that communities were simply atomistic collections of individuals, where the virtuous had one view on the scope of local government and the nonvirtuous another. To them, communities were sets of conflicting potential and actual interest groups. In this clash of interests they knew exactly where their primary loyalties were: to the downtown businessmen, to the central business district, and to the established neighborhoods where the old-time residents lived.[9]

These men saw four other major interest groups in the community: the industrialists, the merchants of the competitive Longacre business section, the residential neighborhoods where newcomers predominated —including the Longacre district—and the unionized blue-collar workers of Oretown. The industrialists were viewed generally as men who neither belonged to nor did their fair share for the community. Most of the major industry established during the war was located in fringe areas outside the city. One of the four members of the Orthodox Conservative clique had been the Mayor right after the Second World War, when an annexation of a major portion of this industry occurred, over the bitter protests of the industrialists. The Oretown clique was not pleased about the fact that one of Oretown's largest mining companies, since it was outside the city, did not pay any municipal property tax. Yet their attitude toward the industrialists was one of wariness rather than open hostility because of their more or less promanagement sentiments, which resulted from their feelings about organized labor, and their desire that Oretown be known as a city where the merchants were as happy to serve people living outside the city limits as they were to serve city-dwellers.

Another factor that may have contributed to the Orthodox Conservatives' suspicious attitude toward the industrialists was that many of the managers of these mostly absentee-owned industrial firms lived in the suburbs and even in nearby Big City. The civic, social, cultural, and—perhaps most unkindly—retail shopping activities of these industrial executives were carried out not in Oretown but in Big City.

The development of a Longacre business district meant additional direct economic competition for three of the four inner-clique Conservatives. These new business rivals and newcomers in underdeveloped and underserviced residential sections of town also competed for local-government services and facilities. Organized labor posed a threat, in their minds, because even though its members traditionally were inactive politically, the union leadership, in an effort to establish the municipal utility and during the competition that followed, had proved to be active and apparently effective in directing union funds and influence in matters of community concern.

Before the Second World War, Oretown's local government was not much larger than that of little Farmdale. It was dominated by the one large industrial firm; periodically, but on the whole unsuccessfully, small businessmen and "Populist" public-power agrarians challenged its domination. By the 1950's, the Orthodox Conservative merchant clique of Main Street viewed City Hall as an institution to be run by and in the business and residential interests of the downtown merchants. They felt that they deserved local political control because the industrialists had failed to perform their civic obligations and because a disproportionate share of the fiscal resources of local government was contributed by each downtown merchant, compared to the share contributed by each factory worker. The best local government was the least; however, when local government programs were needed or desired by the Main Street businessmen, they should be provided efficiently and cheaply under close fiscal supervision by those men.

During the period of unpleasantness in city politics from 1948 to 1952, the respectable merchants found it necessary to administer a series of defeats to those who had invaded their natural political monopoly. They would not compromise with those who had used city government unwisely, that is, in the interests of nonmerchant segments of the community. Respect could be regained for the principles of nonpartisanship, efficiency, low taxes, and the absence of spoils politics in local government only by returning to power the merchants and their organizational arm, the Chamber of Commerce.

The Orthodox Conservative inner clique had a sense of solidarity; the group consisted of comparably well-educated, knowledgeable men of business and the professions. As businessmen and as civic- and service-organization leaders, they felt that their experience and skills were superior to those of the working class. They felt that younger business and professional men who were unwilling to serve in apprenticeship roles in the civic-governmental area or industrial executives who disloyally lived outside the town were not acting in a manner befitting their occupational and social positions. Those who set up stores in the Longacre section, engaged in marginal business operations through advertising gimmicks and give-aways, and approved of municipal power were beyond the social pale.

Classifying the Orthodox Conservatives of Oretown according to sense of cultural class is difficult because, compared to other political ideologists, they were on the borderline between middle and high. On the one hand, they felt that the cultural level of the working-class people in Oretown was below their own. They also took pride in the feeling that they represented the continuation of the native American philosophy of conservatism. On the other hand, they felt some satisfaction that their cultural orientations and pursuits were local rather than cosmopolitan, Western rather than Eastern, and representative of the established citizens rather than of the newcomers to Oretown. Their recreational and entertainment patterns of life reflected this sense of being average or middle cultural class. Because of their sense of superiority relative to working-class people and their sense of cultural continuity, we will tentatively put them in the "high" category in their sense of cultural class, but with those qualifications.

In Petropolis, we find a variant of Orthodox Conservatism in the White four-man inner clique, which proudly used the symbol "conservative" as a primary self-identification. In this clique were an industrialist, two bankers, and a manufacturer-banker; there were no proprietors or retail merchants. All four, like their counterparts in Oretown, were members of the Chamber of Commerce; but, unlike Oretown's Chamber of Commerce, the organization in Petropolis represented primarily industrialists, financiers, and larger proprietors. The merchants had their own organization, an association of retail and wholesale businessmen. One of these four men had once been a prominent official in a national association of bankers in Washington, D. C.

Like the Orthodox Conservatives of Oretown they believed that what was good for business was good for their community; but by business they meant large-scale industry and finance rather than retail trade. They seemed little concerned with the plight of the latter in the general downward economic trend in Petropolis; nor were they concerned with the deteriorating economic position of White or Negro labor in manufacturing. They were all bitterly antiunion in their philosophy.

The two industrialists, in fact, were true believers in surplus and cheap labor, partly because these factors contribute to prosperity for business, and therefore for the community, and partly because they provide the necessary conditions to strengthen the moral fibre and enterprise of working people. To them, poverty was a punishment for sins or a deserved consequence of individual moral failings.

Local government, in their eyes, could not do much for them or for the business community of Petropolis, but it could do considerable harm. Certain housekeeping services had to be provided, but fiscal conservatism should be maintained in providing them. If the poor, particularly the hated Negro–White-labor political machine, were to get complete control of City Hall, the property tax would skyrocket as the result of mismanagement, corruption, and frivolous expansion of local government. A stable tax rate and socio-political structure were important to this clique of Orthodox Conservatives. The stable tax rate should be as low "as it once was," and the socio-political structure should be restored "to what it used to be." In this over-whelmingly Democratic city, all four men were registered Democrats and identified themselves as such at the local level. One regarded himself as a strong Democrat, one as a "not-so-strong" Democrat, and two as Independents at the national level.

The planning and zoning functions of local government, the public-housing program, and the efforts of City Hall to help attract new industry all were to be curtailed, if not eliminated. Under no condition should visionaries be permitted to engage in urban redevelopment or renewal through government, or to expand programs of public works, public welfare, or "boondoggle" public monuments such as a government center. If minimal local government could not meet all desirable community needs, these needs should be satisfied by private efforts. Welfare should be moved from the public domain to the private.

The restorationist outlook of these four conservatives in regard to the net scope of local government also applied to the social and political order. The pre-New Deal period was their time of utopia. Most Negroes had known their place and the White labor unions never would have dared to enter either local politics or an alliance with PESNEG's radical and unrepresentative Negroes. The latest result of New Deal socialism, the Supreme Court's school-desegregation decision in 1954, was unconstitutional, unnatural, and immoral, since the

Negro race was biologically inferior; the decision had to be resisted by all legal means short of force. They felt that it would be many years before the Negro subcommunity would be prepared by secular and religious education to receive from the White subcommunity the status and opportunities that a few radical Negroes, a handful of power-oriented White politicians, and a hypocritical North had stimulated Negroes in Petropolis to demand prematurely.

Three of the four men actually believed that Negroes are inferior to Whites "by nature" in regard to such traits as responsibility, morality, ambition, and even intelligence; the fourth thought that 90 per cent of Negroes were inferior to Whites in these respects. Three of the four men approved—two "strongly"—of the notion that the Supreme Court's power to rule on segregation be taken away by Constitutional amendment. Two of the four inner-clique conservatives disapproved of the Mayor's new biracial race-relations group; two were undecided.

The Orthodox Conservatives of Petropolis differed from those in Oretown in two respects. Those in Petropolis not only wanted White industrialist-financiers to rule in the local polity rather than proprietors and professional men, but they also had a higher sense of cultural class than the Orthodox Conservatives of Oretown. The former participated in a country club in their residential suburb, but they also felt culturally superior to every other interest group in Petropolis, White or Negro. For these people social and cultural class sentiments were intertwined and indistinguishable.

Metroville's single White clique, identified through the nominations of the White Manifest Leaders, also was conservative, but of the type that we call "progressive conservative." The members of this inner clique were three of the leading industrialists of the city. They were directors or top officers of a large number of major glass-manufacturing and banking concerns, including the very largest economic enterprises in Metroville. Not only did they serve on interlocking boards of directors, but they also had interlocking kinship connections. All three men were born in Metroville and their fathers were all wealthy industrialists. In Petropolis, none of the four Orthodox Conservatives in the inner clique had such social backgrounds. Two were from professional homes and two were from the lower middle class; only one was a native of Petropolis. In Metroville, the three men identified themselves as Democrats locally, but "Independents" nationally. In fact, all three were early supporters of Eisenhower for the presidency. One reported that he had considered joining the Republican party.

These men believed, as did the Jeffersonian Conservative clique in

Farmdale, that the community—like the nation—had a single legitimate interest: the collectivity, an organic unity, rather than a community of conflicting interests. In the view of the Progressive Conservatives of Metroville, the community was a collectivity or organism consisting of mutually interdependent social, economic, and racial parts. In contrast, the Jeffersonian Conservative clique of Farmdale viewed the community as a set of generally self-reliant, autonomous, propertied individuals, pursuing substantially common objectives. Both sets of conservatives agreed, however, that the community had a single, organismic interest, even though in Metroville it was a function of mutually interrelated parts and in Farmdale a function of basically identical individuals.

For the Progressive Conservative clique, each part of the community had its natural place; the leading citizens, the men who directed the economy of the city and who owed an obligation to the city that had provided the setting for the exercise of their natural talents, were its brain as well as its heart. The aristocracy were the guardians of the community's interests, in an almost Platonic sense, instead of each property-owner's being the guardian of his own interests and thus of the community's in the "invisible hand" sense of Adam Smith. The Progressive Conservative clique of Metroville was not interested in being popular with the citizens at large; but neither was it averse to allowing the public to see its guiding hand.[10]

The sense of *noblesse oblige* of the select few, of the class which possessed wisdom as well as economic, social, and political power, was complemented by their belief that organization by any other sector of the organismic community to dissipate their controlling, guiding, and directing functions was subversive. This applied equally to proprietors, factory workers, or Negroes. Efforts by these latter citizens to organize and "make demands" of, rather than "submit requests" to, the beneficent leadership were assumed to result from either an easily corrected oversight on the part of the rulers or foreign, communist-inspired plots by un-American subversives.

The Progressive Conservatives' view that civic troubles were caused by foreign, northern, radical agitators seemed to be more than rhetoric. They had a deep-seated belief that demands for substantial changes in one or another aspect of the community decision-making system could not have originated locally, but must have come from outsiders bent on destroying the finest fabric of American community life.[11] When outside organizers tried to form a union in the city's largest industrial firm during the Second World War, and some of the top officers of the local were said to have allegiances to the Radical Left, their foreign-conspiracy theory of civic conflict seemed to them to be confirmed.

The chief officers of the company, one of whom was one of the three inner-clique Progressive Conservatives, had decided that if they had been paying sufficient attention to the morals and guidance of their workers, the workers would have rejected union advances at the outset. So management instituted a program of worker education in "labor-management relations," consisting of courses and seminars for the workers, supplemented by religious and spiritual counseling. An improved paternalism, higher wages, better working conditions than were necessary in economic-power terms alone, and a refined management intelligence-collecting operation were considered sufficient guarantees that the workers would perform their economic and civic roles properly.

Metroville's Progressive Conservative clique differed from the Orthodox Conservatives in Oretown and Petropolis in that it did not consider the community to be a congeries of greater or lesser interests that had to be reckoned with, or even fought, in making policies that set the scope of local government. The citizens were expected to contribute to the best of their abilities to the voluntary fund-raising campaigns for community charities and cultural facilities that were endorsed, sponsored, or initiated by the White civic-political leaders of Metroville. The latter knew that they themselves could be relied upon to contribute more than their fair financial share to such ventures. The citizens also were expected to support the programs and revenue measures of the local government that were approved by this civic leadership, whose property taxes paid for the bulk of the costs of city and county government in the city and in the country.

The conservatism of the inner clique in Metroville was "progressive" in another respect. During the previous decade, part of their progressivism had been manifested in their valuation of consumption, particularly of "culture," in the setting of a puritan dedication to hard work and the industrious life. Their pride in their community and in themselves, their cosmopolitanism,[12] and their regard for their national, regional, and local images all seemed to play a part in their desire that the entire community partake of the fruits of civic life in the affluent society. Voluntary, privately organized activities were preferable when possible; but these attitudes gave their conservatism the progressive quality of using local—as well as state and national —government when they felt it appropriate to initiate a civic program. To be sure, they were as aware of local government's potentiality to facilitate their business and industrial needs. But a restricted or contracted local government was not high in their ideological scale of values nor in their ideological rhetoric, as was the case with the Orthodox Conservatives of Petropolis.

Race relations seemed more harmonious in Metroville than in Petropolis, at least on the surface. This difference in open conflict reputedly resulted from the differences in racial beliefs and actions on the part of such Manifest Leaders as the inner clique in Metroville. However, the differences in racial perspectives that were found to exist were at variance with those presumed to exist by informants in the subcommunities of Metroville.

The Progressive Conservative inner clique in Metroville shared an image of the natural inferiority of Negroes. All three men approved of stripping the Supreme Court of its race-relations jurisdiction by Constitutional amendment. Two of the three disapproved of stopping desegregation either by withholding state funds from school districts that began to desegregate, closing the schools in such an event, or "resisting with force any attempts to mix Negro and White children in the same schools." The third member of the inner clique strongly approved of closing the schools altogether if necessary, "rather than have Negro and White children go to school together." He also approved of withholding state funds from school districts that desegregated, and "if need be," of using force to resist desegregation. He disapproved of Harmony House, although the two other clique members approved of it. In fact, one of the latter had worked for its establishment in Metroville.

It should be recalled that, by Time M, Metroville already had token desegregation. The schools had not been closed, state funds had not been withheld, and force had not been used by any citizen in an effort to block school desegregation. The attitudes of the two men in favor of token desegregation differed from the attitudes of the resistant clique member. The former were opposed in sentiment to desegregation, but they actively supported the Supreme Court decision, at least in regard to school desegregation. The latter was opposed to desegregation. His political ideology was similar to that of White Supremacists, but it was overlaid with a Progressive Conservative ideology. Although such a combination of feelings was not common among the White Manifest Leaders of Metroville, it was possible for a person to adhere to both ideological orientations at the same time.

Before the Second World War, possible "public" needs of Negroes in Metroville were ignored almost totally by the political leadership. Private charity was the rule; the transfer to the municipality of the privately donated general and mental hospitals for Negroes was one of the few exceptions to the practice of dispensing charity from individual Whites to individual Negroes. Commonly, the channel through which such charity flowed was that of master to domestic servant. With the unsettling events of the Second World War, it became impossible for White political leaders to ignore the Negro subcommunity and some of its aspirations. Led by one of the three members of the present inner clique of Progressive Conservatives, most of the White guardians adopted the general policy of reestablishing orderly relations between the racial subcommunities. The outlook became a more or less progressive adaptation of the "White man's burden" attitude. Efforts were made to improve the education, economic opportunities, and civic responsibilities of at least the minority of industrious, earnest, moral Negroes. The White leadership did not hesitate to use the municipal government, or even federal funds, for such projects as Negro public housing during the postwar period.

The resistant member of the inner clique, and a few fellow White civic leaders, felt that a restoration of the Negro subcommunity to its "natural" position, subservient to the White community, was the preferable policy. This was to be accomplished by a demonstration of firmness by the ruling class. The decisional preferences of this racial restorationist in regard to the matter of school desegregation were even more conservative or reactionary than the comparable preferences of the active-racist Orthodox Conservative clique in Petropolis. However, he had gone along generally with the policy preferences of his peers, even in regard to the decision to initiate token school desegregation. It was his intransigence and active leadership role in the mental-hospital-expansion decisional process that had resulted in the reversal of the position of the special hospital committee described in Chapter 6.

His deviance from his inner-clique peers in racial attitudes brought about some cleavage and instability in the inner clique and in the larger Progressive Conservative political-leadership group, where his policy attitudes put him in the minority. On the other hand, he shared many of their "Progressive Conservative" perspectives and, in fact, had been one of the most active leaders in establishing the policies of Progressive Conservatism in Metroville. However, even though he became increasingly opposed to desegregation, he still is considered to have been a Progressive Conservative and is so classified as of Time M, since he lacked the pervasive, preoccupying, racial-superiority sentiments that marked the White Supremacists in these Southern cities. He is, though, referred to below as "resistant."

The racial attitudes of the other two inner clique members were "progressive" when contrasted to those of the Orthodox Conservatives in Petropolis. The "White man's burden" perspective was coupled to an aristocratic conception of the ruler's duty in Metroville, but these two race-relations "progressives" recognized that as time passes most things change. In Petropolis, the White Orthodox Conservative inner clique did not seem to feel that adjustments and readjustments in the relations of the two racial subcommunities needed to be made over a period of time. In a sense, they had a utopian's timeless perspective. The race-relations situation could be returned to what it had been; or if restoration were impossible, the existing relations between the two subcommunities could be frozen indefinitely.

All four men in the Orthodox Conservative clique in Petropolis bitterly opposed desegregation. They favored stripping the Supreme Court of its authority to rule on desegregation. None of them approved of using force to prevent school desegregation, but only two disapproved, and neither one strongly, of closing the schools, if necessary. One person said that this should be done "only as a last resort after trying other methods." The fourth was undecided. All were working actively to prevent any school desegregation, and in this they contrasted with the accommodation policies pursued by two of the three Progressive Conservatives of Metroville. However, we shall not label the Orthodox Conservative inner clique in Petropolis White Supremacists, since that label is reserved for political ideologists who make White Supremacy the central, overriding, all-embracing feature of their political life. This was not the case with any of the four Orthodox Conservatives of Petropolis.

In summary, then, the conservative clique in Petropolis was an interest-oriented set of Orthodox Conservatives with White Supremacy race-relations perspectives; the conservative clique in Metroville was a community-oriented aristocracy with racist sentiments, which generally was accommodating in its race-relations policies. Except for the hospital decision-making process, the restorationist in that inner clique did not let his dissident racial-policy preferences overwhelm his otherwise Progressive Conservative views in political decision-making.

All these manifest political-leadership inner cliques are called "conservative" because they shared a belief that the institutions of local government should be under the guidance and leadership of one or another segment of the community that had more economic power than any other. Their opinions varied as to which segment of the more affluent ought to have such political roles, as well as in their conception of the fundamental character of their communities. There was also some variation in their sense of social and cultural class and in their views of the proper scope of local government in the community. Compared to the inner cliques whose ideologies will be described, some of these variations seem minor; but they did appear to affect political decision-making, decisional outcomes, and the scope of local government.

Competition to Conservatism in Farmdale

One of the two Farmdale Manifest Leaders regarded by both informants and the other Manifest Leaders as a policy deviant was Councilman Cox, a small businessman whose low income was reflected in the location of his residence and business on the "other" side of the tracks. He was a self-appointed spokesman for his less articulate neighbors in this less desirable section of the city. His neighbors brought their troubles to him and he passed them on in the form of demands to his fellow councilmen and the Mayor. Periodically, he made demands that local services such as street paving and repairs be diverted to his section of town from those sections that had been improved already. This was regarded by his Manifest Leader peers as his major policy "peculiarity." A minor peculiarity was his articulate concern with the local tax rate and the costs of municipal government. All of his fellow councilmen were fiscal conservatives, but they sometimes found his proposals to save even more of the taxpayers' money rather unrealistic.

The second Manifest Leader, increasingly renowned for his deviant stance in political decision-making, was Kenneth King, the editor-publisher of the weekly newspaper. His deviance was restricted to policy views regarding the local economy; he urged particularly that the local government give active assistance to the search for new industry and aid in the establishment of a Chamber of Commerce devoted to that purpose. His fellow Jeffersonian Conservatives still regarded him as a conservative in his basic principles; they gave no indication that he had become any softer on socialism than he had been when he took an active role in the postwar defeat of a local public-power movement. But his repeated warnings that the local government and his fellow businessmen must bring in new industry or perish increasingly were thought eccentric; they were not seen as products of the clear vision of a businessman who saw no other way to survive economically.

Mr. King's editorial and personal urging that the municipal water supply be expanded apparently had some impact during the authoritative-consideration stage of that decisional process in which a compromise was worked out. He had been a political leader in that process, and he continued to press for a greater expansion of the water facilities than had been provided in that compromise. When he also continued to urge that a Chamber of Commerce be established to bring in new industry, severe social and economic sanctions were used effectively against him. His fellow Manifest Leaders feared that through his paper he might stimulate the revival of the dreaded postwar Community Conservationists or, at the least, the development of an anti-Jeffersonian, more modern brand of boomer Orthodox Conservatism, such as had been witnessed among the merchants of Oretown some years earlier.

Competition to Conservatism in Oretown

In Oretown, the Orthodox Conservative inner clique was faced with rival cliques of Manifest Leaders, as well as individual dissidents like those in Farmdale. With the election of Mayor French in 1952, the Orthodox Conservatives who had assisted in his election found that they had not backed a high-spirited youth who would quickly learn to accept their counsel and guidance. Instead, Mayor French was an articulate proponent of a divergent ideology and the central figure in a four-man, rival inner clique. Mayor French was a young attorney who, as of 1953, decided, as had many another young attorney, that election to local office was one good path to an established legal practice and a possible state or national political career.

Another member of the Community Conservationist inner clique was an administrator of a special local-government district in Oretown. He felt that his career prospects would be enhanced by developing a strong program in his district through local intergovernmental cooperation with City Hall. The third member was a junior executive in one of the city's largest mining companies. The junior executive suspected that his position with his employer was endangered by his local political activities, but at this time he was in the process of finding a more satisfying career. The fourth member of the inner clique was the least ideologically oriented, but his love of strategic planning and tactical operations made the time he spent in his political leader role well worth the loss of income that it might have brought him in his small business. Besides, he suspected that his political contacts actually would increase rather than decrease his business.

The political ideology of these men was in the process of development during Time E to M. In an inchoate form, it was present as of 1953; at that time it resembled the doctrines of a textbook in municipal government more than a program of political action. This divergent ideology, Community Conservationism, was not wholly at odds with the Orthodox Conservative ideology. Both valued nonpartisanship, efficiency, honesty, and a civil-service system in city government. Although the members of the Orthodox Conservative inner clique were all Republicans and three of the four Community Conservationists were Democrats of the liberal variety at the state and national levels, these differences in party identifications did not distinguish the local political ideologies of the two groups. In fact, the fourth member of the Community Conservationist inner clique was an official in the county Republican hierarchy.

To the Community Conservationists, the community was a collectivity of mutually interdependent parts. Although they were aware of interests and interest groups, they believed that these interests were compatible and convergent. In this, they resembled the Progressive Conservatives of Metroville more than the Orthodox Conservatives of either Oretown or Petropolis. The latter saw interests as bound to conflict in the pursuit of scarce resources. Like the Progressive Conservatives of Metroville, the Community Conservationists of Oretown had their eyes on a future marked by sufficient growth in goods and services to satisfy all. The middle-aged, Orthodox Conservative inner clique of Oretown seemed to have been so molded by economic scarcity that they were preoccupied with getting their fair share of the pie. The more optimistic, abundance-oriented young Community Conservationists felt no reason to doubt their ability to increase the size of the pie.

The community-of-scarcity outlook of the Orthodox Conservative inner clique contrasted with the community-of-abundance outlook of the Community Conservationists of Oretown. This was reflected in their respective views of local taxes: the Orthodox Conservative clique wanted the cost of local government to be as low as possible and their own share of these low taxes to be as small as possible; the Community Conservationists were not low-tax people; nor did they seem very concerned with who paid how much, so long as needed programs of community conservation were provided. These latter, particularly three of the four members of the inner clique, seemed almost selfless in their disregard of the personal economic costs of their community-service activities and almost cavalier in their unconcern with their personal tax bills.

We have designated this latter political ideology "community conservation" partly because, as we have said, like the Progressive Conservatives of Metroville, theirs was a communitywide, essentially collectivist ideology, rather than an individualistic ideology such as the Jeffersonian Conservatism in Farmdale, or an interest-oriented ideology such as the Orthodox Conservatism in Oretown and Petropolis. However, in contrast to the Progressive Conservative clique in Metroville, the Community Conservationists of Oretown believed that the constitutional representatives, the formal authorities, should rule; rather than the industrialists-financiers, rather than men of commerce or retail businesses, rather even than the propertied, the Community Conservationists believed that the entire public, through its representatives, should participate in ruling. Setting and shifting the scope of local government were tasks that had to be performed within the political organization of the community in the public interest; as a general principle, the public interest cannot be identified with one or another segment of the community.[13]

The Community Conservationists of Oretown had a distinctive set of preferences about the scope of local government. These were connected intimately to their view of the community as a series of potentially harmonious and integrated, mutually interdependent parts. First of all, they believed that life in a community produced a profit or surplus that a set of isolated individuals could not attain. Some portion of this surplus had to be reinvested in public programs and improvements to make the profit grow, as well as to increase the resources to be distributed to and consumed by the private sectors of the community. Moreover, there are certain valuable tangible and intangible goods and services that had to be provided through the offices of local government whether or not all citizens recognized their value. These included education for young and old, recreation, aesthetic enjoyment of surroundings, the reduction of noise, dirt, and congestion, and the joy of working together for the good of all.[14] Cooperative action included efforts to solve immediate problems and work out plans for the future, in order to prevent problems and to raise the level of living. Community cooperation was particularly pleasurable, as well as necessary, after a period of community discord and conflict or in the face of external threats. During the Lovegren administration of 1948–1952, Oretown had suffered a violent four-year period of overt political conflict. The postwar civic progress in nearby Big City seemed to add to the feelings of inferiority of Oretown's citizens and to promote envy and a companion sense of suspicion and even fear of their neighboring city.

Merchants, real-estate developers, professional men, and city officials feared that they might lose customers, clients, and taxpayers to Big City. The Community Conservationist inner clique foresaw the possibility that Oretown might be absorbed eventually by its increasingly metropolitan neighbor through consolidation or merger. To them it seemed possible, since the benefits of independence gradually were being overshadowed by the costs of living in a community which was deteriorating as a result of internal conflict and a breakdown in civic pride, as well as through local government's failure to function as it should. Large-scale metropolitan organization had, in fact, a certain appeal to these Community Conservationists; but they wanted consolidation out of strength, not weakness; out of negotiation between respected equals rather than a merger in which a superior city took over an inferior city to solve problems that the latter could and should have solved by itself.

The term "conservationist" was part of the classificatory label for this inner clique because their views and values about their community resembled, in many respects, those of traditionally designated conservationists in regard to natural resources. Natural-resource conservationists believe that the citizens of the United States and future generations have a collective interest in proper resource utilization. The guardians of this public interest are the experts in resource administration. Depending on conditions and trends, their major emphases may vary from preservation or maintenance of an existing pattern of natural resource use, to improvement in the supply and a shift in resource-consumption patterns, to a renewal of resource bases. The natural-resource conservationist not only must have experts in resource management deciding and implementing the policies that give content to the meaning of "proper" resource utilization; but they also must have sympathetic, cooperative citizens working with and for them. Such active citizen support, based on "natural interests," is particularly necessary when "selfish interests" act to despoil or ravage natural physical resources for short-term private profit in contravention to the long-term public interest.[15]

The inner clique of Community Conservationists found themselves at odds with the Orthodox Conservative inner clique of Main Street merchants, as well as with other sectors of the community in certain cases regarding the proper scope of government. Both cliques supported the city-manager form of government. But to the Conservatives this meant, among other things, a city manager who would understand and treat as a matter of priority the needs of the downtown businessmen. To the Community Conservationists, a strong city manager was essential; but he had to be free of commitments to any particular special interest group.[16] These two inner cliques had conflicting decisional preferences regarding such matters as whether or not the municipal utility should take over the private utility, or vice versa. To the one, a well-run municipal utility had great community benefits, as in Big City; to the other, the municipal utility was socialism, regardless of the fact that, in the neighboring Republican-dominated city, the businessmen seemed pleased with their electricity rates, which were among the lowest in the nation.

Annexation of fringe areas which had no city services and areawide health and sanitation problems was favored by the Community Conservationists. To annex such areas in the interests of the entire community, a major Oretown mining company had to be included in the annexation. A good citizen must pay his share of city taxes. If annexations took place which did not include this industrial firm and its highly assessed properties, undue and unexpected cost to the city-dwellers or to those in the newly annexed area might result, and the service benefits contemplated might not be possible; in the view of the Community Conservationists, such a situation would be seriously detrimental to Oretown.

The Orthodox Conservative clique disapproved of annexation of the area that included the large industrial firm. They preferred not to share their voting rights with a set of lower-class people who voluntarily settled in and contributed to conditions of squalor, primitive living, and potential disease. Removing this blight from the nearby landscape was not considered to be worth the costs that the city and its taxpayers would incur for sewers, streets, and other city government facilities and services. Supporting the annexation of the large industry would make the Orthodox Conservative merchants appear anti-industry to its managers; they had no intention of allowing the industry to be annexed. Even more important in their probusiness ideology was the fact that annexation of this area would permit the municipal electric utility, whose area of operations was restricted to the city limits, to compete with the private utility in another area. The Orthodox Conservative clique had not given up their hope that the private utility would be able to eliminate this socialistic intrusion in Oretown.

Another example of differences in policy perspectives related to differences in the political ideologies of the Community Conservationists and Orthodox Conservatives was in regard to urban planning and guided development. The Conservatives regarded city planners with suspicion, but recognized that zoning and planning could serve the interests of businessmen in their commercial and residential locations.

To the Community Conservationists, zoning and planning were necessary for the construction of the good community. The Progressive Conservatives of Metroville, incidentally, resembled Oretown's Community Conservationist clique in recognizing the possibilities for guiding community development; but they resembled the Orthodox Conservative clique of Oretown in that they treated city planners with disdain and thought the planners ought to be subsidiary agents and servants of industrialists and financiers.

At this time, the rhetoric of the Community Conservationist clique was distinctly liberal as well as community conservationist. Part of this liberal rhetoric was directed against the industrialists because they did not share in community affairs and take the proper "long-range" view on such matters as annexation. They directed another portion of their rhetoric against the opponents of the municipal utility. The Orthodox Conservatives were more upset by the latter attacks than by the charges that industrialist participation in civic life was unduly low. They also felt that the city's major industrialists were not cooperating sufficiently; but they did not appreciate epithets such as "big business" when applied by the Community Conservationists to any of Oretown's businessmen.

Some of these differences in policy perspectives between the Community Conservationists and Orthodox Conservatives are apparent in the items they reported as "most" and "least" important to a community. All four members of the Community Conservationist inner clique ranked "community spirit or attitude of the people" or "willingness of the people to undertake and support action to meet community needs and problems" as one of the three most important factors in community life. Only one of the four Orthodox Conservative clique members considered this factor to be of comparable importance; another selected this item as among the three *least* important factors. Business or employment opportunity on the other hand was ranked one of the three most important factors in the eyes of only one Community Conservationist but was one of the three most important factors to all four of the Orthodox Conservatives.

During Time E to M, the Community Conservationist inner clique did not push for annexation, a substantial strengthening of urban planning, or a quick victory for the municipal utility. They felt that healing the wounds of the body politic and the generating of community consensus, harmony, and cooperative action were of prime concern; the initiation of civic-improvement programs could then follow. They did not preclude the possibility of working with the Orthodox Conservatives, since there was potential and actual overlapping in their ideologies, along with the aforementioned differences. Natural-resource conservationists, particularly under conditions of political weakness, will work with some special interests against other, more dangerous, common foes. At Time E, after the election of Mayor French, the Community Conservationists and Orthodox Conservative inner cliques of Oretown faced a political opposition which necessitated periodic mutual cooperation to defeat an even more undesirable enemy. Pragmatism was the dominant principle of the Community Conservationists during this period of underdeveloped doctrines and relative political weakness.

In spite of their differences in political ideology, the Community Conservationists and Orthodox Conservatives of Oretown did cooperate —successfully, as it turned out—in the political decision-making process regarding the location of a municipal parking lot in the downtown area. Their mutual opponent was a group of people who represented the interest of the newer Longacre retail-trading center. They also cooperated in working for the new sewage-disposal plant, and in efforts to create a community hospital.

The third political-leadership clique, led by three men who were not among the Manifest Leaders, had been identified by informants as a set of influential men who held different views about the appropriate scope of local government than did the other cliques.[17]   In fact, these three men constituted the inner clique of a group that had aspired to political-leadership positions during Time E to M, but whose efforts to attain a share in political power were frustrated in all but one decision-making process. At the center of this clique was former Mayor Lovegren. The second in command was his staunch supporter, Councilman Longacre. The third was the top labor-union official in Oretown, who had arrived in the community after the Second World War and joined the Lovegren camp.

The labor-union official was a Democrat; Councilman Longacre was a Republican; and former Mayor Lovegren was a registered Republican but a self-identified Democrat. It was not their state or national partisan orientations that earned their political ideology the title of "liberalism"; rather it was their conceptions of the character of their community, of who should rule, their sense of social and cultural class, and their views about the proper functioning of, the scope of, local government.

This Liberal inner clique saw Oretown as a set of conflicting interest groups, as did the Orthodox Conservatives. Even though Mr. Lovegren and Councilman Longacre were relatively affluent—the former was a retired merchant and the latter an active real-estate developer

—they felt that they represented the "little man" of Oretown, who was forgotten, ignored, or treated shabbily by the well-to-do.[18]   These "little men" included labor, whose interests the labor-union official in the Liberal inner clique felt were his primary concern, the residents and merchants living in the newly developed Longacre Area, and the poor people of Oretown in general.

In the view of the Liberal inner clique the local government was safe only in their own hands and those of their friends.   Unless they held elective office, their strong needs for personal political status would not be satisfied.   In governmental positions, they could keep the costs of local government low and see that it functioned to serve the needs of their own "have-not" supporters.

The municipal utility was their pride and joy.   They had defeated some of Oretown's most powerful men in a no-holds-barred contest in establishing the utility.   Yet this victory was never secure.   When Lovegren was defeated in the 1952 election for Mayor, the question arose as to what the "good government" crowd in the French administration and the Orthodox Conservatives of Oretown might do with their control of the city's affairs.   The issue between public and private power seemed to activate rank-and-file members of the labor unions in Oretown so that the union official in the Liberal inner clique was extremely anxious that the private utility not emerge victorious when the issue was resolved.

Organized labor traditionally had been against the city-manager form of government.[19]   The union official in the Liberal clique was hostile to the manager system in Oretown, as were his two colleagues in the Liberal inner clique.   Their dislike of Mayor French and his fellow Community Conservationists was rooted in an antipathy to the latter's advocacy of a strong city manager and an autonomous administrative decision-making process.   To them, administrative officials appeared to be pawns of the business community.   They were dead set against increasing the political distance between their less affluent citizen supporters and the government.   They opposed the manager system and the stress on the importance of professional public administrators by Community Conservationists as a political-power grab by these inaccessible, unresponsive, and irresponsible people.

These Liberals strongly opposed any attempt to deprive them of the opportunity to exercise their self-acquired political leadership skills in defending their own interests and those of the less privileged against the privileged, vested interests.   The members of the Orthodox Conservative clique considered political leadership to be a somewhat onerous and unrewarding necessity, which political circumstances forced on men who would have preferred to discharge their general civic duties in other ways. For the Community Conservationist clique, political leadership was a means to a somewhat grander set of personal or community ends. For two of the three men in this Liberal clique, the exercise of political influence in acquiring political power, particularly under conditions requiring conflict and an atmosphere of conspiracy, seemed to be what made local politics so important to them.

The labor-union official was the weak link in this Liberal clique. He was not without a certain sort of militancy, but this was not underpinned by a personal need for political influence. Like the other members of the Liberal clique, he lacked any elaborate conception of a positive program whereby local government might function to advance labor's interest even if public power and industrial development were endorsed.[20] His emotions were on the side of liberalism. He liked its antibusiness and anti-industry rhetoric, and found in the electric-power issue a meaningful return on his and his union members' participation investment. If such returns decreased or disappeared, some formal recognition that labor was a respected interest group in Oretown and a more liberal rhetoric on the part of the Community Conservationists conceivably could combine to eliminate organized labor's representation in the Liberal clique. This would leave the Liberals without a direct connection to any mass base at all in their efforts to return to a manifestly powerful position in the political leadership. These assessments and thoughts did not originate with the analyst; they were conscious considerations by members of all three political-leadership cliques.

The two businessmen in the Liberal clique regarded themselves as typically middle class; the labor-union leader felt that he was regarded as of lower-social-class status by most of the civic leadership of the community. However, all three felt that they were regarded by the "respectable" segments of the community as men of very low cultural class. For example, their anti-city-manager sentiments were treated with haughty scorn and derision by their political opponents. The Liberals felt that this was indicative of the general inferiority which their intellectual "betters" attributed to everyone else's ideas. The Community Conservationists also regarded themselves as members of the middle class in social-structural terms, but felt that they had access to the modern truths of proper community organization and life patterns. Their sense of being members of a nationwide, highly respected cultural class, rooted in intelligence, high levels of education, expertise in the management of public affairs, and in selfless concern with the common good, stands in sharp contrast to the Liberals' feelings of being treated as ignorant men whose ideas were scorned.

According to our informants, the one Manifest Political Leader who had no fixed commitments to any one of the rival Manifest Leadership inner cliques was Wilbur Rake, an attorney at law. This uncommitted Manifest Leader was respected by members of both the Orthodox Conservative and the Community Conservationist inner cliques and in turn respected them; but this was not true of the Liberal clique. In this sense, he had commitments; but because neither his political ideology nor his political participation committed him to either the Orthodox Conservatives or the Community Conservationists, he is classified as an uncommitted Manifest Leader. He came from a well-to-do merchant family, and was a Republican of "liberal" persuasion by background and inclination. Rake was an early supporter of a municipal utility for Oretown. He was active in community controversies and retained the respectful admiration of all participants except those in the Liberal clique.

His political ideology was eclectic and pragmatic. In fact, he represented an ideological position that was a composite or merging of Orthodox Conservatism and Community Conservation but that did not have the doctrinaire attitudes of either of these inner cliques. Some portion of his political status and political influence seemed to derive from the aura that emanated from the self-confident, skilled legal craftsman and some portion from his renowned abilities at negotiation and compromise. There were other uncommitted men among the Manifest Leaders of Oretown, but none who had quite the same entrée into the inner circles of both the Orthodox Conservatives and the Community Conservationists.

Competition to Conservatism in Petropolis

Petropolis also had a clique of White Manifest Leaders whose political ideology diverged from that of the Orthodox Conservatives. The informants were correct in suggesting that this opposition to conservatism was a coalition of two inner cliques. The combination is termed the Community Conservation-Liberal clique because of the ideologies of its two parts.

In the Community Conservation clique were Mayor Plunkett, Eben Bacon, Jr., the scion of one of Petropolis' first families, and a wealthy woman of another leading family who was active in women's organizations, welfare work, race relations, and local politics in Petropolis. The three were very concerned about the vicious circle in which they felt the community to be caught. In their eyes, several factors contributed to increasingly severe racial, economic, and class antagonisms, which in turn led to further deteriorations in the community conceived as a collectivity: an archaic double community based on racial division; people and groups working against each other to the detriment of everyone; a civic leadership of disproportionately older men resistant to changes; the absence of long-range planning; and the underdevelopment of a middle class.

In contrast to the short-range goals of the Community Conservationists in Oretown, this clique felt that immediate major moves had to be made to expand the scope of local government to stop further deterioration in community spirit, and to avert further damage to the public interest. Although they had no integrated master program of decisional preferences, they were more consciously committed than their counterparts in Oretown to the doctrines of Community Conservation and to a set of civic-improvement policies. They felt that successful programs of improvement in race relations, including the initiation of school desegregation and the development of better biracial civic leadership, were needed urgently. Improvement of the economy through new industry and redevelopment of the central business district were of the highest priority. Improvements in urban planning and general urban redevelopment and local-government reorganization, particularly annexations of highly assessed industrial areas and consolidation of the city and county school systems, were considered important supplementary means of returning Petropolis to a state of community cooperation and effective collective action.

In Oretown, the strategy of the Community Conservation clique was a defensive one of trying to preserve a minimal level of community integration in order to prevent a complete breakdown in the civic, political, and social orders of the community. Anarchy had to be avoided and the Liberal threat of personal government eliminated before programs of community improvement, redevelopment, and renewal could be initiated through a local government which represented the public interest. Of course, this difference in the two cliques of Community Conservationists was a matter of degree; but it can be illustrated in the matter of municipal parking lots. In Petropolis, the Community Conservationists considered the building of a series of parking lots around the downtown business district a top priority project. This would be of immediate benefit to the merchants; but because of the collective, interdependent nature of the community it would also benefit all citizens; it would improve the entire retail-trading sector of the economy; and it would help to restore civic pride and serve as a magnet to new industry looking for a dynamic city with a modern, pleasant downtown business district. In Oretown, one municipal parking lot was proposed for the downtown area. Oretown's Community Conservationists felt that this shift in the scope of government would have rather limited benefits and consequences in the community. In this and other matters, the Community Conservationists of Oretown were pragmatic in an individual, policy-oriented sense; their counterparts in Petropolis were programmatic or multiple-program oriented.

The Community Conservationists of Petropolis were allied to a Liberal group, the leadership of which resembled the Liberal inner clique in Oretown in their view of the community as a set of competitive interests which they, as the representatives of the interests of the less affluent, lower-status citizens, should rule. Both men in the Liberal clique were more programmatic than their Liberal counterparts in Oretown. Their decisional preferences resembled those of Liberals at the national level. In fact, they viewed the potentialities of local government's role in the local economy and the local social structure much as they viewed the potentialities of the federal government in the national socio-economic structure.

According to the Liberal clique, slum areas were obvious and extensive, particularly in the Negro neighborhoods, but also in White and racially mixed areas. Little low-cost private housing was available to buyers; in fact, after the Second World War, no major, minimally priced housing subdivisions had been built, partly because loans for such developments were difficult to obtain locally. Therefore, it was necessary to expand the local government's public-housing program. Automation in the city's manufacturing plants was contributing to a chronic unemployment situation. The local government's policy position was a crucial determinant of whether or not new industry would come to Petropolis, whether or not it would be high-wage, unionized industry, and whether or not it would be Northern firms coming South to escape unions and union-scale wages.

The Liberals felt that the hospitals operated and maintained by the county government in Petropolis for Negroes and the poorer White citizens were inferior to the private hospitals available to wealthier, upper-class Whites. The levels of education for the residents of the urban fringe were inferior, preventing Whites and Negroes from understanding their true working-class interests and preserving attitudes of racial intolerance and mutual distrust that weakened the Liberal cause.

Since oppression of labor by management knew no bounds, apart from considerations of morality and social justice, the White Liberal in his own interest had to fight for and with the subordinate Negro sub-community. Without education or with inferior education, the Negro constituted another major source of low-wage competition to the White worker. It was necessary that the city government take the lead in breaking the bonds that bound the Negro. The city also should consolidate with the county government, since, because of the traditional conservatism of rural residents and of the White county officials, the latter probably would lag behind. So went the political thinking of the White Liberal clique in Petropolis.

The man who was most articulate in his New Deal-like, intellectual liberalism was the labor-union official. He was a highly educated writer for the local labor newspaper who served as one of the top officers of the local Democratic party. The chairman of the local Democratic party was his fellow Liberal in this clique. The latter, a small businessman, was neither as programmatic nor as committed to the interests of organized labor and racial equality. But both men believed that the political success they both desired could best be obtained through control of the Democratic party and, eventually, of the city and· the county governments. A voting bloc comprised of White and Negro organized labor and PESNEG, with its rank-and-file political workers, was essential to the Liberal clique in order to control the Democratic party and maintain at least some access to city government. This political force would be led by the Liberals with the assistance of the Community Conservationists, whose only chance of success in their community objectives was dependent upon the political organization led by the Liberals. This was the hope of the Liberals and, in some measure, the already present reality of Petropolis' politics.

A working alliance and coalition of sorts existed between the Liberal and Community Conservationist cliques. The latter group was electorally supported by the former. The Liberals, in turn, were given support by the latter in their Democratic party contests and appointments to agencies of local government. Although they agreed in general about what shifts in the scope of local government were desirable, the coalition was an uneasy one, particularly since the Community Conservationists felt that they needed to gather support from certain crucial Conservatives—especially those on the city council—in their efforts to shift the scope of local government, sooner rather than later. Working relationships between the two cliques also were strained somewhat because the Liberals had been publicly associated with what the Community Conservationists regarded as corrupt and immoral political tactics.

Both men in the Liberal clique had a sense of being treated as members of a culturally deprived class. The labor-union official felt that the White civic leadership considered his composite socio-cultural position far beneath their own; the businessman Liberal still felt that he had social entrée to all but the very highest social-class groupings. His feeling of cultural rejection seemed to be rooted in the fact that, immediately after the Second World War, the Orthodox Conservative political leadership had rejected his bid to enter their restricted ranks. He had tried as a representative of the respectable younger businessmen in the community to become a member of the inner circle of Orthodox Conservative political leaders, and had propounded policies of civic improvement supported by a number of the younger business and professional men of Petropolis. He and his policies finally were disapproved by that leadership. Their Community Conservationist inner-clique allies, on the other hand, were all three of significantly higher socio-economic positions and style of life, but did not identify themselves as such. They, like their counterparts in Oretown, were people with a high sense of cultural class, especially in regard to their political morality. Such differences in the sense of political- and cultural-class position between the Liberals and Community Conservationists, rather than any differences in social-class identification, contributed in some measure to instability in this political-leadership coalition.

The Negro Leadership clique of Petropolis consisted of three men who, with other Negro Leaders, constituted a leadership group that usually worked with the Conservationist-Liberal alliance. They were Liberal in political ideology, although not unsympathetic to the aims of the Community Conservation ideology, the pursuit of which by the Community Conservationists could further their primary goal: the advancement of the Negro subcommunity.

These three men were all highly educated, wealthy, top executives in Negro brokerage, investment, and lending institutions. They were not Negro racists or Supremacists. They considered themselves to be part of a community that was treated as an inferior socio-cultural caste. Their ideological orientations were complicated by the fact that they felt considerable social distance between themselves and lower-class Negroes, even though they had racial sentiments, sympathies, and bonds with all Negroes. They had a strong sense of being culturally and socially superior to both Negro and White lower-class people, and at the same time of being treated by most Whites as a culturally inferior group. They had come to believe that the way to break down some of the racial barriers separating upper-class Whites from upper-class Negroes was to increase the economic and political influence of larger numbers of well-educated professional, white-collar, and even blue-collar Negroes in their subcommunity. Liberalism, they believed, was a more appropriate political ideology than Community Conservation for wresting the necessary political and economic advantages from the Orthodox Conservative and White Supremacist groups of Petropolis. Community Conservation seemed to them a somewhat utopian political ideology for the Petropolis of the 1950's.

These men reflected the merging of the earlier "go slowly" and "act quickly" wings of the Petropolis Negro Leadership.[21] One man had been a key figure in the cautious group that had dominated PESNEG for many years. He was now serving on the city school board. Another was the single Negro on the City Council. The third was an official of the local Democratic party and the head of the NAACP's political committee. All three were top leaders of PESNEG. Although none of the three spoke radically in public, as did a few other Negro Leaders of Petropolis, they all were committed to immediate and substantial progress for Negroes through the local political process.

These three Negro Leaders were closer to the White Community Conservationist clique than to the White Liberal clique, even though social relations were not of the most intimate, informal kind. However, it was the latter with whom they worked most closely in the all-important tactical planning regarding local government and Democratic party elections. A major strain in relations between White and Negro Liberals stemmed from the fact that many of the White rank-and-file unionists were segregationists. The latter did not feel that the labor-union official in the Liberal clique represented their political or racial views. At the same time, rank-and-file Negro unionists resented the fact that the union locals were segregated. Neither of these factors, however, had stopped electoral cooperation between large numbers of White labor-union members and Negro voters.

The counterpart to the uncommitted lawyer in Oretown's Manifest Political Leadership was John Leek, the uncle of Eben Bacon, Jr. of the Community Conservationist clique. He was not so privy to the Orthodox Conservative inner clique's deliberations as was his Oretown counterpart, partly because of his nephew's political activities and partly because of his own less than strictly conservative views. The economy of Petropolis had become his special interest, particularly strengthening the industrial base and making the Laboratory Locus a reality. His involvement with the Community Conservationists was sporadic and it was guided by these interests. He and his nephew were close, but the latter was more wholeheartedly involved in the whole range of decisional processes. Moreover, the uncle was separated from the Liberal clique and the Negro Leadership by a gulf of both social and political status. There was a disinclination to work with the former and a lifetime of custom making it difficult to work closely with the latter.

Competition to Conservatism in Metroville

In Metroville's relatively like-minded Progressive Conservative Manifest Leadership, there was one man identified as a policy deviant. He was Williston Russell, III, a respected attorney and elder patrician. He was a Progressive Conservative whose deviance lay in his "progressivism" regarding race relations. He went far beyond any other Manifest Leader in advocating the dissolution of racial barriers. He was regarded by some other Manifest Leaders as their voice of conscience. His actions, more than anyone else's, reputedly were responsible for the White Leadership's postwar efforts to reestablish more harmonious race relations instead of embarking on a path of vengeance toward the entire Negro subcommunity. The political decisional outcome of initiating public-school desegregation in Metroville also reportedly resulted largely from his active influence. His Progressive Conservatism smacked of Liberalism to the White inner clique of Manifest Leaders, particularly to the White resistance-oriented clique member. This dissident pointedly refrained from nominating any of the inner-clique trio and none of them named him as a person of similar policy views.

The Negro Leadership inner-clique trio in Metroville consisted of a minister who was the one Negro on the city council, another minister who had been his predecessor on the city council, and a Negro educator. The latter two men were Progressive Conservatives, apparently through resignation and the lack of other political ideologies represented at the White Manifest Leadership level. The term "accommodating" was used, quite surreptitiously, by a few of the younger, militant Negroes of Metroville in speaking disparagingly of these two men, particularly of Samuel Best, the educator. The former councilman, Reverend Meeter, was noted for his activities against the efforts of the left-wing labor union in the Negro subcommunity during the Second World War. Samuel Best was known for his successful efforts to gain major financial and other support for his school from the city's wealthy White industrialists.

The present Negro city councilman, Councilman Vida, who was also the only Negro on the city school board, was a Progressive Conservative in his political actions and interactions. However, his Progressive Conservatism overlay a Liberal political ideology. The latter was not dominant, since he hoped that substantial gains could and would be made by the Negro subcommunity over the next few years through full cooperation with the White Progressive Conservative political leadership. He also was aware of the absence of a strong White labor movement and the extensive political apathy in the Negro subcommunity, which was reflected in much more limited voter registration than among Petropolis Negroes. He felt that he was a close friend of his Negro councilman predecessor, although not of Samuel Best. Best, in turn, said that Reverend Meeter was a close friend but that Councilman Vida was not. Some political and social distance existed between the more Liberal Councilman Vida and the more accommodating Samuel Best.

Only three White men were chosen by the Negro Leader clique in Metroville from a long list of names which included all of the White Manifest Leaders as men with similar views about the needs, policies, and the future of the city. All three Negro Leaders nominated Williston Russell, III, the policy dissident with the most articulate equalitarian race-relations attitudes. One member of the Negro clique, Samuel Best, also named Mayor Peterson and the Manifest Leader in the White inner clique with the *most extreme White dominance sentiments*. Moreover, Samuel Best named this White influential patron as one of his three closest friends. In his turn, this White Manifest Leader said that he had close contacts and worked closely with Negro Leader Samuel Best, but did not name the latter as either someone with similar policy views or as a close friend.

The relations between the Negro and White Leaderships will be discussed further in Chapter 10. In the next chapter, we shall trace the political-group affiliations of the remaining Manifest Leaders in each community and describe something of the characteristics and perspectives of these larger political-leadership groups, including each inner clique.

NOTES

1. Robert O. Schulze refers to such nominated leaders (without any further operations to establish their degree of participation in decision-making) as

"public leaders." The questions used to obtain the initial nominations were substantially those of Schulze, questions 1, 2, and 5, as listed in his "The Bifurcation of Power in a Satellite City," Appendix B, in *Community Political Systems*, ed. by Morris Janowitz (New York: The Free Press of Glencoe, Illinois, 1961), p. 74. See Appendix A for our operational definitions of Manifest Leader and Latent Leader.

2. See, for example, the arguments in Nelson W. Polsby, "Community Power: Some Reflections on the Recent Literature"; Raymond E. Wolfinger, "A Plea for a Decent Burial"; and William V. D'Antonio, Howard J. Ehrlich, and Eugene C. Erickson, "Further Notes on the Study of Community Power," all in *American Sociological Review*, Vol. 27, No. 6 (December 1962), pp. 838–854.

3. It cannot be emphasized too strongly that different answers to such questions as: "How large is a community's leadership?" are frequently due to variations in the (often implicit) definition of leadership.

4. By "significance" here, we mean importance, particularly in regard to the functioning of political systems. Small variations might have major effects (and reflect major differences) in the politics of different communities. Very little is known about the importance of "small" percentage differences that are real and not due to sampling or other errors.

5. Harry Scoble used a variant of this sociometric technique to identify leadership "factions" in Bennington, Vermont. See his "Leadership Hierarchies and Political Issues in a New England Town," in *Community Political Systems*, ed. by Morris Janowitz, pp. 126–135. See also F. A. Stewart, "A Sociometric Study of Influence in Southtown," *Sociometry*, Vol. X (February 1947), pp. 11–31; and Delbert Miller, "Decision-Making Cliques in Community Power Structure," *The American Journal of Sociology*, Vol. 54 (November 1958), pp. 299–310.

6. In Farmdale, the three men in the so-called inner clique received such an overwhelming proportion of the nominations by the Manifest Leaders that the frequency of their nominations constituted a natural sort of "significant break in the list" of the kind used by Edwin H. Rhyne, "Political Parties and Decision Making in Three Southern Counties," *American Political Science Review*, Vol. LII, No. 4 (December 1958), pp. 1091–1107. In both subcommunities of Metroville and in the Negro subcommunity of Petropolis there was less concentration of nominations. The sizes of the inner cliques do not define the universes of clique members. The reader should be alerted to the fact that others might have been included as members of inner cliques if they had been nominated by a very few other Manifest Leaders. This simple frequency-of-nominations criterion can be improved upon when necessary by more complex operational definitions of inner-clique membership, but it proved to be useful in distinguishing sets of relatively self-conscious ideologists who were regarded by their fellows as intragroup leaders and performed as such, as the following pages indicate.

7. See Arthur J. Vidich and Joseph Bensman, *Small Town in Mass Society* (New York: A Doubleday Anchor Book, 1958), pp. 30–43, 119–121, and 310–311; and Robert C. Wood, *Suburbia: Its People and Their Politics* (Boston: Houghton Mifflin Company, 1959).

8. See Louis Eisenstein, *The Ideologies of Taxation* (New York: The Ronald Press, 1961).

9. See Harmon Sigler, *The Politics of Small Business,* Chapter IV, "Ideologies and Conflicts" (Washington, D. C.: Public Affairs Press, 1961), pp. 36–67; and Francis Sutton et al., *The American Business Creed,* Chapter 17, "The Creed Analyzed: Strains and Ideology" (New York: Schocken Books, 1962), pp. 347–383.

10. See the description of business-class control and "Family *X*," Robert S. Lynd and Helen Merrell Lynd, *Middletown in Transition* (New York: Harcourt, Brace and Co., 1937), pp. 74–90.

11. See W. Lloyd Warner, *The Corporation in Emergent American Society,* Chapter 1 (New York: Harper and Brothers, 1962), pp. 8–13.

12. See Robert Merton, *Social Theory and Social Structure,* Chapter X (Glencoe, Illinois: The Free Press, 1957), pp. 387–400.

13. For a recent statement of the importance of the public interest as a guide to national decision-making, see George A. Graham, *America's Capacity to Govern* (University, Alabama: University of Alabama Press, 1960). Cf. Glendon Schubert, *The Public Interest* (New York: The Free Press of Glencoe, 1960).

14. See *The Exploding Metropolis* by the Editors of Fortune, particularly Chapter 1, by William H. White, Jr., pp. 1–31, and Chapter VI, by Jane Jacobs, pp. 140–168 (Garden City: Doubleday Anchor Books, 1958).

15. See K. William Kapp, *The Social Costs of Private Enterprise* (Cambridge, Mass.: Harvard University Press, 1950).

16. See Jeptha J. Carrell, *The Role of the City Manager* (Kansas City: Community Studies, Inc., 1962).

17. Although each of these three men had been nominated by the panels, none of them received enough nominations as being influential in policy-making to be included as Manifest Leaders. However, they were more frequently nominated as men of distinct policy views, and as opposing others named in the latter connection.

18. For the role of individual small businessmen and something about their motives in several struggles over the city-manager form of government, see Edwin K. Stene and George K. Floro, *Abandonment of the Manager Plan* (Lawrence, Kansas: University of Kansas, 1953).

19. Recent studies that have pointed to the basis of such attitudes include: John H. Kessel, "Governmental Structure and Political Environment: A Statistical Note about American Cities," *American Political Science Review,* Vol. LVI, No. 3 (September 1962), pp. 615–620; E. L. Sherbenou, "Class, Participation, and the Council-Manager Plan," *Public Administration Review,* Vol. XXI, No. 3 (Summer 1961), pp. 131–135; and Stene and Floro, *op. cit.*

20. This is not far from the picture of the views of labor-union officials in Lansing, Michigan, in 1957 as described by William H. Form and Warren L. Sauer, "Organized Labor's Image of Community Power Structure," *Social Forces,* Vol. 38, No. 4 (May 1960), pp. 323–341; and see the references cited therein. See also William Form and Delbert Miller, *Industry, Labor, and Community* (New York: Harper and Brothers, 1960).

21. See James Q. Wilson, "Two Negro Politicians: An Interpretation," *Midwest Journal of Political Science,* Vol. 4, No. 4 (November 1960), pp. 346–369; and his *Negro Politics* (Glencoe, Illinois: The Free Press, 1960).

9

THE POLITICAL-LEADERSHIP GROUP STRUCTURES

When we map the group affiliation of the remaining Manifest Leaders, we find that in Farmdale there were one group of Manifest Leaders, with one political ideology, and two individual dissidents.[1] One of the two dissidents, Councilman Cox, was a "lone wolf"; the other, Mr. King, believed that he shared policy views with the other Manifest Leaders, but they did not indicate that they thought he did.

In Metroville, apparently, there was also only one distinct group; this group had subgroups at the Manifest Leadership level. The Negro Leaders had the following indirect connections to the White Manifest Leaders. Although the one White dissident refrained from saying that his views were similar to those of the members of the White inner clique, other White Manifest Leaders identified members of the inner clique as sharing their policy views and were identified as such by one or more of the inner clique, or both. Moreover, other White Manifest Leaders named the dissident, and he named them as having policy views in common with his own. The Negro Leader inner clique indicated that White inner-clique members had similar views to its own, but was not so mentioned by them; members of the Negro Leader clique also indicated that the White dissident had similar policy views to their own. Nonclique Negro Leaders named members of the Negro Leader clique, the White dissident, members of the White inner clique, and other White Manifest Leaders as having similar policy views. Only the White dissident indicated sharing policy views with both inner-clique and non-inner-clique Negro Leaders.

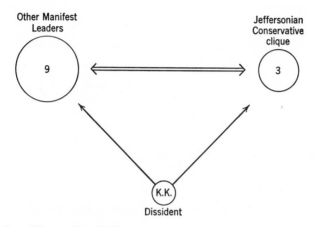

FIGURE 9.1 *Farmdale: Manifest Leadership group structure.*

A central figure in this constellation of subgroups was the White Progressive Conservative dissident whose views on race relations were extreme in the direction of active accommodation. Mr. Russell was the man most frequently nominated—White or Negro—by the Negro Leadership as one of the most influential men in Metroville. The White Manifest Leadership ranked him as influential less frequently than ten other White Manifest Leaders. Moreover, this dissident Progressive Conservative was nominated by the Negro Leaders more frequently than was any member of the Negro Leader clique as a person with whom they shared policy views; White Leaders ranked him lower in this regard.

There were individual Negro Leaders whose political ideology was clearly more Liberal than the ideology of Councilman Vida. However, in terms of their own reported working relationships with others at the Manifest Leadership level, their views all were related, indirectly through their own Negro Leader clique or through other

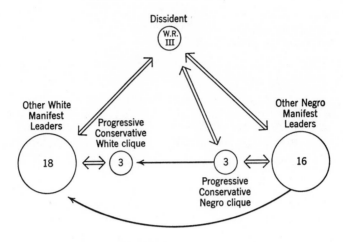

Key: W.R. III = Williston Russell, III
      ⟺   = Reciprocal choices
      ⟶   = Direction of nonreciprocal choices

FIGURE 9.2 *Metroville: Manifest Leadership group structure.*

White Manifest Leaders—particularly Mr. Williston Russell, III—to the single grouping of Manifest Leaders for whom the Progressive Conservative White inner clique constituted the political-ideological core. This picture of the group structure at the Manifest Leadership level in Metroville does not imply that the subgroups of White and Negro Manifest Leaders were committed as self-consciously or as wholly to the political ideology of Progressive Conservatism as were the three members of the White inner clique. However, no political ideologies other than Progressive Conservatism were represented by distinct and separate groups at the Manifest Leadership level in Metroville.

In Petropolis at the Manifest Leadership level, in contrast to both Farmdale and Metroville, we find three political ideologies represented by groups of men, one competing against a coalition of the other two. Twenty of the White Manifest Leaders not yet discussed were identified by one or more of the Orthodox Conservative inner clique. A number of them also felt that they had views similar to those of John Leek, the uncommitted Manifest Leader; the feeling was reciprocal. Nine other White Manifest Leaders were uncommitted: they either did not indicate that they had views similar to those of any inner-clique member, or, more frequently, they named members of both the Orthodox Conservative and Community Conservationist inner cliques.

The Community Conservationist clique was weak numerically, compared to other groups of White Manifest Leaders. Besides their identification with and by the uncommitted Leek and two of the other uncommitted White Manifest Leaders, they said that only two of the other twenty White Manifest Leaders were people with whom they shared policy views. Moreover, the latter identifications were not reciprocal. None of the non-inner-clique White Manifest Leaders named either member of the Liberal clique, who were both allied with the Conservationists, as a person of similar policy views. The Community Conservationists in the Manifest Leadership were in these ways politically closer to other Manifest Leaders than were their Liberal allies, but both wings of that alliance viewed Orthodox Conservatism as the opposition ideology.

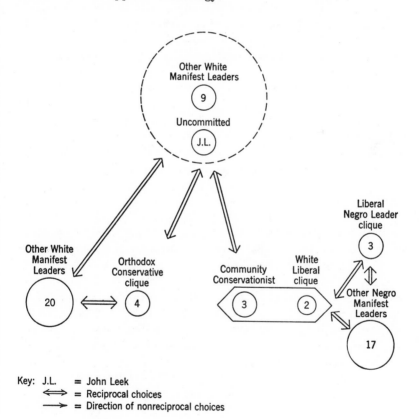

Key: J.L.   = John Leek
    ⟺ = Reciprocal choices
    ⟶ = Direction of nonreciprocal choices

FIGURE 9.3 *Petropolis: Manifest Leadership group structure.*

The Conservationist-Liberal clique coalition identified and were identified by the Liberal Negro Leader clique as men with similar views. The other Negro Leaders were related in the same manner to the Conservationist-Liberal clique coalition. No White Orthodox Conservatives identified any inner-clique Negro Leader as a person with similar policy views, and vice versa. One other Negro Leader, George France, a very wealthy executive of a large loan company who had in earlier years been the chief counsel of moderation to his fellow Negro Leaders, was regarded as a man of similar policy views by two non-inner-clique White Orthodox Conservatives. France also was viewed as a close friend by the same two White Leaders. Two of the three Negro Leaders in the inner clique were named as "close friends," one by four and one by all five Conservationist-Liberal clique members, and also by two of the White Manifest Leaders who claimed similar views with Orthodox Conservative clique members.

Since these apparently were the only points of direct relationship between the Orthodox Conservatives and the Negro Leadership, they deserve closer examination. The wealthy Negro Leader, George France, clearly was more conservative and less liberal, as well as more of a gradualist, in his political ideology than were his Negro Leader confreres. He and two of the three inner-clique Negro Leaders were the only Negroes ranked by the predominately conservative White Manifest Leaders as among the thirty men of most influence in policy-making in Petropolis. France and these two others were the only Negro Leaders named as close friends by any of the Conservative White Manifest Leaders, and he was the only Negro Leader named by the latter as a person with whom they shared similar policy views. However, his fellow Negro Leaders did not rank George France as among the most influential policy-makers in Petropolis.[2]

Another Negro Leader and member of the inner clique, Lou Griffin, was not named by the White Manifest Leaders as among the thirty most influential policy-makers. Griffin, however, was regarded by his fellow Negro Leaders as one of the three most influential men, White or Negro, in local affairs, and as one of the four most influential men, White or Negro, in school affairs in Petropolis. The White Conservationist-Liberal clique coalition named Councilman Standish as the Negro Leader with whom they had similar policy views; he was another member of the Negro Leader inner clique. He was regarded by his fellow Negro Leaders not only as the most influential man in Petropolis in local-government affairs, but also as the number-one man to whom they would go for advice in regard to local-government affairs.

The fact that two of the three members of the Liberal Negro Leader clique also were named as close friends by two conservative White Manifest Leaders indicates something of the ability of the former to work with the latter when, in their view, such cooperation would further their political goals. This testified to their political skills in maintaining this sort of friendship image in the eyes of even a few conservative White Manifest Leaders. Although the Negro Leader clique was Liberal in its political ideology, it proudly pointed to its ability to maintain necessary working relationships with Orthodox Conservatives on the infrequent occasions when such relationships were useful or necessary in informal politics, and with members of the City Council and school board in more formal, official situations. It is such Negro Leaders as these men who were responsible for placing advertisements for their business establishments in the radical, White Supremacist weekly newspaper in Petropolis, a self-confident act.

However, the points of direct, interpersonal connection between the White Orthodox Conservatives and the Negro Leadership were primarily with and through George France. France was not a man of top political status for the other Negro Leaders. His unsuccessful efforts to be the first Negro elected to a county-government post resulted from pressures from his fellow Negroes who wanted a candidate most likely to attract votes from Whites. His decision to run did not overcome his low status with the less cautious Negro Leaders, although it did signal a narrowing of the gulf between the gradualist and more militant wings in PESNEG. There is a parallel here to the relationship between Negro Leader Best and his White peers and "friends" among the White Leadership of Metroville; but the two situations actually were very different.

Samuel Best, the Negro educator in Metroville, was in many ways George France's counterpart. However, a most important difference is that Best was at the very core of the Negro Leadership of Metroville, whereas France was a marginal member of the Negro Leadership of Petropolis. Not only was Samuel Best one of the three members of the Negro inner clique of Metroville, but the other Negro Leaders ranked him more frequently than any other Negro Leader—and only slightly less frequently than Mr. Williston Russell, III—as a man whom they considered to have views most like their own about the needs, policies, and future of their city. Moreover, he was tied for first place with Negro Councilman Vida as the man with whom the other Metroville Negro Leaders worked most closely on community projects or policies. Thus, the Negro Leader in Metroville who felt himself close to the most racist member of the Progressive Conservative inner clique, and in fact was nominated by another member of that clique as having similar policy views, was a member of the Negro Leader inner clique and a man of active political influence with many other Negro Leaders. His counterpart in Petropolis, though related in comparable but less central ways to the White Orthodox Conservatives, was a far more peripheral member of the Negro Leadership.

In Oretown's political group structure at the Manifest Leadership level, almost equal numbers of Manifest Leaders were affiliated with the Orthodox Conservative and Community Conservationist cliques. Another one-third, like Wilbur Rake, were uncommitted. None of the non-inner-clique Manifest Leaders indicated that they had any sympathetic working relationships with the Liberals led by the three-man Latent Leader clique. A few of the Manifest Leaders who apparently had been members of the Liberal group prior to Mayor French's election in 1952 were now affiliated with the Community Conservationists. These findings confirm the impression that, even though other members of the Liberal group were still serving in the City Council, the substantial Liberal loss of power and top political-leadership positions—for instance, the office of mayor—was related, during Time E to M, to a rapid growth of the new group of Community Conservationists which had attracted supporters away from the Liberals, as well as from the ranks of the Orthodox Conservatives.

In summary, the multi-group structure at the Manifest Leader level was similar in Petropolis and Oretown in at least three ways, compared to the single-group, individual-dissident structures in Metroville and Farmdale. First, both Petropolis and Oretown had sets of competitive political ideologies represented by distinct groups of men. Second, a number of Manifest Leaders had overlapping memberships in otherwise distinct Orthodox Conservative and Community Conservationist cliques in both of those cities. The third point of similarity was the relative isolation of the Liberals from others in these two Manifest Leaderships. At the same time, the position of the Liberals in Oretown's Manifest Leadership differed from the position of the White Liberals in Petropolis's Manifest Leadership in the last respect. In Petropolis the White Liberals not only were associated directly with the Community Conservationist clique, but they also had close ties with the Liberal Negro Leadership.

Another point of difference was the proportion of Manifest Leaders who were associated directly with the Community Conservationists in Oretown and Petropolis. In Oretown, ten of the thirty-one non-inner-clique Manifest Leaders said that they shared policy views with one or another Community Conservationist but with members of no

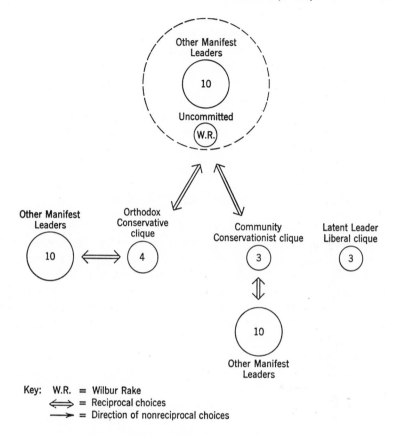

FIGURE 9.4 *Oretown: Manifest Leadership group structure.*

other inner clique; in contrast, none of the thirty-one non-inner-clique White Manifest Leaders of Petropolis reported common views solely with that group. The inner clique of Community Conservationists thus had a numerically broader independent base among the Manifest Leaders of Oretown than the Community Conservationist inner clique of Petropolis had among its White Manifest Leaders. In contrast, the latter were organizationally affiliated with, and more dependent upon, the small White Liberal clique and the more numerous Negro Liberal Leaders. We shall now turn to the political perspectives and characteristics of these groups at the Manifest Leadership level.

Because of the perceived central positions of the inner cliques and the affiliations of Manifest Leaders with one or two inner cliques or none at all, Manifest Leaders are classified under the ideological label of the inner clique with which they were reportedly affiliated, or as uncommitted. Working relationships between people of reportedly similar views are treated as an indication that the Manifest Leaders were to some extent sympathetic, participating members of the political group or groups labeled with the ideologies of their inner cliques. The extent to which policy perspectives and decisional preferences were homogeneous within each of the groups was investigated rather than assumed. This is reported on in the following pages when the perspectives of the political groups are compared within and among the communities.

THE ONE POLITICAL-LEADERSHIP GROUP IN FARMDALE

The characteristics of Farmdale's Jeffersonian Conservatives, including the inner clique, are substantially what they were reported to be in the description of the Manifest Leaders in the previous chapter. If Councilman Cox is treated as outside the Jeffersonian Conservative group, the one low-income Manifest Leader is removed from that group. Every one of the Jeffersonian Conservatives in the Manifest Leadership of Farmdale was involved in the discussions of every one of the decisional processes during Time E to M, except for the matter of approving the proposed state-highway relocation to bypass Farmdale, which was deliberated by only the inner-clique trio. Not every one of these Manifest Leaders participated actively in the discussion of every process; but their presence in a relatively small group when these matters were being discussed made them a much more involved group than even the active influentials, who in turn discussed these matters more frequently than the citizens of lower political-influence rank.

While active influentials normally discussed particulars regarding civic-improvement matters, particularly in the housekeeping subcategory, Jeffersonian Conservative Manifest Leaders discussed particular needs in the setting of their general policy or decisional perspectives which were intimately related to their political ideology. These perspectives were negative in regard to any increases in the net scope of local government in the local economy, or in general; these negative attitudes were reaffirmed periodically in their deliberation and consideration of decisional questions. Discussion about elections and candidates occurred in a similar context. Whereas the active influentials and the citizens as a whole seemed to be concerned with the personality and morality of particular candidates, the Jeffersonian Conservatives tended to discuss these attributes in the context of their ideological orientations. They periodically talked about local taxes in both specific and general terms, unlike the active influentials, who discussed taxes infrequently, and unlike the citizens who discussed the subject in most general terms.

The miscellaneous items most frequently mentioned by the active influentials in Farmdale were related to such things as water pollution, flood control, and irrigation. When discussed by the Jeffersonian Conservative Leadership, they were treated as matters for consideration by individual firms, farmers, and farm organizations. The role of the local government in the reorganization of the economy was not discussed extensively by the citizens at large nor by the active influentials. But it was considered extensively by the Jeffersonian Conservative Manifest Leadership group. The possibility of local government helping to attract new industry finally was decided through the defeat of demands for the extension of city services to a prospective industrial firm and for municipal assistance in establishing and cooperating with a chamber of commerce. The latter would presumably put Farmdale on the road to industrial development.

The Jeffersonian Conservative group paid a great deal of attention to Main Street. They felt that the more merchants were suffering, the more likely that some of them would become receptive to demands for new industry and for the municipality to take over the street-lighting program from the private utility and expand it. One of the younger Jeffersonian Conservatives, as he put it, kept his "ear to the ground" to assess the extent to which individual merchants of Main Street discussed "dangerous" proposals. By Time E, the group had begun to give more attention to collective action through one of the existing service clubs to help the merchants. By doing this they hoped to avoid further demands on local government in this area.

Councilman Cox was regarded as dissident by his fellow Manifest Leaders partly because he acted as a representative of a section of the community rather than in the interests of the whole community, and partly because he rejected the intragroup decision-making norms of the Jeffersonian Conservatives. Two of these primary norms seemed to have been the assessment of the probable future impact of policy formulations on the net scope of local government as the criterion to be used in establishing decisional preferences; when that criterion resulted in doubt as to the proper decisional outcome, the judgment of one of the inner-clique trio was to be taken as correct. Councilman Cox stated that he regarded his own judgment as infallible.

There were other Jeffersonian Conservative Manifest Leaders with

special policy interests, such as a dedicated natural-resource conservationist who advocated more and better local parks. These demands were disposed of by channeling them through either the service
clubs or the county and state government. The natural-resource
conservationist invariably complied with such suggestions.

In contrast to the situation among Farmdale's active influentials,
the Jeffersonian Conservative group did not represent personally any
political interest in favor of expanded municipal programs of housekeeping services, such as the water supply, street lighting, or street
paving. It was noted in Chapter 7 that one of the three active influentials in the sample, who turned out to be among the Manifest Leaders,
represented the views of the entire Manifest Leadership in actively
opposing, with other Manifest Leaders, the demands of another active-
influential merchant for additional street lighting for the central business district. The active influential who had taken an active part in
defeating demands for the establishment of a chamber of commerce
was also a member of the Manifest Leadership and had represented
the perspective of the whole group in his actions. The three active
influentials who were also Manifest Leaders, as well as one active
influential who proved to be a Latent Leader, were all members of
the Jeffersonian Conservative political-leadership group. Their approval of the *status quo* thus was rooted in a political ideology that
placed great value on the small community.

The one Manifest Leader who favored parks and recreation did not
provide a point of access for those who demanded a municipal recreation program. That Manifest Leader, as well as some of the small
businessmen who predominated among the other Manifest Leaders,
seemed to be pursuing, in the service of closely fitting political and
economic interests, policies advantageous to small businessmen. Small
businessmen could reason, and some of these men did, that community
growth could lead to increased competition and thus damage their
economic interests.

But other small businessmen in the same Manifest Leadership group
were conscious of pursuing their ideology—or their ideological "interest"—in a way that violated their own conceptions of their economic
interests, defined in both short- and long-range terms. The latter,
like Mr. King, felt that the way to greater wealth was to increase
sales through expansion in the size of the city and in the number of
resident customers. Advertising was viewed as a futile device for
doing much to help retail trade; new industry with its payrolls and
purchasing power was the only way to increase significantly their
economic fortune. But to these men, unlike Mr. King, new industry

and community growth were evils to be avoided at almost any cost.

The small businessmen among the Manifest Leaders were, to be sure, relatively affluent. They did not have the sorts of financial difficulties faced by Mr. King and other more marginal merchants of Main Street. But affluence is basically a relative conception: not even the most affluent of these men, including the few who also had extensive real-estate holdings in Farmdale, had incomes approaching those of the wealthiest Manifest Leaders in the White subcommunities of either Metroville or Petropolis. They were well off compared to others in Farmdale, and this may have been their standard of comparison. On the other hand, as soon as small businessmen with presumably comparable economic roles—or in Max Weber's sense, comparable economic-class positions—are thought to be distinguishable on the basis of their socio-psychological, comparative frames of reference, such "purely" economic-interest variables as occupation and income become more complex socio-psychological variables.

For some of Farmdale's Manifest Leaders, there was a close fit between their self-defined economic and political interests. But for others there seemed to be a hiatus, if not a conflict, between these interests. In the one case, their political ideology, Jeffersonian Conservatism, was congruent with their closely fitting politico-economic interest; in the other case, the same ideology fitted their political interests more closely than their economic interests. It cannot be expected that many people can adhere to an ideology that is inconsistent with their self-conceived economic interests, even though logic-tight compartments in the "normal" mind are known to psychologists. But these instances of sacrifice of self-conceived economic interests to political ideology existed, as did the distinct possibility that political ideology had shaped the economic interest of others.

What is significant here is that other small businessmen with comparable incomes in the Farmdale random sample aspired to bigger and better businesses; neither they nor their more marginal fellows of comparable economic roles discussed, to any great extent, the possibility that their economic interests might be pursued politically. Instead, they dwelled on alternative courses of self-help as the answer to their economic problems. If there were an automatic, direct connection between economic position or even economic interest and political interests, we would have expected to find that some of the economically dissatisfied had political interests in the sort of municipal government efforts to stimulate the economy that were apparent in other cities. This is not to suggest that all of the small businessmen in Farmdale were now firm believers in Jeffersonian Conservatism, particularly those who had been active Community Conservationists or more Orthodox Conservatives before Time E. This does not agree with the findings. What we do mean to suggest, and more will be said about this in Chapter 11, is the importance of the political leadership, a significant portion of which was ideologically oriented, in the actualization of potential political interests based on economic interests and position, as well as in the definition of economic interests for occupants of particular economic positions.

THE ONE POLITICAL-LEADERSHIP GROUP IN METROVILLE

In Metroville, the economic optimism of the White citizenry and, to a somewhat lesser extent, of the White active influentials was reflected in the perspectives of the White Manifest Leadership. The relative pessimism of Negro active influentials and of the Negro citizens of lower political-influence rank was not reflected in the perspectives of the Negro Leaders. The latter were less optimistic than the White Manifest Leaders in their evaluations of the state of economic opportunity in Metroville; but they were much more optimistic than other Negroes. Negro Councilman Vida was the only Negro or White inner-clique member who was pessimistic in his evaluation of economic opportunity in Metroville; this indicated his general, atypical, private policy restiveness (Table 9-1).

Although the White Manifest Leaders were relatively optimistic about the local economy, they viewed job opportunities for the citizens as one of the "most important community issues, problems, or projects" (Table 9-2). Next to the current hospital issue, economic conditions were their primary concern. This was in sharp contrast to the relatively low ranking given to the state of the economy by their Negro Leader counterparts, by both White and Negro active influentials, and by the rank-and-file citizens of both subcommunities. This concern with the city's economy was a feature of their Progressive Conservative orientation which identified the welfare of Metroville with prosperity in their own industrial and financial enterprises.

More than half the White Manifest Leaders had become active in efforts to acquire new industry. However, their efforts were not directed toward the municipal government, but partly to the county government and primarily to the Chamber of Commerce. These activities did not involve many of the Negro Leaders in comparably active roles.

The White Manifest Leaders of Metroville were not as active in industrial promotion as Petropolis' White and Negro Manifest Lead-

TABLE 9-1 Political Perspectives of Categories in Metroville

	White		Negro	
	Manifest Leaders N = 22	Active Influentials N = 5	Manifest Leaders N = 19	Active Influentials N = 2
Rating of economic opportunity in community				
Very good	23%	0%	32%	0%
Good	73	60	42	0
Not very good	5	20	21	100
Do not know	0	20	5	0
	101%	100%	100%	100%
Involvement in attracting new industry				
No concern	9%	0%	21%	0%
Discussed	32	80	68	100
Activist role	59	20	11	0
Do not know	0	0	0	0
	100%	100%	100%	100%
Spending local tax money to attract new industry				
Approve	54%	60%	79%	50%
Undecided	14	20	16	0
Disapprove	32	20	5	50
Do not know	0	0	0	0
	100%	100%	100%	100%
Rating of downtown business district				
Very good	18%	0%	11%	50%
Good	45	60	58	50
Not very good	36	40	32	0
Undecided	0	0	0	0
	99%	100%	101%	100%
Favor increased city taxes, if necessary, to rebuild downtown business area				
Yes	45%	60%	89%	0%
No	50	40	11	0
Do not know	5	0	0	100
	100%	100%	100%	100%

ers. There was also more opposition to spending tax money in this area among Metroville's White Manifest Leaders than among any other category in Metroville except Negro active influentials. The three members of the inner clique were opposed, one very strongly, not only to the idea of using local tax funds, but also to the attraction of new industry to either the city or the immediate surrounding area. Rather than increase unnecessarily the demand for labor in and around

TABLE 9-2   Rank Order of Most Important Community Issues, Problems, or Projects to the Manifest Leaders in Metroville

Subject Category *	White Manifest Leaders N = 22	Negro Manifest Leaders N = 19
Economic conditions	2.0	5.5
Race relations	3.5	2.0
Housekeeping services	6.0	3.5
Community planning	6.0	1.0
Health	1.0	3.5
Education	3.5	5.5
Governmental organization	6.0	—

* The subject categories were listed, included, and assigned a rank only if 30% of the Manifest Leaders mentioned an item in the category.

Metroville, they preferred that the more rural parts of the county with marginal farming operations have new industrial job opportunities. None of the three felt that the local economy afforded less than satisfactory economic opportunities for the citizens, so that the needs of their own firms for plentiful and relatively inexpensive labor did not seem to them to conflict with the collective needs of Metroville. The Negro Leaders, on the other hand, while inactive in the existing activities to bring some new industry to Metroville, were most approving of the notion of shifting the scope of local government in the direction of helping finance such activities.

Since the income level of the Negro citizens was low, their occupations were generally menial and unskilled, and they were under- and unemployed, how is it that at least the two so-called "progressives" in race relations in the White Progressive Conservative inner clique apparently viewed the economic circumstances of Negro citizens with equanimity? This was not a matter of unawareness; it was a facet of their "gradualistic" perspectives on race relations. They felt that every relaxation of racial barriers must wait until Negroes were clearly ready for more equal treatment. In regard to the role of Negroes in the economy, they felt that most Negroes were in jobs that suited them by training and disposition, and that unemployment, for example, was due more to laziness and irresponsibility than to lack of opportunity.

These two White inner-clique Progressive Conservatives, although referred to earlier as active accommodators, were technically active racists according to our racist-accommodator measure. This measurement was made after the decisional outcome to provide token desegregation in Metroville. They had been most active and influential in reaching that outcome but then took the position that "token" desegregation meant exactly that and not massive or even moderate desegregation. They felt not only that most of the "responsible" Negroes, particularly the Negro Leadership, were satisfied fully with the decisional outcome, but also that the Negro subcommunity as a whole was satisfied with its economic opportunities as well as with such important items as public housing for Negroes, of which both of these men approved.

Their race-relations attitudes, however "conservative," stand in sharp contrast to the sentiments of the third member of the White Progressive Conservative inner clique. All three men took a "states' rights" position in approving the removal by Constitutional amendment of the Supreme Court's power to rule on local segregation practices. As we indicated earlier, two of the men disapproved of withholding state funds, closing schools, or using force, if necessary, to prevent school desegregation, but the third member approved of those policies.

Besides Mr. Williston Russell, III, the noted accommodator, one-third of the entire set of White Progressive Conservatives were active accommodators. The White Manifest Leaders as a whole were more like the accommodating White active influentials than the more racist rank-and-file White citizens in their attitudes toward school desegregation (Table 9-3). They were much more approving of Harmony House than the White citizens as a whole, but less so than the White active influentials. The Negro Leadership, on the other hand, entirely approved of Harmony House, the majority "strongly."

Both Negro active influentials were classified as active racists, and 17 per cent of the Negro citizens of lower political-influence rank were active or potential racists. In contrast, the Negro Leaders were entirely active accommodators. The Negro Leadership was actually rather optimistic about job desegregation in the future. Forty-two per cent were very optimistic in predicting that 5 years hence "Negroes and Whites will be working side by side on the same sorts of jobs in factories and businesses in Metroville *much more than now.*" An additional 47 per cent predicted "a little more than now." The Negro Leadership was more optimistic in this regard than Negro citizens at large.

TABLE 9-3   Race-Relations Perspectives among Categories of White Citizens in Metroville

Attitude toward Desegregation Policies	Manifest Leaders N = 22	Active Influentials N = 5	Political-Influence Substructure N = 293 *
Amend Constitution			
Approve	27%	20%	48%
Undecided	32	20	28
Disapprove	41	60	24
	100%	100%	100%
Withhold state funds			
Approve	5%	20%	34%
Undecided	14	0	21
Disapprove	82	80	45
	101%	100%	100%
Close schools			
Approve	5%	20%	30%
Undecided	9	0	20
Disapprove	86	80	50
	100%	100%	100%
Use force, if necessary			
Approve	5%	0%	11%
Undecided	0	0	9
Disapprove	95	100	80
	100%	100%	100%
Attitude toward Harmony House			
Approve	59%	80%	32%
Undecided	27	20	57
Disapprove	14	0	10
	100%	100%	99%

* The numbers responding to each item actually ranged from 248 to 272 with the respondents unable or unwilling to answer the questions ranging from 21 to 45.

In regard to civic-improvement matters, a majority of the White Manifest Leadership approved of public housing. There was a smaller minority of dissenters than among the White active influentials (Table 9-4). The most racist of the inner clique was undecided about the value of public housing for Metroville. The Negro Leadership gave even greater support to public housing than the very supportive Negro subcommunity at large.

The most racist member of the White inner clique felt most strongly about the mental-hospital issue in accordance with his racist perspectives. The rank-and-file White citizens, as well as the active influentials, had divided sentiments. Equal proportions favored expansion

TABLE 9-4 Civic-Improvement Perspectives of Various Categories in Metroville

	White		Negro	
	Manifest Leaders N = 22	Active Influentials N = 5	Manifest Leaders N = 19	Active Influentials N = 2
Attitude toward public housing				
Approve	63%	60%	95%	50%
Undecided	9	0	5	50
Disapprove	19	40	0	0
Do not know	9	0	0	0
	100%	100%	100%	100%
Preferred outcome of hospital modernization				
Expand on present site	50%	0%	26%	50%
Improve present hospital and build branch	18	60	5	0
Build entirely new White hospital	32	20	47	0
Don't care	0	20	5	50
New integrated hospital *	0	0	16	0
	100%	100%	99%	100%
Attitude toward school consolidation				
Approve	86%	80%	69%	50%
Undecided	0	0	21	0
Disapprove	14	20	5	50
Do not know	0	0	5	0
	100%	100%	100%	100%
Involvement in school consolidation				
No concern	27%	60%	21%	100%
Discussed	50	20	68	0
Influenced others	14	20	5	0
Very active	9	0	5	0
	100%	100%	99%	100%

* This was an unsolicited response to this forced-choice question.

of the White hospital on its present site, improving the present hospitals and building branch hospitals for future overflow, and building an entirely new White hospital in a non-Negro area. The White Progressive Conservative Leadership as a whole was comparably divided, with only one-third in favor of the segregation plan, building the new White hospital in a non-Negro neighborhood.

Although the Negro citizenry contained a higher proportion of people who did not care one way or another, almost half the Negro Leaders reluctantly approved the plan finally adopted by the White Progressive Conservatives. *All three members of the Negro Leader inner clique joined in this approval.* A distinct minority of the Negro Leaders rejected all three of these proposals when asked by the interviewers to choose the one they preferred. Individually and spontaneously they declared that they preferred any plan that would combine the separate Negro and White hospitals into a single integrated community mental institution; this course never was considered seriously by the White Progressive Conservative authorities.

More than one-third of both the White Manifest Leaders and White active influentials regarded Metroville's downtown business district as not very good, compared to less than one-sixth of the White citizens at large (see Table 9-1). However, the three inner-clique White Progressive Conservatives rated the central business district as good or very good. Moreover, at least half of the White Manifest Leaders, including the inner-clique trio, were opposed to the idea of increasing city taxes to rebuild this area of the city. Although majorities of nonclique Manifest Leaders and active influentials were receptive to a municipally sponsored program of downtown redevelopment, the strong feelings of the inner clique and of others in these categories that this was a matter for merchants to handle themselves resulted in a consensual acceptance of the leadership's rejection of merchants' demands for such a program. Moving traffic quickly was a feature of a progressive community which was supported by the entire Manifest Leadership, over the objections of some merchants who decried the prohibition against on-street parking. The concern with blight and the beauty of buildings had not been extended to the deteriorating stores of downtown businessmen by some of the Manifest Leaders who otherwise thought that the city's aesthetic appearance was a proper concern of their municipal government.

As one example of the perspectives of the Manifest Leaders in Metroville toward governmental reorganization, we may take the matter of consolidation of city and county schools. The White and Negro Manifest Leaders approved of the idea even more than did the rank-and-file citizens of both races, who approved more than they disapproved. The only White Manifest Leader who strongly disapproved was the "resistant" White member of the Progressive Conservative inner clique. The White active influentials also approved. However, of the White Manifest Leaders who were most active in this decisional process, two approved of school consolidation; another approved but "saw the objections to it"; a fourth disapproved because the school system then would "become a political football"; and the fifth was the strongly disapproving member of the inner clique. The approving Negro Leaders, active influentials, and citizens at large all were relatively inactive in this political decision-making process.

Before drawing any conclusions from these findings, we shall mention something about the policy concerns of the White and Negro Manifest Leaders of Metroville (see Table 9-2). The major difference between White and Negro Manifest Leaders in the extent of their policy and decisional concerns is that proportionately more of the White Manifest Leaders mentioned matters of governmental reorganization, particularly school consolidation, than did the latter. The mental-hospital decision-making process topped the list of such concerns for the White Manifest Leaders; the Negro Leaders were less concerned and Negro rank-and-file citizens were unconcerned. The citizens at large in the White subcommunity were concerned less than were the White Manifest Leaders but more than were the White active influentials. It was a matter of primarily spectator concern for the citizens and a matter of personal activity and involvement for the leadership.

Community planning and guided development, particularly the need for additional public and accessible private housing, was the most frequently mentioned concern by the Negro Leadership; the state of race relations was concern number two. A smaller proportion of Negro citizens at large also ranked these two matters as their primary concerns. Both Negro active influentials were concerned with race relations; housing conditions, housekeeping services, and the quality of education were their only other concerns. Apparently the White Manifest Leadership was concerned with the widest variety of political decision-making matters, while the other categories of citizens in both subcommunities left local economic matters almost entirely in the hands of these industrial and financial chief executives for whom economic conditions had been the primary concern.

As befitting affluent men of industry and commerce, the White Progressive Conservative Leadership stressed as values—that is, the "most important factors in any community"—education, the opportunity to advance economically, the community spirit of the big companies, and labor relations (Table 9-5). The extent to which people took pride in their community also was selected as an important value by a larger proportion of the White Manifest Leadership than of the White citizens at large. The condition of race relations was not a primary value for the White active influentials, but it was of more concern to the White Progressive Conservative Leaders than it was to the White citizenry.

The Negro citizens as a whole considered schools to be of greatest importance, followed in order by availability of adequate housing, opportunity for economic advancement, and the responsiveness of city government to people's wishes. However, both the Negro Leaders and the Negro active influentials ranked the state of race relations as their primary value. The responsiveness of the city government to people's wishes was valued next most frequently by the Negro active influentials, but not by the Negro Leaders. The latter ranked opportunity for economic advancement as being as important to them as race relations, even though they did not seem to be actively involved in working toward or immediately concerned with large-scale

TABLE 9-5   Ranking of Factors as among the Three Most Important in Any Community by Various Categories in Metroville *

	White			Negro		
	Manifest Leaders N = 22	Active Influentials N = 5	Political-Influence Sub-structure N = 285	Manifest Leaders N = 19	Active Influentials N = 2	Political-Influence Sub-structure N = 203
Opportunity for economic advancement	2.0	3.0	3.0	1.5	3.5	2
Schools	1.0	1.0	1.0	3.0	3.5	1
Availability of adequate housing	8.0	4.5	3.0	4.5	—	3
Friendliness of people	9.0	—	3.0	7.0	—	6
Race relations	4.0	—	6.0	1.5	1.5	5
Responsiveness of city government to people's wishes	7.0	2.0	5.0	4.5	1.5	4
Community spirit of the big companies	3.0	—	7.5	7.0	—	9
Labor relations	5.5	—	7.5	—	—	7
People's pride in the community	5.5	4.5	9.0	7.0	—	8

* No rank order was assigned if 10 per cent of the category did not select the item as among the three most important factors in any community.

job opportunities or job advancement for Negroes, compared to their concerns with housing and various noneconomic aspects of race relations. Apparently the Negro Leadership relied, in a moderately optimistic manner, on the White Manifest Leadership and those associated with that leadership in local government positions and on the biracial Harmony House, in which some of the latter participated, for continued, if piecemeal, progress in improving opportunities for Negroes to advance economically within the existing economic structure. In this and in other policy areas, the Negro Leadership manifested no militancy of the sort shown by Petropolis' Negro Leaders.

Several points should be considered about the Manifest Leadership level in Metroville. First, although the political ideology of both inner cliques and of most other Manifest Leaders was Progressive Conservative, not every member of the single political group was a Progressive Conservative. Specifically, there was a minority of Liberals among the Negro Leaders. There was also a politically and socially meaningful racial differentiation at this level of the political power structure. However, a single functioning political-leadership group existed at the Manifest Leadership level that bridged this White-Negro separation and these ideological differences. Neither the White Orthodox Conservative Manifest Leaders nor the Liberal Negro Leaders constituted political groups distinct from a Progressive Conservative group. How the Manifest Leaders as a whole functioned as a single political group led by Progressive Conservatives, even though other ideologies were represented, is discussed in the next chapter.

A second point is that these policy and decisional perspectives were not, in fact, identical, even among the Progressive Conservative Manifest Leaders. Not only was there the minority opposition to public housing, for example, but there were distinct differences and even sharp conflicts in the decisional preferences of equally Progressive Conservative Manifest Leaders; the dissident was simply the best-known case.

Some of these differences were epitomized by the comparatively extreme racism of the one member of the Progressive Conservative inner clique. Others were reflected in the attitudinal differences toward spending local tax money to acquire new industry, to improve the mental institution, or to consolidate the schools. Ordinarily, decisional outcomes that became authoritative policy were accepted with good grace. But Progressive Conservatism as a political ideology offered only vague guidelines as to preferred policies and decisional options. The "collective interest" was of concern to the Manifest Leaders, but it frequently had to be hammered out according to personal interpretations before it could be accepted as policy to be pursued by adherents of Progressive Conservatism.

A good example of this is to be found in the area of race relations. For the most part, the Progressive Conservative orientation was toward peaceful race relations through the gradual relaxation of racial barriers, where possible on an individual basis or, if necessary, on a collective basis, in areas of token rather than "bread-and-butter" significance. White Supremacy as a political ideology was frowned upon, and the espousal of White Supremacy sentiments by the White inner-clique member, particularly on the mental-hospital issue, caused considerable discomfort, since it violated the spirit of Progressive Conservatism as interpreted by most Manifest Leaders. Yet racial accommodation in the spirit of Progressive Conservatism was sufficiently ambiguous to provide for "legitimate" disagreement as to the proper perspectives to be taken by an adherent in a policy matter.

Another point worth noting in summary is that the tenet of Progressive Conservatism that considered the organization and reorganization of the local economy a matter for private management in the collective interest, rather than for municipal government, had several consequences. The interest of the Negro subcommunity in economic opportunity was channeled through the privately organized and operated Harmony House, which had no police powers but simply the power of persuasion. Such an arrangement was approved not only by the Negro Progressive Conservative inner clique but also by almost the entire Negro Leadership. A share of the profits made by the largest firms in Metroville was devoted to public purposes through privately organized charities. The result was that the industrial executives maintained control of certain areas of civic improvement that were potentially within the scope of local government, and retained leverage to influence the local government in regard to other matters of civic improvement.

The community-planning and guided-development functions were regarded by the leadership as being inextricably tied to the organization of the local economy, and to its informally responsible, public-spirited management, from which the community at large, or at least the two segregated subcommunities, derived collective benefits. Thus the municipal zoning and planning operations at City Hall were viewed primarily as useful tools and adjuncts of corporate planning and, thereby, as in the collective community interest. The Progressive Conservatives did not denigrate aesthetic values but fitted them to the priority needs of industry and business so that slum clearance and urban redevelopment simultaneously could satisfy multiple values.

These conceptions led to majority approval by the White Progressive Conservative Leaders of public-housing programs; the local government was viewed as a proper subsidiary agency of these self-conceived guardians of the community. Another result of these conceptions was the development of the belief by some that the county government could be trusted to serve as the agent of the civic-political elite in such functions as helping to attract *suitable* new industry to the area. It should be noted that the decisional preferences of the senior industrial executives in the White Manifest Leadership, including the three in the inner clique, were in some ways less "progressive" than those of the Progressive Conservatives of other occupational positions. This can be seen clearly in the attitude toward the necessity of spending local tax money to attract new industry to the area: of the twelve men who approved of the idea, only two were senior industrial executives; the other ten were financiers, professional men, and junior industrial executives. The ten men who either disapproved or were undecided about the wisdom of spending money to attract new industry were all senior officers in the city's largest industrial firms. The financiers saw a convergence in their corporate needs to lend, invest, and make money through relocating new, diversified industry in Metroville and the needs of people in the community for additional job opportunities. Three of the four financiers approved of spending local tax money to help attract new industry, two strongly; the fourth, although he disapproved of this role for local government, was very active in efforts to attract industry to the outlying areas of the county.

These findings suggest that in Metroville there was actually a closer fit between economic and political interests at the political-leadership level than in Farmdale. In Chapter 8, it was suggested that the absence of merchants among Metroville's White active influentials may have been detrimental to the political interests of this sector of the community. This also can be said about the absence of merchants from the ranks of the White Manifest Leaders. However, their adherence to a Progressive Conservative ideology as they defined it, instead of a simple economic interest, apparently was responsible, at least partially, for such decisional preferences as support of public housing, the endorsement of the county government's efforts to obtain new industry, and token desegregation; and, as we shall see, the industrial executives among the White Manifest Leaders of Petropolis supported the spending of local tax money to help attract new industry, as did the financiers of that city. Although economic role or position can and does seem to shape economic and political interests, the shaping may vary both in degree and in kind from community to community.

THE MULTIPLE POLITICAL-LEADERSHIP GROUPS IN PETROPOLIS

We now shall consider the characteristics and perspectives of the several groups of Manifest Leaders in Petropolis. Partly because comparable data on some of the perspectives of the Negro Leaders were not available and partly to clarify the similarities and differences between the perspectives of the Negro Leaders and those of their White allies, we shall present the findings for the Liberal Negro Leaders separately from those of the White Community Conservationist-Liberal coalition. However, both that White coalition and their Negro Leader associates are regarded as members of one group that ordinarily in community politics was opposed to and by the Orthodox Conservatives, whose ideology already has been described. The coalition consisted of the two inner cliques; no other White Manifest Leaders reportedly were affiliated only with them, while twenty of the thirty non-inner-clique Manifest Leaders were affiliated with the Orthodox Conservatives.

The five members of the White Community Conservationist-Liberal group were younger than the Orthodox Conservatives or the uncommitted. Two of the former were under 35 and none were over 55 years of age. In contrast, the majority of the Orthodox Conservatives and uncommitted were men over 55. Petropolis' Negro Leadership was an older group of men than their White allies. An age difference distinguished the predominantly middle-aged Negro Leaders from their older White counterparts in Metroville. An age difference in the reverse direction also distinguished the White and Negro segments of the Community Conservationist-Liberal group in Petropolis. If age differences constitute some sort of barrier to easy communication and close, trusting associations—which may not always be the case— the difficulty Metroville Negro Leaders had in communicating and working with their White counterparts, who were separated by a racial and socio-economic gap, may have been accentuated by the age gulf. The age difference also may have reinforced a noticeable difficulty in the working relationships between the Negro and White Leaders of similar ideological persuasion in Petropolis. The more senior citizens among the Negro Leaders tended to be somewhat sceptical of the political judgment and strategy of their younger White friends; similarly, the White Orthodox Conservatives stressed, in an even more extreme fashion, the political immaturity, wrong-headedness, and deviant political behavior of their "young whippersnapper" White opponents. White Orthodox Conservatives had been known to remark that political agitation emanating from the Negro subcommunity must have originated with the very young, irresponsible Negro youths rather than with the Negro Leaders of more advanced age, who they "knew" in earlier years had been followers of a proper Booker T. Washington philosophy.

Financiers, but not industrial executives, were to be found within both racial wings of the Conservationist-Liberal political group. Organized labor was represented personally by Fred Ames, the White Liberal; but no other union official or blue-collar workers were found among either White or Negro Liberal members of that group. In contrast, industrial executives were either uncommitted or, more usually, members of the Orthodox Conservative group. More than one-quarter of the latter were industrial executives; such men and financiers together constituted more than half the Orthodox Conservative group. However, proprietors were almost as numerous as industrial executives and financiers among the Orthodox Conservative Manifest Leaders. Proprietors were represented in the White Conservationist-Liberal group by Mayor Plunkett and John Jay; the one housewife in the Manifest Leadership, the wealthy Mrs. Ann Burgett, also was in that group. The occupations of the Negro Leaders were described earlier, in Chapter 8, as being representative of the financier—that is, brokerage, investment, and lending companies—proprietorial, and professional segments of that subcommunity.

Besides these differences in the age, industrial-executive, labor-union, and housewife representation between the White Orthodox Conservatives and the White Conservationist-Liberal group of Manifest Leaders, there was also a striking difference in their party identification. Although the members of both groups identified themselves as Democrats in their local party affiliations and ordinarily were active in local Democratic party affairs, at the national level their identification as partisans differed: almost half the Orthodox Conservatives identified themselves as independent or Republican in national politics, compared to 20 per cent, one of the five, Independent Mrs. Ann Burgett, of the White Conservationist-Liberals.

This is interpreted as an indication of the extent to which the differences in ideologies between the inner cliques were manifested in an associated, consistent difference, in the expected direction, of partisan loyalties.[3] Disenchantment with the program and policies of the nationally more liberal Democratic party had gone even further among Metroville's White Progressive Conservatives than among Petropolis' Orthodox Conservatives, on the basis of this indicator; but it seemed to be present to at least some degree for the latter. It also may have been a factor in the difficulties that some of the Orthodox Conservatives encountered in working actively in, and for control of, the local Democratic party organization, a significant organization in Petropolis' community politics. In Metroville, on the other hand, the lack of strong attachment to the national Democratic party platform did not prevent the Eisenhower Democrats among the White Progressive Conservative Manifest Leaders from firmly controlling the local Democratic party organization.

Petropolis' Liberal Negro Leadership had a distinct minority of men who were disenchanted still further with what was to them a too conservative Democratic party dominated by Southern Conservative Democrats; they had become active members of the local, minority Republican party. However, the overwhelming majority of the Negro Liberal Leaders were still active Democrats, locally as well as nationally. The minority of Republicans were among the most vocal, militant Negro Leaders; this did not strengthen the Conservationist-Liberal group when political decision-making was limited to registered Democrats, as occasionally was the case.

These differences in national partisan orientations also constitute indirect evidence of the validity of the identification of the membership of these groups, based on the perceptions of presumedly knowledgeable citizens or the Manifest Leaders nominated by them; they also help to justify the sociometric procedures used to establish the group affiliations of other Manifest Leaders with the inner cliques. A more direct test of the validity of treating these groups as distinctive and as sharing different political orientation can be made with self-reports of voting—or, in the case of men ineligible to vote in municipal elections because of residence in the suburbs, preferences—in the 1957 Petropolis mayoralty election. In that election Mayor Plunkett, a member of the Community Conservationist inner clique, had defeated Ralph Todd, his Orthodox Conservative inner-clique counterpart, in a bitter contest. The members of the Conservationist-Liberal group were all Plunkett voters; the members of the Orthodox Conservative group were Todd voters. Of the twenty Orthodox Conservative Manifest Leaders who answered the question, seventeen reported voting for Todd, two did not vote, and one refused to say how he had voted. Of the ten uncommitted Leaders, five voted for Todd, three voted for Plunkett, one did not vote but said that he would have voted for Plunkett, and one refused to say for whom he had voted.

In Petropolis, as in Metroville, identifying Manifest Leaders as members of one or another group, when not uncommitted, does not mean that every member shared each clique's political ideology in the consistent, self-conscious, relatively pure form in which it was held by inner-clique members; but this self-reported divergence in vote between Conservationist-Liberals and Orthodox Conservatives lends a certain credibility to the classification of the political-group memberships of the Manifest Leaders. Not all of the Negro Leaders were asked whom they voted for in that mayoralty election, but it would be most surprising if everyone of that category had not voted for Plunkett.[4]

The subject discussed most by Orthodox Conservatives and the uncommitted as the "most important issues, problems, or projects facing Petropolis at the present time" was economic conditions, particularly the need for new industry (Table 9-6). It followed race relations as a primary concern of Conservationist-Liberals. It also was a subject frequently discussed by the Negro Leaders; but it ranked behind community planning, particularly the need for more public housing and additional private housing for Negro citizens, and race relations generally, in frequency of discussion. The need to improve the economy by strengthening its industrial base was a subject of primary

TABLE 9-6 Rank Order of Most Important Community Issues, Problems, or Projects to the Manifest Leader Groups in Petropolis *

	White Manifest Leaders †			Negro Manifest Leaders
	OC N = 20	Unc N = 7	CC-Lib N = 5	N = 20
Economic conditions	1	1.0	2.0	3
Race relations	3	2.5	1.0	2
Housekeeping services	2	2.5	—	—
Community planning	—	4	3.5	1
Health	—	—	—	—
Education	—	—	—	—
Governmental organization	—	—	3.5	—

* The subject categories were listed, included and a rank assigned, only if 30% of the Manifest Leaders mentioned an item in the category. The N's in this and following tables exclude those not responding to particular items.

† OC   = Orthodox Conservative

  Unc   = Uncommitted

  CC-Lib = Community Conservationist-Liberal

concern to the various groups in the Manifest Leadership just as it was of central concern to the citizens, especially the Negro citizens.

In Metroville, the Negro Leaders were concerned more with other policy matters in their discussion, while the White Progressive Conservatives were concerned primarily with preserving or expanding economic and job opportunities within the framework of the existing industrial base.

The Orthodox Conservatives of Petropolis were less optimistic about economic opportunities than were the Progressive Conservatives of Metroville (Tables 9-1 and 9-7). However, they were far less pessimistic than the Conservationist-Liberals, the Negro Leadership, or the citizens at large in both subcommunities. Only one of the four members of the Orthodox Conservative inner clique was active in the efforts to acquire new industry for the city, although the larger group of Orthodox Conservative Manifest Leaders were relatively active in these efforts. They even approved of spending local tax money for this purpose, but all four members of the inner clique opposed it.

The Liberal Negro Leaders and the White Conservationist-Liberals were equally active in efforts to acquire new industry and opposed demands that the local government not participate in accomplishing that goal; but these groups had a striking sense of urgency related to a more pessimistic view of local economic trends than did the Orthodox Conservatives. Opportunity for economic advancement was selected by the Conservationist-Liberals as frequently as was "people's pride in their community" as one of the three most important factors in any community (Table 9-8). The Orthodox Conservatives selected schools more frequently than economic opportunity; moreover, the latter was selected as a primary value by twice the proportion of Conservationist-Liberals as of Orthodox Conservatives. One hundred per cent of the Conservationist-Liberal group of White Manifest Leaders approved local government's spending of tax money to assist in bringing new industry to Petropolis, if this were necessary.

Thus, the Conservationist-Liberals agreed with the views held by both the active influentials and rank-and-file citizens of the White subcommunity of Petropolis about the state of the local economy and what needed to be done to improve it. The Orthodox Conservative inner clique was less in accord with the economic-improvement perspectives of the White citizens at large. Even in regard to the Locus Laboratory, which would bring new industry near but not into Petropolis, the unanimous "strongly approve" attitude of the Conservationist-Liberals resembled the strong support given to this plan in the White subcommunity; only one of the inner-clique Orthodox Conservatives

TABLE 9-7   Political Perspectives of Categories and Groups in Petropolis

| | White | | | | Negro | |
| | Manifest Leaders * | | | Active Influentials | Manifest Leaders | Active Influentials |
	OC N = 20	Unc N = 6	CC-Lib N = 5	N = 37	N = 20	N = 33
Rating of economic opportunity in community						
Very good	15%	50%	0%	13%	10%	9%
Good	75	50	60	58	55	27
Not very good	10	0	40	24	35	55
Do not know	0	0	0	5	0	9
	100%	100%	100%	100%	100%	100%
Involvement in attracting new industry						
No concern	5%	0%	0%	24%	10%	6%
Discussed	25	17	20	40	25	58
Activist role	70	84	80	35	65	35
Do not know	0	0	0	0	0	0
	100%	101%	100%	99%	100%	99%
Spending local tax money to attract new industry †						
Approve	70%	50%	100%	95%		
Undecided	5	0	0	3		
Disapprove	25	50	0	3		
Do not know	0	0	0	0		
	100%	100%	100%	101%		
Rating of downtown business district †						
Very good	25%	17%	0%	22%		
Good	45	33	20	49		
Not very good	30	50	80	27		
Undecided	0	0	0	3		
	100%	100%	100%	101%		
Favor increased city taxes, if necessary, to rebuild downtown business area †						
Yes	55%	50%	80%	76%		
No	40	33	0	19		
Do not know	5	17	20	5		
	100%	100%	100%	100%		

* OC   = Orthodox Conservative
  Unc   = Uncommitted
  CC-Lib = Community Conservationist-Liberal
† Comparable data unavailable for these Negro respondents.

TABLE 9-8   Ranking of Factors as among the Three Most Important in Any Community by Various Categories and Groups in the White Subcommunity in Petropolis *

	Manifest Leaders †			Active Influentials	Political-Influence Substructure
	OC N = 20	Unc N = 7	CC-Lib N = 5	N = 37	N = 302
Opportunity for economic advancement	2.0	1.5	1.5	3	2
Schools	1.0	1.5	3.0	1	1
Availability of adequate housing	8.5	—	6.0	8	7
Friendliness of people	4.5	3.5	—	6	5
Race relations	8.5	6.5	4.0	4	4
Responsiveness of city government to people's wishes	7.0	6.5	—	2	3
Community spirit of the big companies	3.0	6.5	6.0	8	9
Labor relations	6.0	6.5	6.0	8	8
People's pride in the community	4.5	3.5	1.5	5	6

* No rank order was assigned if 10 per cent of the category did not select the item as among the three most important factors in any community.
† OC   = Orthodox Conservative
  Unc   = Uncommitted
  CC-Lib = Community Conservationist-Liberal

strongly approved and one disapproved completely of the Locus Laboratory.

The uncommitted White Manifest Leaders were most optimistic about the condition of the local economy, but they were actively involved in promoting new industry. Their feelings were mixed about spending local tax money in these efforts: half of them approved and half disapproved of such a policy. On the other hand, all but one strongly approved of the Locus Laboratory plan. In contrast to the divergence noted in Metroville's Manifest Leadership, the evidence is that the senior industrial executives in the Manifest Leadership were no more opposed than any other occupational category, including bankers and financiers, to this fiscal role for local government.

Metroville's Negro Leadership was relatively optimistic about economic opportunity, compared to the pessimism of the Negro citizens at large. They were not active in efforts to acquire new industry. In sharp contrast, the Negro Leaders of Petropolis were more economically pessimistic and much more active in regard to strengthening the industrial base of their city (see Tables 9-1 and 9-7).

The Orthodox Conservatives resembled the active influentials and the rank-and-file White citizenry in regarding the downtown business district as adequate or very good (see Table 9-7). The uncommitted were disposed to view the downtown business district as "not very good"; the Conservationist-Liberals were most negative in their evaluation of this part of town. However, the Orthodox Conservatives, including all four members of the inner clique, and the uncommitted were less willing than either the active influentials or the rank-and-file citizens in the White subcommunity to increase city taxes to rehabilitate the central business district. The Conservationist-Liberals in the White Manifest Leadership favored this notion. Since only 25 per cent of the White citizens at large and 20 per cent of the White active influentials were opposed to increasing city taxes for redeveloping the downtown business district, the Conservationist-Liberals seemed to have popular support for their preference for downtown redevelopment as well as for the improvement of the municipal functions of community planning and guided development as means of improving the Petropolis economy.

Of the several political-leadership groups in Petropolis, only the White Conservationist-Liberals and the Negro Liberals mentioned matters of community planning and guided development as a topic of relatively frequent policy deliberation (see Table 9-6). The Negro Liberals, like the Negro Progressive Conservatives of Metroville, predominantly discussed public housing and the need to relax residential bars: the White Conservationist-Liberals primarily discussed the need to improve the municipal-planning function and make it more autonomous. Neither category of community planning and guided development was of such conversational concern to Orthodox Conservatives, but the uncommitted deliberated both matters. These aspects of civic improvement were stressed by White and Negro Community Conservationists and Liberals in the Manifest Leadership; although these matters had not excited a very large proportion of either the active influentials or the less influential segments of the White subcommunity, they were of at least conversational concern to both of these portions of the Negro subcommunity as well as to the uncommitted White Manifest Leaders.

The Conservationist-Liberals and the uncommitted favored such civic-improvement matters as public housing, with a majority of each "strongly" approving them (Table 9-9). Although none of the Orthodox Conservatives strongly approved public housing, almost two-thirds did approve. Two of the four inner-clique Orthodox Conservatives were undecided; the other two disapproved. Public housing was an extremely popular program among the White citizens of Petropolis

TABLE 9-9   Civic-Improvement Perspectives of Various Categories and Groups in Petropolis

	White				Negro	
	Manifest Leaders			Active Influentials	Manifest Leaders	Active Influentials
	OC N = 20	Unc N = 6	CC-Lib * N = 5	N = 37	N = 20	N = 33
Attitude toward public housing						
Approve	65%	100%	100%	82%		
Undecided	15	0	0	5		
Disapprove	20	0	0	13		
Do not know	0	0	0	0		
	100%	100%	100%	100%		
Attitude toward school consolidation †						
Approve	90%	50%	100%	54%		
Undecided	0	33	0	27		
Disapprove	10	17	0	19		
Do not know	0	0	0	0		
	100%	100%	100%	100%		
Involvement in school consolidation						
No concern	15%	33%	0%	30%	5%	30%
Discussed	50	50	40	46	30	45
Influenced others	30	0	20	22	20	15
Very active	5	17	40	3	45	9
	100%	100%	100%	101%	100%	99%

* OC   = Orthodox Conservative
  Unc   = Uncommitted
  CC-Lib = Community Conservationist-Liberal
† Comparable data unavailable for these Negro respondents.

as well as among their Manifest Leaders. Although comparable interview data were not obtained from the Negro respondents, public housing evidently was a frequent subject of conversation and something the Negro subcommunity clearly approved.

School consolidation, another policy advocated by the Community Conservationists, was approved not only by their White Liberal allies in the Manifest Leadership, but also by the Orthodox Canservatives (Table 9-9). The uncommitted were either opposed or undecided. This was an example of a policy favored more by the White Manifest Leadership as a whole than by either the active influentials or the citizens at large in the White subcommunity. There is no comparably systematic information on the attitudes of the Negro Leaders and subcommunity in regard to school consolidation. Except for the Negro Leadership, the Community Conservationists in the Conservationist-Liberal coalition were the most active political-leadership clique in this decision-making process. According to reliable but unsystematic reports, the Negro Leadership was active but divided on this issue: to one set of Negro Leaders, school consolidation was a way of gaining widespread school desegregation in the future and an improved public school system for Negroes as well as Whites; to the other, school consolidation seemed likely to delay desegregation in the city's school system.

In regard to race relations, there was a sharp division between the Conservationist-Liberals and the Liberal Negro Leadership on the one hand and the Orthodox Conservatives on the other. The Negro Leaders, like their racial counterparts in Metroville, were all active accommodators, as were the White Conservationist-Liberals. Sixty-three per cent of the uncommitted were active racists; only 13 per cent were active accommodators. Eighty per cent of the Orthodox Conservatives, including the four members of the inner clique, were active racists; another 10 per cent were potential racists. Thus the Orthodox Conservatives in the Manifest Leadership of Petropolis were even more racist in orientation than the predominantly racist White subcommunity.

Among the White Progressive Conservatives of Metroville, where school desegregation already had been initiated, the proportion of active accommodators was higher than among the Orthodox Conservatives of Petropolis; there was also more opposition to extremist segregationist policy preferences (see Tables 9-10 and 9-3). However, among Petropolis' Orthodox Conservatives there was less disposition to withhold state funds, to close the schools, or to use force to block desegregation than among the rank-and-file White citizens or the White active influentials there.

The greater degree of accommodation sentiment among the Conservationist-Liberals than among the Orthodox Conservatives or the uncommitted was evident also in the attitudes of these groups toward the Negro political organization, PESNEG, and toward the newly established biracial municipal commission to improve race relations. The Conservationist-Liberals unanimously approved both, whereas only half the uncommitted and less than half the Orthodox Conservatives approved either. The municipal race-relations commission actually received "strong" approval from 80 per cent of the former; only two of the twenty-six Orthodox Conservatives and uncommitted who reported their attitudes gave equally strong approval.

TABLE 9-10   Race-Relations Perspectives among Political Categories and Groups of
White Citizens in Petropolis

	Manifest Leaders			Active Influentials	
Attitude toward Desegregation Policies	OC N = 20	Unc N = 6	CC-Lib N = 5	N = 37	N = 317 *
Amend Constitution					
Approve	65%	83%	0%	65%	61%
Undecided	0	0	0	14	18
Disapprove	35	17	100	22	21
	100%	100%	100%	101%	100%
Withhold state funds					
Approve	0%	17%	0%	30%	36%
Undecided	45	0	0	8	23
Disapprove	55	83	100	62	41
	100%	100%	100%	100%	100%
Close schools					
Approve	10%	17%	0%	35%	34%
Undecided	25	17	0	5	16
Disapprove	65	67	100	59	50
	100%	101%	100%	99%	100%
Use force, if necessary					
Approve	0%	0%	0%	11%	13%
Undecided	15	0	0	3	9
Disapprove	85	100	100	86	78
	100%	100%	100%	100%	100%
Attitude toward PESNEG					
Approve	45%	50%	100%	54%	39%
Undecided	30	17	0	24	41
Disapprove	25	33	0	24	20
	100%	100%	100%	102%	100%
Attitude toward municipal biracial committee					
Approve	40%	50%	100%	64%	36%
Undecided	20	33	0	32	49
Disapprove	40	17	0	3	15
	100%	100%	100%	99%	100%

Key: OC   = Orthodox Conservative
        Unc   = Uncommitted
        CC-Lib = Community Conservationist-Liberal
* The numbers responding to each item actually ranged from 299 to 312 with the respondents unable
or unwilling to answer the questions ranging from 5 to 18.

Two of the four Orthodox Conservative inner-clique members disapproved of, and the other two were undecided about, both organizations.

We find, then, that in Petropolis the accommodating White political-leadership group, the Conservationist-Liberals, not only was opposed in its outlook on race relations by other White Manifest Leaders, but also faced a relatively racist set of White active influentials and a racist-minded White subcommunity. In Metroville, the accommodating attitudes of the substantial minority of White Progressive Conservative Leaders and the token-desegregation policy of the majority of leaders were in accord with the feelings of the White active influentials, even though in their race-relations sentiments the White citizens at large resembled the actively racist White citizens in the political substructure of Petropolis.

Returning to the subjects of policy deliberation, we find that although Conservationist-Liberals primarily were concerned with race relations and their improvement, and the Negro Leaders discussed housing conditions and other matters of race relations most frequently, the Orthodox Conservatives discussed both the state of the economy and various matters of housekeeping services more frequently than they did race relations (see Table 9-6). Race relations was also more frequently considered "one of the three most important factors" in a community by Conservationist-Liberals than by Orthodox Conservatives (see Table 9-8). Whether or not the Community Conservationists stressed improvements in race relations because this seemed the only way to improve the entire community and provide social justice, and whether or not the White Liberals, particularly John Jay, thought that improvement of the Negro subcommunity was the way to pursue power, the fact remains that this political coalition was active in concert with the Liberal Negro Leadership. They sought to shift the scope of local government so that it would function to increase economic, social, and governmental opportunity for Negroes. In general, they were opposed in these pursuits by the Orthodox Conservatives.

In this city of racial politics, the Negro Leadership had become optimistic about the future course of Negro-White relations. Whereas 42 per cent of Metroville's Negro Leadership thought that there would be "much more" job desegregation within 5 years, 70 per cent of the Petropolis Negro Leaders felt equally optimistic. There was much less optimism about the future of economic opportunity for Negroes in Petropolis in both the active-influential and rank-and-file segments of that subcommunity.

Housekeeping services had been improved by the government in the area of Petropolis where most of the upper- and upper-middle-class Negroes, including the Negro Leadership, lived. Public housing was a reality; and urban renewal, although not yet accepted, promised additional housing benefits for Negroes. The new municipal commission on race relations provided a few Negroes with opportunities for some social and political interaction with Whites, as did the biracial Committee on Industrial Development, the local Democratic party, and other informal political organizational settings. Even though school desegregation still was thwarted by the active opposition of the Orthodox Conservatives, and even though Petropolis had an active, organized, radical White Supremacy movement with connections to the Orthodox Conservative Manifest Leadership group, politically the Negro wing of the Conservationist-Liberal coalition in Petropolis trusted the city administration and was optimistic about its policies.

The small number of Community Conservationists were optimistic about the future of Petropolis, but they were pessimistic about its current condition and present trends. Their high valuation of "people's pride in the community" was indicative of the direction they felt needed to be taken to restore Petropolis to the first rank of cities in Southern State.

One other small but significant, organized political-leadership group existed among the White Latent Leaders of Petropolis. Its formal organization, PECORR (Petropolis Committee on Race Relations), was so small that none of its members happened to be selected for interviewing. Like the Liberal clique in Oretown, none of the leaders of this group had been named with sufficient frequency to make the Manifest Leader list, since they were not known widely enough as individuals to be named by many informants as the inner clique or key men; but their organization, PECORR, was named as a political-leadership group, and we shall regard it as such. Its members acquired their limited political-leadership positions in the decisional process which resulted in the removal of John Jay and Fred Ames from office in the local Democratic party. They probably also shared in the unit of political power that accrued to the contributors to the decisional outcome not to initiate public-school desegregation by Time *M;* but they had no political-leadership positions in that process. Their chief spokesmen were two young professional men, and their membership was recruited primarily from lower-class people in Petropolis and the rural fringe. It was a true White Supremacy organization in political ideology. A few Orthodox Conservatives contributed funds but did not join officially. They preferred to remain members of a

White Supremacy-minded, upper-class, Orthodox Conservative group, rather than a less respectable, more single-minded ideological group.[5]

In their alliance with both White and Negro Liberals, the Community Conservationists were pitted politically against the Orthodox Conservatives and the White Supremacists in PECORR. They felt that they should expand their political support in the White subcommunity, particularly in the face of increasing barrages of propaganda from White Supremacists that they were too friendly to Negroes and even too radical. This led them to work for the support of the uncommitted in the Manifest Leadership and in lower political-influence strata in the White subcommunity, and to compromise and accommodate themselves to the more pliable members of the Orthodox Conservative group. This weakened somewhat their own coalition with White and Negro Liberals, even though some of the latter were not entirely averse to this stress on political togetherness. However, the Negro Liberals in general felt that this orientation on the part of their well-meaning, younger White colleagues was somewhat naïve politically; they were also sensitive to the militancy in the political-influence substructure of their subcommunity, particularly among the young Negroes. Our findings confirm the youthful character of Petropolis' Negro active influentials (see Chapter 8, Table 8-1).

It is clear from the foregoing picture of the political perspectives of the Orthodox Conservatives that the ideological position of the inner clique was more consistent than were those of other members of their group. But even though they were explicit in applying their ideological doctrines to decisional and policy questions, the fact that two of these four men were undecided about public housing for Petropolis suggests something of the divergence in policy preference from their ideological prescriptions. Their attitudes on particular policies may have resulted in part from their sensitivity to the popularity of proposals or programs that they opposed. This seemed to be a factor not only in public housing but also in regard to municipal support for efforts by the Committee on Industrial Development to attract new industry to Petropolis.

In any event, it is apparent that a number of Orthodox Conservatives agreed with various policy formulations advanced by the Conservationist-Liberal group. This extended beyond agreement to maintain an active local-governmental industrial-promotion campaign. The Orthodox Conservative inner clique found it extremely difficult, except at election time, to maintain a united front against the Plunkett administration, since the latter formulated such policies as the establishment of a state-supported technical training center to provide training for workers; otherwise the industrial corporations themselves might have had to provide such training. Even extreme Orthodox Conservative industrialists found such a center to be in their immediate economic interests: it would reduce their own costs and facilitate the introduction of labor-saving, highly productive automation. Their pocketbooks seemed sometimes to overrule their antigovernment sentiments.

Moreover, the Orthodox Conservative inner clique held to a political ideology wherein the respected industrialists and financiers would maintain key political decision-making leadership roles. However, among the Orthodox Conservative Manifest Leaders were a majority of men with other, somewhat lower-status occupational positions. When the Community Conservationists formulated a set of policies designed to stimulate existing retail business—for example, expansion in the municipal parking lot program—some of the merchants among the Orthodox Conservatives did not reject the proposal automatically, even though it was backed by the Negro-White labor "machine." On the other hand, Community Conservationists could not count on support from the merchants among the Orthodox Conservatives and uncommitted when, as happened periodically, they attempted to protect the roles of professional public administrators who, in the making of administrative decisions, had injured the interests of the merchants.

There was thus a tension within the ranks of the Orthodox Conservatives that contributed to a comparable tension within the ranks of the Conservationist-Liberal group. The Community Conservationists continued to hope that their program of civic and economic improvements would appeal to the less doctrinaire opponents among the Orthodox Conservatives, as well as to the uncommitted. Since they were averse to community-disrupting political conflict, they tried to avoid activating their opponents in political decision-making even when, as was usually the case, they could not expect conversion and active support from them. For somewhat different reasons, both Negro and White Liberals were opposed to such aspirations on the part of the Conservationists. The Negro Leaders, with a few exceptions, were sceptical because they thought that it was wasted effort to try to convert White Supremacists, which most of them believed many of the Conservatives were. Tactical considerations might dictate temporary political accommodations, but they were resigned to the necessity of progressing by means of forcing their opponents to surrender in major political battles. The White Liberals agreed with their Negro associates, but they also worried that in return for support of such decisional preferences as relocating new industry in Petropolis, the Orthodox Conservatives would exact unacceptable concessions—for example, that new industry would be nonunion in character—from their Community Conservationist allies.

Despite the periodic crossing of the ideological boundaries between these political groups, the interrelatedness of certain political interests, and the hopes of the Conservationists that the Orthodox Conservatives would one day join the ranks of a united, single political leadership led by Conservationists, we shall continue to treat the groups as analytically distinct. During Time E to M, their spokesmen and strategists were successful in maintaining, substantially inviolate, the integrity of their groups. They maintained the affiliations of most of their respective group memberships in pursuing what they each regarded as basically hostile political philosophies and programs in distinct organizational settings. Although members of each group did interact with each other directly and through the uncommitted leaders, the Orthodox Conservatives and the splinter group of White Supremacists adhered to the view that the Conservationist-Liberal alliance was the political enemy; this view was—within the aforementioned limits—generally reciprocated.

Finally, the importance of John Leek, the central uncommitted Manifest Leader, must not be overlooked. His special concern was improvement of the industrial base. He advocated an expansionist role for municipal government as one among many devices to promote industrial development; in this he worked closely with his relative, Eben Bacon, Jr., and with Mayor Plunkett, two of the three members of the Community Conservationist clique. He was respected and liked by many others in the Manifest Leadership: Orthodox Conservatives, other uncommitted Leaders, and Negro Leaders. Although none of the inner clique Orthodox Conservatives considered Leek a close friend, one felt that he and Leek shared similar views. Neither John Jay nor Fred Ames, the two White Liberal Manifest Leaders, felt that Leek was a close friend; but Jay thought that he shared policy views with Leek "50 per cent" of the time. Therefore, Leek's usual advocacy of decisional preferences advanced by the Community Conservationists, in addition to those that related to strengthening the economic base of the community, seemed to dilute opposition to those preferences. He was a prototype of the uncommitted who was periodically wooed by the various groups in Petropolis' politics.

THE MULTIPLE POLITICAL-LEADERSHIP GROUPS IN ORETOWN

We turn now to the multigroup political-leadership structure of Oretown. None of the Manifest Leaders were members of the Liberal clique—the latter were all Latent Leaders. The picture of the Mani-

fest Leadership's characteristics derived from treating them as a single
category changes dramatically in some respects when the characteristics of the two groups of Manifest Leaders are compared. Oretown's
Manifest Leadership contained a higher proportion of men under 35
years of age than any other Manifest Leadership. This was almost
entirely due to the youthfulness of the Community Conservationist
group of Manifest Leaders. Forty-six per cent of the members of that
group were under 35 years of age, compared to but 14 per cent of the
Orthodox Conservatives and 9 per cent of the uncommitted. However,
Oretown's Orthodox Conservatives were younger than their ideological
counterparts in Petropolis: they were predominantly a middle-aged
group, whereas more than half those in Petropolis were over 55 years
of age.

One of the two women among the Manifest Leaders belonged to
the Community Conservationist group; the other was uncommitted.
All the Orthodox Conservatives were male. The Community Conservationists were less wealthy than the Orthodox Conservatives.
Thirty-eight per cent of the former made less than $6,000 per year,
and 38 per cent made more than $10,000 per year. The comparable
figures for the Orthodox Conservatives were 7 and 79 per cent. Only
27 per cent of the uncommitted had incomes as high as $10,000 per
year.

Almost one-third of the Community Conservationists had not attended college, compared to one-quarter of the uncommitted and less
than one-tenth of the Orthodox Conservatives. On the other hand,
largely because of the professional men in their ranks, the Community
Conservationists had the highest proportion of people with post-
graduate professional education. Thus the Community Conservationists were younger, of more varied educational attainments, and
of distinctly lower incomes than the Orthodox Conservatives.

It was primarily the Community Conservationists who gave Oretown's Manifest Leadership its appearance of being a leadership of
newcomers in this city of relatively few long-term residents. The
Orthodox Conservatives and the Liberals for the most part represented
the small segment of the prewar population. Two-thirds of the
Orthodox Conservatives and Liberals, slightly more than half the uncommitted, but only one-third of the Community Conservationists
had lived in Oretown more than 10 years.

The occupational backgrounds of the Orthodox Conservatives and
Community Conservationists differed as well. Half the Orthodox
Conservatives were proprietors, including the editor of the Oretown
newspaper. Four, 23 per cent, were industrial executives—three of

these represented the community's largest mining company and one the private utility—and three were professional men, 21 per cent. The Community Conservationists were primarily professional men— 54 per cent—including two attorneys, two professional public administrators, and an educator. In addition, one of them was a junior executive, one a senior banker, and one a small financier. There were only two proprietors, 15 per cent, in their ranks. The eleven uncommitted Manifest Leaders included five proprietors, four professional men, one banker, and one housewife.

The proprietorial-industrialist Orthodox Conservatives were predominantly Republican, by a ratio of 6:1. There were slightly fewer uncommitted Republicans, but the Community Conservationists were equally divided in their partisan identification. The four members of the Orthodox Conservative inner clique were Taft Republicans. Three of the four members of the Community Conservationist inner clique were Adlai Stevenson Democrats; the fourth was a "liberal" Republican. However, the inner clique of the Community Conservationists was bipartisan in its political role, since it interacted in the mixed set of partisans which constituted the Community Conservationist Manifest Leadership group. The Liberal clique was also of mixed partisan character. The union official was an active Democrat, former Mayor Lovegren was a small businessman who identified himself as a Democrat but was a registered Republican, and Councilman Longacre was an active Republican party worker.

In contrast to the Community Conservation clique in Petropolis, the Community Conservation clique in Oretown, during Time E to M, followed a strategy of defense, of trying to preserve a minimal level of community integration to prevent a complete breakdown in the civic, political, and social orders of the community. Perhaps as a reflection of this, the Community Conservationist clique stressed as one of its most important values "community spirit or attitude of the people" and "the willingness of the people to undertake and support action to meet community needs and problems" more than did the Orthodox Conservative clique. The latter stressed business or employment opportunity. This difference characterized the value orientations of the respective groups.

Almost half the Community Conservationists felt that both "community spirit" and "willingness of the people to undertake and support action . . ." were among the three most important factors in any community where they preferred to live; 29 per cent of the Orthodox Conservatives selected the former and only 7 per cent selected the latter (Table 9-11). The uncommitted agreed that community spirit

TABLE 9-11   Factors Selected as among the Three Most Important in Any Community by Various Political Categories and Groups in Oretown *

Factors	Manifest Leaders			Latent Leaders	Active Influentials	Political-Influence Substructure
	OC N = 14	Unc N = 11	CC N = 13	Lib N = 3	N = 101	N = 612
Opportunity for economic advancement	93%	45%	64%	67%	72%	67%
Schools	64	64	70	33	60	60
Availability of adequate housing	7	27	0	0	25	26
Community spirit	29	55	45	0	11	10
Willingness of people to understand and support action to meet community needs and problems	7	9	45	0	11	11

* The percentages are the proportions selecting each factor from a longer list of factors as among the "three most important in any community."
Key: OC = Orthodox Conservative
        Unc = Uncommitted
        CC = Community Conservationist
        Lib = Liberal

was important, but the Community Conservationist message that collective, supportive citizen action was urgent apparently did not have much impact on them or on the citizens at large. The Liberals did not select either factor as among the most important community conditions. Information collected through interviews indicated that the Liberals felt that the "right" political leadership—that is, their own political leadership—would ensure a good community and that all the citizens had to do was to elect the appropriate men to office and vote in the appropriate manner on whatever measures these elected officials submitted to them for their approval.

The Orthodox Conservatives stressed economic opportunity as one of their primary values more than any other leadership group—even more than the active influentials or rank-and-file citizens. The Community Conservationists and uncommitted were the only sets among all these categories of leaders and influentials who more frequently selected schools as a more important community value than economic opportunity.

The general disregard by all leadership groups of the local economy as a pressing subject for local-government attention can be inferred from the ratios of optimists to pessimists in regard to economic opportunity. Among the citizenry in Oretown, the optimists, who rated economic opportunity as "very good" or "excellent," outnumbered the pessimists by a 2:1 margin. Among the active influentials the opti-mist-to-pessimist ratio rose to 9:1. The comparable ratios for the Orthodox Conservatives, Community Conservationists, uncommitted, and Liberals were 7:0, 8:1, 6:1, and 3:0. Whereas one-fifth of the rank-and-file citizens rated economic opportunity in the community as "not very good" or "poor," only one-tenth of these political leaders, including the Latent Leader Liberals, were comparably pessimistic about the local economy.

None of the political-leadership groups in Oretown were highly satisfied with the condition of "planning for community development." One-fifth of the citizens at large and almost one-quarter of the active influentials were somewhat or very dissatisfied with this function; the proportion of comparably dissatisfied in the political leadership groups ranged from one-quarter of the uncommitted to almost one-third of the Community Conservationists, one-third of the Liberals, and one-half of the Orthodox Conservatives. The Orthodox Conservatives were dissatisfied with plans which originally had been made by former Mayor Lovegren's administration in order to create a municipal utility; they also disliked the continuing bitter competition between the utilities. However, some of the Orthodox Conservatives were dissatisfied with their own ideological brethren—the industrialists rep-resenting the largest corporations in Oretown—for their inactivity in planning with other Orthodox Conservatives for the future of the community, and also for their negative attitudes toward such deci-sional questions as annexing the area in which one major mining plant and equipment were located to avoid sharing city tax burdens.

The Orthodox Conservatives were dissatisfied particularly with the municipal program of street construction and maintenance, as were the citizens at large and the active influentials. Almost two-thirds of the Orthodox Conservatives, compared to less than one-third of the Community Conservationists and uncommitted and none of the Liberals, reported, when asked specifically, that they were dissatisfied in this regard. The Liberals took pride in the extensive street-paving program initiated by the Lovegren administration. The Orthodox Conservatives not only resented this accomplishment and made caustic references to the inferior quality of materials used and the work it-self, but they also resented what they considered to be a dispropor-tionate amount of street paving in Councilman Longacre's subdivision, at the expense of repairs in the more established sections.

Another of the typical disputes between the Orthodox Conservatives and the Community Conservationists centered on the public schools. The Superintendent, an Orthodox Conservative Manifest Leader, had developed good working relationships with Main Street. One hundred per cent of the Orthodox Conservatives responded to a question about how the school officials would react if the respondent contacted them about a local community problem by selecting the statement "They would try to understand my problem and do what they could about it." Forty per cent of the Community Conservationists and two of the three Liberals selected instead answers that indicated distrust of, or cynicism about, these school officials.

The Community Conservationist opposition to the school system's chief administrative officers centered in a feeling that the latter overemphasized physical plant, athletics, and the maintenance of a low school-tax rate, and that in so doing they neglected more important matters which were admittedly costly: curriculum improvement and better pay and better working conditions for teachers. The efforts of the Community Conservationists to replace the Superintendent were resisted by the Orthodox Conservatives. The Liberals were not actively involved in this controversy. The fight over the Superintendent divided the school board, on which one other Orthodox Conservative and one Community Conservationist served. This conflict in school politics did not facilitate the development of consensus between the two groups, a consensus that was particularly important to Mayor French's Conservationist city administration.

The foregoing description of the political perspectives of the groups at the political-leadership level in Oretown were obtained in comparable, standardized interviews, and were supplemented by less comparable depth interviews and by less systematic observations such as we were able to obtain in Farmdale. Several conclusions can be drawn from that various noncontradictory information. The relatively self-conscious political ideologies held by each inner clique gave each larger group a distinctive central tendency in its ideological leanings. Variations in the degree of ideological commitment by the membership of each group, and the flexibility allowed by each ideology to its adherents in choosing among decisional choices, contributed to the unpredictability of Oretown politics. As in Petropolis politics, it was difficult to predict which group would support and which group would oppose particular policy formulations at the leadership level. Perhaps the greatest degree of predictability came from the opposition of all other leadership groups and individuals to the Liberals. The Orthodox Conservatives and Community Conservationists felt that fiscal and personal irresponsibility would prevail, as they felt it did from 1948 to 1952, if Liberals held local governmental office, and that organized labor would have undue influence at City Hall. The hostility was mutual, except that the labor-union member of the Liberal clique did not oppose the members or the preferences of the members of the other political groups out of hand.

In several decisional processes, a working alignment of Community Conservationists and Orthodox Conservatives against the Liberals was noticeable. This was in part due to the role of uncommitted leaders, particularly Mr. Wilbur Rake. The latter did not have the same degree of political status nor did he attempt to exercise his political influence as frequently as Mr. John Leek, his uncommitted counterpart in Petropolis; but his disposition to compromise and work with members of otherwise opposing groups facilitated these cross-group coalitions in particular decisional processes.

Political competition between Orthodox Conservatives and Community Conservationists continued partly because the inner clique of the latter group frequently made use of liberal rhetoric, their power position was basically promunicipal, they favored greater and more autonomous decision-making powers for local government in its community-planning and guided-development functions, and they were quite willing to increase local taxes to pay for various civic improvements, even though these were not at issue in the decisional processes of Time E to M.

The Orthodox Conservatives seemed to be of two general types, which represented two sometimes conflicting economic interests: the retail merchants and other small businessmen, and the senior industrial executives. The political ideology of Orthodox Conservatism advanced by the inner clique and other members also was at variance with the ideology held by the industrialists: the four small businessmen in the inner clique advocated for Oretown a political leadership of small businessmen, particularly retail merchants, whose stake in responsible, efficient, inexpensive local government was great. They had become disillusioned with the prospect of inducing the industrialists to participate actively in ruling; indeed, as we have noted, many of the industrialists lived and participated in the civic, social, and political life of Oretown's larger and more cosmopolitan neighboring city. The merchants and city residents among the Orthodox Conservatives wanted as broad a property-tax-paying base as possible; but the mining companies, whose executives for the most part lived in the suburbs, had an interest in remaining outside the reach of the city's property tax.[6]

The industrialists among the Orthodox Conservatives included the official of the private utility. A number of the merchants in the Orthodox Conservative group had come to regard his dedication to the principle of private ownership as a rather costly business for them. They had begun to feel that, instead of engaging in a competitive battle, the private utility might support the efforts of Mayor French to set up a citizens' group to study the electric-power situation and recommend a peaceful solution in the community's interest.

The other three top industrialists among the Orthodox Conservatives felt that the rulers should be representatives of the interests of the industrial backbone of the city; they shared the sense of high social class with their Orthodox Conservative brethren in Petropolis. This, along with their actual social isolation from the other Orthodox Conservatives, helped to maintain a political distance between these two subgroups. This distance dated from the Second World War, when retail merchants replaced the industrial representatives in local office; the merchants were then successful in their postwar annexation efforts directed at some of the industrial properties. The new set of industrial managers of absentee-owned corporations that arrived in Oretown during and after the Second World War felt that if others would not rule in their interests they might as well refrain from political participation, except when their corporate interests were directly at stake.

It also should be remembered that Mayor French's candidacy had been backed by Conservative Main Street merchants as the least of three evils. The Orthodox Conservatives still felt that there was hope for the French administration as the latter learned that it needed continuous help in competition with the Liberal group. Moreover, the tenets of Community Conservation as a political ideology had not developed as they had in Petropolis by Time M, which was actually five years earlier in Oretown than in Petropolis. The disposition of Community Conservationists to work with Orthodox Conservatives against the Liberals for programs that they felt would benefit the entire community and their feeling that numerous uncommitted people could be enlisted in their causes mitigated the competition between these two political groups somewhat. Whether or not the frequent breakfasts, lunches, dinners, and meetings of other kinds between members of these two groups in the concerted effort to raise funds for a community hospital would reduce the political competition still further would be known after Time M.

THE POLITICAL-LEADERSHIP ROLES OF THE INNER CLIQUES: IDEOLOGY AND INTERESTS

Political leadership, as the term is used here, denotes both positions, in a structural, static sense, and roles, in a functioning, dynamic sense, of people in community power structures as political decisions were made during a particular period of time. On the basis of our procedures, the classification of political leaders as members of inner cliques distinguished some political leaders from others by their political status. Men of the political-leader inner cliques were regarded by others as in some sense central political figures who stood for or embodied political programs, perspectives, or preferences of some importance in community politics. Analysis revealed that these men were extremely articulate and had relatively well-developed political ideologies which were important to them in their roles as political leaders in decision-making. The analysis further revealed that the inner cliques played special political roles that further differentiated them from other members of the political leadership; it also explained this relatively special political status compared with that of men who had other political roles as members of their respective Manifest Leaderships.

As we reconstructed the political decision-making processes during Time E to M in each community, it became apparent that the inner cliques did three things more consistently than most other political leaders: first, they propounded general doctrines of their political ideologies; second, they applied those doctrines to decisional questions and announced the "proper" decisional preferences and outcomes to others; third, they acted as the chiefs of staff, the planners of the broad strategies to be followed by members of their groups, in the making of the political decisions that would affect the scope of government in their communities. The classification of some political leaders as members of inner cliques required arbitrary cutoff points, arbitrary inclusion of some but exclusion of others. Therefore, it is understandable that some political leaders who were observed to have participated in such roles on occasion were not included; in general, the inner-clique members and some of their closest associates seemed to have played such roles more than other leaders.

Because of the political status accorded each inner clique by members of their political groups, each of these larger groups had more of an ideological character than it might have had if the members of the inner cliques had played less ideologically oriented roles. The ideology-minded inner cliques sometimes were faced with the difficult task of deciding the political interests that would benefit certain economic interests, as well as the political interests that were consistent with ideological tenets. This task was sometimes complicated further by the need to develop strategies that promised political success, particularly when their political interests or those of some of their members seemed to dictate a decisional preference that was contrary to ideological considerations.   The inner cliques seemed to be pre-occupied with adjusting interests and ideology, not only when ideology was contingent rather than prescriptive for particular policy matters, but also when interests of their members were at odds.

The picture sometimes drawn by so-called power-elite analysts of a single-minded political leadership representing the interests and ideology of the "haves" but not the "have nots" is not a valid picture, even of the two communities with the single political-leadership groups, Farmdale and Metroville.   In Farmdale the ideology propounded by the Jeffersonian Conservative inner clique did not serve the economic interests of the merchants who needed community growth to alleviate their financial problems, nor were the latter's economic interests incorporated into political interests, as this point of view suggests.   In Metroville, the economic and political interests of the "haves" differed considerably, as the analysis of the preferences of financiers and industrial executives illustrated.   Also, within that single political-leadership group were a diversity of viewpoints on the appropriate functioning of local government in race relations.

For strategic and other reasons, the Orthodox Conservative inner clique of Petropolis, which was so ideologically opposed to municipal and national government involvement in the local economy, did not actively oppose efforts by the Plunkett administration to assist in helping to attract new industry to the community.   To establish whether the political interests of the industrial sector of Petropolis really differed from those of the industrial sector of Metroville—as the greater approval of such a program in the former than the latter community by industrial executives among the Manifest Leaders suggested—a special study was conducted.   Samples of industrial executives, besides those in the Manifest Leaderships, were interviewed in each city.[7]   It was found that Petropolis' industrial executives who were not in the Manifest Leadership, and who were a politically inactive group, were actually like the industrial executives of Metroville in overwhelmingly disapproving of, for example, spending local tax money to attract new industry to their community. Such a hiatus in Petropolis between the industrial executives in the political-leadership group that was most opposed to the prolabor Liberals and the industrial executives in the powerless stratum of the power structure contradicts the power-elite theory, which identifies economic and political interest with the decisional preferences of an economic, ideological, or interest group's representatives in a political leadership, particularly in regard to business and industry.

Pluralists could point to the same finding as illustrative of their proposition that compromise is likely to take place in a competitive politics, since victory goes to the side with broad support rather than to the side that remains doctrinaire in pursuing either narrowly defined political interests or an ideology of limited popular appeal. However, the maintenance of political hostility between the competitive political groups in both Oretown and Petropolis would seem to contradict the pluralist conception of American community politics as being marked by consensual compromises on the part of heterogeneous political interest groups interested in short-range goals rather than longer-range political philosophies. Such hostility resulted, for the most part, from aversion to one another's political ideologies, and most decisional outcomes were a function of victories and defeats, not of compromises. The pluralist idea that community politics is a politics of purely political interests rather than of political ideologies cannot be maintained, even in the two multiple-political-leadership-group communities of Oretown and Petropolis. The actions of the several groups were influenced by their strongly ideological centers, that is, their inner cliques; therefore, they were distinguishable on the basis of ideology as well as interests.

Certainly in the communities with one political leadership group, Farmdale and Metroville, the centrality of ideological considerations and the "underrepresentation" or absence of representation of particular political interests at the Manifest Leadership level violated the pluralist conception. Similarly, the power-elite conception that single political-leadership groups are always unified, single-minded, and monolithic in political decision-making was not valid for Metroville. That there can be disputes even within the intimate ingroup that constitutes the inner clique of single-group political leaderships, and that these disputes have significant consequences for decisional outcomes, is attested by the situation in Metroville's White Progressive Conservative group during Time E to M. This was particularly evident in race-related decisions, as well as in the differences between the financiers and industrialists among the White Manifest Leaders in regard to decisions about the role of local government in improving the economy. That certain potential interests can remain potential and may not be "heard" by a responsive political leadership, or that the preferences of the group are not embodied even in part in decisional outcomes, is attested by the situation of the merchants and of the Negro subcommunity in Metroville. Their interests were "heard" to the extent that they were compatible with the tenets of Progressive Conservatism as these were interpreted by the ideological authorities in that leadership group.

We suggested above that each political-leadership group had more of an ideological orientation that it might have had if the men playing the inner-clique roles had been less ideology-minded. Actually, the finding that the members of each inner clique were more articulate, self-conscious ideologists than were most of the other political leaders affiliated with their groups makes it unlikely that the groups could have been less ideology-minded than they appeared. In other words, there seems to be a general pattern that ideologists obtain inner-clique positions and, consequently, political groups become less groups of men with similar interests than groups with relatively developed ideologies and interests. With the exception of one member of the Community Conservationist inner clique in Oretown who was primarily a master strategist and secondarily a committed ideologist, all of the members of the inner cliques in the four communities acted as chiefs of staff for particular political ideologies. The extent to which these men seemed to enjoy their strategist roles and the ways they played them varied. Some, like Mayors May, French, and Plunkett, obviously enjoyed the public stage which their inner-clique roles permitted them. Others, like Judge Catis in Farmdale and William Polk in Metroville, preferred an "elder statesman" role, whereas the inclination of Eben Bacon, Jr. was to be in the thick of organization-of-political-support activities, serving as a chief tactician in obtaining preferred decisional outcomes.

We might speculate at this point that men of strong ideological leanings seem to be pushed by others into inner-clique roles, even if they do not like to make political strategy, so long as they are not disinclined to such tasks. To speculate further, there seems to be an inclination for the less ideology-minded to want articulate ideologists to interpret their political worlds; similarly, strong ideologists seem to feel a need to organize others politically in pursuit of the utopias incorporated in each ideology. In any event, the political-leadership structures of all four communities had one or more political groups marked in some measure by the ideological attachments of their inner cliques.[8]

The existence of the inner cliques and, to a lesser extent, other Manifest Leaders resulted in another exception to a pluralist thesis. This thesis is that not only are people motivated politically by interests, but that specialization in political interests is the rule. Generalists, men of diverse political interests in regard to a variety of decisional subjects, are, in the pluralist view, far outnumbered and even overshadowed in importance by men of special political interests, that is, political particularists. There were more particularists than generalists among the citizens at large, active influentials, and Manifest Leaders in the four communities. But the higher one looked in the political-influence structure the greater was the proportion of generalists to particularists. However, a fact of great significance was the finding that, in their special leadership roles of strategic planning to protect and advance their political ideologies, the inner cliques were in all four communities generalists. Although outnumbered by political leaders of special interests, these small chiefs of staff acted to maintain their respective political groups as informal organizations concerned with the scope of local government in its manifold aspects. This gave the political-leadership groups a broad focus of political attention of the kind that is usually associated with political parties rather than with political interest groups.[9]

Certain of the apparent discrepancies mentioned at the end of Chapter 7, between the political perspectives of active influentials on the one hand and decisional outcomes and visibility of groups in decision-making on the other, can now be better understood. For example, it would appear that both ideological and strategic considerations of the White Liberal Leaders of Petropolis dictated their alliance with Negro political forces and led them, despite the racist sentiments of their White active-influential associates in the labor movement, to active, visible support of decisional outcomes opposed by anti-Negro groups. It would also appear that the anti-public-housing sentiments of White active influentials in Metroville found little support in the White Manifest Leadership. Public housing for both White and Negro citizens had become part of the accepted policy meaning of Progressive Conservatism. Economic conditions had been of concern to the Negro citizens of Metroville in a private, economic frame of reference rather than a public, political one. Although Metroville's Negro Leaders, when asked, approved of governmental efforts to improve the industrial base, they, like Negro active influentials, ranked economic conditions relatively low on their list of most important community issues, problems, or projects. Since the Negro Leadership appeared to be relatively unconcerned with the state of the economy, the absence of Negro involvement in decision-making pertaining to the economy is more understandable.

However, this still does not explain why such political interests in the economy were less developed among Metroville's than Petropolis' Negro Leaders; nor why, since there were matters of priority concern to the Negro Leadership of Metroville, such as housing and racial segregation, they were so much less involved in political decision-making than their racial counterparts in Petropolis. Whether or not such differences resulted from Metroville's Negro Leaders' having greater confidence and trust in the White Progressive Conservative Leadership than Petropolis' Negro Leaders had in their ideological enemies, the White Orthodox Conservatives and the White Supremacists, or whether or not there was a difference in the degree to which legitimate or illegitimate sanctions were feared in the two Negro subcommunities, remains to be explored.

In the next chapter, we shall continue to describe and compare the group structure of the four political leaderships in order to classify each power structure by type. Of particular interest are the settings in which members of the political-leadership groups engaged in the authoritative consideration of political decision-making, that is, acted in their roles as political leaders; the relationships between Latent Leaders from each random sample and the sets of Manifest Leaders; and the roles of government officials in the political leaderships of the four power structures.

NOTES

1. The operational definitions of leadership groups and dissident individuals are contained in Appendix A.
2. It would seem that Negro Leaders had probably considered George France one of their ranks in previous years. Therefore, since he was nominated by White Manifest Leaders at the time of our study but not by Negro Leaders, the indication would seem to be that the White subcommunity had failed to keep up to date on changes in the Negro subcommunity. Because of a major demonstration, and, hence, visible change in the composition of the Negro Leadership in Tallahassee, Florida, it was reported that White and Negro Leaders concurred on their identification of the "New Leaders." See Lewis M. Killian and Charles U. Smith, "Negro Protest Leaders in a Southern Community," *Social Forces,* Vol. 38, No. 3 (March 1960), pp. 243–257.
3. A comparable analysis of leadership in Bennington, Vermont, has revealed similar differences in partisanship, age, and other characteristics between and among three factions identified by sociometric techniques. See Harry Scoble, "Leadership Hierarchies and Political Issues in a New England Town," in *Community Political Systems,* ed. by Morris Janowitz (Glencoe, Illinois: The Free Press, 1961), pp. 117–145.
4. *Ibid.,* pp. 131–134.
5. It is difficult but sometimes possible to obtain valid information on such relationships. See Floyd Hunter's comment on the difficulty in *Community Power Structure* (Chapel Hill: The University of North Carolina Press, 1953), p. 147.
6. One of the major differences between Oretown and Bennington, Vermont, as described by Harry Scoble, was the absence of executives and managers of the nationally owned plants in the latter community among the Manifest Leaders. The attitudes of the leadership toward such men in Bennington were similar

to the attitudes of some of the merchants toward the industrial executives outside and even within the Orthodox Conservative group in Oretown. Harry Scoble, *op. cit.*, p. 139. Cf. Roland J. Pellegrin and Charles H. Coates, "Absentee-Owned Corporations and Community Power Structure," *The American Journal of Sociology*, Vol. LXI (March 1956), pp. 413–419.

7. Robert O. Schulze's operational definition of "economic dominants" was revised slightly to identify industrial executives and financiers to be interviewed. Robert O. Schulze, "The Bifurcation of Power in a Satellite City," pp. 73–74. We reduced Schulze's figure of 75 workers to 50 workers and did not use the capital-worth-assessed-valuation criterion. See Schulze in Janowitz, *op. cit.*

8. In discussions of interests and ideologies as motivating forces in political behavior, it is frequently overlooked that the production, distribution, and consumption of ideological symbols may itself be of value to people. While some people may not themselves be self-conscious, articulate, sophisticated ideologists, they may enjoy being consumers of particular ideological messages.

9. One of the disputes between "power elitists" and "pluralists" is whether political leaderships are active participants in a variety of decisions—issues or scope areas—or whether leaders specialize in those issues or scope areas in which they have the strongest interests. Floyd Hunter did not claim that there was no specialization in Regional City on the part of the political leadership, but his critics have frequently charged that such was his thesis and that he was wrong. The assertion that in such cities as Regional City there are no generalists in the political leadership is disproven by a new study of Regional City. See Kent Jennings, *Community Influentials: a Study of Elites* (New York: The Free Press, forthcoming 1964). Our findings of a minority of generalists in political-leadership groups are comparable to Dahl's findings in New Haven. He describes the Mayor as the central generalist in an "executive-centered coalition." Robert A. Dahl, *Who Governs?* (New Haven: Yale University Press, 1961), pp. 203–205. See also Floyd Hunter's review of Dahl's *Who Governs?* in *Administrative Science Quarterly*, Vol. 6, No. 4 (March 1962), pp. 517–519. Arthur J. Vidich and Joseph Bensman describe how and why a few "general leaders" are drawn into decision-making regardless of their special interests, as well as detailing the need for more particularistic interests and more specialized role-playing. See their *Small Town in Mass Society* (Garden City: Doubleday Anchor Books, 1960), pp. 266–269.

10

TYPES OF POWER STRUCTURES: *Time E to M*

Thus far we have described something of the characteristics and perspectives of the groups at the political-leadership level in the four communities as of Time M. A picture of the interrelationships of groups, individual dissidents, and uncommitted leaders during Time E to M also was begun. We turn now to a somewhat more complete, comparative description of the intra- and intergroup relations at this political-leadership level of the community power structures. We shall pay special attention to these groups' patterns of functioning in the important authoritative-consideration stages of political decision-making during Time E to M as revealed by the historical reconstruction of the decisional processes occurring in that period (see Chapter 6).

TWO VARIATIONS ON ONE PATTERN OF LEADERSHIP IN DECISION-MAKING: FARMDALE AND METROVILLE

There were striking similarities in the organization and operation of the political leaderships in little, quasi-rural Farmdale in Western State and in much larger, biracial, industrial Metroville in Southern State; this was apparent in the authoritative-consideration stage of political decision-making during Time E to M. Differences in the power structures of these communities will be noted, but generally they resembled each other more than they resembled either Oretown or Petropolis; the latter in turn resembled each other on the two major classificatory factors determining type of community power structure.

Farmdale

The authoritative-consideration stage has been defined as the stage of action by the political participants who have the last chance, the final voice, in selecting one or another from a set of two or more possible outcomes as the policy that defines the scope of government for a succeeding time period.

The men who have contributed purposefully and successfully to the selection of a decisional outcome during this period of political decision-making are designated the political leaders of the community power structure. The locus of this stage in Farmdale was more frequently than not in a private organizational setting of the single group at the political-leadership level. In Farmdale, thirteen of the fourteen political decision-making processes that took place during Time E to M were deliberated and decided in three private, nongovernmental settings.

The approval of the state's proposal to bypass the community with a new highway was made by the Jeffersonian Conservative inner clique, meeting in a social setting. The social interactions at each other's homes provided the members of the inner clique, who were also kinfolk to each other, with a setting that was used frequently prior to or during the consideration of specific decisional questions by the larger group of Jeffersonian Conservatives. A second setting in which most of the selected set of decisional processes were considered authoritatively was the informal "poker club." Here the Manifest Leaders, except for Councilman Cox and Kenneth King, and sometimes invited guests met regularly to consider the political business of the community. A third setting was the board-of-directors meetings of one of the most prestigious service clubs; all the Manifest Leaders but Councilman Cox and Mr. King (who had been expelled) met to consider decisional options on occasion there.

As we noted earlier, the Manifest Leadership of Farmdale contained the highest proportion of elected authorities of any of the four communities. Inner-clique member Bill May was the Mayor, and two other Manifest Leaders, in addition to the sometimes dissident Councilman Cox, served on the city council. A number of the political decision-making processes reached the city council during this period, but the decisional outcome actually had been selected beforehand. Once the outcome had been agreed upon in one or another private setting, formal or informal local-governmental compliance was a foregone conclusion. The substantial overlapping of the Manifest Leadership and the elected officialdom in Farmdale was one of the differences in the patterns of decision-making between the substantially similar community power structures of Farmdale and Metroville.

On a rare occasion, the city council itself might directly receive a policy formulation. These demands would sometimes come from a councilman. The Mayor or another councilman ordinarily would refer the matter to a council committee for further study. Deferring demands for shifts in the scope of local government was the usual procedure, except when they were rejected out of hand in the light of an earlier, clear-cut agreement that a particular scope of government in fact should be maintained and not shifted. In the substantial majority of the political decision-making processes during Time E to M, policy formulations that resulted in demands were deliberated in one or another of the aforementioned private organizational settings. Occasionally policy formulations occurred in one of these private group settings and were at once deliberated and the demands immediately disposed of by authoritative consideration, a considerable overlapping or telescoping of decisional stages. But most policy formulations and demands were followed by a relatively distinct, developed stage of policy deliberation by the Jeffersonian Conservative group or one of its subgroups. The ordinary outcomes of the sets of political demands made during Time E to M for net or internal shifts in the scope of local government were negative. The single political group of leaders was successful in its opposition to such demands.

One of the younger Conservative Manifest Leaders specialized in gathering information.[1] He consciously tried to be aware of incipient policy formulations or actual demands expressed by members of the business community. The many voluntary formal organizations in Farmdale served as settings for the leadership to learn, at an early stage of political decision-making, of problems that could lead to policy formulations for undesirable shifts in the scope of local government, or of demands that were in the policy-deliberation stage at the "under-leadership" level of the community power structure. These voluntary organizations, particularly the subsidiary political organizations among them, also served as vehicles for the leadership to organize political support from active influentials and less influential citizens in opposing undesirable demands.

Besides the poker club, two or more Manifest Leaders regularly attended meetings of ten organizations in the community. At least 10 per cent of the membership of each one of these ten were active political participants, according to our sample survey. Thus, the Manifest Leadership was in close touch with the politically active segment of the citizenry of Farmdale.

The political leadership's direction and guidance of the subsidiary political organizations provided a means for coopting dissidents who favored a more expanding, active local government and community. In addition, direction and guidance of these organizations facilitated the gathering of political intelligence, organizing political support among the citizens, and diverting political to civic energies and enterprises; they also provided a setting for applying severe deprivational social sanctions. One of the most active spokesmen for a newly organized fraternal organization which supported the establishment of a municipal park-and-recreation program was brought into the leading service club by several Manifest Leaders who hoped by doing this to moderate or eliminate the recreational-facility demands emanating from this lower-middle- and lower-class fraternal organization, to which the Manifest Leaders had little direct access. The organization had been formed by this active influential with the assistance of Councilman Cox and a few of his friends from the other side of the tracks. In this small town of numerous formal organizations, the Jeffersonian Conservative group had a network of offices and organizations in which to participate with the citizens in order to obtain their own decisional preferences and to combat any "undesirable" decisional preferences of the latter.

Historical reconstruction of the fourteen political decision-making processes, through reports by the Manifest Leaders themselves and by others whom they mentioned, confirmed that non-Manifest Leaders attempted to exercise political influence on and through individual Manifest Leaders, and vice versa. The Manifest Leaders felt that the non-Manifest Leaders did have some impact on their decision-making behavior, ordinarily through strengthening and reinforcing decisional preferences and dispositions to act in particular ways in selecting particular decisional options. Some of these apparently influential men made their impact on decisional outcomes, obtaining a share in political power, in the settings of authoritative considerations—that is, as Latent Leaders.

Just before Time *M*, the city council authoritatively considered one set of decisional demands which had not been considered in its particular form in any of the aforementioned private-organization settings: the demand for the annexation of certain residential areas. Thus, every member of the city council, including the non-Manifest Leaders, deserved the classification of Latent Leader. A majority of the city councilmen were also regular members of, or invited on occasion to "play cards" in, the poker club.

In analyzing why such a small proportion of active influentials in the Farmdale random sample proved to be Latent Leaders (see Chapter 8) we found the usual reason was that the decisional outcome not to shift the scope of local government was contrary to their demands for such shifts. About one-third of the active influentials were not classified as Latent Leaders because they did not have direct access, through discussion, either to officials or to civic leaders in Farmdale. A few of the active influentials not so classified had been active politically, not in a decision-making process, but in a more general role. Sometimes they expressed their satisfaction with the existing minimal scope of local government and with the men who administered the city's affairs. For example, respondents reported discussing how nice it was to live in a small community with an appropriately limited and comparatively inexpensive local government. Sometimes they directed demands for what they considered specific "administrative" decisions to men such as the municipal employee who was the chief administrative officer, the *de facto* city manager; hence, they were classified as being involved in administrative but not political decision-making.

Besides the three active influentials who turned out to be Manifest Leaders, a fourth active influential was classified as a Latent Leader. He was a lawyer who was also the part-time city attorney. Like the Manifest Leader–active influentials, he was an ingroup member of the Jeffersonian Conservatives. He was a charter member of the poker club and an active participant in the other authoritative-consideration settings controlled by that group; in his official, appointive capacity he had direct entry into the formal-government settings. His legal practice was the largest in town, and he had a retainer from the private utility and the major mining company in town, in addition to his small salary from the municipal government. He was opposed to community growth, and personally concerned about the influx of attorneys he foresaw as an inevitable consequence of urbanization and industrialization. Jeffersonian Conservatism was a political ideology he understood and fully supported.

There seemed to be relatively little specialization in the political roles played by either Manifest or Latent Leaders. The exceptions were Judge Catis, the elder statesman and a direct, two-way communicator between the community and the state government, the aforementioned younger Manifest Leader who specialized in gathering political intelligence among the businessmen of Main Street, and, of course, the inner clique. Even the city attorney was not regarded by other political leaders as the monopolist of legal opinions and information, although he was the recognized authority on drafting ordinances.[2]

Most of the leaders played multiple roles in making political decisions, both inside the leadership group and in interaction with nonleaders. For example, every member of the Jeffersonian Conservative political group engaged in the self-conscious exercise of political influence inside and outside his voluntary associations; such activities were directed toward increasing the level of satisfaction with the limited scope of local government.

Such efforts were partly directed against the possible regrouping of the Community Conservationists, who had been in political-leadership positions up to Time *E*. Apparently there were no other aspiring, competitive leadership groups vying with the Jeffersonian Conservatives in this period. Both Councilman Cox and Kenneth King were regarded as individual dissidents, but neither aspired to compete with the single ideology represented most articulately by the Jeffersonian Conservative inner clique. Kenneth King had attracted a few followers, but they had attempted to get the political leadership to accede to their demands, rather than regarding themselves as a competitive leadership group.

The fact that most of the active influentials had been thwarted in their efforts to shift the scope of local government meant not only that they were not members of the political leadership, but also that they were in fact without political power during this period. Although they probably did have more political influence than those lower in the political-influence structure, they acquired no more political power than the two-fifths of the citizenry that did not participate politically at all. Some of the citizens lower in the political-influence structure may have contributed something to one or another decisional outcome and acquired some share in the units of political power assigned during this period when they, like the Latent Leaders in the sample, assisted in resisting shifts in the scope of local government. A few citizens apparently did contribute, although not in the authoritative-consideration stage and therefore not as political leaders, to the affirmative decisional outcome to relax the enforcement of traffic and parking regulations in Farmdale, thereby deserving to be credited with a share of political power.

However, during Time *E* to *M*, the distribution of political power among the citizens was limited, since the pattern of decisional outcomes of demands to expand and to shift internally the scope of local government was negative. The degree of the leadership's responsiveness to the sets of demands made during Time *E* to *M* to shift the scope of local government was relatively low. The men who emerged as the political leaders of the community power structure as a consequence of their successful roles in the period immediately prior to each decisional outcome were sometimes also aided by supportive counter-demands to maintain the existing scope, but the demands in favor of particular shifts outnumbered the counterdemands in a number of the decisional processes. Members of the political leadership primarily responded to the dictates of their political ideology, particularly as that ideology was propounded and the decision-making strategy developed by the inner clique of the Jeffersonian Conservatives.[3]

Metroville

In Metroville, as in Farmdale, the overwhelming majority of the decision-making processes during Time E to M were considered authoritatively in private, nongovernmental settings. Although policy formulations suggesting shifts in the scope of local government were generated and at first deliberated most frequently in official govern-mental agencies, in all but four of the twenty-three decisional proc-esses the decisional outcomes emerged from the authoritative consider-ation of choices in private settings.

These settings included the informal social and business milieus in which the Manifest Leaders relaxed and worked together. The fabric of these settings was woven tightly, both because of the mutual eco-nomic enterprises in which most of these men were engaged and be-cause of their kinship ties. Eleven of the twenty-two Manifest Lead-ers were related to each other by blood or marriage. This close group of men of great wealth and high social position had access to each other's homes and offices; they also belonged to the same exclusive country clubs and cultural organizations.

Their master political organization, corresponding to the "poker club" of Farmdale, was the Committee for Better Government. Established during a time of community crisis after the Second World War by a group of economically and socially important men, its various committees corresponded to various local governmental units and the group constituted a private analogue of the municipal govern-ment. It did not meet regularly as did the much smaller "poker club" of Farmdale. Instead the Progressive Conservative inner clique and a few of the closest associates of its members constituted the ac-tive, continuing core of the organization; they surrounded themselves with various study groups investigating and formulating policies in areas that seemed from time to time to need improvement. Com-mittees of this organization constituted the bulk of the personnel of special citizens' committees officially appointed by the Mayor to make recommendations on matters involving major public expenditures or shifts in the scope of local government.

A decade earlier Gerald Smith, Sr., one of the Conservative Leaders at the time of our study, had been one of the key founders of the Committee for Better Government. In Chapter 5 we mentioned that he had talked to a leading civic club when that organization was founded. This typified the roles played by members of the White Manifest Leadership when, in their view, the organization of political support required their personal appearance and prestige in political decision-making. One of the inner-clique members, Samuel Trump, II, and one other Manifest Leader specialized in relationships between the community and the state capital or Washington, D. C.; otherwise the Manifest Leaders played the sorts of diverse roles in decision-making that their counterparts in Farmdale played.

However, the Manifest Leaders did not serve in elective posts in municipal government. One did serve as an elected county-government official, in a post traditionally filled by one or another of them. Others served on a number of the many municipal appointive commissions; this provided a direct bridge between the public and private government. For example, having a member on the city-county planning commission permitted the decisional processes involving the question of shopping-center construction in fringe areas and an increase in the authority of the city council relative to the planning commission in rezoning matters to be considered authoritatively in these official settings rather than in private settings. Other members of the commission not in the Manifest Leadership looked to the Manifest Leader on the planning commission to provide information about the desires of other important leaders in order to avoid endangering their own goal of further development of a more autonomous planning process based on expert, professional guidance.

Consideration of the decisional process involving zoning and the power of the planning commission in the formally authoritative city-council setting similarly was facilitated by the presence of an elected city councilman who was a senior officer in one of the Manifest Leadership's largest corporations; in the corporate hierarchical structure, he was under Samuel Trump, a member of the Progressive Conservative inner clique. The councilman was regarded by his fellows as Mr. Trump's representative in municipal affairs. The somewhat marginal member of the White Manifest Leadership, Mr. Williston Russell, III, played a comparable personal role in his capacity as city attorney.

Perhaps the most important agent-principal relationship in city government was that between Mayor Peterson and the inner clique

Polk. Of somewhat lesser but still great importance was the relationship between the City Manager and the Manifest Leadership. Neither the Mayor nor the City Manager was nominated sufficiently often to appear on the list of Manifest Leaders. Both men, as well as the eight city councilmen, were Latent Leaders, although involved in a smaller proportion of the political decision-making processes than most Manifest Leaders during Time E to M.

It was William Polk who had coopted Mayor Peterson and had then become his chief mentor soon after the latter had first been elected on a "beat the elite" platform in the early postwar years. The other Manifest Leaders' dislike and distrust of Mayor Peterson, the "rabble-rouser," were reduced substantially over the years as he conformed to the demands of the man to whom he accorded a devoted political status; this is attested by the fact that the Mayor tied with Mr. Polk and Mr. Trump, II, among most frequently nominated men to whom the White Manifest Leaders said they would turn for advice on local-government matters. Only the City Manager and the third member of the Progressive Conservative inner clique, Harold Allen, Sr., were nominated more frequently as potential advisors. The White Manifest Leadership as a whole regarded the City Manager as a strong person, able both to monitor Mayor Peterson's political activity and to guide him in decision-making. Every one of the White Manifest Leaders "approved" of the City Manager, almost one-third of them "strongly." Two disapproved of the Mayor, two more were undecided, and none of them strongly approved of him, including his inner-clique advisor.

The Mayor's subordination in his political-influence relationship with his mentor was recognized by the White Manifest Leaders. In fact, only his mentor, of all the Manifest Leaders, nominated him as one of the "ten people who can get a major policy or project adopted in Metroville." The three members of the Progressive Conservative inner clique were ranked one, two, and three among the men most frequently nominated in this regard by the other White Manifest Leaders.

The City Manager was hand-picked by the White Progressive Conservatives and was regarded as a trusted administrator of municipal affairs. His advice on administrative matters was accorded a high degree of political status by the Progressive Conservative clique, and the Manifest Leadership named him even more frequently than members of the inner clique as a potential advisor on local-government affairs. To the question, "If you wanted some advice on what can or should be done in regard to local government or community welfare, whom would you go to?", he responded that he would probably go to some of the business leaders.[4]   In regard to spending local tax money to attract new industry to Metroville, he suggested that industrial promotion was a matter for the Chamber of Commerce and local industry and not for the local government.

The relationship of the Mayor and the City Manager to the Negro Leadership also should be understood.   The Negro subcommunity gave Mayor Peterson solid electoral support, partly because they considered him a relatively independent friend of the Negro, and partly because he was one of the chief points of contact between the White Progressive Conservatives and the Negro Leadership.   The latter apparently believed Mayor Peterson when he took credit for the former's decisions to improve the Negro subcommunity in various ways.   The Negro Leadership ranked the Mayor more frequently than anyone else as one of the three most influential persons in local-government matters and as the man to whom they would turn for advice in regard to such matters.[5]   The City Manager was ranked next most frequently as one of the three most influential men in local-government matters and slightly behind Councilman Vida, one of the inner clique of Negro Leaders, as a potential advisor.   The White Manifest Leader named most frequently as the man with policy views similar to those of the Negro Leaders was Williston Russell, III; but the Negro Leaders seriously overestimated his political influence by nominating him most frequently as one of the ten men, White or Negro, who could get a major policy adopted in Metroville.   The asymmetrical relationship between Negro Leader Samuel Best and the Mayor's political mentor, influential William Polk, has already been noted.

Thus, some of the Negro Leadership's most direct channels of personal access to local government were through a Negro councilman who somewhat hesitantly accepted a "go slowly" Progressive Conservatism; two other even more cautious inner-clique Negro Leaders, one of whom seemed infrequently to question the political cues given him by the restorationist key White Progressive Conservative; a Mayor perceived as a friend of the Negroes but who actually took the same positions as did that White political leader; and a City Manager who saw his political role as the effectuator or administrator of decisions properly made by the White business and civic "elite."   The White Manifest Leader in local government to whom the Negro Leadership also accorded very high political status, Williston Russell, III, was more truly their "friend," but he was accorded little status in political decision-making by the White inner clique of Progressive Conservatives.   Stirrings of discontent were apparent by Time *E* (1957) among some Negro Leaders and among Negroes not recognized in their own subcommunity as Leaders. These discontented Negroes still had to contend with this distinctive, tightly woven network of informal White political leaders, White formal authorities who were Latent Leaders, and Negro Leaders at Time M (1958).

One of the ways that Mayor Peterson and the City Manager maintained a working relationship with members of the Negro Leadership was through appointment of the latter to various municipal commissions and agencies; these relatively numerous municipal appointive positions already have been mentioned. A comparable relationship existed between the Negro Leadership and the city school board. The Mayor had appointed Negro Councilman Vida to serve on that board. The Negro Leaders ranked Councilman Vida and the White School Superintendent, a Latent Leader not in the random sample, more frequently than anyone else as influential and as potential advisors in school affairs. The School Superintendent, like the Mayor, accorded the highest positive political status to White Manifest Leaders and to those board members who, like the aforementioned White city councilman, were senior officers in the city's largest corporations. The Negro Leaders in their political roles in city government thus were surrounded by White politicians who accorded high political status to members of the White Progressive Conservative inner clique and their close associates.

The socio-economic "aristocracy" of White Progressive Conservatives, particularly the inner clique and their closest associates in the Manifest Leadership, were one step removed from the political demands that emanated from the White and Negro citizen substructures. They relied on the Mayor, the City Manager, other elected municipal-government officials, and some of the White Manifest Leaders with special interests who served as appointive officials on municipal commissions and agencies to handle frequently routine administrative demands and relatively simple political demands, and to bring to the Progressive Conservative group those matters that required their personal intervention. To be sure, policy formulations contemplating shifts in the scope of local government emerged periodically as political demands from friends of the Manifest Leaders or from the Manifest Leaders themselves. This means that they could be raised immediately in a setting of the White Progressive Conservative group and disposed of efficiently in a political decision-making process wherein the stages of decision-making were monopolized by the Manifest Leaders themselves and selected Latent Leaders. Ordinarily, demands made by Negro Leaders were directed to the Mayor or City Manager by or through Negro Councilman Vida, or they were transmitted directly in a "hat in hand" manner. On occasion, Mr. Williston Russell, III, served as a direct link into the Progressive Conservative group.

The White Manifest Leaders tended to belong to relatively exclusive community organizations. Two or more White Manifest Leaders regularly attended four of the five associations classified as subsidiary political organizations. Two or more members of the Negro Leadership belonged to fifteen community or subcommunity organizations. These included all four Negro subsidiary political organizations. These, like those of their White counterparts, provided for the Negro Leadership an additional set of formally organized, voluntary associations with limited membership which were more exclusively leadership organizations than they were composite organizations of leaders and other citizens, as had been the case in Farmdale. This points to the greater associational self-sufficiency and personal distance between the political leadership and the White and Negro citizen substructures in Metroville than in Farmdale.

The organization to which the greatest proportion of Negro Leaders belonged in Metroville was Harmony House, one of the eleven community organizations to which the White Manifest Leaders belonged. Its activity in behalf of greater job opportunities for Negroes, for example, was rigidly circumscribed by the policies set by those Manifest Leaders who were the policy-makers for the largest industrial firms in the city.[6] The Democratic party organization was one of the patently political organizations to which Negro Leaders belonged and in which they held office. Its White chairman was a younger businessman, a non-random-sample Latent Leader, and a close friend and distant relative of a large number of the White Manifest Leaders. He was covertly an active racist, and one of his closest advisors was his fellow-racist member of the White Progressive Conservative inner clique, William Polk.

The Latent Leaders from the random sample of Metroville's White subcommunity included three of the five active influentials. One White active influential who has *not* been classified as a Latent Leader was a woman who knew many Manifest Leaders but who was not a member of any organizations to which Manifest Leaders belonged. She did not participate in any political decision-making process. Moreover, to illustrate her distance from the political leadership, she regarded "the League of Women Voters" as the most important decision-making group in local politics. Another active influential who was not classified as a Latent Leader was a youngish man who was a real-estate developer. He was a close friend of Mr. Williston Russell,

III, and a member of the country club to which the White Manifest Leaders belonged. He had both indirect and potentially direct access to authoritative-consideration settings of Manifest Leaders, but he did not participate in any of the decision-making processes during Time E to M.

One of the three Latent Leaders in the White random sample was a retired life-insurance-company executive who considered himself a close friend of six Manifest Leaders, including all three members of the inner clique, as well as of the Mayor and City Manager. He had worked closely with Mayor Peterson in getting the community's blue laws repealed. He was a member not only of the Manifest Leaders' country club, but also of two other of their civic organizations, and served as an appointed member of one of the more important municipal-government commissions.

The other two White Latent Leaders were women, both newcomers to Metroville. One, whose husband was a junior executive in one of the city's few large absentee-owned industrial corporations, knew ten of the twenty-two White Manifest Leaders personally, and belonged to the country club and to one of their cultural associations. She had been actively urging the creation of an urban-redevelopment program, not to provide additional industrial- or business-expansion sites but because she was concerned with the plight of Negro slum-dwellers and was interested in the "city beautiful."

The other woman Latent Leader was a recently arrived Northerner, and an active member of the Republican Club of Metroville. Her husband was a professionally trained technician in another of the largest manufacturing firms. She knew no Manifest Leader personally, nor did she belong to any of the latter's organizations. She had no idea of the important people in decision-making in regard to local-government matters in the community. Her attitudes towards the civic elite were reflected in her voluntary comment that she did not like "the control of the community by a few big firms." This woman was a school teacher who, although in favor of school consolidation, worked against that in favor of the measure to pass a bond issue for school construction.

Although only three people in the small White sample were classified as Latent Leaders, projecting that finding for the White population as a whole means that probably there were more White Latent Leaders than White Manifest Leaders. The smallest fraction, although not an inconsiderable number, probably had direct access to the private social settings in which the small number of Manifest Leaders engaged in authoritative consideration with such Latent Leaders. Another fraction participated in those settings that were quasi-public and dominated ordinarily by Manifest and Latent Leaders who were not elected government officials. The special citizens' committees appointed by the Mayor to make recommendations about recreational matters and the question of how to improve the municipal mental institutions operated in such settings. Other Latent Leaders served as appointed members of formal local-government commissions and agencies. Perhaps the largest number of Latent Leaders obtained a measure of political power as leaders in those decisional processes involving special elections. The proponents of immediate financial support for schools, of improvements in the water and sewage-disposal systems, and of expressways, during Time E to M engaged in successful electoral-leadership roles. Some of the active opponents of increased taxes for recreational facilities were Latent Leaders in the pre-election authoritative-consideration stage which came after other Latent Leaders had joined Manifest Leaders to defeat demands for municipal swimming pools.

Only one of the two Negro active influentials was classified as a Latent Leader. He not only engaged in what he termed "inquisition of candidates" for local office as an active member of a poorly organized Negro voters' association, but he also worked to turn out Negro voters in support of the school bond issue and against school consolidation. The other Negro active influential did not participate in any of the twenty-three political decision-making processes during Time E to M.

It was noted earlier that Negro and the White citizens of Metroville did not participate politically more than did the relatively apathetic citizens of Farmdale. Even highly educated Negro citizens did not participate very much in activist roles, nor did they attend meetings where policy or decisional matters were discussed. This pattern held even for the Negro Leaders in Metroville. Although one of their inner clique was an elected city councilman, and they felt they had access to the Mayor, the City Manager, and to Williston Russell, III, as well as to other individual White Manifest Leaders, 42 per cent of the Negro Leaders said that they had not taken an active part in any local-government or community matter in the past year, and 32 per cent reported that they had neither played an activist role nor attended any meeting where such matters had been a major subject of deliberation.

When participating politically in Metroville, the Negro Leadership, like the Negro rank-and-file citizens, seemed to concentrate not on the political decisions, to which they had little direct access at any stage, but on particular administrative matters of Negro-subcommunity welfare. This attitude was similar to that of a number of the active influentials in Farmdale. Included among these matters were particular housekeeping and recreational-facility improvements, access by individual Negro families to existing public-housing units, and admission to White schools by individual Negro petitioners. These were considered proper subjects of demands addressed to administrators such as the City Manager and the School Superintendent, although in some cases they were intended and interpreted as covert, generalized expressions of dissatisfaction with the dominant White political leadership. Such subjects of administrative demands were analogous to the concern individual Negro citizens felt about economic opportunity, which they considered to consist of individual problems amenable to solution by the action of private and economic, rather than public and political authorities, if amenable to solution at all. The Negro Leaders apparently made demands, and served as representatives of other Negro citizens with similar demands, in administrative decision-making processes involving petitions for particular housekeeping, recreational, public-housing, and desegregation benefits. However, the Negro Leaders apparently were not concerned very much themselves, nor as intermediaries of others, with economic problems, except in a personal, individualistic kind of charity role.

However, by Time M, a handful of the White Progressive Conservative Leaders had begun to suspect that the frequency with which some "administrative" demands, particularly in regard to school desegregation, were being made and passed on by Negro Leaders reflected an increased Negro discontent, at least on the part of a few "troublemaking agitators" in the Negro subcommunity. The political, social, and cultural distance between the White and Negro Manifest Leaders prevented the former from observing the discontent first-hand, as the political leaders in Farmdale did in assessing the political perspectives of their citizens.[7]

The White Political Leadership was personally closer to the county than to the municipal government; this was typified by the Manifest Leader who was carrying on the tradition of serving as an elected member of the governing body of the county. Although White Latent Leaders served as relatively trusted delegates or surrogates in municipal-government posts, the White Manifest Leadership was somewhat more removed from the White political-influence substructure in the city than from that of the county. This difference is perhaps a partial explanation of the political distance that we found put even city-dwelling White citizens farther from their municipal than from their county officials. There was evidence that the postwar trend of a unified leadership concerned with the community in both its county and municipal aspects had begun to be reversed. Before the Second World War, political leaders had been concerned with the county and cared little for what went on inside the predominantly working-class city. The political distance of Metroville's White citizens might also have been due to the opinion of some White citizens that the Mayor was more pro-Negro and pro-White-labor than a representative of the Progressive Conservative Manifest Leadership. This lack of valid political information might explain partially the heavy anti-Peterson vote in 1957 among White citizens.

The socio-economic gap between the White Manifest Leadership and the rank-and-file White citizens, the traditional political apathy of the latter, and the associational distance between that leadership and even the upper-middle-class White citizens also caused the White Manifest Leadership to be uncertain as to the character and magnitude of political discontent, particularly on the part of city-dwelling White citizens, with such policies as further city growth through additional annexations and such racial accommodation policies as token desegregation. The White Progressive Conservatives assumed that the county-dwellers were more antiannexation and anti-Negro than the city-dwellers. At the time of the school desegregation decision there had been in Metroville no organized counterpart to the White Supremacist PECORR of Petropolis. Neither William Polk nor any of the other White Manifest Leaders had developed by Time M the sorts of financial or other supportive relationships with a newly formed White Supremacy organization in Metroville that individual Orthodox Conservative Manifest Leaders had developed with PECORR in Petropolis. The White Manifest Leadership assumed on the basis of the absence of violence when desegregation was initiated and the seemingly widespread political apathy in the White subcommunity, the latter being a correct impression according to our findings of relatively limited distributions of political participation and political influence in both Metroville subcommunities, that control of the political system was still very much in their hands.

The monitoring of the political perspectives of merchants and of labor-union people in Farmdale by the close contacts of the Manifest Leadership with those segments of the community in a voluntary associational setting was accomplished to a lesser extent, although in equivalent ways, in Metroville. For example, one White Manifest Leader, a banker who was sympathetic to new industry in the city, served as the head of a Chamber of Commerce committee to take charge of plans to evaluate the need for, and move ahead with, private actions to stimulate business in the downtown section. In this he was supported by the sons of two other White Manifest Leaders. The industrial executives in the Manifest Leadership kept their ears close to the ground in their own manufacturing enterprises to hear and, if necessary, head off any prounion activities, or more militant unionism, on the part of their workers. Their positions as the heads of these "involuntary" associations, the corporations, provided these men with a channel for identifying and doing something about the local political dangers they foresaw from the rise of a politically active labor movement. It was not the White citizens of Liberal, prounion persuasion that the White Manifest Leadership were most unsure about politically, but those of less Progressive, more Orthodox Conservative views and Negro Liberals.

The intermediate White Latent Leadership and a substantial curtain of color, age, and socio-economic status lay between the White Manifest Leadership and the Negro Leadership. The more "equalitarian" younger sons and relatives of these White Manifest Leaders might have provided some direct points of contact across the racial barrier, as did young Eben Bacon, Jr., in his political interactions with Negro Leaders in Petropolis, but this was not allowed by their White elders. Nor had the predominantly middle-aged Negro Leadership developed to any great extent a personal political-status relationship of the kind that elderly Negro Leader Samuel Best had established with William Polk; this crossing of the color barrier apparently was possible in Metroville only between men of the same generation.[8] Samuel Best was less typical of Negro political discontent than were other Negro Leaders in Metroville. Moreover, the very young and the blue-collar workers were not represented in the Negro Leadership of that subcommunity, including its Latent Leader segment. The Negro Leadership in Metroville was apparently quite out of touch with the particularly politically discontented, more militantly inclined Liberal elements among the young people of that subcommunity.

The Negro Leadership of Metroville was for the most part personally uninvolved in any of the political decisions made during Time *E* to *M*. When the community of Metroville is viewed as having a single political system and single structure of political power, we find that some of these so-called Negro Leaders had restricted political-leadership roles and that others had none at all in the community power structure. Some of them shared in the political power accruing to the politically participant contributors to decisional outcomes, but, like the one Negro Latent Leader, in the particular role of campaigning in special elections. Negro Leader Samuel Best urged Negro citizens to vote for a bond issue to improve the street system of the city, the item he mentioned as the fourth most important community problem in Metroville. He was one of those privy to deliberations at the authoritative-consideration stage wherein William Polk led the White Leadership to reverse itself and support the racist mental-hospital proposal. Samuel Best also deserved to be accorded a share in political power in that decision because of his subsequent active support of Polk's successful move.

The few decisional processes referred to the White and Negro citizens in elections afforded them their greatest opportunities to participate in authoritative consideration and thereby acquire political-leadership roles. Only a few citizens had access to the relatively closed, private settings controlled by the White Manifest Leadership and the formal governmental settings that were open to some actively interested citizens. These same electoral decisions were also the most accessible channels for the average citizen to acquire some share of political power during Time E to M. However, only a small minority of the small number of eligible voters turned out. Although a small proportion of White and Negro voters, unlike their fellows in Farmdale, earned political power in these specific electoral roles, it would appear that the distribution of political power was extremely limited in the body politic of Metroville.

The several elections on special measures illustrate several matters of importance about the power structure in Metroville during Time E to M. First, such decisional questions as those involved in the defeat of the recreational measures and the matter of school consolidation signalled some change in the traditional pattern of political decision-making. In both of these cases and in the case of the mental-institution matter, demands for shifts in the scope of local government were deliberated and political support was organized early in these processes by official agencies of local government. These included the municipal recreation and mental-health commissions and the lay advisory board in the city school system. In all of these cases, counter-organizational efforts directed by Manifest Leaders had to be used to stop certain highly educated White and Negro citizens from successfully pursuing decisional outcomes which the leaders deemed undesirable. In earlier years, the scope of local government in regard to such matters as recreational and mental-health facilities had been within the province of informal authorities whose private, large-scale donations ordinarily were sufficient to finance any shift in scope that was deemed desirable or to block those deemed undesirable.

Metroville politics thus witnessed the development of an organization-of-political-support stage in decision-making in which citizens serving as or working with appointive authorities pursued their mission most seriously and independently, to the point of conflict with important Manifest Leaders in a small fraction of the decisional processes. This was epitomized by the White woman Latent Leader who worked with a citizens' committee in support of the two school measures. Her openly critical opinions about the established industrial-civic rule were also, we suspect, a change of potential significance. Such opposition also was evidenced by the informal and unsuccessful efforts of some Negro citizens to marshall electoral support behind the recreational measures.

The actions of the second White woman Latent Leader indicated another change in the power structure. Her active participation in the local Republican party was deviant behavior for members of the political leadership, even though an increasing number of leadership members had begun to identify themselves with the Republican party. How many more women were actually in the political leadership is difficult to estimate on the basis of this small sample. But this one woman represented a significant break with the postwar traditionally male leadership of Metroville. Formerly, certain major "cultural" and charitable projects had been regarded as nonpolitical and were assigned by the political leadership to women. To find women such as this Latent Leader independently expressing themselves on such matters as the need for urban redevelopment, even at the country club, a setting in which political matters traditionally were reserved for discussion by male members, must have been a shock to these men. Although there was little indication that having women active in Metroville's politics would mean any departures from preferred policies, their presence, even in relatively nonpublic, latent roles, marked another departure from the past in the functioning of the political leadership of the power structure.[9] Although such women introduced an element of unpredictability for the male political leadership, that leadership still resembled Farmdale's male leadership, since women in Metroville had not gained access to the men's locker room in the country club, the executive suites, or the luncheons held for purposes of political discussions in the downtown clubs, hotels, or restaurants.

These same decisional processes attested the conflicts in preferences among the Manifest Leaders themselves. The mental-institution problem was the most extreme example of a difference in decisional preferences leading to a bitter controversy within the single group of Progressive Conservatives. However, even apart from such race-related issues, complete consensus in policy perspectives was not the norm in the political leadership of Metroville. Although individual views and values were legitimized by referring them to and asserting their congruity with the political ideological doctrines of Progressive Conservatism, the resolution of intragroup conflict made it necessary for members of the group to exercise their political influence upon one another; they had to use sharp exhortations, quiet bargaining, friendly persuasion, social sanctions, implied economic threats, and promises of economic and welfare rewards, the latter directed most frequently by White political leaders to their Negro counterparts.

Many Manifest Leaders considered the mental-hospital issue unprecedented in its bitterness and the unwillingness of individual Manifest Leaders to compromise with other Manifest Leaders. In this issue, as in a number of the other decisional processes, the decisional preferences of the Manifest Leadership diverged, to some extent, according to whether the Leaders were active in the county domain or in city affairs. Although only a small minority of White Manifest Leaders, when asked specifically, disapproved of the Mayor, the disapproval that existed was concentrated among those most involved with the county government. The Mayor's mentor, William Polk, was at one pole; the county commissioner Manifest Leader was at the other. Polk's White resistance sentiments seemed to be at the source of his intransigence. The county commissioner's fiscal responsibility to his more tax-conscious county constituents and his desire to maintain his personal political-influence position in the Manifest Leadership seemed to make him adamant in his opposition. Whether or not this cleavage presaged a county-city split in the political leadership of Metroville and instability in the community power structure could not be answered before Time M.

However, the single Progressive Conservative group still existed at Time M. Whatever the degree of internal discord, and this should not be unduly exaggerated, no member of the Progressive Conservative group in Metroville, White or Negro, seriously saw himself leaving the group or starting a competitive group. Two of the three White Latent Leaders identified themselves as members of the Progressive Conservative political-leadership group; the third was distant and critical, but even he was not involved in a group aspiring to replace or turn out the current leadership. The Negro Latent Leader, who was so hostile to the dominance of the White subcommunity that he was at least verbally an active racist, actually believed himself to share policy views with six White Manifest Leaders. He also considered himself to be a close friend of Mayor Peterson, Negro Councilman Vida, and two White Manifest Leaders, including racist William Polk.

A small group of White citizens of modest means and low social status had formed a White Supremacy organization during Time E to M, after the decision to initiate token desegregation was announced publicly. This organization had neither connections with nor support from any of the White Manifest Leaders. Its members had adopted a policy of watchful waiting to see what the outcome of administrative decision-making in individual desegregation cases would be, before deciding whether they dared to strive for community political-leadership positions as a competitive group.

Similarly, the more militantly inclined Liberal Negro citizens were trying to decide whether or not they could displace the present Negr Leaders from their seemingly impotent positions in the communi,y power structure. There seemed little possibility that they could secure leadership positions, since they would be opposed by the strong White industrialists and financiers, and could not rely on the support of the politically passive and alienated members of the Negro subcommunity; there was no strong organized-labor movement in the White subcommunity with which they might ally themselves, as had been possible during the immediate postwar effort to topple the rulers by means of an integrated political movement of minority groups. By Time M, political Liberalism in Metroville was more a memory than an organized political ideology competing with Progressive Conservatism. The latter's dominance of the leadership of the community power structure was intact.

A COMPETITIVE PATTERN OF POLITICAL LEADERSHIP IN DECISION-MAKING: PETROPOLIS AND ORETOWN

During Time E to M in both Oretown and Petropolis, Liberals were competing for political-leadership positions with Conservatives. In these two communities there was substantially greater competition for political-leadership positions than in Metroville and Farmdale. Individual dissidents and internal cleavages were noticeable in the latter cities, but in both Oretown and Petropolis the political dissidence and competition took the form of political warfare between contending groups. These groups differed in their general political ideologies, as well as about particular decisional preferences. The political battleground more often extended into the city council or the city school board meetings than remained in private settings.

Petropolis

None of the groups at the Manifest Leadership level in Petropolis escaped the intragroup politics that marked Metroville's and, to a lesser degree, Farmdale's solitary political-leadership group. As we have already remarked, policy and decisional preferences and ideological sentiments ranged from consensual, clear-cut positions taken by inner-clique members to diverse, uncertain, and sometimes conflicting positions taken by more marginal members of the group. This was most obvious for the Orthodox Conservative group, which had the largest membership among the identified White Manifest Leaders of any political group. However, intraclique disagreements and intraclique political-influence relationships were evident in every leadership clique during Time E to M. In addition, there were several uncommitted members of the Manifest Leadership whose support in political decision-making was sufficiently attractive to the contending political groups to moderate decisional demands or positions on occasion; this blurred somewhat intergroup differences.

For example, the Community Conservationists, partly as a matter of political ideology related to the declining economy and partly as a matter of strategy, had developed a relatively consensual set of decisional preferences cross-cutting contending political groups in regard to the need for local-government activity in industrial promotion. Such privately organized groups as the Committee on Industrial Development served to provide settings for multiple-political-group support for the city administration's active attempt to reorganize the economy and revive the community.

The Community Conservationists, in political alliance with White and Negro Liberals, moderated what might have been an even more conflicting and contentious local politics. Mayor Plunkett himself was a leading spokesman of the Community Conservationists. Since his projected role for the city government included stimulation of retail trade and the development of a more independent community-planning function, he felt that relationships between City Hall and the merchants should be improved to gain the latter's active support and to avert opposition to his program from that quarter. He also felt that race relations should be improved. This led him and his fellow Conservationists to try to bridge the political groups.

Since the authoritative-consideration stage took place in formal-government settings, and City Hall politically was controlled through the electoral process, any political group could control such groups as the appointed bureaucracy and the appointive city school board, if it could gain predominant electoral support. Just as the Orthodox Conservatives seemed to be in unchallenged control of the county government and therefore could maintain or shift its scope with little difficulty, comparable control of City Hall was regarded as a political plum within the reach of Orthodox Conservatives or Liberals.[10] Public offices were distributed equally among Orthodox Conservatives, Community Conservationists, and uncommitted Manifest and Latent Leaders, while neither White nor Negro Liberal political leaders had their "fair share" of such offices.

Although there was one elected Negro Councilman and one appointed Negro city school board member, the Negro Leadership of Petropolis had a different relationship to the Mayor and City Manager than the Negro Leadership had in Metroville. In Metroville, the Negro Leadership had been content to accept appointive positions on formal, if generally ineffective, municipal-government boards and commissions. They had come to rely for administrative largesse on the Mayor and City Manager as well as on their Negro councilman; they also relied upon the Progressive Conservative decision-makers in the White subcommunity rather than participating actively in decision-making themselves. In Petropolis, the Negro Leaders exercised an option that had not been developed by their Metroville counterparts. Although they accepted appointments to the newly created race-relations commission established by the Mayor prior to Time M, they held relatively few *appointive* positions in city government. Instead they held office and worked actively in PESNEG, in the local NAACP, and in the local Democratic party organization led by the White Liberal clique among the Manifest Leaders. In sharp contrast to the 42 per cent of the Negro Leaders of Metroville who had responded negatively when asked whether or not they had actively participated in any local-government or community issue during the last year or so, only 5 per cent of the Negro Leaders in Petropolis gave this response. Only 10 per cent of the Negro Leaders of Petropolis, compared to 47 per cent of the Negro Leaders of Metroville, reported that they had not attended a meeting or gathering at which city-government matters had been a major subject of consideration.

There was an independent, formal associational underpinning of the divergent, competitive groups at the political-leadership level. PESNEG, as a subcommunity political organization, had no real counterpart in Metroville's Negro subcommunity.[11] It was not only a manifestly political organization, but it also was active in trying to maximize Negroes' opportunities for economic advancement. Its counterpart in this latter function in Metroville was the biracial, but White-controlled, and far less militant Harmony House. The industrial unions not only were extensive, but they also were relatively well organized in Petropolis. The separate, segregated locals were subsidiary political organizations which had a voters' league, primarily for Whites, that compared to the electoral apparatus of PESNEG. The Negro and White labor-union leaders overlapped and worked together in the local Democratic party leadership. They were represented in the Manifest Leadership by the White Liberal two-man clique, who were the chief officers in the Democratic party until an unfavorable decisional outcome removed them from office, and by the Liberal Negro Leadership.

The Community Conservationists were numerically weak at the Manifest Leader level. Unlike the Liberals, they lacked independent associational bases, that is, subsidiary political organizations of which they were the officers or leaders and to which citizens at large belonged. The City Manager was not a close political ally of Mayor Plunkett and the Community Conservationists. He was uncommitted and admitted a strong desire to maintain a peaceful, primarily administrative decision-making process at City Hall; this desire was reflected in his quiet opposition to substantial or innovative shifts in the scope of local government unless and until he learned that these were not controversial. For example, he resisted the Mayor's program of creating a stronger, more autonomous city planning department because he knew that a number of the Orthodox Conservatives disliked governmental planning. In another instance, he opposed the proposed urban-renewal program for the Negro slum area, a most important policy formulation of the Community Conservationists, because he wanted first to find out whether or not the Negro Leadership and the Orthodox Conservatives both would go along with it.

Knowing of his independence from the Mayor, the Negro Leaders had developed direct working relationships with the City Manager. In fact, they selected him more frequently than the Mayor, but less frequently than Negro Councilman Standish, as someone to whom they would go for advice on local-government matters, even though they selected the Mayor more frequently than the Manager as one of the three most influential men in local-government matters. The City Manager, while an "active accommodator," disapproved of both PESNEG and the new biracial municipal race-relations agency. He took the point of view that segregation was not currently at issue and that such problems would solve themselves when Negroes were better off economically. However, he did not make the mistake of other White Manifest Leaders in selecting George France as one of the three most influential Negro Leaders. The real "who's who" of the Negro Leadership was well known to him.

Lou Griffin, the member of the inner clique of Negro Leaders who headed the political committee of the local NAACP, was accorded high political status by his fellow Negro Leaders, but by only one White Manifest Leader beside the City Manager. Only Fred Ames, the Liberal union leader among the Manifest Leaders, volunteered that Lou Griffin was one of the ten most influential policy-makers in Petropolis, a man with whom he had the closest contacts and shared similar policy views, and whom he considered a close friend. The Negro Leader to whom White Manifest Leaders frequently looked was George France, venerable president of one of the Negro sub-community's largest loan companies, who in earlier years had been the leading proponent of a "go slow" political policy for PESNEG. Frank Eldon, a member of the present Negro Leader inner clique, was the most cautious, least militant of the Negro Leaders of high political status.

Mr. France's spokesman role and political perspectives have been compared to those of Negro Leader Samuel Best in Metroville. George France was named by two of twenty White Orthodox Conservative Manifest Leaders who responded to the question as a man whose views about the needs, policies, and future of Petropolis were most similar to their own. He was named by four White Orthodox Conservatives but by none of the White Community Conservationists or Liberals as a person with whom they had worked closely on community projects; two of these Orthodox Conservatives considered him a close friend. He was regarded as a friend by four of the five White Conservationist-Liberals; but they did not accord him the political status which they did other Negro Leaders, particularly Negro Councilman Standish.

Mr. France's political perspectives contrasted sharply with Mr. Griffin's. To France, one of the few Republicans in the Negro Leadership, the three most important issues facing Petropolis were downtown redevelopment, the quality of the public schools, and urban renewal. To Griffin, an active, strong Democrat, the most important issues were public-school integration, elimination of racial restrictions in employment, and an urgent need for better municipal planning. Whereas Mr. France rated race relations as "good" in Petropolis, Mr. Griffin rejected the most extreme listed alternative, "not very good," and substituted a more negative one: "very poor—quiet on the surface but very poor relations." Mr. France's Republicanism kept him out of the local Democratic party, one of more important political organizational settings of the Negro Leadership. This indicated France's marginal and indirect political-influence relationship in such political decision-making processes as the two involving the selection of the top officials of the Democratic organization. Mr. Best's strong Democratic party identification, on the other hand, had no such political implications in Metroville.

Although George France was actually ideologically a Liberal and, by Time *E*, more of a believer in independent political action by leaders of the Petropolis Negro subcommunity than was Samuel Best in Metroville, the biggest difference between the two was in their positions in their respective Negro Leaderships. Best was accorded relatively high political status not only by White Manifest Leaders but also by his fellow Negro Leaders. France, on the other hand, was apparently a man of waning political influence among his fellow Negro Leaders.[12] None of them named him as one of the men to whom they would go for advice on local-government matters. Instead they named Negro Councilman Standish most frequently as a potential advisor, followed by the City Manager and Mayor Plunkett. Even though Frank Eldon was an inner-clique member, his fellow Negro Leaders were still somewhat uneasy about him because, like France, he had pursued a very cautious policy in earlier years.

Apart from Mayor Plunkett, no other White Community Conservationist was named by a Negro Leader as a potential advisor, not even Eben Bacon, Jr. The latter had in fact served in this capacity on occasion, but this illustrates the weak, sporadic working relationship between the Community Conservationists and the predominantly Liberal Negro Leadership. The White Liberal clique had closer working relationships to the Negro Leadership. Yet the distance between White labor's rank-and-file and the Negro subcommunity created something less than a united front or solid coalition between the White and Negro Liberals.

The Community Conservationists acted as a well-organized, forceful team when they went into action on particular decisional processes. But their intragroup organization was of an intermittent character rather than a constantly meeting board of political strategists. They had to rely heavily on the willingness of individual Community Conservationists to involve themselves actively in particular decision-making processes. Members of the Community Conservationist group not named as Manifest Leaders were like the latter in being highly educated, younger people; women were almost as well represented as their husbands in active roles. In Petropolis White women were traditionally interested in the League of Women Voters, a subsidiary political organization. In community and local-government affairs, Mrs. Ann Burgett, the Community Conservationist inner-clique member, relied on members of such female subsidiary political organizations when citizen support for the priority decisional preferences of her political group had to be organized. The more militant antifeminists among the male Orthodox Conservative group pointed to these women in local politics as evidence that the 19th amendment to the Constitution had been a mistake. They were seriously concerned with the strength such organizations as the League of Women Voters gave to their political opponents, a phenomenon that was of increasing concern but not yet a significantly complicating factor in either Metroville's or Farmdale's simpler power structures.

While some of the Orthodox Conservatives continued to try to acquire control of the local Democratic party, they looked more to the executives of the industrial and financial corporations for active support. Many of the latter who participated socially with Orthodox Conservative leaders in an exclusive country club and had close business relations with them were ideological allies but nonparticipants in local politics. These men, when they did participate, attempted to exercise political influence through cash contributions or conversation at the most. It was particularly frustrating for the Orthodox Conservative political leaders to have politically activated so few of the friends with whom they shared both political interests and political ideology in more permanent group roles.

Turning to the Latent Leadership in Petropolis, we found that not only were members of elected and appointive units of local government to be classified as Latent Leaders, but also that 2 per cent of the random sample in the White subcommunity was classified as being in that category. A somewhat different definition of Latent Leader revealed that ten of the thirty-three Negro active influentials, or 4 per cent of that sample, were so classified.

Three of the seven White Latent Leaders identified themselves with Orthodox Conservatives; one with the Community Conservationists; one with members of the Conservationist-Liberal coalition; and two were uncommitted. Such political-group self-identifications or affiliations were based on the choices made by each Latent Leader when asked to select from a listing of all the Manifest Leaders those whose policy views were most similar to his own. The three oldest Latent Leaders were Orthodox Conservatives. One man was an executive in a life-insurance company, another an executive in a variety of businesses, and the third was a lower-level manager. All were active opponents of desegregation, one in favor of having state funds with-

held from desegregated schools and another in favor of force, if necessary, to prevent school desegregation. Two had voted for Plunkett's
Orthodox Conservative opponent. The third lived outside the city,
but reported that he strongly disapproved of Mayor Plunkett. Two
of these three men were members of the country club, a socio-political
center of Orthodox Conservatism.

Two of these three men were also strong Democrats; the Independent stated that the "one-party system" and "labor problems" were
the two "most important issues facing Petropolis." One of the two
Democrats had worked actively to remove John Jay as head of the
local party organization; he also reported his opposition to the labor
unions and PESNEG.

The Latent Leader identified with the Community Conservationist
clique was a middle-aged, well-educated, former social worker who at
the time of the study was a housewife. She was an active accommodator in race relations and supported the Supreme Court decision.
She was an admirer and close friend of Mrs. Ann Burgett, one of the
Community Conservationist inner clique. She not only had voted for
Mayor Plunkett and approved of both PESNEG and the new biracial
municipal race-relations commission, but also commented that the
trouble with Petropolis was the "existing labor monopoly by the big
absentee-owned companies." She was a strong Democrat at all levels.

The one White Latent Leader who identified himself with both Community Conservationist and Liberal White Manifest Leaders was a
young blue-collar worker and active union official. While approving
of Eben Bacon, Jr., and Mrs. Ann Burgett, he did not share Mayor
Plunkett's policy views but actually "disapproved" of him, although
he felt that he had to vote for him against his opponent. This Latent
Leader was an active Democrat and highly involved in the union's
voters' league. He maintained that the reason Petropolis was growing
more slowly than other communities was that "the vested interests
were involved and selfish desires of some to keep it as it is; high wages
and the organization of labor is not a deterring factor in the growth
of Petropolis."

This Latent Leader regarded himself as a close friend of two of
the three Community Conservationist inner-clique members and of
the two members of the White Liberal inner clique. He was not sure
he approved of PESNEG. He was an active accommodator in race
relations, but within limits. Born and raised in Southern State, he
regarded Negroes as by nature equal to Whites in intelligence, but
inferior in morality, responsibility, and ambition. He was uncertain
about the hypothetical plan to amend the Constitution, but he dis-

approved of the other suggested racist alternatives in the event of public-school desegregation. This Latent Leader was almost a prototype of those White unionists who had developed working political relations with the Negro subcommunity, but whose Liberalism was limited in racial matters by their Southern heritage. Thus, the White-Negro Liberal political group was itself a coalition rather than a unitary political force.

The two uncommitted Latent Leaders both identified themselves with Orthodox Conservatives and with Community Conservationists, but not with Liberals. In their own way they also were prototypes of members of the Petropolis political leadership. One was a junior executive in a large firm. He disliked John Jay and worked as an alternate delegate in the Democratic party organization to unseat him. He disapproved of the labor unions and was active in opposing desegregation. He commented that George France was "the right-type Negro," but that "we had better not have a radical kind of NAACP here or else we'll organize a similar White organization."

The other uncommitted Latent Leader was the wife of a factory worker. She disapproved of Fred Ames, the union official in the White Liberal clique, and of two men in the Orthodox Conservative inner clique whom she voluntarily described as "too antilabor." She was opposed to desegregation but wanted to keep the schools open even if they were desegregated. She regarded the woman in the Community Conservationist inner clique as a good person and a friend, but she also identified herself as sharing policy views with leading Orthodox Conservatives.

The Negro Latent Leaders were younger than the Negro Manifest Leaders. Half of them were women, even though there were no women among the Manifest Leaders. One of the five female Latent Leaders was of relatively low status, being married to a factory worker. Three were white-collar working women, two of them social workers. The fifth was a proprietor's wife. Three of the five male Latent Leaders were blue-collar workers, one retired. A fourth was a public-school teacher and the fifth a lawyer who worked for one of the large Negro investment houses.

The Negro Latent Leaders as a whole were between the active influential and Manifest Leadership categories in socio-economic status. One union leader and another union member were in their ranks, while four of the ten Negro Latent Leaders reported that they frequently associated with labor-union officials. Nine of the ten were Democrats; half of them were relatively active in the local party. Four of these five reported that segregation was a major topic of conversation at party meetings. Nine of the ten were also members of the local NAACP, as well as of PESNEG.

The discrepancy we noted earlier between the older, more affluent, business and professional men in the Manifest Negro Leadership and the younger, poorer, blue-collar workers of both sexes among the Negro active influentials was also noticeable among the Negro Latent Leaders culled from the active-influential category. On a variety of policy perspectives the young, the poor, and the working class in the Negro subcommunity as well as specifically at the Latent Leader level of the power structure were understandably more militant in their Liberalism than were most of the Manifest Leaders. Whatever militancy may have been channeled off by such "radical" Manifest Negro Leaders as William Steers, the publisher of the Negro News, was in a sense made up for by the effective participation of these militant categories in the Negro Leadership. Whatever inclinations existed on the part of individual Manifest Negro Leaders to moderate demands in the interest of long-term political success, and there were some, there were pressures from below to press on with the urgent business at hand. This caused some instability within the Negro Liberal group, particularly in its alignment with White Community Conservationists; but whether or not it ultimately would result in any changes in the political group alignments within the community power structure's leadership, only time would tell.

The decisional process in which the Manifest and Latent Negro Leaderships and those lower in the political-influence structure were most likely to have acquired a share of political power was the quasi-electoral process in which extreme White Supremacists were thwarted in their bid to gain the top posts in the local Democratic party. By contributing for the most part through indirect political-influence relationships through Negro Manifest Leader members of the biracial Committee on Industrial Development and through the Negro Leader serving on the City Council, a number of Negro Latent Leaders and others in subleadership positions probably acquired some share of political power in such decisional processes as those resulting in the retention of local government's participation in industrial promotion. Three of the ten Negro Latent Leaders in the sample reported that they had actively participated in attracting new industry to the city; none of them reported being unconcerned and completely inactive. Although the Negro Manifest Leaders were even more active in such decisional processes—65 per cent had activist roles—the level of political participation of the Negro Latent Leadership in Petropolis can be appreciated when compared to that of the Negro

Manifest Leadership in Metroville: only one-tenth of the latter, in response to the identical question, reported that they had played comparable activist roles.

Intergroup and intragroup political-influence relations took place in Petropolis; but in Metroville, only the latter occurred at the political-leadership level. Moreover, decisional outcomes emerged in formal or informal local governmental or quasi-governmental public settings more frequently in Petropolis than in Metroville or Farmdale. Thus political-power relations were more competitive and more public in Petropolis than in Metroville or Farmdale. The "sides" more often than not were shaped by this competition between ideologically self-conscious political groups at the leadership level of the community power structure.

The distance between the political leadership of Metroville and the political substructure was mediated by the controlled local-government officialdom. In contrast, in Petropolis various political groups competed directly for the elective and appointive positions in local government and in political decision-making processes that affirmed or modified the scope of local government. If Farmdale were compared only to Metroville, the political leadership of the latter would appear to have been more competitive than the former. When we compare all three political leaderships at once, Farmdale and Metroville seem to have had consensual power structures and Petropolis' power structure appears to have been more competitive.

It would also appear that political power was distributed more broadly among the citizens as a whole in both the White and Negro subcommunities of Petropolis than it was in either Metroville or Farmdale. There were proportionally fewer citizens who failed to participate politically at all and who did not belong to at least one subsidiary political organization in Petropolis than in either of the other two communities. Moreover, all but the completely nonparticipant citizens in Petropolis had the greatest chance to influence the stream of events that culminated in the decisional outcomes as of Time M.

In Metroville, rank-and-file citizens, particularly Negroes but also Whites of middle- and lower-class status, had fewer channels and less likelihood of making comparable contributions to the more closed, distant, decision-making process; the decision-making process was dominated by the single political group at the leadership level of the power structure. In Farmdale the political leadership was in such close touch with the political-influence substructure that it could avert political demands and, in any event, counter contemplated "undesirable" shifts in the scope of local government by ignoring them or by providing private instead of public resources to satisfy the needs underlying the demands.[13]   In Petropolis, demands went through an authoritative-consideration stage involving considerable competition.

The political groups in Petropolis made successful forays on the marginal members of each other's groups in some decision-making processes; in others, ideological lines were crossed in the pursuit of nonideological interests.   However, the modal outcomes of the processes were not compromises in the sense that commentators sometimes suggest is typical in a polity with competing political groups.   Compromises that minimally satisfied the people making conflicting demands were in fact more frequent in Farmdale, where the political leadership was a more consensual ingroup.   The ideologically self-conscious inner cliques of each group in Petropolis played roles that prevented the sorts of compromised outcomes that might otherwise have satisfied at least some of the rank-and-file adherents of each group.   The character and content of the political ideologies represented by groups at the political-leadership level mitigated against this.   The racially tinged Liberalism of the Negro Leadership and the class-conscious Liberalism of White political leaders on the one hand, and the equal but opposing class consciousness of Orthodox Conservatism on the other, partially were responsible for the continual or nearly continual conflict in decision-making processes.   But this conflict also resulted from the White Supremacy sentiments of leading Orthodox Conservatives.   Relatively consensual decisions such as those regarding the responsibility of the local government for the economic base of the city were made during Time E to M.   Other decisions made throughout the same period, however, triggered off the familiar intergroup political warfare.

PESNEG occasionally endorsed a racist Orthodox Conservative for local office.   By doing this its members hoped to acquire some positive political status if he considered their voting support important to him, and to moderate his racist perspective.   The more militant Negro Leaders opposed this practice, as did the Negro Leadership in general, when it was suggested by their allies, the White Community Conservationists.   Such "compromising" tactics were rejected completely by the politically more rigid White Supremacists of PECORR.   Since PECORR-endorsed candidates were regularly beaten by Community Conservationists, Liberals, and even by Orthodox Conservatives in municipal elections, and since they could not marshall sufficient support to have their own men elected to replace Jay and Ames as the leaders of the local Democratic party, the members of PECORR remained a small, marginal group in both the political-leadership and substructural portions of the community power structure. They had contributed more to the greater complexity and competitiveness of Petropolis' power structure by Time M than had their recently formed counterpart White Supremacy organization in Metroville to the power structure in that community.

The already complex politics of competitive ideologies was complicated further by the situation of such segments of the White subcommunity as the merchants. The attractions of laissez-faire Orthodox Conservatism as an ideology was tempered by the cross-pressures exerted by the aspects of Community Conservation that promised active local-government efforts to improve their economic positions through such projects as building municipal parking lots for the downtown business area. Other aspects of Community Conservation seemed to work against the immediate economic interests of merchants, such as prohibitions against on-street parking; these were opposed by the merchants. White labor's leadership gained political power through their minority participation with White Community Conservationists and the Negro Liberal Leadership. This associated the leading Community Conservationists with a political machine of the worst kind in the eyes of merchants who were otherwise sympathetic to some of their policies. During Time E to M such complexities were not prominent in the politics of either Farmdale or Metroville.

Oretown

Oretown's power structure resembled that of Petropolis more than that of either Metroville or Farmdale: there was a competitive-political-group situation at the leadership level, and political power was widely distributed in the body politic. Oretown was the city of fewest political decision-making processes during Time E to M; but it had the highest proportion of processes characterized as informal, quasi-elections, in which there was relatively extensive mass participation. In both decisional processes concerning the future of the private and municipal electric utilities, channels were open and used by relatively large numbers of citizens in the two settings where citizens could contribute to the decisional outcomes. They could contribute directly and purposefully by taking or switching their service from one or the other utility. In addition to these politico-economic acts, the citizens could exercise political influence upon city councilmen and local municipal-utility commissioners in official settings where authoritative consideration of these processes also took place.

In the quasi-electoral decisional process to establish a community hospital, citizen political participation was extensive. A relatively large number of the citizens also played roles in the authoritative-consideration stage. Thus they became political leaders in this process and in the community power structure. As in Petropolis, units of local government provided authoritative-consideration settings for the exercise and acquisition of leadership roles in decision-making.

Oretown's Manifest Leadership, like the Manifest Leadership in Farmdale, was close to the citizens in terms of common memberships in subsidiary political organizations. Of sixteen voluntary associations in which two or more Manifest Leaders were active members, thirteen were subsidiary political organizations providing direct channels between less participant citizens and the political leadership, and indirect channels from citizens to leaders through the politically participant members of such organizations.

The Orthodox Conservatives in the Manifest Leadership were, with certain notable exceptions, active members in many of these subsidiary political organizations. Neither they nor the Community Conservationists had labor-union officials in their ranks. Even though there were two self-identified Democrats in the ranks of the Orthodox Conservative Manifest Leaders, neither one was active in the local Democratic organization. The Community Conservationists had active organizational Democrats in their ranks; most of them belonged to two of the three service clubs that were subsidiary political organizations. In contrast, the Orthodox Conservatives were concentrated in the most prestigious service club, to which few Community Conservationists belonged. Thus, these contending political groups had somewhat different subsidiary-political-organization bases, even though other such organizations were "bipartisan" or bigroup in the ideological- and political-group perspectives and identifications of their leaderships. The Liberal Latent Leader clique was isolated effectively from the community service and welfare organizations, particularly from those that operated on Main Street. Their subsidiary-political-organization memberships were concentrated in some industrial unions, in the local Democratic party organization, in which they competed with Community Conservationists in exercising political influence, and in the weakly organized local Republican party, in which they were outnumbered substantially by Orthodox Conservative Manifest Leaders.

The several political groups at the Manifest and Latent Leadership level were close to their potential or actual constituents or supporters in the citizenry in Oretown, as was the case with the one political group in Farmdale. These political groups were all represented in the persons of Manifest Leaders in the elective posts in local government. The fact that there were multiple contending political-leadership groups in Oretown and Petropolis and not in Farmdale contributes to the impression that in its political structure Oretown was more like Petropolis than Farmdale.

The Community Conservationists were a larger, better-organized political group under Mayor French than their Petropolis counterparts were under the intragroup leadership of Mayor Plunkett and Eben Bacon, Jr. The Liberals of Oretown, in contrast, were a small leadership group which did not have the relatively firm organizational underpinnings provided the Liberals in Petropolis by White labor unions, PESNEG, and the local Democratic party. The labor unions in Oretown politically were more aware and active than organized labor in either Farmdale or Metroville; but they were less so, and had proportionately fewer officials politically participant and narrower political interests, than their counterparts in Petropolis. Also in contrast to their counterparts in Petropolis, the decisional objectives and goals of Oretown's Community Conservationists and Liberals were less well developed. Their ability to appeal as distinctive political groups was less than it was for the Conservationist-Liberal group in Petropolis.

The Community Conservationists in Oretown failed to develop a working alliance with the Liberals; they regarded the Liberals as their worst enemies. The impulse of Community Conservationists to work with another political group as an expedient tactic was directed to the Orthodox Conservatives, and their coalition against the Liberals helped to blur political distinctions in the eyes of the citizens. The Community Conservationists' commitment to political peace and their desire to "depoliticize" decision-making as they upgraded a more autonomous administrative decision-making process in the community interest made their policy goals even more vague to citizens than those of the Community Conservationists of Petropolis. The latter's identification with "saving the economy" and "redeveloping the central business district" helped them form a public image that was less crystallized for Oretown citizens.

During Time E to M, Oretown's Community Conservationists grew increasingly self-conscious of their own ideological tenets. It should be noted that Time E was 1952 for Oretown and 1957 for Petropolis. During the interim years the doctrines of Community Conservation and their analogues at the national level continued to develop.

The Liberals seemed to be focused on a single issue in Oretown: the conflict between the municipal and the private utility. This issue had less extensive appeal than did the Liberal stress in Petropolis on social reorganization—that is, amelioration for Negroes—industrial promotion, and slum clearance. The reorganization of the local government to give more citizenship status to White and Negro organized labor gave Petropolis' Liberals an appeal not used in a comparable manner in Oretown. First of all the Liberals of Oretown were identified with a section of town, Longacre; and secondly, their public image seemed to be that of men who wanted leadership positions for themselves rather than in the interest of a larger group or "cause." Also, the Liberals of Petropolis acquired a certain political status from those citizens who opposed the "vested interests," as symbolized by the big corporations of the leading Orthodox Conservatives. In Oretown the Orthodox Conservatives were more often small merchants than industrialists and financiers. That image may have retarded anti-Orthodox Conservative feeling among lower-class citizens of that city.

The Latent Leaders of Oretown constituted 2.6 per cent of the citizen sample. According to group identifications and associations, the nineteen Latent Leaders included two Liberals, six Orthodox Conservatives, six Community Conservationists, and five who were uncommitted.

One of the two Liberal Latent Leaders was a union official who served in the important central labor council. But the Liberals did not have a monopoly on labor-union Latent Leaders. A man active in the union in which one of the Liberal clique was a chief officer served self-consciously as a "representative of labor" on the independent elective board that administered the municipal utility. However, he was a Community Conservationist in orientation and political-group identification. Another Latent Leader was an active union man who also supported the Community Conservationists. The potential Liberal support among the working-class citizens thus was shared with the Community Conservationists, at least at the Latent Leadership level.

The Orthodox Conservative Latent Leaders were active in subsidiary political organizations. In contrast, the relative weakness of the Community Conservationists in the associational substructure in the polity was reflected in the fact that only two of "their" six Latent Leaders belonged to a subsidiary organization which served as a center of Community Conservationist strength.

The five uncommitted Latent Leaders were for the most part leaders in the decisional process involving the hospital drive. Two were union members, but only one of them was active. He was also an active Democrat, but concentrated his attention on county rather than community politics.

One of the three other uncommitted Latent Leaders also specialized in county and state rather than community politics. Another restricted her participation to school and neighborhood affairs on Oretown's rural fringe. She was most active in the drive to establish a community hospital. Otherwise she was involved in direct appeals to officials to end their efforts to annex that area to the city. The last uncommitted Latent Leader was active in the hospital drive but otherwise felt himself to be distant from the officials of local government. He belonged to only one (fraternal) organization in Oretown.

Whether or not Mayor French's Community Conservationist administration would develop a larger, stronger political group after Time M by gaining support from uncommitted Latent Leaders or from active influentials will be discussed in a later chapter. Whether or not their Liberal political opponents could be defeated and, if so, whether or not this would mean the development or disintegration of relations between Community Conservationists and Orthodox Conservatives also were unresolved at Time M.

A related unanswered question was whether or not the necessary political cooperation for the Community Conservationists would be forthcoming from the densely settled area outside of town. They considered this area an integral part of the political community, and felt that it should soon be legally annexed. However, there was opposition from the industrialists among the Orthodox Conservative Manifest Leaders whose plants were located in that area, as well as from the relatively poor fringe-dwellers, who were fearful of city taxes. Such people were represented in the sample of Latent Leaders by the lady who was not committed to any existing group of Manifest Leaders. Another question was whether or not the merchants among the Orthodox Conservatives could be induced to work with the Community Conservationists. The desire of merchants on Main Street to lighten their property-tax burdens by distributing them over industries in the fringe areas of the city was a source of potential conflict between the wings of the Orthodox Conservatives. This fact was recognized most clearly by the inner-clique spokesmen of that group and by the Community Conservationists.

Whether or not a continuation of the cooperation that existed during Time E to M between the Conservatives and the Conservationists on particular decision-making processes would push the working class toward the Liberals was a question asked by some Community Conservationists and Liberals. Other questions that arose as the next period of analytic concern approached were whether or not the Community Conservationists, in stressing a greater political role for professional public administrators, would alienate organized labor, whose officials have traditionally distrusted "neutral" city managers and the latter's definition of the public interest, and whether or not the Liberals, by their continued attacks on the city-manager form of government in Oretown, would maintain or even increase their political following among organized labor.

All these questions of political dynamics may be subsumed under one general question: was the competitive power structure in evidence in Oretown by Time M stable or unstable; would the functioning of political-power relations and thus the power structure change from competition to consensus and from a competitive structure to a consensual structure? Comparable questions arise about the other characteristic of the community power structure: was Oretown's competitive *mass* power structure relatively stable, or would it change during the next time period to a competitive or consensual *elite* power structure? We shall explore such questions and comparable ones for the other communities in the following chapter.

These questions imply that the four community power structures have been classified by type. The material presented in this and the two preceding chapters were intended to permit such classification. In classifying the community power structures, which will now be done specifically, we shall summarize some of the more relevant findings reported above.

TYPES OF POWER STRUCTURES

Relative to each other, Farmdale and Metroville had Consensual Elite power structures, whereas Oretown and Petropolis had Competitive Mass power structures during Time E to M. Only two of the four types of community power structures specified in Chapter 3 were thus represented in these four communities (Figure 10.1).

Ideological Convergence-Divergence of the Leaderships

The relative convergence in the political leadership's ideology in Farmdale and Metroville stems from the fact that there was only one leadership group in each community. Neither community even had political groups with divergent, competitive ideologies aspiring to leadership positions. In Farmdale, the Community Conservationists, a competitive political-leadership group prior to Time E, had become disorganized, leaving the field to the Jeffersonian Conservatives. In Metroville, the Progressive Conservatives subsumed within their group

Political leadership's ideology	Distribution of power	
	Broad	Narrow
Convergent	(Consensual Mass)	Consensual Elite Farmdale Metroville
Divergent	Competitive Mass Oretown Petropolis	(Competitive Elite)

FIGURE 10.1 *Power structures in the four communities: Time E to M.*

men who otherwise might have been active in Orthodox Conservative or Community Conservationist political groups.

Liberals in Metroville's White subcommunity were unorganized; Liberals in the Negro subcommunity and its Leadership did not act politically on the basis of their Liberal ideologies but as relatively disciplined members of the inclusive Progressive Conservative group. The White Supremacists were not an organized political group that was part of the political leadership, but some of their sentiments were expressed by a minority of Progressive Conservative leaders. This contributed to internal conflict within the Progressive Conservative group, but it did not result in a divergent political leadership characterized by intergroup competition.

In Petropolis the divergence between political groups was greatest between the right-wing Orthodox Conservative and the small White Supremacist groups and the left-wing Liberals. There was some political distance between the White and Negro Liberals, as well as between the Community Conservationist and Liberal wings of that coalition; but generally this was a relatively consensual alliance. To be sure, there was some intergroup consensus in policy preferences and crossing of group lines in some decision-making processes, particularly on the part of Orthodox Conservatives and Community Conservationists. However, there was more antagonistic competition than consensus, especially between the inner-clique spokesmen of these two groups, compared to the one-group political leaderships of Farmdale and Metroville.

Oretown's leadership was composed of several groups whose ideologies conflicted sharply. The greatest degree of competition by Time *M* was between the Orthodox Conservatives and the newly emergent Community Conservationists on the one hand and the Liberals on the other. However, there was rivalry between the Orthodox Conservatives and the Community Conservationists as well. In both Petropolis and Oretown, the existence of uncommitted leaders lessened somewhat the multigroup ideologically grounded competition, but did not reduce it to the level of consensus found in the political leadership of both Farmdale and Metroville.

Breadth-Narrowness of the Distribution of Political Power

The power structures of Farmdale and Metroville were consensual compared to those in Petropolis and Oretown; but they were also elite structures, compared to the latter, in the distribution of political power among the citizens. There were proportionately fewer citizens in Petropolis and Oretown than in Farmdale or Metroville who did not share in the political power that accrued to those who purposefully contributed to decisional outcomes.

An analysis of data on the attendance at meetings at which local-government or community matters were a major subject of discussion is illuminating in this regard. Some of those who reported being present at such gatherings were engaged in the authoritative-consideration stage of political decision-making. This is particularly the case for the Manifest and Latent Leaders. Most of the issues discussed at such meetings probably were in the political or administrative decisional stages of deliberation, organization of political support, or both, or in the general, pre-decision-making stage of using political influence to maintain the existing scope of local government.

The private settings where decisional alternatives ordinarily were considered authoritatively in Farmdale and Metroville were closed-group settings. In Metroville, where the highest-political-status leaders, the White Manifest Leaders, had extremely high socio-economic status, such political settings were closed to a relatively large number of middle- and upper-middle-class Whites, as well as to most upper-class Negroes. Informal meetings for policy deliberation or organization of political support were held infrequently in the Negro subcommunity, even at the political-leadership level. As we have noted, only 10 per cent of the Negro Manifest Leaders of Petropolis reported that they had not attended a meeting where local-government matters had been a major topic; 47 per cent of the Negro Manifest Leaders of Metroville reported that they had attended no such meeting.

A smaller proportion of the citizens of Farmdale and of the two subcommunities in Metroville reported that they had played activist roles and attended meetings than did the citizens of Oretown and the two subcommunities of Petropolis. Highly educated Negroes in

Metroville had engaged in informal political discussion with friends more often than highly educated Whites; but neither category attended more formally organized political meetings. We assume such meetings were important as places where political demands could be made effectively in a chain of political-influence relations culminating in a decisional outcome. Therefore, one of the contributory factors underlying the assessment that Farmdale and Metroville had elite and Oretown and Petropolis had mass distributions of political power during Time E to M was the small number of such meetings held in the former and the much larger number held in the latter two communities.

For purposes of assessing distributions of political power among communities, the types and character of political meetings attended by citizens is as illuminating as the frequency of such meetings. Almost two-thirds of the political meetings reportedly attended in Farmdale were official meetings of an agency of local government, according to the findings of the sample survey. A comparatively large proportion of those few in the citizen sample attending such meetings did so as official members of municipal agencies. The largest proportion of other meetings attended were of neighbors preparing petitions or deliberating the most appropriate way to remedy housekeeping problems such as a particular street repair or a dangerous traffic condition at an intersection. The few meetings where demands for major shifts in the scope of local government were deliberated usually led to such demands being submitted to the city council for authoritative consideration. Typically, the Mayor and councilmen then would engage in such consideration in a private setting, such as the poker club, from which negative outcomes ordinarily emerged.

In the Metroville White subcommunity almost two-thirds of the relatively few political meetings attended also were identified as those of official agencies. When such meetings were not part of administrative decision-making processes, the political discretion of the officials ordinarily was constrained by their political-status relationships with the prestiged White Progressive Conservatives. The other one-third were identified as meetings of one or another of the formally organized voluntary associations. In the Negro subcommunity the meetings in which citizens had participated in discussions of local-government affairs predominantly were held by neighborhood associations and, less frequently, churches. On occasion the setting was a local Democratic party group, an organization which was firmly controlled by the White Progressive Conservative leaders. The neighborhood and church meetings attested to the political distance of the Negro subcommunity from the processes of political decision-making and, incidentally, to the key roles played by the ministers in the leadership of the Negro subcommunity.

In the Petropolis Negro subcommunity, relatively more people attended both union and Democratic party meetings; these meetings were organizational channels for transmitting messages between citizens and political leaders. The latter frequently attended the meetings and were active participants in the discussions. Many Negro citizens attended meetings of both the NAACP and PESNEG. PESNEG and its important committees ordinarily met in open session, which members and nonmembers attended. Frequently, Negro leaders and the rank-and-file engaged in highly contentious debate on decisional options at the meetings of PESNEG. Group solidarity was obtained and group discipline was imposed in decision-making ordinarily only after a vigorous deliberative process in a kind of developed "democratic centralism." The inner clique guided such deliberations but sometimes acquiesced to more militant demands than they preferred in order to maintain their central position as the leaders within the group.

In Oretown, the political meetings attended by citizens were held in local-government settings and in associations classified for the most part as subsidiary political organizations. There were relatively few meetings like those in Farmdale where neighbors got together in informal groups over minor administrative decisional matters.

The ratio of official local-government meetings to unofficial political meetings was almost 2:1 in Farmdale and in the White subcommunity of Metroville; this ratio nearly was reversed in Oretown and in the White subcommunity of Petropolis. These ratios do not mean that proportionately fewer citizens in the latter communities reported attending political meetings held by municipal agencies, in which settings authoritative consideration was frequently the decision-making norm. The opposite was the case: the citizens of Oretown and Petropolis, besides attending these official meetings more than did citizens of Farmdale and Metroville, attended many more unofficial political meetings. The "private" political meetings attended by citizens in Oretown and Petropolis more often provided channels through which political participants could influence decisional outcomes indirectly than did those in Farmdale and Metroville, since the men who were among those engaged directly in selecting such outcomes were present more often in the former than in the latter communities.

Classifying Farmdale and Metroville as having Consensual Elite power structures and Oretown and Petropolis as having Competitive Mass power structures is an operation that summarizes but does not explain the major differences in the patterns of decision-making of the communities during Time E to M. Such differences include the degree of open conflict in decision-making and the demands openly pressed by both merchants and organized labor in Oretown and Petropolis—and by Negroes in the latter city—compared to the apparent absence of such organized demands by their counterparts in Farmdale and Metroville. We shall now focus on a question that was raised earlier: to what extent, if at all, fears of illegitimate sanctions on the part of these segments of the populations of Farmdale and Metroville explain the differences between their power structures and those of their sister cities. We shall assess the probability in the four communities that such illegitimate sanctions would have been used effectively to thwart legitimate political efforts to shift the scope of government. In other words, we now shall turn our attention to the sense of electoral potency and to the permeability of the power structures, that is, to the regimes, in the four communities.

NOTES

1. This is not to say that other political leaders were not engaged in gathering intelligence. However, the extent to which this monitoring role was consciously played by the young man referred to here was both pronounced and obvious, so that he has been singled out as perhaps the best example of this kind of political-role behavior among the political leaders of Farmdale.

2. Arthur J. Vidich and Joseph Bensman point to the importance of legal skills in the political role of one of their key political leaders in Springdale. *Small Town in Mass Society* (Garden City: Doubleday Anchor Books, 1960), pp. 222, 127–129. Why lawyers in some communities like Springdale and non-lawyers such as Judge Catis in Farmdale become politically important in relating communities to the state government is unclear, as are the reasons for the degree and effectiveness of participation by lawyers in their community's politics and variations therein from community to community.

3. In a variety of ways, Farmdale seemed, during this period, to resemble Springdale in its political leadership. *Ibid.*

4. According to Floyd Hunter the Mayor of Regional City was nominated more frequently by the White Manifest Leaders there in response to a comparable question, but his relationship to key businessmen in the political leadership suggests some similarity to the role of Metroville's Mayor and City Manager as described herein. *Community Power Structure* (Chapel Hill: University of North Carolina Press, 1953), pp. 81 and 102, and Table 2, p. 63.

5. The relationships between Negro Leaders and the Mayor of Regional City were apparently not unlike the corresponding relationships in Metroville.

6. Upgrading of Negro workers, for example, was a policy that was strictly controlled by the major manufacturers and, at best, was a policy of "token" advancement.

7. Evidence of this is apparent from the questions asked of field interviewers by White Manifest Leaders concerning what might be going on in the Negro Leadership of Metroville. With rapport between the interviewers and interviewees equal or even better in Petropolis, the interviewers were told rather than asked by White Manifest Leaders there about current affairs in the Negro Leadership.

8. With the breakdown of plantation systems, the pattern of feudalistic assistance from the "lords" to the "serfs" is disrupted, with consequences that are generally overlooked in the emphasis given to the new freedom serfs acquire. This phenomenon is striking in Latin American and other underdeveloped countries today. Roland J. Pellegrin and Vernon J. Parenton discuss changes in a rural Negro community in Louisiana, and the paternalistic system, which involved frequent and informal interaction between Whites and Negroes, in "The Impact of Socio-Economic Change on Racial Groups in a Rural Setting," *Phylon* (First Quarter, 1962), p. 59.

9. For a discussion of the increasing role of women in New York City politics, see Robert S. Hirschfield, Bert E. Swanson, and Blanche D. Blank, "A Profile of Political Activists in Manhattan," *The Western Political Quarterly*, Vol. XV, No. 3 (September 1962), p. 494.

10. There were private preferences and covert political deliberation by both Negro and White Liberal Leaders for a system of "proportional representation" rather than "token representation," or a division of both elective and administrative positions on the basis of race and socio-economic class. Such demands are sometimes publicly made in cities like New York by religious and racial groups. See Ralph A. Straetz and Frank J. Munger, *New York Politics* (New York: New York University Press, 1960).

11. For a general discussion of Negro local voters' organizations and political leagues in Florida, see Hugh Douglas Price, "The Negro and Florida Politics, 1944–1954," *Journal of Politics*, Vol. 17, No. 2 (May 1955), pp. 198–220.

12. Leading White citizens had some decades earlier assisted Mr. France in setting up his now prosperous business. Negro businessmen, like minority groups everywhere, have often had to rely upon patrons early in a post-emancipation period for assistance in economic enterprises. In the absence of a paternalistic arrangement, Negroes and other underprivileged groups in big cities have frequently resorted to comparable assistance from the White underworld or the entrepreneurs of organized crime. The earlier patron arrangement may be superseded by contractual arrangements on the part of following generations and remain a source of resentment and hostility on the part of the younger generation, partly directed at the recipient of the patronage. This seems to have happened in the case of Mr. France.

13. For a description of how the political leaders in a town about as small as Farmdale averted political demands in a manner comparable to that of the political leadership in Farmdale, see Arthur J. Vidich and Joseph Bensman, *op. cit.*, especially pp. 112–115, 129–131, and 216–217.

11

TYPES OF REGIMES: *Time M, an historical*
analysis of regimes and power structures,
and three models of political systems

Three related sections constitute this chapter. The first section contains a typology of the four regimes according to assessments of the variables defining regimes based on historical observations made during Time E to M. In the second, less recent events extending back to the end of the Second World War are analyzed historically in order to enable us to classify regimes and power structures during those periods. Special attention is devoted in that section to assessing the stability or instability and the changes or stasis in regimes and power structures. The reader will have an opportunity in Chapter 12, which describes something of the regimes and power structures in the one-year period succeeding Time E to M—that is, Time M to $M + 1$—to examine predictions concerning both aspects of these political systems. We shall attempt to present the trends noted from the Second World War to Time E as well as the reasoning underlying the analytic judgments of whether there was relative political stability or instability and, if instability existed, whether or not changes in regimes or power structures were expected.

In Chapter 5, the postwar political histories of the four communities were sketched in narrative, descriptive fashion. In order to classify the types of regimes and power structures that existed by Time M with somewhat more confidence, it proved helpful to reconstruct previous events in terms of a systematic classification of their regimes and power structures during that previous time. The permeability of the power structure dimension is a prediction of future events, and the sense of electoral potency as well as the two defining dimensions of types of power structures are projections of historical situations— events that occurred during Time E to M—into the future—during Time M to $M + 1$, other things being equal. By assessing the values of the variables that determine the classification of regimes and power structures over a substantial period of time, trends may be revealed which bear on their stability and prospects for change. This historical mode of analysis, which is intended to increase both the validity of the classifications and the confidence with which they are made, un- fortunately must be based on observations, measurements, and assess- ments of relevant variables that are increasingly unreliable as the analysis reaches farther back in time. Hearsay, memory, occasionally dubious documentary sources, and contradictory reports pose a diffi- cult set of measurement problems for the researcher of a recent his- torical period. The problems involved in investigating a relatively distant historical period when the political phenomena of interest hap- pened several years to a decade earlier are sometimes insurmountable. The periods of historical interest for us begin in each community with the end of the Second World War.

A particularly difficult problem was the lack of reliable data on the extent of political participation during these earlier years; such data would at least provide preliminary estimates of the distribution of political power among the citizens. Although available voting and registration records were used as clues to the extent of citizen political participation, systematic estimates of the latter could not be made for these earlier periods. Instead, the distribution of political power was inferred primarily from the reconstruction of events through in- formation provided by informants who had participated actively in decision-making and from newspaper accounts and other records that revealed something of the relative size and character of the political leadership; special attention was paid to the Latent Leadership, gov- ernment officials, and others of possible lesser renown than the Mani- fest Leaders. We caution the reader that the following historical analysis may be much less reliable than the analysis for Time E to M.

The third section summarizes a variety of the findings to be reported in the early part of this chapter and findings reported earlier in the book. This summary presents three models of political systems which represent a more dynamic picture of the functioning of the power structures as affected by the regimes than will be suggested by the separate, more static pictures of the power structures and regimes by Time M. While the structural pictures were necessarily derived from observations of the functioning of power relations during Time E to M, an effort was made in these "process" models to see the power structures and regimes in interaction. To do so, it was necessary to reexamine sequences of political events *within* the single period *E* to *M* and to examine, to the extent possible, comparable sequences within each of the several periods of time into which the postwar periods were divided. We turn now to the first section and the types of regimes that existed at Time *M*.

TYPES OF REGIMES: TIME M

The four communities are classified by the type of their regime in Figure 11.1.

The reasons for these classifications follow.

Farmdale—A Guided Democracy

The power structure in Farmdale was impermeable compared to that in the other three communities. The regime was a Guided Democracy, according to our definition. Even though the sense of electoral potency was comparatively high—approximately as high as it was in Oretown and Petropolis and higher·than in Metroville—the power structure appeared to be the least permeable of the four communities.[1]

During the decision-making processes in Farmdale in which demands were defeated for the establishment of a chamber of commerce, the building of a municipal swimming pool, and the establishment of a city recreation program, illegitimate sanctions were applied effectively to proponents of these shifts in the scope of local government. These sanctions were of a severe social and economic character. How-

Sense of electoral potency	Probability of illegitimate sanctions blocking efforts to shift the scope of government	
	Low	High
High	Developed Democracy Oretown Petropolis	Guided Democracy Farmdale
Low	Underdeveloped Democracy Metroville	(Oligarchy)

FIGURE 11.1   *Types of regimes: Time M.*

ever, they did not lower the sense of electoral potency of those against whom they were applied, even though they stopped those individuals from continuing to press their demands. To understand this apparent paradox we must examine in detail the instances in which illegitimate sanctions were used effectively and the position of individuals to whom they were applied.

In both the decisional process regarding a chamber of commerce and that regarding expansion of the city water supply, Mr. King, the publisher who was a dissident Manifest Leader, and several younger allies pressed their demands vigorously in their civic associations and in informal meetings. Mr. King was socially ostracized by many of his former Manifest Leader friends, to the point that he was given a "silent treatment" by some, while efforts were made by his foes to label him as an "eccentric"; finally he actually was expelled from the most prestigious civic club, ostensibly for failing to pay his dues.

Partly because there was a minor compromise in regard to expansion of the municipal water supply and mostly because Mr. King simply could not believe that his former political associates, with whom he shared many Conservative ideological tenets, would resort to such politically motivated, clearly illegitimate sanctions, he maintained an optimism that his demands would be met as soon as they were fully understood by such people as his "friends" in the Jeffersonian Conservative inner clique. Although such social sanctions were accompanied by implied threats to withhold advertising from his newspaper, these threats were not recognized as such by Mr. King. Although he continued to press his demands by buttonholing the men of Main Street, his political position was weakened fatally by the effectiveness of such sanctions on his younger supporters.

One of his most zealous supporters was a young accountant. This proponent of community growth and development was visited by a delegation of Manifest Leaders who made it quite clear that if he hoped to establish a good practice in Farmdale, he would be expected to drop such demands. He could, they suggested, work within established private associations for his goals with and under the guidance of community leaders who knew what was best for Farmdale. Although he understood what they implied, he remained optimistic that he could coopt those who had threatened him effectively by complying until he attained a secure practice as a certified public accountant and became known to the citizens as a public-spirited civic leader. His sense of electoral potency remained high, although he had been blocked effectively for a time from making further political demands by severe illegitimate economic sanctions and clearly implied threats of social ostracism.

Another active young supporter of King's demands was effectively threatened so that he stopped making demands. He was employed by one of the Manifest Leaders, who requested that he disassociate himself from such trouble-makers as King and join a prestigious civic club at his employer's expense. This young man inferred that he might have been discharged if he had disregarded his employer's advice. He was apprehensive that he would be deprived of his livelihood. He suppressed his demands and accepted his employer's offer to pay his dues and support his application for membership in the club. However, he maintained a sense of electoral efficacy, feeling that he and his friends eventually would be recognized when politically influential people in Farmdale realized that new industry was necessary to revive the deteriorating economy of the community.[2]

The man who was pressing for municipal support of the local baseball team was insensitive to the gossip beginning to circulate that he was eccentric. But his demands for a shift in the scope of local government were redirected into demands for support from privately organized community organizations. Such support eventually came forth. This man was the active influential included by chance in the random sample. He was not a Latent Leader because his efforts did not contribute to the shift in the scope of local government in question. The redirection of his demands took place when he was invited to join the same civic club from which Mr. King had been expelled. After doing so, he was treated as a man of foresight and wisdom in recreational matters in the community. His own leadership in a lower-class fraternal organization containing many fellow recreationists was influenced substantially by his newer, more prestigious organizational milieu. He soon found that the efforts of his fraternal organization to raise funds for the ball team were successful through civic benefits endorsed by his newer organization. Thus his attention was turned from the municipality's tax coffers.

Although this man's political demands had been stopped through cooptation and guidance, the political activities of another man pushing for a municipally supported recreational facility were blocked by the application of illegitimate social sanctions. The latter was met by a planned campaign of personal criticism, charging that his well-known charitable and welfare activities could no longer provide an excuse for advocating a costly program certain to raise taxes substantially. He also was ostracized socially; this bothered him considerably. As a member of a religious minority group and one of the few avowed Democrats among the Main Street merchants, he was vulnerable to the campaign of social ostracism and ridicule.

Why did these sanctions, classified as illegitimate by the analysts, block his demands without at the same time reducing his high sense of electoral potency? By Time M he had given up his efforts to gain a favorable decisional outcome, but he retained his complete faith in the democratic character of Farmdale's decision-making processes. He was able to put aside his preferences and to be distracted by other pursuits. Apparently this helped him to consider such sanctions isolated incidents that were not likely to be repeated. He knew nothing about comparable sanctions used against certain of his fellow citizens and refused to examine the motivations of his decisional opponents, even when pressed by an interviewer. His insistence on remaining "innocent" in regard to the political motivations of others helped to preserve for him a picture of other people as basically well intentioned.[3]

The permeability of the power structure in Farmdale has been estimated as relatively low—that is, there was a relatively high probability of illegitimate sanctions blocking efforts to shift the scope of local government—during Time M to $M+1$, compared to the situation in any of the other communities. This assessment assumes that the political leadership was relatively constant and that there was relatively little change in the composition or decisional perspectives of members of the single group of Jeffersonian Conservatives. It further assumes that the decisional preferences and demands of the potentially sanctionable would remain fairly similar during Time M to $M+1$. These assumptions may be better examined when the patterns of stability-instability and stasis-change are considered.

The estimate of the probability of illegitimate sanctions' being used effectively in Farmdale also rests upon the estimate of whether or not the political leaders were prepared to act in comparable situations after Time M as they did during Time E to M, and whether or not reactions to those sanctions would be comparable. We are not using the specific frequency with which these illegitimate sanctions were used effectively during Time E to M as the yardstick for making this assessment. Apparently there were only a few instances of effective illegitimate sanctioning; but there were indications that the sanctioners had been ready to use them in several other instances if they had felt it necessary. However, these few instances, the disposition of the sanctioners to use such sanctions, and the vulnerability of others who were deliberating preferences contributed to the assessment that the power structure was more impermeable in Farmdale than in any of the other communities.

It should be clarified that the evaluation of the sense of electoral potency as relatively high in Farmdale, compared to its condition in the other three cities at that point in time, does not mean that everyone was voting in local elections, although both registration and turnout were relatively high; nor does it mean that everyone had a well-developed sense of electoral potency. In fact, a sizeable portion of the citizenry appeared to be apathetic and indifferent to both the electoral process and political decision-making in general.[4] There was no indication, however, that there was a specific sense of political impotence stemming from or related to the prospect of the use of illegitimate sanctions in either general municipal elections or in political decision-making. Even the most disillusioned Community Conservationist previous leaders, like those aforementioned sanctioned citizens and the numerous marginal merchants and labor-union people interviewed in addition to the respondents who were in the sample survey, gave no indication of electoral impotence similar to that discovered in Metroville.

Metroville—An Underdeveloped Democracy

Metroville's regime was an Underdeveloped Democracy at Time M. Some Negro Leaders, White labor-union officials, and some Liberals of both races freely admitted, when asked in confidence, that they feared illegitimate sanctions if they were to organize political support behind some of their political demands disliked by the Progressive Conservatives. They considered their jobs, their credit, and, in the case of some Negroes, even their personal safety in jeopardy if the political leadership were threatened by rival political groups.

Such feelings were not universal, but there were memory and myth to remind Negroes, militant White unionists, and Liberals of the physical force and violence that had been narrowly averted during the postwar crisis in Metroville. Many Negro citizens and Negro Leaders were averse to the formation of a political group comparable to the Petropolis Negro subcommunity's PESNEG. Instead, a gradualist NAACP chapter was the leading political organization. This was, by itself, a weak means for extensive subcommunity political organization, as the experience of many local NAACP chapters in cities throughout the South attests. The absence of political group competition with the dominant White Progressive Conservative leadership may have resulted in part from this fear of illegitimate sanctions, a sense of electoral impotence on the part of Negro and White citizens.

Some lower-class Whites feared for their jobs; a few upper-class White citizens who might have liked to support or be active in a competitive, more broadly based Community Conservationist political group feared such social sanctions as ostracism. A few White Liberals recognized an even greater difference between their ideology and that of the "ruling class." These Liberals seemed to be quiescent not only because of a sense of pessimism and despair about their prospects of political organization and victory in the foreseeable future but also because of fears of illegitimate sanctions.

Liberals in the Negro Leadership, as well as Negro Progressive Conservative Leaders, were in a comparable situation: they were pessimistic about the prospect of even long-run political success through independent action, and in addition they benefited from cooperation with the city administration and the White Progressive Conservative Leadership. Failure to support Mayor Peterson, they believed, might end the favors they had received during his tenure in office. It should be recalled that some measure of political status went with the offices to which Negro Leaders had been appointed by the Mayor, and that token public-school desegregation had occurred by Time M in Metroville. With the establishment of a large absentee-owned industrial firm, a breach had been made in traditional employment practices. In this firm the first small-scale experiments were made with desegregation in employment—on the assembly line, as well as among the professional, technical workers. Negroes had some hope that this would be a hole in the dike of employment desegregation.

Interwoven with pessimism about their prospects, even in a "fair fight," and appreciation of the benefits that their forefathers lacked and their friends in many other Southern cities still did not have, was a deeply rooted, periodically conscious fear of illegitimate sanctions. Apart from men like Negro Leader Samuel Best, and it may have been true to some extent even for him, the political trust extended to such political advisors as the Mayor and the City Manager was compounded from lack of choice, an ineradicable hope, and real fears. Many felt that the Mayor had betrayed the trust and hope that had been placed with him in his first race for office as the friend of the downtrodden against the White political-leadership group. Even those who trusted him feared that he would be unable to prevent illegitimate sanctions against the group as well as against individuals. Besides personal deprivations, there was a fear that public housing for Negroes might be abolished, hospitalization and medical-care opportunities eliminated, and even their unskilled laboring jobs reserved for White rural immigrants to Metroville.

The sense of electoral potency was considerably lower among representatives of these political groups in Metroville than among their counterparts in Farmdale, Oretown, and Petropolis. Was the pessimism and fear this reflected justified? The tentative answer to this question is negative: compared to the other three communities, Metroville's power structure was closer to the condition of permeability in Petropolis and Oretown than it was to the relative impermeability in Farmdale. In other words, the probability was relatively low that the potentially sanctionable would be met with effective, severe illegitimate sanctions if they tried, during Time E to M, to promote their demands—even to the point of using the electoral process to elect a city administration more disposed than was Mayor Peterson's to support their political demands.

In explaining why this assessment was made—and why it was so difficult to make—and thus why Metroville was classified as an Underdeveloped Democracy, several matters need to be clarified. The potentially sanctionable include those who have been deliberating decisional preferences. Also included are those whose demands have been repressed or suppressed in a policy-deliberation stage as well as those who have tried to organize political support. Some of the observations of such deliberation were made through the sample survey. As in Farmdale, additional interviews were held with specially selected individuals, including labor-union officials, those who were reputedly "radical" or especially "militant" members of the Negro subcommunity, and leaders of the recently founded White Supremacist organization. Such people, with few exceptions, turned out to be more fearful in general of illegitimate sanctions than were their counterparts in Petropolis.

The "sanctionability" of the potentially sanctionable by the potential sanctioners was then roughly assessed. We judge that the potentially sanctionable were relatively vulnerable because their fears were of the nature of self-fulfilling prophecies; they also were insecure economically, since they had no resources to fall back on if they were deprived of their jobs in the major industrial firms in which most of them worked. According to their own reports they were committed to remain in Metroville and not move away. We assume that, for at least a while after Time M, neither the unions nor existing Negro political organizations provided a protective organizational setting for members that would weaken the illegitimate sanctions to the point at which they would become ineffective. The political strength of existing unions could be assessed indirectly from a natural test of economic strength: one of the largest industrial unions struck one of the larger industrial firms in order to retain in its contract a long-accepted arbitration clause which management had decided to discard. During Time E to M, after a strike lasting several weeks, the union capitulated to management's demands.

The potential sanctioners are those who had attained political-leadership positions by Time M. Theoretically, these may or may not have been the same people who had been in the political leadership at Time E. In the case of Metroville, the political leadership apparently had remained fairly constant between Time E and Time M. The assessment was that these potential sanctioners could bring illegitimate sanctions, especially economic ones, to bear against most of the potentially sanctionable; and that these sanctions would prove effective in blocking shifts in the scope of local government. However, the probability that such sanctions would be used in the period from Time M to $M + 1$ was judged to be low, even if the potentially sanctionable were to organize political support behind their demands to the point of forming a competitive political group.

In evaluating the degree of permeability of the power structure, it is not just a question of whether or not the application of illegitimate sanctions would be effective if used; but it is a question of whether or not such sanctions would probably be used if the potentially sanctionable pushed their demands past the policy-deliberation stage after Time M. The greatest difficulty in making this assessment for Metroville resulted from the absence of instances of the applications of illegitimate sanctions during Time E to M. Demands that might have called forth such sanctions had been repressed and not pushed beyond the policy-deliberation stage of decision-making. Thus there is no way to infer from overt acts of this type the disposition of potential sanctioners to use illegitimate sanctions.

Instead, we must assess the disposition of the potential sanctioners in various hypothetical but likely situations in the immediate future on the basis of other sorts of evidence. One is the information obtained from the political leaders themselves about their attitudes as of Time M. Another type of evidence comes from situations prior to Time E in which illegitimate sanctions might have been but were not used. Both types of evidence were used in assessing the permeability of the power structure; it was adjudged by the analysts to be higher in Metroville than a number of the fearful citizens imagined.

We first examined the probable reaction of the political leadership to demands that were being deliberated by the small, extremist White

Supremacy organization formed after the initiation of token desegregation, prior to Time M. We consider it unlikely that illegitimate sanctions would have been used against the members of the organization after Time M, even if they acted illegally in pursuit of a policy of resegregation by terror and violence. Since the Progressive Conservatives had decided to initiate token desegregation in order to preserve peace and law in the collective interest of the community, any effort at violence in reversing this decisional outcome would have met with strong disapproval on the part of most White Manifest Leaders. A city attorney, Mr. Williston Russell, III, was ready to act swiftly as the prosecutor of such lawbreaking; the police were primed by both the City Manager and the Mayor to arrest White citizens resorting to such illegal action; and the county sheriff's office and the state police were ready to support the local authorities. Therefore, such political action on the part of White Supremacists would have been met not by illegitimate sanctions but by the legitimate and probably effective sanctions of established law and order.[5]

We also must examine the possibility of illegitimate sanctions being used against demands from Negro Liberals or White labor-union Liberals. This provides an occasion for reminding the reader of a basic limitation of the classification scheme used for regime types: by Time M, there was no organized group that was the polar opposite of the White Supremacist organization in Metroville. For example, if a Black Muslim organization standing for Negro Supremacy had been formed, the probability might have been higher that illegitimate sanctions would have been used against them, although the effectiveness of such sanctions would have been in question.[6] Or, if a truly left-wing labor-union movement had arisen and its members had begun to make certain demands for radical shifts in the scope of local government, the evaluation of the permeability of the power structure might be different.[7] The evaluation of a power structure as being relatively permeable and thus, relatively, a Developed Democracy does not mean the power structure is completely permeable—that is, open to any political group—or that this dimension of democracy is as developed as it conceivably might be.[8]

There was considerable evidence that the Progressive Conservative political leadership as a whole had become convinced during Time E to M that under their guidance the Negro Leadership and the "respectable" segments of the Negro subcommunity were satisfied with their lot and the progress they had made during the past decade. Their carefully developed plans to improve race relations and labor-management relations in their own corporations had borne fruit. Political or economic demands from the Negro subcommunity or the

White working class that the Progressive Conservatives regarded as extreme or radical were ordinarily interpreted as the work of a militant, extremist individual, probably from the North. We concluded that it was likely that, if extreme demands had been pursued after Time M, the reaction of the White Leadership would have been that these demands were the work of trouble-makers, not of the larger, "law-abiding" segments of the community. Their more responsible fellows could be trusted to handle such people; the political leadership would not have to resort to the use of illegitimate sanctions.

The White Progressive Conservative Leadership in fact prided itself on its cosmopolitanism, an attitude developed after the Second World War. This sophistication included a limited toleration of dissidence. There was no guarantee that tolerance was so deeply rooted that it would not be forgotten if extreme demands were made by a competitive Liberal political group aspiring to leadership positions. However, it seemed likely that it would endure, at least while legitimate and probably effective means of political competition were used to prevent such an opposition from attaining their political goals.

The last major use of illegitimate sanctions in Metroville politics occurred just after the Second World War: White labor joined Negroes in a Radical Left-dominated politico-economic movement. The firm opposition of Mr. Williston Russell, III, and some others prevented the possibility of a violent encounter between the private police forces employed by the major corporations and the unionists. However, militant White and Negro unionists were fired, and many were forced to leave Metroville under duress when they were unable to find employment in other firms in the city. Resort to such tactics after Time M was considered unlikely. It seemed improbable that the demands that were being deliberated by a few militant Negroes would be pushed in the way that they had been earlier.

A Radical Left labor-union organization's seeking a monopoly of the leadership positions in the community power structure was only an academic possibility for Metroville or other cities of Southern State by 1958, Time M. If the more likely strategy of political action through existing subsidiary political organizations in the Negro subcommunity, through mass protests and public demonstrations by Negro citizens, or both were adopted after Time M by the potentially sanctionable, our judgment is that even the illegitimate economic sanctions used in the postwar period would not be attempted except as a last resort; and that, if they were used, they would not be as effective as formerly. We shall examine the prospects that such a strategy might be adopted by Negro political forces after Time M.

There was, of course, some possibility that illegitimate sanctions would be used effectively after Time M. The assessment of a low probability or a relatively permeable power structure assumes that the unlikely could occur. Since contingencies existed in making the assessment and since there were difficulties in assessing the validity and reliability of the evidence that was used, the assessment for Metroville was particularly tentative, as we have said. If the assessment of the probability or permeability dimension is wrong, Metroville had an Oligarchic regime; if it is valid, and we think it is, Metroville's regime was an Underdeveloped Democracy.

Petropolis and Oretown—Developed Democracies

The Consensual Elite power structure in one community, Farmdale, was associated with a Guided Democratic regime; the Consensual Elite power structure in Metroville was associated with an Underdeveloped Democracy. The two Competitive Mass power structures occurred with Developed Democracies in Petropolis and Oretown. In both of the Consensual Elite power structures, power was distributed narrowly, and there was a relatively low degree of political participation. In both of the Competitive Mass power structures, the broad distribution of political power was associated with a relatively high degree of political participation. Before inferring the existence of a causal nexus between and among patterns of extensive citizen political participation, a Competitive Mass power structure, and a Developed Democracy, let us examine the reasons for classifying both Petropolis and Oretown as Developed Democracies.

In both communities, the power structures appeared to be relatively permeable. In other words, the probability that illegitimate sanctions would be used effectively after Time M to block efforts to shift the scope of local government was assessed as relatively low. This is not because certain groups in these competitive political leaderships were not disposed to use illegitimate sanctions, but rather because it was unlikely that such sanctions would be effective. This estimation is based primarily on events that took place during Time E to M.

The sense of electoral potency was adjudged as relatively high in both Petropolis and Oretown. The decisional preferences of every significant political minority group were represented by one or more Leaders. Although decisional defeats were suffered at least once by every such interest group, even White and Negro Supremacists in Petropolis felt free to push as hard as they could in organizing political support behind their demands. Electoral and decisional optimism was not high, particularly for citizens representing extremist points of view in Petropolis and representing extremely Liberal points of view in Oretown; however, this pessimism was not rooted in the fear of illegitimate sanctions being used against them. The fact that these are comparative assessments must be borne in mind.

Although members of the unions in both cities had the protection of an active set of union officials, grievance procedures, and national labor-relations laws, they could not engage in political participation, particularly on the job, without some risks. Nor did such protection afford them complete immunity from the use of political sanctions of traditional legitimacy, for example, granting an employer the right to have employees commit themselves to certain minimal levels of economic performance in the job, if these employees were spending an undue amount of time in political decision-making while being paid for their participation in economic decision-making. Therefore, the relatively high sense of electoral potency was not a condition of complete freedom from fears of illegitimate sanctions, but of relatively great freedom from such fears, compared to the fears of their blue-collar counterparts in Metroville.

The largest firms in both Petropolis and Oretown were absentee-owned. Their managements, while not always apolitical in community politics, were charged with the priority task of making profits rather than pursuing particular political ideologies. This economic mission did not prevent some of the top managerial people of these firms from indulging their own personal inclinations to participate in local politics, as the occupational backgrounds of the Orthodox Conservatives in both cities attest. In fact, their economic mission charged them with participating in decision-making processes wherein certain substantial and immediate corporate interests were at stake. In Metroville there was a greater overlap between the economic and the political hierarchies: the senior officers of the corporations were also the senior, Manifest Political Leaders of the community power structure. Even the top corporate official of Metroville's largest absentee-owned firm was a Manifest Leader.

Proportionately more industrial executives of Oretown were preoccupied with community affairs in the city in which they lived, neighboring Big City. Those in Petropolis were preoccupied with state and national rather than community politics, unlike the situation in Metroville. When the politico-economic leaders of Metroville wanted to check on labor's political activities, they monitored the workers in their own corporations. When the industrial executives of Petropolis and Oretown wanted to check the same thing they tended to look at extracorporate settings. The unions in both Petropolis and Oretown were subsidiary political organizations. They provided an important political milieu for the deliberation and organization of political support behind political demands. Although the unions' political milieus extended into the plants and factories, they had physically separate, independent political-organization centers. In Oretown, these included the union halls; the local Democratic party; the regular meeting places of the Liberals, including several in the Longacre section of town; and the headquarters of the municipal utility. In Petropolis they included the union's voter league; the headquarters of the Democratic party; the editorial office of the labor newspaper; and, for Negro unionists, PESNEG and the NAACP.

One of the most important functions of the unions as subsidiary political organizations seemed to be creating a sense of economic security that contributed to a sense of electoral potency on the part of their members. Another may have been to lessen the disposition on the part of management to use illegitimate sanctions to achieve their political goals. A politicized union could wreak economic havoc in retaliation for politically inspired dismissals that might be accepted by a union or a set of nonunionized workers oriented solely to economic goals. Such obvious considerations were not overloked by the managers of the largest industrial operations in either Petropolis or Oretown.

We have assessed the disposition to use certain sorts of illegitimate sanctions as being relatively low in both Petropolis and Oretown. We have estimated that such economic sanctions as those relating to employment or discharge of workers would be generally ineffective in view of the job security and protective political environments afforded by union membership in these cities. These assessments were based on observations, during Time E to M, that there were few instances of the use of such sanctions or of either repression or suppression of demands as a result of their application. Other illegitimate sanctions, however, were used extensively in the politics of both cities, but they were relatively ineffective and failed to lower the sense of electoral potency of the citizens. These sanctions included boycotts of businesses, social rejection, and ostracism. We shall discuss events during Time E to M in order to clarify the assessment of these sanctions as ineffective.

In Petropolis we found that members of the Negro subcommunity had informally boycotted White merchants. Although these boycotts for the most part were motivated by socio-economic considerations, at least some of the boycotters had political ends in view as well.

Among other goals, they sought to put pressure on those whom they felt were contributing to the decisional outcome not to desegregate the public schools. Not only were most of the boycotted White business-men so impervious to such actions that they did not become politically deactivated, but many of them had encouraged the boycott by refus-ing to serve Negro customers. Certain White businessmen, such as the owners of a radio station catering to a Negro audience and de-pendent in part on Negro advertising, were quite sensitive to the pos-sibility of boycotts. Rather than avoid making any White Suprem-acist political demands they might favor, these businessmen operated in a more covert, less public fashion. Since these men were not actually stopped from pushing their demands—that is, from organiz-ing political support behind them even covertly—a judgment that these community power structures were relatively permeable is warranted.

It is difficult, as Negro informants in both Petropolis and Metro-ville repeatedly emphasized, for a White person to understand the fears any Negro grows up with in Southern and most Northern cities.[9] Lynchings have not and, indeed, cannot be forgotten; nor can those sanctions which lead to hunger or to social degradation. Fear of the Whites is endemic among Negro citizens of America, even in the middle of the twentieth century. For this reason, a more finely drawn ranking probably would place Petropolis below Farmdale and Ore-town, both of which had few Negro citizens, on the sense of electoral potency dimension. Yet the fears of illegitimate political activity on the part of the Negroes of Petropolis were considerably below those of their racial brethren in Metroville. This was manifested in a variety of ways, particularly on the part of the Negro Leadership and Negro citizens who were not recent arrivals from the rural, more traditional caste areas of Southern State. Although fears of illegiti-mate political reprisals are ever-present for Negro citizens in the United States, the degree of such fears is important for the present analytic assessments. We believe that, because of the matter of degree, the inclusion of Petropolis with Farmdale and Oretown as cities of relatively electorally potent citizens is warranted.

What should already be clear is that in Petropolis fears of illegiti-mate sanctions had not succeeded to anything like the same degree as they had in Metroville in preventing Negro citizens from making political demands or participating politically. It is likely that such repression would have been even greater in Metroville if the Negro citizens had been subject to threats such as those printed in the White ‚Supremacist paper in Petropolis. In connection with a boycott being

contemplated by some of the younger Negroes in Petropolis, and as
illustrative of such open threats, a slightly paraphrased portion of a
typical editorial from that paper is as follows:

Only chicken-hearted white merchants would want to sell to Negroes. Let
Negroes dare to start a boycott and we'll boycott them back, but good.
Negroes have nothing themselves anyway—and let the rabble-rousers in
PESNEG start it and we'll take away their jobs, they won't get a loan from
anyone, we'll kick them off of welfare, and let them get their own book-
learning. Negroes who talk about boycotts are Northern communists who
work with ministers, none of whom are worth a damn—and the international
Jewish-Supreme Court conspiracy. Warren, the Jewish sympathizer, and
his court won't be able to do a thing about this—it's outside of their jurisdiction.

The Negro subcommunity's response to this particular threat ranged
from hate to rather bitter amusement at these words of a person who
regarded himself as superior to Negroes. The Negro brokers' advertisements in that very paper were a reflection, not of their weakness
and anxiety, but of their strength and security.

Security is perhaps the key word in understanding the difference
in attitudes towards illegitimate sanctions of both Negroes and Liberal
working-class Whites in Petropolis and Metroville. Those in Petropolis had a relative psychological security, rooted in social and economic
resources that deprived illegitimate sanctions of some of their force.
In Petropolis, the Negro and White factory workers were more secure
in their jobs than those in Metroville. A portion of the Negro upper
class were financially secure because of their investment, brokerage,
and lending institutions. Negro businessmen facing boycotts or other
threats knew that subsidiary political organizations would support
them. They knew that PESNEG or the NAACP would threaten
electoral reprisals if White officials ignored the situation. These and
similar organizations helped to protect them. The White working
class were protected through their unions and the Democratic party.

Few citizens of Petropolis could ignore illegitimate sanctions. But
protective organizational resources were available to them that did
not exist or were not adequate in Metroville. As one Petropolis
Negro Leader put it, the Negroes of Petropolis had learned how to
use "the only two things the White man respects: the dollar and the
ballot." The White financiers wanted to continue the transactions
involving the large sums of capital accumulated by some of the Negro
financial institutions; they knew that the latter had other banking
arrangements available in other communities. But the acceptance by

the White Supremacist newspaper of advertising revenues from Negroes symbolized a relatively general awareness in the Negro subcommunity of the importance of their purchasing power to White businessmen. The Negro Leadership of Petropolis also was well aware that the disciplined Negro vote was significant to White candidates for municipal office, as well as for special measures needing voter approval. The White labor-union leaders were equally aware of the political impact that the less disciplined but still respected labor vote had in Petropolis politics. In Metroville the situation of White labor and of the Negro subcommunity was very different.

Oretown witnessed illegitimate sanctions during Time *E* to *M*. The informally organized boycott was used against the merchants of Main Street and Longacre. Since deep political cleavages existed in the community, particularly those associated with the conflict between the public and private electric utilities, many merchants and professional men expected that support of one side or the other would mean a loss of business. How extensive these boycotts were is not known, but that they existed was an established fact. In some cases they resulted in a shift to more covert political action, as occasionally was the case in Petropolis; but, in general, the use of such sanctions did not prevent people from pushing their political demands.

In both Oretown and Petropolis, as in Farmdale, during Time *E* to *M*, politically inspired, informal social ostracism was practiced in some of the voluntary associations to which the more affluent merchants and businessmen belonged. However, in both Oretown and Petropolis, the formal organization of social groups along political lines had proceeded further and was more widely recognized than it was in Farmdale. In Metroville the "best" formally organized voluntary associations were more exclusive to start with, so that social ostracism for substantial political "deviance" was irrelevant. When members of the ingroup, the Progressive Conservative political leadership, fell out politically over a matter such as the mental-institution issue, a cooling of social relations was noticeable; but the manners and mores of this upper-class set of interlocked kinfolk and business associates made expulsion from the group or social ostracism improper. It was as unthinkable to try to freeze out socially a pro-violence Supremacist in the Manifest Leadership as it was to eject Mr. Williston Russell, III, an "integrationist" in the eyes of some of his social peers.

However, in Oretown and Petropolis, such illegitimate sanctions were not as effective as they were in Farmdale in suppressing political demands. It was not necessary to take up a tactic of political good behavior while trying to work from within, as the young accountant felt forced to do in Farmdale. More friendly, or at least more politically heterogeneous, organizational settings were available in both Oretown and Petropolis to those ejected formally or informally from particular associational settings of their peers. Even Liberal businessmen had optional organizational settings. In Oretown the Liberal businessman could withdraw into "his" section of town, Longacre; if he did not live, work, or go to church there, he could drop by to talk shop with politically congenial fellows in the stores and lunchrooms.[10]

Although there were few Liberals among the White business and professional men of Oretown, there were even fewer in Petropolis. But these few did have associational settings such as the local Democratic party organization serving as both a buffer for social sanctions and an alternative to settings that sometimes became too hostile. We have stressed the formally organized voluntary-association setting and the larger informal social setting because of the psychological-political functions they seem to have served. They functioned not only as channels of communication between the "average" citizen and the political leadership, but also as subsidiary political organizations for the personal-political needs of those who were threatened with illegitimate sanctions.

The presumed function of subsidiary political organizations was to increase the probability of political status of even politically non-participant citizens and hence of political influence for a political participant in community politics. However, these speculations have not been verified by solid empirical findings. Similarly, the functioning of such organizations for the potentially and actually sanctioned must remain for the moment a matter of speculation. The importance of even a single like-minded person for an individual with deviant political ideas suggests the importance of a small group of friends to enable a person to manage the anxieties that sanctions may invoke.[11] Members of even a friendship group may go their several ways when one of their number is the object of sanctions by others in the polity. A politically oriented friendship also may find itself becoming apolitical as illegitimate sanctions isolate it and its individual members from other socio-political settings. The ability of a sanctioned person to continue to express his political demands is thought to be enhanced considerably if he has access to members of a larger association. Obviously a person who has both friendship groups and larger associational-group memberships is in a better position to provide himself with the assurance and support he may need to continue his political action in the face of disturbing deprivations.

We estimate the probability of the effective use of illegitimate sanctions after Time M as relatively low in Oretown and Petropolis because they were not used often and because attempts to use them were apparently unsuccessful. Obviously, political events could prove this assessment wrong. The adequacy of the regime classification is better judged after the assessment of political stability-instability and stasis-change are considered.

STABILITY-INSTABILITY AND STASIS-CHANGE IN POWER STRUCTURES AND REGIMES: SECOND WORLD WAR TO TIME M

To facilitate assessments of the prospects of change in both regimes and power structures during the next year, and to test the kinds of hypotheses presented in the last chapter of the book, the time between the end of the Second World War and Time E in each community was divided into periods of approximately one year in length. We shall not attempt in the following section to discuss specifically the types of regimes and power structures in each of those periods. Instead, the focus is upon changes or trends in the classifications.

Farmdale—Second World War to 1950 (Time E)

From 1946 to 1950, Farmdale was the scene of an open political battle between the numerically superior Community Conservationists and a comparatively small number of Jeffersonian Conservatives in the political leadership. The Community Conservationists had embarked on a program of community and local-government growth. The men in a majority of the elective positions in the city council as well as in the mayor's office supported this program. They also were organized informally in a community-improvement association. From all reports, Farmdale during this entire postwar period was a Developed Democracy. Illegitimate sanctions were not effective and the citizens evidenced a high sense of electoral potency. Many citizens apparently participated in decision-making; a relatively large proportion of them played activist roles in highly competitive processes. Until 1950 the power structure was a Competitive Mass type.

Since immediately prior to Time E a Developed Democracy and a Competitive Mass power structure existed, the conditions during Time E to M of Guided Democracy and Consensual Elite power structure were of uncertain stability. This instability could have resulted in returning Farmdale to a Developed Democracy. But to return to a Competitive Mass power structure would have required the organization and the aspiring to political-leadership positions of either the

Community Conservationists or other political ideologists competitive to Jeffersonian Conservatism. The pre-Time E tradition of grass-roots democracy, with the high voter turnout in the issueless municipal elections at Time E, constituted a potential for mass participation that was lacking in Metroville. We think it unlikely that the ritualistic turnout at the polls would or could have continued at that high level in the absence of more widespread, competitive participation in decision-making. However, since the Community Conservationists seemed to become more and more demoralized and more and more pessimistic about their political prospects, it is unlikely that competition would have returned from that direction. Mr. King continued to press his political demands in the face of the sanctions levied against him; but he was not a Community Conservationist nor a friend of theirs. King's supporters were effectively deactivated, so that the continuation of a Consensual Elite power structure was regarded as a relatively safe prediction.

If illegitimate sanctions such as those that had been used effectively against advocates of an expanded scope of local government were continued or were applied on a wider scale, there was a possibility that they might lose their effectiveness, in view of their unusual character in the postwar history of Farmdale. What was perhaps more likely than a return to a Developed Democracy in Farmdale immediately after Time M was the emergence of an Oligarchy. If political demands had continued to be pushed and met by the sorts of illegitimate sanctions encountered during Time E to M, fears of such sanctions might have been engendered and the sense of electoral potency might have decreased. What to some observers is an essentially Oligarchic character of small-town politics may have been the step beyond Guided Democracy in a movement away from the earlier postwar Developed Democracy.

We might note in passing that, in Farmdale, the prospects of the development of a group consciousness on the part of organized labor and the entry of organized labor into local politics as Liberals, as happened in Oretown in the same Western State, was deemed unlikely. In Oretown this had happened when absentee-owned mining companies and their unions had come to town to develop the mineral deposits in the area. There were two reasons that a more militant unionism was not likely to come to Farmdale. First, there were fewer known mineral deposits in the Farmdale area, although metal-processing firms had expressed some interest in coming to the community. But more important, the political leadership of Farmdale actively opposed such industrial location in their town, and there was little indication that a new policy would be adopted. The political leaders were not inclined to invite new industry and unions to come to Farmdale. This example of the impact of the political on the economic system of a community encouraged stasis and stability in the power structure and regime in Farmdale at Time M.

Metroville—Second World War to 1957 (Time E)

The Consensual Elite power structure in Metroville was a more static, stable structure than that of Farmdale. It had been a Consensual Elite structure since 1946; this meant that by Time M it had existed 12 years, compared to the 2-year duration of Farmdale's Consensual Elite structure by Time M.

Metroville's regime had undergone two changes during the postwar period. During the Second World War, it had been an Oligarchy. As we have already noted about Metroville, it seemed:

. . . an Oligarchy through the 1930's. Just before and during the Second World War, the Negro subcommunity was allowed to organize political support through such organizations as the local chapter of the National Association for the Advancement of Colored People (NAACP) in order to request that White government officials shift the scope of government in various ways. Prior to that time such organizational activity and such petitioning probably would have provoked the same reaction as did efforts by Negroes to nominate candidates both before and during the war: effective illegitimate sanctions. The difference in the degree of oligarchic control from the thirties to the forties was significant, although the immediate postwar situation still warranted the Oligarchy classification for this regime.

Not even the few formally organized voluntary associations that were classified as subsidiary political organizations in the Negro subcommunity during Time E to M could have been so classified before the war. In that earlier era they were in fact as well as manifestly service agencies for health, welfare, religious, and social needs of Negro citizens, who were almost completely apolitical.

During the Second World War, with the establishment of the labor union, a sudden politicization of the Negro subcommunity and White workers resulted in the obliteration of subcommunity barriers and the political integration of the lowest portion of the White social structure and Negro citizens. The sense of electoral potency seemed to rise dramatically, but it was fragile and short lived. This was probably a period of Guided rather than Developed Democracy, since illegitimate economic sanctions and legitimate political sanctions succeeded in averting major shifts in the scope of local government. These sanctions returned Metroville to a condition of a relatively low sense of electoral potency and to Oligarchy.

During that period the power structure in Metroville remained Consensual Elite, since the threat to the single political-leadership group of what was then Orthodox Conservatism was unsuccessful. The Radical Left did not succeed in gaining either political decisional victories or political-leadership positions nor in broadening the distribution of political power among the citizens. This classification does, however, illustrate the usefulness of more complex classificatory schemes than our fourfold typology of power structures permits. The Consensual Elite power structures, both before and after the rise of the Radical Left, were very different in some respects from the structure that existed during that period of abortive competition. On the other hand, we may continue to use the simple classificatory scheme without great loss, since the purposes of the present analysis are limited.

The immediate postwar Oligarchy also was of a somewhat different character from the almost feudal type that prevailed during the prewar period. A few Negroes remained politically active; the biracial Harmony House was created as a subsidiary political organization; and a local NAACP and a handful of other voluntary associations also became subsidiary political organizations. The fear of illegitimate sanctions made these organizations merely settings in which policy deliberation was followed by a respectful petitioning of local-government officials. But even this weakly developed network of political meetings was a development from the prewar Oligarchic regime, where the "Uncle Tom" type of political-influence relations existed between a handful of individual Negroes and White political leaders.

The development of a Progressive Conservative political ideology by the leadership replacing the earlier, more rigid White Supremacist-Orthodox Conservative one contributed to this more modern type of Oligarchy. The newly gerrymandered wards assured the Negroes one city councilman of their own to whom they could directly present petitions. But in 1949 the relatively unified political elite faced the election of Mayor Peterson, who had marshalled sufficient votes from the Negro subcommunity and lower-class Whites in a "rabble-rousing" anti-vested-interests campaign that once again generated a sudden rise in the sense of electoral potency on the part of the politically, economically, and racially underprivileged.

The political leadership had begun by this time to develop its Progressive Conservative programs of community improvement. It has been noted (in Chapter 5) that these leaders opposed Peterson in the primary but endorsed him in the general election against his Republican opponent. Such strategic considerations as loss of some community confidence in Democratic Metroville if they endorsed a Republican was reportedly one of the reasons given for endorsing Peterson. Another was their increasing commitment to improving the lot of minority groups, Negroes and the poor Whites, as the best way to avert the development of either a competitive Radical Left or, more likely, competitive Liberal groups. The Progressive Conservatives believed that they could acquire influence over Peterson and the forces of protest that he represented without using illegitimate sanctions of the kind used against active supporters of the earlier Radical Left group. However, they stood ready to use such sanctions if their efforts failed, or if they were unable to block undesirable shifts in the scope of government through their representatives on the City Council —even if they failed to persuade Peterson himself.

Their efforts were successful. The Mayor quickly came to believe that he could not shift the scope of government without the active cooperation of the still consensual White political leadership. Instead of competing with them, he developed cooperative working relations with them in political decision-making. As we already have described, one of the inner-clique Manifest Leaders succeeded in persuading the Mayor to accept the point of view of the Progressive Conservative group. The power structure remained Consensual Elite, since political decision-making still was restricted to the very few, and the distribution of power remained restricted. The regime had changed, however, from an Oligarchy to a Guided Democracy.

The Progressive Conservative political leadership seemed, after Mayor Peterson's cooptation, disposed to give their policies of guided, minimal relaxation of racial barriers one last chance. Even though they, and particularly the younger and newer members, were opposed increasingly to the use of illegitimate sanctions, they were prepared to use them, if necessary, to block undesirable shifts in the scope of local government. The Negro Leaders, many of whom were appointed to positions on municipal commissions which yielded some political status, had become wary once again of illegitimate sanctions. These were in general very cautious men, since the more militant of the Negro Leaders had moved from the city when the union lost its struggle. The proportion of ministers in their ranks is partly explained by the fact that ministers were economically secure and, hence, relatively invulnerable to the illegitimate economic deprivations which had been used effectively against the blue-collar Negroes in the ranks of the militant union leadership.[12]   The Negro Leadership and remaining White union leaders had maintained a relatively higher sense of electoral potency than they had had during the prewar years; this was reinforced when Mayor Peterson ran successfully for reelection. Once again he represented himself, although in a milder manner, as a friend of the poor and powerless.

During the period between 1951 and 1954, slowly but steadily changing dimensions resulted in a change in regime from Guided Democracy to Underdeveloped Democracy.   The sense of electoral potency began to fall off as more members of the Negro and White minority groups in Metroville perceived no basic changes in their political system.   But at the same time, the Progressive Conservatives' aversion to the use of illegitimate sanctions grew stronger.   Such sanctions were incongruent with their desire to have the city known nationally as the most culturally progressive one in the state.   Thus we make the tentative classification of Metroville as an Underdeveloped Democracy, not only during Time E to M, but also during the immediately preceding period of approximately 4 years' duration.

The recent period of stable change in both classificatory dimensions of the regime type had culminated, on the one hand, in an apparently static state of a relatively low sense of electoral potency but, on the other, in a continuing change towards increasing permeability of the power structure.   At Time M, one potential source of change in the classification of Metroville as an Underdeveloped Democracy seemed to be the cleavage in the power structure between accommodating and racist Progressive Conservative leaders, as in the mental-hospital decision.   In the development of such a competitive political leadership, it seems likely that the Negro Leadership and at least some White Liberals in the working class would join forces and stimulate mass participation on one side, with White citizens of the opposite persuasion on race-relation matters on the other side; conceivably, this could have led to a Competitive Mass power structure.   Whether or not such a competitive power structure became a mass or remained an elite structure, the sense of electoral potency could rise and change the regime from an Underdeveloped to a Developed Democracy.   But this sequence of change was judged unlikely because of the demonstrated inclination and ability of the Progressive Conservatives to close ranks when their unity seemed to be threatened by intragroup disagreements.

An even greater potential source of change in Metroville's regime was thought to be the development of a political leadership group of Community Conservationists.   It was noted earlier that highly educated White newcomers to Metroville were not members or, if they were, not central members of the Progressive Conservatives. Two women among the Latent Leaders with such characteristics had political perspectives that seemed to be based on Community Conservationist rather than Progressive Conservative premises. The upper-middle-class activists on the side of improved recreational facilities and school consolidation, either at once or following school improvements, as well as the supporters of urban redevelopment for other reasons than simply providing the glass industry and other businesses with new sites, suggested the increasing importance of such orientations in Metroville's politics.[13] However, there was little evidence that such people would organize their own political group at any point in the immediate future. Nor was there any evidence that the Progressive Conservatives and a group of Community Conservationists would not work out an accommodating relationship so that the political leadership would consist of convergent groups and remain consensual. However, if such a group did develop, it might lead to an increased sense of electoral potency and Developed Democracy as a result of the broadening of the political leadership.

The development of a Community Conservationist-Liberal alliance, with or without Negro participation, seemed quite unlikely. Nor was there any indication on the basis of this analysis of periods prior to Time E that an independent, competitive Negro or Negro-White Liberal political group, with effective mass participation through public protests and demonstrations, would be created during Time M to $M + 1$. The rise of the Radical Left seemed to have occurred as a result of an unusual combination of circumstances unlikely to be duplicated in the foreseeable future.

We might mention in passing that the Mayor was concerned with the overt criticism that he had encountered from fringe-area residents and some city-dwellers over his active support of the last large annexation; he also was concerned with what he and certain White Manifest Leaders had identified as an increased grumbling and discontent from somewhere in the Negro subcommunity. However, these did not seem to indicate a likely change in either the type of power structure or the type of regime during the next period.[14]

Too little is known of the consequences of migration patterns for community political change or instability to assess them here. But we might mention some of the more relevant findings in passing. A striking pattern was the outflow from Metroville of young Negroes, particularly those with high-school or higher levels of education. This was evident from U. S. Census data and confirmed by the sample-survey findings. The latter revealed, for example, little difference in the educational status of Negro adults of various ages, suggesting that the younger Negroes with college training were leaving the community at a rapid rate. Younger adults were, however, much more likely to have had 2 to 4 years of high-school education than older adults in the Negro subcommunity at Time M—60 per cent of those under 35 years of age and 10 per cent of those over 35 years of age had that amount of formal education. Those under 35 years of age were much more disposed to leave the community than those over 35 years of age. This was evident in the responses to the question: "Would you leave Metroville if you had a satisfactory opportunity to do so?" Seventy-three per cent of these younger adults replied affirmatively, compared to but 47 per cent of the older adults.

It was to be expected that younger adults would be more disposed to leave a community; but this finding was due only slightly to age and for the most part to level of education. It was the high-school- and college-educated Negroes of all ages who were most disposed to move from Metroville, whereas the young adults of low education were almost as likely to respond "no" to this question (rather than "don't know") as were the older people of equally low education. Since the younger adults were the most highly educated, it appeared that the Negro subcommunity was likely to lose a disproportionate number of just those citizens most disposed to militant political action.

There is, of course, a potential gap between preference or aspiration on the one hand and opportunity and action on the other. The younger Negro adults of Metroville had not joined their peers who had already moved from the community, many of them to Northern cities. How many "satisfactory opportunities" would arise and be acted upon is unknown, as are the long-term political consequences of this selective emigration on the part of the more highly educated young Negroes. Conceivably, the most energetic, potentially most militant Negroes were being drawn from the community, leaving behind those most likely to endure the political *status quo*. It is possible, on the other hand, that the relatively well-educated younger Negroes who did leave Metroville in their search for more adequate opportunities were those least likely to act politically in a fashion that could endanger their prospects of upward socio-economic mobility and the attainment of respectability. It may be, though, that if those who wanted to leave found less opportunity to do so in the future—under such conditions, for example, as an increasing degree of unemployment in the nation—underemployment in Metroville of the increasingly well-educated, more economically skilled youthful Negroes would contribute to political tensions and instabilities of the kind associated with political instability in various underdeveloped countries that have segments of the population trained beyond the capacity of the economy to absorb them. In any event, there was at Time M little reason to assume that the immediate future would see much change in the net emigration of highly educated Negroes, nor much change in the relatively high proportion of well-educated younger adults remaining in the community. Since various, contradictory speculations might be offered, it was assumed here that this migration pattern did not provide a condition likely to lead to community political change in the immediate future, although it was a factor that created more political instability than might have existed with another kind of pattern.

We might mention here also what was happening during Time E to M insofar as the patterns of White migration were concerned. A disproportionate number of the White newcomers to Metroville were relatively highly educated, although, as we shall see, far less so than was the case in Petropolis. The same trend existed in the White as in the Negro subcommunity, but to a lesser degree: the highly educated young people were leaving the community; but the White subcommunity, unlike the Negro subcommunity, was also experiencing an influx of relatively well-educated newcomers.

Anti-Negro sentiments in Metroville were related to both educational level and length of residence. Since the newcomers were more highly educated than old-timers, their movement into the community was a force for the preservation of a Progressive Conservative attitude on racial policies rather than a force for the strengthening of the political forces pushing for a more Supremacist set of policies. Newcomers, whether accommodating or racist in outlook, were, however, not politically active. While these newcomers would in time become "old-timers" in the White subcommunity, their relatively accommodating perspectives, assuming they were maintained, did not suggest any immediate changes in the community's power structure or regime.

Petropolis—Second World War to 1957 (Time E)

Petropolis' Developed Democracy and Competitive Mass power structure had endured longer than had the Underdeveloped Democracy of Metroville. This type of regime had existed since about 1947 and this type of power structure since about 1949. During the 1930's Petropolis witnessed the development of subsidiary political organizations both in the Negro subcommunity and in the White working class that did not come to Metroville until much later. When they eventually did develop in Metroville, they were not as extensive as those in Petropolis. Led by the relatively wealthy Negro businessmen, the drives to register Negro citizens and to develop political organizations extending into the grass roots made continual progress and were regarded as substantial successes by the end of the Second World War. Relatively secure labor-union officials in the well-organized industries joined with the politically conscious Negroes in a coalition that, during the postwar years, was to enjoy substantial victories in local politics.

A regime that once had been Oligarchic had become, even before the Second World War, an Underdeveloped Democracy. Fear of illegitimate sanctions was slow to subside, so that political influence first was generated in the increasingly frequent political meetings wherein White candidates would come to the Negro Leadership for quiet endorsement in their campaigns for local office. Yet this newly found feeling of political potency was so overshadowed by fear of illegitimate sanctions, even on the part of senior officers of the largest investment companies, that the "go slow" wing of the Negro Leadership, even during the war period, completely dominated more militant Leaders, whose sense of electoral potency had become relatively high.

Until the end of the war, the power structure in Petropolis was a unified structure dominated by an all-White Orthodox Conservative group. Immediately after the war the first stirrings of opposition came from two directions. One was reflected in the political demands emanating from within the Orthodox Conservative group itself for net shifts in the scope of local government desirable for business interests. The other also came from the business community, but from men who, while relatively unself-conscious about their own ideological positions, were Community Conservationists. With strong opposition from the Orthodox Conservatives, particularly from industrialists and some of the financiers, these developments were controlled, the political leadership remained consensual, and the distribution of power remained elite.

During the next few years—approximately 1947 to 1949—the regime became a Developed Democracy and the power structure changed from a Consensual to a Competitive Elite structure. It is possible that the structure had become Competitive Mass in type by that time, with relatively high voter turnout and public protest meetings on several decisional matters; but because of the uncertainty and inconclusiveness of the data we shall reserve the label "mass" for the next period. At the beginning of that period, some Community Conservationists had been elected to the city council by defeating Orthodox Conservative opponents, with the political support of Negro and White labor. That election campaign seemed to mark the beginning of a high sense of electoral potency on the part of those who earlier had feared illegitimate sanctions. The high sense of electoral potency remained stable and unchanging through Time M.

The Community Conservationist-Liberal coalition in this period gained some of their decisional objectives, thus sharing political leadership positions with Orthodox Conservatives. For example, an extremely large, costly, diversified set of civic-improvement programs was authorized by the voters in a special election. On such other matters as gaining recognition for the newly unionized municipal employees, whose fear of illegitimate sanctions had been so reduced that they had dared to organize City Hall, and the demand for legislation to require subdivision developers to absorb the cost of utility installations instead of the local government, the opposing Orthodox Conservatives were the victors. During this period, the successful election of John Jay and Fred Ames as the chief officers in the local Democratic party organization was accomplished by White and Negro Liberals. Although a costly bond issue for improving the schools was passed with strong labor-union support over the opposition led by Orthodox Conservatives, a proposed public-housing program was defeated without a public vote when the city council succumbed to pressures from real-estate and taxpayer interests to reverse its earlier support of the proposal.

After the election of a Community Conservationist as mayor in 1949, Petropolis not only maintained its Developed Democracy but also witnessed the relatively permanent establishment of a Competitive Mass power structure. With the election of Mayor Plunkett, another Community Conservationist, in 1951 and his subseqent reelections, Petropolis experienced no change significant enough to warrant a reclassification of its Developed Democratic regime or its Competitive Mass power structure.

To return for a moment to an important feature of quite different power structures in the two cities of Southern State during Time E to M, we should note that the impulse towards the development of relatively independent, autonomous political organizations in the Negro subcommunity occurred first, in a stronger fashion, and more successfully in Petropolis than in Metroville. One might speculate that this had something to do with the Petropolis Negro Leadership's more direct contact, in their cosmopolitan and extracommunity relationships, with the sweep of national political Liberalism, as well as with their relatively greater economic security. During the 1930's and 1940's, Petropolis seemed to be more of an "open" political system; its Negro subcommunity as well as its White working class had more and better-developed channels through which political messages arrived from the national political system than did these categories in Metroville.

But this historical analysis also indicates that fears of illegitimate sanctions which, if they had continued, might have weakened the subsidiary political organizations in Petropolis or created pressures for a more radical political movement than occurred, and which might have fixed Petropolis for a longer period of time as an Underdeveloped Democracy, did not substantially disappear until another political event had occurred. The Negro subsidiary political organizations in Petropolis did not wither or weaken, and the sense of electoral potency became high, at the point in time at which White citizens joined them as fellow Liberals and allies against an Orthodox Conservative political group. This might have resulted from an accidental juxtaposition of political phenomena with no cause and effect connection, but it deserves closer examination.

During the brief period of Guided Democracy under the attack led by the Radical Left, and during the even briefer period of Developed Democracy under the protective shield of Mayor Peterson's Liberal rhetoric, Whites in Metroville had been active politically in concert with Negroes; but in neither case did these Whites have the capacity to continue their common political front with their Negro allies. In Petropolis, the political skills of White citizens as well as their accessibility to organizational milieus and positions from which their Negro allies were substantially excluded seemed to have contributed to the rise in the sense of electoral potency on the part of both Negroes and working-class Whites which had occurred but had not endured in Metroville. A similar phenomenon will be mentioned shortly as it was observed in Oretown.

Even though the relationship between two racial parts of the Liberal political group in Petropolis was not perfect, and there was an even greater tenuousness in the alliance between the Community Conservationists and Liberals, it seemed that their sympathetic orientations toward one another gave to each a degree of political optimism. It gave the Liberals of both races a more solid foundation for their sense of electoral potency than would have been the case without such mutual support. The major sources of political instability appeared to originate with the period preceding Time E to M. They included this racial cleavage and the political flirtations of Community Conservationists and Orthodox Conservatives.

The Community Conservationist-Orthodox Conservative flirtation had first occurred in the immediate postwar stirrings of Community Conservation, which in time became a more distinct political ideology for some citizens. However, the movement of the Community Conservationists back and forth over these years, first to the Orthodox Conservatives and then to their Liberal allies, did not threaten to change the type of power structure from competitive to consensual even though it seemed to be a pattern of political instability. At no time did this pattern seriously suggest that a single coalition of Community Conservationists, Orthodox Conservatives, and Liberals, not to speak of the White Supremacist political group, was about to be born. Nor did this pattern of instability threaten to give way to a considerably less competitive set of relationships between and among these groups, another way in which a consensual power structure is created without a merging of formerly competitive groups. Even when the local economy's major industry was endangered by the possibility of product substitution from an industry located elsewhere, and even when the economy, particularly in its manufacturing base, began its serious postwar decline, both occurring in the period preceding Time E, such political cooperation did not come anywhere near realization. Cooperation in particular decision-making processes such as the creation of a municipal center for the training and upgrading of the skills of workers had parallels during these earlier postwar periods, but they always were followed by intense conflicts in other decision-making processes.

Since the effective merger of the two wings of Petropolis' Negro Leadership, the militants and moderates, there appeared at that time to be no serious threat that the younger, lower-class people among the Negro active influentials and Latent Leadership would replace the older, higher-status Manifest Leadership. The latter were still more moderate than some of the former, but the developed procedures of "democratic centralism"—that is, full and frank discussion in the group but compliance with the decision reached by the leadership of the group—suggested that no such split would occur in this group. The failure to obtain desegregation by Time M created some strain between the more and less militant members of the Negro Liberal group; but even the lawsuit to strike down the state's plan to permit selective desegregation in the cities of the state obtained the reluctant approval of the inner clique and most others, although not that of

George France. The direct action taken by a small group of younger Negroes and a Negro minister to desegregate a candy store was looked upon by many Negro Liberal Leaders with disfavor, but there was little indication that this signified the beginning of a split in the group.

In any event, none of these presumedly unlikely events would be likely to lead to a change in either the power structure or the regime. This historical analysis generally gives the analyst little reason to qualify or be less confident in portraying Petropolis as a Developed Democracy at Time M, nor in predicting that it would continue to have a Competitive Mass power structure in the next time period.

The migration pattern for Petropolis Negroes was strikingly similar to that of Metroville's Negro subcommunity. The most highly educated Negro youth had been leaving Petropolis at a relatively rapid rate, although the younger people who remained were generally better educated than the older adults. While the youngest adults, those under 25 years of age, were as disposed to leave Petropolis as were their counterparts in Metroville, Negroes between the ages of 25 and 34 were much less disposed to leave Petropolis than their counterparts in Metroville. Sixty-two per cent of the youngest Negro adults in Petropolis indicated that they would leave if given a satisfactory opportunity to do so, compared to 47 per cent of the 25–34 year olds there. The comparable figures for Metroville were 75 and 72 per cent, respectively. Although family incomes were slightly higher in the Negro subcommunity of Petropolis than in Metroville, the rate of unemployment and conscious concern about the obvious economic decline in the community was higher in the former than in the latter. The somewhat greater disposition of Negro adults in the 25-to-34 age bracket to remain in Petropolis than in Metroville may be related to the greater degree of political development in the former than in the latter, to the attractiveness of employment in the major Negro investment and brokerage businesses, or both, even though job possibilities in those enterprises were relatively restricted. Such inferences are not weakened by the finding that Negro adults of medium and high education levels in this age category in Petropolis were particularly less disposed to leave than their counterparts in Metroville, while there was little difference among the poorly educated youth.

We are not so much concerned here with the reasons Negroes in Petropolis wanted to leave or remain in the community, nor with the reasons for the difference in disposition to leave on the part of Negroes in Petropolis and Metroville. Rather, we are interested in the consequences of particular patterns of migration to the community's political system. To the extent that the highly educated Negro adults in this 25-to-34 age category were disposed to remain in Petropolis because of the local community's economic attractiveness to them, it might be that they had a stake in "gradualism" not shared by equally highly educated Negro youth who were potential emigrants. If, on the other hand, this age group was disposed to stay because of their evaluation of the political system as dynamic, as affording opportunities to acquire, maintain, and enhance their political dignity, their remaining in the community could be a source of continued pressure for a militant and consequently competitive politics. In either case, there was little reason to interpret the Negro migration pattern as likely to cause a major change in either power structure or regime type.

In the Petropolis White subcommunity, the bulk of the newcomers were highly educated. Almost two-thirds of the residents who had been there for less than 6 years had at least some college education, compared to less than one-third of the White citizens of Petropolis who had resided there for 6 or more years, and less than one-third of the White newcomers in Metroville. Apparently, the economic decline in Petropolis meant that moderately educated, skilled or semi-skilled, potential newcomers were selecting other communities in which to settle in preference to Petropolis. Business executives of established corporations were the ones still moving to Petropolis. Racist sentiments were closely related to both level of education and length of residence in Petropolis. For example, the poorly educated newcomers were in favor of, or uncertain about, amending the Constitution to strip the Supreme Court of its power to pass on segregation by a 6:1 ratio—that is, "strongly approve," "approve," and "undecided," compared to the "disapprove" and "strongly disapprove." The comparable ratio for equally poorly educated old-timers—those who had lived in the community for more than 5 years—was 14:1. For the highly educated newcomers the proportion disapproving that policy was 59 per cent, while for the equally well-educated old-timers it was 30 per cent.

It was noted in an earlier chapter that the more racist of the highly educated White citizens of Petropolis were disproportionately in active-influential positions. The fact that the highly educated newcomers were much more accommodating in their race-relations perspectives suggests that if and when they rose in the political-influence structure, they might contribute to a lessening of the political competition that was rooted in some measure in racial divisions. The existence of such a category also suggested that there was a prospect of the Community Conservationist White political leaders developing greater strength than they had yet been able to achieve as an independent political group. Yet there was apparently little prospect of the more elderly, old-timer Orthodox Conservative group opening its ranks to any major degree to the younger, highly educated, more accommodating, business-executive and professional group of newcomers to Petropolis. Nor was there any way to predict whether a continued trend in the net immigration of highly educated accommodators would speed up any reorganization of the political leadership toward a more moderating, more consensual structure.

These notations on the migration patterns and trends of Negro and White citizens in both Metroville and Petropolis were offered here to indicate that in assessing the degree of political instability and the prospects of political change, no controlling reason could be found in these data to assess either political system as likely to be substantially different in the period after Time M from what it was during Time E to M. At the same time, the comments about the political implications of migration patterns suggest the need to obtain more valid and reliable information pertaining thereto for improving estimates of political stability and instability and making predictions about political change or stasis.

Oretown—Second World War to 1952 (Time E)

Oretown's political history during the 1920's, 1930's, and early 1940's was that of a relatively Developed Democracy, alternating periodically with an Oligarchic political condition; the power structure seemed to be Consensual Elite. These patterns related to Oretown's one-company-town character during those years and the periodically Populist and Liberal political character of a portion of its populace.

An alliance of merchants and managers from the dominant industrial firm constituted the membership of a single Orthodox Conservative political leadership with strong Jeffersonian Conservative leanings in that era. Periodically, a movement led by farmers on the outskirts of the community pushed for the creation of a publicly owned electric utility and for other net increases in the scope of local government. They invariably were defeated in their former demands and ordinarily were unsuccessful in the latter.

By the end of the Second World War other mining companies had moved into a rapidly growing Oretown. The merchants and their brand of Orthodox Conservatism, which included by then the decisional preference to annex industrial properties, had taken over City

Hall.[15]   A Consensual Elite power structure and a Developed Democracy existed until 1948.   After the election of a mayor and of several city councilmen who identified themselves as Liberals, the power structure became at Time E, and remained to Time M, Competitive Mass in type; the regime continued to be a Developed Democracy. As in Petropolis, leading Liberals were small businessmen, marginal proprietors, and dealers in land: investors, developers, and other real-estate entrepreneurs.   Their personal desire for political status, their enjoyment of the exercise of political influence, and their need for political power were reinforced by their recognition of the substantial economic benefits to be gained by retaining certain local-government policies and shifting others.   They organized a Liberal group, including labor-union officials, to compete with the Orthodox Conservatives.   This signified for the first time the development of an opposition group to the merchants and industrialists who had dominated the Consensual Elite power structure for years.

The major source of instability for the power structure in Time M to $M + 1$ was in a twofold possibility: the Liberal political group could be so severely defeated by an alliance of Conservationists and Conservatives that they would disintegrate or remain a permanently powerless minority group (like the Community Conservationists in Farmdale during Time E to M); and this coalition could be maintained, so that the power structure would become Consensual once again.   The Orthodox Conservatives had given evidence during the 1946–1948 period that they pursued certain policies which the Community Conservationists considered to be in the collective, public interest; this would have made such a change in the power structure more likely than it would be otherwise.   However, at Time M a permanent coalition still seemed a rather remote possibility.

To weaken or permanently destroy the Liberal group in the immediate future, their opponents would probably have had to do something about the fact that two of the city councilmen were committed, outspoken Liberals; they were not coming up for reelection for two years after Time M.   The political history of Oretown is that of a community in which minority groups, and sometimes majorities, frequently had used the devices of direct democracy to permit popular participation in the authoritative-consideration stage of political decision-making.   Although recall of these Liberal councilmen could be attempted, past attempts to recall officials had rarely been successful, although they had frequently been made.   There was little prospect of a change in Oretown's established regime from Developed Democracy to another type or of a change in Oretown's power structure from a Competitive to a Consensual type during Time M to $M + 1$.

If the Community Conservationists in collaboration with the Orthodox Conservatives could accomplish their priority goal of reducing the rate and conflicting character of political decision-making, while strengthening the administrative decision-making process, there was a prospect that the power structure might change, if not from Competitive to Consensual, at least from Mass to Elite. If the cooperative political decision-making process for a new hospital had marked a new period of collaboration and consensus, whether or not it eliminated the Liberal–anti-Liberal political-leadership competition, a trend might have been established toward less extensive political involvement on the part of the citizens as they developed greater political trust in the political leadership.

There are several reasons for regarding such a change in the type of power structure during the next time period as unlikely. It was inferred, on the basis of observations made during Time E to M, that the controversy between municipal and private electric power was not about to be resolved, resulting in a predicted high level of political participation and a relatively broad citizen sharing in political power, at least for this decisional process. The fact that Liberals were, and were likely to remain, on the city council, thereby giving them a public-spokesman position from which to interest and activate citizens to convert administrative into political decision-making processes, also mitigated against such a change from a Mass to an Elite type of power structure. Besides these evaluations, the postwar and the prewar political history of Oretown suggests that the pattern of periodic citizen participation in politics through the devices of direct democracy and in other ways was not about to be broken suddenly. A pattern of failures of mass citizen participation to accomplish goals of substantial or innovative shifts in the scope of local government meant that those with such decisional preferences had not attained a share in the analytically accorded units of political power. But the victors ordinarily had to and did marshal substantial mass support behind their preferences, so that the result was a relatively broad sharing in political power. The Community Conservationists may have put Oretown on the road to an Elite Power structure in a Developed Democracy setting, but the analysis of the political history of that community leads us to evaluate such a change as unlikely to occur in the immediate future, if ever.

Figure 11.2 is a summary classification of the types of power structures and regimes revealed by the historical analysis of the postwar periods through Time M. Periods beyond Time M ranging from 3

	1946–1947	1947–1948	1948–1949	1949–1950	1950–1951	1951–1952	1952–1953	1953–1954	1954–1955	1955–1956	1956–1957	1957–1958
					(E to M) *							
Farmdale, Western State												
Power Structures	-5 CpM	-4 CpM	-3 CpM	-2 CpM	-1 CsE	0 CsE						
Regimes	DD	DD	DD	DD	Gu	Gu						
							(E to M)					
Oretown, Western State												
Power Structures	-6 CsE	-5 CsE	-4 CpM	-3 CpM	-2 CpM	-1 CpM	0 CpM					
Regimes	DD	DD	DD	DD	DD	DD	DD					
												(E to M)
Petropolis, Southern State												
Power Structures	-11 CsE	-10 CpE	-9 CpE	-8 CpM	-7 CpM	-6 CpM	-5 CpM	-4 CpM	-3 CpM	-2 CpM	-1 CpM	0 CpM
Regimes	Un	DD	DD	DD	DD	DD	DD	DD	DD	DD	DD	DD
												(E to M)
Metroville, Southern State												
Power Structures	-11 CsE	-10 CsE	-9 CsE	-8 CsE	-7 CsE	-6 CsE	-5 CsE	-4 CsE	-3 CsE	-2 CsE	-1 CsE	0 CsE
Regimes	Olg	Olg	Gu	Gu	Gu	Gu	Gu	Un	Un	Un	Un	Un

* Time E to M refers to the time periods beginning with the municipal elections prior to the first set of sample surveys and ending with those surveys, which is approximately one year in every community (period 0) except in Farmdale, where it is two years (periods -1, 0).

Key:

Power Structures	Regimes
CpM = Competitive Mass	DD = Developed Democracy
CsE = Consensual Elite	Un = Underdeveloped Democracy
CpE = Competitive Elite	Gu = Guided Democracy
	Olg = Oligarchy

FIGURE 11.2 Power structures and regimes by time periods in the four communities.

years in the two Southern cities to 8 years in Oretown and 9 years in Farmdale are discussed in the next two chapters; these, along with Figure 11.2, will be used in the final chapter for the purpose of testing various hypotheses, including some about the relationship between power structures and regimes. That relationship constitutes, for our purposes, a partial description of a political system and is of central concern in the next section.

THREE MODELS OF POLITICAL SYSTEMS

We have constructed three models of political systems, since the power structures and regimes of Oretown and Petropolis were similar, and Farmdale and Metroville had similar power structures but dissimilar regimes (Figure 11.3).

These system models refer to the effects of particular combinations of power structures and regimes on the decision-making processes whereby policy formulations become political demands when deliberated—the demands may or may not be pushed into an organization-of-political-support stage, if they are not then in such a stage—decisional choices emerge, and outcomes are selected.

Citizen Activation and Leadership Roles

All four communities are at least partially "open systems," as we have had occasion to note earlier. This means that political stimuli may enter the community from outside, either from other communities or from a "higher" level of government and politics of which these community political systems may be regarded as subsystems. Such stimuli may enter the community in several ways: a message may be sent from an outsider to an insider; an outsider may move to the community and become an insider; or an insider may himself obtain

| | **Regimes** | | |
Power structures	Developed Democracy	Underdeveloped Democracy	Guided Democracy
Competitive Mass	Oretown Petropolis		
Consensual Elite　·		Metroville	Farmdale

FIGURE 11.3 *Power structures and regimes: Time E to M.*

information that is being circulated outside. The messages, however they enter the community, may be political in character or they may become political after they enter. Political stimuli may, of course, be substantially generated within the political community through an innovation made locally or at such a temporal distance from earlier stimuli from the outside that an analyst feels it is more useful to classify the political stimuli as local in origin.

In all four communities, political demands arose from both inside and outside sources. Individuals in each community's power structure formulated and then deliberated political demands with other individuals, creating the pressures that constituted the impulses to shift the scope of local government, whether successful or not by Time M. These people were probably not, in the majority of political decision-making processes in all four cities, members of the political leadership in either Manifest or Latent positions. The demands that were not repressed from fears of illegitimate sanctions, as some were in the Underdeveloped Democracy of Metroville, and those that were not repressed from feelings of political weakness at some point reached the men who became or remained the political leaders. In the two Consensual Elite power structures Manifest or Latent Leaders then disposed of the demands, ordinarily with little public notice. In Farmdale decisional outcomes were usually negative; that is, the minimal scope of local government was maintained and even internal shifts in the traditional patterns of local government's functioning were blocked. In Metroville some of the decisional outcomes were positive and some were negative, as already indicated; the one most public issue was the mental-hospital decision. White citizens followed the developments in this decision with great interest but with no knowledge of the major race-relations premise underlying the decisional outcome.

In the two Competitive Mass power structures, the demands that reached the political-leadership level from citizens in nonleadership positions were treated differently, apart from the outcomes themselves. First, a number of intracommunity political demands were picked up by members of one or another of the political groups aspiring to or already at the political-leadership level. In their roles as ideological spokesmen and the chiefs of staff for their political groups, members of the inner cliques or their associates would begin to organize mass, public support from the sectors of the citizenries that they thought might contribute to the pressures for or against particular shifts in the scope of local government. It was ordinarily at this point, and this was the second difference, that relatively extensive citizen participation would begin. Subsidiary political organizations served as settings for the mobilization or conversion of supporters or potential opponents. This seemed to be the general sequence of events during Time E to M, and in those cases of political decision-making in which organization and counterorganization of political support during Time E to M simply had carried over from a preceding time period, not only in Oretown and Petropolis, but also in Farmdale during its pre-Time E Competitive Mass power-structure periods.

The political systems of the communities with the Competitive Mass power structures thus differed in at least two ways from those with Consensual Elite structures, especially in the political roles of their respective leaderships as these related the leaderships to the political substructures. There was a tendency in Oretown and Petropolis for the authoritative-consideration stage in political decision-making to take place more frequently in an open, public setting and the decisions to be of a public-issue character. A closed, private setting with restricted decisional conflict was more characteristic of Farmdale and Metroville. This does not mean that government officials in their formally authoritative capacities and settings were never the political leaders in decision-making in Farmdale and Metroville, but that this was more frequently the case in Oretown and Petropolis. Nor does this mean that there was a smaller proportion of elected government officials in the political leaderships of the Consensual Elite than in those of the Competitive Mass power structures, since there was an extensive overlap in Farmdale. It does mean, however, that in Farmdale and in Metroville there was a greater tendency than in Oretown and Petropolis for outcomes already to have been selected by the time the formal authorities publicly engaged in authoritative consideration in their official forums, even though in Farmdale government officials were among the active participants in the *de facto* private authoritative-consideration settings; or, if not, there was less likelihood of political decisions' becoming public issues in the former than the latter power structures.

The political roles of the political leadership in the Competitive Mass power structures differed from those of the political leadership in the Consensual Elite power structures in two respects. In the former, as in the latter, the political leaders were the participants in authoritative consideration, but the political leaderships in the Consensual Elite structures did considerably less to stimulate the citizens to become involved in political decision-making than did those in the Competitive Mass structures. Secondly, the stages of political decision-making tended to be more highly developed and temporally distinct in the Competitive Mass power structures than in the Consensual Elite. This resulted in a difference in the pattern of roles of these two sets of political leaders. The political leaders in Petropolis and Oretown spent more of their time and energies in more distinctive deliberative and organization-of-political-support stages. They were trying to build the mass support that they felt was needed in the public authoritative-consideration settings to influence the officials of local government whose actions would result in decisional outcomes.

Of comparable importance in the Competitive Mass power structures was the need to develop political support in the political-influence substructures to threaten opponents with electoral defeat. In the Consensual Elite power structures, the impulse to bring political demands to the attention of the citizens as voters and as active supporters in decision-making was less pressing, since there was no competitive political group to the Jeffersonian Conservatives in the one community or to the Progressive Conservatives in the other. Therefore, in the Competitive Mass power structures, there was a continual need to activate or acquire adherents from among the citizens; and there was a need to control and guide the relatively few participating citizens in political decision-making in the Consensual Elite power structure.

These differences in political roles of those in the Competitive Mass and Consensual Elite power structures should not obscure a general pattern in the four communities: relatively few citizens initially made political demands. There was a relatively broad distribution of political power, at least in some political decisional processes, in the two mass power structures. The overall distribution of political power in the two elite power structures during Time E to M was relatively narrow. This did not result from a more widespread generation of policy formulations and demands by a politically conscious citizenry for shifts in the scope of local government in the former than in the latter. Rather it seems that in the Competitive Mass power structures there was, over time, a flow of demands from a few citizens in the substructure to members of an aspiring or actual political-leadership group. In turn, this group transmitted back to a larger proportion of the citizens these or reshaped demands which the citizens could take on as their own. On the other hand, a political leader might monitor the outer world or his local community, and borrow or innovate a political demand himself that he then transmitted to the citizens to assimilate as their own political demand. In either of these processes, competitive political groups would, if they opposed the demand, mobilize their own supporters or potential supporters in the citizenry in opposition to such demands.

In contrast, the political leaders who received political demands from other citizens or generated their own political demands in the Consensual Elite power structures less frequently sent activating political messages back to substantial proportions of the citizens for the sort of public support considered necessary in the Competitive Mass power structures. The classifications of these types of power structures indicate that in neither of the consensual power structures was there a competing political group to contribute, through opposition, to this politicizing function in the citizen substructure. The intragroup conflicts, noticeable particularly in Metroville, did not operate in the same way. The two-way flow of political demands was not absent in either Farmdale or Metroville, but it was much more restricted.

In Metroville, the organization of political support by municipal-government appointive officials and the counterorganization efforts of members of the Progressive Conservative Leadership in the school consolidation and recreational processes during Time E to M extended this two-way flow of political demands towards the pattern in the Competitive Mass power structures. In the mental-hospital issue White citizens entered the process as spectators but with some potential for becoming active contributors to the pressures that were developing for and against a new White facility. In Oretown, and to a lesser extent in Petropolis, during Time E to M, the Community Conservationists went out of their way to mediate conflicting demands so that they would not increase or reinforce existing levels of citizen political controversy. However, although these patterns of political decision-making were not completely different in the two types of power structures, there was sufficient dissimilarity to further distinguish the functioning of the Competitive Mass power structures from the Consensual Elite.

The political systems in Oretown and Petropolis, compared to those of Farmdale and Metroville, seemed to have no major impediments to the process in which demands of individuals, acting for themselves, friends and associates, or political interest groups, ordinarily became contested issues between opponents from ideologically hostile political camps. The regimes in the different political systems of Farmdale and Metroville constituted distinct major impediments to the development of such a process. In the Guided Democratic regime of Farmdale, demands were defeated before decisions became public issues, before the decisional preferences became widely held political interests, and before they could serve as the cement for any potentially competitive political-leadership groups. In that political system, potential political demands either remained prepolitical and private, took the form of diffuse political discontent, or became specific, administrative decision-making demands. Illegitimate sanctions when demands became actual demands for shifts in the programs and policies of local government were available to avert public issues.

In the political system of Metroville, the Underdeveloped Democracy, characterized by the fear of illegitimate sanctions, retarded political demands as well as the formation of an independent, competitive political-leadership group, a vital feature of the political systems of Petropolis and Oretown. Fear of the sorts of sanctions that were used in Farmdale helped to maintain the Consensual Elite power structure and mitigated against a Competitive Mass power structure in Metroville. However insufficient—that is, however important other factors may have been—an increase in the sense of electoral potency seemed to be a necessary condition for the development in Metroville of the type of political system found in both Petropolis and Oretown.

A Developmental Model

The model of the political systems of Oretown and Petropolis may be extended into a developmental model by examining the sequences by which Oretown's power structure became Competitive Mass during 1948 and 1949 and Petropolis' during 1949 and 1950. In Oretown, it seemed that the Consensual Elite power structure first became Competitive. A divergent political group of relatively small size aspired to positions of political leadership, and successfully contested a major decisional process. Then the power structure quickly became Mass as larger numbers of citizens were drawn into decision-making processes. In Petropolis, the Consensual Elite structure first became, and remained for a time, a Competitive Elite structure. After about two years, the structure became Mass in character as the system operated to extend political power among the citizens in the manner described above. This suggests that if Developed Democracy did become the regime in Farmdale, Metroville, or both after Time M, the political systems would not automatically become like that of Oretown and Petropolis: they would not necessarily have Competitive Mass power structures.

If the type of regime that functions as a major impediment to the development of the political system characterizing Oretown and Petropolis were changed appropriately, the rise of a competitive political group would be facilitated but not ensured, at least not immediately. The sufficient conditions for the development of such a system would seem to lie in such a problematic competitive situation. The existence of relatively widespread potential political interests, such as the Negro subcommunity's concern with economic conditions in Metroville or the concern with specific housekeeping-service improvements in Farmdale, would seem to constitute conditions that would facilitate the rise of a competitive Liberal group in the former and the return of a competitive Community Conservationist group in the latter. Such interests also would seem to constitute conditions for the relatively swift broadening of political power among the citizens, if such political group competition were established. But there is apparently no necessary direct relationship between Developed Democracy and a Competitive Mass power structure.

The nexus referred to above among extensive citizen participation, a Competitive Mass power structure, and Developed Democracy—these patterns characterized the political systems of Oretown and Petropolis during Time *E* to *M*—apparently develops in a sequence: from competition to extensive citizen participation to a mass distribution of power in a setting of Developed Democracy; but the nexus does not always, however, proceed to that point. In both communities during the postwar period, although there were no instances of political systems that had Competitive Mass power structures with other than Developed Democratic regimes, there were instances of political systems with Developed Democracy and other than Competitive Mass power structures. We shall return to this point in the next two chapters, where there is occasion to examine the developmental model again as the political systems of Farmdale and Metroville became after Time *M* like the system in Oretown and Petropolis as of Time *E* to *M*, and to examine a change in the political system in Oretown from one of Developed Democracy and a Competitive Mass power structure to one of Developed Democracy and a Consensual Elite structure.

To the extent that the foregoing models of political systems are valid, there is reason to believe that several of the theoretically possible political systems are empirically unlikely, if not impossible. Such systems are those in which regimes of any kind are associated with a Consensual Mass power structure. In other words, a Consensual Mass power structure would seem to be improbable. The reason for this is the presumed importance of ideological competition in marshalling citizen support in electoral and public decision-making. In the absence of such organized competition, there would seem to be little need for the development in a political system of processes for bringing about mass distributions of political power, even in the absence of regime impediments. Further consideration of the empirical absence in all four communities from the Second World War to Time M of this logical possibility is postponed until the final chapter, which encompasses periods after Time M, in order to determine first whether or not a Consensual Mass power structure, a preference of Community Conservationists in both Oretown and Petropolis, did develop.

A Limitation of the Models

One of the major limitations of these models of political systems should be noted at this point. They are restricted, specifically, to patterns of political rather than of administrative matters. Particularly in the political system of Metroville during Time E to M, which had a Consensual Elite power structure, the relatively well-developed administrative apparatus at City Hall had more extensive relationships to White and Negro citizens than the estimated distribution of political power among the citizens suggests. Demands for administrative shifts in the scope of local government also were in evidence in Farmdale during Time E to M. In the process of administrative decision-making in the three political systems during that time, the features of polyarchy so stressed by pluralists, such as bargaining, compromises, responsive "hearings," and the relatively great degree of satisfaction of demands by citizens and interest groups, were noticeable.

In matters of administrative decision-making, which, by definition, were matters not considered by participants to involve very important, value-laden, general shifts in the scope of government, members of political groups were more disposed to bargain and compromise with each other. In the systems with multiple groups, there was in administrative decision-making less a politics of ideological conflict than a politics of individual and group political interests. The processes wherein relatively large numbers of citizens were drawn into the fray by the competitive political-group leaders were processes in which the "important" political decisions were made rather than the "technical" administrative decisions.

In all three types of political systems, fringe members of political groups, so-called "professional politicians," and professional administrators all felt freer to cross those group lines and act expediently rather than on ideological principle in administrative decision-making.

But this does not eradicate the very great differences among those systems in regard to political decision-making. In the political system of Farmdale some Manifest Leaders were local government officials; there was a rigid control over the extent to which administrative decision-makers had freedom of action. In Metroville's political system, the control exercised by the Manifest Leaders over government officials, both through political influence of the Manifest Leaders on the government officials and through political status accorded by the latter to the former, constituted comparable controls over administrative decision-making. The fact that administrative demands frequently were limited by fear of pushing them into the political realm was a distinctive feature of that political system. The importance of local government positions to the contending political groups in the political systems of both Oretown and Petropolis attested the distinctive character of that system. They sought to control appointive positions through their elected officials, a matter of public politics.

Pluralist and Power-Elite Theses Reassessed

It is these differences in political systems, and in the relationships between the administrative and political realms, that indicate a need to revise the pluralist concept of polyarchy in, and the power-elite view of, American community politics. The political systems of both Farmdale and Metroville during Time E to M attested the existence of at least two exceptions to the presumed pluralist norm of fully free politics. The exception in the small town of Western State was not a matter of fear of dissent in a conformist atmosphere, but rather of dissent stilled by the functional equivalent of force—that is, illegitimate economic and social sanctions. Whether or not that system would yet develop a regime of Underdeveloped Democracy or even Oligarchy to support a Consensual Elite power structure, or whether or not Farmdale would redevelop a political system like that of Oretown and Petropolis as of Time E to M, will be discussed, but are irrelevant to this point, which refers to the period at hand.

In Metroville, the pluralist image of the rejection by political leaders of the legitimacy of force or its equivalents is largely valid. But a point made more frequently by the power-elite school is also valid: fears of such sanctions were relatively widespread. However, such fears did not, as that school has maintained, result from an accurate understanding of the lengths to which a "power elite" would go to maintain their positions and policies.

The existence of the secret ballot and civil liberties protected from local-government infringement by an independent judiciary did not guarantee, as some pluralists would maintain, political systems with regimes of Developed Democracy. Nor did "democratic elections" *per se* result in either mass citizen political participation or relatively widespread distributions of political power. It was not the development of a competitive two-party system, a feature stressed by pluralists, that resulted in the competitive politics associated with relatively extensive citizen participation.[16] In the *de facto* one-party community of Petropolis, two wings or factions of the one party constituted an important battleground; but the primary policy deliberation and internal authoritative-consideration centers of leading political-group protagonists were outside of party settings. In Oretown, although the two parties were involved in the major political competition in this formally nonpartisan city, the major battle lines were drawn outside the party organizations.[17]

Electoral victories were important in both Oretown and Petropolis. However, elected officials acted not as independent individuals, compromising with anyone and everyone to maximize their chances of re-election, but as members of one or another relatively cohesive group, trying to stay in office with a sufficiently large number of like-minded officeholders to advance the political goals of their group. It was the chief administrative officers, the city managers, in those polities who tried to avoid group commitments and policy positions that would endanger their tenure.[18]

A pluralist conception of polyarchy needs substantial revision and elaboration, even for those community political systems closest to the image of competitive, multigroup politics. Similarly, a power elite version that considers, in our terms, a Consensual Elite power structure to be associated with something other than a Developed Democratic regime as the pattern in American community politics also needs revision. Not only do the political systems of Oretown and Petropolis reveal the importance of elections and public office in political decision-making, but these systems also require the rejection of the power-elite thesis that at the top of all such power structures are small sets of men of top socio-economic power who pursue substantially *status quo* political policies. To be sure, the prominent Manifest Leaders in all four political systems were, as categories, people of affluence and high social standing. But in Oretown and Petropolis less privileged and even underprivileged groups were represented personally in the Manifest and Latent portions of the political leadership. Even in Farmdale the citizens at large were well represented among the active influential portion of the political influence structure. Metroville was the closest to the power-elite image of integrated, overlapping political and socio-economic superstructures.

A final word is in order upon a theme stressed both by pluralists and power elitists. A polyarchal system is valued by pluralists partly because many people presumably have memberships in numerous interest groups, thereby weakening their potential militancy or extremism and producing consensus-building group "disloyalties"; another reason is that groups log-roll and otherwise accommodate themselves to each other, thereby producing pluralistic tolerance. Thus, political interest groups tend to make moderate demands; elected officials comply, to some extent, with the demands that are most important to those making them. The sort of system that assertedly results is a happy blend of self-restraint and a scope of government that shifts responsively to community needs and problems. Analysts who see a power elite rather than polyarchy as the American norm bemoan those "elite systems" for these reasons: they are more monolithic, less responsive to demands of disadvantaged groups, and have more fixed scopes of government dedicated to preserving the socioeconomic *status quo* than less elite, more "representative" systems. To some extent, the expectations of both schools of thought are at variance with our findings.

During Time E to M there was some evidence that in the Developed Democracy and Competitive Mass systems of Oretown and Petropolis, some, though not all, demands were moderated—there was very restricted overlapping, multiple interest-group memberships, some key uncommitted people, and some log-rolling—and there was compliance to some demands by elected officials—ordinarily when they themselves made or supported demands or were outvoted by others. But in both pluralistic power structures sharp political conflict, decisional checkmates, and frustrating failures to shift the scope of local government occurred. On the other hand, significant shifts in the scope of local government did occur in "power-elite" Metroville during Time E to M.

In the more Competitive Mass Developed Democracy of Petropolis, Negro citizens were unable to obtain even token desegregation, although they were relatively well organized and politically militant. In the similar political system of Oretown, the extraordinary conflict between the municipal and private utilities remained unresolved. As is apparent in observations of totalitarian nation-states, if the needs, interests, and ideologies of the rulers dictate large-scale shifts in the scope of government, such shifts may occur more expeditiously than in competitive democracies. Farmdale's rulers adhered to a *status quo* ideology; but the Progressive Conservative ideology of Metroville's political leadership resulted in some major shifts in the scope of local government that would be unexpected on the part of a more *status quo* Orthodox Conservatism, such as that of some of the industrialists-financiers of Petropolis. Public controversy was minimal; certain segments of the citizens were ignored, or their needs were taken into account only insofar as they happened to resemble those of the ruling group; but the latter's identification of their own needs with those of the community at large resulted in some large shifts in the scope of Metroville's government. This was one of the unexpected but by now understandable characteristics of that political system during Time E to M.

Before leaving this comparative analysis of these political systems as of Time M, we will present data that bear on one more dimension of political systems: information levels. These data derive from survey responses of citizens and Manifest Leaders in the two subcommunities of both Southern cities concerning who were the most influential men in local government policy-making and (for all but Petropolis' Negro citizens and Leaders) which group, generally, was the most important in the making of decisions in the community. The latter alternatives were: the mayor and council, the voters, the businessmen, the out-of-town companies, the leading civic organizations, the banks and insurance companies, the county commissioners, the labor leaders, the Negro Leaders, and, in Metroville only, the largest firms.

A comparative analysis of the newspaper coverage of local politics in both cities revealed a comparable degree of information in Petropolis and Metroville, with two exceptions noted below, even though in the former there were more newspapers representing diverse political viewpoints than in the latter. What our findings illuminate is how the two types of political systems produce, and in turn seem to be reinforced by, different degrees of citizen political information or ignorance. The latter, as used here, refers to a condition in the body politic wherein citizens are misinformed about important aspects of their politics, of their power structures and regimes, apart from the specific matter of expectations of illegitimate sanctions. Such misinformation was due here primarily to certain political structural conditions. By "due to political structural conditions" we simply mean resulting from the way the political system functions, especially in regard to the patterns identified above as major analytic components of the system models.

One striking gap or distortion in the political information of both

White and Negro citizens in Metroville was their failure to apprehend the influence position of William Polk, an inner clique Progressive Conservative Leader. No Negro citizen in the sample, and very few White citizens, mentioned him as among the most influential men in local government policy-making. The mayor was named most frequently by both White and Negro citizens. One-third of the Negro Leaders named Mr. Polk in this connection, more than the number naming Negro Councilman Vida or Mr. Williston Russell, III, and only slightly fewer than those naming the mayor and city manager. Almost three-fourths of the White Leaders named Mr. Polk, more than named anyone else, as among the most influential men in local politics.

In Petropolis, the citizens, Negro and White, also named their mayor more frequently than anyone else as among the most influential, but in this their judgment corresponded to both the Negro and White Leaderships'.

This finding indicates that the citizens in both cities had similar perceptions of an overlapping formal and informal authority structure, but that in the one case they were right and in the other they were wrong. In Metroville, the polity where they were wrong, the political leadership, particularly the White portion thereof, was not misinformed.

On the other item, the analytic assessment is that the alternatives "the mayor and council" and "the voters" were relatively more accurate responses in Petropolis, while "the businessmen" and "the largest firms" were relatively more accurate responses in Metroville as valid pictures of the composition of the political leaderships. Such an assessment corresponds to the judgments of the respective White Leaderships. In Petropolis, 68 per cent of the White Manifest Leaders picked the mayor and council or the voters as the most important in the making of decisions while one-fifth selected the businessmen or out-of-town companies. Exactly 68 per cent of the White Manifest Leaders of Metroville selected the businessmen and the largest firms, while only 16 per cent picked the mayor and council or the voters, an almost perfect reversal of the Petropolis pattern. Once again, the White citizens of both cities resembled each other in perceiving the mayor and council or voters as the most important decision-makers, which meant that the picture of the power structure in the minds of the Metroville citizenry, including Negro citizens, were at sharp variance with the view of the White Leadership there.[19]

The Negro Leaders of Metroville were midway between the White and Negro citizens on the one hand and the White Leadership on the other in their conceptions of who were the most important decision-makers in the polity. While one-third of these Negro Leaders did pick the largest firms or businessmen, more than half of them picked the mayor and council or voters.

The aforementioned differences in cognitions hold even when citizens' level of education is held constant. Although in Metroville the highly educated were slightly more disposed to select the largest firms or businessmen as most important decision-makers than were the less educated, they resembled the latter much more than they resembled the White Leadership in these images.

Whether or not the reasons for this involve wishful thinking and/or fear of making closer inquiry into the matter,[20] the Negro Leaders shared with the citizens of both subcommunities, although to a somewhat lesser extent, a picture of their polity that was at substantial variance to that held by those who were in fact the powerful leaders.

To what extent such differences were due to differences in the degree to which the mass media organs in the two cities intended to misinform is difficult to estimate accurately. Our tentative assessment is that the Metroville mass media men did not differ very much from their Petropolis counterparts in regard to the intention to deceive their citizenries, or to relate less than the whole truth about political decision-making as they understood it. Although the media in Metroville did not report adequately on the political roles of such men "behind the scenes" as William Polk, nor on the private settings in which authoritative consideration of political decisions took place (the two exceptions referred to above), the differential degree of citizen and minority group misinformation was fundamentally a function of the different kinds of political systems in the two cities.

The images of citizens in Petropolis who conceived of the mayor and council and/or the voters as the most important decision-makers in that city were automatically validated by the character of that political system, as in Oretown. The mayor and council there were important figures in political decision-making; authoritative consideration as well as other stages of decision-making occurred frequently in accessible public settings, and there was sharp electoral competition among opposing political groups. In Metroville's political system, on the other hand, another set of forces were at work. There was relatively little reason for political leaders to become public figures as candidates themselves, or as active campaign managers or influential backers of candidates, in the noncompetitive situation. When that occurred in such situations as Farmdale's, with a Consensual Elite power structure and a Guided Democracy regime, there was little impetus to making public, or having it made public, that certain private settings constituted the loci of authoritative-consideration stages. In Farmdale, as in Petropolis and Oretown, the citizens' views of the mayor and council or voters as most important in decision-making were also automatically validated by the overlapping of the formal and informal authorities in the political leadership of the power structure, but the view of such settings as city council meetings as the most important loci of decision-making is not as valid a conception in the former or in Metroville as in the latter two communities.

By "little reason for" and "little impetus to" making things known to citizens, we simply mean that as the normal course of political decision-making varies by political system, the information obtained by citizens from first-hand experience, indirectly via an informal word-of-mouth grapevine, or from newspapers will ordinarily vary as a natural, automatic consequence of the different decision-making patterns. Where citizen participation in decision-making is widespread, citizens are more likely to obtain information personally or from participant acquaintances than are citizens in systems with little participation. When reading newspapers in political systems like Petropolis, the citizen is more likely to obtain valid information than he is when reading papers in Metroville, because equally conscientious coverage of governmental personnel and settings is likely to reveal actual patterns of political leadership in one system but not in the other. To obtain equally valid information in the other setting, coverage not only would have to be "overconscientious" or "abnormal," in the sense of observing nongovernment people in private settings as well as officials in public settings, but also would be abnormally difficult. It is one thing to get information from closed meetings of government officials; it may be much more difficult to obtain access to political meetings of informal authorities. To obtain equally valid information in such different political systems as those of Metroville and Farmdale on the one hand and Petropolis and Oretown on the other, the resources that need to be invested may differ significantly; the political structural conditions make it "easier" in the former than in the latter.

One might ask whether the citizens in Petropolis "really" knew that their mayor and council or that the voters were relatively more important than they were, for example, in Metroville. Are not their responses simply the expression of what Americans in every community are taught to believe, just as in Metroville one meets with the same kind of image of the centrality of electors and the elected for the same reason? Our only response to that is to present an analogy. Few of us have personally observed that the world is round or that micro-organisms cause diseases. When we act on the basis of that knowledge, however, various useful consequences follow. Moreover, these are facts that we have come to expect have been verified by various scientific observers whose separate methods lead to corroborating findings. When citizens personally participated in the mass politics of Petropolis and Oretown, they were simultaneously testing their perceptions of political reality for themselves and creating that reality for other citizens as well. To the extent that citizens were nonparticipants in the elite power structures of Metroville and Farmdale, they were contributing to the myths in which they believed.

One might prefer to view the conceptions of the locus of decision-making power in Metroville as indicative of a state or condition of political manipulation, rather than of political ignorance or misinformation. To the extent that the informal authorities of Metroville purposefully concealed or purposefully failed to pronounce their identities, and to the extent that they and the formal authorities in Farmdale purposefully maintained privacy in their authoritative consideration of community decisions settings or purposefully failed to proclaim to the citizenry that such settings were in use, one might prefer to assess the resulting condition as manipulation. Although silence may be as effective a way to manipulate consciously as speaking untruths, to use the term for the political leadership in one type of system and not for that in another implies a significant difference in character or style that we do not think exists.

We would submit that those responsible for the misinformation in the two communities could not be expected to pronounce or proclaim in that fashion and that they were no less honorable and no more devious than their political leader counterparts in the other two cities. We would say, instead, that one of the consequences of the workings, and one of the contributions to the maintenance, of these different kinds of political systems is a different degree of political information in the respective bodies politic, quite apart from the manners, mores, and morals of the particular people in the political leaderships. In politics, as in economics, a person may have to shoulder a very great and sometimes superhuman or impossible burden to reach a goal that a person in another system may be able to reach with a minimum of effort, even assuming that the two people are similar in character and perseverance. To expect the political leaders in systems like Metroville's and Farmdale's to have informed their citizens to the extent that citizens were informed in systems like Petropolis' and

Oretown's would be expecting the former to conform to a standard of behavior far different than that actually adhered to by the latter, or by almost any set of political leaders in the most Competitive Mass–Developed Democracy systems.[21] While personal character had little to do with such consequences of systems as citizen information levels, particular people, or even a particular person, can make a marked impact on the character of the political system itself and on the course of development from one type of system to another within a community over time. Our interest in further understanding of the dynamics of the foregoing models of these political systems, as well as of their instability and changeability, led us to continue our observations of people in politics in the four communities in the succeeding time periods, the subject of the next two chapters.

NOTES

1. It should be remembered that assessing citizens as having a high sense of electoral potency does not mean that they have to feel confident that they can win or attain their decisional objectives but simply that they do not expect illegitimate sanctions to be used against them if they participate politically.
2. Clearly, if such "terror" had not been momentary, or if it had had politically depressing impacts on others, or both, the regime might have been classified as an Oligarchy rather than as a Guided Democracy.
3. It should be clear from the foregoing analysis of individual reactions to the use of illegitimate sanctions in Farmdale that individual personality plays an important part in the effect that sanctions have on the political behavior and orientations of those to whom they are addressed. The evaluation of such sanctions and the extent to which they lower an existing high sense of electoral potency is a complicated process which may profit from joint research inquiries by psychologists and political analysts. The subsidiary-political-organization milieu may have had something to do with both the ineffectiveness of illegitimate social sanctions and the disposition of potential sanctioners to apply heavier illegitimate sanctions or to use more legitimate measures such as cooptation. The reactions of particular individuals who are sanctioned may or may not be solely or even primarily a matter of deep-rooted personality attributes such as ego-strength or fear of social avoidance. They may be due to a socio-psychological complex of factors, such as the psychological recognition of socially and economically real alternative resources that can be substituted for the threatened or actual deprivations.
4. Although there were more citizens in Farmdale than in the other communities who knew who the most important decision-makers were, approximately one-third of the respondents in the random sample were unable to name any individual, group, or position.
5. Floyd Hunter indicated that in Regional City in 1950–1951 open acts of violence were more condemned than in earlier years. In Metroville some

7 years later, the kinds of Klan activities he describes, and the participation of city employees in that organization, were not possible and would have been met by swift, legal reprisals should they have been attempted. See Hunter, *Community Power Structure* (Chapel Hill: University of North Carolina Press, 1953), pp. 146–147.

6. Such an organization might well have evidenced a relatively high sense of electoral potency, given the dynamic character of their political movement, and been oblivious to illegitimate sanctions that would be effective with members of less cohesive political organizations.

7. Floyd Hunter describes the case of a social worker's being fired, apparently for involving his organization in "partisan politics," *op. cit.*, pp. 190–193. He not only was apparently a Progressive party supporter but also allowed that party to use space in his association's building. The point here is that this might not have happened if the particular party had not been involved in the particular election. No such events occurred during 1957–1958 in Metroville. For other instances of Hunter's references to illegitimate sanctions, see *ibid.*, pp. 112, 144–147, and 176–179.

8. It is conceivable, and some have so argued, that a perfectly permeable power structure could sooner or later convert a Developed or Underdeveloped Democracy into an Oligarchy. This is basically the argument of those "democrats" who would withhold or withdraw civil liberties from Communists.

9. Every White citizen ought to read the testimony of James Baldwin on this point. See *The Fire Next Time* (New York: The Dial Press, 1963).

10. The situation in Farmdale as of 1950–1952 resembled that of small towns as described by Robert C. Wood, *Suburbia: Its People and Their Politics* (Boston: Houghton Mifflin Co., 1959), pp. 266–289.

11. See S. E. Asch, "Effects of Group Pressure upon the Modification and Distortion of Judgments," in *Group Dynamics: Research and Theory*, ed. by Dorwin Cartwright and Alvin Zander (Evanston, Illinois: Row, Peterson and Company, 1953), pp. 151–162.

12. In a discussion of the replacement by a New Leadership of an Old in the Negro subcommunity of Tallahassee, Florida, Lewis M. Killian and Charles U. Smith point out that three of the six Old Leaders had jobs in the state-supported school system, but none of the New Leaders did. Among the five New Leaders were three ministers. See their "Negro Protest Leaders in a Southern Community," *Social Forces*, Vol. 38, No. 3 (March 1960), pp. 253–257. Vernon J. Parenton and Roland J. Pellegrin comment that a White pastor who had moved into a Negro community in Louisiana not only initiated unheard-of social-welfare programs but also, apparently as a militant Liberal, helped to organize a labor union among sugar-cane workers. See their "Social Structure and the Leadership Factor in a Negro Community in South Louisiana," *Phylon*, Vol. XVII (First Quarter, 1956), pp. 74–78. That militancy on the part of Negro ministers is not an automatic consequence of their relatively secure position, and that this matter of fears of illegitimate sanctions needs to be more fully investigated, is suggested by Floyd Hunter's reports of the perceptions by other Negro Leaders of Negro ministers in Regional City's subcommunity, *op. cit.*, pp. 117–118. See also Ruth Searles and J. Allen Williams, Jr., "Negro College Students' Participa-

tion In Sit-Ins," *Social Forces*, Vol. 40, No. 3 (March 1962), pp. 215–220; and *New York Times* (Western Edition), Jan. 19, 1963, p. 4.

13. Floyd Hunter reports a comparable intragroup split in Regional City's White Manifest Leadership group on the matter of public housing. *Op. cit.*, pp. 224–225. For a split between Regional City's city and county leadership, see Hunter's discussion of the "Plan of Development," a plan to permit the city to annex fringe areas, *ibid.*, pp. 216–219.

14. Whether this analytic assessment was wrongly made, or whether related, unexpectedly swift changes took place in the next period of time, the reader may judge for himself from the discussion of the next period, Time M to $M + 1$, Chapter 12.

15. Oretown's historical economic development was not unlike that of Cibola, as described by Robert O. Schulze. See his "The Bifurcation of Power in a Satellite City," in *Community Political Systems*, ed. by Morris Janowitz (New York: The Free Press of Glencoe, 1961), pp. 19–81.

16. Edwin Hoffman Rhyne, on the basis of a study of county politics in a southern state, questions the assumption of a coalescing type of relationship between the local political power system on the one hand, and the party and governmental systems on the other, particularly as it rests on the presumed consequences of two-party competition or definition of democracy as, among other things, a political system with two competitive parties. See his "Political Parties and Decision Making in Three Southern Counties," *American Political Science Review*, Vol. LII, No. 4 (December 1958), pp. 1091–1107. Allan P. Sindler, in a discussion of Louisiana's state politics, points to the political functions served by a factional system with one party and the lack of systematic investigation of various kinds of two-party politics. See his "Bifactional Rivalry as an Alternative to Two-Party Competition in Louisiana," *American Political Science Review*, Vol. XLIX, No. 3 (September 1955), pp. 641–662. For summaries of studies that bear on possible bases of competition in community politics other than two political parties, see Robert E. Lane, *Political Life* (Glencoe, Illinois: The Free Press, 1959), Chapters 18 and 20. For a description of competitive groups based on other than local political party competition in a variety of Florida cities, see Gladys M. Kammerer and others, *City Managers in Politics* (University of Florida Monographs, *Social Sciences*, No. 13, Winter 1962).

17. That competitive local parties can serve as the centers of, or settings associated with, competitive political-leadership groups is clear from such studies as William J. Gore and Robert L. Peabody, "The Functions of the Political Campaign: A Case Study," *Western Political Quarterly*, Vol. XI (March 1958), pp. 55–70. In Farmdale there was virtually no local Democratic party, and the local Republican party, while better organized and a subsidiary political organization for the Orthodox Conservatives, was not often used as a setting for community politics. In Oretown the local parties were somewhat more organized and involved in the legally nonpartisan elections than in Farmdale, although less well organized and less distinctive in municipal politics than the two "local mass caucuses" described by J. Leiper Freeman in Bay City. See his "Local Party Systems: Theoretical Considerations and a Case Analysis," *The American Journal of Sociology*, Vol. LXIV, No. 3 (November 1958), pp. 282–289. Although the Orthodox Conservatives tended to be associated with the Republican party, the local political-leadership

groups were generally multiparty in their community operations. Petropolis, although also legally nonpartisan, had a striking factional division in the local Democratic party which was closely related to the competition between the political-leadership groups in the community's politics. Struggle for control of the local Democratic party was a central controversy in the municipal politics of Time E to M. The intraparty fights resembled Stackton's two-party system, as described by Peter H. Rossi and Phillips Cutright, "The Impact of Party Organization in an Industrial Setting," in *Community Political Systems*, pp. 81–116.

18. E. E. Schattschneider, an analyst of political parties and an intellectual predecessor of the community-politics "pluralists," does not see the major parties at the national level as sharing a single set of decisional preferences but as bidding for the electoral support of a variety of interests in pursuit of electoral victory where "the process ends with a narrow margin of difference." See his *Party Government* (New York: Rinehart and Company, 1942), p. 92. During Time E to M the competition that was found in Oretown and Petropolis was between and among ideologists who differed in emphasis rather than on the principle of value allocations in the community. Such differences are "minor" compared to, for example, differences between the competing groups and the Radical Left. However, our emphasis is upon what appeared to be major differences in the eyes of political leaders concerning their own and other political perspectives in the two sets of communities. Our estimate of "major differences" rather than of "narrow margin of difference" accords with Robert H. Salisbury's criterion of groups tending to "view the other as an unholy conspiracy aimed at destroying its opponents." *Western Political Quarterly*, Vol. XIII (June 1960), pp. 498–507. The important point is that relatively sharp competition was found in two of our cities in the period of interest even though electoral success was important to the competitors where, presumably, bidding for electoral support minimizes ideological and decisional differences.

19. The one major difference between the White and Negro citizens of Metroville was in the greater inability of Negro respondents to answer the question at all. More than 25 per cent of the latter said that they did not know, compared to about 13 per cent of the former.

20. A hint of the extent to which American citizens generally may feel constrained to act politically for fear of being sanctioned is contained in Gabriel A. Almond and Sidney Verba, *The Civic Culture: Political Attitudes and Democracy in Five Nations* (Princeton: Princeton University Press, 1963), Tables 9, 10, and 12, pp. 120, 122. Although they used a somewhat ambiguous question, and limited it to discussion of politics, it is sobering to note that they found that even in the United States more than one-quarter of the highly educated and half the poorly educated considered themselves less than perfectly free to discuss politics. What the proportion is among racial, occupational, and ideological minorities can only be imagined—well-known, individual acts of political courage notwithstanding. Investigation of such important regime dimensions as fears of illegitimate sanctions tends to be slighted in relatively developed national democracies on the assumption that most citizens are either psychologically secure, healthy, and free of political fears of a neurotic or realistic character or have a relatively constant and politically insignificant level of such anxieties. Comparative community

studies within nation-states as well as comparative cross-national studies of diverse political systems are in order to examine the usefulness and validity of such assumptions.

21. As we shall see, consensual power structures are possible in settings of Developed Democracy, with, presumably, such misinformation conditions. Without building such dimensions as citizen information levels into regime typologies, an option indicated in Chapter 1, *supra,* it is natural for some to criticize democracies with such conditions while others may counter by stressing different dimensions of democracy that may be in a "better" state. It is also understandable that different values placed on the importance of such dimensions, particularly by proponents of different types of political systems, may lead to quite different evaluations of a particular system. Different views about the nature of man and the polity may lead some to charge manipulation because they feel that political leaders have the duty to be "better" than is the norm or than is thought possible in some types of systems. Others may insist that such charges signify naïvety or deceitfulness on the part of people who are themselves manipulated or manipulators in Guided Democracies or Oligarchies. Decisions about human moral capabilities in political systems that differ in degree if not in kind are as difficult to make as is the choice of terms for such dimensions as "information levels" that may vary in connotation by the level and kind of political moral standards held.

12

NATURAL EXPERIMENTS: *Time M to M + 1*

Our analysis of the political systems of the four communities has led to their classification in two basic typologies: power structures and regimes. These may be considered *post facto* hypotheses about the political relationships of citizens during a time period immediately prior to the investigators' establishment of a field research staff to observe ongoing processes in these "laboratory" communities. In the ensuing time period, however, during and after the intensive measurement and observation of community politics took place, an opportunity was available to test the validity of our classifications—that is, test these hypotheses as to the nature of the four political systems.

The test was carried out in the following manner. During the two years following the first set of measurements which were made through the sample surveys and interviews, designated earlier as Time M to $M + 1$, three decisional processes were selected for analysis in each community. These three were chosen on the basis of their being the most likely to change power-structure and regime aspects of each political system and the scope of local government, considering their potential impact on a wide sector of the population. For each of these decisional processes, an outcome was predicted. The predictions were based on our assessments at Time M for the period Time E to M of the character of each power structure and regime. If our predictions about the outcome of the decisional processes were correct, the classifications or the hypotheses about the nature of the political systems—on the basis of this test—would not need modification. If the predictions proved to be wrong, then the classification of the power structure, of the regime, or of both would have to be amended, that is, the classificatory "hypotheses" would have had to be rejected; otherwise, changes since Time M in some or all of the variables determining type of power structure and regime must have produced the unexpected results. This provides an occasion to evaluate the predictions of change or stasis made in the previous chapter, which will increase our understanding of political-system dynamics. Although Time M to $M + 1$ in the four communities is divided into two periods ($+1$ and $+2$, Figure 13.1) of 1 year each for the classificatory and hypothesis-testing purposes of the final chapter, the 2-year periods are treated herein as the period of "natural experiments."

By concentrating on decisional processes occurring within a relatively short period immediately following Time E to M, we were able to control, in effect, a number of important variables. This permitted this testing of hypotheses about the dynamic interrelationships of the political variables. That is, the major defining characteristics of the social structure and ecology of the communities did not change detectably during these 2-year periods, nor did the government institutions. Thus, the observer is "free" to concentrate on the interrelationships of the political-system variables in which he is most interested; this is sometimes more easily accomplished with natural experiments or current case studies than with historical studies that encompass longer periods of time in the past.

FARMDALE: TIME M TO M + 1

Outline of Decisional Processes in Farmdale during Natural-Experiment Period

First Decisional Process—Increase-sales campaign
  Policy Demanded—A privately organized retail sales campaign specifically to divert the demands of some businessmen for local-government action to halt the deterioration of the local economy
  Category of Decisional Process—Economic reorganization
  Predicted Outcome—Demand will be carried out in such a way that it will preclude governmental involvement in economic amelioration of the community
Second Decisional Process—A new streetlight system
  Policy Demanded—A new streetlight system to encourage evening shopping and to discourage the drift of local trade to neighboring communities

Category of Decisional Process—Civic improvement; economic re-
organization
Predicted Outcome—Demand will be defeated
Third Decisional Process—A new zoning code
Policy Demanded—A new code to guide orderly development of the
city and to discourage marginal developments
Category of Decisional Process—Civic improvement; economic re-
organization
Predicted Outcome—Demand will be realized

Although the Jeffersonian Conservative leaders had successfully
countered the threat to the *status quo* inherent in the chamber-of-
commerce movement, they still sensed that a certain anxiety in the
business community about economic conditions required more positive action on their part. Thus, they began quietly to "talk up" a
campaign to increase sales in Farmdale to see if the merchants were
attracted to the idea. Before long, the campaign had taken concrete
form. The leaders delegated most of the day-to-day activities of a
new "increase-sales" organization to merchants in such a way that
the whole idea appeared to have developed spontaneously. So carefully had it been planned, however, that the most scarcity-minded
of the small businessmen had been given roles that ensured them a
small profit through participation. Efforts were even made to coopt
Mr. King, the dissident newspaper publisher, by indicating to him
the amount of special advertising that would be placed in his paper
as part of the campaign. But the efforts to attain unanimous support
were not completely successful; the troublesome newsman used the
campaign as an illustration of the need for a permanent organization
to engage in systematic efforts in behalf of business stimulation. Not
only did he suffer the loss of the prospective new advertising, as the
new sales organization gave its advertising brochure to a printer in
a nearby city, but he also found himself losing regular advertising.

After some hesitation about the application of such severe economic
sanctions—the Jeffersonian Conservatives assumed that the loss of
advertising might bankrupt Mr. King unless he gave in quickly—
merchants discontinued their advertising in his paper. Although he
depended on such advertising revenues to stay in the black, Mr. King
surprised the sanctioners. Instead of becoming "properly respectful"
of the policy preferences of the "sound" citizens of the city, he began
to go outside the city for advertising. He retaliated where it hurt
his fellow merchants the most. At the same time that major efforts
were underway to increase trade in Farmdale, the local newspaper was

carrying advertisements that told Farmdalians about bargains in the stores of neighboring cities. Although Mr. King's sense of electoral potency was not diminished, he was forced to discontinue his attempts to influence local policy; he spent every spare minute on the road trying to replace the lost revenues. Thus he was successfully deactivated, as his younger friends had been. The regime remained a Guided Democracy for approximately a 3-month period after Time M.

If the increase-sales campaign succeeded in enlisting the interest and participation of most of the local businessmen, whatever contentment they may have felt that some action was being taken to stimulate the local economy appeared to have faded with the end of the campaign. Within a very short time, there were unmistakable signs that the Main Street community was percolating with worry over business conditions. Although most of those who were worried had no ideas about the appropriate public or private action, a few of the formerly active Community Conservationists joined some Jeffersonian and more Orthodox Conservative merchants in demanding governmental action to stimulate commerce by establishing a modern streetlight system. This was designed to facilitate and encourage evening shopping; some merchants thought this should be the first step in the development of a more positive relationship between the local government and the business community in pursuit of improvement of the local economy. Although they agreed with the ideology of the Jeffersonian Conservatives in some respects, these particular merchants held a markedly different view about the role of local government in the local economy. The Jeffersonian Conservatives would not condone even indirect public pump-priming or other governmental activities to expand the total amount of wealth in the community; but the streetlight proponents believed that one of the proper functions of local government was to help to create conditions that would maintain or improve the private economic base of the community.

After the proponents of street lighting had organized a petition to the City Council embodying their demand, the ensuing decisional process took an unusual course, compared to the processes occurring during the prior period. It was unusual for a group of people to dispute a policy of the Jeffersonian Conservative leaders. Since the dissolution of the Community Conservationists as an organized political group, dissident businessmen had acted as individuals. It was also unusual for such a group's spokesman to be a prominent, well-respected member of the community. The spokesman for the streetlight proponents belonged to the leading civic club, and had a long history of participation in civic activities. He was thus a difficult person to oppose with illegitimate sanctions.[1] Moreover, since sanctions had been directed against the publisher and others during the past months, further activity of this sort might have become too visible, too repressive; it might have created a wave of antagonism against the sanctioners. As a result of such reflection by members of the political leadership, sanctions were not used to block this demand.

Aside from his unassailable social position, the spokesman also commanded a resource that had been scarce among those dissenting from the policies of the Jeffersonian Conservatives during Time E to M. He had copious information about the policy he was proposing: its cost, methods of financing, and the legally required relationship between public and private funds. He had met with the representative of the electric utility prior to the presentation of the petition in order to acquire and organize this information. Thus, he was able to press his demand before the city officials and interested citizens in cogent fashion, step-by-step. His opponents were unable to impede him by calling for "further study" on every point or by pointing to aspects of the proposal that were incongruent with legal requirements. Through this preparation, he managed to keep the proposal before the public, that is, he prevented it from being easily tabled or transferred to a committee for consideration "at some future date," and encouraged its continuous consideration before the whole city council at regular meetings where it was likely to receive maximum publicity.

The political skill of this man was indicated by the moderate approach he took to the problem. He did not call for sudden, vast new spending policies in order to provide the new light system. Rather, he suggested that the individuals in the affected area be assessed to cover costs of installation and initial operation; the city then would assume operation gradually over the years. Although formerly apolitical, this man had sympathized with the policies proposed by Community Conservationists. He found himself suddenly a leader of a resuscitated group which was hostile to important aspects of the ideology and policy perspectives of the Jeffersonian Conservatives. The morale of the dispirited Community Conservationists suddenly revived when they saw their cause unexpectedly carried forward by such an able person.

The most unusual aspects of the process followed. During the extraordinarily well-attended council meetings, which were exceptionally well-reported in Mr. King's newspaper, the Mayor began to indicate his disapproval of the demand. The spokesman of the Main Street dissidents debated with him logically and forthrightly. When the Mayor informed the petitioners that the electric company was not authorized to bill the individual merchants in the manner suggested, his adversary rebutted him with the correct statement of the detail of the law. When the Mayor finally fell back and staked the outcome on his personal authority by saying that in his judgment the city should not agree to having lights installed "at this time," his opponent asked the city to begin to make plans to build a reserve fund for the purpose. The Mayor replied that he would rather delay further expenses for another year, and was met with flat disagreement. At the next meeting, called to settle the question, the Jeffersonian Conservatives showed that they had yielded. The improved streetlight system began to be installed almost immediately.

Immediately after the conclusion of this decisional process, another one occurred which was also unusual in its publicly visible character. The Jeffersonian Conservative group had been working for several months on a new zoning code to bring the regulations up to date in accordance with changes in land use that had occurred since the Second World War. The planning commission, composed entirely of Jeffersonian Conservatives, had viewed this project as a matter of civic preservation, a way of maintaining and improving the value of living in their quiet community. The new code submitted to the city council for adoption included such changes as the addition of a tourist-commercial zone, which would limit such "marginal" establishments as motels and diners to a relatively small area; the restriction of new gas stations to a very circumscribed area; and the provision that all new businesses had to provide off-street parking facilities. The last-mentioned provision was exactly opposite to the policies in force in the other three communities, where the local government had assumed the cost of providing off-street parking as a means of stimulating the downtown business district and as a useful civic convenience. The new provision in the Farmdale code would have discouraged new businesses, in that the expense of getting started would thenceforth have had to be augmented by the acquisition of scarce land for parking purposes. But it was not this provision that led to a political issue; rather it was the first two of those mentioned above.

What had appeared to be a civic-improvement or preservation policy to the Jeffersonian Conservatives, that is, the limitation of low-order establishments catering to the tourist trade through a change in the previously unenforced municipal regulatory ordinance, was viewed as governmentally imposed restrictions on private property by a number of other landowners. A few of the most doctrinaire Jeffersonian Conservatives felt that even a zoning ordinance was a violation of ideological prescriptions, while a few others acted only on the basis of economic interest. The newly revived Community Conservationists were generally in favor of controlling land use by zoning. But they felt that the proposed zoning change was a blow to a vital part of the local economy and against the general public interest. Petitions were circulated among the few property-owners in the affected areas who felt that the new provisions restricted them from the best use of their land. Since the local economy was relatively undeveloped, the use of land bordering the highway for motels and service stations was one of the most obvious ways of making that land profitable. Those adversely affected hired an attorney from a larger, neighboring city to present their objections to the city council. In a public hearing attended by a score of unhappy property owners, the attorney emphasized that the new code would be "legislating new service stations out of the picture," as well as imposing great difficulties on the already existing ones.

The opponents of the code wrapped themselves in a doctrine that was ordinarily very close to the hearts of the Jeffersonian Conservatives themselves. They maintained that the code would result in the government's virtually confiscating private property, the rights of property owners, or both. An eloquent public statement of their case by an attorney from out of town, and hence not subject to local pressures, made a covert counterattack difficult. The protest was by no means a mass movement, but it would have been extremely difficult for the Conservatives to try to sanction a score of citizens fighting for their economic lives and protected by traditions that were widely shared in the community. As a result, the Jeffersonian Conservatives once again yielded, and the offensive provisions of the code were deleted. The victorious property owners did not know—but the Conservative leaders did—that within the decade, the motels, diners, and service stations dependent on the tourist and normal intercity commercial traffic could not be expanded much farther with the opening of the relocated highway bypassing Farmdale. In short, though the dissidents "won" on this zoning issue, they already had lost a far more basic battle in the highway-relocation decision.

The current issue illustrates that the Conservatives still had a monopoly of information on some decisional questions. This gave them an extremely important strategic advantage in local politics. For example, on this issue, they would have preferred to adopt the zoning provisions restricting "undesirable" land use. Even though the highway relocation promised to prevent this type of development in the future, the Conservatives would have preferred to prevent it as of that moment in order to preclude having to deal later with a central strip of the city filled with useless establishments. Still, as sole possessors of the information about the highway relocation, they were able to adapt their strategy in the face of opposition to the zoning provisions. They yielded on a matter about which others felt strongly, thus lowering the level of discontent in the community. They allowed gas stations to continue to be built on the "doomed" highway, knowing that the earlier decision would insure ultimate success.

The course of this decisional process suggested that those dissidents most likely to be able to check or defeat the Jeffersonian Conservatives would be people with a high degree of educational attainment or high occupational status. These would give them resource bases for the acquisition and use of information on policy questions. On the basis of our experience in the other three communities, we would have expected to find that ideological opponents of the Conservatives with such socio-economic characteristics were Progressive Conservatives or Community Conservationists, rather than Liberals. Partly on the basis of that expectation, we would also have expected that political competition in the future in Farmdale probably would be relatively restrained, such as that between Community Conservationists or Progressive Conservatives and Orthodox Conservatives, rather than that between Liberals and any of the others. All of this was predicated on the assumption that other relevant conditions, such as the political apathy of the labor unions, would not change. If such a change did occur, it might promote the development of a Liberal leadership group. That did not happen but competition did return.

In each of these processes, we predicted that the Jeffersonian Conservatives would control the authoritative-consideration stage, because they had done so during Time E to M, and because they had demonstrated their effectiveness in sanctioning potential rivals in the past. Although they did control the decision in the first process, the desired effect of the increase-sales campaign—the prevention of an increased scope of government in the local economy—was short lived. The decision on the streetlight system increased governmental involvement in business stimulation, which means that our prediction was incorrect. Again, on the third decision, we were proven incorrect, as the zoning code was modified to eliminate provisions desired by the Jeffersonian Conservatives. Because of the "unusual" aspects of the last two decisional processes, which we have described, we conclude that the major defining characteristics of the local political system— the type of regime and the type of power structure—were changing.

The open presentation of demands to the city council indicated the continuation in Farmdale of a high sense of electoral potency. The variable that seemed to have undergone change was the probability of effective use of illegitimate sanctions. During the first decisional process, illegitimate sanctions were effective in stopping the publisher's demands for a shift in the scope of government. During the second and third processes, such sanctions were not brought into play. As a result, we judge that the community had changed from a Guided to a Developed Democracy by the middle of the natural-experiments period, that is, by the end of period +1.

In none of the decisional processes was there actually massive citizen participation. Thus, we still judge the community as being toward the "narrow" rather than the "broad" end of the distribution-of-power continuum. There is no evidence that the opponents of the zoning-code provisions constituted a single aspiring political-leadership group with an ideology divergent from that of the Jeffersonian Conservatives. Rather, they seemed to be interested only in specific provisions of the code. These dissidents did not maintain themselves as a group after gaining a redress of grievances.

On the other hand, the proponents of the new streetlight system did press their demand for a change in the scope of government as one part of a general set of desired changes in the relationship between government and the declining economy. Although they shared some of the policy perspectives of the Conservatives, they differed strongly in this area. The Community Conservationists of Farmdale did not have as high a sense of cultural superiority as their fellows in Oretown or Petropolis, but they shared with the latter a conception of the community as a collectivity that was antithetical to the individualistic conception of the Jeffersonian Conservatives. Their success in participating in the authoritative-selection stage, their power in the decision, and their renewed self-consciousness as a group aspiring for political leadership, particularly in this area of local politics, indicate a change in the other variable determining type of power structure. The ideology of the political leadership seemed to have become divergent rather than convergent. Therefore, we must reclassify Farmdale as a Competitive Elite structure.

However, the local elections of 1954 showed that opposition to the policies of the Jeffersonian Conservatives as represented by Mayor May had not extended to presenting a rival slate of candidates for election to City Hall. In 1952, the Mayor was reelected without opposition. The councilmen elected with him, while not of his political group, did not adhere to ideologies divergent from his. In the absence of electoral competition, it seemed unlikely that the apparently new Competitive Elite power structure would change in the direction of a Competitive Mass structure. Whether it would return to a Consensual Elite or remain a Competitive Elite power structure was a question more to the point.

The use and effectiveness of illegitimate sanctions and the decisional outcome in the decisional process involving the increase-sales campaign confirmed the classification of Farmdale's regime and power structure as of Time M. But the earlier forecast that no change would take place in either dimension of the political system, and that, if there were a change, the community would become an Oligarchy, proved to be wrong. For one thing, the continued application of such sanctions was more unpleasant and upsetting to the sanctioners than had been supposed; perhaps this was because they had used them so sparingly and for a relatively short period earlier: starting at Time E, two years prior to Time M. Second, the disposition of the sanctioners to apply illegitimate sanctions against people of "their own kind" was less than had been assumed. Third, some of the sanctioners became more worried than expected about a revival of a competitive opposition group that might take their case to the polls and obtain majority citizen support for a rival slate. It was not the existence of an electoral process *per se* that was a factor in the change in that regime variable. Rather it seemed to be the existence of such a process in the context of concern that a potential opposition group was about to use elections to change the probabilities of decisional outcomes as well as the identities of the current political leadership.

From the point of view of the potentially sanctionable, their disposition to reorganize under new leadership had been seriously underestimated. The analysts had not appreciated how important a role a single individual, the spokesman for the improved streetlight system, could be in the development of a competitive and effective political-leadership group and, hence, in changing a community's power structure from a Consensual to a Competitive Elite. This is not to suggest that a single aspiring political leader, even a well-known civic leader, can always or even usually be so successful; but it does signify the possibility of such success if a combination of theoretically important conditions or circumstances exist. The latter would include the relative inexperience and fragile disposition of potential sanctioners to continue to sanction illegitimately. It also would include such factors as the existence of an ideological political group currently unorganized but formerly well organized—that is, from the Second World War to

Time E, 1950; a recent history of competitive politics; the use of elections and their evaluation as important in setting or shifting the scope of government; official governmental settings as authoritative-consideration settings; and the existence of a network of subsidiary political organizations wherein a potentially competitive group could deliberate and organize political support behind their policy formulations.

We shall return to the matters of stability and change in Farmdale's political system in the next chapter. However, we should note the fact that Farmdale's political system during the natural-experiments period had become more like Oretown's and Petropolis' systems during Time E to M insofar as it now had a Developed Democracy; but it did not have the Competitive Mass power structure that characterized those other two systems. This Developed Democracy-Competitive Elite combination is another example of a regime–power-structure pattern already observed through the postwar historical analysis; it was characteristic of Petropolis' political system during two successive periods, 1947–1948 and 1948–1949. Whether or not in Farmdale, as in Petropolis during those periods, this pattern constituted a transitional political system and would turn into a Developed Democracy-Competitive Mass system of conceivably greater stability we also shall see in the following chapter.

ORETOWN: TIME M TO M + 1

Outline of Decisional Processes in Oretown during Natural-Experiment Period

First Decisional Process—Annexation of North Oretown
  Policy Demanded—City should annex fringe areas to eliminate serious flood and health problems
  Category of Decisional Process—Civic improvement; economic reorganization
  Prediction—Demand will be defeated
Second Decisional Process—Recall of two councilmen
  Policy Demanded—Strengthening of the concept and institutions of "good government" and the council-manager plan by recalling two councilmen who have actively opposed both
  Category of Decisional Process—Governmental and political reorganization; economic reorganization
  Prediction—Demand will be defeated

Third Decisional Process—Mayor's power advisory committee
  Policy Demanded—City should begin to make plans, as directed by
  the committee, to end the major community controversy by having the municipal utility purchase the facilities of the private
  electric utility
  Category of Decisional Process—Political reorganization; economic
  reorganization
  Prediction—Demand will be defeated

Sewage and drainage problems in North Oretown became so severe
in early 1954, after Time *M*, that demands were made by some residents of the area for annexation to the city of Oretown. An attempt
earlier that year to incorporate the area as a municipality and thereby
to provide for sanitation and storm sewers had been stopped short by
the announced opposition of the *X* Company, one of the largest employers in the region. The *X* Company had resisted all efforts to
resolve the problems of the area by taxing it to provide funds for
housekeeping services. The company already had its own services,
such as fire and police protection and a septic-tank system for sewage
disposal. When petitions were circulated calling for an election to
annex the area to Oretown, Mayor French and the rest of the Community Conservationists decided that the time had come to support
the demand. They felt that the problems spoke for themselves,
and that the only way to resolve them was for the city to annex the
area to provide the needed services. They were concerned primarily
with improving the community. To the *X* Company's objections,
they answered that the latter should pay taxes just as every other
community member should.

The *X* Company led the opposition to annexation, allying themselves with the other industries in the Oretown area in a campaign
based on the unfairness of forcing the company to pay city taxes.
The industries viewed this as an unjustified economic deprivation,
and they treated the problems of the area as a secondary matter.
The other opponents also perceived the question primarily in economic
terms. These included farm owners who were outraged that their
pastures should be treated as a source of revenue for a municipality,
and small property owners who had built outside the city limits precisely to avoid paying city taxes. Many of these people were so
marginal economically that they preferred to live amid health dangers
rather than increase their annual costs. The private electric utility
opposed annexation to avoid competition from the municipal utility,
which legally could operate only inside the city limits.

The opponents of the annexation organized a political-advertisement and letters-to-the-editor newspaper campaign. But the proponents appeared to believe that rationality and community foresightedness would carry the day; accordingly, they did not do much campaigning. Apparently, however, the same forces that had discouraged annexation in the past were operative again, for those in the area voted more than three-to-one against the proposal. Economic considerations also seemed to be of primary concern within the city, since the measure was voted down there by a substantial margin in a light turnout.

However, during the ensuing winter severe floods beset the area. Property damage and various health problems resulted. The proponents of annexation again circulated petitions to call an election; again they were opposed by the same constellation of forces. The proposed area was redrawn, omitting those sections voting most heavily "against" the prior year. The "second-time-around" emotions seemed to be even stronger than before. A group of women in North Oretown threatened to boycott any merchant who opposed annexation, thereby discouraging the sensitive retailers among the Conservatives from openly joining their industrialist and private-utility allies in the ranks of the opposition. However, their most important subsidiary political organization, the Chamber of Commerce, acted to deter the annexation proceedings by calling for a postponement during which a committee might study the matter. Since the city council was in the midst of the recall controversy involving mismanagement charges in a city department, the officials were willing to grant the "cooling off" period. The Mayor appointed a fact-finding committee representing both sides in the dispute plus noncommitted people; the committee hired two firms to make studies of different aspects of the problem. These were financed by the local industries. Some months later, however, the controversy was revived when the two consulting firms disagreed on whether the X Company should be included in the annexation area, and the Mayor's committee found itself divided on the question. The council then voted to place the matter on the ballot, with the X Company included but with other areas most strongly opposed to annexation excluded.

The local industries campaigned concertedly on the issue that Oretown was acquiring a reputation of hostility to industry, its lifeblood, because of this injustice to the X Company. Privately, industry spokesmen revealed their distaste for the kind of people who lived in North Oretown: "No self-respecting person would stay there." They believed that any person who had settled in the area should have known what the conditions were, and that asking local government to tax industry to change these conditions was immoral. The Mayor replied to the industrialists' campaign by pointing out that problems of the area required solution and suggesting that the industries were overlooking community interests in their zeal to avoid further costs. Thus the Conservatives and Community Conservationists were sharply divided on the issue. Although the Conservationists managed to win a tiny majority of the voting inside the city, the Conservatives again won a majority in North Oretown, thereby triumphing in the decisional process as they had the previous year, and during the Time E to M period. The outcome of the decisional process was as predicted. Moreover, the character of the process appears strongly to confirm the typing of the power structure as competitive. No effective illegitimate sanctions were used to block demands for a shift in the scope of government; and clearly the sense of electoral potency remained high. The perspectives of the leadership were divergent, and there were a great many citizens who influenced the shaping of the decisional outcome.

A second decisional process during this period also was marked by a high degree of conflict, and the final demise of the Liberals. Ever since Mayor French's election in 1952, he had had to contend with a city council that might on any matter, and on some matters did, oppose him. The Liberals on the council, diametrically opposed to the ideology of the Community Conservationists, were stung by the Mayor's public proposal that ward lines be abolished and councilmen elected at large to better represent the whole community: he also suggested that councilmen, and the mayor, serve 2-year rather than 4-year terms. Their resistance to the whole concept of manager government and independence of administrators in local decision-making led to an attempt in the first half of 1955 to recall them.

The city council, immediately prior to the recall, included four members who frequently were hostile to the Community Conservationist position and two who generally supported it. The leading members of the majority group were Liberal Councilmen Longacre and Thomas. When a department's missing records were discovered, the Liberals attempted to discredit the city manager, while the others absolved him. Shortly afterward, the manager announced his intention to resign. The Liberals acted at the next council meeting to fire him immediately, then succeeded in obtaining a replacement, currently a merchant in another community. He appeared on the job early the next morning. The Community Conservationists expressed shock that action was taken so abruptly, first in firing the manager without demonstrated cause and second in hiring a replacement without calling for applications from qualified professional administrators. The Liberals counterattacked by charging their opponents with an attempt to cover up the missing city records.

Shortly thereafter, the recall was initiated by the Community Conservationists and supported by the Conservatives. The recall petitions attacked the two Liberal councilmen for opposition to the city-manager form of government.

While the Conservationists were preoccupied with reorganizing Oretown politically to eliminate the influence of special interests and to develop a consensus behind community planning and development, the Conservatives were anxious to remove from public office men who had brought class conflict into local politics, had identified themselves too closely with the socialistic municipal utility, and who represented a new business area that threatened the central business district. The two leadership groups worked closely with each other in this endeavor; but, as on most recent public issues, the Community Conservationists performed the publicly visible roles and the Orthodox Conservatives stayed behind the scenes.

An effort was made to mobilize the civic clubs in a drive to acquire sufficient names on petitions to call the election and then to campaign for the recall itself. The recall coalition found that most clubs, lodges, and professional associations preferred to "stay out of politics," even though they favored recall; but several organizations made themselves available for this purpose. The Liberal councilmen were unable to find any civic organizations to support them. The Democratic party was the one organization most likely to be useful to the Liberals, since it was led by men friendly to them by virtue of a common strong commitment to public development of hydroelectric power. When the Mayor, who was also a local Democratic party official, intervened to assure the party workers that public power was not at issue, this potential base of political influence was lost to the Liberals. As a result, the only organized group supporting them was an alter ego of the municipal utility called the Committee to Preserve Good Government. This group was certain that the recall was really an attack on the city's municipal utility by the private utility and its allies.

The outcome was a shattering defeat for the Liberals. In a large turnout, the recall was successful, by a margin of three and one-half to one. The Conservatives and Community Conservationists had won overwhelmingly. This continued the pattern of constant political success when these two groups were in coalition during Time E to M. The outcome, just prior to the end of Time M to $M + 1$, had removed the Liberals from any official forum, a process of attrition that had begun with Mayor Lovegren's defeat in 1952. In the course of the campaign, there had been much interaction and cooperation between the two leadership groups, which presented the prospect of increasing convergence in the future, particularly since members of both had come to the conclusion that a protracted high level of controversy had damaged the community sorely and that the time had come for unity in behalf of the common good. However, important members of both groups still had not forgotten their mutual hostilities and hopes for the other's political demise. Aside from this possible but not-yet-realized movement toward consensus at the leadership level, the decisional process itself confirmed Oretown's political system as having Developed Democracy and a power structure in which masses of citizens participated in decision-making.

A less dramatic but significant aspect of the election was that sectionalism seemed to be on the wane as a political factor within the city. Whereas the Longacre section had "spawned" the Liberals since its annexation to the city after the Second World War and had been the strongest locus of support for the municipal utility, it was here that the Liberal councilmen met their heaviest rejection at the polls in 1955. Apparently the section was becoming integrated into the city, socially and politically, as well as legally. The power issue and the special needs of that district may have ceased to be as salient to residents there as they once had been. If this were the case, a prediction might be made that among the citizens in general, as well as among the political leaders, a new consensus was developing. Whether or not this was in fact the case, and what its effect might be on the extent to which the citizenry would participate in decision-making—that is, whether a Consensual Mass power structure would prove to be impossible, as suggested by the models presented in the previous chapter—will be investigated in the next chapter.

It would be a mistake, however, to suggest that Oretown was already moving consistently toward a Consensual Mass type of power structure, as the third decisional process indicates. Neither side in the electric-power issue had prevailed in the Time E to M period; each had been able to block the efforts of the other to ruin its competitor. So pervasive was the acrimony associated with those decisional processes that the Community Conservationists decided that the issue must be resolved if the community were to progress at all. As a first step, the Mayor appointed an advisory committee to investigate three alternatives: sale of the private utility's facilities to the municipal utility; sale of the municipal utility's facilities to the private utility;

and maintenance of competition. The committee represented moderate opinion. It elected as its chairman Attorney George Keel, an active young civic leader. He had business associations with the Conservatives, had served as attorney for the recall committee, and was a proponent of public development of hydroelectric power in all regions, as well as a supporter of the municipal utility.

The Mayor expected that his committee would produce a report suggesting purchase of the private utility's facilities by the municipal utility as the means of ending their cutthroat competition and restoring harmony to the community. He planned to use the report to strengthen his request to the citizens for action in the desired direction. Attorney Keel organized the committee, conducted the investigation, and produced the report virtually by himself. This was a matter of choice on his part; the other members apparently acquiesced, relieved to be rid of an extremely time-consuming and delicate task. When the report was completed, it evidently failed to meet the Mayor's expectations, for it was never acted upon. Six months later Keel was retained by the private utility's supporters.

Keel came to the conclusion that the private utility had acted honestly earlier when the city officials were attempting to arrange for municipal purchase of its rival utility. The price the private utility had asked at that time was approximately the same as the one Keel figured independently 6 years later. As a result, his report concluded that the city should hold a bond election to authorize purchase of the private utility's holdings. The recommended price was close to the 1949 figure and included the purchase of the water system owned by the company. These two provisions were unacceptable to the municipal utility's supporters, the Mayor, and his group of Community Conservationists, who believed that the price was far too high and that the water system was inadequate and should be treated as a separate question. As a result, the city council tabled Keel's report after almost no discussion of it; it was filed away, never to be revived. Keel later enthusiastically joined the ranks of the private utility adherents, becoming an outspoken Orthodox Conservative in ideology and action and a vigorous opponent of the Mayor on a variety of matters.

The outcome of the decisional process thus was as predicted: the first step in a projected plan to end competition in the distribution of electric power through acquisition of the private utility's facilities was defeated. Clearly, the process illustrated the existence of continued divergence in the ideology of the community leadership. It seems less likely that Attorney Keel would have taken the steps he did if a leadership group in competition with the Community Conservationists had not existed. Though this is a matter of conjecture, it would seem that Keel, or at least one of less integrity, courage and independence, might have found it much more difficult to oppose the Mayor and alienate his whole political group had there not been another group with whom he could become affiliated and from whom he could gain support in his future political activities. Stated another way, we can say that Keel would have been much more liable to sanctions through an economic boycott of his law office and social ostracism had there not been a group of political leaders in competition with the Mayor's group. In any case, the third decisional process, like the first two during this period, demonstrated nothing that would lead us to reject our classification of Oretown as a Developed Democracy with a Competitive Mass power structure by Time M. Nor would it lead us to reject the earlier prediction that Oretown would maintain such a system during Time M to $M + 1$.

One of our forecasts and one decisional prediction were proven wrong; another decisional prediction was correct but for the wrong reason. The forecast made in the previous chapter and the decisional prediction both concerned the Liberals. Given the historical pattern of, for the most part, unsuccessful attempts to recall officials in Oretown, successful relationships between Liberal leaders and organized labor, and Liberal strength in the Longacre section of town, we had not expected that they would be eliminated from political-leadership positions, nor that their opponents would obtain sufficient votes to recall them from the city council. One consequence of the mistaken forecast was that we were not prepared for the lessening of political-leadership-group competition—although the power structure was still competitive—by the end of Time M to $M + 1$. Besides the weakening of Liberal support from Longacre, and apparently from organized labor, we had failed to anticipate both the strategy of the Liberals' opponents in planning a recall election and the well-organized efforts of the Community Conservationists and Orthodox Conservatives in reaching the grass roots and influencing people to go to the polls. The recall campaign was cast in terms of "corruption in government" and unfair favors for special interests. Apparently this helped remove or overcome in a number of citizens' minds the Liberal defense that the recall represented an undercover attempt to eliminate inexpensive public power.

The prediction that the city's plans to end the electric-power controversy would be defeated was correct, but not because we could predict Mr. Keel's actions. It had been expected that the Liberals would succeed in blocking any such actions in the city council, which, of course, they were not able to do after being dismissed from office. The fact that the decisional outcome was predicted correctly for the wrong reason does contribute to clarifying some of the changes in, and instability of, the power structure, although the changes were not sufficient to warrant reclassification of the structure by the end of Time M to $M + 1$.

Before revisiting Oretown in the following chapter, we turn to the two Southern communities during the Time M to $M + 1$ period.

PETROPOLIS: TIME M TO M + 1

Outline of Decisional Processes in Petropolis during Natural-Experiment Period

First Decisional Process—Establishment of the technical training center
   Policy Demanded—City and county to provide funds for the construction of a building to house the training center
   Category of Decisional Process—Economic reorganization; social reorganization
   Prediction—Demand will be realized unless it involves desegregation, in which case it will be defeated
Second Decisional Process—Formulation of an urban-renewal plan
   Policy Demanded—City should formulate an urban-renewal plan as a first step in developing an urban-renewal program
   Category of Decisional Process—Economic reorganization; civic improvement; governmental reorganization
   Prediction—Demand will be defeated
Third Decisional Process—School desegregation
   Policy Demanded—City school system should desegregate
   Category of Decisional Process—Social reorganization
   Prediction—Demand will be defeated

The Community Conservationists believed that they had won a major battle when one of the state-supported technical training centers was awarded to Petropolis at the close of the Time E to M period. Economic development was, for this group of leaders, the only way in which the community might lift itself out of its depressing slump. In a zealous campaign, preparatory to applying for the center, they had surveyed the relevant needs and plans of the community's current and prospective industries. This had involved a mailed questionnaire, which the recipient firms were asked to complete and return. The application's acceptance by the state commission depended, in part, on the completeness of the information. The extreme slowness with which the questionnaires were returned indicated that other prominent community members were not so convinced of the importance or the desirability of the center. This had prompted Eben Bacon, Jr., to make an extremely strong statement, carried in the press; he stressed the need for the center and the fact that the businessmen, the source of many complaints about declining economic conditions in Petropolis, would be directly to blame if the application were delayed and the city lost its opportunity for a center. The business community was affected sufficiently to insure the adequacy of the application. Petropolis got its center.

The Community Conservationists then were shocked to discover that further obstacles lay in their path. Unless action were taken to put the center into operation within a certain period, the tentative award would be transferred to another community. Yet the Committee on Industrial Development was relatively slow about offering land to the school board as a site for the center; and the board itself was slow in selecting personnel to plan the site and the building, and slow to set a date for the bond election necessary to provide funds to construct the building. In order to expedite the matter, Eben Bacon, Jr., systematically contacted the people responsible for necessary action at every step of the way, tactfully urging them to "get on the ball"; he even suggested the most efficient and appropriate means by which this might be done. That he was successful in this endeavor testifies both to his political influence and to his political status in the community.

To that point in the decisional process concerning the establishment of the center, the Community Conservationists had encountered no open, active opposition to their proposal. In their zeal to insure the success of the center, they had neglected to consult Negro Leaders. The Community Conservationists sought civic improvement through economic development. They literally had forgotten about the social aspects of the prospective institution. Suddenly, in the late summer of 1958, the issue of desegregation loomed as the most difficult obstacle yet encountered. As the date for the necessary bond election was announced, Negro Leaders demanded to know what the center's admission policy would be. It became instantly apparent to the Community Conservationists that Negro support or opposition would be the decisive factor in the whole process. Their reasoning was as follows: there almost certainly would be a light turnout for this special election, inasmuch as most citizens would not be aware of the importance of the center. There was a constant core of "no" voters on every electoral matter involving increased expenditures and taxes. To offset the latter, it would be necessary, as in several past cases, to mobilize the Negro vote. The center was an adult-vocational-education operation and, hence, under the jurisdiction of the city school board. If it was to be segregated, the Negro Leadership, from either choice or the pressure from below, would oppose the bond issue. Increasingly, Negroes for whom desegregation was a most important goal had risen to demand that the leaders stand firm in behalf of that policy. One such man was William Steer, the militant editor of the local Negro newspaper. He wrote an editorial about the technical-training center, the gist of which was "desegregation or else." Since available funds would permit the construction of only one building with one set of equipment per specialty, separate but equal facilities were impossible.

One of the Community Conservationist inner clique then approached the chairman of the school board, an adamant opponent of desegregation and political friend of the Orthodox Conservative leaders, and put the problem before him. The chairman replied that while he was very much in favor of the center, he was unalterably opposed to races' mixing, as were other board members. The Community Conservationists contacted him again to present the following points in favor of a nonsegregationist admission policy and to summarize the probable lineup of interests on the bond issue mentioned above: (1) the heads of all major civic organizations were committed to supporting the board in the event of adoption of such a policy; (2) desegregation in Petropolis' public schools was bound to occur within a fairly short period anyway, so the board might as well choose the time and place for its first occurrence, rather than having the time and place forced on them; (3) this was a particularly apt place to begin to desegregate, since only adults were involved in the center, participation was voluntary, and persons were to be selected on the basis of good moral character. With the decision hanging in the balance, segregationist Board members decided to compromise and omit race as a relevant characteristic for admission if admission were restricted to adult males. The White woman was thus protected from the dangers of biracial social contacts in a vocational-education setting, even at the cost of her occupational future. This compromise proved acceptable to most of the Negro Leaders, who regarded it not as a compromise but as a major defeat for White Supremacy and the forerunner of public-school desegregation throughout the school system.

No overt organized opposition to this decisional outcome was observed in the community except, to some small degree, from the direction of White Supremacist PECORR. Leaders of PECORR insisted that the racial purity of adult White males should not be sacrificed simply to save Southern White womanhood. The bond election was decided affirmatively by a substantial margin in a light turnout; the solid Negro vote in favor accounted for the margin of victory. A number of Whites, their economic and racial perspectives in conflict, did not vote at all.

Our decisional-outcome prediction, therefore, was partially incorrect. It is necessary to determine whether the error resulted from incorrectly classifying the power structure or regime, or whether changes had occurred in the conditions determining these types. An examination of the ideology of the leadership shows that there was a shift in the race perspectives of some Orthodox Conservatives in crucial decision-making roles. In deciding that, in a limited area and under unusual conditions, improvement in the economic situation was more important than their dislike of desegregation, they had begun to rebuild their ideology, at least on a temporary basis. Their willingness not to oppose and, in some cases, even to support the center despite its admission policy placed them closer to the ideological position of the Community Conservationists than ever before. The change in perspective, then, appears to account for the error in prediction, even though this change in one of the defining dimensions of the power structure was insufficient to warrant any reclassification of the power structure.

So general had dissatisfaction with economic conditions become in Petropolis that demands for amelioration became increasingly widespread on the part of the business and professional men. The merchants' own organization was not active and the Chamber of Commerce was ineffective in its activities in the face of a continuous accumulation of studies sponsored by the Community Conservationists that documented various aspects of the decline. These factors impelled some of the younger merchants and businessmen to form a new organization, formally attached to the merchants' organization, named the Core City Committee. It was their purpose to commission a professional investigation of present and future business conditions, and to use the resulting report as the basis of a program for contemplating municipal and private associational action, which they would lay before the public, to revive the downtown area. The officers of the CCC were a group of younger men; they worked closely with the inner-

clique Community Conservationists and the uncommitted John Leek.
One "young Turk," well known for his efforts in behalf of economic
development and civic improvement, ran unopposed on a platform
composed substantially of the CCC objectives for a city council position in the May 1959 election. In this election the Orthodox Conservatives tried unsuccessfully to get a member of their group to oppose
Mayor Plunkett in his successful bid for reelection. With the popular
technical training center coming to Petropolis and with developing
plans for stimulating trade and improving the industrial base of the
city, his potential opponents felt that the Mayor's popularity was at an
all-time high and that it was wiser to wait until 1961 to oppose him
at the polls.

One of the most significant characteristics of the new civic association was that it included several Orthodox Conservative leaders among
its members. These were mainly retail merchants, rather than the
financiers and industrialists who provided the core of that political-
leadership group. During Time E to M, the four inner-clique Conservatives had stated their opposition to downtown redevelopment.
Although there were a number of civic organizations that included
members drawn from more than one leader group, the special, manifestly political purpose and sense of urgency surrounding the formation of the CCC suggested that its broad representation might reflect
new patterns of interaction and values within the community's political leadership.

The report of the CCC was somber in tone and called for bold action to revitalize the downtown area. Clear warnings were given that
inaction would result in the loss of a major proportion of trade to
new suburban shopping centers. The newspapers gave a great deal of
publicity to the CCC and its report. It was in this sort of environment that urban-renewal proposals were revived. The Community
Conservationists felt that urban renewal would fulfill a wide variety
of functions. Most important, it would be a significant step in the
rehabilitation of the downtown area, a matter that had been discussed
but not acted upon for many years except for the municipal-parking-
lot program. As such, it would strengthen the economic base of the
community. In ridding the city of a slum, urban renewal would be
attacking a major social problem, as well as meeting the demands of
many in the Negro sector. It would turn an area that drained the
city's tax resources into a tax producer. Finally, and not least important, urban-renewal activities might bring together elements in
the community that for over a decade had been warring.

The Community Conservationists had been extremely worried about the "bad name" of Petropolis in the state and among business circles generally. This "bad name" had derived from the prominence of Negro and labor leaders in local politics. Although they had made or instigated public statements that labor-management relations in Petropolis were as good as they were in many communities with a much lower proportion of workers in unions, the Community Conservationists knew that the majority of firms moving to Southern State were looking, in part, for a nonunion or weak-union community. It was rumored that prospective industrial firms interested in Petropolis were being warned away by certain Conservatives who used the Negro-White labor "machine" as a symbol of what awaited industry in their community. As efforts for the rehabilitation of the downtown area were shaping up, it seemed that an urban-renewal program also might be a means of developing cooperation and consensus among formerly hostile or distant political groups. A dramatic community-wide effort to reshape the city might go far to remake the poor image of the city held by outsiders, and thereby might make the task of attracting new industry considerably easier. The Liberals took no strong position on urban renewal, even though they generally approved it because of particular provisions of the plan, such as public housing for poor Negro families.

Previous efforts on the part of Mayor Plunkett and the Community Conservationists to develop an urban-renewal plan had died quickly under the attack of Conservatives and even the city manager, but the situation seemed to have changed. There was a new city manager, and some of the Conservatives seemed to have changed their position on the matter, apparently impressed with the scope of the current and prospective economic decline; others perceived urban renewal as a way in which the severe traffic problem could be alleviated. Others still were ideologically opposed to "spending," the intervention of the federal government in the local area, and the creation of a new unit of local government with some autonomy to deal directly with Washington, D. C. The Conservatives faced a disintegration of "resolve" among some of their former political associates, and the movement of many of the younger businessmen into the camp of the Community Conservationists.

The Conservatives had not allowed these younger men access to the authoritative-consideration stage, that is, into leadership roles in decision-making; nor had the older Conservatives accorded much political status to them, even in policy-deliberation stages of decision-making in the past. The development was somewhat reminiscent of the immediate postwar period, when the Conservatives had been so impervious to the demands of younger civic leaders for a share in the making of decisions that new leadership groups had been formed in reaction. The current crop of Community Conservationists were distinctly younger men; through the CCC and a new urban-renewal agency they offered their youthful peers, who ordinarily rose to positions of leadership in the Orthodox Conservative group after 15 or 20 years, the prospect of immediate prominence in Community Conservationist-oriented subsidiary political organizations. Those who jumped at or more cautiously accepted this prospect were brought into intimate settings wherein the Community Conservationists had "natural" organizational channels for impressing these men with their general ideology. A number of younger men who originally had leaned toward the Orthodox Conservative viewpoint joined the ranks of the leaders of the Community Conservationist political group, with others constituting a much larger rank-and-file membership than the Community Conservationists had been able to muster by Time M. The dependable understructure of the Orthodox Conservative group underwent an unexpectedly rapid reduction in size. The Orthodox Conservatives were aware and concerned about this development, stimulating further efforts on their part to develop accommodations and policy consensus with the Community Conservationists. The more tenured Community Conservationists also were aware of the mistrust their newer colleagues had in their alliance with the Liberals, particularly the White Liberals. However, these younger businessmen of Petropolis were distinctly less racist in outlook than their older associates; they tended to support the Community Conservationist stress on continued social reorganization to improve the position of the Negro in the interest of the whole community. The rapidity of these shifts in the group structure was unexpected and unpredicted.

Some of the most doctrinaire anti-urban-renewal Conservatives were attracted by the notion of clearing out the unsightly Negro slum area, even through this particularly undesirable method of slum clearance. Interests cut across ideological sentiments in the Orthodox Conservative camp. Thus the demand for the preparation of an urban-renewal plan as the first stage in an urban-renewal program was successful.

The ensuing plan called for the rehabilitation of a Negro slum which bordered the downtown business area; the creation of a new, distinguished residential area which was planned to attract professional personnel associated with the Laboratory Locus; a modernized street grid to improve traffic flow, facilitate trade, and provide more parking facilities; and the expansion of the downtown commercial district. The Negroes in the affected area were promised public housing on a scale commensurate with their needs; this provision evoked the approval of Negro Leaders for the plan as a whole. Though this was but the first stage in an anticipated larger-scale urban-renewal program, and opposition might develop in the latter stages, there was, during the latter part of period +2, no strongly organized opposition to the demand that a plan be formulated.

The unorganized opposition had a very interesting character. As with the technical training center, the extreme White Supremacists voiced some opposition. The race issue was less prominent in urban renewal than in the technical training center, but in both of these and other matters, extreme White Supremacists seemed to be increasingly vocal in their opposition, on additional grounds as well: unnecessary tax increases, bureaucratic ignoring of people's desires, and socialism. These declarations seemed to reflect an increasingly Radical Right-White Supremacy mixture of ideologies, apparently addressed particularly to the inhabitants of the fringe areas surrounding the city, and to the more rural county folk. That their fringe-dwelling audience was, at Time M, potentially most receptive to anti-governmental-expenditures messages can be inferred from the following table (Table 12-1). Dividing the White respondents in the

TABLE 12-1   Attitudes of White Citizens in Petropolis toward Tax Increase for Downtown Redevelopment, by Educational Level * and Place of Residence: Time M

Downtown Redevelopment Attitudes

	Support	Undecided	Oppose	Totals %	N
City-dwellers					
Low education	59%	10%	31%	100%	74
Medium and high education	66%	11%	23%	100%	164
Fringe-dwellers					
Low education	31%	21%	48%	100%	29
Medium and high education	65%	16%	18%	99%	55

* Those citizens who had not been to high school were classified as having low education, with those who had attended high school for at least one year classified as having medium or high education.

Petropolis sample survey into those with less than a high-school education and those with more, we find that the most opposition to a tax increase, if necessary, for downtown redevelopment came from the poorly educated fringe-dwellers. The same table shows that for every other city- and fringe-dwelling category there was considerably greater approval than disapproval—in fact, a majority. This Community Conservationist policy with its widespread public support, which was even stronger among the active influentials, did not seem to provide what seemed to be a developing Radical Right movement with a particularly promising opportunity to supplant the Orthodox Conservatives as the leading opponents of big, socialist, municipal-government programs.

The predicted decisional outcome thus did not occur. Even though urban renewal had been resisted successfully during Time E to M and, therefore, was expected to meet defeat during Time M to $M + 1$, forces in support of the demand were augmented by at least some leaders who had opposed it in the past; and the lack of opposition from any leadership group changed the power relations. The initial resistance to urban renewal was overcome by the increasing pressures exerted on opponents by the segments of the community that supported the proposed program. As with the decision on the technical training center, this decisional process revealed a decreasing amount of conflict among the leadership groups of Petropolis, particularly between Community Conservationists and Conservatives. The apparent narrowing of the political distance between the two groups seemed reinforced by the absence, in the May 1959 elections, of a Conservative candidate against the Mayor, in marked contrast to the situation two years before. Thus, one of the power-structure variables—ideology of the political leadership—seemed to be changing in the direction of convergence.

However, there were still sharp differences between the Liberals and the Conservatives. As the Community Conservationists and Conservatives moved closer together ideologically, the former appeared to move away from the Liberals. The prospects that an organized Radical Right political group might emerge and, if so, that its members might obtain political-leadership positions, were most uncertain. Whether or not these developments were definite and whether or not they would result in damage to the Liberal-Community Conservationist electoral coalition remained to be seen. The decisional process revealed no detectable change in the variables determining regime type.

In the spring of 1959, a set of demands for desegregation of the Petropolis city schools was made again. Overcrowding in the Negro schools had increased seriously, and when the school board appeared to view as a solution the reopening of a decrepit building that had once housed White students, Negro citizens were incensed. A large delegation appeared before the board to argue that the old "jim crow" school should not be used, to seek a solution in complete desegregation, and to do so through public hearing and proceedings, rather than by resort to court cases, one of which was pending. The demand had been formulated by PESNEG, and was endorsed by the PTA's and the local branch of the NAACP. The school-board chairman reiterated his belief that the community was not ready for integration. Some weeks later, a delegation reappeared before the board to repeat and renew their demands. It was composed of both moderate and militant Negro Leaders, who spoke strongly against using the old school to accommodate the overflow from the Negro schools.

During the summer, the school board felt compelled to file a brief asking that the law suit brought by Negro petitioners for a court order to force the school board to make plans for desegregation be dismissed, on the grounds that the plaintiffs had not exhausted their administrative remedies. In view of the renewed demands by the Negro delegation for "administrative remedies," the board felt itself to be under such pressure that it might consider initiating some desegregation. The pressure was increased when the sole Negro member of the school board urged that steps be taken to begin desegregation. Comparing the situation to Metroville, he suggested that Petropolis was capable of taking the same sort of steps.

In late summer, some 200 Negro students sought reassignment to White schools in a coordinated "administrative" action to obtain the desired outcome in this political decision-making process. This was the largest number of such requests ever made in any city of Southern State; it was a set of actions reaching down into the substructure of the Negro subcommunity. All but a handful were denied, and these were to be acted on within a few days. As anticipation mounted, the board announced that approximately ten of the students would be reassigned to White schools, including one of the students whose family had participated in filing the court case. While there was some disagreement within the board on some of the decisions—each request for reassignment was treated individually—it is worth noting that some of these "administrative-political" decisions were unanimously in favor of reassignment. Many Negro and some White citizens shared in the political power accruing to those who purposefully contributed to the pressure that led to the desegregation outcome. Desegregation proceeded uneventfully, if in a token fashion.

Thus, the outcome of the decisional process again was counter to the prediction. As in the other two processes, the factor of change was the attitude and behavior of the Orthodox Conservatives. Consistent opponents of desegregation in the past, they always had acted to prevent it through the majority's opposing it on the school board. However, in the present case, the choice was between accepting token desegregation or provoking a judicial decision that would almost certainly constitute a political defeat, as well as a fierce propaganda battle between the White and Negro subcommunities. This would have been, in the eyes of some of them, the *coup de grace* to the national reputation of the community. Furthermore, intransigence on the part of the Conservative leadership might have allowed the full burden of blame for the trouble to fall directly on themselves, with the result that they would be further isolated politically in the community. As has been noted, the younger members of the Main Street sector were being increasingly drawn into the ranks of the Community Conservationists, as were some members of the Conservative group, on such matters as downtown redevelopment. The Orthodox Conservatives also found themselves without the kind of state-government support that the White Supremacists of Little Rock and other Southern communities had had in their initially successful efforts to thwart court orders.

Finally, in contrast to the situation in Metroville prior to desegregation, the leadership of the Negro subcommunity was united publicly in organizing political support on behalf of desegregation, so that there was no opportunity for the Conservatives to use "Uncle Tom" allies to evade the demand. This was the case even though a small number of younger Negro Latent Leaders had taken the initiative away from the Manifest Leaders in this decision, as they had in the candy-store and school-law-suit processes. There seemed to be a new militancy in the Negro Leadership which had increasingly made the established Negro Leaders more a set of "formal" authorities for the Negro subcommunity in political decision-making and, in appearance, less Liberal—or, relative to these new demands, more cautious than they had seemed in the previous period. Thus, with the Negro Leadership making the demand, supported tacitly by many Community Conservationists and White Liberals, and opposed publicly by no leaders, a major step toward social reorganization of the community was made through local-governmental action.

Once again, whereas the decisional outcome appeared to reflect an increasing convergence in decisional perspectives within the political leadership, there was no apparent change in the other major variables. We conclude that the classification of Petropolis as a Developed

Democracy and Competitive Mass power structure by Time M was confirmed by the natural experiments; the regime remained unchanged, while the power structure, still a Competitive Mass type, was undergoing some change within the leadership in such a way as to draw two of the three groups, the Orthodox Conservatives and the Community Conservationists, closer together.

METROVILLE: TIME M TO M + 1

Outline of Decisional Processes in Metroville during Natural-Experiment Period

First Decisional Process—Change in policy concerning desegregation of the schools

    Policy Demanded—Continued, gradually increasing school desegregation

    Category of Decisional Process—Social reorganization

    Prediction—No such political decisional process will occur (the policy will be realized within the domain of administrative decision-making), but if it does occur, demand will be realized

Second Decisional Process—Construction of a new mental hospital

    Policy Demanded—County government should construct a new hospital for Whites in a new section of the city, giving the Negroes the renovated former White asylum

    Category of Decisional Process—Civic improvement; social reorganization

    Prediction—Demand will be realized

Third Decisional Process—Annexation

    Policy Demanded—City should annex bordering suburban areas

    Category of Decisional Process—Civic improvement; economic reorganization

    Prediction—Demand will be realized

After one year of token desegregation at a Metroville high school, a small group of Negro parents demanded that their children also be reassigned to the desegregated school. They assumed that there would be a continuation of administrative decision-making on such requests, based on the rules used by the school board the previous year. Inasmuch as the petitioning parents lived in the same area as the successful petitioners of a year earlier, and inasmuch as the same process of NAACP selection of a small number of "appropriate" students to present to the board had been followed, a process based on **an agreement** between the Negro Leadership and the board, the Negro parents expected an affirmative decision from the board.

Unexpectedly, from the Negroes' standpoint, the board refused the request, though at the same meeting it permitted token desegregation at the elementary-school level. Refusing to reaffirm as a basis of assignment policy the distance between a student's residence and the schools, the board cited a general criterion that included best interests of the child, efficient administration, and the general welfare. The decision reflected a redefinition of token desegregation within the White political leadership of the community. Concerned that changes were occurring too quickly in the traditional relationships between the races, the leaders decided that token or "gradual" desegregation should not mean a continuously increasing rate of desegregation. As a result, the board, which had accepted the leaders' formulation of the first desegregation policy, also accepted the modification. With the outcomes of these administrative decisions, a new and unpredicted political decisional process was initiated by the formulation and deliberation by Negro citizens of plans for a new decisional outcome on general school-desegregation policy.

Shortly after this, the board announced another decisional outcome reinforcing the new definition of token desegregation. The voters during Time *E* to *M* had been called on to approve a bond issue for constructing new classrooms. Even though some Negroes opposed it on the grounds that the new schools would be segregated, the Negro Leadership supported it, and the Negroes in general responded in a strongly affirmative way at the polls. Now the school board announced a change in building plans. Where no new Negro high school had been envisioned in the plans set before the voters in the spring, the new plans included one such school in precisely that area where the Negro families who had petitioned for their children's reassignment to White high schools lived. The construction of a high school for Negroes in that area undoubtedly would slow down, if not eliminate, the reassignment of Negroes to White schools.

The change in plans had been made by a committee of the board in a meeting which had not included one of its members, Councilman Vida, the only Negro on the board. Stung by what he considered to be the second consecutive act of betrayal by the board, he called for a series of open meetings in the Negro sections, in order that the board might apprise itself of sentiments among that part of the population. Reportedly, the meetings were agreed to only after he threatened to hold them on his own if the board failed to cooperate. The meetings were held, but they did not result in a change in the board's decision. The White board members were in an extremely defensive position throughout these meetings, and the opposition of the Negro community to the decisions was unmistakably demonstrated. At the conclusion of one of these meetings, Councilman Vida suggested to the audience that the board and other local government agencies would need Negro support in future bond issues, as they had in the past. This overt statement of the potential power inherent in an organized, dissident Negro electorate was a significant new element in the politics of Metroville.

The decision not to permit continuous desegregation was different from what we had predicted. It was expected that once the Negro community had expressed its displeasure, the White Progressive Conservatives would change the building plans to permit somewhat more desegregation. But the racist point of view seemed to be hardening among these White Leaders. This change appears, however, to have resulted entirely from the Progressive Conservative leadership's definition of the concept of desegregation. The power-structure variables do not appear to have undergone changes. No new leaders appeared in the course of the decisional process and there was no effective mass participation in the decision—the open meetings did not affect the decisional outcome. On the other hand, the successful demand that the meetings be held, the large-scale expression of dissidence that occurred during the meetings, and the scarcely veiled threat of organized Negro opposition on future referenda suggest the development of a more efficacious orientation toward the electoral process among the Negroes. If these appearances were not misleading, Metroville seemed to be moving in the direction of a Developed Democracy within one year from Time M.

As these decisions were being taken by the board, another decisional process that affected relations between the races was gaining momentum. At Time M, the community leadership finally had closed ranks behind a demand that the county government should establish a new mental hospital for Whites in a "respectable" location in the city and renovate the old White hospital for use by Negroes. This would have required an election to authorize the issuance of a multi-million-dollar bond issue. However, the county commissioners were ambivalent about the proposal. They shared the perspectives of the leadership on most matters; but while some of them were actual members of the leader group, one of them had been the single dissident in the earlier decision to construct the new facility on a new site. He and others still felt considerable pressure from rural constituents against the idea; therefore, they procrastinated. When other White

Progressive Conservative leaders prevailed upon a team of "non-partisan," mental health experts to "announce" in favor of their proposal, the commissioners compromised. Instead of calling immediately for a bond election, they put a set of choices on the ballot and called an advisory election.

The only organized force in the straw vote was a group organized by William Polk and other White Progressive Conservatives, known as the Citizens for Better Mental Care (CBMC). Their publicity campaign seemed to carry the day in the absence of much voter interest or adverse publicity, and the proposal to build the new hospital on a new site was overwhelmingly approved.

A bond election to provide the millions of dollars for the new hospital was then called for the following spring, 1959. This was the largest amount ever asked by the commissioners in such a referendum. Once again, there was virtually no open, organized opposition at the outset of the campaign; the proponents carried on a vigorous campaign through CBMC. Throughout the lengthy period preceding the election, there was little mass communication of dissident viewpoints on the hospital question, despite the very large amount of money involved. The only public forum used by the opponents was the letters-to-the-editor column of the local newspapers, which ran a number of indignant or questioning letters, most of which were ignored by the hospital forces. These letters were more than countered by the barrage of "pro" letters received and published as a consequence of a letter-writing campaign organized by members of CBMC.

The only public figure to suggest the need for more information and to sound a critical note was a relatively fringe member of the Progressive Conservatives, a junior executive of a local radio station. Two weeks before the bond election, he posed some questions about the site for the new hospital and the amount of money that might be obtained from the federal government and from private donors. None of these points, he suggested, had been the subject of public discussion or information on the part of the CBMC; yet all of them might vitally affect the final cost, and could conceivably make possible a reduction in the cost of the new hospital to the citizens. He juxtaposed these questions on the air in a program with a general position favoring the bond issue. The Mayor was quick to leap to the attack, stating that the *only* issue was whether or not the hospital should be built. The issues raised by the radio executive, he charged, were irrelevant and designed to confuse the voters.

The commentator was visited by a group of his fellow White Leaders who said that his position had threatened the success of the bond election. They indicated that Negro voters reportedly were now hostile to the proposal, and that any additional opposition engendered by the radio station and other media might be sufficient to defeat the new hospital. In effect, they delivered an ultimatum to him to cease those kinds of broadcasts. Since the leaders involved were politically and socially close to the station owner, this threat implied a severe sanction. With some uneasiness, and knowing that others among the Manifest Leaders felt his questions were appropriate ones that they would like to see answered even though they would not openly oppose CBMC's efforts, he continued to ask the same kinds of questions on his program. The earlier split in the White Progressive Conservative group over the hospital issue apparently had not yet healed. The newspaper supported the bond issue editorially, but repeated some of the radio commentator's questions.

The campaign by the CBMC was accelerated in the period before the election, with many spot announcements on radio, sizeable newspaper ads, and the use of television. The extensiveness and intensiveness of the campaign were unparalleled in the political history of the community. Speakers broadly representative of the community civic and political leadership were used, including the entire city council, except for the sole Negro member, Councilman Vida. At Time M, Vida had approved of the new-White-hospital proposal. Bitter over being "betrayed" in the school-admission cases and the school-building program, he had decided, reluctantly, to shed his Progressive Conservative orientation and act thereafter independently on his Liberal, race-conscious attitudes.

His deviant behavior was associated with rumors that the Negroes would oppose the bond issue because of their desire for one mental hospital for all citizens and because of their dissatisfaction with the school board's decisions of the previous fall. Although such Negro Leaders as Samuel Best were prominent members of CBMC, the local NAACP organized a last-minute propaganda campaign urging Negroes to vote "no." The division of opinion among the Negroes was reflected in a sharply divided vote within the Negro ministers' association, which, nonetheless, endorsed the bond issue. Another source of opposition was some rural sections of the county. In these sections, voters were opposed to moving the hospital to a site less convenient for them than the present city location, and they seemed to be unhappy over the cost. On the day before the election the radio commentator editorially urged the citizens to vote on this important issue, but suggested that they vote the way their "own minds directed" them. His failure to endorse the bond issue indicated that the threatened sanction had not been effective.

The bond issue was passed. The turnout was heavy, compared to the small proportions of votes cast in past special elections. City voters overwhelmingly approved, but a majority of the county voters disapproved. The Negroes were more opposed than other city voters. The decisional outcome appeared to be a personal triumph for the Mayor, who had championed the proposal despite his past reliance on the Negro electorate. It also was a victory for William Polk, who had formulated the demand against the opinion of his fellow political leaders, won most of them over to his position as passive or active supporters, and then effectively organized the campaign for public support.

In the aftermath of this election, Negro Councilman Vida announced for reelection on a platform that demanded the election rather than appointment of city-school-board members, better race relations, and other more specific policies. He stated publicly that race relations were deteriorating, and that the community needed to consider the possibility and consequences of serious deterioration in the future.

The decisional outcome was as predicted. However, the decisional process had some characteristics that differed significantly from characteristics of past decisions. These differences suggested that the community's political system was undergoing some major changes, particularly in the variables affecting regime type and somewhat less so in the variables determining type of power structure. First of all, the bond election was an indication that major civic improvements probably could not be accomplished any longer solely through private donations and private action. Community growth and rising costs had raised the cost of new facilities beyond the amount that even the economic leaders and old families of Metroville felt they could afford to give. To the extent that the public was now being asked to participate in paying for such facilities, it seemed that the electoral process, in the form of referenda, would be used more frequently. With increased demands on the public pocketbook, more opposition to the policies of the leadership might develop, particularly in the form of a growing body of "no" voters. To the extent that elections occurred more frequently, there would be more opportunity for the public to participate in electoral decision-making. And the more public the process of decision-making was, the more likely it was that representatives of other perspectives would appear in various stages of decision-making. What we are suggesting is a growing potential for mass participation in decision-making and a wider distribution of political power in Metroville.

Although the decisional process reflected no actual change, there was an increasing potential for change in one power-structure variable:

leadership ideology. There was clearly a potentially aspiring Negro Liberal leadership group, but it was not yet organized. A set of independent Negro Liberals had broken away from Progressive Conservative fellow Negroes; but they hesitated to form a competitive group because their newly found sense of electoral potency had done nothing to clarify what such a group could accomplish. Nor had a man yet appeared to lead in the formation of such a group. Councilman Vida, the logical possibility, had no such aspirations. Since the White Progressive Conservatives remained together as a group, and since they were victorious, there were no new leaders and no possibility for divergence from that quarter. Though one White Manifest Leader had taken an independent position, he did not oppose his fellows directly on a matter of ideological significance, but rather on matters of morality in tactics: he wanted fuller and franker disclosures so that the citizens could vote intelligently. Those few White Progressive Conservative leaders who still opposed the hospital expenditure simply sat this election out. The whole process, including those portions of it occurring in the Time E to M period, reveals a consensual leadership which continually, although barely, survived internal strains toward divergence in policy if not ideological perspectives.

With regard to the other power-structure .variable, the distribution of power, the electoral campaign revealed considerably more public participation during Time M to $M + 1$ than in the past. A large number of citizens were involved in the CBMC campaign; they organized publicity, contacted voters, and arranged for transportation to the polls. This order of participation was necessary to the favorable outcome of the election; those who engaged in it must be considered to have had power in the electoral decisional process. However, it must be remembered that formulating the demand and the selection of the decisional options on this large-scale project involved only a few leaders, operating in a setting far removed from the citizens. Finally, it is notable that there was an unusual amount of independent, although for the most part unsuccessful, political activity on the part of the Negro subcommunity, thereby continuing the pattern established in the school-desegregation matter. Therefore, we feel that Metroville's power structure remained a Consensual Elite structure during Time E to M, compared to those of Oretown and Petropolis; however, it was a much less stable structure by the 1959 municipal election, 1 year after Time M.

One of the variables determining regime type reflects great change. There appeared to be a sharply increased sense of electoral potency, particularly among a portion of the Negro Leaders. The Negroes were divided in their sympathies on the hospital vote. But the activities of such a leader as Negro Councilman Vida, who, during the desegregation decisional process, publicly had pointed out the importance of the role of Negroes in bond elections and had refused to endorse the hospital bond issue, and of the leaders of the NAACP who organized a last-minute countercampaign, reflected a rising belief that the Negroes could be mobilized effectively in political decision-making without being deterred by illegitimate sanctions. The White leadership had not used illegitimate sanctions in response to protests and active opposition to their policy preferences in the school-desegregation and mental-hospital issues; this restraint, together with the appearance of top White Leaders on television asking, in effect, for their votes, seemed to alert the Negro subcommunity, as well as poor Whites, to the new era in Metroville politics in which illegitimate sanctions by the White leadership were unlikely. The absence of illegitimate sanctions against the Negroes in these processes indicates the correctness of the classification of Metroville as an Underdeveloped Democracy rather than an Oligarchy as of Time M. But 1 year later Metroville seemed to have become a relatively Developed Democracy.

The earlier prediction of a continuation of Underdeveloped Democracy in Metroville was based in part on the expectation that there would be no drastic changes in the policies of active racial accommodation pursued by the White Progressive Conservatives, particularly in regard to the pace of school desegregation. What was not expected was the increasing intragroup influence of a few leaders whose less accommodating perspectives made an impact on school-desegregation policy. The chief administrators did not adhere to a policy of administrative decision-making; they did not follow their own set of rules, designed, in fact, to control the degree of desegregation, that presumably were to be applied in a relatively straightforward, technical fashion in particular instances of application by Negro children for admission to White or minimally desegregated schools. Instead, they viewed the decisions in relation to their general political significance and violated their own technical criteria in making the decisions in accord with more racist preferences of particular Progressive Conservative leaders. Furthermore, we had not expected that the White political leadership would conclude that the initiation of token desegregation at the elementary-school level warranted the development of a new pattern of segregation at the high-school level by a change in already announced plans for new school sites. Nor had there been a correct assessment of probable Negro reaction to any sharp setbacks in their slow advances in regard to social reorganization; consequently, our forecast in this regard was not correct. Although a few Negro Liberals outside of the Negro Leadership reportedly had expressed their discontent privately during Time E to M, the number of such men who did not feel politically impotent and who did not fear illegitimate sanctions had been underestimated. Not enough of them felt this way to make the assessment of the fears of illegitimate sanctions and the Underdeveloped Democracy classification erroneous as of Time M. But they apparently functioned effectively "underground" as active influentials in the following year to stimulate a lessening of such fears to an extent that was not appreciated and was unpredicted at the time the regime was classified.

Mayor Peterson had no trouble in obtaining renomination in the primary and victory in the election of 1959. His enemies in the Democratic party, as well as his Republican opposition, seemed to be demoralized by his successful, active role in the highly publicized mental-hospital decision. By emphasizing his close association in that effort with such a prestigious group of civic leaders, and implying that his political status among the political leaders was unrivaled, he seemed to take the spirit out of his opponents, who campaigned against him in a seemingly half-hearted manner. Increasing disillusionment with his performance did not split the Negro vote, since there was nobody else acceptable in the contest. The recently organized White Supremacists strongly disapproved the decision to initiate desegregation at the elementary-school level; but they approved wholeheartedly of the rejection of so many applications to transfer from all-Negro schools to those nearer their homes. They also approved of the plans for the new Negro high school. They seemed to be somewhat undecided about the hospital issue: they approved the decision to move the White institution out of an increasingly Negro neighborhood, but did not appreciate the costs of constructing the new hospital. For some of these relatively poor people, race was the only factor that counted; but for others their pocketbooks created something of a dilemma for them.

With one more major civic improvement accounted for, the leadership of Metroville began to work toward yet another one. The community was already something of a model of progress in Southern State, and the leaders were anxious to improve its reputation regionally and even nationally. As the census year, 1960, approached, and another city in Southern State threatened to surpass Metroville in total population, civic pride was engaged. Annexation of suburban areas seemed to be the best way of emerging victorious in this competition without resorting to unselective attraction of major new industry.

The addition of these residential areas would strengthen the tax base of the city and allow a number of further improvements to be made that would render the city even more attractive to new businesses and industries of the "right" kind. As population density in these areas had increased, problems of sanitation had developed, so that annexation also was considered desirable as a public-health measure. Essentially, however, annexation would symbolize to the citizens and to outsiders continuous community progress.

The major annexation just prior to Time *E* had been accomplished by means of an election held inside and outside the city. However, Metroville could annex fringe areas by means of an ordinance. The Metroville City Council passed such an ordinance, but actual annexation would depend on the approval of city voters of a bond issue to finance extension of city facilities to the areas proposed for incorporation. A multi-million-dollar bond issue was to be submitted to the city voters; this was by far the largest amount ever requested—the somewhat smaller, but still very large, hospital bond issue had been a countywide measure.

A groundswell of opposition began to develop. Manned largely by fringe-area residents, the ranks of opponents included two city councilmen and two county commissioners. Their difficult task was to convince the *city* electorate to vote against the bond issue. They formed an organization, Citizens Opposed to Compulsory Incorporation (COCI), which campaigned primarily on two issues: (1) that city taxes, as well as those of fringe residents, would increase with annexation, and (2) that the democratic right to vote had been denied the fringe-dwellers, who were being forced into the city against their will and without right of appeal. The same two issues, denial of the right to vote and imposition of high taxes, were to become the rallying cries of the opposition to urban renewal and other civic improvements in both Metroville and Oretown in the future. The popularity of the COCI cause was attested by the large number of fringe-area residents who joined the organization, made small contributions to finance publicity, and contacted friends living in the city to influence them to oppose the bonds. The theme of rising taxes was emphasized and re-emphasized. The opposition councilmen stated that the corps of city employees, such as the police force, was inadequate for the city, let alone for an increased area. With constant pressure in favor of salary increases for these underpaid people, as well as the normal cost of extending facilities, taxes were bound to rise. It is interesting to note that the wards which elected these two councilmen voted heavily against the Mayor in the 1959 election, indicating the possibility of a general sentiment in these districts against costly civic improvements.

The contentious publicity campaign waged by both sides was unprecedented in Metroville. The mental-hospital campaign had been a most unusual effort, but there had been only one position publicly represented. Radio and newspaper ads, billboards, and television programs were used extensively by both the "pro's" and the "anti's." The opponents stressed in their propaganda that the proannexation organization had "big money" available, and were "powerful forces with unlimited funds," whereas they, the opponents, were little people who had scraped together small contributions. The little people's campaign was referred to as a "crusade."

The proannexation organization stressed that there would be no tax increases associated with a successful annexation. They promoted the concept of community progress, and suggested that those living in the suburbs were selfish people, unwilling to pay their share of the costs of a fine community. The ads were signed by several Progressive Conservative leaders and other prominent community members.

Civic associations and neighborhood groups became additional settings for the organization of political support. The proannexation people were able to use as spokesmen the professional city personnel and quasi-official and official boards, such as the planning commission. The Mayor took a prominent part in their activities. The opposition gained its most important official supporter at the last moment when a Progressive Conservative Manifest Leader who was a county commissioner announced that he was against the bonds in a local newspaper story. Plainly torn by cross-pressures, he apologized publicly to his friends, the other Progressive Conservative leaders, but stated an obligation to speak out in favor of his rural constituents, who strongly opposed annexation. The Mayor bitterly attacked his action.

Mayor Peterson, with trepidation, had wagered on a successful annexation campaign. During Time E to M, he had complied with advice that additional annexations be delayed until detailed feasibility studies were made because of his own worries about the resentments caused by the last annexation in the fringe area. Although the bond issue for the new annexation was to be voted on only by city-dwellers, the Mayor was concerned that resentment might, in the next election, result in reversing his last narrow margin of victory. The Mayor had mentioned his interest in consolidation of the city and county government even before Time M; this was a policy formulation that he did not push, so that it did not become a decisional process involving political power. But his known interest in the matter was interpreted by county officials as another indication of the Mayor's urge toward governmental reorganization that would put him on top of a single metropolitan monolith, and this increased the city-county fissure over annexation.

The Mayor's worries had some basis in fact; the antiannexation forces had real opportunities in their campaign to marshal the votes of city-dwellers in the appropriate direction. This can be inferred from the findings shown in Table 12-2. At Time M, the entire White-subcommunity sample, both city and fringe residents, had been asked about their attitudes toward city-county school consolidation and city-county governmental consolidation. Although school consolidation had been defeated, primarily as a result of citizen support for immediate school improvements, the White citizens at large and the White active influentials had favored the idea of city-county school consolidation. In contrast, 40 per cent of the White-subcommunity sample disapproved of city-county governmental consolidation; 30 per cent were undecided; and 30 per cent approved. The fringe-dwellers were least approving and most undecided: only 16 per cent approved; 42 per cent were undecided; and 42 per cent were opposed. Among the residents of the city, opinion was divided more evenly between the supporters and opponents of governmental consolidation.

If these attitudes toward governmental consolidation may be interpreted as an indication of sentiments towards the new annexation issue, it would seem that the Mayor had something to be bitter about when a high-political-status figure among the Progressive Conservatives announced his opposition to the proposed annexation bond issue. It was possible that opponents of annexation could reach sympathetic and uncertain White citizens below the level of those who had been active influentials during Time E to M—four of the five in the sample had approved of, and the fifth was undecided about, governmental consolidation—if they could set up a real grass-roots set of channels of communication of a kind unknown in recent years in Metroville

TABLE 12-2   Attitudes of White Citizens in Metroville toward City-County Government Consolidation, by Place of Residence: Time M

	Approve	Undecided	Disapprove	Totals	
				%	N
City-dwellers	36%	25%	39%	100	222
Fringe-dwellers	16%	42%	42%	100	90

politics. This was also an inference from these findings. The result of the bond election suggested that their intensive endeavors to do this met with at least some success.

Citizens of the city, in the biggest turnout seen for a special election, narrowly voted down the annexation. The wards of the two dissident councilmen provided a disproportionate share of the "no" votes. In a postelection statement, the chairman of the COCI announced his intention to maintain his organization intact as an "advisory group" to work for the appropriate scope of city and county government. A new political grouping, the Radical Right, organized in the wake of this decisional process. In the ensuing meeting of the city council, the Mayor reproached the two opposition councilmen for the conduct of their campaign against annexation. In the course of the discussion, the city's policy of supplying water below cost to the biggest users, the major industries, was questioned. This was perhaps the first time since the days of the Radical Left that the Progressive Conservatives' policies were questioned publicly, with the implication that the city administration might be performing special favors for industry.

Thus the decisional outcome was opposite to the prediction; the decisional process reflected momentous changes in the political system since Time M. One of the leading Progressive Conservatives actually had deserted his fellow Manifest Leaders on a major issue of "progress" and had emerged on the winning side; this suggested that the leadership finally had divided into two parts: a more racist but still Progressive Conservative city-centered group and a county-centered, more Orthodox Conservative group. The Progressive Conservatives considered the entire metropolitan area, the city and a very large part of, if not the entire, county, as the community which had a single interest to be advanced by the men of great wealth. Those of more Orthodox Conservative leanings felt that there were two areal interests, the city and the county outside the city; they felt that the rulers of the county protected the stake of the county's residents in "home rule" and low taxes and thus opposed the city's interests in expansionist governmental reorganization and costly but unnecessary programs symbolic of cultural and community "progress."

The victory of the organized opposition, and the statement of intention to continue organized local political activity indicated that a new and, in its first test of strength, successful political leadership group had emerged. The difficult decision of formerly Progressive Conservative county-oriented leaders to develop an independent, more Orthodox Conservative group to plan strategy and deliberate policies apart from their city fellows apparently was motivated in large part by a desire not to lose their political influence with their constituents to the new, more reactionary, Radical Right group that joined those against the annexation. As in Petropolis, the newly arisen Radical Right was characterized by an integral mixture of that ideology and White Supremacy. The White Progressive Conservatives' continued support of the Mayor, with his notorious Negro and White blue-collar-worker support, threatened, in the eyes of some county leaders, to push the fringe- and county-dwellers into the arms of the new Right. The verbal battle between the Mayor, the leading public representative of the civic-improvement forces, and the low-tax-oriented councilmen suggested the possibility of a polarization developing within the city between these two political groups. Finally, there had been a high degree of mass participation in the campaign and an unprecedented turnout at the polls to decide the referendum. In short, the power structure appeared to have become mass in character. The Competitive Elite structure that had emerged after Time M had been succeeded within a year by the Competitive Mass structure.

The absence of effective illegitimate sanctions and the demonstrated high sense of electoral potency on the part of the opposition marked the community, at least as of that point in time, as having maintained and strengthened the community's Developed Democratic regime. Even a few repressed White Liberal labor-union leaders seemed, by the end of Time M to $M + 1$, to have become so pessimistic about their political prospects that they had moved into an apolitical rather than an electorally impotent state, in the sense of fearing illegitimate sanctions. Instead of their sense of electoral potency's rising as a reflection of their Liberal or organized-labor orientation, a number of other White Liberal unionists were becoming newly politicized as supporters of the Radical Right's efforts to deal a mortal decisional blow to City Hall and the "elite." The phenomenon of nationally oriented Liberals in the working class supporting the local political activities of the Radical Right in Oretown is explored in some detail, with more adequate data, in the next chapter. The antiannexation forces provided an opportunity for the poor Whites, White labor, and White Supremacists to release accumulated frustrations and vent hostility against the "ruling class" for the first time in a decade in a decisional process that was not simply a regularly scheduled municipal election in Metroville.

Whether or not the successful activation of the Radical Right would unite the White Progressive Conservatives again, what the Negro Leadership would do under the present conditions, and whether or not the political system would revert to an earlier type of power structure, regime, or both are questions considered in the next chapter. Toward the end of that chapter is a chart containing the classifications of the power structures and regimes of each community's political system during the natural-experiment periods.

NOTE

1. The natural-experimental approach consists primarily in making observations in the field in each community as events unfold, taking advantage of the primarily—and necessarily—historical approach used to conduct the sample surveys and other interviews to reconstruct patterns during Time E to M. A model for the "natural-experiments" period was the landmark study by Harold Gosnell, *Getting Out the Vote: An Experiment in the Stimulation of Voting* (Chicago: University of Chicago Press, 1927). See also Samuel J. Eldersveld, "Experimental Propaganda Techniques and Voting Behavior," reprinted in *Political Behavior: A Reader in Theory and Research*, ed. by Heinz Eulau, Samuel J. Eldersveld, and Morris Janowitz (Glencoe, Illinois: The Free Press, 1956), pp. 210–217. For a research design approaching the experimental controls obtained in these two studies, see the report on Oretown in the next chapter. The method used to collect data in the present chapter might be labelled for each community "the theoretically guided, multiple, current case study" method to distinguish it from the usual case study in political science. The latter tends to be guided by implicit theoretical considerations, focused on a single decision in a given community or organization, and in the nature of an historical reconstruction of more or less recent events that occurred sometime in the past, before the analyst began to make his observations. Peter Rossi terms the latter "decision sociometry" when used systematically with a sociometric technique, although that term could also cover the approach used here. See his "Theory and Method in the Study of Power in the Local Community" (unpublished paper delivered at the annual meeting of the American Sociological Association, New York, August 1960). For both its methods and its subject, see Peter Rossi and Robert Dentler, *The Politics of Urban Renewal* (New York: The Free Press of Glencoe, 1961).

13

THE COMMUNITIES REVISITED: *a new politics*
of discontent and the rise of the Radical Right

After the periods discussed in the previous chapter, each community was visited again. In Metroville and Petropolis, the investigation that took place during the 1-year period we report on was conducted primarily through secondhand reports and newspaper accounts of observations made by people on the scene. During a 7-year span in Farmdale, periodic observations were conducted by researchers in the community itself; a sample survey of the businessmen was done in the middle of that span, in addition to the necessary newspaper perusal.[1] The researchers kept Oretown under close, continuing, personal observation in the field, and during Periods 7 and 8 returned to do a panel study involving a random-sample survey, reinterviews with a subsample, and interviews with special samples of relevant populations.[2] What was learned from revisiting the four communities constitutes the substance of this chapter. Special attention once again was given to the regime and power-structure components of their political systems during these periods. The narrative deals only with those decisional processes and elections that most clearly illustrated changes in or the maintenance of the regimes and power structures; the classifications of both during these periods of revisiting and the prior natural experiment periods are summarized toward the end of this chapter in Figure 13.1.

In three of the communities during these revisiting periods, local Radical Right groups become important in community politics. Some of the leaders of these groups were officially in the national Radical

Right movement; they brought to their communities the sorts of messages contained in the literature produced and distributed nationally by particular Radical Right organizations.[3]   Moreover, it was apparent that others of the local leaders read and subscribed to such materials.   The strength of the Radical Right needed to be assessed in a better way than analysis of available electoral statistics permitted.   For this reason, among others, the large-scale study was undertaken in Oretown during these periods.   Of particular analytic interest was the Radical Right's attraction in the new politics of discontent, especially at election times, of blue-collar workers and the poor who traditionally were Liberal and Democratic in their national political behavior.   The analysis of that phenomenon is presented in the long section on Oretown in the latter part of this chapter.

FARMDALE: PERIODS 3 THROUGH 9

The organization and success of the group of dissident businessmen during the natural-experiment Periods 1 and 2 in Farmdale heralded a shift in regime type to Developed Democracy and in power-structure type to Competitive Elite.[4]   During Periods 3 through 6 this "loosening up" of the political system continued.   The dissident businessmen expanded their demands into a Community Conservationist program. They wanted to keep conflict to a minimum in the community, but they were willing to provoke the Jeffersonian Conservatives in attempting to break the latter's control of the civic-association network by organizing new service clubs and senior and junior Chambers of Commerce.

In organizing the latter, care was taken to assure the troubled and angry Jeffersonian Conservatives that these organizations would not attempt to duplicate the services performed by the latter's key civic club; nor would their meetings and activities conflict with those of the older organization.   This moderate approach made it extremely difficult for the Conservatives to attack the new organization directly without appearing excessively power-oriented and monopolistic.   Furthermore, the Community Conservationists were able to enroll a few of the Jeffersonian Conservatives as members of the Chamber of Commerce, which, while moderating their program, strengthened their ability to implement some of their political demands.

These demands included a policy of economic development, which would attract new commercial and industrial enterprises, and such secondary policies as zoning revision and modernization of the water system, which were designed to promote this development.   The Chamber of Commerce held meetings to identify local economic needs, to consult experts on ways of satisfying them, and to generate local support for the emerging policies.

A junior executive of Farmdale's leading industrial firm was a leader in the initiation and development of the Chamber of Commerce and of joint Chamber–local-government industrial-expansion activities. This indicated acceptance by the town's single most important employer of the need for economic growth, regardless of its impact on the local labor market.

The manner in which industrial development was pursued indicates the adjustment that was made between the old leaders who sought to maintain the Jeffersonian virtues of Farmdale and the ascendant leaders who desired economic growth. The Chamber of Commerce saw to it that representatives of potential new companies were introduced throughout the business community in an effort to achieve consensus on their "desirability." The potentially negative features of every new firm, such as the type of labor it might attract, the fumes its plant might emit, and the cost of extending municipal services to its site, were considered carefully. Thus, by the end of 1958, only two new industrial developments seemed likely for the immediate future; both actually were major expansions of already established plants. Many other companies had been contacted by the Chamber of Commerce, but the negotiations had not been concluded. Plans for industrialization were being made at a moderate pace. It appeared unlikely that Farmdale would become a boomtown.

The Jeffersonian Conservative-dominated local government moved very slowly to facilitate these demands. They had so many public pressures concentrated behind them through the new subsidiary political organizations that the Conservative officials were influenced to go along, if reluctantly. This reversal of past decisions represented a substantial victory for the Community Conservationists. In 1956, after years of uncontested elections, the city council election became competitive. Candidates who were favorable toward policies of Community Conservation were elected, adding to the impetus of the new demands. There was so much ferment in the political system that meetings were held on rehabilitation of the most dilapidated sections of the city; one of the means suggested for dealing with the problem was a federal-local cooperative urban-renewal venture. This came to little; but the fact that such a suggestion could be made and discussed, and a federal bureaucrat brought in for consultation, indicates the revolutionary nature of the politics of these periods compared to those of Time E to M.

The deaths of two of the three most influential inner-clique Jeffersonian Conservative leaders during this period may have weakened the Conservatives. Although new, younger leaders were recruited by the group, they were less dyed-in-the-wool Jeffersonian Conservatives and were more willing to try to work with the Community Conservationists. However, their perspectives also were conditioned by the long tenure of the high-political-status triumvirate, the Jeffersonian Conservative inner clique. The two deceased Conservatives often were referred to as if they were alive and hovering over the decision-making process. Mayor May retained a high degree of respect in the community. Even those who diametrically opposed his policies spoke of him as a "good mayor," or suggested that "Farmdale is lucky to have him." The Community Conservationist Chamber of Commerce president, who had deplored the Mayor's resistance to cooperation with the Chamber in industrial promotion, declared to the interviewer: "I'd vote for him again." This esteem for the upholders of the old order tended to retard policy change.

However, the frequency of meetings and the high rate of political discussion on both sides of issues led us to conclude that the power structure had become Competitive Mass in type by the end of Period 3, 1955. The limited data available on popular participation during this period provides evidence to support this conclusion. A survey of a random sample of business and professional men conducted two years later, in 1957, showed a much higher rate of discussion than had prevailed among the business and professional men in the sample survey of 1952: only 53 per cent reported even occasional discussion of local-government matters with friends in 1952; by 1957 the proportion had risen to 85 per cent.

By the 1958 mayoralty election, Mayor Bill May had decided to leave public office after serving several 2-year terms. Only one candidate came forth: the new city treasurer. Identified with the old guard, but a member of the Chamber of Commerce and a moderate, he helped to draw Conservatives and Community Conservationists together. The new city council predominantly represented the Community Conservationists, and the wheels of local government began to turn more rapidly in matters of policy change to accommodate and promote economic development of the community. Unable to resist the new movement, ex-mayor May finally joined the Chamber of Commerce. This indicated a willingness to cooperate on the part of the old hard-core Conservatives, who were becoming less Jeffersonian than Orthodox in adjusting to this time of change. The political leadership of the community developed into a coalition. Harmony once again became characteristic of Farmdale politics. The frequency of political meetings appeared to decline, and decisional processes once again became consensual. Policy formulations emerged at the leadership level and moved through local-government and civic-association channels without controversy and without provoking much citizen participation. Occasional bond measures for implementing a Community Conservationist policy were passed with little opposition. Thus, we conclude that, during Period 7, Farmdale's power structure had shifted once again, this time to Consensual Elite.

The rise of Community Conservation was not followed by an emergence of the Radical Right, as happened in Oretown, Metroville, and Petropolis. Though there were isolated outcries against local government's violation of individual rights, there was no organized movement reflecting this perspective. Unlike the situation in the other communities, Community Conservationist policies in Farmdale did not involve major increases in local-government expenditures. The community was so much smaller than the others that it did not require the same sort of public improvements. Such new policies as industrial promotion represented significant shifts in the scope of government, but were not implemented as "crash programs" lavishly financed by the Chamber of Commerce and local tax revenues; relatively small amounts of money were involved. Thus taxes did not rise appreciably as a result of the new policies, and the less affluent were less affected than their counterparts in the other communities.

A further factor that may have discouraged the rise of a Radical Right group was that Farmdale did not have a large corps of professional public administrators who might have symbolized "dictated" decision-making and big government. Since local officialdoms were composed of friends and neighbors, they maintained one aspect of a sense of intimacy in local government. The converse seemed to be true in the other three communities; it apparently was related to a growing sense of political alienation, on which Radical Right movements thrived. The Community Conservationists in Farmdale did not seem to have quite the sense of cultural superiority, particularly in regard to the political culture, that characterized the Community Conservationists in the other communities. Finally, the utterances of local leaders and public officials still emphasized such symbols as traditional efficiency in government, responsiveness to grass roots, and reliance on private problem-solving. Thus the political climate was more soothing to the potential constituency of the Radical Right than it might otherwise have been. The Consensual Elite power structure was maintained during Periods 8 and 9.

Throughout all of these post-Time M periods, while the power structure underwent three changes, the regime remained a Developed Democracy. In their concern with preventing or slowing down major undesirable shifts in the scope of government, the Jeffersonian Conservatives gave little thought to the use of illegitimate sanctions. The question of their use had become academic once competition had returned to the political leadership.

Postscript from Farmdale

Although these post-Period 9 events are not subject to the analysis that follows, we shall mention them briefly here. A decade after the decision had been reached in private to approve the state's plan to have the major highway bypass the community, the residents of Farmdale saw that the actual construction of the bypass was underway and would have major implications for their tourist trade. A sense of crisis spread through the merchants on the highway and on Main Street. Efforts to attract new industry were redoubled. Almost 15 years after it had first been proposed, a bond issue was approved overwhelmingly by the voters to modernize and expand the municipal water system, an essential element in attracting new industry. The Jeffersonian Conservative plea for the small town was lost in the public outcries for the urgent need to do something.

Since other communities in Western State were competing for new industry, the immediate prospects for reorganizing the industrial base were not good. A county fair was proposed as a way to bring tourists to Farmdale and as a device for putting the community "on the map" for prospective new industry. The Community Conservationist's political leadership quickly approved, and made available every resource of municipal government to assist the venture. But demands to modernize the fire department were turned down. The political leadership desperately tried to preserve the community in the face of the reality of the economic impact of the highway bypass. Yet they could not recommend doubling the municipal tax rate, which was the estimated cost of replacing the volunteer firemen with paid city employees. Farmdale's future was a question being discussed by many citizens, but one which we cannot answer in the present volume.

METROVILLE: PERIOD 3

In Metroville, the increased citizen politicization that characterized the natural-experiment periods continued through 1961, Period 3, becoming even more pervasive. Two major factors seemed to be associated with this condition, which was so different from the consensual, paternalistic atmosphere of the previous decade. The first factor concerned the general orientation of the public to the scope of government; the second concerned the changing perspectives of Negroes toward the scope of government.

After years of continuous expansion as part of the comprehensive program of the dominant Progressive Conservative leaders, the voters refused to support major shifts in the scope of government that required major expenditures. The first stirring of the hitherto quiescent citizens against the costly Progressive program was noticeable in the mental-hospital issue, during Period 1; the suburban and fringe residents in particular showed resistance. In the late spring of 1960, these rural and suburban elements successfully had propagandized and organized the less affluent among the city voters to defeat the annexation-related bond issue. This blocked the Progressive Conservatives' goals of maintaining Metroville as one of the state's four largest cities and the rationalization of governmental services in the metropolitan area.

As the Progressive Conservatives required more and more frequent voter support in approving major capital outlays, their organization became inadequate to the political task. The electorate grew uncontrollable and vetoed costly shifts in the scope of government. Although the competition once again unified the temporarily divided Progressive Conservatives, this group of leaders found such a reaction to their rule incomprehensible. They had not adjusted their strategies effectively with regard to conversion and mobilization of voters. In this, the Progressive Conservatives strongly resembled the Community Conservationists of Oretown and Petropolis, as we shall see.

The catalyst of the voter reaction was a united congeries of Radical Right groups whose most sensational feat had come in the defeat of annexation in Period 2, 1960. After that time, they had organized to contest one decisional question after another, sometimes successfully and sometimes not. But they had not lost in any decisional process in which the electorate participated in the authoritative-consideration stage. For example, the Radical Right, assisted by other activists who had been instrumental in the defeat of the annexation proposal, had succeeded in blocking an urban-renewal program for months after the political leadership had appeared to have the matter decided. Through representatives on the council and in letters-to-the-editor columns of the local press, the opponents demanded that the program be voted on by the general electorate. They managed to force the

Mayor to delay calling a final vote on the matter in council. In the interim, threats were made to file a court suit contesting the legality of aspects of the program. Finally, when a court ruled in a related case that such aspects were legal, the Mayor brought the question before the council, which voted to avoid further delay and to authorize the program. This was one of the last decisional processes in which the Progressive Conservative position was supported overwhelmingly by the council, since the 1961 elections recast the membership substantially. In a sense this was a costly victory: the Radical Rightists were provided with grist for the propaganda mill. Here, the Rightists claimed, was another example of efforts by the Mayor and his supporters to deny the people their inalienable right to vote on matters of importance. Expropriation of private property through taxation and ceding local authority to the federal bureaucracy without representation became battlecries of those most cynical about City Hall and the aristocracy. Surely there must be something wrong with a program foisted on the people without their consent.

Ignoring the people was the cry first raised by the opponents of annexation, with reference to the fact that the city legally—but, according to them, immorally—could annex a fringe area without a vote of the area's residents. Moreover, even after the contested settlement of the related urban-renewal issue, Mayor Peterson announced that he was considering annexation again. However, this time he favored handling the measure through a special act of the legislature, a legal possibility in that state. This announcement, which was not acted on further by the Mayor, raised the oppositionist ardor of the Rightists even more. Not only were the local officials bypassing the fringe-area citizens, they were not even going to consult the citizens of Metroville itself.

The issue of direct democracy and its alleged violation by City Hall and the civic-political leadership through *de facto* reorganization of local government to deprive citizens of their electoral "rights" was made even more intense by two further decisional processes during this period. These also concerned governmental reorganization, specifically of the school system. As part of their desire for efficient administration, the Progressive Conservatives finally initiated a school consolidation campaign. Both city and county school boards supported this goal. But there was some difference of opinion as to whether the resulting unified school board should be appointed or elected. The Progressive Conservatives were able to organize the issue in such a way as to postpone this decision until the matter of consolidation itself was decided. The Rightists opposed them on the grounds that this was simply another step in the creation of big government: control would be given to administrators and removed yet another degree from the citizens. The Negro subcommunity leaders also took a stand in opposition; they feared that further county administrative control—Negroes had never attained direct representation in the county—would weaken their influence in the schools and curtail future progress in desegregation.

At first it appeared that the Progressive Conservatives would be victorious in this matter; but their school-consolidation plans came to an abrupt halt when the Radical Right and the Negroes used their primary weapon, the vote, in effective opposition. Before consolidation was possible, the voters in county and city would have to approve a rise in property taxes. In a heated campaign, the low-tax, anti-big-government, anti-Progressive Conservative forces, together with the Negroes, defeated the tax hike. The margin was well over two to one in the city and even greater in the county. Taxes were maintained at their current level, and the consolidation program was prevented. The voters seem to have been so mobilized by the continuing debate between the major contestants that the leadership of the opposition forces appeared to be riding a surging wave of protest. A relatively large number of Rightist Latent Leaders and, to a lesser degree, the Negroes managed the successful electoral campaign.

That the contest would continue seemed indicated by one of the last issues to arise during Period 3. One of the elected White councilmen, reflecting Rightist views, and the one Negro councilman together sponsored a proposal to change the mode of selection of the city school board from nomination by the mayor with council approval to popular election. These men successfully guided the council, which authorized a petition to the city's state legislative delegation to propose an act at that level to permit this change. However, that delegation was dominated by Progressive Conservatives who refused to act on the council's request, thereby defeating the demand. Since the inaction of the delegation in effect blocked a demand to expand the role of the citizens as electors in community decision-making, the defeated forces became even more enraged than they had been, and more committed to strengthened political organization for ultimate victory.

The 1961 local elections, the point in time that marked the end of Period 3, seemed to bring the outstanding issues into focus, an unusual characteristic for mayoralty and councilmanic elections in Metroville. So inflamed had the opposition to the incumbent Mayor become that he chose not to seek reelection. A number of candidates announced for this position and for seats on the council. Political feeling was so intense that a variety of interest groups, long since unrepresented in a campaign for office, entered candidates. The Radical Right was not represented by its strongest potential candidate in the mayoralty primary because its chief spokesman on the council chose to withhold his candidacy until a future election. The Progressive Conservatives supported for this position a young man, new to politics, whose rhetoric was tailored to mollify some of the outraged citizens: he declared himself in favor of consultation with all affected citizens in any further consideration of annexation. However, several more Orthodox Conservative candidates tried to obtain the nomination. Another White candidate ran on a Liberal platform, attacking the city-manager form of government, and supporting an income tax on a progressive basis and a reduction in regressive property taxes; he advocated popular voting on annexation and equal job opportunities for Negroes. His share of the vote was quite small, but it was significant that a White Liberal should attempt an overt organization of political support in behalf of his demands. No such phenomenon had occurred for well over a decade in Metroville politics.

One of the most dramatic events in the primary process occurred when it appeared that the Negro subcommunity might for the first time run its own candidate in the Democratic mayoralty primary. Because of the large number of White candidates in the contest, a block vote might have proved successful in the primary. At the last moment, Progressive Conservatives met with the potential Negro candidate, who publicly announced his decision not to run in return for an undisclosed concession to his subcommunity. Apparently, this involved an agreement by the Progressive Conservatives to support local reapportionment, so that Negroes would receive a larger proportion of seats on the city council. This "deal" was negotiated from the following calculations: realistically, the Negroes could not hope to win the general election for a candidate of their race; furthermore, any such attempt might generate hostility and reprisals among the White majority. Finally, they were far more opposed to the White Supremacist Rightists than to the relatively moderate Progressive Conservatives, and they did not want to swing the election to one of the former group's candidates. The fact that Negroes and White Radical Rightists had found themselves on the same side in several decisions did not signify any lessening of the hostility they felt for each other. The Progressive Conservatives needed, as they had in the past, Negro votes to elect their candidate. The alliance was definitely a limited one, as we shall indicate below; but it ensured the Democratic mayoralty nomination for the White Progressive Conservative candidate.

The Progressive Conservatives were increasingly Republican at the national and even at the state level. They found themselves in a difficult local position. Traditionally, they had ignored the local Republican organization; but they now worked desperately to convince the increasing number of Republican voters in the White middle and upper classes to vote against the Republican candidate for mayor in favor of their own Progressive Conservative Democratic candidate. The difficulties they had had in working for Mayor Peterson in earlier elections without publicly announcing that he was their candidate and not an independent Democrat working for Negro-White working-class interests were not eliminated with his retirement. Nor could they speak as local Republican officials against some of the Radical Right candidates running for the council as Republicans. Their earlier decision not to leave the local Democratic party organization was coming home to roost. Even the most Supremacist of the White Progressive Conservative leaders had to succumb to the pressures by their fellows to swallow their pride and their policy preference; they had to try to work out a new accommodation with the Negro subcommunity in order to obtain Negro votes for their mayoralty candidate. In the absence of any realistic alternative, the Progressive Conservatives did overcome their White Supremacist sentiments in this conflict. Otherwise, they would have had to join the leaders of the Supremacist Radical Right, an obnoxious alternative for these dignitaries.

The new militancy among Negroes which was first detectable in the mental-hospital bond-election campaign expressed itself in a surprising manner in the primary election for the Council position from the Negro ward. Incumbent Councilman Vida, by then considered by Progressive Conservatives the most dangerously extreme Negro Manifest Leader, campaigned phlegmatically against two Negro opponents. The first was a Latent Leader who had participated in a successful sit-in demonstration which we shall describe briefly. The second was a newly active representative of a militantly Liberal position in Negro politics. His campaign called for equal opportunities for Negroes in a variety of specific economic and social contexts: public housing, fair local apportionment for Negroes, an urban-renewal emphasis on basic Negro problems rather than amenities and business sites for affluent Whites. In a heavy turnout, the politically neophyte Liberal won by a substantial margin. He proceeded to organize political support in behalf of the demands outlined in his platform.

In the general mayoralty election, the White Progressive Conservative Democratic candidate barely defeated his Republican opponent; the victory resulted from a huge majority in the Negro precincts, since the Republican won in most of the White ones.   A large minority of council seats were won by Conservative Republican candidates.   The Democratic councilmen included the Radical Right leaders, Progressive Conservatives, Community Conservationists, and the Negro Liberal.   The new Mayor thus faced a council situation of a large number of extremely hostile members, who would require careful mayoral strategies and maneuvering.   The Negro Liberal councilman found that his support was necessary to the new Mayor.   As a result of his bargaining position, rapid progress was made through appointments by and pressures from the Mayor to increase opportunities available to Negroes in public employment and office.   Furthermore, the Mayor and council already were taking preliminary steps to consider reapportionment of its seats in order to provide more equitable Negro representation, although it appeared unlikely that this proposal would be approved without protracted conflict.

It was clear that Metroville had remained a Developed Democracy in the time following the natural-experiment period; in fact, the regime seemed to have become more solidly established.   The sense of electoral potency was high for a range of interests, which included some that had been dormant and repressed, to the extent that such general interests as that of the Negro subcommunity and the Radical Right seemed to be represented by various congeries of political subgroups, often in alliance within the limits of the larger interest, but currently maintaining subgroup distinctions.   The city council, now the locus of authoritative consideration in many decisional processes, represented a range of political groups, ideologically characterized as Progressive Conservative, Community Conservationist, Liberal, and Radical Right.   There was no manifestation of the threat or use of potentially effective illegitimate sanctions.   In the highly politicized atmosphere, it appeared doubtful that such sanctions would have been effective, since allies were available to any sanctioned or threatened party, and a variety of groups existed as protection for those who formerly were more susceptible to sanctions as individuals.

Just before the end of the natural-experiment period, a most important incident occurred in Metroville which strengthened the rising sense of electoral potency in the Negro subcommunity; its repercussions extended into the revisiting period.   Traditionally, in Metroville and the other communities, teenagers and young people were not active participants in community politics.   Thus, the researchers' attention and the sample surveys were focused on adult politics.   Then a group of young Negro high-school and college students staged a sit-in in Metroville.   After strong initial resistances on the part of the Mayor and the White political leadership, the public demonstrations, police arrests, the growing threat of forceful retaliation by White Supremacists, and national notoriety of the worst sort led to the successful desegregation of some lunch counters. This youthful set of new Negro Leaders openly accused the older Negro Leaders, including the local NAACP, of having done nothing and of dragging its feet in a disrupting manner in this major decisional victory.[5] Most of these young activists returned to their studies and to political inactivity after this event, but they had left their mark. Fears of illegitimate sanctions on the part of older Negroes became in some measure shame over such fears. Impetus thus was added to the organization of older Negro Liberals. Such men as Councilman Vida appeared to be too moderate compared to the other two Negro candidates, even though he had led the first movement directed against the White political leadership in the school-desegregation matter. It should be noted that the youthful sit-ins occurred after the stirrings had already begun in the Negro subcommunity, but it is problematical whether the Negro revolt would have gone as far as it did or as soon as it did if they had not happened.

The Negro Liberal movement replaced the individualistic political Liberalism in the Negro subcommunity. After its break with the Progressive Conservatives, this group became the first disadvantaged Liberal group in any of the four communities that was able to compete politically and that did not include (White) Liberal businessmen in its leadership. It is difficult to determine whether or not this was an exception to an earlier noted rule, or whether the general pattern consisted of several "accidental" cases, including this latest "deviant" case. But certain relevant conditions of this last case should be noted.

The emergence of an organized Liberal Negro group occurred at a time when Metroville's own Negro youth acted on the basis of messages coming into the adult and the youthful portions of the subcommunity from the outside through the Negro national magazines, through the extracommunity contacts of individual Negroes, particularly the ministers, and through individual Negro newcomers. The flow of such messages continued to increase; they told with fervor of a chain reaction of heroic, frequently successful, instances of dramatic social reorganizations in other communities in the South. At the same time, the White Progressive Conservatives, who had been becoming less accommodating, suddenly extended the olive branch, but on radically new terms. A détente was accomplished, after a period of decision-making moves parallel to those of the Rightists; a *de facto* coalition was formed between the new Negro Liberal group and the White Progressive Conservatives. Whether or not the Negro Liberal group would or could have survived for very long without such a White ally to provide a way of continued sharing in political power was also problematical, since a long-term collaboration with the White Supremacist Radical Right was impossible.[6] And whether or not the newly developed sense of electoral potency could have continued on the part of such a permanent, powerless political minority group is, we think, doubtful. But these are academic questions, since the unexpected had occurred; the Developed Democracy regime had become stronger, rather than weaker, by the end of Period 3.

So contested were the decisional questions, so many were the positions represented by leaders or aspiring leaders, so high was the voter turnout in election after election, so pervasive was public consideration of decisional options that it is safe to conclude, though we lack systematic data, that political participation was both extensive and intensive. The issues appeared to be ones to which a large proportion of the populace were highly sensitive: taxes, big government, elite dictation, bureaucratic conspiracies, violation of democratic rights, the structure and substance of the educational system, the position of the Negro.

The leadership had not reverted, after the natural-experiment period, to the Progressive Conservative monopoly situation of Time E to M. Instead, the Radical Right maintained its organization and a share of the political-leadership positions. Although they were victors on questions such as school consolidation and higher school taxes, they were losers on several other matters. The state of the electorate was such that their leadership positions appeared safe for the foreseeable future. The Progressive Conservatives had been successful in a number of issues, thereby maintaining a share of the community political leadership; but their position seemed severely threatened, and their sense of strategy sorely tried. It seems clear that they would have to develop and maintain new lines of communication to the citizens if they were to recoup their political fortunes. So few were these lines of communication during Time E to M, so few were the subsidiary political organizations in which other than Progressive Conservative Leaders were members, that the task appeared extremely difficult. This estimate seems reinforced by the consideration that the Community Conservationists—with whom the Progressive Conservatives shared many perspectives—in none of our other communities had fared much better in relations with that great bulk of their communities who had a sense of middle or low cultural class.

Besides these contending leadership groups, there were the Negroes, whose leadership situation was still unstable. The established Negro

Progressive Conservative Leaders seemed out of place in the new, more militant politics. Latent Leaders had emerged in the sit-in demonstrations. Some of them remained active Liberals. Negro activists had contributed effectively to the defeat of school consolidation; some of them were probably Latent Leaders. The new Liberal Negro councilman so far had been effective in bargaining for the support of influential Whites in the matter of Negro representation in local government. Although the Liberal group had not yet formed a stable, recognized, inner clique to develop long-range strategy to wrest the necessary concessions from the White Progressive Conservatives for a program of economic, civic-improvement, social, and governmental reorganizations, their critical position was such that the chances for some extensions of their power in important political decisions seemed excellent.

The distribution of victories in decisional processes were such that they reflected the sharing of power, although not equally, by all these groups. The availability of channels for the citizens to contribute to decisional outcomes, and their heavy use of these, indicated a wide distribution of power. By virtue of the ideologically divergent leadership and the mass contributions to decisional outcomes, we estimate that the power structure had at long last become Competitive Mass. The political system in the major features of the model resembled the Competitive Mass-Developed Democracy systems of Petropolis and Oretown.

PETROPOLIS: PERIOD 3

The increasing cooperation between Community Conservationists and Orthodox Conservatives that was characteristic of the natural-experiments period continued and grew firmer after that time. But the alliance between the Community Conservationists and the Liberals tended toward disintegration. An overwhelmingly important issue reflected this clearly. The Community Conservationists initiated a proposal to consolidate the government of the city and the county. The goals were rationalization of governmental services, more equitable financing of such services, and planned urbanization of the fringe and rural areas of the county, including provision for the creation of conditions especially attractive to new industry. The plan mobilized a wide range of leaders of varying ideologies. Several uncommitted leaders, including the highly influential John Leek, actively endorsed the plan because of its relation to industrial development. Many others, including young Orthodox Conservatives and uncommitted leaders, sought to support the image of a progressive city that would be created nationally and regionally by the success of the plan. Several Orthodox Conservative Manifest Leaders heartily and actively supported the plan because the structure of government it contemplated would reduce the political influence of the Liberal Negro-White labor coalition, which lacked organization and electoral strength outside Petropolis' city limits. The Conservatives felt that there would be enough county voters, traditionally more conservative and racist than the city voters, to overwhelm the Liberal electorate.

All these elements combined to organize a subsidiary political association in behalf of the plan. It coordinated the campaign, directed speakers to civic groups, and generally served to increase collaborative interaction between formerly distant or hostile political leaders.

Two groups predictably became active in opposition: the Liberals and a variety of ultra-Conservative county residents. Since this governmental reorganization threatened the basis of their political influence, the Liberals were zealous in their counterorganization; they devoted more effort to this measure than to any other in their political history. The Negro sector of the Liberal leadership worked far more quietly, perhaps because the Negro subcommunity was easily mobilized and partly because the essentially upper- and upper-middle-class Negro Leadership did not want their public image to be that of opponents of progress. Though the labor unions were split on the question, the great bulk of them backed the Liberal leadership.

The county residents included a small number of rank-and-file citizens and political leaders who supported the plan. But many in that area were aroused in opposition. Their spokesmen included increasingly prominent Radical Rightists who saw in the plan a number of evils: it represented big government and big taxes, concentration of political power, accentuation of administrators' control, increased urban planning, and other measures violating citizens' rights. Radical Right sentiments prevailed over White Supremacy sentiments, since the proposal was widely understood to diminish Negro political influence in the city, if adopted. As in Metroville on school consolidation, governmental consolidation was opposed independently by deadly enemies: Supremacist Radical Rightists and Negro-White labor Liberals. The Radical Right of Petropolis did not appear to be as highly organized as the Radical Right of Metroville, however, nor were their voices the most prominent raised on the side of the *status quo*. The county leaders who would stand to lose their positions under consolidation almost unanimously opposed it, as did Conservative farm groups who feared uniformly high tax assessment and property valuation throughout the county.

The supporters of the plan threw a tremendous amount of resources into the campaign. They bought large and frequent newspaper ads and television time and distributed pamphlets. They publicized the fact that among those actively backing the plan were a large number of people who, over the years, had been honored for their civic devotion and leadership. However, they seemed unable to reach the great bulk of citizens whose cultural experience had been such that it prevented them from having or appreciating the values of "rationality" in government, professional urban planning, and political decision-making in the general interest. Much of the campaign activity of the "progressives" seemed to be directed to those who already supported the plan, not to the nameless, civically undistinguished mass of residents.

The plan was defeated by a tremendous margin in both city and county. This was a sharp defeat for Mayor Plunkett, the Community Conservationists, their Orthodox Conservative associates, and various uncommitted leaders. Power was shared by White and Negro Liberals, Radical Rightists, and the nonideological voters who feared higher taxes, urban planning, and diminution of their base of political influence. The decisional process that encompassed virtually the whole Community Conservationist program had been overwhelmingly lost. A major factor in the loss seemed to be that those leaders had tried to substitute a broadened civic leadership for a political organization with firm lines of communication to, and commitments from, the mass of citizens of low cultural class: the Negroes and the White industrial working class.[7]

Though defeated on the plan, the Community Conservationists, a relatively large number of Orthodox Conservatives, and industrially oriented uncommitted leaders proceeded to initiate another demand, which unified their ranks further by gratifying a common value: maintenance and promotion of the industrial base of the economy. Even though a technical study had shown that residential users of water had been paying proportionately several times the fees paid by industrial users, these men proposed that industrial rates be reduced further as an inducement to present industry to remain in the community and for new industries to enter. The management of the city council's deliberation of the question jointly by inner-clique members of both the Community Conservationist and Orthodox Conservative leadership groups indicated how consensual were the new relations between these groups.

The Liberals were divided on the issue. They sought the strengthening of the industrial base of the community, while, at the same time, they favored progressive taxation in government and payment for municipal services according to ability to pay. Most of these leaders acquiesced, though one labor representative stood out in opposition. The Community Conservationists and their new allies were therefore successful. They hoped that this action would serve to improve the reputation of Petropolis in the eyes of industry, a reputation these leaders feared had been damaged severely by the local political activities of the militant Liberal leadership and the highly conflictful character of local politics.

The 1961 local elections indicated that the structure of the political leadership was undergoing a drastic change. The former Democratic party leader, Liberal John Jay, announced his candidacy for mayor, in opposition to Conservationist Plunkett. The Liberals thereby expressed their unhappiness over the new alliance between Plunkett's group and their arch-enemies, the Orthodox Conservatives.

The Negro Liberals were thrown into a dilemma. Plunkett and the Community Conservationists had accorded them status in difficult times, and always had been constructive in their race-relations orientations and behavior. Nonetheless, it was through their alliance with the Liberal machine that the Negro subcommunity had gained most of its victories over the past dozen years. At the last moment, PESNEG decided to support John Jay, believing, apparently, that Plunkett had been "backsliding," that Jay had proven his friendship consistently, and that their future prospects were best secured through maintaining ties to disadvantaged White labor rather than with the increasingly distant, advantaged Community Conservationists.

Plunkett was reelected by a relatively narrow margin after a hotly contested campaign. For the first time in the political history of PESNEG, a large portion of the Negro electorate had not accepted the decision of its leadership. This reflected to some extent the private disagreement of some of the leaders of PESNEG with the majority's endorsement. Negro voters split almost evenly in voting for mayor, and an unusually large proportion failed to vote; this resulted in Plunkett's narrow victory.

Actually, a *de facto,* internal reorganization of the Negro Leadership had continued to take place during these periods. Literally only a handful of highly educated, young adult Negro Latent Leaders had continued to develop a more radical set of demands for social and governmental reorganization in Petropolis. They developed a substantially independent political-leadership organization with numerous young Negroes, of college and high-school age, and with some White college students. Working as local units of increasingly militant national Negro civil rights organizations, they were providing a leadership that the Negro Liberal Leadership in PESNEG could neither control nor effectively oppose. That Manifest Liberal leadership found its freedom of action in authoritative-consideration stages of decision-making increasingly reduced. From its vantage point, the newer Negro Leaders were almost a Radical Left group in their goals, strategy, and tactics; yet in the absence of a direct challenge to its leadership of the subcommunity, the officials of PESNEG dared not openly resist this manifestation in Petropolis of the national Negro revolt. Thus, at a time of increasing accommodation between White Community Conservationists and Orthodox Conservatives, made possible in some measure by the increase in racial-accommodation tactics of the latter, further sharp splits were appearing in the working alliance of the former with the Negro Leadership.

It should be noted in passing that the development of a newly militant minority of Negro Leaders based on ordinarily prepolitical youth differed in two respects from the youthful uprising noted in Metroville. In the latter city, the young people found themselves facing a more openly resistant older Negro Leadership than that in Petropolis. Furthermore, the children of Petropolis' Negro subcommunity found themselves working with a small but politically astute set of young Negro adults, whereas in Metroville the rebellion by the Negro children had no such support, and the adult Negro Liberals who succeeded them as aspirants to the political leadership of Metroville were not the men of the militant civil-rights organizations as they were in Petropolis. It is conceivable that the noticeable pattern in our findings of a disadvantaged group of Liberals, whether moderate or more radical, attaining or maintaining political-leadership positions in a community's power structure only when they have joined with a set of somewhat more advantaged colleagues might, if it is valid, be superseded by a pattern of the disadvantaged joining with such extra-community allies as the Department of Justice or national civil-rights organizations. If so, it would appear that the prospects were higher in Petropolis than in Metroville for a more militant Negro Leadership to maintain political-leadership positions at least for some period of time, even without a working alliance with local White political groups.

What Plunkett's reaction to PESNEG's decision would be was impossible to predict. That his administration would continue to need Liberal support was indicated by the results of the council election, in which a large proportion of Liberal-supported candidates emerged victorious. He would not look to the Radical Rightist citizens in the White subcommunity for support, nor would it have been available had he tried. They had to sit this election out, since they saw no basic distinctions between Liberals and Community Conservationists; the Rightists considered them equally deficit-spending, integrationist, socialists, with traditional upholders of the Conservative order inexplicably deserting to the enemy camp—as had happened with so-called Liberal Republicans, renegades at the national level.

The sense of electoral potency remained high in Petropolis. Illegitimate sanctions were not in evidence, and, as was now the case in Metroville, the use or threat of such sanctions appeared to be ineffective because of the protection afforded the potentially sanctionable by competing subsidiary political organizations and leadership groups. Thus, the regime appeared to have been maintained as a Developed Democracy.

The leadership was divergent in ideology. During this period, at least one decisional outcome was won by each of the contending groups. Liberals and a variety of ultraconservative Latent Leaders were victorious in the consolidation affair; Community Conservationists and Orthodox Conservatives were successful on the matter of water-rate changes. Such was the enmity between Orthodox Conservatives and Liberals that it appeared unlikely that the Conservationists of the newly enlarged center could arrange a consensus or working arrangement between their new associates on the right and their former associates on the left.

Participation in the consolidation issue had been high throughout the community; this indicated that at least that large segment of "anti" voters had shared power in the outcome. There is no reason to believe that the distribution of power had become any more narrow than in previous time periods. Hence, we conclude that the power structure continued to be Competitive Mass in type.

ORETOWN: PERIODS 3 THROUGH 8

Increasing Leadership Convergence

In the discussion of the successful recall of the two Liberal city councilmen in Period 2, we mentioned the possibility that Oretown's power structure might have been moving from a competitive to a consensual type. At that time we noted:

In the course of the campaign, there had been much interaction and cooperation between the two leadership groups, which presented the prospect of increasing convergence in the future, particularly since members of both had come to the conclusion that a protracted high level of controversy had damaged the community sorely and that the time had come for unity in behalf of the common good.

It was also noted that the Longacre section of the city, which earlier had given the Liberals strong support, was becoming politically integrated into the city. Following the recall, there was continued political change in the direction of a more consensual and a more elite power structure, so that, by the end of Period 3, the power structure in Oretown was Consensual Elite. It remained so for about 4 years, until Period 7.

After the recall of the Liberal councilmen, a new city manager was hired. He differed very much from his immediate predecessors both in political ideology and in his conception of the proper role of the city manager. The new city manager, Mr. Jackson, was ideologically a Community Conservative; he was hired by Mayor French and the other city councilmen partly because he shared their ideology. He had been trained in the politics of a big city, and was politically sophisticated. Because of these training experiences and because of his political ideology, he viewed the appropriate role of a city manager as that of a leader in political decision-making—albeit a quiet, almost invisible leader—and the monopolist in important administrative decision-making. He was a strong but not a domineering man, and he felt that Oretown needed a strong city manager. His predecessor had felt that a city manager should leave "policy-making" to the elected officials. Jackson believed with his fellow Community Conservationists in Oretown that a number of matters that traditionally had been the subjects of political decision-making ought to be subjects of administrative decision-making and within the domain of the public administrators. He believed, even more than most of his fellow Community Conservationists, that community conflict should be replaced with community quiescence, if not consensus, because a city manager could not operate effectively in the center of severe political conflict. He felt that if a community's political leadership were to become consensual, there would be no need to fear a "Populist" citizenry's periodic intervention in political or administrative decision-making and their thwarting of appropriate shifts in the scope of local government.

In particular, City Manager Jackson felt that there were three urgent conflict-reducing tasks of the highest priority in Oretown. One was the elimination of serious competition between the Community Conservationists and the Orthodox Conservative merchants on Main

Street. He believed that if these political groups reciprocally recognized each other's legitimate short-term interests, an identical long-term interest in community improvement would lead to a cooperative instead of a competitive relationship between these two centers of political influence. He felt that the hostility between the Orthodox Conservatives, who represented the major industries in Oretown, and Mayor French's administration, especially in the matter of annexation of the area in which much major industry was located, could and should be eliminated. Further, he believed that the public-private power issue had to be resolved, but that if the first two objectives were accomplished the third would follow. He shared the view of his fellow Community Conservationists who had been in Oretown for longer periods of time that if the small businessmen who had served as the leaders of the Liberal political group could be prevented from obtaining electoral success, the cleavage between the large blue-collar and smaller white-collar segments of the community would disappear.

Mayor French agreed, although somewhat reluctantly and with some skepticism about the prospects of success, to follow City Manager Jackson's advice to refrain from criticizing the "selfish" attitudes of the industrialists in their antiannexation position. A major effort was made under City Manager Jackson's .direction to establish personal and social relations and a channel of direct political communications with the senior industrial executives who had been so influential in the electoral defeat of annexation in the area north of Oretown. At the same time, an effort was made in the service-club and civic-group settings dominated by the Orthodox Conservatives to solidify the close working relationships that had developed between the Community Conservationists and the former group during the successful recall campaign.

As these efforts were under way, the municipal elections of 1956 were approaching. The voters were to be asked in that election to approve two bond issues for improving library facilities and the physical structure of the city hall. Funds were to be requested to build a new city library to replace the inadequate existing library facilities and for the construction of a new city hall. It was felt that the latter would improve the working conditions of city-government employees and that it would stand as a visible monument of civic progress that, much like the new community hospital, might contribute to an urgently needed increase in civic pride on the part of Oretown's citizens. The campaign to raise sufficient funds to build a community hospital had been successful. An attractive but inexpensive structure had been built to provide, for the first time, hospital facilities for the citizens within the city itself.

At the beginning of 1956, during Period 3 and almost 9 months before the election, Mayor French announced that he would not run for reelection. After serving 4 years as a part-time mayor who had actually devoted many more hours to the position than the financial remuneration warranted, Mayor French found that his income had suffered severely. He felt that he could not afford to run again and that it was his duty to alert his fellow citizens to the need for a replacement. In the middle of the summer of 1956, the Mayor made his decision final and public. A relative newcomer to Oretown, Mr. Roland Terch, decided that he would like to be mayor. He was a businessman who, during his postwar residence in Oretown, had not been very active in community political or civic affairs. He identified himself as a Republican, but was not active in the local Republican organization; nor was he a member of any of the service or civic clubs in the community. However, he was a close friend and neighbor of one of the officials of the private power company. Another of his close friends was attorney George Keel, the man who had become an advocate and a defender of the private utility after his chairmanship of the advisory committee appointed by the Mayor to recommend a solution of the private-versus-public electric-power controversy.

Mr. Terch's candidacy was popular with the officials of the private utility and with leading Orthodox Conservative members of Main Street. At about the same time, a strong supporter of Mayor French on the city council decided to enter the race for mayor's office. This man was a Democrat, a businessman, and a Community Conservationist in political ideology. Although Mayor French preferred one of his closer associates, he agreed that this councilman should run, even though the latter was something less than dynamic in his public appearances. Of particular significance to the Mayor was a petition nominating this councilman for the mayoralty that was circulated by one of the inner-clique Orthodox Conservatives. A somewhat conservative, active member of the Community Conservationists was then induced by Mayor French and others to serve as this councilman's campaign manager to seal what seemed to them a united electoral front on the part of the Conservatives and Conservationists.

The business community, however, now had two candidates from which to choose. A meeting of Main Street merchants was called to see if business support might not be obtained for one rather than split between the two. At this meeting the supporters of Roland Terch convinced the overwhelming majority present that he would be the better candidate. Mr. Terch also had the support of City Manager Jackson. Jackson felt that Mr. Terch would be a cooperative man with whom to work and that his candidacy would help to solidify relations between City Hall and Main Street more than would the candidacy of the Democratic Conservationist councilman. This disagreement over strategy within the Community Conservationist group, between the City Manager and the Mayor, was to produce an unexpected candidacy and a most unusual election.

When former Mayor Lovegren announced his candidacy, he pointed out that Mr. Terch had the support of the private utility. Mr. Lovegren once again had strong support from the union chiefs. Mr. Terch hoped that eventually the competition between the private and municipal utilities could be resolved by the municipal utility's paying a fair price for the private utility's facilities in Oretown. In the interim, he suggested, the two companies could share their facilities, thereby eliminating unnecessary duplication. Electricity rates might be raised by about 10 per cent in the interest of both companies. Terch was a strong supporter of the city-manager form of government and in favor of the continuation of the programs and policies of the French administration.

The councilman who was running for mayor was a more enthusiastic supporter of the municipal utility. He was not concerned particularly with the quick settlement between the two utilities, apparently because he felt that this competition guaranteed the lowest possible utility rates for the citizens of Oretown. He also was a supporter of the record of the French administration, for which he worked as a city councilman. Both Mr. Terch and the city councilman strongly supported both the library and city-hall bond issues.

Mr. Lovegren campaigned on the following complex of issues. The first and foremost issue was the private-and-municipal-power-company competition. Lovegren was entirely on the side of the municipal power company and referred to Mr. Terch as a "private company" man. He identified all of his opponents, including Mayor French, as advocates of monopolistic private power. Lovegren ran on his record as the man who had brought to Oretown cheap electric power and as the man responsible for all of the civic-improvement programs initiated during his and Mayor French's administrations. He attacked Mayor French for improving fire protection with funds that had been earlier set aside to help purchase sites for new industry. He attacked the city manager and, by implication, the city-manager form of government. He concentrated his attacks on City Manager Jackson, his "exorbitant" salary, the inability of the citizens to reach the city manager, and Jackson's attendance at professional meetings at the city's expense. Lovegren took no position on either of the bond issues, but he made strong antitax statements throughout his campaign. A repetitive theme of the Liberals in Oretown during Mayor Lovegren's administration, 1948 to 1952, and thereafter was the need to make civic improvements and at the same time lower local taxes. Oretown's tax level already was lower than the tax levels of many other smaller and larger cities in Western State. Both school and municipal taxes were comparatively low, and the need to increase taxes to make needed community improvements was a central feature of the Community Conservationist program.

About 1 month before the 1956 election, a group of leading Community Conservationists urged Mayor French to run again. They suggested that they could organize a write-in campaign that would give him the victory in November. This group included the councilman candidate's campaign manager. He felt that, since he was unable to raise funds for the councilman because the business community was supporting Mr. Terch, and because Mr. Terch would probably lose to former Mayor Lovegren, Mayor French had to run and win or else see the work of the last 4 years be completely undone. City Manager Jackson did not agree, because he felt that either Mr. Terch or the city councilman candidate would defeat Mr. Lovegren.

One of the factors that finally induced Mayor French to run again at this late stage was his observation that the city employees of the independent municipal utility district were campaigning actively for Lovegren. This suggested to him that his administration had not succeeded in developing the sort of effective, cohesive municipal organization that was so vital to the success of his program. If the employees of the municipal utility still thought that its preservation was most likely under Mr. Lovegren, Mayor French concluded that he was still very far from his goal of ending the community's conflict-producing utility competition through a consensual, peaceful victory for the municipal utility. Two weeks before the election, Mayor French publicly announced that he agreed to run as a write-in candidate for the office of mayor; his city councilman associate withdrew from the race in his favor.

Mayor French's organization swung into action in a variety of ways. Petitions in which they declared their support of Mayor French were circulated among the citizens. The hope was that this would stimulate the petition signers to write in Mayor French's name on election day. The local radio station carried numerous announcements that the voters should "write in French" on election day. Sample ballots with French's name written in were sent to almost every household just before the election. Mayor French appeared on a variety of television programs with Democratic candidates running for partisan office in other races. Lovegren's campaign did not gain momentum with Mayor French's belated announcement. Roland Terch did increase his campaign activities and seemed to rely on a telephone campaign set up by the local Republican organization. In those telephone calls, the Republican party workers urged the election of Terch but the defeat of the library and city-hall bond measures which Terch had supported publicly. Although this was a legally nonpartisan election, the local party organizations were important subsidiary political organizations during the campaign.

City Manager Jackson's prediction that former Mayor Lovegren would run last turned out to be correct. Mayor French received a plurality of votes, running about 30 per cent ahead of Mr. Terch and 50 per cent ahead of Mr. Lovegren. The library bond issue was passed narrowly; the city-hall bond issue was defeated narrowly. The Longacre section, which had been the area of strongest Liberal-Lovegren support, seemed to have been split: in one of the two precincts, Mr. Lovegren won a plurality of the votes; in the other, Mayor French was the electoral leader. In one of those precincts both bond measures were defeated substantially; in the other both were approved by substantial margins. Immediately following the election, serious efforts were made to heal the breach between the supporters of Roland Terch and Mayor French. This breach had been reinforced by the role of the two antagonistic local party organizations, but at the same time it had been minimized by both French's and Terch's directing their campaigns against Lovegren instead of each other.

The Community Conservationists now felt that they no longer had to worry about organized labor, since Mayor French had proved a strong vote-getter among blue-collar workers. Continued efforts were made to woo labor-union officials away from the Lovegren camp, particularly Donald Scott, one of the members of the Liberal inner clique. Lovegren's defeat in 1956, together with the successful recall of the two Liberal councilmen a year earlier, brought about the complete collapse of Lovegren's Liberal political group. Donald Scott accepted an appointment to a local-government commission, and the activities of other labor-union leaders seemed now to be regarded as substantially irrelevant in Oretown's politics. Mayor French, City Manager Jackson, and other Community Conservationists assured the merchants of Main Street that Mayor French's campaign had not been directed against Mr. Terch, but against the possibility of Mr. Lovegren's return to office. They suggested, in fact, that, since Mr. Terch now had acquired some experience in politics, and hopefully would continue to be involved in community affairs in the next four years, they might give him their full support in 1960. Developments in the still extant annexation questions gave additional impetus to the increasing convergence of the Orthodox Conservatives of Main Street and the Community Conservationists in and outside City Hall. In this political decision-making process and in the building of a consensual political leadership, City Manager Jackson played a crucial role.

Six months after coming to Oretown, City Manager Jackson received petitions from the residents of North Oretown for the city to hold another election to annex this area. He took the position that another election was premature unless there was more evidence that an election there would be successful. Mr. Jackson decided that it was imperative to gain approval of the annexation from Oretown's large X mining company, which was located in that area and which had been firmly opposed to any annexation of their property. Jackson first persuaded Mayor French to stop making anti-industrialist statements. He then brought the Mayor and the top executive of the X Company together, and, after a long period of developing social relations, they reached political accord.[8] During Period 4, the company announced that it no longer would oppose the annexation of this area, including their valuable industrial plant and equipment, to the city. This announcement followed another "technical" survey by an engineering firm, initiated by Jackson, which recommended annexation as the most sensible way to solve the sewage, drainage, and health problems of that area.

Relations were now better between City Hall and the industrial segment of Oretown. There also was a corresponding improvement in relations between the merchants of Main Street and City Hall. Many merchants looked with favor upon the proposed annexation because they foresaw an improvement in their own tax position when the valuable industrial properties were included in the city's tax base. At the same time, the French-Jackson city administration began to explore seriously with the private utility the possibility of the city's paying what both parties would consider a fair price for the facilities of the private utility, and thus ending the private-municipal power war. These events and the active involvement of the city manager in many of the Main Street civic and service clubs led to a new and almost unprecedented level of cooperation between Orthodox Conservatives and Community Conservationists. It seemed, in fact, that as time passed additional numbers of Orthodox Conservatives became Community Conservationist in orientation.

The Rise of the Radical Right

Mayor French felt that the time was ripe for the city to increase in its population and area through the annexation of the large problem-ridden area north of Oretown. The city manager was exceedingly cautious in regard to the annexation. He repeatedly recommended postponing another election until the residents of that area clearly indicated that another annexation election would have favorable results. He was concerned about two things: the tremendously complicated problems that the professional public administrators would face in making the large-scale sewage and other improvements that a newly annexed area of this character would require; and the bitter opposition which he sensed from among a number of the residents of this area, particularly those owning farmlands that would be subject to city property taxes for services that owners felt they did not need or want.

During Period 5, a number of the residents of the fringe area north of Oretown requested again that the city hold an annexation election. In the meantime, the city planning commission had recommended that the city annex the area including the largest industrial properties but excluding some of the land with the rural uses. This was a somewhat smaller area than a number of the advocates of annexation desired to see included. But it accorded with City Manager Jackson's preferences for not taking into the city people who would be opposed to such an action and who might constitute an anti-municipal-government group after annexation. This time the annexation election was postponed because another matter that the French administration considered more urgent was on the ballot for a November vote. After a long negotiation, the private utility company agreed with the city on a fair price for their properties. If the voters would approve a bond issue to buy out the assets of the private utility, the private-municipal electric power issue would come to an end in Oretown. The bonds were to be repaid out of the projected revenues of the municipal utility and no local tax increase was involved.

In the course of pre-electoral negotiations, the various groups in the current political leadership became ever more consensual as they worked together to solve what all parties agreed was the community's most important problem. The management group in the private utility were under orders from their home office outside of the community to try to reach an agreement so that the company could get rid of a unit that was damaging to the overall company profits at a price that would satisfy the company's stockholders. The Orthodox Conservative businessmen involved in the negotiations foresaw substantial community benefits in the cessation of this fight over the principle of private ownership, whose ultimate outcome they saw, with regrets, was now a foregone conclusion. Because of the private utility's decision, they agreed with the Community Conservationists that the more quickly the outcome could be settled, the more quickly a mutually beneficial, cooperative relationship could be established among the various segments of the community to whom the electric-power issue had been more important than normal economic and social relations. There seemed little doubt in the minds of any of the negotiators that the voters would approve the revenue bonds.

The power bonds, however, went down to defeat by a very narrow margin in the election. Informal opposition had been noted immediately prior to the election, but the failure of the voters to act "rationally" in turning down a chance to end an "unnatural" competitive situation was puzzling to Oretown's political leadership. The opinion among the political leadership was that a number of the voters had been under a misapprehension in that they believed that a vote for revenue bonds would mean an increase in their local property taxes. A number of the voters also were thought to be unaware of what educated people understood to be in economic terms a "natural monopoly." And then there was the usual, "irrational" set of "no" voters who took a perverse pleasure in obstruction.

However, analysis of the electorate's behavior revealed that the dominant motivation of the voters who voted to defeat the proposal was a simple, logical interpretation of economic principles, no matter how "irrational" it may have seemed.[9] Many voters not only had begun to take the conservative motto that "competition is good" seriously, but a large number of them also felt that however "unnatural" this competition was, it was the best guarantee against a single surviving utility's raising its electric-power rates. The defeat of this measure reinforced consensus among political leaders and further motivated them to work closely together in spite of the fact that their ideologies differed.

In the meantime, a new political decision-making process was being born. This was a question of whether or not Oretown's local government should participate in an urban-renewal program under the authorization of federal and state legislation. Apart from its future impact on the issue of private or municipal electric power, annexation, and other political decision-making processes, it marked the beginning of the end of the newly developed Consensual Elite power structure in Oretown.   Its end occurred some 4 years after the initiation of the urban-renewal decision-making process and will be noted at the end of this chapter.   In Period 3, one of the professional planners in the area had suggested that the new federal-local partnership program of urban renewal might provide a means of solving some of North Oretown's major problems.   An Orthodox Conservative businessman initiated by letter a series of contacts between interested parties in Oretown and appropriate federal officials in Washington, D. C., and in the regional headquarters of the Housing and Home Finance Agency to explore the possibilities.   In Period 4 a planning grant was obtained from HHFA, and Oretown's urban-renewal program was initiated formally.

An area inside the city limits was selected for renewal instead of the problem-ridden fringe area of North Oretown.   This was an area of mixed land uses.   It was primarily a residential area, which suffered from a condition of what planners refer to as "blight" and substandard housing.   A number of industrial structures were interspersed with the homes in this not particularly attractive part of town.   A plan which would cost almost a million dollars was developed, in which a new "super-standard" residential area would be created through demolition and clearance of some of the most deteriorated residential and all of the industrial structures.   A new school would be built; an attractive, multiacre park would be located there; and space would be reserved for "semipublic" uses—that is, for church sites or civic-organization buildings.   A portion of the area was reserved for multiple-family apartment units.   One of the major, articulated desires of the citizens and public administrators most active in deliberating the priority functions of the proposed urban-renewal program was the creation of a fine residential neighborhood that would produce its fair share of local taxes at a minimal cost to the citizens of Oretown.   It was expected that the building of a new school in this area and the installation of a variety of municipal facilities and services would substantially pay for the city's one-third share of the total cost.   In fact, it appeared that the federal government would provide almost 99.9 per cent of the cash funds needed to undertake the project.

It was imperative that the advocates of this urban-renewal program obtain the cooperation of the independent recreation district and of the independent school district.   A chief public administrator of the recreation district and prominent Community Conservationist was active at the outset in support of the urban-renewal program, ensuring the district's cooperation.   The top administrator in the school district that included Oretown had been an Orthodox Conservative Manifest Leader during Time *E* to *M*. During Periods 1 and 2, the natural-experiments period, he had been succeeded in office by a young Community Conservationist. The latter influenced the school board, which initially had resisted the program, to agree to cooperate fully.

A citizens' advisory board for urban renewal had been formed under the active leadership of Mayor French. It was composed of a cross-section of citizens, including a representative of organized labor and several representatives of the Orthodox Conservatives of Main Street. In the meantime, the politically astute Mr. Ben Kelly, the small businessman member of the Community Conservationist inner clique, had become the new president of Oretown's Chamber of Commerce. A "local-government committee" of the Chamber was formed for the purpose of initiating reviews of the budgets of the individual units of local government, which the Chamber membership could then endorse or disapprove. This constituted an effective organizational merger of Community Conservationists and Orthodox Conservatives; each budget was endorsed as it came to the Chamber's attention. This did not mean that Orthodox Conservative opposition to local-government spending and increased taxes ceased. For example, George Keel actively opposed the proposed school budget as unnecessarily large, and urged the individual local-government units to agree informally to an overall limit on spending and taxes and to work out necessary budget cuts. Such attempts by Mr. Keel and other individuals were defeated in the Chamber of Commerce.

The active proponents of urban renewal hoped that the program would improve consensus and increase civic pride in the community, as had happened when the community hospital was built. At the outset, they were careful to anticipate expected anti-urban-renewal arguments. With endorsement from the city's central labor council, no extensive opposition was expected from the nationally liberal, Democratic working class. For the "unreconstructed" Orthodox Conservatives who might oppose this government-spending program, it was to be stressed that President Eisenhower had asked Congress to approve the urban-renewal program. Public housing, the citizens were to be assured, was not contemplated in the program. The local realtors would handle the property transactions and the local banks would finance the program on short-term notes. The government would serve only as the guarantor. The small net costs to the city presumably would allay the fears of those concerned about an expanding, expensive local government. Recognizing that a number of aged people with very low incomes were living in the urban-renewal area, the active supporters of urban renewal assured themselves and others that adequate private housing at low cost was available to these soon-to-be-dispossessed people. However, at about the same time, the county government began to formulate a public-housing program especially for low income, aged people; the first projects were to be located in Oretown's fringe area. The advocates of urban renewal who had been most concerned about the relocation of the aged from the renewal area now ceased to worry.

Although an election on the urban-renewal program was not necessary by federal, state, or local law, and had not been contemplated when the program had been initiated, an unofficial, advisory vote of the citizens of the city was scheduled for sometime during Period 6. Although no bond issue was necessary to finance the city's share of the program, it was felt that an expression of substantial citizen support at the polls would be beneficial. As the election approached, a small businessman living in the renewal area began an active anti-urban-renewal campaign. This man was not a member of the Orthodox Conservative political group, although he was a strict Orthodox Conservative by political ideology. Nor did he have social entree or belong to any of the subsidiary political organizations dominated by the merchants of Main Street. The last time this man had come into public prominence was just prior to Time *E*, when he spoke against and threatened to pass petitions to abolish the city-manager form of government. He charged, at that time, that the city-manager form of government was unnecessarily costly, that it had resulted in unnecessarily high taxes, and that it was undemocratic. Because of his violent opposition to a Liberal political ideology, he had not joined Mayor Lovegren, who also was opposed to the city-manager form of government and high taxes, at that time.

With the assistance of an articulate, well-educated associate from neighboring Big City, this man revived his earlier charges, this time directing his fire at the proposed urban-renewal program. A number of small organizations characterized by a Radical Right political ideology already had come into existence in Oretown and in the surrounding area. These organizations were subsidiary local chapters of national Radical Right associations. This man and his close associates brought them into Oretown's community politics for the first time.

After a short but bitter campaign, the advocates of urban renewal defeated their opponents in the municipal election on the program by a narrow margin. The voters responded to the intensity with which the pro and con urban-renewal campaigns were waged by turning out in numbers even larger than had turned out for the city-council-men recall election of 1955.   The victors congratulated themselves that they had had sufficient foresight to organize the various segments of the community as well as they had.   But they were taken aback at the apparently widespread receptivity of Oretown's citizens to the antigovernmental ideological appeals of the Radical Right spokesmen for the opposition to urban renewal.   They were also somewhat baffled in regard to which segments of the community had proved to be susceptible to what they regarded as the irresponsible propaganda of the Radical Right.   Their explanation was that too many of the friends and supporters of their Community Conservation programs had stayed home from the polls, while the chronic dissenters—"aginners," as they called them—had turned out in droves.   On the other side, the strength of their electoral support, even in this losing cause, convinced the Radical Right leadership that their prospects were bright for capturing political-leadership positions, and for acquiring political power, in future decision-making in Oretown's community power structure.

The Lower Classes and the Radical Right

Two months after this election, a new sample survey was conducted in Oretown in order to assess the dynamics underlying this surprisingly close vote.   Using the same procedures that were used at Time M, the Manifest Political Leadership was identified at the same time. Only 3 per cent of Oretown's Manifest Leaders strongly disapproved of the urban-renewal program.   Some 86 per cent of the Republican and Democrat Manifest Leaders approved the urban-renewal program; half of these Leaders approved "strongly."   In contrast, only 43 per cent of the citizens at large, voters and nonvoters, approved of urban renewal and only 13 per cent approved "strongly."   One-quarter of the citizens disapproved; the proportion of "strongly" disapproving citizens was identical to the proportion of those who "strongly" approved. Almost one-third of the citizens at large were undecided about the merits of urban renewal.[10]

Citizen attitudes towards urban renewal and voting for or against it did not follow political-party lines (Table 13-1).   In fact, the only difference in the urban-renewal attitudes of partisans was the slightly greater approval of urban renewal by those who identified themselves as Republicans than by those who identified themselves as Democrats or Independents.   Since the Radical Right led the opposition to urban renewal in terms of Conservative Republican principles, was the absence of "party-line" cleavage an indication that the proponents of

TABLE 13-1   Attitudes in Oretown toward Urban Renewal, by Partisan Self-Identification *

Partisan Identification	Approve	Undecided	Disapprove	Totals %	N
Republicans	48%	31%	22%	101	107
Democrats	43%	33%	24%	100	208
Independents	43%	25%	32%	100	87

* The Approve category contains the "strongly approve" and "approve"; the Undecided category includes those who "don't care," and the Disapprove category contains the "strongly disapprove" and "disapprove" of urban renewal in this and the following tables. This and the following tables are based only on survey date from residents of the city itself, except for Tables 13-10 through 13-13, which also include fringe-dwellers.

urban renewal had been successful in attracting bipartisan support .from the citizens and removing ideological considerations? If so, what citizens for what reasons were opposed to urban renewal? Was the Radical Right correct in its assessment of widespread citizen support for its ideology in both its national and local community referents?

We find that national liberalism-conservatism in Oretown actually did at this time follow party lines. Republicans were more conservative than either Democrats or Independents. This measure of political ideology is based primarily on attitudes toward the appropriate scope of the federal government. National political ideology, independent of party identification, is also a function of social or cultural class position, so that, for example, the lower the level of education, the more liberal were Oretown citizens, whether they were Democrats, Independents, or Republicans (Table 13-2). Thus, Democrats were more liberal than Republicans, both because there was an ideological difference between these partisans and because more working- and lower-class citizens of Oretown were Democrats than were Republicans.

If national political ideology has played a role in shaping urban-renewal attitudes, we would have expected the more liberal self-identified Democrats to be more approving of urban renewal than the generally more conservative Republicans. However, this was not the case. We found that at low and high levels of education, citizens who were liberal nationally approved more of urban renewal. But these relationships were reversed among those with moderate levels of education, resulting in an unexpected overall relationship between national ideology and urban-renewal attitudes. The more conservative the respondents, the more they approved of urban renewal, although this relationship was very weak.

Three factors contributed considerably to an explanation of these somewhat anomalous findings, and explained, to some extent, the differences between the supporters and the opponents of urban renewal. These factors are: position in the cultural-class structure as indicated by educational level; political cynicism; and attitudes toward a central ideological and policy preference of Community Conservation, namely, the disposition to increase local taxes, if necessary, to make community improvements.

The higher their educational attainments, the more approving the citizens were of urban renewal (Table 13-3). Almost twice as many of those who at least had begun a post-high-school education as of those who had no formal education beyond high school supported urban renewal. This relationship is stronger than similar relation-

TABLE 13-2   National Political Ideology in Oretown, by Partisan Self-Identifications and Educational Level *

			Totals	
	Liberal	Conservative	%	N
Republicans				
Low education	48%	52%	100	21
Medium education	56%	44%	100	16
High education	23%	77%	100	22
Democrats				
Low education	69%	31%	100	39
Medium education	59%	41%	100	41
High education	42%	58%	100	12
Independents				
Low education	61%	39%	100	18
Medium education	63%	37%	100	27
High education	50%	50%	100	4

* Respondents with one or two years of high school are included with the less-than-high school respondents in the low-education category to increase the number in this category. This weakens the relationship apparent in this and in the following tables.

TABLE 13-3   Attitudes in Oretown toward Urban Renewal, by Educational Level

Educational Level	Approve	Undecided	Disapprove	Totals %	N
Low	35%	38%	27%	100	190
Medium	46%	28%	26%	100	158
High	67%	19%	14%	100	84

ships between occupation and income level on the one hand, and urban-renewal attitudes on the other. This suggests that common values and evaluations shaped by educational environments and experiences —that is, common positions in the cultural-class structure—was more of a determinant of such political attitudes than position in the socio-economic structure. The difference between those who had and had not been to college is especially noticeable in a variety of comparable situations.

Regardless of national political ideology, educational level had an independent impact on urban-renewal attitudes. Thus, the college-educated liberals and conservatives both approved more of urban renewal than their less educated ideological fellows (Table 13-4). Variously educated conservatives supported urban renewal more than did the less educated liberals. Thus, even though those who had higher educational levels tended toward conservatism and Republicanism, and conservatism indicated opposition to urban renewal

TABLE 13-4   Attitudes in Oretown toward Urban Renewal, by National Political Ideology and Educational Level

	Approve	Undecided	Disapprove	Totals %	N
Liberals					
Low and medium education	38%	30%	32%	100	103
High education	93%	7%	0	100	15
Conservatives					
Low and medium education	46%	20%	34%	100	61
High education	63%	24%	13%	100	30

among the most poorly and most highly educated—but not among the moderately well educated—the considerably higher educational levels of Republicans than of Democrats countered the potentially greater opposition to urban renewal among Republicans. The Community Conservationist and Orthodox Conservative advocates of urban re- newel, generally highly educated themselves, talked during the cam- paign with highly educated Democrats and Republicans, who were disposed already toward urban renewal, regardless of their national ideological leanings.

What were the bases, if any, besides that of low cultural-class posi- tion itself, for the appeal of the Radical Right's anti-urban-renewal, ideological propaganda? The two major themes in the Radical Right's anti-urban-renewal campaign were that such a program was a social- istic, undesirable extension of the scope of the federal government into properly local affairs, and that it represented a violation of local citizen opinion by dictatorial, unresponsive city officials who were attempting to usurp political power and improperly invade private decision-making domains. Although the first argument may have reinforced or created anti-urban-renewal attitudes among national conservatives, particularly those of lower cultural-class position, the latter found a more receptive audience among those who were polit- ically cynical or distant than among those who were more trusting of their city officials.

The politically distant were proportionately more numerous among the most poorly educated; the moderately educated were the most cynical. The college educated were the most politically trusting of any educational category.

In general, the politically trusting approved more and disapproved less of urban renewal than the politically cynical. The politically distant were the most undecided or apathetic about urban renewal (Table 13-5). That the poorly educated were the most politically distant accounts in some measure for their indecision. As educational

TABLE 13-5   Attitudes in Oretown toward Urban Renewal, by Political Cynicism

| Political Cynicism | Approve | Undecided | Disapprove | Totals | |
				%	N
Trusting	56%	29%	15%	100	178
Cynical	38%	26%	36%	100	195
Distant	34%	48%	18%	100	58

level increased, so did approval of urban renewal—within each of these "political culture" categories. Education made the most difference for the politically trusting, much less difference for the politically cynical, and practically no difference for the politically distant (Table 13-6). However, within each educational category, the politically trusting were invariably more supportive of urban renewal than were the politically cynical or the politically distant.

One reason, then, for the relationship between educational level and attitudes toward urban renewal is that the different educational categories had different social-psychological relationships to their city officials. These differentiations in an aspect of the sense of cultural class affected this decisional preference. We shall pursue other possible meanings of educational and cultural-class differences insofar as they may explain that part of the education–urban-renewal-attitudes relationship not explained by the different political-cynicism-trust-distance orientations of the different educational categories. It is interesting to note that national liberals turned out to be less politically trusting of Oretown's city officials at this time than national conservatives. Since this was the case at every educational level, including the lowest, and since the least well educated were the

TABLE 13-6 Attitudes in Oretown toward Urban Renewal, by Education and Political Cynicism

	Approve	Undecided	Disapprove	Totals %	Totals N
Low Education					
Trusting	42%	45%	13%	100	71
Cynical	32%	25%	43%	100	87
Distant	25%	56%	19%	100	32
Medium Education					
Trusting	58%	21%	21%	100	66
Cynical	40%	27%	33%	100	73
Distant	28%	50%	22%	100	18
High Education					
Trusting	78%	15%	7%	100	41
Cynical	49%	26%	26%	101	35
Distant *	—	—	—	—	—

* Percentages are omitted because of the small numbers.

most liberal in their national political ideology, the strongest opposition to urban renewal from the least educated was more understandable.

In an effort to establish whether this national-liberalism–political-mistrust nexus was specific to Oretown and traceable, in part at least, to the anti-local-Liberal political sentiments of the Community Conservationists and Orthodox Conservatives who had dominated City Hall for almost four years, or whether this was a more general phenomenon, these relationships were investigated in nearby Big City. In that city, there was no such relationship among the moderately or highly educated, although there was a comparably strong relationship between level of education and attitude toward urban renewal. Among the poorly educated, the liberals were less politically trusting and more distant than the conservatives, although both national ideological groupings were equally cynical. In Big City, there was not at the time these data were collected, nor had there been since the Second World War, a political-leadership group comparable to the Liberals of Oretown. Nor had there been an issue such as the private-municipal power conflict or urban renewal to invoke national liberal and conservative ideological doctrines in community politics. The hypothesis that national liberals were likely to be politically mistrusting in Oretown, because of the political misfortunes of the national-and-community-oriented Liberal political-leadership group, is not disproven by these findings in the neighboring community.

This is not to suggest that the Community Conservationists of Oretown did not include in their ranks nationally oriented liberals. Mayor French himself belonged in that category. But the defeated Liberals brought their national ideological rhetoric and doctrines to community politics, particularly to the emotion-stirring private-public power issue. Concern for the tax burdens of the poor, of the working men, and, not coincidentally, of the more marginal property owner and entrepreneur, was a liberal theme reiterated by the Liberal inner clique before their group met with defeat and disorganization. By 1959 the Community Conservationists and, to a lesser extent, their confreres among the Orthodox Conservatives had as a central tenet of their ideology and decisional program the spending of local tax monies and, if necessary, the increasing of property taxes, the chief source of local revenues, for desirable programs of community improvements, renewal, or rehabilitation in the public interest. The Radical Right had become the new trustee of the public purse in Oretown and the protector of private property against "confiscatory" taxes there, whether levied by local, state, or federal officials.

The urban-renewal program was characterized by the Radical Right as an unnecessary program that would have to be paid for by the city's taxpayers, either through their federal income taxes or through local property taxes that would be used to finance the municipal improvements for which Oretown was planning to receive credit as its one-third share of the cost of that program. Although taxes and costs were relatively minor themes in the campaign against urban renewal, the local tax sentiments of the citizens, as indicated by the findings of the sample survey, did much to explain citizen opposition to urban renewal—particularly among the poorly educated.

The citizens were asked to indicate their attitude toward "increasing local taxes, if necessary, to improve city services." Neither the amount nor the type of tax increase was specified, nor were the city services identified specifically. This ambiguous, almost "projective" type of question elicited responses clearly indicating that the relationship between tax-mindedness and urban-renewal attitudes was as strong as that between the latter and political cynicism. The linear relationship was such that almost three-fifths of those citizens who .approved such tax increases approved of urban renewal, compared to half of those who were undecided and less than one-third of those who were opposed to such tax increases (Table 13-7).

Attitudes towards this tax-increase item were related to educational level: the poorly educated were most opposed. Differences in education still made a difference in urban-renewal attitudes, regardless of tax-increase attitudes, although the difference was relatively small for those opposed to such tax increases (Table 13-8). Because those with less than some college education were considerably more opposed to such a city services tax increase, another portion of the less educated's greater opposition to urban renewal is explained.[11]

TABLE 13-7   Attitudes in Oretown toward Urban Renewal, by Attitudes toward Increasing Local Taxes to Improve City Services

Increase Local Taxes, if Necessary, to Improve City Services	Urban Renewal			Totals	
	Approve	Undecided	Disapprove	%	N
Approve	58%	25%	17%	100	157
Undecided	49%	35%	16%	100	110
Disapprove	30%	33%	37%	100	166

TABLE 13-8 Attitudes in Oretown toward Urban Renewal, by Attitudes toward Increasing Local Taxes to Improve City Services and Educational Level

Increase Local Taxes to Improve City Services	Urban Renewal			Totals	
	Approve	Undecided	Dis-approve	%	N
Approve					
Low education	48%	34%	17%	99	58
Medium education	59%	20%	21%	100	61
High education	72%	19%	9%	100	32
Undecided					
Low education	38%	44%	18%	100	45
Medium education	50%	29%	21%	100	38
High education	64%	28%	8%	100	25
Disapprove					
Low education	24%	37%	39%	100	87
Medium education	37%	31%	31%	99	70
High education	30%	10%	60%	100	10

Liberals were less trusting of city officials than were conservatives. Similarly, fewer of them supported this Community Conservationist tax-increase disposition. This was true for people of all education levels, although the difference between highly educated liberals and conservatives was small. Thus, the lower the level of education, the more frequently was found a combination of liberalism, political mistrust, and opposition to tax increases for improvement of city services.

There was a substantial overlapping in attitudes of political mistrust and opposition to the hypothetical tax increase at every educational level in Oretown. The independent impact of this tax attitude was noticeable when we also found that it was related to urban-renewal attitudes for both liberals and conservatives at every level of formal education. We have noted already that, among the moderately educated, the more liberal citizens were more opposed to urban renewal than the more conservative citizens. We now find that this was due almost entirely to the greater opposition to local tax increases among the liberals than among the conservatives, and not to the greater disposition of conservatives as national ideologists to favor the program more than their liberal counterparts at this educational level.

TABLE 13-9   Attitudes in Oretown toward Urban Renewal of Citizens with Selected Patterns of Attitudes toward Increasing Local Taxes to Improve City Services, Political Cynicism, and Educational Levels

	Urban Renewal				
				Totals	
	Approve	Undecided	Dis-approve	%	N
A. Low education, "Approve" or "Undecided" re increasing local taxes to improve city services, and politically trusting	52%	43%	5%	100	42
B. Low education, "Disapprove" of increasing local taxes to improve city services, and politically cynical	24%	26%	50%	100	46
C. Medium education, "Approve" or "Undecided" re increasing local taxes to improve city services, and politically trusting	59%	22%	19%	100	54
D. Medium education, "Disapprove" of increasing local taxes to improve city services, and politically cynical	33%	29%	38%	100	42
E. High education, "Approve" or "Undecided" re increasing local taxes to improve city services, and politically trusting	81%	17%	3%	101	36

We may summarize this analysis by looking at educational level, political cynicism, and attitudes towards increasing local taxes, if necessary, to improve city services, as they interacted to affect urban-renewal attitudes. Each one of these factors produced greater or less opposition to urban renewal independently of the others.

The people most opposed to urban renewal were the poorly educated, politically cynical citizens who were opposed to increasing taxes to improve city services (Table 13-9, B). When their poorly educated fellows regarded the city officials as responsive to the citizens and at the same time approved or were open to the possibility of local tax increases to improve city services, outright opposition to urban renewal almost disappeared. With these political orientations, the poorly educated supported urban renewal far more than did their more highly educated fellows who were antitax and anti-city-officials on the same measures (Table 13-9, D).[12]

The Radical Right found the most sympathetic citizen support for its anti-urban-renewal campaign and continued postelectoral opposition among the working class; those with low levels of education in whatever occupations; such segments of the citizens as the aged, who were less educated than younger adults; those who were politically cynical about or distant from their city officials; and those who were opposed to spending local-tax monies on civic-improvement programs of the kinds advocated by the relatively "free-spending" Community Conservationists.[13] The Community Conservationists found their citizen allies among the better-educated citizens of Oretown, among those who felt that the city officials were responsive to the citizens, and among those who were disposed to see local taxes increase, if necessary, in the interest of civic improvements. The urban-renewal issue had not brought about the sort of partisan and national ideological cleavages which the Radical Right had hoped would bring them victory at the polls in the urban-renewal election. On the other hand, the Community Conservationists appeared to be surprisingly weak insofar as citizen support for such civic-improvement programs as urban renewal was concerned; the weakness was most evident in the numerically large lower- and middle-class segments of the community.

A Crucial Test of the Political-System Models

By the time of this urban-renewal issue and the resulting birth of the Radical Right as an aspiring political-leadership group opposed to the Community Conservationist-Orthodox Conservative or Main Street-City Hall alliance, the analytic assessment was that Oretown's power structure had become a Consensual Elite structure and its regime type remained a Developed Democracy. Even though the Liberals had become disorganized and relatively quiescent, there was no observable increase in either fears of illegitimate sanctions or in the probability of such illegitimate sanctions' being used by the new leadership. Although there was still minority Orthodox Conservative opposition to the decisional preferences of the Community Conservationists, the level of cooperation between these two formally competitive leadership groups had risen substantially. The relatively cooperative working relationships between these two leadership groups had survived even this recent determined effort by the new political group, the Radical Right, to attain a share of political power in Oretown. The distribution of political power had become and remained more elite and less mass in character than during Time E to M and the natural-experiment periods. This assessment is based on an analysis of the extent to which the citizens at large participated with some probability of attaining political influence and making a contribution to one or more decisional outcomes during Periods 3 through 6. The assessment may be illustrated in one regard by a comparison of citizen participation in Oretown from Time M to about the end of Period 6, the summer of 1959. These data were obtained from sample surveys conducted at the beginning and the end of this approximately $5\frac{1}{2}$-year time span.

There was a noticeable decrease of citizen political participation between 1953 and 1959. The proportion of the community samples, in both the city and the fringe area, reporting no discussion at all with city officials, civic leaders, or friends, no active part in decision-making, and no attendance at a political meeting of any sort increased from 18 to 35 per cent from Time M to Period 6. Although some of the differences in particular political participation items are small for one or another of the educational categories, in every one of the three level-of-education categories on all five political-participation items there was a drop-off between these two points in time (Table 13-10). There was a relatively heavy decrease in the extent to which the citizens of Oretown reported discussing local government or community affairs with friends, civic leaders, and local government officials. This decrease in policy or decisional discussion was greater for the less educated than for the well educated in their respective friendship groupings, but there was even a decrease in such discussion with friends among the well educated. There were substantial decreases in such discussion with civic leaders and local-government officials among the well educated as well as among the less educated.

TABLE 13-10   Political Participation Rates * by Educational Level in Oretown at Time M (1953) and Period 6 (1959)

Political Participation Items	Time M (1953)			Period 6 (1959)		
	Educational Level			Educational Level		
	High, %	Medium, %	Low, %	High, %	Medium, %	Low, %
Discuss with friends	93	86	68	86	68	45
Discuss with leaders	52	34	23	35	15	7
Discuss with officials	40	18	16	25	13	4
Attend meetings	21	13	11	18	12	6
Activist role	24	10	10	16	8	2

* The percentages refer to the proportions of respondents in each educational category who reported that they at least "occasionally" discussed local-government or community matters with the specified others or who had attended at least one meeting wherein such a matter had been a major subject of deliberation or who had taken a more active part in policy-making.

A major prediction had been made that, with the increasing consensus at the political-leadership level of the power structure, there would be a movement toward an elite structure manifested in decreased political participation by the citizens at large. That prediction was based on the observed absence of a Consensual Mass power structure in any of the four communities from the Second World War to Time M (and during the natural-experiment periods) and on the theoretical grounds derived from the political-system models presented in Chapter 11. The prediction was most important in its theoretical significance: its inaccuracy would have forced us to reject or to modify drastically the models of political systems so far formulated. But the aforementioned findings were consistent with that prediction and increased our confidence in these theoretical models of political systems.

At the same time, another prediction was made in regard to the character of the newly consensual political leadership. Because a central tenet of Community Conservationist ideology in Oretown was that citizens had a civic duty to express their support of their city government by voting and thereby minimally to discharge their basic citizen obligations, it was expected that participation at the polls would decrease less than political discussion, attendance at political meetings, and participation in more activist roles. This prediction is borne out by the data, which indicate that the citizens at every educational level reported voting more regularly in the sample survey of 1959 than in that of 1953 (Table 13-11). The well educated reported a level of voting that was even higher than that reported by the equally educated, electorally high-participant citizens of Farmdale 6½ years earlier. Those with medium levels of education now ranked with their educational counterparts in Farmdale and in Petropolis' White subcommunity. The poorly educated citizens of Oretown reported a voting rate that was higher than that reported at Time M by the poorly educated, not only in Oretown but in every other community or subcommunity. A comparison of the voting statistics for local elections in these two periods bears out the increased participation of the citizens of Oretown at the polls.

The pattern first observed in Farmdale during Time E to M of high voting rates with low nonelectoral participation was also the pattern in Oretown by Period 6. The habit of going to the polls and voting, even in relatively "issueless" campaigns, may have contributed to the maintenance of a high voter-turnout rate in both Oretown and in Farmdale, but it is doubtful that this was the only, or even the major, factor producing this pattern in Oretown during this period. High voting rates actually increased over these years. Therefore, we suspect that this was, at least in some measure, due to the central belief of the Community Conservationists that citizens should vote, and to their repeated proclamations of that belief in their respective official and unofficial positions in the several units of local government.

We will examine now, through the data collected in the two sample surveys, two possibilities specifically relating to the substantial decrease in nonelectoral citizen political participation in Oretown be-

TABLE 13-11   Voting Rates * in Local Elections in Oretown at Time M (1953) and Period 6 (1959), by Educational Level

Educa-tion	Time M (1953), %	Period 6 (1959), %
High	84	90
Medium	68	72
Low	63	69

* The percentages refer to the proportions of citizens in each educational category who reported that they "sometimes" or "always" voted in local elections.

tween these two points in time when the political leadership had changed from competitive to consensual. In examining the support of and opposition to urban renewal among the citizenry, the relatively high level of political cynicism among the moderately educated and the relatively great political distance of the poorly educated from their government officials were noticeable. This suggests the possibility that the sharp drop in political participation between Time M and period 6 may have been due to increases in the sense of political distance, to increasing political cynicism on the part of the citizens, or to both. Inspection of the responses of the citizens in these two samples in regard to their feelings of political cynicism-distance-trust reveals that there was only a slight increase in the degree of political cynicism from the prior to the latter points in time. This increase in political cynicism was, in fact, almost entirely due to a shift in feeling on the part of fringe dwellers.[14]

· At Time M, the citizens both inside the city and in the fringe area who were politically distant were the least politically participant of all. This was the case at every level of education. Although the difference was small among the well educated, the politically cynical at every educational level were more highly participant than were the politically trusting. By Period 6, the time of the second sample survey, the politically distant were still the least politically participant but there was little difference between the politically cynical and trusting in regard to their degree of political participation. The drop-off in political participation did not result from the slightly higher level of political cynicism. Political participation dropped off almost equally sharply for the politically cynical, the politically trusting, and the politically distant. The drop-off in participation was somewhat sharper for the fringe residents. But this aspect of the general shift from a mass to an elite power structure in Oretown was fairly general in both areas of the community, and at every level of the social structure. A political participation index, consisting of the three discussion items, the meeting-attendance item, and the activist-role item, reveals that there was a considerably sharper drop-off in political participation between these two periods in time for those lowest in the social structure, even though the decrease was substantial even in the middle and upper social-structure levels.

If the hypothesis that decreased participation resulted from increased political cynicism or political distance on the part of the citizens had been supported, an alternative hypothesis derived from the political-system models would have been weakened. The alternative hypothesis was that, with the increasing consensus at the political-leadership level and with decreasing opportunities and narrowing channels for citizen participation in decision-making, nonelectoral participation would decrease without sharp increases in political cynicism or distance. Underlying this alternative hypothesis was the assumption that the newly consensual political leadership was building a more elite power structure in a manner that was sufficiently satisfying to the citizens to avert a substantial rise in citizen political frustration. The data do not contradict this alternative picture of political dynamics.

The changes in the structures of political influence in Oretown over these years can be seen even more clearly when the distribution of political influence in 1959 is compared to its earlier distribution at Time *M*. The index of political influence used to identify the active influentials at Time *M* was constructed in the same manner for 1959 (Table 13-12). Since citizen political participation had decreased, it is not surprising to find that memberships in subsidiary political organizations had also decreased substantially. Fifteen per cent of the citizens had belonged to two or more such organizations at Time *M* compared to only 3 per cent in 1959. The proportion of citizens belonging to no subsidiary political organizations increased from 50 to . 85 per cent over this period of time.

The proportion of citizens at the bottom of the political-influence structure doubled; the proportions at the top decreased sharply from Time *M* to 1959. The active influentials became proportionately a much smaller category by 1959, and their characteristics were different from those of the active influentials at Time *M* (Table 13-13).

Oretown's earlier active influentials had been more representative, in socio-economic characteristics, of the citizens at large than the ac-

TABLE 13-12   Index of Political Influence in Oretown at Time M (1953) and Period 6 (1959)

Political-Influence Score	Time *M* (1953)	Period 6 (1959)
3	14%	4%
2	29	8
1	39	53
0	18	35
Totals %	100	100
N	738	500

TABLE 13-13 Distribution of Selected Characteristics in Oretown among the Active Influentials at Time M (1953) and Period 6 (1959)

Characteristic	Time M (1953) N = 102	Period 6 (1959) N = 20
Sex		
Male	59%	75%
Age		
Over 55 years	22%	30%
Under 35 years	25%	25%
Occupation		
Managerial-		
Professional-		
Proprietorial	10%	60%
Blue-collar	46%	30%
Housewives	29%	5%
Farmers	—	—
Income		
Over $10,000	7%	15%
Under $4,000	31%	5%
Education		
College	23%	50%
Less than 2 years		
high school	35%	—
Length of residence		
Less than 10 years	67%	50%
Party identification		
Democratic	55%	30%
Republican	36%	50%
Independent	7%	20%
None	2%	—

tive influentials in any other of the research communities or subcommunities. This was no longer the case. The active influentials at the top of the citizen political-influence structure were, in 1959 compared to Time M, much better educated. They were predominantly proprietors, professionals, and executives. There were far fewer Democrats and fewer women in their ranks.

The political leaders of Oretown now were surrounded by a set of upper-class and upper-middle-class active influentials; the minority of the active influentials who were of lower-class status were not particularly sympathetic to Community Conservationist proposals. There was a consistent, strong relationship between educational level, for example, and position in the structure of citizen political influence. There was also the strong relationship between level of education and attitudes towards urban renewal. The active influentials would have been even more supportive of the Community Conservationist-Conservative leadership alliance if the poorly educated active influentials had not proved to be entirely lacking in pro-urban-renewal sentiments. That leadership had not been able to bring into positions of active influence the minority in the working class who supported such programs.

Moreover, the more upper-class supporters of the leadership alliance were underrepresented among the active influentials. For example, there was a minority of well-educated citizens opposed to urban renewal. These people were disproportionately numerous at the active-influential level, so that disapproval of urban renewal was considerably stronger among the well educated at that level—38 per cent disapproved—than among the well-educated citizens at large, of whom 14 per cent disapproved. These patterns suggest that the organizational base of the increasingly consensual Manifest Leadership was somewhat less unified in its perspectives than the shift over time to a more uniformly upper-class set of active influentials might suggest, reflecting the efforts of the competitive Radical Right to enter the political leadership and thereby change the power structure to competitive.

The picture of a more elite power structure developing in such a way as to avert sharp increases in citizen political frustration is a less stable, simple picture if these attitudinal cleavages at the active-influential level are kept in mind. The potential for increased political participation and change from a Consensual Elite to a Competitive Mass power structure would seem to be greater to the extent that a consensual leadership's organization of the informal structure of citizen political influence is not monolithic—as it apparently was not, even by 1959. Assuming that anti-urban-renewal attitudes constituted a basis of potential support for the aspiring Radical Right, it was clear that potential support for that group was restricted neither to the citizens at the bottom of the community's political-influence structure nor to the lower class, but was also present at the active-influential level of that structure by some citizens of various socio-economic positions.

A Return to Competition

After the narrow success of the campaign for urban renewal, the way seemed clear for those in favor of annexing the large area north of Oretown to proceed with plans for the annexation. City Manager Jackson still resisted an annexation election, because he sensed the increasing political mistrust of City Hall among residents of that area (noted above when the political attitudes of the citizens were compared through the two sample surveys). These research findings attested to the political acumen of the city manager in comparison to that of some of his fellow Community Conservationists. Among the latter were those who felt that there would be no serious opposition to annexation in that fringe area because it was now so obviously in the public interest to become part of the city in order to make needed improvements in the interest of the health and welfare of all citizens. A more detailed analysis of the survey data collected toward the end of Period 6 revealed that the greatest increase in political cynicism on the part of the residents of this fringe area was among the well educated. These were the citizens who proved to be the most articulate opponents of annexation.

A new annexation election was scheduled for Period 7, to be held both inside the city and within the fringe area to be annexed. In the meantime, the Radical Right stepped up its anti-urban-renewal campaign. They began to direct their fire at the city's new housing code, which was an ordinance passed by the city council in compliance with the federal government's requirement that a city have such a code as part of its "workable program" to be eligible for urban-renewal funds. The Community Conservationists strongly approved of the housing code, since its requirement that home owners maintain their residences in accordance with professionally promulgated housing standards would check the development of slums and blighted areas and avert the need for future urban-renewal programs in residential areas. They also favored the code because it would be a useful tool in maintaining what they considered to be an aesthetically pleasing community. The Radical Right spokesmen pointed to the housing code, particularly in its inspection and enforcement provisions, as the clearest example of the real objective of the proponents of urban renewal: to expand government's dictatorial powers.

Between the urban-renewal election and the scheduled annexation election, the Community Conservationists became a less organized political group. This was most noticeable in the plans that several of the key public-administrator members of this group began to make in regard to their future occupational positions. City Manager Jackson, James Watt of the recreation district, who was an original and still active member of the Community Conservationist inner clique, and the young, dynamic supervisor of the urban-renewal program all began to look for positions in other communities. These men had begun to feel that Oretown was entering one of its periods of "negativistic" citizen reaction to needed shifts in the scope of local government. They did not realize that their Community Conservationist messages were failing to make an impact, particularly on the working class in Oretown, but they had begun to feel that, however inexplicable, the increasing citizen opposition to some of their most important programs constituted a serious threat to their professional careers and a personally frustrating phenomenon.[15]

The city residents voted overwhelmingly in favor of annexation in the special election of 1960 but the residents of the annexation area itself approved of the proposal by a margin of less than 1 per cent. After almost a decade of political decision-making on this matter, the city of Oretown expanded significantly in both area and population with this annexation. At this time, City Manager Jackson left Oretown, and his successor was faced with the large-scale technical and political problems of improving and integrating the newly annexed area into the city. Mr. Jackson had not underestimated the scope of the political problems that annexation would bring to City Hall, as future events proved.

As the municipal elections of 1960 approached, Mayor French decided not to run for a third 4-year term. Led by him, the Community Conservationists at and around City Hall and the merchants of Main Street decided that Mr. Roland Terch would be their candidate for mayor. One of Western State's leading Radical Rightists announced his candidacy in opposition to Mr. Terch. Mr. Terch ran on a platform of continuing the French administration's major programs. His opponent ran on a platform of slashing city taxes, reducing substantially the scope of local government in order to revive free enterprise, and ending urban renewal and the county's public-housing program. As the election approached, the Community Conservationist-Orthodox Conservative alliance campaigned strenuously, because they felt that the election of a leading spokesman of the Radical Right as mayor would mean the end of civic progress in Oretown. Besides the mayoralty candidate, the Radical Right had members running for council positions.

When the ballots were counted, Roland Terch had become the new mayor of Oretown. Three of the six city councilman posts, however, had been won by men who were either Radical Rightists in political ideology or voted in an anti-Terch, "administration" direction. In less than 1 year, Mayor Terch exercised his authority to vote when there was a tie in the council more than a dozen times. Three of the councilmen consistently voted Community Conservationist, whereas the other three councilmen voted against them. Mayor Terch's ballot was the difference between victory and defeat, political power and no political power, for the Radical Right in these decisional processes. Prior to this election, the Radical Right had obtained decisional victories that had earned them political power and a share of the leadership positions in what had become, by the end of Period 7, a Competitive Mass power structure.

After the municipal elections of 1960, in Period 8, the Community Conservationists suffered a major, public political defeat when a handful of the residents in the urban-renewal area prevented city inspectors from enforcing the housing code by refusing them permission to inspect their dwellings. The Mayor and his supportive city councilmen felt that public opinion might be opposed to the legitimate authority of City Hall if it tried to enter the residences of these uncooperative citizens. The housing code in its entirety would soon become subject to political decision-making, with a public vote affording those in the newly annexed North Oretown area an electoral opportunity to express their feelings about the recent annexation and the Terch administration.

Negotiations between and among officials at City Hall, at the municipal and private utilities, and on the part of leading merchants of Main Street culminated in an agreement to submit to the voters toward the end of Period 8 a new proposal that revenue bonds be approved and sold for the purpose of the municipal utility's buying out the facilities of the private utility. This provided the occasion for the Radical Right, through initiative petitions, to schedule a vote at the same time on whether or not the citizens should repeal the city's new housing code. A vociferous campaign was conducted by the opponents of the housing code, who constantly reiterated that repealing the housing code would estop future urban-renewal programs and possibly prevent the present urban-renewal program from being completed. Just before the election, some of the most active proponents of repealing the housing code also urged the citizens to vote against the electric-power bonds. The opponents of the Radical Right for the most part urged the voters to retain the housing code and approve the power bonds.

With the entry into Oretown's politics of the Radical Right as an organized political-leadership group, some of their chosen targets were visibly upset, especially by what they regarded as slanderous attacks and vicious, invalid name-calling by this new political force. By the time the Radical Right made its next move, such vituperation had become mutual. If the Radical Right had by then become the sole political-leadership group, there would have been a question about the state of the permeability of the power structure or the probability that illegitimate sanctions would be used in the future. Since this had not happened, Oretown's regime remained that of a Developed Democracy. While political hate and antagonism were at a new high, the power structure remained permeable and the sense of electoral potency was high. The current electoral decision-making processes attested to the absence of either condition of Oligarchy in Oretown's regime.

The results of the voting on these two special measures attested to the success of the Radical Right in maintaining political-leadership positions in Oretown's community power structure. The housing code was repealed, with the voters casting almost twice as many ballots for repeal as against. The proposed electric-power bonds went down to defeat by a margin of less than 1 per cent. The voters from the newly annexed North Oretown area voted against the housing code by about ten to one and also contributed disproportionately to the defeat of the power bonds.

Immediately after the election on the housing code and on the power bonds, a sample of the citizens in the city who had been interviewed first in Period 6 were reinterviewed.[16] These reinterviews revealed that more of the opponents than supporters of the housing code and of the power bonds had turned out to vote. This was the case at both the low and medium levels of education, although not among the numerically small segment of well-educated citizens. Forty-nine per cent of those with less than a college education who said they wanted to keep the housing code actually voted, compared to 68 per cent of the comparably educated who wanted to see the housing code abolished. The same variables that had affected citizen attitudes toward urban renewal shaped citizen preferences for and against the housing code and the power bonds.

There was a strong relationship at every educational level between the earlier attitudes toward urban renewal—measured during Period 6 —and current attitudes toward both the housing code and the power bonds. For example, among the poorly educated citizens who had earlier approved of urban renewal, almost 50 per cent were in favor of keeping the housing code; among the poorly educated who had disapproved of urban renewal, 92 per cent were in favor of abolishing the housing code. Among the moderately well educated who had approved of urban renewal, 63 per cent wanted to keep the housing code; among the equally educated who had disapproved of urban renewal, 72 per cent wanted to abolish the housing code. Among the well-educated citizens of Oretown who had earlier approved of urban renewal, some 70 per cent wanted to keep the housing code; 80 per cent of the well educated who had earlier disapproved of urban renewal wanted to see the housing code abolished.

Opposition to the housing code and to the power bonds, attitudes which were strongly interrelated, was again centered among the citizens of lower socio-economic status, among the citizens who disapproved of increasing taxes to improve city services, among the politically cynical, and among those of liberal national political ideology.

This liberal-conservative national ideological cleavage was comparable to the relationship found between national ideology and attitudes toward urban renewal some two years earlier. In both cases, among the well-educated citizens, the liberals had the expected attitudes; that is, they approved of urban renewal and the housing code more than did the highly educated conservatives. Among the poorly and moderately educated, however, there was an even stronger relationship in the opposite direction, so that overall the more liberal citizens were less supportive of urban renewal and were more in favor of abolishing the housing code than were conservatives. It may well be that among the better-educated citizens, the political rhetoric of the Radical Right had touched national ideological orientations, whereas the antitax and "protect the poor and the elderly" themes in the anti-housing-code and anti-power-bonds campaign messages of the Radical Right had touched humanitarian and financial self-interest sentiments of the lower class.

During these reinterviews, the respondents were asked to select which of four reasons was the most important one in their vote to abolish the housing code in the event that that had been their electoral choice. Only a small minority said that their major reason for voting to abolish the housing code was that this would stop future urban-renewal programs, one of the four alternatives offered. An equally small minority selected as the most important reason for their anti-housing-code vote the option "it is something the politicians and bureaucrats want but not the people." The less educated citizens selected that reason proportionately more than did the better-educated citizens. The option "it invades private property rights" was the most frequently selected choice, but there was a direct relationship between educational level and choosing this reason. A substantial majority of the better educated, half of the moderately well educated, but only a minority of the poorly educated selected this as their reason for wanting to see the city's housing code abolished. The second most frequently selected reason for voting to abolish the housing code was that "it hurts elderly and poor people most." Here there was an inverse relationship between educational level and the frequency with which this last choice was selected. More than half of the poorly educated who said they had voted to abolish the housing code selected this as their most important reason for so voting. About one-quarter of the moderately well educated selected this as reason number one for their anti-housing-code vote; only one in ten of the well educated who had voted to abolish the housing code selected this option as their most important reason. These findings suggest that the Radical Right's interpretation of the housing-code election as evidence that their ideology was sweeping the community was somewhat off the mark.

In the 2-year period between the end of Period 6 (1959) and the time of the housing-code election (1961), citizen approval of urban renewal had declined. Using the same attitudinal measure for the same respondents at these two times, the proportion approving urban renewal was discovered to have dropped from 46 to 39 per cent. Although the anti-housing-code vote was not for most of the citizens a vote to stop further urban-renewal programs because the latter were ideologically undesirable, a hostile attitude to the active proponents of the urban-renewal program and a companion sympathy for the underdog did relate most strongly to citizen decisional preferences in the housing-code voting. Eighty-eight per cent of the citizens who agreed "strongly" or "somewhat" that "the people behind urban renewal in Oretown are trying to push people around" were in favor of abolishing the housing code, compared to only 23 per cent of the citizens who disagreed "strongly" or "somewhat" with this statement (Table 13-14). This relationship held for citizens of every educational level.

The feeling that those behind urban renewal in Oretown were pushing people around was more prevalent among the citizens of both low and medium educational levels than it was among the well educated. Mistrust of local officials and anti-local-tax sentiments were also still stronger among the blue-collar and middle-class citizens than among the citizens of upper-class status. Between 1959 and 1961 there was a small but noticeable increase in disapproval of tax increases to im-

TABLE 13-14   Attitudes in Oretown toward the Housing Code, by Attitudes about the People behind Urban Renewal

"The People behind Urban Renewal in Oretown Are Try-ing to Push People Around."	Housing Code		Totals	
	Abolish	Keep	%	N
Strongly or somewhat agree	88%	12%	100	82
Slightly agree or disagree	46%	54%	100	24
Strongly or somewhat disagree	23%	77%	100	78

prove city services.   Whether or not the political activity of the Radical Rightists had contributed to or caused such attitudinal shifts in the citizenry, their ability to tap an increasingly low sense of cultural class on the part of the masses of Oretown's citizens mitigated against the sort of supportive citizen action and attitudes so important to the Community Conservationists in the latter's strivings to serve the community they conceived of as a collectivity with a single, classless interest.

The Radical Right seemed to find an increasingly sympathetic audience among the large segment of the citizenry that was not so much attuned to the antigovernment, pro-private-enterprise doctrine but to the charges that political decision-making was being usurped by administrative officials and that both political and administrative decision-making were being monopolized by a small group who felt that everyone's political preferences but their own were inferior.   Although the Radical Right ideology was shared by few of its electoral supporters, numerous citizens were given an opportunity in the housing-code and power-bonds election to express their hostility to the attempted imposition of policies which had been formulated and deliberated by men who seemed to regard themselves as a select political-cultural class.[17]   Some citizens who were quite unsympathetic to the national orientations of the Radical Right but who voted on the housing code and power bonds in the "Radical Right direction" were provoked by the apparent disregard by men at City Hall and on Main Street of the financial implications for those without great wealth and by the disregard for the most vulnerable citizens, in the pursuit of the aesthetically pleasing, rational, and politically consensual community—all central values of the Community Conservationists.

Although similar factors were operative in affecting both attitudes toward urban renewal—when measured 2 years earlier and when measured again in 1961—and attitudes toward the housing code, the pre-election campaign itself had an observable impact on housing-code attitudes. The opponents of the housing code not only turned out to vote more than did the housing-code supporters, but the former reported in the set of reinterviews that they urged others to vote against the housing code more than did the latter.

The well-educated citizens urged others to vote one way or another more than did the less educated. Thirty per cent of the former were active in this way, compared to 18 per cent of the poorly educated. The poorly educated who had 2 years earlier disapproved of urban renewal were, however, as active in this regard as the well educated of whatever urban-renewal sentiment.

Position in the political-influence structure as of 1959 was even more strongly related to attempts to influence others about the housing code some 2 years later. Almost two-thirds of the active influentials urged others to vote in the housing-code election, compared to 60 and 44 per cent of the citizens who had ranked in descending order in the next two political-influence strata, and 3 per cent of the citizens in the lowest stratum of the political-influence structure. Although the proponents of abolishing the housing code were in a small minority among the active influentials, the greater frequency with which they attempted to influence other citizens resulted in almost an equal number of active influentials' urging others to vote to abolish and to vote to retain the housing code, according to the findings of this second set of interviews.

The failure of the Conservationist-Conservative political leadership to develop a more supportive set of active influentials thus had its consequence in this and the electric-power bonds decisions, where the same pattern was found. The distance between that leadership and citizens of lower-class status also had comparable consequences. More than half the citizens reinterviewed immediately after the housing-code election who were in favor of abolishing that code reported that they had been urged in a personal, social, or organizational setting to vote one way or another on the housing-code measure. The impact of these contacts in gaining political influence for one side or another in the housing-code election may be seen in the following findings: Among those who in 1959 had disapproved of urban renewal were relatively few who were contacted by housing-code supporters. However, those few reported that they were in favor of keeping the housing code. The other anti-urban-renewal citizens, who were urged to vote against the housing code or were not contacted at all, were in favor of abolishing the housing code by overwhelming margins.

Contacts from the anti-housing-code people among those who had earlier approved of or been undecided about urban renewal also made a significant difference in their attitude towards the housing code (Table 13-15).

These contacts made even more of a difference among the citizens of low education (Table 13-15). If this election demonstrated anything about the differences in the organizational character of the competitive political-leadership groups, it demonstrated the greater effectiveness of the grass-roots organization of the Radical Right. That organization was particularly effective in converting and inhibiting citizens who were earlier predisposed to vote in the Community Conservationist direction, especially the citizens toward the lower end of the socio-cultural structures who had become even more removed from the political organization extending from City Hall.[18]

Oretown's political system had thus changed from a system with a Competitive Mass power structure during Time E to M and the natural-experiment periods to a system with a Consensual Elite power structure, but then back again to its earlier type. Throughout these periods the regime remained a Developed Democracy. We can see more clearly that the early postwar period of Developed Democracy associated with a Consensual Elite power structure was a possible pattern. Even though that type of power structure changed again by

TABLE 13-15 Attitudes in 1961 in Oretown of Citizens Approving or Undecided about Urban Renewal in 1959 toward Housing Code, by Anti-Housing-Code Contacts

| | Housing Code | | | |
| | | | Totals | |
Approved or Undecided about Urban Renewal	Abolish	Keep	%	N
Urged to vote against housing code	63%	37%	100	27
	(82%) *	(18%)	(100)	(11)
Not contacted	38%	62%	100	78
	(41%)	(59%)	(100)	(37)

* The figures in parentheses refer to the comparable proportions for poorly educated citizens who earlier approved or were undecided about urban renewal.

Period 7, it had been maintained for about a 4-year period. Thus we have a clearer picture of how a political system characterized by a Developed Democratic regime can exist with other than Competitive Mass types of power structures. After Time M, Farmdale offered examples both of the Developed Democracy-Consensual Elite and the Developed Democracy-Competitive Elite patterns; Metroville offered after Time M an example of the former; and Petropolis offered in earlier postwar periods examples of the latter. The classifications of the types of power structures and regimes in the post-Time M natural-experiment and revisited periods are summarized in Figure 13-1.

It would seem that hortatory efforts of the kind made in Oretown during Periods 3 through 6 on the part of Community Conservationists to involve masses of citizens as active supporters of their policies—that is, to have a Consensual Mass power structure other than on election day—were unlikely to succeed, at least in the absence of Oligarchy. The political-system models suggest that, when there is a Consensual political leadership, the dynamic influences that involve citizens as sharers in political power are missing. In the absence of sharp political competition, there seems to be a natural tendency for citizen political participation to subside; subsidiary political organizations contract, and a consensual or convergent leadership thinks of the community not as a complex of political-influence strata with different cultural and socio-economic classes to be cultivated for their active political support, but as a mirror-image of the already active supporters of that leadership. A return to a Competitive Mass power structure thus seems to be the "natural" change to take place next should a change occur in a Consensual Elite power structure. But we shall leave such analyses for the next hypothesis-testing chapter.

Postscript from Oretown

Although beyond the purview of the periods providing data for testing hypotheses in the next chapter, another natural opportunity to assess the pulling power of the Radical Right in the citizenry came in the early spring of 1962. Specifically, events at that time permitted an assessment of the strength of the Radical Right in community politics when that political group attempted to recall both Mayor Terch and one of his city-councilman supporters on the ground that these men showed themselves unresponsive to the will of the people by continuing to support the current urban-renewal program after the voters had abolished the city's housing code. In the Radical Right's campaign to recall these elected officials, national ideological themes

Table across time periods: 1950-1951, 1951-1952, 1952-1953, 1953-1954, 1954-1955, 1955-1956, 1956-1957, 1957-1958, 1958-1959, 1959-1960, 1960-1961

	1950-1951	1951-1952	1952-1953	1953-1954	1954-1955	1955-1956	1956-1957	1957-1958	1958-1959	1959-1960	1960-1961
Farmdale, Western State	(E to M)*		(Nat. Exp.)†					(Revisited)‡			
period	−1	0	+1	+2	+3	+4	+5	+6	+7	+8	+9
Power Structures	CsE	CsE	CpE	CpE	CpM	CpM	CpM	CpM	CsE	CsE	CsE
Regimes	Gu	Gu	DD	DD	DD	DD	DD	DD	DD	DD	DD
Oretown, Western State			(E to M)	(Nat. Exp.)				(Revisited)			
period			0	+1	+2	+3	+4	+5	+6	+7	+8
Power Structures			CpM	CpM	CpM	CsE	CsE	CsE	CsE	CpM	CpM
Regimes			DD	DD	DD	DD	DD	DD	DD	DD	DD
Petropolis, Southern State								(E to M)	(Nat. Exp.)		(Revisited)
period								0	+1	+2	+3
Power Structures								CpM	CpM	CpM	CpM
Regimes								DD	DD	DD	DD
Metroville, Southern State								(E to M)	(Nat. Exp.)		(Revisited)
period								0	+1	+2	+3
Power Structures								CsE	CsE	CpM	CpM
Regimes								Un	DD	DD	DD

*"Time E to M" refers to the time periods beginning with the municipal elections prior to the first set of sample surveys and ending with those surveys, which is approximately 1 year in every community (period 0) except Farmdale, where it is 2 years (periods −1, 0).

†"Natural Experiments" refers to Time M to $M + 1$, the two 1-year periods (+1, +2) discussed in Chapter 12.

‡"Revisited" refers to the periods after period +2 discussed in the present chapter.

Key: Power Structures

CpM = Competitive Mass
CsE = Consensual Elite
CpE = Competitive Elite

Regimes

DD = Developed Democracy
Un = Underdeveloped Democracy
Gu = Guided Democracy

FIGURE 13.1 Power structures and regimes, by time periods, in the four communities

were continually stressed. Whether or not these themes would have their intended impact on the working class, and whether they would be sufficient to overcome an extensively organized Community Conservationist-Orthodox Conservative effort to avert what the latter regarded as the greatest threat yet to civic peace and progress, was at that time still an open question.

Mayor Terch and his councilman colleague, in their campaign to defeat the recall, stressed the fact that they were responsive to the wishes of the people. They committed themselves to submitting voluntarily to popular vote any future urban-renewal or public-housing programs which the city government considered desirable. This self-imposed restriction in itself constituted a victory for the Radical Right. In an election marked by an extremely high voter turnout, the attempted recall was defeated by approximately a 60-40 margin. In a number of the precincts in the newly annexed North Oretown area, the voters were overwhelmingly in favor of the recall. The Radical Right's effort to capture City Hall had failed; the city council still consisted of an uneasy balance between Community Conservationists and Radical Rightists, with the Mayor still in possession of the authority, the legitimate potential political influence, to cast the decisive tie-breaking ballot which would determine decisional outcomes and political-power allocations.

Although the Radical Right had suffered a major defeat, there was little indication that the redeveloped Competitive Mass power structure could be changed in the immediate future. The Community Conservationists and their Orthodox Conservative allies, who had worked as a well-organized political group in their successful opposition to the recall, were no longer "running scared." They became less well organized quickly thereafter as the Radical Right leadership withdrew temporarily from political decision-making in the community in order to consider their future political strategy. The Radical Right incorrectly interpreted the citizen support they had received as an indication that their national-local ideology was still on its way to becoming the dominant ideology of citizens in every portion of the social structure. At the same time the Community Conservationists interpreted the election, again incorrectly, as evidence that "the responsible citizens" had rallied to defeat an almost psychopathic negativism stimulated by "rabble-rousers" on the far Right. There was little appreciation at City Hall and on Main Street of the attitudinal cleavages underlying the citizens' voting behavior, or of the dynamics of a politically relevant cultural-class system which followed, but was not identical to, the social or economic structure in Oretown. A growing gulf was beginning to be sensed between the upper political cultural class and the relatively large class of citizens whose local-community political decisional preferences differed from those of the Community Conservationist and Orthodox Conservative spokesmen in that upper class. But ideas about how to reach the lower cultural classes and bridge or reduce the gulf were noticeably absent, both at City Hall and in the Chamber of Commerce.

The city manager was not the sort of "politician" that his predecessor, Mr. Jackson, had been, although the latter had not been any more innovative than the former in developing a permanent organization at City Hall whose roots would reach the rank-and-file industrial workers as well as the industrial executive echelon of this lunch-bucket community. Advocating extreme caution in political decision-making, neither the new city manager, nor Mayor Terch, nor any of their fellow Community Conservationists were prepared to advocate any new program contemplating major shifts in the scope of local government. When in 1962 a city budget appropriation for a study of ways to improve the central business district of Oretown was not matched by contributions from the merchants of Main Street, it appeared that the Community Conservationist dynamism at City Hall was at an end—at least for the while.

Some of Oretown's leading Community Conservationists joined at this time with a group of their ideological counterparts in neighboring Big City in organizing a new, formal association that was to focus on metropolitanwide instead of intracommunity problems. Modeled after a subsidiary political organization in a larger metropolis of Western State, the founders of this new metropolitan group purposefully enlisted both cooperative and hitherto uncooperative leading citizens of an Orthodox Conservative ideology. The immediate stimulus for the founding of this organization was the rise of a Radical Right group in the neighboring city comparable to, and interconnected with, the organized Radical Right leadership group of Oretown. Another factor was the increasing attention paid by public administrators, political scientists, and Community Conservationists nationally to metropolitan rather than single-community problem solving. Whether or not the various study groups of this new metropolitan association could or would try to reach the grass roots in either of these two cities, wherein the Radical Right had been so successful in eliciting electoral support to thwart Community Conservationist programs of civic improvement, was questionable. The Radical Right in Oretown's neighboring city had led a successful campaign to defeat that city's proposed urban-renewal program, and it had succeeded in other decisional processes as well. There was little evidence that the Community Conservationists in Big City were any more aware of, or had any better plans to deal with, what proved to be working- and lower-class electoral support for the Radical Right in that city— revealed by a panel study there—than were the Community Conservationists and their Orthodox Conservative allies of Oretown.

It would seem that the next move in the Developed Democracy of Oretown would be made by the Radical Right. But it was unclear for the moment what political demands would be made and what political decision-making processes would be triggered off from that direction to stimulate the functioning of what now seemed to be a relatively stable, Competitive Mass power structure changing in a cyclical but stable fashion from conflict to quiescence. It has been pointed out that, during the two decades prior to the Second World War, Oretown's power structure was generally Consensual Elite in type, but at times it seemed almost to become a Competitive Mass structure. This was due in part to the periodically Populist and Liberal political character of a portion of its populace. Although by the 1960's Developed Democracy had replaced the earlier alternating Developed Democracy-Oligarchy pattern in the type of regime, a comparable power-structure pattern was discernible which was due in part to the periodically Populist and Radical Right opposition to the ruling Community Conservationist-Orthodox Conservative coalition. Whether or not Oretown would maintain that rhythmic pattern for another decade or more we must leave for the unfolding of future events to determine, and perhaps for another book to describe.

NOTES

1. There have been relatively few community studies on which researchers have actually returned to communities to appraise socio-economic or political changes, or both, over time. A recent study of community politics in which an analyst returned to reappraise an earlier study and to assess possible political changes is reported in M. Kent Jennings, *Study of Community Decision-Making* (New York: The Free Press of Glencoe, forthcoming), following Floyd Hunter, *Community Power Structure* (Chapel Hill: University of North Carolina Press, 1953). Such revisitings by sociologists and anthropologists include: Robert and Helen Lynd, *Middletown* (New York: Harcourt, Brace and Co., 1929) and *Middletown in Transition* (New York: Harcourt, Brace and Co., 1937); James West, *Plainville, U.S.A.* (New York: Columbia University Press, 1945), and Art Gallaher, Jr., *Plainville Fifteen Years Later* (New York: Columbia University Press, 1961); Robert Redfield and Alfonso Ville Rojas, *Chan Kom: A Mayan Village* (Chicago: University of Chicago Press, Phoenix edition, 1962); Robert Redfield, *A Village that*

Chose Progress: Chan Kom Revisited (Chicago: University of Chicago Press, Phoenix edition, 1962); and Oscar Lewis, *Life in a Mexican Village: Tepoztlan Restudied* (Urbana: University of Illinois Press, 1963). Recent political studies which through historical reconstruction have identified major changes in political leadership include: Robert O. Schulze, "The Bifurcation of Power in a Satellite City," in *Community Political Systems*, ed. by Morris Janowitz (New York: The Free Press of Glencoe, 1961), pp. 19–80. A study focusing on changes in the political leadership more through a reconstruction of political decision-making is Roscoe C. Martin, Frank J. Munger, and others, *Decisions in Syracuse* (Bloomington, Indiana: Indiana University Press, 1961), and note especially pp. 305–307 therein.

2. See Donald T. Campbell, *Experimenting, Validating, Knowing: Problems of Method in the Social Sciences* (New York: McGraw-Hill, forthcoming); and Richard C. Snyder, "Experimental Techniques and Political Analysis: Some Reflections in the Context of Concern over Behavioral Approaches," in *The Limits of Behavioralism in Political Science*, a symposium ed. by James C. Charlesworth (Philadelphia: The American Academy of Political and Social Science, October 1962), pp. 94–123. For a series of articles dealing with the analysis of change through time, see Paul F. Lazarsfeld and Morris Rosenberg, editors, *The Language of Social Research* (Glencoe, Illinois: The Free Press, 1955), Section III, pp. 206–283.

3. An interesting series of essays on the Radical Right is contained in Daniel Bell, *The New American Right* (New York: Criterion Books, 1955).

4. See Figure 13.1 for the classification of Farmdale's and the other communities' power structures and regimes during these revisiting periods. In the present chapter, the periods referred to are all after Time M, although the $+$ symbol is omitted from the text.

5. For a study of the upper-middle-class backgrounds of Negro college students in Greensboro and Raleigh, North Carolina, see Ruth Searles and J. Allen Williams, Jr., "Negro College Students' Participation in Sit-Ins," *Social Forces*, Vol. 40, No. 3 (March 1962), pp. 215–220. They valued respectability and achievement, affirmed equal opportunity, and selected nonviolent protest as an acceptable means of demonstrating. Thus, what we would regard as a sense of belonging to a low cultural class or caste, which is not stressed by Searles and Williams, may be related weakly, not at all, or inversely to social-class characteristics for certain groups. It may lead to Liberalism, or Negro Supremacy or separatism, and Whites to the Radical Right. See E. U. Essien-Udom, *Black Nationalism* (New York: Dell Publishing Co., 1964).

6. For earlier comments on the possible importance of White allies for Negro Liberals, see Chapter 11. Although of perhaps crucial importance in particular protests, the value of assistance from the U. S. Department of Justice might ordinarily be too short-term and specific to replace local White allies, whether those allies are respectable White businessmen, White politicians, or even the White underworld. In neither Petropolis nor Metroville were faculty members of the White colleges either White Manifest or Latent Leaders as members of the Liberal political group. This may not have been specific to the biracial character of their communities, but it may have reflected a pattern of academic intellectuals entirely involved in their Liberalism as spectators or active participants in national politics and relatively unconcerned with local politics. A possible exception is in the very

biggest cities. See Delbert C. Miller, "Town and Gown: The Power Structure of a University Town," *The American Journal of Sociology*, Vol. LXVIII, No. 4 (January 1963), pp. 432–443.

7. See John C. Bollens, editor, *Exploring the Metropolitan Community* (Berkeley and Los Angeles, University of California Press, 1961), especially, Chapter 13, pp. 282–316; and the discussion of group support of and opposition to charter reform, Robert O. Schulze, *op. cit.*, pp. 53–61; and Advisory Commission on Intergovernmental Relations, *Factors Affecting Voter Reactions to Governmental Reorganization in Metropolitan Areas* (Washington: The Commission, May 1962).

8. See the attitudes of the Kane-Abbel company, those of the executives of U. S. Motors, and the issue of annexation in general, as described by Robert O. Schulze, *op. cit.*, pp. 61–66; and Amos H. Hawley and Basil G. Zimmer, "Resistance to Unification in a Metropolitan Community," *Community Political Systems*, editor Morris Janowitz, pp. 146–184.

9. Morris Janowitz, Deil Wright, and William Delany concluded that lower-social-strata groups demand extensions of the scope of government's welfare services and yet feel that the costs imposed by the government are not worth the services currently rendered. *Public Administration and the Public —Perspectives Toward Government in a Metropolitan Community*, Michigan Governmental Studies, No. 36 (Ann Arbor: Bureau of Government, Institute of Public Administration, University of Michigan, 1958), p. 40.

10. Although the urban-renewal program had been approved in the municipal election by a bare majority, 64 per cent of those interviewed who had a definite opinion were, by the time of the survey, on the "pro" side. Some of those who reported they were undecided or actually approved of the program may have changed their attitude, while others may have expressed an attitude at variance with their "real" attitude as expressed in the more private voting booth.

11. Oliver P. Williams and Charles Adrian, in *Four Cities* (Philadelphia: University of Pennsylvania Press, 1963), find that in four medium-sized Michigan cities, precincts composed predominantly of low-income property owners consistently voted more negatively on referenda involving local expenditures and bond issues than did other precincts, regardless of the type of political process predominant in the community. In Oretown, the majority of the working class, as well as of other citizens, owned homes or were buying them. Home owners or buyers favored local property-tax increases less than did renters, but it was those currently buying homes who most favored urban renewal. The most antagonistic were the poorly educated home owners, that is, older, long-term residents, whereas the home buyers tended to be the younger, more highly educated newcomers. It is useful and revealing to note that anti-urban-renewal attitudes did not result simply from fears that their own homes might be the next to go or that their local property taxes would increase because of the city's one-third contribution to the cost of the program, both themes of the anti-urban-renewal forces.

12. Insufficient attention has been paid in recent years to what may be relatively large numbers of "deviants" in the working class in terms of such political orientations as these. Although a necessary corrective for a variety of romantic views of the proletariat and *petit bourgeoisie*, a current fad is to document or explain relationships between "undemocratic" attitudes and

lower- or working-class status. See, for example, Seymour Martin Lipset, *Political Man* (Garden City, New York: Doubleday & Company, 1960), Chapter IV, "Working-Class Authoritarianism," pp. 97–130.

13. With increasing age, attitudes toward urban renewal became less favorable for the poorly educated, but not for the moderately educated. Overall, the relationship between age and urban-renewal attitudes was primarily a function of the relatively low educational levels of older citizens compared to that of younger citizens.

14. In the second sample survey in Oretown in Period 6, the fringe area was restricted to the relatively large area north of town which had been the subject of consideration for annexation to the city. In making comparisons on shifts in political cynicism of fringe-dwellers, and in Tables 13-12 and 13-13, fringe-dwelling residents living outside that area who were included in the sample survey at Time M are excluded from the tabulations.

15. These men feared an increasing conflict among narrowly defined interests, or what Oliver P. Williams has called an "arbiter" type of government. In Williams' terms, City Manager Jackson in particular seemed to be oriented toward a local government that was both an instrument of community growth and a provider of life's amenities, whereas his successor was more oriented toward a combination of the latter and a caretaker kind of government. See his "A Typology for Comparative Local Government," *Midwest Journal of Political Science,* Vol. V (May 1961), pp. 150–165.

16. Two hundred twenty-two randomly selected respondents from the 440 respondents interviewed in the random sample of adult city-dwellers interviewed at the end of Period 6 were re-interviewed at this time.

17. The development of both the housing-code issue and the earlier urban-renewal issue fit in general the model of the development of public issues presented by James S. Coleman, *Community Conflict* (Glencoe, Illinois: The Free Press, 1957), especially pp. 8–9 and 10–14. For an interesting case study of community controversy over urban renewal, see Peter H. Rossi and Robert Dentler, *The Politics of Urban Renewal* (Glencoe, Illinois: The Free Press, 1961). See also Julia Abrahamson, *A Neighborhood Finds Itself* (New York: Harper and Brothers, 1959); Martin Millspaugh and Gurney Breckenfield, *The Human Side of Urban Renewal* (New York: Ives Washburn, Inc., 1960); and Kurt W. Back, *Slums, Projects and People* (Durham, North Carolina: Duke University Press, 1962).

18. See the comparable interpretation of the motivations of "anti-" voters by John E. Horton and Wayne E. Thompson, "Powerlessness and Political Negativism: A Study of Defeated Local Referendums," *The American Journal of Sociology,* Vol. LXVII, No. 5 (March 1962), pp. 485–493. See also Wayne E. Thompson and John E. Horton, "Political Alienation as a Force in Political Action," *Social Forces,* Vol. 38, No. 3 (March 1960), pp. 190–195.

14

CONCLUSIONS

Since the end of the Second World War, there has been growing recognition that urbanization and industrializaton produce a staggering accumulation of physical and social problems in the local community. Community Conservation has become the ideology of more and more political leaders who have tried to solve these problems and to introduce greater amenities into urban community life. Because Community Conservationists have become important in so many communities and because the situation in American communities is analogous in some respects to that at the national level, the ideology is of increasing importance in American political life. In the present study, Community Conservation was significant in three of the four communities; in the fourth, Metroville, the Progressive Conservatives had moved so much in the direction of Community Conservation that they were becoming indistinguishable from Community Conservationists.

In association with the ascendance of Community Conservationist leaders, we have found the Developed Democratic regime type also ascendant. In 1946 and the ensuing years, three of our four communities were characterized at one time or another by other types of regimes; but by the end of our observations in 1961, all four were Developed Democracies. Developed Democracy is the ideal regime in the eyes of Community Conservationists. Community Conservationists believe in conditions that maintain and support a widely understood, permeable power structure. In other words, they desire conditions that maintain and support opportunities for political mobility. Their ideal type of power structure is Consensual Mass. They believe that the citizens should participate broadly and actively in political decision-making, particularly voting, and especially in elections for representatives as well as for measures. But so committed are they to the essential rightness of Community Conservationist values that they desire prior consensus among political leaders on such matters as local-federal cooperation in urban renewal, annexation of fringe areas, rationalization of metropolitan-area government, beautification of the city, and professionalization of the public service. However, this does not rule out all forms of political competition from their image of the ideal politics. They expect differences in emphasis and opinion among good citizens, sometimes manifested in competitive electoral campaigns and open public debates, and even in contested decisional processes. But in their view, there should not be division among the political leadership over the general Community Conservationist ideology and program, since these are based on the public interest and aim to improve the community physically and culturally through the most "rational" means. Furthermore, Community Conservationists value highly harmony and unity—"pulling together." They regard local community affairs as essentially nonpolitical, and tend to associate controversy with "politics." An additional factor reinforcing the value of harmony is many communities—in our study Petropolis and Oretown in particular—is the nationwide competition among communities for new industries. Conflict is thought to create a highly unfavorable community image to outsiders, an image that might well repel any prospective industry.

Although we have found Community Conservation and the Developed Democratic regime generally dominant in our four communities, nowhere did we encounter the "ideal type" of power structure, Consensual Mass. This current deviation from the Community Conservationist ethic seems to be the result of the rise of a political group that the former neither foresaw nor now seems to understand: the Radical Right has become important; it is locked in battle with the tenets and forces of Community Conservation, producing in two of the four communities a Competitive Mass type of power structure and reinforcing that structure in a third community. The Radical Right has reacted against a continuously expanding scope of local government with its attendant growth of bureaucracy and professionalization, and against the Community Conservationist emphasis on the collectivity rather than the individual. In the South, since the Supreme Court decision of 1954, this resistance has been based in some measure on antipathy to the use of government to reallocate social status between the White and Negro subcommunities. Emotions focused first on school-desegregation decisions, but sit-ins and other demands for desegregated public or quasi-public facilities have now become involved.

The Radical Right has been at a disadvantage in the competition with Community Conservation: the latter is supported generally by the mass media, by upper-middle-class civic morality, and by the ideological climate emanating from the White House, whether the incumbent be an Eisenhower or a Kennedy. Feeling acutely that they are the representatives of "the true values" but are ignored by the powerful, the Radical Right has gained some power at the local level by exploiting the major weakness of their opponents: their distance from such culturally marginal groups as the working class, the aged, the small property owner with a fixed income, and the small farmer. These people are unlikely to have the college education that is increasingly the hallmark of the Community Conservationist; they are unlikely to participate in those social activities that produce or maintain the political orientations of the "normal" civic leadership of most American communities. Beyond this, particularly in the small and medium-sized communities such as those we have studied, these people as small property owners share a sensitivity to taxes that provides the Radical Right a point of access, a place to begin a political conversation. The property tax is now by-and-large a regressive tax. Since much of the Community Conservationist program requires heavy expenditures, the success of that program is largely dependent on "selling" the small property owner on its desirability. However, it is here that the Radical Rightists frequently have been able to do a better job of political organization than the Community Conservationists. The mobilization of culturally marginal groups by Radical Right ideologists has been most apparent in decisional processes involving bond referenda.

The Radical Right, however, was not very successful in penetrating the political leadership in Petropolis, the only one of our four communities in which a Liberal leadership group existed. Apparently, the Liberal political organization, dependent numerically on labor-union members and focusing on social and economic amelioration, won the support of a sufficiently large proportion of the working class to thwart the Radical Right, whose appeal to the working class as a marginal group has been largely negative with regard to the scope of government.

In tracing the development of these leadership groups and the types of regime and power structure with which they are associated, we deal with phenomena that apparently are taking place in a large, though presently undetermined, number of United States communities. In this chapter, we will present and test a series of interrelated hypotheses that specify relationships among some of the major political-system variables—regime, power structure, leadership groups, and the scope of government—and between these variables and the social and economic systems. This treatment will not be exhaustive, and many conceivable relationships between these variables will not be investigated. But the hypotheses are designed to account for similarities and differences in some of the more significant aspects of the political systems of the communities we have observed.

Some of the hypotheses omitted here were tested earlier with data from the four communities during Time E to M. Others that might have been presented were not because sufficiently comparable data were not available. Because limitations of space precluded the specification of many other hypotheses that might have been tested in this chapter, the primary purpose of what follows is to illustrate how the approach used herein can contribute to the further development of empirically based political theory of community political systems— whether those communities are local, state, or national. The reader is invited to formulate additional hypotheses for testing with the findings reported earlier in the book or that might be applied in future comparative studies of political systems.

The years between the Second World War and 1961 were divided into fifteen time periods in each of the four communities. For each period, regimes and power structures were classified by type, and such other variables as scope of government were assessed. These classifications and assessments were made largely on the basis of voting statistics, newspaper stories, and informal interviews. The data for the periods prior to Time E, on balance, were much less systematic, reliable, and valid than those used for the analysis of the E-to-M, natural-experiments, and revisited periods. The danger of using such data seemed to us overbalanced by the value of an analysis over a period of time in which certain variables, in effect, can be controlled while the interaction of others is observed. This more dynamic type of analysis yields greater insight into the sources of change and stability in politics, and can serve as something of a model for future studies of political systems which look to the recent past, to an unfolding present, or to both for their data (Table 14-1).

Hypotheses will be presented regarding the following: the existence and emergence of Developed Democracy; relationships between regimes and power structures; changes within power structures; the formation of political-leadership groups; the internal organization of political-leadership groups; shifts in the scope of government; relationships between governmental structure and power structure; and some relationships between the social and economic systems and the local political system.

THE EXISTENCE AND EMERGENCE OF DEVELOPED DEMOCRACY

Hypothesis: The existence of competitive electoral opportunities for citizens to select public officials or decisional outcomes is a sufficient condition for the existence of Developed Democracy.

Test: Cases of non-Developed Democratic regimes
Farmdale, -1, 0
Petropolis, -11
Metroville, -11 through 0

Rejection of this hypothesis would require evidence that non-Developed Democratic regimes exist in association with electoral situations of competition among candidates or decisional options.

In Farmdale and Petropolis, such regimes existed during limited periods. In Farmdale, no decisional outcomes were decided at the polls during this time in special elections, nor was there competition for local public office.

In Petropolis, elections for local office were uncontested in 1947. A major bond proposal designed to provide for comprehensive improvement of public facilities was managed consensually by the Conservative leadership. However, shortly thereafter, during Period -10, frustrated Negro and labor elements began to be more assertive in politics: Negroes because they continued to be denied status by the Conservative leadership and the Conservative leadership's policy of markedly discriminatory allocation of funds for White and Negro education; and labor because of the unwillingness of the Conservatives to recognize a city employees' union. The union leaders decided to organize an electoral campaign to authorize more funds for the city's school system. The bonds were opposed by the Conservatives but were endorsed overwhelmingly. This success, plus the victory in a party election of a new local Democratic leadership sympathetic to labor and the Negro subcommunity, became associated with a rapidly rising sense of electoral potency on the part of these large sectors of the population. The change in orientation of formerly marginal groups transformed the regime from an Underdeveloped Democracy to a Developed Democracy. These sets of data from Farmdale and Petrop-

TABLE 14-1   Power Structures and Regimes, by Time Periods, in the Four Communities

	1946–1947	1947–1948	1948–1949	1949–1950	1950–1951	1951–1952	1952–1953	1953–1954	1954–1955	1955–1956	1956–1957	1957–1958	1958–1959	1959–1960	1960–1961
					(E to M)*		(Nat. Exp.)†					(Revisited)			
Farmdale, Western State	−5	−4	−3	−2	−1	0	+1	+2	+3	+4	+5	+6	+7	+8	+9
Power Structures	CpM	CpM	CpM	CpM	CsE	CsE	CpE	CpE	CpM	CpM	CpM	CpM	CsE	CsE	CsE
Regimes	DD	DD	DD	DD	Gu	Gu	DD	DD	DD	DD	DD	DD	DD	DD	DD
							(E to M)	(Nat. Exp.)				(Revisited)			
Oretown, Western State	−6	−5	−4	−3	−2	−1	0	+1	+2	+3	+4	+5	+6	+7	+8
Power Structures	CsE	CsE	CpM	CpM	CpM	CpM	CpM	CpM	CpM	CsE	CsE	CsE	CsE	CpM	CpM
Regimes	DD	DD	DD	DD	DD	DD	DD	DD	DD	DD	DD	DD	DD	DD	DD
												(E to M)	(Nat. Exp.)		
Petropolis, Southern State	−11	−10	−9	−8	−7	−6	−5	−4	−3	−2	−1	0	+1	+2	+3
Power Structures	CsE	CpE	CpE	CpM	CpM	CpM	CpM	CpM	CpM	CpM	CpM	CpM	CpM	CpM	CpM
Regimes	Un	DD	DD	DD	DD	DD	DD	DD	DD	DD	DD	DD	DD	DD	DD
												(E to M)	(Nat. Exp.)		(Revisited)
Metroville, Southern State	−11	−10	−9	−8	−7	−6	−5	−4	−3	−2	−1	0	+1	+2	+3
Power Structures	CeE	CsE	CsE	CsE	CsE	CsE	CsE	CsE	CsE	CsE	CsE	CsE	CsE	CpM	CpM
Regimes	Olg	Olg	Gu	Gu	Gu	Gu	Gu	Un	Un	Un	Un	Un	DD	DD	DD

* Time *E* to *M* refers to the time periods beginning with the municipal elections prior to the first set of sample surveys and ending with those surveys, which is approximately one year in every community (Period 0), except in Farmdale, where it is two years (Periods −1, 0).

† Natural Experiments refers to two-year periods (+1, +2), discussed in Chapter 12.

Key: Power Structures

    CpM = Competitive Mass
    CsE = Consensual Elite
    CpE = Competitive Elite

    Regimes

    DD = Developed Democracy
    Un = Underdeveloped Democracy
    Gu = Guided Democracy
    Olg = Oligarchy

olis indicate that the latter type of regime does not occur in the absence of electoral competition, and that the emergence of electoral competition is associated with the emergence of Developed Democracy.

Metroville's political history, however, provides evidence of a different sort. From Periods -11 through 0, the regime was not a Developed Democracy; but there were frequent contests in mayoralty and other elections for local office. Furthermore, many of these were heated contests. During the first successful mayoralty campaign of Mayor Peterson, his appeal to the downtrodden against the "ruling elite" was explicitly made and reiterated. Specifically, the Negro subcommunity and the less affluent sectors of the population generally experienced a rising sense of electoral potency, a belief that his election would promote desirable shifts in the scope of government. The Progressive Conservative leaders at that time were willing to accept the victory of Peterson in the Democratic primary rather than fight it in the general election and risk the demise of the Democratic party organization. But they were unwilling to acquiesce in the shifts in the scope of government for which the candidate campaigned. Hence, after his election, the probability remained high that the political leaders would act illegitimately to stop shifts. The absence of a competing organization supporting Peterson and based on his electoral constituency meant that such sanctions probably would have been effective in their impact upon policy deviants. As time passed, the sense of electoral potency of those who had supported Peterson declined as it became apparent that Peterson would not develop such an organization to make a broad attack on the problems of the Negroes and the poor. To the contrary, he had come to terms with the group against whom he had campaigned so bitterly. Meanwhile, the Progressive Conservatives' political orientations were changing toward a more accommodating, moderate position. Their predisposition to use illegitimate sanctions diminished as they became increasingly cosmopolitan and increasingly concerned with the community's image in the nation. The decline in the Negro sense of electoral potency was accompanied by a decline in the probability of the effective use of illegitimate sanctions. The regime gradually changed from Guided to Underdeveloped Democracy. So disillusioned had the Negroes become that their sense of electoral potency remained low, even in the bitter, competitive mayoralty campaign of 1957 (in which Peterson was attacked as the "Negroes' candidate"), although their vote gave Peterson the margin that allowed him narrowly to win despite much White opposition.

Therefore, the evidence available from three of the communities is mixed.   The total number of cases (by time periods) weigh against the hypothesis, and we reject it, although it is supported in two of the three communities.

Hypothesis: For the emergence of Developed Democracy, it is necessary for a group that is ideologically divergent from the prevailing political leadership to aspire to leadership through public office or in political decision-making.

> *Test:* Emergence of Developed Democracy
> Petropolis, −11 to −10
> Farmdale, 0 to +1
> Metroville, 0 to +1
> Non-Developed Democratic Regimes
> Farmdale, −1 through 0
> Metroville, −11 through −1

To test this hypothesis, we shall examine those three cases in which the regime changed to a Developed Democracy from some other type. We shall compare them to those cases where Developed Democracy did not exist for two or more periods.

Between Periods −11 through −10 in Petropolis, the regime changed from Underdeveloped Democracy to Developed Democracy, as was described in the previous section.   Associated with this change was the emergence of a new group aspiring to political leadership, the Liberals.   The Liberals combined the ideological interests of many Negro subcommunity leaders and White union leaders in a coalition that became known as "the machine."   Shortly thereafter, an allied but separate leadership group emerged among the moderate, younger businessmen: the Community Conservationists.

In Farmdale the regime changed from Guided Democracy to Developed Democracy between Periods 0 and +1, as a Community Conservationist leadership group formed to contest the policies of the Conservatives.   Previously, the latter had monopolized the political leadership of the community.

The Metroville regime shifted from Underdeveloped Democracy to Developed Democracy from Period 0 to Period +1.   Associated with the change was a rising protest on the part of Negroes who were angry over the Progressive Conservatives' recent decisions about school desegregation and the maintenance of segregation in mental health facilities.   Negro Leaders, formerly subservient or acquiescent to the Progressive Conservatives, now began to strike out independently in local politics.   Their ideological position combined aspects of both Community Conservation and Liberalism.   Their ideology and leadership-group structure were diffuse, but they constituted an identifiable aspiring political leadership group in opposition to the prevailing one. The next year (Period +2) another ideological orientation was represented by an aspiring leadership group: the Radical Right. This group organized the diffuse opposition among fringe-area residents and the less affluent urbanites to the costly civic improvements demanded by the Progressive Conservatives.

Hence, in all three of the cases where Developed Democracy emerged, an ideologically dissident aspiring political leadership group also emerged to compete with the established leaders.

There were only two cases in which a non-Developed Democratic regime was maintained for more than one period. In neither of these cases was there a dissident aspiring political leadership group. In Farmdale during Periods −1 and 0, the one dissident young accountant who was interested in organizing a political leadership group that would be ideologically distinct from the Conservatives was threatened with illegitimate sanctions. He decided, at least as a temporary strategy, to join the Conservatives and to cease his opposition before a dissident aspiring leadership group was ever formed. We detected some political complaints in the community, particularly among residents of the less affluent part of town—about the poor conditions of streets and sidewalks—and among the merchants—about the decline in retail trade. This was a form of political interest group activity at a low level of articulation and organization. However, the complaints did not lead to effective action, since there was no group of aspiring leaders to channel the opposition to the prevailing conservative policies. Similarly ineffective in the absence of such leadership between Periods −11 and −1 were the merchants of Metroville, disadvantaged by the parking bans and traffic regulations which had been implemented by the Progressive Conservatives; the Negroes, who opposed poor housing and slum conditions; and those fringe-area residents who opposed the rising costs of "good government."

However, at the beginning of the period encompassed by our research in Metroville (−11), there was a brief appearance of an ideologically dissident aspiring political-leadership group that was not followed by the hypothesized change in regime. A Radical Left group that had risen to leadership of the union attempting to organize the community's largest industrial plant challenged the Progressive Conservative political leadership with regard to virtually the whole scope of local government. They struck the plant; their picket line was manned by workers of both races in a dramatic challenge to the ruling group. This rather sudden development and an effort to capture City Hall subsided quickly, however, when the charge was publicized that the

Radical Left controlled this union movement. Rank-and-file support dwindled rapidly, and the Radical leadership withdrew from the community, some by choice and others because of pressures directed against them. Their demise was so complete that no semblance of the former Radical Left leadership group reappeared. The Oligarchic regime was maintained.

Thus, with one partial exception, the evidence supports the hypothesis. The presence of conflicting political interests in a community does not appear sufficient by itself to raise the sense of electoral potency of minority groups to a high level or to lower the probability of effective illegitimate sanctioning—that is, to change the regime from some less democratic form to Developed Democracy. In our four communities, this change occurred only where competition emerged between ideologically divergent political-leadership groups. The partial exception, the case of the Radical Left aspirants in Metroville, suggests a qualification to the hypothesis: the ideologically dissident aspiring political-leadership group must exist for more than a few weeks if a democratic change in regime is to emerge. If such a group of aspirants endures only for a brief period, this apparently is not sufficient time to provide for the development of a firm sense of electoral potency on behalf of minority-group members. Nor does this temporary existence of a dissident group provide a sufficient basis for the marshalling of resources to enable the minority-group members to withstand severe illegitimate sanctions. In short, the brief appearance of such a group does not lower the sense of vulnerability to, nor the effectiveness of, such sanctions, a necessary but insufficient event.

REGIMES AND POWER STRUCTURES

Hypothesis: A Competitive Mass type of power structure is sufficient but not necessary for the existence of a Developed Democratic type of regime.

Test: Competitive Mass power structures
        Farmdale, -5 through -2, $+3$ through $+6$
        Oretown, -4 through $+2$, $+7$ through $+8$
        Petropolis, -8 through $+3$
        Metroville, $+2$ through $+3$
    Other types of power structures
        Farmdale, -1 through $+2$, $+7$ through $+9$
        Oretown, -6 through -5, $+3$ through $+6$
        Petropolis, -11 through -9
        Metroville, -11 through $+1$

If the hypothesis is to be supported, the evidence must show that Developed Democracy exists wherever a Competitive Mass type of power structure exists, and that Developed Democracy exists also in some situations where the power structure is of another type. The evidence does indeed bear this out. During thirty-one periods of Competitive Mass power structure among the four communities, the type of regime was Developed Democratic, without exception. However, during the twenty-nine periods of non-Competitive Mass power structure, fourteen were also periods of Developed Democracy.

The existence of a Competitive Mass power structure, by definition a situation characterized by an ideologically divergent political leadership and widespread citizen participation in decision-making, provides an atmosphere in which illegitimate sanctions are discouraged, or rendered ineffective if used, and in which the sense of electoral potency of the citizens is promoted. But these are not necessary conditions for Developed Democracy. We already have discussed the matter of the conditions under which a Developed Democracy may emerge from another type of regime. But where Developed Democracy already exists, power relations may be relatively consensual and the bulk of the citizens inactive without the regime becoming markedly unstable. For example, in Farmdale during Periods +7 through +9, there was (1) a coalition political leadership of the only two former leadership groups in the community, the Conservatives and the Community Conservationists; (2) the scope of government was being expanded continuously, thereby meeting the needs of formerly dissatisfied groups, and, at the same time, the tax rate was declining; (3) the community was still so small that there was no demand for the hiring of a large corps of professional public administrators and no need for public acquisition of private property for such purposes as slum clearance, urban redevelopment, or street reorganization to alleviate traffic problems; and (4) because of these last factors, there was no significant development of a feeling of low-cultural-class identification on the part of the propertied and economically marginal people who in other communities provided recruits for the Radical Right. The citizens appeared to be satisfied with the nature of local government and politics, and their sense of electoral potency remained high. This brief period of consensus during a democratic regime did not appear to raise the probability, in any detectable way, that illegitimate sanctions would be used.

In Oretown, after the defeat and disintegration of the Liberals and the coalescence of other leaders during Periods +2 and +3, the power structure became Consensual Elite. So conditioned had the populace become to political mobilization that, while participation declined markedly, the sense of electoral potency remained high, and there was no resort to illegitimate sanctions. At other times, where Developed Democratic regimes were found in association with Consensual Elite power structures, there was competition between an established group of political leaders and an ideologically dissident group of aspiring leaders who had not yet gained power in a decisional process. In these situations, the succeeding time period showed a change to a competitive power structure, since the aspiring groups were in all cases successful in at least some of their policy-making ventures.

Hypothesis: A regime of Developed Democracy is necessary for the existence of a Competitive Mass type of power structure.

Test: Same test as for the cases of Competitive Mass power structures, page 657.

As we indicated above, all instances of Competitive Mass power structures occurred in association with a Developed Democratic regime. Where there was no such regime, no case of such a power structure was found. Hence the evidence supports the hypothesis.

We find that only under conditions of Developed Democracy is there a political leadership composed of two or more ideologically divergent groups—plus other, unaffiliated leaders. Only where such a competitive leadership exists are there channels and stimuli for political participation that would attract large-scale citizen involvement. Where conditions for Developed Democracy do not exist—for example, where the sense of electoral potency is low—the mass of citizens are not likely to be involved actively in politics. Either they fear illegitimate sanctions in the event of their participation, or, in the absence of issues cast in ideological terms, they remain apathetic or lack a channel through which they might influence decisional processes. In either case, the distribution of power is narrow. If they lack such a channel, it is probably the result of a political leadership monopoly. This absence of competition at the leadership level may or may not result from a high probability of illegitimate sanctions; in either case, the power structure is consensual.

If the sense of electoral potency is high and the probability of illegitimate sanctions is also high, one of three developments may occur. If, as a result of the high sense of electoral potency, there is a relatively continuous stream of demands for a shift in the scope of government, the leaders may change their disposition to use such sanctions to block the shift because they fear that overuse or continuous use might provoke a more harmful consequence than loss of the particular decisional outcomes at stake. In such a case, the regime will become a Developed Democracy and the power structure will tend toward mass participation and competition among leaders. If the dissident demands are simply blocked, the power structure will remain consensual; in the absence of competition among established leaders, widespread participation will not occur, and power will not be widely shared. If dissidents try to organize but are sanctioned effectively, the power structure will remain consensual. And, since in the absence of competing organizations there will be little opportunity for mass participation in decisional processes, the power structure will remain elite.

Hypothesis: If the regime is other than a Developed Democracy, the power structure will be Consensual Elite.

Test: Cases of non-Developed Democratic regime
Farmdale, −1 and 0
Petropolis, −11
Metroville, −11 through 0

In all fifteen cases among the four communities in which the regimes were Guided Democracies, Underdeveloped Democracies, or Oligarchies, the power structures were Consensual Elite. Thus the evidence strongly supports the hypothesis. For an analysis of the impact of non-Developed Democratic regime conditions on the power structure, see the immediately preceding section.

In Farmdale during Periods −1 and 0, the high probability of illegitimate sanctions kept potential, aspiring political-leadership groups from organizing in behalf of their demands to shift the scope of government. Since no such organization existed, and since there was no way in which to actualize dissident political values, the Conservative leadership was left with a virtual monopoly in the field of political organization and communication. There was no channel through which a large number of dissatisfied citizens might participate effectively in decisional processes.

During the periods of Oligarchy in Metroville (−11 and −10), attempts by the Radical Left to shift the scope of government were utterly defeated; the union organizational base of the dissidents was destroyed; and the aspiring political leaders had to leave the community. There was no further attempt during this period to organize in behalf of dissident demands, and the paternalistic leadership opened no channels through which the citizens might influence decisional processes.

Although following the election of Mayor Peterson in 1949 his supporters' sense of electoral potency was temporarily high, the leaders became more disposed to use illegitimate sanctions. We believe that such sanctions would have been effective; therefore, we have classified the regime as a Guided Democracy. Neither Mayor Peterson nor other aspiring leaders attempted to organize an ideologically distinct political group; thus, there was no opportunity or stimulus for the mass of citizens to participate in decisional processes, and the power structure remained Consensual Elite. During the ensuing periods, the scope of government began to shift to meet some of the needs of the Negroes through such measures as public housing and the improvement of streets in Negro areas. But Peterson and Negro Leaders hinted repeatedly that if any attempt were made to speed the shift in scope or to change it radically, severe sanctions would be used, and the gains already made would be lost or jeopardized. As a result, no Negro Leader organized political support behind such demands during these periods, and the Negro subcommunity remained quiescent. This and the city officials' failure to move faster contributed to a decline in the Negroes' sense of electoral potency. Labor was even quieter, since it had been hit the hardest during the days of attempts to organize, in Period −11. The dissidents lacked both a channel for participation and a high sense of electoral potency. Therefore, the power structure remained a Consensual Elite type through Period 0, even though the Progressive Conservative leaders became less disposed to use sanctions toward the end of this relatively long period of time.

In Petropolis during the Underdeveloped Democracy of Period −11, there was a traditional carry-over of a low sense of electoral potency on the part of politically submerged groups such as the industrial workers and the Negroes. Thus the distribution of power remained narrow.

In summary, unless the probability is low that sanctions will be used, it is unlikely that a dissident political group will produce aspiring political leaders to compete effectively with the existing leadership in decisional processes. In the absence of such effective competition, the power structure is consensual. There will also be a relatively small amount of mass participation in decisional processes, since the dissidents will not have been able to develop an organization. Thus the power structure will be elite. This explains the presence of Consensual Elite power structures in Oligarchies and Guided Democracies, where the probability of sanctions is high.

But even where the probability of sanctions is low, the sense of electoral potency may also be low from fears of sanctions carried over from a previous period, just as relevant groups may be cynical or habituated to political inactivity even without a sense of electoral impotence. None of these conditions generate mass political participation.

A last hypothesis concerning changes in power structure and regime type, which will not concern us further here, is as follows:

Hypothesis: Changes in regime and changes in power structure tend not to occur in association.

Test: Thirteen periods in which some change occurs; three show changes in both regime and power structure.

Most changes in power structure and changes in regime do not occur in association. Although changes in regime dimensions often eventually lead to changes in power structure dimensions, and vice versa, at any point in time a change in one tends not to be associated with a change in the other.

POWER-STRUCTURE DYNAMICS

Since there were no examples of Consensual Mass power structures in the four communities, we will not directly develop hypotheses about that type of power structure, although related hypotheses will indicate why there were no such power structures. In the introduction to this chapter, we suggested some reasons for the empirical absence of this type of power structure—the ideal type in the ideology of Community Conservationists—in recent times in communities of the United States. Apparently, only when aspiring leaders who are ideologically divergent from the established leaders become active do large numbers of citizens become involved in decision-making so that the distribution of power becomes widespread. A political leadership representing only a single ideology does not seem to have sufficient "drawing power" to stimulate enough citizen participation to distribute power broadly. In other words, issues do not appear to stimulate mass participation unless they are cast in terms of ideological competition. In short, our empirically based observation is that a competitive political leadership is necessary, although insufficient, for the existence of a power structure of the mass type. From this we derive the following hypotheses and tests.

Hypothesis: If the leadership changes from competitive to consensual, the distribution of power will change from mass to elite.

Test: Changes from competitive to consensual leadership
      Farmdale, -2 to -1, $+6$ to $+7$
      Oretown, $+2$ to $+3$

In the three cases where the leadership changed from competitive to consensual, a change occurred in the distribution of power from mass to elite. Thus the available evidence supports the hypothesis.

In Oretown from Period $+2$ to $+3$ the leadership changed from a situation of competition between Liberals, Community Conservationists, and Conservatives to one in which the Liberals had been destroyed as a leadership group and the two remaining groups had coalesced; Community Conservationist values became increasingly dominant. The distribution of power shifted sharply from the mass end of the continuum to the elite, as we indicated in the previous chapter when Oretown was revisited and another sample survey was made. The development of a consensual leadership was associated with a change in the subsidiary-political-organization structure of the political system. The Democratic party and the labor unions had been relatively independent channels of political influence when the Liberals were a leadership group. These channels declined in importance under the coalition leadership. The civic associations, dominated by the upper middle class, and the governmental advisory boards, staffed by lay citizens, became much more important. The political process became more tightly structured and less spontaneous —a matter of formal meetings, committees, and prearranged agendas. The survey data from 1953 and 1959 tend to confirm this picture of drastically declining informal discussion of local political matters.

However, this "bureaucratization" of the political process may contribute to the instability of a Consensual Elite power structure, at least in a Developed Democracy. With the decline in participation over a period of time in Oretown, there were signs of growing alienation in the community. An unorganized but electorally potent group of dissidents, labeled "aginners" in the local newspaper, became apparent in the community. Resentful of the high degree and character of organization of the political process and the perspectives of the Community Conservationist leaders, they began to organize their own political group, which later emerged as the Radical Right. This injected an element of organized opposition into the community. This opposition produced, in time, a new power-structure type, Competitive Mass.

In Farmdale, the coalition between Community Conservationist and Conservative leaders developed during Period $+7$. The widespread political activity and conflict characterizing Periods +3 through +6 gave way to a harmonious, accommodative politics in the latter period. With the leadership in agreement, decisional processes tended to occur within the leadership stratum of the community, and general citizen participation seemed to decline.

Another change from a competitive to a consensual leadership occurred in Farmdale, between Periods −2 and −1, not through an amalgamation of formerly competitive groups, but through the decline and disorganization of the Community Conservationists. The surprise write-in election of Bill May over the incumbent mayor further discouraged the Community Conservationists and deprived them of their primary public forum. The ascendant Jeffersonian Conservatives proclaimed a period of accommodation and consolidation of gains that seemed to soothe agitated political emotions in the community. At the same time, they increasingly restricted political decision-making to their own ranks. Decisional questions were referred less often to the general citizenry for consideration, and few channels existed for participation, except through the Conservative-dominated subsidiary political organizations. With the disappearance of the Community Conservationists as an ideologically distinct political-leadership group, citizen participation declined and the power distribution became more elite.

Hypothesis: If the distribution of power changes from elite to mass, the leadership will either remain or become competitive.

Test: Changes from elite to mass power structures
      Farmdale, +2 to +3
      Oretown, −5 to −4, +6 to +7
      Petropolis, −9 to −8
      Metroville, +1 to +2

In every case in which the power structure changed from elite to mass, either competition within the leadership was maintained, or the leadership became competitive. Therefore, the available evidence wholly supports the hypothesis.

In Farmdale, the Community Conservationist leaders who had "cracked" the power structure during Period +1 began to develop a subsidiary political organization which would mobilize their supporters throughout the community. Competition between them and the Jeffersonian Conservatives seemed directly responsible for activating the citizens. This resulted in the more widespread distribution of power. The change in distribution of power in Petropolis between Periods −9 and −8 occurred in the same fashion. The rise of the Liberal group and the competition between Community Conservationists and Conservatives at the leadership level contributed to the mobilization of the citizens in a series of sharply contested decisional processes.

The organization of an aspiring Liberal leadership group in Oretown at the end of Period −5 was followed by the mobilization of the Democratic party and the labor unions in Lovegren's successful campaign for mayor. The protracted period of conflict over the utility and the "good government" issues that followed, in which first the Liberals and then the Conservatives were victorious, marked a redistribution of power in which a large proportion of the citizenry shared. The rise of the Radical Right as an aspiring leadership group during Period +6 led in the ensuing period to the mobilization of the lower cultural class which was opposed to the costly "good government" programs of the Community Conservationist-Conservative coalition. The decline in popular participation that had taken place following the fall of the Liberals was now reversed. The power structure became mass in type.

Similar developments occurred in Metroville between Periods +1 and +2. A Radical Right leadership group arose to channel the inchoate, ineffective opposition to Progressive Conservative policies. A diffuse but growing Negro independence in politics was molded and developed by a new leadership group composed of Negro Community Conservationists and Liberals. In the highly conflicting political controversies that followed, the power structure became mass in type.

Hypothesis: If a Developed Democratic regime exists, a Competitive Mass type of power structure will be more stable if the competitors represent high and low cultural classes than if the competitors represent the same general cultural class.

Test: Farmdale, +3 through +7
Oretown, −4 through +3
Petropolis, −8 through +3

There were two cases in which the competitors represented the same general cultural class. These were Farmdale during Periods +3 through +6, and Oretown during Period +2. In each of these cases, the power structure changed from Competitive Mass to Consensual Elite.

Where the competitors represent high and low cultural classes, relatively sharp feelings of deprivation are present in politics. These maintain or intensify the emotions of the participants and produce clearly demarcated political camps (Oretown, −4 through +1; Petropolis, −8 through +3). Where the competition is within a single cultural class—usually the high cultural class—there is a strong tendency toward coalescence. The competitors tend to have a high rate of interaction, socially and in civic associations, which discourages constant conflict. They share a similar community life; members of the competitive groups are accustomed to joint committee work on community projects, and associated informal daytime meetings. Liberals and Radical Rightists feel uncomfortable as "deviants" in such environments. They come to feel that they have no voice in a "bureaucratized" politics, even though they have the opportunity to participate in formal hearings and meetings. Participation in those channels is likely to be less effective than participation in the informal settings out of which may come the announcement of a community project. Common outlooks are developed or reinforced in such settings to which everyone does not have access.

Another factor is that the immediate interests of the Conservatives frequently are served through Community Conservationist policies. An example of this is urban redevelopment, a typical Community Conservationist policy which often receives support from the generally Conservative business community because of the real estate, design, banking, and construction business it generates. Furthermore, such programs, as well as highway grids, parking systems, and other similar, typically Community Conservationist policies make central business districts more attractive and thereby may strengthen the financial situation of this business sector. These considerations may encourage Conservatives to support Community Conservationists, despite their hostility toward governmental intervention in these areas.

Finally, Conservatives and Community Conservationists tend to value harmony in local affairs; overt, protracted conflict is politically obstructing as well as unpleasant to them. Liberals and Radical Rightists frequently become involved in conflict because their demands require modifications of the *status quo.*

These three factors—intensive social interaction, communality of interests, and desire for harmony—brought the two initially competitive segments of the high cultural class into increasing agreement in Oretown, Farmdale, and Petropolis. In Oretown and Farmdale, the coalition of the Conservative and Community Conservationist leadership groups led to a change in power-structure type from Competitive Mass to Consensual Elite (Oretown, +2 to +3; Farmdale, +6 to +7). In Petropolis, there was increasing agreement within the high cultural class, but the power structure remained competitive because of the racial factors in local politics and because of the presence of Liberal leaders whose low-cultural- and socio-economic-class interests continued to conflict with the interests of the Conservatives and Community Conservationists.

FORMATION OF POLITICAL-LEADERSHIP GROUPS

Hypothesis: A Liberal leadership group will emerge if (1) labor-union leaders see the community as politically relevant and as composed of interest groups, and (2) if some business or professional men ally themselves politically with these labor leaders.

Test: Farmdale, all periods
Oretown, all periods
Metroville, all periods
Petropolis, all periods

In Farmdale, at no time during our study were the local labor-union officials oriented toward local politics as representatives of a working-class interest group; nor did they seem to see local politics as involving the interplay of occupational interest groups. Furthermore, at no time were even the most dissatisfied, expansion-oriented businessmen disposed toward the organization of a political-leadership group supported by a class-conscious working class. Thus, neither condition necessary for the formation of a Liberal leadership group was present in that community.

In Metroville, the radical nature of the labor-union movement during Period −11 seems to have prevented organized labor from forming an alliance with any segment of the business-professional community. So deep was the impact of this economic-political movement that even a decade later there was no apparent possibility of such an alliance, although many other changes in the community had effected an "opening up" of local politics.

Throughout the periods of our study, both conditions necessary for the establishment of a Liberal leadership were present in Petropolis. The labor leadership had a strong sense of identification with a working class that felt deprived by the economic leaders of the community. They were aware that desirable shifts in the scope of government could alter this situation to some degree. The availability and initiative of disgruntled businessmen, represented by John Jay, led to the establishment of a Liberal political-leadership group.

In Oretown a similar situation existed, although the labor leaders had a less strongly developed sense of the community as being politically relevant for interest groups. But businessmen such as Lovegren and Longacre fostered this conception effectively enough to develop a Liberal organization, principally on the basis of the public-power issue.

However, from the 1952 mayoralty election on, Oretown's labor leaders became less and less oriented to social-class differences in local political interests. Concurrently, union leaders were gaining political status as a normal part of the local political process. Mayor French, victorious in 1952, strengthened his political organization by appealing to labor leaders on a basis different from that used by Lovegren in the previous period. By appointing union officials to advisory committees and other positions of politico-civic leadership, he encouraged them to develop a Community Conservationist, rather than a Liberal, ideology. Hastened by the loss of electoral support from the workers, the Liberals lost power.

It is clear why labor leaders, with their organized access to masses of potential voters, are of critical importance in the dynamics of Liberal political-leadership groups. But it is not quite so obvious why businessman allies are so necessary. Because businessmen have both high prestige and high political status in the local community, they add an element of political respectability which the labor element of the Liberal group ordinarily lacks. Because of the propensity of businessmen to participate in civic, occupational, and fraternal associations, they acquire skills in interpersonal and intergroup relations and in the organization of community projects that are not as easily learned within the labor sector. Without the support of businessmen and, therefore, without the resources of status and organizational skills, the labor leadership of Metroville was unable to influence local politics, despite the legacy of class consciousness developed during the strike days of Period −11.

The recent rise in Metroville of a Negro Liberal leadership group was a phenomenon occurring from a single racial subcommunity. Neither labor-union leaders nor businessmen from the White subcommunity were involved. How effective and stable such an independent Liberal political leadership group in the community power structure would prove to be is still uncertain. To what extent its maintenance over time depended on the continuation of a multigroup competitive White leadership, including an active Radical Right, is unknown. While it was an atypical development, relative to the present hypothesis, its occurrence suggests that the more usual conditions may not hold for community political systems marked by biracial power structures, at least of the kind found in Metroville in most recent periods.

Hypothesis: Where there is a political-leadership group that conceives of the community as a collectivity, the Radical Right will organize to become another leadership group, unless there is also a Liberal leadership group. If, however, an existing Liberal group includes Negro Leaders or White Leaders sympathetic to Negroes, the Radical Right will organize to become another leadership group.

Test: All four communities

Those who view the community as a collectivity, Progressive Conservatives and Community Conservationists, are concerned with its public image. In order to raise community prestige and to increase the amenities of community life, such people support civic improvements—such as urban renewal, new public buildings, or beautification of the downtown area—and good government, including institutionalizing the planning process and professionalizing the public service. Both civic improvement and good government are costly, at least in the short run. Taxes increase—particularly, in the local community, the property tax. The increase is felt as a burden by the small property owners, a feeling often exacerbated by the milieu in which civic improvements and good government are realized. That is, the small property owner, as well as other culturally "marginal" citizens, sees the situation as one in which "civic progress" is being managed, directed, or imposed by college- or professionally trained administrators who view his particular problems only in relation to "the community welfare" as they define it. The administrators and the civic leaders constituting the Progressive Conservative or Community Conservationist political-leadership groups believe that democracy has been institutionalized in the civic-improvement process because open hearings are held on proposals; because a ramified advisory committee structure recruits the "normal" leadership of the community to help plan and manage the civic improvements; and because the offices of the public administrators involved are open at specific periods to anyone with a complaint, a problem, or a desire for more information.

However, those who oppose civic improvement and "good government" policies are often frustrated by these formal opportunities for expression of grievances and point of view. At open hearings, skilled, educated administrators and civic leaders can present their point of view eloquently and as in the interest of the total community. The dissident, frequently less well-educated and less skilled in interpersonal relations, is in the position of upholding a selfish interest and trying to block progress. He feels increasingly "pushed around, unconstitutionally, by Big Government." He has not participated in the advisory committees that have shepherded the particular civic improvement through the earlier stages of the decisional process because he is not known as a civic leader. He does not interact informally with the rest of the civic leadership, and he is uncomfortable in their presence.

The culmination of this difference in values and consequent failure of communication is the mobilization by Radical Right ideologists, sometimes of upper socio-economic class, of the frustrated small property owners and others among the less affluent citizens who resist a heavier tax burden. So strong is the emotional reaction of the low cultural class to civic improvements and good government, and so forceful are such symbols as bulldozers knocking down a substandard home in behalf of civic progress, that these ideologists are able to contest effectively the entire influence of the civic leadership and their subsidiary political organizations, such as "clubs," occupational associations, and lodges, in some of the decisional processes in which these issues are involved. In the course of some of these civic improvements, for example in the case of urban renewal, real-estate interests may realize a substantial profit, and planners and other professional public administrators may gain prestige, from implementing a major civic improvement. So great may be the gap between Community Conservationists and those of low cultural class that many of the latter, although progressive or "liberal" in national politics, follow the Radical Right and its low tax program locally. As a result, those communities in which the regime is a Developed Democracy, and in which there are either Progressive Conservative or Community Conservationist leaders, also tend to generate a competing Radical Right political-leadership group. The Radical Right can gain a position of leadership through the electoral process, either by organizing campaigns against bond referenda for civic improvements or by electing a few officials who will delay and harass attempts to "improve" the community. This was the pattern in Oretown during Periods +6 through +8 and in Metroville during Periods +1 through +3. Since the aspiring Negro Liberal political-leadership group developed after the rise of the Radical Right in Metroville, its existence did not provide a real test of the second part of this hypothesis, nor of the qualification of the first part.

The Radical Right did not develop in Oretown until the Liberal political leaders had lost their power and their positions of leadership and finally no longer were even an aspiring political-leadership group. That the Radical Right can appeal effectively to the low cultural class only in the absence of a Liberal group of political leaders also is suggested in Oretown by the fact that Radical Right spokesmen ran for city-council positions but were defeated by Liberals. After the dissolution of the Liberals, the Radical Right spokesmen were able to win some city-council elections and also to become a political-leadership group in the community's power structure.

Although there were Community Conservationist political leaders in Petropolis, the existence of a Liberal group retarded the acquisition by the Radical Right of similar positions and power. The situation was similar to that in Oretown, but it was even more pronounced in Petropolis. The Liberals had developed an organization based on the labor unions which served to tie them to a sizable section of the working class. Their electoral machine was successful in electing many Liberals to city office and in providing them a public forum which further reinforced their ability to prevent the acquisition of power by the Radical Right. Since the Liberal ideology includes the proposition that government should be used to benefit socio-economically disadvantaged groups, and since Liberals in power can provide some such benefits to these groups, the effectiveness of the Radical Right is limited in using "Big Government" as a negative symbol about which to rally the disadvantaged elements of the population. However, since the Liberals were a biracial leadership group in Petropolis, the Radical Right was able to attract more of the low cultural class on the basis of its strong racist appeal than might otherwise have been possible. During Period +3, the Radical Right, drawing its main strength from fringe-area residents, mobilized voters against the consolidation proposal, partly on the basis of preventing the city-based Negro-labor machine from extending its sway into the fringe and rural areas of the county.

All of these tests have offered evidence in support of the hypothesis. But the one remaining community, Farmdale during Periods +1 through +9, does not. During this time, a Community Conservationist leadership group broke the leadership monopoly of the Conservatives. The competition lasted through Period +6, when the two groups coalesced. Despite the rising strength of the Community Conservationists, no Radical Right citizen acquired a leadership position and no Radical Right interest group appeared to be developing in the community. Why did Farmdale's politics deviate from the expected pattern?

There are a number of factors that seem to be responsible for the deviation. Perhaps the most important one was that the Jeffersonian Conservative leaders had long been upholders of individual initiative and had strongly opposed Big Government, federal "giveaway" programs, a burgeoning professional public-administrative corps, public housing, and anything else that smacked of socialism or worse. By Period +6 they had changed their perspectives sufficiently to cease opposing every demand that the scope of local government be shifted to meet such needs as that for new industry, a better water supply, and cooperation with the Chamber of Commerce's economic-development activities. But they still gave lip service to many slogans and beliefs cherished by the Radical Right. At the same time, the Conservatives differed from the Radical Right in their self-perceptions. The Conservatives of Farmdale saw themselves as members of a respected cultural class. They felt no need to destroy the power of the molders of community values, since they still thought of themselves as those molders. Their sympathy with basic Radical Right values regarding the scope of government won them the support of people in the community who had similar values, and since they already held high positions in the power structure, a Radical Right group did not organize to try to gain power in decisional processes.

The small size of the community also made individual efforts in politics appear to be more fruitful than in a more complex, highly urbanized community. Individualism did not seem a frustrated ideal in Farmdale. This was related to another factor associated with the size of the community: the absence of need for an extensive professional public service. The public officials remained part-time elected officials, not professional administrators with a university-bred set of values and styles which were different from those of the local citizens. The officials seemed far more approachable than planners and other administrators seemed in Oretown and Metroville. Hence, potential Radical Rightists did not seem to feel so much frustration locally as in these other communities.

Despite the continuous expansion of the scope of government during Periods +1 through +9, the shifts did not entail a sharp increase in the tax burden. Rezoning to facilitate the introduction of new industry cost nothing. Cooperating with the Chamber of Commerce's program to advertise the virtues of the community to prospective home owners, employers, and merchants did not require unusual amounts of public funds. In fact, the low tax rate had declined further during one of these years. The tax situation, then, also discouraged the feeling of oppression that in other communities was reflected in the rise of the Radical Right. What we suggest here is that Farmdale may represent one type of small community in the United

States where Radical Right sentiments are not likely to be focused locally.

A related hypothesis emerges from this investigation.

Hypothesis: Where "good government" becomes institutionalized, strong cultural-class conflict will be generated.

Test: All four communities

In all of our communities but Farmdale "good government" became institutionalized. In the three cities, this seemingly progressive step was followed by the outbreak of sharp cultural-class conflict, but this did not occur in Farmdale. The dynamics of this development followed closely those described in the preceding section. The institutionalization of "good government" involved some or all of the following policies: adoption of the city-manager form of government, commitment to urban planning, and annexation of fringe areas. The less affluent saw these primarily in terms of costs; ideologists of the right maintained that these policies were evidence that government was trampling the rights of citizens; and ideologists of the left said they reflected government's insensitivity to the real needs of the socioeconomically deprived.

Oretown provides examples of these reactions. When the Conservative leadership in power after the Second World War attempted to meet the backlog of urban problems that had developed with community growth during the 1940's by rationalizing and professionalizing the governmental structure, the Liberals rose up in opposition. Although the primary interest of the Liberals was municipal power, a continuing but unrealized goal was the destruction of the city-manager form of government. The demise of the Liberals left the leadership to the Community Conservationist-Conservative coalition by the end of Period $+3$. A series of decisional processes then resulted in such outcomes as the annexation of fringe areas and urban renewal. In the course of these moves the role of public administrators became increasingly important. The reaction to these policies led to the formation and rise of the Radical Right, a process which has been described above.

In Metroville, the continuous institutionalization of "good government" under the aegis of the Progressive Conservatives took longer to generate a strong cultural class conflict because the Radical Right feared illegitimate sanctions until Period $+1$. The use of the whole "ideology of good government" by the proponents of annexation in 1960 stimulated a very strong reaction among Radical Rightists.

In Petropolis, the Community Conservationists increasingly favored such aspects of good government as consolidation of city and county government and of school systems. Such policies would have diluted the political power of the Negro-labor coalition by adding in local elections large numbers of rural and urban-fringe residents opposed to the Liberal groups. This led to the bitter mayoralty-election campaign of 1961, based on the conflict between high and low cultural classes.

The policy that seemed to illustrate this cultural difference most clearly was annexation. To both Community Conservationists and Progressive Conservatives, the fringe areas seemed the locus of city problems that required rationalization. The demands of fringe-area residents who opposed annexation were considered selfish interests, blocking the path of progress. To those residents, annexation appeared a coercive measure which would result in the levying of heavy taxes by men who had no understanding of the suburbanite's position. The annexation of a large Oretown fringe area by the margin of a handful of votes resulted in the addition to the city electorate of a mass of voters who were mobilized by the Radical Right to defeat every bond issue that arose and even to reverse some of the good-government policies adopted in the past, such as the housing code. This situation was not foreseen by the Community Conservationists. Such unanticipated consequences reflected a wide gap between cultural classes.

INTERNAL ORGANIZATION OF THE POLITICAL-LEADERSHIP GROUPS

We now have investigated some of the conditions under which various kinds of competition may occur between political-leadership groups. The internal organization of these groups also may reveal some uniformities among these four communities.

Hypothesis: Various types of political-leadership groups have characteristic subsidiary-political-organizational bases.

Test: Conservative groups in all four communities
Community Conservationist groups in all four communities
Liberal groups in Petropolis and Oretown
Radical Right groups in Petropolis, Metroville, and Oretown

The Community Conservationists and the various Conservative groups all use the civic-association network as subsidiary political organizations. One common aspect of their cultural-class perspectives is participation in community organizations in behalf of civic improvement, civic welfare, or both. This is not merely a socio-economic status difference between them and the other groups, for the Radical Right leaders often are recruited from the same socio-economic status level; but the latter belong to a different cultural class, and their alienation is reflected in their nonparticipation in, or nonacceptance by, the civic-association network.

The advantages inherent in the use of the civic-association base are its respectability and its superficially nonpolitical character. So traditional are the activities of such associations in American community life that their political function frequently is overlooked, even by those who use them in this fashion. Political-leadership groups with a civic-association organization base operate most effectively in the absence of public conflict, because their adherents perform their political functions adequately in the normal course of their civic activities, whereas the potential adherents of other groups tend to be inactive or unaware of decisional processes in the absence of controversy. At the same time, a limitation of this organizational base, under some conditions, is that it does not mobilize the great mass of citizens; under other conditions that is an asset.

Liberal political-leadership groups rely primarily on two subsidiary organizations: the local Democratic party and labor unions. Both of these have access to large numbers of voters, and as long as the Liberals can maintain this base, they are virtually assured of some power in the community. The disadvantage of this organizational base is that it is not particularly effective in decisional processes that do not involve elections. Because of the relatively low rate of participation of Liberal leaders and followers in the civic-association network, the Liberals tend to be represented less than Conservatives and Community Conservationists in the intermediate stages of decisional processes, such as policy deliberation. Even when Liberal leaders hold public office and are better represented in these stages, they usually are outnumbered by political leaders belonging to higher cultural classes, and deliberations frequently occur in civic-association surroundings—such as the meetings of the Chamber of Commerce. These factors may create a moderating influence on Liberal leaders. They are so removed from their mass supporters that they are likely to become less extreme in their perspectives if offered civic and political status by their political foes. Another disadvantage inherent in this party-labor organizational base is that it is manifestly highly political, and, as such, it may attract constant criticism from the mass-communications media, which, under certain conditions, can constitute a strong enough cross-pressure on the Liberal rank-and-file to diminish its support.

The Radical Right relies neither on a party nor on civic associations. As a radical group, it organizes new associations that are distinctly and overtly political. These often bear names symbolic of their traditional values, such as Voters for Constitutional Government. These subsidiary organizations are kept mobilized to use systematically all available constitutional channels to win decisional outcomes. Even where a decision apparently has been reached and the process apparently has come to an end, the Radical Right will tenaciously seek additional means to prolong the matter until a favorable outcome is reached. For example, in Oretown, systematic preparations for urban renewal were organized by the Community Conservationist-Conservative coalition for more than 2 years before the initiation of the program. So great an outcry was raised by the Radical Right about the "bypassing" of the people in the decision that the coalition agreed to an advisory vote on the issue. This they narrowly won, and the program began. The Radical Right then turned to the courts, waging long-drawn-out suits that ultimately proved unsuccessful. Finally, they were successful in calling for a referendum on the municipal housing code which was required as a basis for the urban-renewal program. The code was revoked in this election, throwing the partially completed urban-renewal program into confusion at the time our observation of the community ended.

Letters-to-the-editor columns and pamphlets frequently are used to maintain the alertness of Radical Right supporters, since the editorial policies and pages of local newspapers usually are controlled by Conservatives or Community Conservationists. A resource of the Radical Right leadership is fanaticism, which keeps its subsidiary organizations constantly alert and ready to be mobilized.

Because the Radical Right is alienated from the civic-association network, its leaders do not participate even as much as the Liberals in the formulation and consideration of policies that take place in the civic-association milieu. Consequently, the Radical Right is likely to be involved in fewer stages of fewer decisional processes than are the other leadership groups. As in the case of the Liberals, this deficiency is less where Radical Right leaders hold public office. Radical Rightists are most effective in decisional processes involving elections, as are the Liberals.

One variation on these patterns occurs when Community Conservationists attempt to obtain labor-union support in their efforts to construct a communitywide coalition. In Oretown, where this was attempted, some labor leaders cooperated in this venture and received prestigious public positions for doing so. But the union membership tended to lose interest in the resulting consensual politics, so that the labor leaders gradually lost the support of the subsidiary political organization for which the Community Conservationists approached them. Furthermore, as the ideological perspectives of these union leaders became less liberal, the working class became available to appeals from the Radical Right, a development that we have analyzed in previous sections of this chapter.

SHIFTS IN THE SCOPE OF GOVERNMENT

Hypothesis: There is no general relationship between shifts in the scope of government and type of power structure and regime.

Tests: All four communities

The direction and extent of shifts in the scope of government are a function of (1) the ideology of the various political groups and their perception of community problems, and (2) the pattern of group composition of the political leadership. Among our four communities, extensive shifts occurred under every type of power structure encountered and under every type of regime. How is this to be explained?

There are four general ideological categories of leadership groups that emerged during the course of this study: Community Conservationists, Conservatives, Liberals, and Radical Right. Of these groups, only one has a rigid ideological position on the scope of government: the Radical Right. This group opposes any extension of its scope and strives continuously for its contraction. Community problems are perceived only in terms of the encroachment of big government. If we had a much larger sample of political periods in a much larger sample of communities, we might find a situation in which the Radical Right monopolized the political leadership, a situation in which we would expect contractions in the scope of government.[1] In the absence of this "special" kind of case, we find no general relationship between regime type or power structure and shifts in governmental scope. All the other leadership groups have contingent perspectives. This results in irregularities in the shifts in scope.

For example, the Jeffersonian Conservatives, the Conservative leaders of Farmdale, were ideologically as strongly opposed as the Radical Right to extensions of the scope of government; but they did not react so inflexibly to concrete situations as did the latter. As an advantaged cultural class, they disliked conflict because it was "political," in the most negative sense of the term. If it came to a choice between open conflict, the public marshalling of political influence in a competitive decisional process, and avoidance of conflict by compromising to permit some extension of the scope of government, they tolerated extension. This, essentially, was what happened in the natural-experiment period when the Community Conservationist group demanded that streetlights be provided for the downtown area of Farmdale. When the Conservatives ascertained that they could not defeat the demand without embroiling themselves and the community in open, bitter conflict, they gave in. Jeffersonian Conservatives do not give in, of course, when the demanders can be countered in a publicly invisible way—that is, when the conflict is confined to a few active participants—for this does not politicize the community as a whole.

The Liberals, who ideologically tend to support extension of the scope of government, as a general principle, may oppose a particular extension, depending on the needs such government action would meet. For example, during Period 0 in Oretown, the Liberals opposed a demand that the city build a public parking lot in the downtown area to promote shopping in that district. Liberal opposition was predicated on the basis that building such a lot, in effect, would be subsidizing one group of merchants at the expense of the whole community. The merchants they represented, those of the Longacre district, provided their customers with parking facilities at their own expense. The Liberals failed in this endeavor and the scope of government was expanded despite their efforts.

A final example involves the Community Conservationists. Although they tend to support expansion of the scope of government to resolve urban problems and improve the community, use of the government is contingent on available choices. Thus, Community Conservationists in Oretown supported private development of a community hospital because this seemed the most expeditious way of getting a hospital; but they were ready to demand a government-operated hospital if the private efforts failed.

Shifts in the scope of government, then, depend on what groups constitute the political leadership at a given point in time and on what the ideology of these groups is in relation to their perception of specific community problems. These findings force us to reject a frequently encountered assumption in the field of political science that political competition leads through compromise to a widespread distribution of power, as the competing groups gain partial gratification of their demands. Translating this assumption into the form of a hypothesis in our terms, it is:

Where the regime type is Developed Democracy and the power-structure type is Competitive, net shifts in the scope of government occur continuously, relative to the rate of such shifts under other regime and power-structure conditions.

Perhaps the greatest shifts in the scope of government occurred in Metroville during the long period when, under varying regime conditions, the Progressive Conservatives were the only political leaders of the community. Great shifts occurred in such directions as the rationalization of government structure, the extension of services through the metropolitan area, accommodation of future growth in contemporary traffic plans, desegregation of public facilities, etc. In fact, such a major shift as desegregation of public schools occurred without organization of Negro support behind demands for it and earlier than in Petropolis, where there were widespread, organized Negro demands for it and where the power structure was Competitive Mass and the regime Developed Democracy. The least shift in the scope of government occurred in Oretown, where intense competition between a set of political-leadership groups under Developed Democratic regime conditions frequently produced policy deadlock and mutual vetoing.

THE IMPACT OF GOVERNMENTAL STRUCTURE ON TYPE OF POWER STRUCTURE

Hypothesis: The financial structure of local government is a factor that promotes the Competitive Mass type of power structure.

Test: All four communities

Because local-government officials usually cannot carry out programs involving major new expenses without gaining prior approval of the citizens in a bond election, the financial structure of local government promotes citizen participation in decisional processes. Therefore, as urban development and decay occurred in all four communities, the citizens had an increasing opportunity to participate in the authoritative-consideration stage of the decisional processes. Of course, the organization of the policy choices that finally appear on the ballot may reflect the high concentration of political influence among a small group of leaders, as was the case in Metroville. But over time, the necessity of obtaining public approval for new expenditures provides a continuing opportunity for effective mass participation. In Metroville, the increasing use of the electoral process in decision-making promoted more sustained competition and conflict than had occurred ever before. Perhaps because of the high legitimacy surrounding the electoral process in this country, as opposed, for example, to "back-room deals" and other less visible phenomena of day-to-day politics, dissidents felt free to organize electoral support in behalf of their demands as well as to engage in other kinds of political activity. Because of its public, highly visible nature, the electoral process generates more widespread communication than other political processes. In any case, the increasingly frequent use of the electoral process to decide the scope of government in Metroville was associated with the development of the organization of dissidents, both Negroes and Radical Rightists, which in turn contributed to the development and maintenance of a Competitive Mass power structure.

In Oretown the frequent bond elections associated primarily with the projects of the Community Conservationists facilitated the expression of dissident sentiments and the organization of a political-leadership group in competition with the ruling coalition. In Petropolis, the combination of bond elections and the strong electoral machine of the Liberals contributed to the ability of the latter to sustain themselves as a leadership group during a period when they had few other political resources.

Only in Farmdale, for reasons we already have described, was there relatively little electoral activity, even though the turnouts for the few elections were high. Interestingly, Farmdale was the only community to have something other than a Competitive Mass power structure by the end of our study.

SOME RELATIONSHIPS BETWEEN THE SOCIAL AND ECONOMIC SYSTEMS AND LOCAL POLITICS

Hypothesis: If the major economic units in a community are home owned, the regime type is more likely to be other than Developed Democracy and the power structure type other than Competitive Mass.

Test: Metroville and Farmdale (home ownership)
Petropolis and Oretown (absentee ownership)

Viewed over all the periods of our study, the evidence seems to support the hypothesis. Petropolis and Oretown, whose economies were characterized by absentee ownership, had more periods of Developed Democracy and Competitive Mass power structure than the other two communities, whose economies were characterized by home ownership, although the difference between Oretown and Farmdale was small. The economic leaders of Metroville and Farmdale were members of the single group of political leaders in their respective communities which discouraged political competition. The prominence of these people in Metroville's political leadership influenced some groups in the community to refrain from making demands because they feared illegitimate economic sanctions. So distant were the political leaders from the citizens there that these fears immobilized some large groups, even though the probability of the use of sanctions actually was low.

However, definite changes gradually appeared in these relationships. While the economic base in both Farmdale and Metroville remained essentially the same, the ideology of the economic leaders changed. In Metroville, the overlapping economic and political leadership became increasingly oriented to Community Conservationist values nationally, and toward promoting their community in the eyes of the nation as a paragon of modern, urban America. The leaders themselves saw this change primarily as a matter of their desire for rational government in an increasingly complex urban environment. But their increasingly cosmopolitan outlook and adoption of community-improvement values also led to a change in their disposition to use illegitimate sanctions to block opponents in local politics. So subtle was this transformation that, as we have mentioned, various potential and actual interest groups in the community failed to comprehend that such sanctions probably would not be used, and thus the regime type remained Underdeveloped Democracy for a rather long period of time.

Dramatic changes also occurred in the perspectives of the economic leaders in Farmdale, where the owner of the largest industry had been a member of the Conservative leadership group. Increasing cosmopolitanism characterized the son who inherited the top management of the dominant industry. As this industry became even more important in the local economy, as it expanded and employed an ever larger proportion of the local labor force, the top management seemed to lose interest in local affairs. Concurrently, the middle-level management took an active role in the activities leading to the establishment of the Chamber of Commerce and organized support in behalf of shifts in the scope of government to encourage the development of new industries in the community. In short, the locally active managers of the largest industry acted with the economic needs of the community in mind, rather than simply the desire of that industry to have a favorable labor situation. The political consequences of this activity on the part of one of the second-level managers and others allied with him were the transformation of the regime type to Developed Democracy and of the power-structure type to Competitive Elite and later to Competitive Mass. Finally, in Period +7, a consensual form of power structure evolved; but only after the Conservative leaders had been defeated repeatedly on major issues and finally had modified their political perspectives sufficiently to cooperate with the Community Conservationists.

Thus, we pose for future studies the following hypothesis, suggesting a change in the relationship between patterns of ownership and local politics.

Hypothesis: The pattern of ownership (home or absentee) of the major economic units in a community has decreasing importance for the type of regime and power structure.

Hypothesis: Economic growth, decline, or *status quo* trends are not related to type of regime or power structure.

Test: All four communities

Metroville and Oretown experienced gradual economic growth over the whole period of our study. There was no relationship, however, between the two regime and power-structure types; Oretown had a Developed Democratic regime and a Competitive Mass power structure, while Metroville had a non-Developed Democratic regime and a Consensual Elite power structure during much of this time.

In Farmdale, the economy was in relative equilibrium over time. But there were several changes in power-structure type and some changes in regime type, none of which seemed directly related to trends in the economy.

Petropolis was the one community in which economic conditions deteriorated markedly over time; but it was also the most stable community in regime and power structure type. The decline began after the advent of Developed Democracy and a Competitive Mass power structure; it had no relation to their development.

Thus we have no evidence of any general relationships between economic trends and such political change.

Hypothesis: There is no relationship between community size and either regime or power-structure type.

Test: All four communities

A general hypothesis stemming from sociological research is that pluralism tends to occur more often in larger, more complex societies than in smaller, simpler societies. Following from this, we might expect that the politics of small communities would tend to be more "closed" and monopolistically controlled than the politics of larger communities; that is, we might expect to find a regime type other than Developed Democracy and a power-structure type other than Competitive Mass more frequently in a smaller than in a larger community. However, the smallest and the largest of the four communities, Farmdale and Metroville, showed more deviation from the Developed Democratic regime and Competitive Mass power structure than did the two intermediate in size, Oretown and Petropolis. This indicates the absence of any relationship between size and these political characteristics.

Our findings suggest that such variables as the probability of illegitimate sanctions sense of electoral potency, distribution of power, and ideological diversity operate independently of such ecological factors as size. On the other hand, particular case studies of community politics suggest a pattern of closed politics and monopolistic control in small communities. Furthermore, it seems much easier in small communities for a small group of leaders to control political information and potentially relevant organizational bases—such as the civic clubs—than in somewhat larger communities. It is possible that Metroville's closed politics resulted from its paternalistic Southern traditions and its continuing history of dominance by a few old families, despite its relatively large size compared to our other communities. For these reasons, we expect that a comparative study of a large number of communities, controlled for size, might indicate a relationship between size and type of regime and power structure. Nonetheless, on the basis of our more limited comparative study, we also would expect to find that types of regime and power structure vary in considerable degree, regardless of size.

Hypothesis: There is no relationship between rate of community growth and type of regime or power structure.

Test: All four communities

The two Western communities, Farmdale and Oretown, grew at a much faster rate than either of the Southern communities, of which Metroville was growing faster than Petropolis. Oretown was expanding at a much faster rate than Farmdale.

Oretown's growth seems to have contributed directly to its highly competitive, open politics. And yet the needs generated by rapid growth were not translated automatically into political demands and turbulence. This awaited the development of a leadership group, the Liberals, which formulated and articulated demands for a rapid expansion of the scope of government, and then developed subsidiary political organizations through which they might exert effective influence in decisional processes. In Farmdale, the leadership group which, in the immediate postwar period, favored an expansion in the scope of government to meet the needs of a growing population was defeated and disorganized through the strategies adopted by the Conservatives. Here, the most important factors were political and not ecological.

Metroville grew faster than Petropolis, but its politics was more consensual and more controlled than that of Petropolis. Among the critical factors in Metroville's political system were also the perspectives and organization of the Progressive Conservative leaders; that is, the factor of rapid growth did not contribute to political conflict as might have been expected.

We conclude that growth rate may provide a potential basis for conflict and competition in politics, but that conflict and competition seemed to be related more directly to other political factors.

In this chapter, we have attempted to present hypotheses which summarize some of the most significant relationships among the most important variables treated in our study. We view this theoretical statement as quite provisional, and we believe that continuous, experimental, comparative research will be necessary to refine, reject, verify, or extend these hypotheses.

Since research is often not continuous and dissimilar in the area of local politics, it is extremely difficult for us to place our four communities in the universe of American communities. The greatest gap between our study and the "real world of local politics" is that we have not included a major metropolitan center in our investigation. Yet we have reason to believe that in many respects the difference between the politics of a major metropolis and the politics of our four smaller communities is more apparent than real. For example, the rise of the Radical Right in the United States, which we have investigated in some detail, appears to be a phenomenon based in small- and medium-sized communities. But the recent politics of such major urban centers as Detroit and Los Angeles reveal political dynamics that can be better understood through the use of concepts developed in this study. In both cities mayoralty elections pitted essentially Community Conservationist candidates against Liberal candidates. The Liberals won, even though the bulk of the civic leadership and prominent labor-union and Democratic party leadership were on the other side, because they appealed largely to the mass of the discontented— Negroes, the unemployed, and variegated members of the low cultural class—with whom the Community Conservationist had little contact or political status. These are the groups that we have found most frequently supporting the Radical Right. But our analysis shows that the potential base of dissidents is essentially a low cultural class, which may tend either to the Radical Right or to the Liberals. In the major urban centers of the United States, the traditions and organization of Liberalism are more highly developed than are those of the Radical Right. The presence of a proportionately large, deprived Negro constituency also promotes a politics of competition between Community Conservationists and Liberals, rather than between Community Conservationists and the Radical Right. But the essential point is that this kind of political dynamic, the defeat of an administration's civic improvement tax program, voter rejections of school budgets and bond issues, or the frequent defeat of metropolitan government-consolidation proposals throughout the United States, can be better understood if investigators use a framework such, as ours, whether the community being studied is an Oretown or a Los Angeles.

Another major blind spot of the present volume has been the lack of focus on the federal character of American community politics. American political communities are open systems not only in reference to their economies and societies, but also in reference to the political systems in which they are embedded: the state, the region, and the nation-state. Political theory-building would profit in various ways from the construction of models of communities that recognize inputs from such large systems as blocs or groupings of nation-states, just as it would profit from the development of models that specify possible circular flows of events from and to communities and from and to the state or national levels. These constitute some of the most intellectually exciting, potential developments in comparative community studies. We trust that colleagues will join us in such tasks, as other colleagues study more intensely a variety of particular political processes within communities that we have been able only to touch on in passing or have had to ignore completely.

A CONCLUDING WORD

We have in this book purposefully tried to subject our own political values to the test of political truth. This does not mean that we are unaware that our values shape our research, from the selection of problems for study through the choice of major variables to the interpretation of findings, including the acceptance or rejection of hypotheses and the assumption of the risk of being wrong in so doing.

It may not be out of place here to suggest that we share an apprehension that one of the many reasons the world may witness the final holocaust is the sparsity of valid, reliable, and relevant knowledge of what constitutes political systems called "democratic," what they do and do not do, and how they work. We have a strong preference for Developed Democracies, yet we think that we, like many of the most articulate proponents of such regimes, have at best a very partial understanding of their limitations and their strengths, of the conditions for their establishment, maintenance, and growth, or of the conditions under which they may disappear or remain at an unsatisfactorily low level of development.

Our values led us to explore the possibility that what we term a relatively Consensual Mass power structure can be developed in a Democratic political regime. One of the major political problems of our time is that posed by the need for a viable "collectivist" ideology, that is, one that does conceive of communities as collectivities, which at the same time encourages individual dissent and innovation and that supports and maintains the permeability of power structures. The dangers generated by increasingly interdependent and interacting sets of collectivities demand a concern for the survival of groups and the preservation of their interests at the same time that the increasingly sophisticated and effective techniques for political indoctrination and totalitarianism make the dangers to the individual in that enterprise greater than ever before. The increasing urgency of the eternal human dilemma, namely, the need for both individualism and group-oriented welfare policies, demands of the political analyst a much greater effort than ever before if the chain-reaction that might be started between polities leading to the final physical chain-reaction is to be avoided.

We are profoundly disturbed not only by the state of American democracy and political culture, as we understand it, but also by the apparent complacency of so many democratic theorists as well as propagandists. Of particular importance to us is the need to understand the conditions under which it may be possible to integrate such marginal groups as Negroes and others of low cultural class into Democratic regimes, and to understand the conditions under which a more widespread distribution of political power and political dignity can occur in which such groups can share. These conditions are particularly complex in an age that seems to put a premium on expert knowledge available to few citizens for the making of political as well as other kinds of decisions, an age whose technology produces automation and massive unemployment, atom bombs and massive anxieties, and which still finds the demands of political minorities for full integration into power structures and regimes met by massive resistances. The complexity of the physical world has not stopped the production of knowledge in physical science. The complexity of the political world cannot stop an increasing knowledge of the relationships between rulers and ruled, of the processes of political respect, reaction, and revolution. It is to such ends that we urge continual comparative research on community political systems.

NOTE

1. Although the format of this chapter may suggest an adequate testing of hypotheses for all communities in the United States, the writers are fully aware of the limitations imposed by the size of the sample, the relatively short time span covered in each community, and the fact that many of the hypotheses have not been developed, and may prove to be more or less valid, for studies that are broader than ours with respect to sample, time, and country. Yet the logic of empirically grounded theory suggests that as studies improve in quality and scope, their findings ought to consider those of less adequate studies rather than adopt a strategy of forbearing to test hypotheses or to make implicit rather than explicit tests until the better studies have been done. Moreover, even small-scale studies may permit an exploration in some depth of dynamics and theoretical relationships that the large-scale studies cannot easily manage. This does not constitute, however, an argument for smaller rather than larger studies, nor is it an argument for the case study rather than the "many cases" study. The problems of validity and reliability of findings in regard to American community politics will not begin to be solved until larger studies than ours are undertaken.

APPENDIX A   OPERATIONAL DEFINITIONS

This appendix describes the general procedures used by the authors in conducting their sample surveys and the operational definitions they used for the major variables referred to in the text.

We have not attempted to describe every aspect of our methods. For example, technical calculations of sampling errors have been omitted, as have computations of statistical significance in the tables. Since our research designs for various portions of the study have developed considerably during the past few years, we feel that statistical tests might lend an unwarranted aura of precision and authority to some of the findings. We have purposefully portrayed other findings as real or actual when such tests have indicated that they may have emerged by chance.

Such analytic decisions rest on our feeling that at this stage in the development of empirically grounded theory of comparative political systems it is premature to insist on a level of assurance that most political and social research cannot yet justify. We feel that it is more important to utilize as systematically as possible a theoretical framework in ordering and presenting data that have a certain internal consistency, even at the risk of pursuing theoretical dead ends, than to abandon prematurely a theoretical direction to avoid accepting a false hypothesis or rejecting a true one.

Although we feel strongly that studies of political phenomena need to be made and reported prior to the solution of many of the methodological problems that bear directly on the validity of such studies, we believe that the kind and quality of political knowledge needed for the implementation of political ideals depends ultimately on more attention to, and more adequate solutions of, such technical problems. It is to this end that we present the lengthy "semi-technical" discussion and comments that follow, trusting that the integral interdependence of political theory and research methodology will be more appreciated than it sometimes is by students of politics.

SAMPLE SELECTION, TIME M

At Time M, the authors used area-probability random samples to describe and compare the citizenries of the four communities.[1] We obtained maps of each city from such sources as planning commissions and utility offices and from these maps numbered the community's blocks consecutively. Extensive cruising was carried out to determine whether very large or very small blocks should be divided or combined before being assigned numbers. Next, a previously calculated number of blocks was selected from a table of random numbers. Then, using a type of cluster sampling, we chose two or three households from each block to obtain a specified number of interviews. In Farmdale, for instance, we acquired a list of dwelling units from utility and city-directory listings and supplemented it with surveys of the blocks. After each block had been mapped and addresses obtained for each dwelling unit, including multiple-family dwellings, every nth unit was selected for an interview.

The third stage in the sampling operation consisted of selecting adults to be interviewed within the selected dwelling units. Ordinarily the interviewers were instructed to interview one male and then one female adult, choosing the head of the household when this rule permitted such a choice. If no male was in residence the interviewer was instructed to interview three females in succession so that the male-female selection rule would obtain.

For areas outside of each city maps, including aerial-survey maps, were gathered. An effort was made to draw a boundary line around the fringe areas whose population ordinarily shopped in the community itself or in a shopping center within a mile of the city limits. This boundary line was determined by purposive interviews in the fringe areas designed to establish such shopping patterns. In Farmdale, for example, each person in the initially designated sampling area was asked where he did his "regular family shopping." Seventy per cent responded that they shopped regularly in Farmdale, 11 per cent said in both Farmdale and the nearest big city, 10 per cent said in the nearest big city, and 9 per cent said in smaller communities outside of Farmdale. When these respondents were classified according to distance from the larger city, a direct relationship emerged between shopping in Farmdale and proximity to the larger city.

We then divided the fringe areas into smaller areas of approximately the same number of dwelling units as in the more sparsely populated blocks inside the city; numbered them and selected the necessary number of areas at random; listed the dwelling units in each selected area; and chose two or three of those units for interviews. In Farmdale, a listing of every dwelling unit in the selected fringe area was available from a recent map showing the location by address or postal-route number of each unit. The sample of dwelling units in that community's fringe area was drawn at random from the list.

In order to obtain an acceptable proportion of completed interviews —that is, at least 84 per cent—the interviewers sometimes had to call as many as seven times at the designated dwelling unit to find a suitable respondent at home. The proportion of completed interviews, however, was maintained at 84 per cent or more of those selected in the sample.

A special sampling problem existed in the two Southern cities, where we wished to obtain independent samples of both the Negro and White subcommunities. White respondents were sampled and interviewed first, after excluding all-Negro blocks from those to be sampled. If a dwelling unit selected for the White sample was occupied by Negro residents, another dwelling unit was drawn from the same block. Every effort was made to identify areas occupied by Negroes before drawing the block sample for the survey of Negroes. However, some Negroes living in generally White neighborhoods probably were not interviewed, introducing a bias into the Negro samples.

For the Oretown panel study conducted in 1959, a systematic sample was drawn from utility-company lists, and every listed multiple-family dwelling was noted on planning-commission maps. After these maps were checked, every dwelling unit was numbered in a clockwise fashion around every block, moving in a serpentine fashion from block to block. Every nth house was then selected for an interview with an adult householder. The fringe area outside the city was mapped and divided into small areas, and the sampling procedure described earlier was applied to obtain the desired number of interviews.

The interviews conducted in Oretown 2 years later were obtained from a subsample selected at random from the original respondents. If a person had moved away, died, or could not be reached to complete an interview, a substitute was drawn from among the original respondents. The findings reporting relationships at the latter time are based on the answers of respondents who were interviewed both times.

It should be stressed at this point that because of the nature of sample surveys and the necessity of doing two samples in each of the Southern communities, Time M represents at least a 3- to 4-week period—it took that long to complete the interviews for particular samples. Therefore, to say that Time M was a specific "point" in time and of exactly the same duration in each community is an analytic fiction that is unavoidable. The interviews with Manifest Leaders ordinarily involved an even greater time lag; in Oretown, they were treated as Time M measurements even though they were completed months after the citizen sample. In analyzing the data, the variable character of Time M was borne in mind, even though it was treated conceptually as a particular point in time. If interviewing staffs could be as large as possible within the limits of efficiency and manageability, and special categories of respondents such as Manifest Leaders could be interviewed at the same time as the rank-and-file citizens, the difficulty posed by naturally occurring events during the time of such measurements would be minimized.

SAMPLE REPRESENTATIVENESS, TIME M

Table A-1 compares educational characteristics of the samples obtained at Time M with those reported by the United States Census of 1950 for Oretown and 1960 for the Southern cities. Comparable census information was not reported for communities as small as Farmdale. Generally the reported differences were slight; the largest difference was the underrepresentation of the least-educated citizens and an overrepresentation of the moderately well-educated citizens in the Petropolis Negro sample, assuming that the census figures are the standard of accuracy. Other such comparisons yield comparably close sample and census distributions.

Since minor discrepancies existed between the census figures and our sample surveys in the distribution of such characteristics as formal-education level, the representativeness of the samples for purposes of valid comparative analysis might legitimately be questioned. Care had to be exercised to avoid searching for explanations of variations in such matters as political participation rates, which actually may have been similar but appeared to differ from community to community because of biased samples.

If we were to assume that the census figures were more accurate than our own and were to ignore the differences that might have resulted from changes between the time of the census and the time of our surveys, a pattern would emerge indicating that the sample surveys underrepresented slightly the poorly educated and overrepresented slightly the better educated. Although the bias tended to be consistent, the opposite pattern appeared in the case of college-educated Metroville Whites, and there was no overrepresentation of the highly educated citizens of Oretown. A relatively large underrepresentation

TABLE A-1   Percentage Differences in Educational Achievement Reported for the Communities in the United States Census and in the Sample Surveys at Time M *

Community	0 to 6 Years	Educational Level	
		7 to 12 Years	13 Years or More
Oretown			
% difference between 1954 sample and 1950 Census report	−4 †	+4	=
Petropolis			
% difference between 1958 sample and 1960 Census report			
Whites	−3	−2	+5
Negroes	−12	+10	+2
Metroville			
% difference between 1958 sample and 1960 Census report			
Whites	−3	+8	−5
Negroes	−1	−1	+3

* These data are reported for people 25 years of age and over to make the survey data comparable to the Census reports. The samples actually include citizens 21 to 25 years old as well.

† The + or − represents the direction the percentage in the sample deviates from the percentage in the Census.

of the poorly educated was found in the sample of the Negro subcommunity of Petropolis. Data are presented in the next section bearing on the question of whether these possible sample biases affected the important rank-ordering of the six samples on political participation levels (Chapter 7).

THE VARIABLES

Variable I: Political Participation

To measure political participation as of Time E to M, the respondents in the sample surveys were asked the following questions:

Items: 1a.   How often have you seriously discussed local government or community matters with friends during the past year? Often. Once in a while. Not at all.

1b. and 1c.   The above question was repeated with the substitute phrases: "with civic or community leaders"; "with city or county officials."

2.   Have you attended any meetings or gatherings during the past two or three years in which city government metters were a *major* subject of consideration? Yes or no.

3.   Have you taken an active part in any local government or community issue during the past two or three years? Yes or no.

If the respondent answered "yes" to Item 2, he was asked what group held the meeting.

The following statement was read to all respondents before they answered Item 3: "Another way in which people engage in public affairs is to take an active part in some issue that arises. By active part is meant doing things to get a decision made in a particular way by securing signatures, holding or attending special meetings, speaking to groups, calling on people, and the like." If the response was "yes" to Item 3, the respondent was asked what the issue was, and what sort of action he took.

Analysis of the answers to these questions indicated that those responding affirmatively ordinarily could describe their participation or the meeting attended; this may signify validity of the responses.[2] The questions were originally asked before the element of time became theoretically important to the authors. After the first sample survey, analysis of the content of the responses to the follow-up questions for Items 2 and 3 indicated that respondents rarely answered in the affirmative in regard to events occurring more than 1 year prior to the time at which the questions were asked. In more recent years, these items have been worded consistently to refer to "during the past year."

In all six samples there were positive relationships between educational level and political participation. In twenty-four of thirty possible relationships for the five participation items in the six samples, there were linear relationships between the two variables indicating that the highly educated participated more than the moderately well educated, and that the latter participated more than the poorly educated. In four of the other six relationships the highly educated participated more than the moderately well educated, but those with little education participated as much as or more than those with a moderate amount of education. In the two remaining relationships, the highly educated participated slightly less than those with little education, in one case, and less than the moderately well educated in the other.

Even though a number of individual relationships were slight, the pattern was that higher educational attainment was positively related to higher political participation. However, not only were the two exceptions in the Negro subcommunity of Metroville important (indicating positive political interest but nonparticipation in organization-of-political-support stages of decision-making), but the magnitude of these relationships on particular items varied considerably from sample to sample. The larger the range, the greater was the distance between the political-participation rates of those with much and those with little education. Concerning discussion with friends, for example, the percentage difference between those with much and those with little education varied from 25 per cent in Oretown to 47 per cent in the Negro subcommunity of Metroville. Concerning the activist role, the difference between those with much and those with little education varied from 1 per cent in the opposite, unexpected direction among Negro citizens of Metroville to 44 per cent among Negro citizens of Petropolis.

It is of some interest to note that for the first and third discussion items the range was greatest among Negroes of Metroville, whereas on the second discussion item, as well as on both remaining items of political participation, the range was greatest among Negroes of Petropolis. Closer inspection of Table A-2 indicates that all of these relatively great differences in participation were due primarily to the relatively high participation levels of the highly educated in these two subcommunities on the respective items, and not to the relatively low participation of those with little education. In contrast, the most restricted ranges were to be found among Negro citizens of Metroville on the attend-meetings and activist-role items; but this was largely due to the relatively low participation rates of the highly educated compared to the rates of the highly educated on these same items in the other samples.

On the basis of the same composite rank-ordering participation index that was used to compare the relative degrees of participation from community to community, citizens characterized by similar levels of education were compared from community to community. The order for the samples holds for each educational category, with one exception. Highly educated Negroes in Metroville were tied with highly educated Whites in Petropolis in the rate of their political participation. We can analyze this more carefully from the data in Table A-3,

TABLE A-2 Political-Participation Rates of Educational Categories as Deviations from Cross-Community Averages, and Intracommunity Ranges between High and Low Education Categories *

Political-Participation Item	Oretown Whites				Petropolis Whites				Petropolis Negroes				Farmdale Whites				Metroville Whites				Metroville Negroes			
	High	Me-dium	Low	Range	High	Me-dium	Low	Range	High	Me-dium	Low	Range	High	Me-dium	Low	Range	High	Me-dium	Low	Range	High	Me-dium	Low	Range
Discuss with friends (64%)†	+29	+22	+4	25	+23	+7	−17	40	+26	+6	−7	33	+14	−4	−21	35	+16	−3	−26	42	+29	−6	−18	47
Discuss with leaders (29%)	+23	+5	−6	29	+26	−2	−10	36	+53	+18	−4	57	+12	−14	−17	29	+24	−2	−21	45	+38	−4	−13	51
Discuss with officials (18%)	+22	=	−2	24	+25	+4	−1	26	+18	+1	−7	25	+9	−6	−5	14‡	+21	−1	−9	30	+26	−9	−11	37
Attend meetings (9%)	+12	+4	+2	10	+9	+1	−3	12	+34	+18	+1	33	+8	−4	−3	11‡	−1	−7	−8	7	−5	−2	−7	(−)2‖
Activist role (9%)	+15	+1	+1	14‡	+9	=	−6	15	+37	+6	−7	44	+15	−1	−5	20	+5	−5	−3	8‡	−5	−7	−4	(−)1‖

* The rates are the differences and directions—plus, minus, or equal—in percentage points between the proportion of the particular educational category participating to the specified degree and the average participation rate of the six samples calculated for each participation item. Ranges are the absolute percentage-point differences between the rates of the high and low education categories. The degree of participation specified for the discussion items is at least once in a while and for the other two items an affirmative response.

† (%) = Cross-community average.

‡ The relationship is slightly curvilinear.

‖ The relationships are curvilinear and the highly educated are slightly less participant than one other educational category, a finding denoted by the symbol (—).

which is a rearrangement of the data in Table A-2; participation rates are presented sample by sample according to educational level. By holding educational level constant, we can focus on similarities and differences in political-participation rates, item by item, of people from the several communities and subcommunities who have a common degree of formal education.

In twenty-six of thirty instances, those with little education had minus scores—that is, below the composite sample averages. The number of minus scores for the moderately educated was sixteen out of thirty. In only three of the thirty cases did the highly educated obtain minus scores. This points up the overall relationships of educational level to political participation.

If we look at this table horizontally, we can see that the participation scores for Farmdale, Metroville Whites, and Metroville Negroes tended to be lower for those with a low or moderate amount of education than they were for the comparably educated in Oretown and the two subcommunities in Petropolis. This was most pronounced for the moderately well educated: all fifteen participation scores for the former samples were minus scores, compared to but one of fifteen for the latter samples. Three of the four positive scores obtained by citizens with little education were in Oretown and the fourth in the Negro subcommunity of Petropolis. However, except for the one item of discussion

TABLE A-3   Political-Participation Rates as Deviations from Cross-Community Averages, and Cross-Community Ranges, by Educational Level

Educational Level	Ore-town	Petropolis		Farm-dale	Metroville		Range
		Whites	Negroes		Whites	Negroes	
High							
Discuss with friends	+29	+23	+26	+14	+16	+29	15
Discuss with leaders	+23	+26	+53	+12	+24	+38	41
Discuss with officials	+22	+25	+18	+9	+21	+26	15
Attend meetings	+12	+9	+34	+8	−1	−5	39
Activist role	+15	+9	+37	+15	+5	−5	42
Medium							
Discuss with friends	+22	+7	+6	−4	−3	−6	28
Discuss with leaders	+5	−2	+18	−14	−2	−4	32
Discuss with officials	=	+4	+1	−6	−1	−9	13
Attend meetings	+4	+1	+18	−4	−7	−2	25
Activist role	+1	=	+6	−1	−5	−7	13
Low							
Discuss with friends	+4	−17	−7	−21	−26	−18	30
Discuss with leaders	−6	−10	−4	−17	−21	−13	17
Discuss with officials	−2	−1	−7	−5	−9	−11	10
Attend meetings	+2	−3	+1	−3	−8	−7	10
Activist role	+1	−6	−7	−5	−3	−4	8

with friends, the ranges seemed to be relatively restricted for those with little education, indicating that there was not much variation in the participation rates of those with little education. The variation in the proportions of citizens participating in activist roles, for example, was only 8 percentage points for those with little education. For the highly educated the comparable variation was 42 percentage points.

Again looking horizontally, we find that both the highly educated Whites and the highly educated Negroes in Metroville participated relatively little on both the attend-meetings and activist-role items. It is on the three discussion items that the highly educated Negroes of Metroville participated most. Thus, the high position of the highly educated Negroes of Metroville on the composite participation index resulted from their high participation on the discussion items, even though they had not participated much on the other two participation items.

It would appear that the possible sample biases would not have affected appreciably the general political-participation rank-order of the communities and subcommunities. The Negro Metroville sample would have ranked at the bottom of the list even more certainly if that sample had not possibly had a slight bias in overrepresenting highly educated respondents. The possible slight overrepresentation of highly educated Whites in Petropolis, if corrected, would not have reduced that subcommunity's political-participation rank to that of the Metroville White subcommunity. A presumably more representative sample of the Negro subcommunity of Petropolis would have lowered its political-participation rank below that of Oretown's (with which it had been tied). Whether it would have been higher than, equal to, or slightly lower than that of the Petropolis White subcommunity is uncertain, but it clearly would still have been much higher than that of Farmdale and both subcommunities of Metroville.

Variable II: Subsidiary Political Organizations

To classify associations as subsidiary political organizations, the authors adopted the following procedures. An index of community political participation was constructed for each community, and each respondent was assigned an index score. Respondents were given one point for an affirmative answer to any of the three forms of Item 1— that is, for responding that they had seriously discussed local-government or community matters with friends, civic or community leaders, or city or county officials. No more than one point was possible, even if a respondent had responded affirmatively to all three forms of this discussion item. A second point might be earned by responding affirmatively to Item 2, and a third point by responding affirmatively to Item 3.

A fourth point was given to those who responded that they voted "often" or "once in a while" rather than "not at all" to the question "How often do you vote in local elections (city or county)?" Those respondents with three or four points were classified as active participants.

Each respondent was also asked: "Do you belong to any organization or association?" Categories of organizations and associations probed for were: civic or fraternal, neighborhood, farming, labor, religious, political, professional, social, general, and others. Each member's political-participation-index score was noted. Those associations listed by two or more of the respondents in which 10 per cent or more of these member respondents had scores of 3 or 4 points on the political-participation index were classified as subsidiary political organizations.

Church membership and political-party identification were excluded from these operations. Groups or associations within churches and local party organizations or clubs were included. Although membership in labor unions might be regarded as involuntary, labor unions were included. Membership in labor unions or their locals was treated as membership in a subsidiary organization within a community. White and Negro samples were classified separately for each of the Southern cities.

To assess the degree to which members of subsidiary political organizations were involved in community political decision-making, we tabulated the responses of members in the White samples of Petropolis and Metroville to the following question: "Have you personally worked in these organizations on any important community problem, policy, matter, or issue?" There were more affirmative responses to this question in Petropolis than in Metroville, but within both cities members of subsidiary political organizations responded affirmatively more often than members of nonpolitical subsidiary organizations. Combining the data from both samples, we found that 42 per cent of the members of subsidiary political organizations responded affirmatively to this question, compared to 25 per cent of the members of nonpolitical organizations. The difference was noted for respondents at every level of political participation except the lowest (i.e., no participation).

Such findings suggest the need to investigate the extent to which— and conditions under which—members of subsidiary political organizations are most likely to obtain political influence and political power in community decision-making; the kinds of members most likely to obtain such influence or power; and the influence the active participants have on ordinarily nonparticipant citizens. Research on the comparable functions of families and friendship groups is also needed.

Comments: Subsidiary political organizations are defined differently than they usually are in political science and sociology. Such organizations are most often classified as political, social, civic, fraternal, business, labor, and so forth. Such manifest purposes may be ascertained on the basis of provisions in the organization's constitution, by-laws, or the individual interpretations of members.

In communities, however, organizations may have political purposes and tasks at the same time that they serve nonpolitical needs. They may serve as important centers for political participation, influence, and power relations even though these tasks are not included in the organization's constitution and even though they may not be recognized as such by the organization's members.

Members of associations formally organized for economic, social, or civic improvement, or for mutual benefit of any kind, may engage in political action with other association members. A political participant's action is more likely to influence the stream of events that constitute a community political decision-making process if the action in the first instance reaches another individual. Receptive individuals are more likely to be reached by the originator of the political action because they are more likely to be found in such an organization than in associations that are not—in these functional terms—political. Thus subsidiary political organizations serve to make indirect as well as direct political-influence relations in community power structures more likely.

This means that analytically a subsidiary political organization is a milieu wherein organizational participation functions in a way that increases the likelihood that politically participant members will be accorded positive political status by other members, and hence, political influence. Nonmembers also may see an organization as a center of political activity if some of the members of that organization are active political participants. This may increase the prospects that nonmember targets of politically participant members will accord the latter political status and thus political influence. In these and other ways, a subsidiary political organization increases the likelihood that the political participation of members will influence the political decision-making processes of the community.

Just as studies of American national politics have pointed up and offered reasons for the importance of the formally organized voluntary association in that politics, we have had occasion in all four of our cities to be impressed by the importance of such organizations in community politics, for similar reasons. In the city as in the nation, highly active political participants, particularly those who feel strongly about maintaining or changing the scope of government, are unlikely to put aside their political sentiments and behavior when they are in formal associational environments. The nonpolitical purposes or tasks of some of these associations may in fact shape political attitudes and decisional preferences of members as well as be shaped by them. When members of associations participate in politics, other association members may take their acts into account partly because of the affection or respect felt for their fellows. This dynamic, of course, would tend to hold true, and even more so, among members of generally more intimate family or informal-friendship groups.

What might be called the political-status "halo effect" of membership in subsidiary political organizations would seem to be greater than the comparable halo effect of membership in equally large but more apolitical formal associations, or in smaller, however political, family or informal-friendship groups. By this we mean that as an association comes to be thought of, correctly or incorrectly, by government officials and/or by civic leaders if not by the general public, as a setting wherein highly active political participants are acting politically, the disposition of government officials and civic leaders to take an individual member's political acts into account may increase. So, too, might we expect that in general there is a positive relationship between the proportion of politically active members in an association and the perceptions by officials and civic leaders of the larger polity of the political character of the association.

One reason for this seems to be that members of such organizations are thought to represent the decisional preferences of the other members of the association, or some significant fraction thereof. In addition, those to whom political participants communicate may explicitly or implicitly, consciously or unconsciously, identify the participants as belonging to an organization that has a relatively politically active membership. A presumption may be created in the minds of the recipients of the communication that other activists as well as other politically non-participant members may be induced to engage in political decision-making. Whether this presumption is valid or not is irrelevant to this process of generating political status.

Membership and participation in subsidiary political organizations may contribute to the political status, and to the political influence when political participation occurs, of members of such organizations, for an allied reason. Sensitivity to, or fears of, political pressures and sanctions is but one of the bases of political status and political-influence relations. Respect or deference may be another. One of the ways that respect for a person or for a person's judgment in regard to civic affairs is generated in modern America is by people's participating voluntarily in organizations that are concerned with improving aspects of life in a community. This respect or disposition to defer to a person's judgment or abilities in regard to various features of community life may be generalized or transferred to a person's political judgment, attitudes, or preferences in regard to the scope of local government. We assume that this process is particularly common in civic organizations that are subsidiary political organizations, wherein the respect generated by members' associational activity may be transferred to their composite politico-civic judgment. A member of a subsidiary political organization may thus gain respect from non-members for his political actions; that is, he may acquire political influence, via such processes of generalization, transference, or what we termed the political-status "halo effect."

Defining subsidiary political organizations on the basis of these sorts of assumptions means that not only manifestly political organizations such as the city council, budget committees, taxpayers associations, and groups formed for such special purposes as electing certain types of officials or for the adoption by government of particular kinds of policies and programs will probably fall in this category, but others as well. Even some of the foregoing voluntary associations may not qualify if, for whatever reasons, insufficient numbers of members are active politically. Even manifestly political associations may over time become relatively apolitical as members pursue as primary endeavors the satisfaction of their needs for social, affectionate, or fellowship relations, for economic benefits, or for educational satisfactions. It has been noted on occasion, rightly or wrongly, that in these days of an expanded, active federal government even local political-party organizations or clubs have become more than ever a source of social satisfactions and less of a setting wherein economic or welfare needs of people were satisfied in the interest of the political needs and purposes of the political leaders of the organizations or clubs. Such possibilities do exist, and the definition of subsidiary political organization used herein provides for these possibilities. One consequence of this functional conception of a political organization is that as political participation varies over time, so may the classification of organizations as subsidiary political organizations. Our operational definition of subsidiary political organization thus builds in this possibility.

Among those associations classified as subsidiary political organizations were those that were voluntary, in that membership was not automatically attained at birth or at a designated chronological age, but was awarded on the basis of the initiative of the individual. Some sort of admission procedure had to exist over which current members had some degree of control which established whether or not a particular person could become a member according to the organization's rules. Therefore, membership established solely through self-identification would not qualify an association as a potential subsidiary political organization. For example, political parties with which people might identify themselves were not eligible to be classified as subsidiary political organizations.

Local party units, committees, or clubs which controlled admission to their ranks to some degree were eligible to be classified as subsidiary political organizations. Churches were ineligible because of the large element of almost automatic entry at birth or later in life, although admission procedures may exist and more or less strict expulsion procedures may make retention of membership for many purposes far from a simple matter of self-identification. Associations of ministers, however, or voluntary groupings within churches were eligible for the designation.

Labor unions are ordinarily quasi-voluntary, even in areas of union or closed shops. Economic circumstances may in many areas reduce their voluntary character for men who simply cannot be adjudged free to find a nonunion job. At the same time such opportunities are not always absent, particularly if a working man is willing to endure economic sacrifices to avoid membership in a labor union. We include labor unions in all four cities as eligible for classification as subsidiary political organizations. Associations of businessmen, merchants, and professional men are eligible, as are civic, fraternal, recreational, civic-improvement, and educational organizations.

Corporations, partnerships and other forms of business organizations or firms were not considered eligible. They are formally organized voluntary associations and a case could be made for their eligibility as subsidiary political organizations. There are clearly firms whose managers do not leave their political activities to their after-office hours nor hide their membership in a firm when acting politically outside the firm. Nor is corporate identification always disregarded by others, even when a manager tries to identify himself solely as a citizen. However, since our estimates of political influence for this analysis could not be very refined or precise, the fact that there were in our four cities associations of business and professional men and women eligible to be classified as subsidiary political organizations means that many business and professional men and women could have been credited with some increase in the probability of their political participation's leading to political influence. Labor unions, on the other hand, were more frequently the only subsidiary political organization, when so classified (in three of the four cities) to which blue-collar workers belonged.

Treating labor unions as eligible for the subsidiary-political-organization category may be used to clarify the conception of such organizational milieus as increasing the likelihood that political acts of members will have impacts on others, directly or indirectly. Political influence has been conceived in most general terms as the according of political status to, the taking into account of, a political participant's attitudes as a direct or indirect consequence of the latter's acts. A more detailed specification of political-influence relations might include a statement of whether the "taking into account" process was positive or negative. A person may be described as exerting positive political influence on another if the other's attitudes or actions are affected in the direction intended by the actor. If a political participant's actions lead to changes in the attitudes or actions of the other which are not only unintended but in some ways contradictory to the intentions of the actor, the relationship may be thought of as negative political influence. Both positive and negative political influence may be embedded in an affectionate or hostile, respectful or fearful, personal or impersonal context, although one would expect certain relationships between the kind of influence and context.

Political-status relations may be described similarly in terms of their positive or negative character depending on the extent to which the taking into account results in greater convergence or divergence in the mind of the person according political status between his own political attitudes and those of the person whom he is taking into account. Political-status relations may also be positive or negative regardless of the motives or feelings of the person according the status to the other.

In a community with labor unions that are classified as subsidiary political organizations but are resented and disliked by a political leadership of businessmen who may be antiunion in general and/or because the particular unions are perceived to be political organizations, union activities may generate disrespect and not respect, defiance rather than deference. Political participation by members or officers of the "political" union may have an adverse effect on the political leadership of the community's political organization; it may lead to political decisions that are even less desirable than earlier decisions in the eyes of the labor union's membership and leadership.

In such a situation membership in the subsidiary political organization would still be enhancing the prospects of a politically participant union man's being accorded political status and acquiring political influence with the community's political leadership, although the status and influence may be regarded as negative rather than positive in character. Alternatively, such a political leadership of businessmen may accede to demands made by much-disliked union leaders for fear of the political or economic consequences of doing otherwise. Political influence may be positive but exercised in the context of dislike and fear.

We were not uninterested in the kinds of political influence that political participation is likely to have brought members of various subsidiary political organizations. Our first concern in the present analysis was to identify those who were more likely than others to have acquired political influence because of memberships in subsidiary political organizations, regardless of whether that influence was likely to be positive or negative relative to preferred decisional outcomes.[3]

The methods used herein to classify, and the particular operational definitions of, subsidiary political organizations need to be improved. Because we worked with community samples, it is quite likely that a number of small voluntary associations (apart from very informal social groups) were omitted from the list of subsidiary political organizations in each city. Moreover, even large organizations represented in the lists of respondents' organizational memberships may have been misclassified because such a small fraction of their memberships were identified through those random-sampling procedures. Future investigations might well compare the relative advantages and costs of obtaining lists of members of all the formal associations in a community and then sampling the memberships for this classificatory purpose. Additional investigation of other percentages than the criterion of 10 per cent of the members needing to be active political participants to classify organizations as subsidiary political organizations is also an obvious need. The investigation of other criteria than simple membership (such as regular attendance, etc.) is in order. The complex phenomena involved in the concept of a subsidiary political organization deserve to be pursued with far more research resources than have hitherto been devoted to this theoretically important matter.

Variable III: Political-Influence Index: Active Influentials

The index of political influence as of Time M was constructed in the following manner. On the basis of responses to the political-participation items, respondents were assigned a score of zero on the index if they had not responded "often" or "once in a while" to Item 1a, b, or c, and if they had not responded "yes" to Item 2 or 3, regardless of their subsidiary-political-organization scores. If they responded positively to at least one of these two sets of participation items, but did not belong to any organization classified as a subsidiary political organization, they were assigned a score of one point on the political-influence index. Those who received only one point for their affirmative answers to the political participation items (a maximum of one point was possible for Items 1a, b, and c, with one point possible for Items 2 and 3, individually) and who belonged to one or more subsidiary political organizations were assigned a score of two on the political-influence index. All respondents who received two political-participation points and who belonged to one or more subsidiary political organizations were assigned a score of three points. These individuals became our "active influentials."

Comments: It should be remembered that the political-influence index is subject to the same assumptions that underly the measurement of political participation and membership in subsidiary political organizations. As further research clarifies the probabilities that political participation will lead to political influence, and the meaning of participation in subsidiary political organizations, more useful indexes of political influence can be constructed. However speculative the two probabilistic assumptions underlying the political-influence index used here may be—that is, that the more people participate politically, the more likely they are to exercise political influence; and that the more such action takes place in settings wherein other political participants are present, the more likely it will be that the individuals will exercise more political influence than persons outside such settings—they seem sufficiently reasonable to warrant their being used as they have been in this study.

Indices of socio-economic class position seem to rest on foundations that are as uncertain and speculative as those supporting the index of political influence. Using indicators of such variables as formal education, occupation, and/or income to assess the degree of social status accorded people by others would seem to be similar to using the indicators of political influence as a measure of political status (as defined herein). However, indices of socio-economic class are frequently used as measures of what we would term social influence, and to that extent need as much further investigation as does the index of political influence.

One of the revisions that our data have suggested for the future formulation of indexes of political influence is the assignment of points for participation in particular, selected political decision-making processes. The index would then be less a general political-influence index, and more a specifically political-decision-making-influence index. On the other hand, an analyst might want at least two indexes of political influence, one a general measurement and the other a more specific measurement. To the extent that research becomes more intensive and refined, a multiple set of such indexes relating to various categories of decisions—scope areas, institutional areas, and so forth—would appear useful.

One consequence of more specific indexes of political influence would be to make the proportions of people at the active-influential and upper strata of more particularistic indexes smaller, unless the criteria for such categories were considerably attenuated, suggesting the need for much larger samples than were used in this study. The fact that there were such small numbers in the active-influential stratum, particularly in Metroville, already point to this need. Although such small numbers make very unreliable some of the descriptions and comparisons of the kind used, for example, in Chapters 7 and 9 in regard to the active influentials and Latent Leaders, and subject certain findings to the most severe sampling errors, we felt that it was more useful to proceed with a theoretically relevant analysis than to wait for better data.

It was noted in Chapter 7 that the perspectives on race relations on the part of White citizens in Metroville who were high in the structure of political influence differed radically from those who were high in the socio-economic structure (as measured by level of education). Even though there was in general, as described in Chapter 7, a positive relationship in most samples between positions in the political-influence structure and those in the socio-economic structure, there were other instances of deviation between the political perspectives of the highest strata in both structures. This bears on a fundamental point in regard to the use of the political influence index, namely that political theory needs to be developed with the use of such political classification schemes independently of social-structure analysis. By this we do not mean that relationships between the two structures should not be investigated, nor that the two are likely to be independent of each other. Rather, the use of such political-structure portraits as revealed by indexes of political influence should proceed, however inadequate particular indexes of such structural positions may be, without assuming that indexes of social structure automatically or under even "unusual" conditions either reflect or underly those of political structure.[4]

Variable IV: Political Decisions and Authoritative-Consideration Stages

Two randomly and independently selected stratified samples of officers of formally organized voluntary associations and elective and appointive officials of local government provided information about each community's policy problems as of Time *M*. In each community twenty people were selected for the first panel and seventeen for the second, except in Farmdale where the panels totaled twenty-five members. At least two people representing each of the following areas were included on each panel: education, municipal government, business and the professions, and civic or service activities. The remaining nine and twelve members were selected from among the heads of social-welfare, fraternal, special-services, veterans, social, country-club, and religious associations.

Members of both panels were asked such questions as "What, in your opinion, are the most important problems, projects, or issues facing [the community] at the present time?" If the respondent indicated that there were none, he was prompted by the interviewer: "Weren't there any important policies decided, or projects undertaken?" (in reference to the prior 1-year period, except in Farmdale, where the period was 2 years). And finally, "Are there any others you can think of?" The responses to these questions were then supplemented by the research team by examining newspapers and minutes of the city council and other local-government agencies.

Then three, four, or five apparently well-informed citizens in each community were asked to do the following: (1) to classify the responses of the two panels according to whether or not the most active participants in those matters in the community thought that the "problems, projects, or issues" involved local government; and (2) to indicate whether the items gleaned from the newspapers, minutes, or other sources, or any other items not mentioned by panel members were important policy matters involving local government, and whether these items had been decided or allowed to die during the past year(s), or whether they were still being considered.

For the period prior to Time *E*, the authors selected decisions and established their importance through interviews, the space accorded issues in the newspapers at the time they were extant, and other such means. These included individual scrapbooks and materials such as diaries, sometimes discovered in a fortuitous manner, and analysis of other miscellaneous documentary materials in the files of voluntary associations, in annual reports and messages from mayors, etc. In this manner, a reconstruction of political decisions was made year by year for each community. An effort was made to include in those listings such decisions as the three authors independently rated as being as important to participants as the decisions selected by the panels of informants at Time M. To make that judgment, the analysts necessarily relied on such indicators as the evaluations of the informants, stress on matters in the newspaper, etc.

When the three authors disagreed on such ratings, each offered, in as neutral a manner as possible, reasons for his own judgments. Every effort was made to avoid arguments, intimidation of each other, or a fixed commitment to an initial classificatory position (a set of coding rules continued for the authors' analytic judgments on a variety of measures to be described below). Such a procedure resulted in an initially high degree of agreement on the part of the analysts, and as time passed there tended to be an even higher degree of consensus on such interpretative coding judgments, which may have been a consequence of increasing (conscious or unconscious) understanding of, and commitment to, a single standard of judgment, the unconscious development of a pattern of dominance among the coders such that one person's standard of assessment was used by one or both other coders unintentionally (which is not incompatible with the first point), or the development of a need to "give in" because of time or other pressures.

The authors kept in touch with events after the Time M interviews through additional interviews with selected informants and visits from time to time by one or another member of the research group. Oretown was the site of practically continuous observation.

In gathering and coordinating our data for the book, we included in the final set of universes of political decisions "during the past year" (Time E to M) the following: those items mentioned by two or more of the thirty-seven members of the two panels which were considered political (i.e., as relating to the scope of local government) by the well-informed citizens; those items identified by the analysis of documentary sources which were classified by at least one of the latter as a relatively important policy matter involving local government; and those items mentioned for the first time by one or more of the well-informed citizens. Most of the items found in newspapers and other documentary sources were mentioned by two members of the two panels. A few of the items mentioned by the panels were eliminated as "nonpolitical" by the well-informed citizens. For example, all matters regarding local education were eliminated except for those relating to school consolidation and desegregation.

For each political decision-making process in each city, the formal authorities were identified—ordinarily the city councils, but sometimes a planning commission or other local-government agency. Whether a political decision was still being considered in such a setting or had been disposed of earlier—since Time E but prior to Time M—in such a setting, an attempt was made to discover with whom the formal authorities individually or collectively were interacting. The authors ascertained who the active participants were at the time that the matter was still "undecided." If a decisional outcome had not yet or apparently would not reach a set of formal authorities, those who had the last chance to select the outcome were identified, as well as the settings in which their authoritative consideration took place.

Much the same procedure was used, although less systematically and more unreliably, for the pre-Time E periods, relying primarily on the memories of a smaller number of selected informants. For the post-Time M periods, a comparable procedure was used, supplemented by "case study" reports prepared by members of, or assistants on, the research staff. Such reports were more in the form of week-to-week or month-to-month, and, in some cases, day-to-day field notes made by the researchers.

Comments: Only one general comment will be made in regard to identifying and describing political decisions and their stages, particularly the authoritative-consideration stage. The absence of conventional rules or standards for classifying political decisions and their stages makes any such operations as those described above most difficult. Although there has been much historical research on "political decision-making" with attention to what we have referred to as the authoritative-consideration stage, such studies have tended to take formal, institutional definitions as adequate guidelines for describing "reality," or else implicit rather than explicit criteria have been used to guide the analyst. This may make comparisons difficult for analyses undertaken by the same researcher or actually impossible when decision-making analysis is undertaken by different analysts. The effort to reconstruct past decisions was subject to the usual difficulties of memory, recall, and inadequate record-keeping. Even the more recent historical reconstructions of Time E to M and the on-going historical documentations during the post-Time M periods were less satisfactory than we had hoped or expected before they were attempted. Given the theoretical significance of such data, further research needs to be done, at least until minimally accepted standards of judgment and measurement become conventions accepted by researchers.

Variable V: The Political Leaderships: Latent Leaders

Two sets of Latent Leaders were identified systematically for the Time E to M periods through the following procedures. First, Latent Leaders were culled from those classified as active influentials in each random sample by their responses to the following questions about their active participation: "What was the nature of the issue, and what was the nature of your activity?" (asked only if they answered "yes" to Item 2: "Have you taken an active part on any local-government or community issue during the past 2 or 3 years?")

To be classified as a Latent Leader, an active influential had to have answered "yes" to Item 2; he then had to have indicated that he had been active in one or more of the set of political decisions that the analysts had decided were extant during the year preceding; and his description of the "issue" and the nature of his activity must not have indicated that his desires were completely frustrated by the outcome of the decision as of Time M. In addition, the active influential had to say "often" or "once in a while" to Item 1b or 1c.

Latent Leaders were also singled out by identifying the active participants in the authoritative-consideration stage of political decisions through historical reconstruction, and ascertaining, where possible, the decisional preferences of those active participants to establish which of them were apparently contributing purposefully to the decisional outcome as of Time M—that is, those who were at least minimally satisfied with the outcome as of that time. The particular intention in identifying Latent Leaders in this manner—that is, those who may not have been part of the random sample—was to establish whether particular sets of city officials were also Latent Leaders.

Variable VI: The Political Leaderships: Manifest Leaders

At Time M, in every community but Oretown, the first panel of "informants" was asked the following questions—or a slight variation in Farmdale:

Suppose a major project were before the community that required decisions by a group of leaders that nearly everyone would accept. Which people would you choose, regardless of whether or not you know them personally?

In most cities, certain persons are said to be influential "behind the scenes" and to have a lot to say about programs that are planned, and projects and issues that come up around town. What persons in [this community] are influential in this way or are influential in being able to stop particular community policies? Are there any other people with whom these leaders work that have not been named so far and should be included in a list of community leaders? [5]

In Farmdale, the first panel of informants was asked questions which differed in some respects:

Whom do you regard as the most influential persons as far as having a say or determining what decisions shall be made in regard to local-government matters? Whom do you consider the best informed and best qualified to judge whether existing or proposed policies are good or bad in regard to local-government matters? Whom could you go to among your personal acquaintances, or persons you feel you could go to, for advice as to what should be done in regard to local-government matters? Of all the people in your community, whom do you regard as the generally most influential?

Persons mentioned by one or more of these panel members were listed in alphabetical order and shown to members of the second panel for their selection of the "twenty or twenty-five generally most influential people."

In the White subcommunities of Petropolis and Metroville, the numbers of people named by the first panel in response to these questions were ninety-eight and seventy-two, respectively. Alphabetical listings of those nominees were then shown to the members of the second panels with the following comments:

We have talked to a number of people in [this community] who have given us a list of people whom they consider to be important in community policy-making. We would like you to look at this list and indicate which of these people you would consider to be among the twenty or twenty-five *most important* people in this regard. By most important people we mean people who can get a major policy or project adopted in [this community]. You may feel free to add anyone whom you think is important in community policy-making who is not on this list.

The nominations of the second panel were tabulated and individuals receiving five or more votes were regarded as the potential Manifest Political Leaders. Two of the forty-three nominees in Petropolis and two of the twenty-five nominees in Metroville were Negroes, also nominated by Negro nominees as among the most influential Negro Leaders. These four individuals have been treated analytically as Negro Leaders rather than included in the White Manifest Leader category. In Farmdale there were sixteen potential Manifest Leaders.

In Oretown a somewhat different procedure was used to identify the potential Manifest Leaders. Forty people were named at least twice by the panel members. In addition, eleven nominees who were named only once were added to the list. The second set of panelists was told: "We want you to tell us as best you can how influential each person listed is. How much influence does he have on policy formation and in getting things done?" The choices offered for each person were: very high, high, medium, low, very low. The thirty-eight people receiving five or more votes as "very high" or "high" were classified as potential Manifest Leaders.

In the Negro subcommunities two smaller panels of informants—totalling twenty in Petropolis and nineteen in Metroville—were used to identify potential Negro Manifest Leaders or Negro Leaders. The two potential Negro Leaders nominated by the panels of White informants in each city were also nominated by the Negro panelists and included in the foregoing figures. Although White citizens were nominated by the Negro panel, they were not included in the potential Manifest Leader categories.

The following operations were then performed for each set of potential Manifest Leaders. Negro nominees were not included because no comparable, systematic data were available. The potential Manifest Leaders were questioned to ascertain whether they had participated in at least one of the political decisions defined as occurring in the particular community during Time E to M. The decisional preferences of these respondents were then ascertained in order to assess whether they were at least partially satisfied with the outcome of the decisional process or processes in which they had participated. In most instances the information was obtained through interviews with these nominees, but in a few cases they were not interviewed and selected informants who had participated actively in the particular decisional process were asked whether the nominee had appeared to be satisfied. Finally, the decisional processes were reconstructed to identify authoritative-consideration stages, which were used to decide whether the potential Manifest Leaders—if they had apparently been active participants in at least one decisional process and had preferences that accorded minimally with the outcome—had participated in this stage. This reconstruction provided the data for the inference in the text that the Negro Leaders of Metroville probably did not perform political-leadership roles in the power structure of the total community, whereas the Negro Leaders of Petropolis, or a substantial proportion of them, acted as leaders in the polity as a whole during Time E to M.

All of the potential Manifest Leaders in Farmdale, Oretown, both subcommunities of Metroville, and the Negro subcommunity of Petropolis were interviewed. Eighty-two per cent of the White potential Manifest Leaders in Petropolis were interviewed; three partial interviews and data from other sources were obtained for the rest. On the basis of these interviews and other data the authors concluded that of the sixteen potential Manifest Leaders in Farmdale, fourteen were actual Manifest Leaders; of the forty-one potential Manifest Leaders in the White subcommunity of Petropolis, thirty-nine were actual Manifest Leaders; of the twenty-three in the White subcommunity of Metroville, twenty-two were actual Manifest Leaders. The number remained the same in Oretown and in the Negro subcommunities. That number was maintained for analytic purposes, but a general reevaluation was made when assessments were later offered of the political power of the Negro Leaders of Metroville.

The interview questions used to ascertain whether the potential Manifest Leaders had actively participated in political decision-making during Time E to M and what their decisional preferences were varied somewhat from community to community. Ordinarily the questions used to classify Latent Leaders, about matters in which the respondents had participated, were used, as well as the questions on attendance at meetings. In Farmdale each potential Manifest Leader was questioned about the degree of his activity and his preferences in regard to the selected set of decisional processes. In Oretown these respondents were asked to "list, as near to ten as you are able, those problems or issues that you regard as the most important in your community today or during the past two years." They were then asked to indicate how active or inactive they had been on each, the choices being: very active, somewhat active, somewhat inactive, and very inactive. They were also asked for each matter mentioned in which they had been "very active" or "somewhat active": "Would you tell us whom you worked with most closely?" In addition, they were asked specifically for the degree of their activity in regard to three of eight selected political decisions.

In both subcommunities of Metroville and in the White subcommunity of Petropolis the potential Manifest Leaders were asked, in addition to the activist-role and attend-meetings questions, "Is there any particular community policy matter on which you are now working closely with any persons on this list?" The list contained all of the names of the people nominated at least once by either the first or second panel in response to the questions used to identify the potential Manifest Leaders. We then tried to determine how much the potential Manifest Leaders had participated in three political decisions. They could choose one of the following answers: "I have not been concerned one way or another and have pretty much remained on the sidelines"; "I have become quite interested and have discussed the subject on many occasions with friends and acquaintances"; "I have become very much concerned and actually have tried to influence my friends and acquaintances one way or another whenever the subject came up"; "I have felt the decision was very important and have become actively engaged in support of one or the other side by helping get signatures, making special calls on the individuals, writing letters, talking to officials, speaking to groups, or some other means of seeking to affect the outcome."

The same three decisional outcomes were used to try to determine the decisional preferences of potential Manifest Leaders. In this case the answers could be: strongly approve, approve, undecided, disapprove, strongly disapprove. If we failed to obtain responses from the potential Manifest Leaders we accepted the decisional preferences ascribed to them by informants who reported being their friends, and who indicated that they had "worked closely on community projects or policies" with the particular potential Manifest Leaders. In effect, the data on decisional preferences were the final criteria necessary for potential Manifest Leaders to be classified as probable Manifest Leaders.

In Petropolis, the decisional preferences of the potential Negro Leaders were obtained through responses to the question: "Have you personally worked in PESNEG on any important community problem, policy matter, or issue?" or through reports of leading members of PESNEG. The nominees' positions on decisional processes considered in that setting were used as the criterion for distinguishing among the potential and the probable Manifest Leaders.

To clarify the operational definition of Manifest Leader, the five cases of potential Manifest Leaders (i.e., those receiving five or more nominations by the second set of panelists) who were not classified as probable Manifest Leaders and were therefore excluded from the Manifest Leader category will now be discussed briefly. In Farmdale a man who was nominated as an influential person frequently enough to be included among the 16 potential Manifest Leaders also was included by chance in the random sample. He was classified as an active influential (according to the operational definition specified under *Variable III*), but neither as a Latent Leader, nor, finally, as a Manifest Leader. He was active in the decisional process concerning the establishment of a municipal park-and-recreation program. As described in Chapter 11, he had actively participated in the authoritative-consideration stage unsuccessfully, and by Time M he had been coopted in such a way as to substitute a nonpolitical demand for his defeated political demand.

The second man who was nominated but who was not finally classified as a Manifest Leader was referred to in Chapter 6 as a civic leader who had advocated unsuccessfully a community swimming pool as a needed civic improvement. He was widely known as a man who could be counted on in various civic welfare activities; he headed up innumerable campaigns to raise money for such purposes. However, in his one attempt to gain political power in decision-making during Time E to M, his leadership activities were frustrated by his friends and associates who saw a community swimming pool as an unnecessary, costly frill. In fact, as described in Chapter 11, effective illegitimate sanctions were brought to bear against him by some political leaders.

In Metroville, the one potential White Manifest Leader of the twenty-three so nominated by the second panel who was not classified as a probable Manifest Leader was a minister. His church had a high-status congregation, to which more than 40 per cent of the other White Manifest Leaders belonged. He was not only spiritual advisor for such men, but he participated in a variety of their social settings wherein some of the political decisions were authoritatively considered. He belonged to and participated actively in Rotary and the chamber of commerce. His political activity was restricted to the two decisions during Time E to M concerning recreational facilities, and the mental-hospital decision-making process. In all three he was on the losing side.

This minister believed in racial equality, and indicated that Negroes were the same as Whites in intellectual capacity, responsibility, morality, and ambition, adding on each of the last three attributes the phrase "other things being equal." He explained that comment by saying that Negroes would be socially equal to Whites when they were "given a chance at education, decent living, and so forth." His own self-reports, and those of others, attested to his purposeful inactivity in the decision to initiate school desegregation (as well as the administrative question regarding particular Negro applicants for admission to White or mostly White schools) because of his desire to maximize his long-run influence and from a feeling that it would be better if that outcome were to come from others, as it actually did. Thus, he was not accorded any political power during Time E to M, and was not classified as a probable Manifest Leader. This was the classificatory decision even though it was apparent that he had purposefully tried to exercise political influence in regard to the general matters of racial attitudes of his congregation (including the substantial number of White political leaders) and desegregation through his sermons, in private moral counseling, and in "social" conversations.

The other two potential Manifest Leaders who did not make the final list of Manifest Leaders were two women in Petropolis. One woman had apparently been active in political decision-making prior to Time *E*. She was the executive secretary of a social-work agency in Petropolis, in close touch with a variety of male civic and political leaders. The other woman, although active in the Junior League, the Girl Scouts, the YWCA and other civic and service organizations, was also not an active participant in political decision-making during Time *E* to *M*. Although her civic activities resulted in frequent mention in the newspaper, and although her community prominence brought her into close association with a wide range of male civic and political leaders, she was less than fully informed about her community's political structure. She named the League of Women Voters in Petropolis as the organization that was "the most influential in the making of important decisions affecting the whole community," which, as a statement of political reality rather than a hortatory statement, was, in our opinion, erroneous.

The sixth case, that of Kenneth King, one of the probable Manifest Leaders although a dissident in Farmdale's Manifest category of fourteen members, is informative about the difficult analytic decisions in applying the operational definition of Manifest Leader. His failure to obtain significant shifts in the scope of local government's activities regarding the economic base of the community by Time *M* was accompanied, as described in Chapter 11, by the use of illegitimate sanctions directed against his political-decision-making activities. Yet he was accorded some political power as a leader in the decision wherein a minor compromise was reached on the question of expanding the water supply. This analytic assessment was difficult to make for several reasons. By the time that the authoritative-consideration stage in that decisional process was reached, Mr. King was being treated as an outsider by the insider political leaders. It was difficult to assess the extent to which he had participated in that stage in helping to shape the outcome. It was also difficult to assess the degree of satisfaction with that compromise on the part of Mr. King. In interviews, his reports vacillated between having been extremely dissatisfied and having been moderately dissatisfied with the outcome. In both cases the doubt was resolved in his favor, so to speak, thus making him a Manifest Leader. His case also clearly underlines the fact that a single person may, given the concepts and operational definitions used herein, be a political leader in a community's power structure in regard to one or more decisional processes but not in regard to others, and he may even be without political power in those other processes.

Comments: There are some unresolved conceptual ambiguities which should be noted. Should units of decision-making power be assigned to include passive individuals in groups engaged in authoritative consideration, to "front groups," committees, and collectivities of various sorts, whose function seems to be lending an air of legitimacy to decisional outcomes? [6] Should the individuals playing these roles be classified as leaders? Such groups or individuals seem to rate a relatively high position in the political-status structure if their role-playing is successful, and they may be described in terms of the political status they may have with others. The questions seem to come down to whether or not such groups have freedom of action, and how to measure degrees of such freedom. Perhaps a dichotomy —freedom of action or no freedom of action—would be a step toward solving this problem if subjective impressions could be superseded by more satisfactory measurements.

The conceptual definition of Manifest Political Leaders is not intended to be inclusive of all political leaders in a given time period, but, rather, to be inclusive of the universe of those who are probably political leaders and are so known to selected informants. Given the fact that the universe is bounded by informants' perceptions or conceptions, any change in the identity or number of informants, or in the standard of consensus or agreement used to include or exclude nominees, means a potentially different universe and a different set of Manifest Leaders. A political leader may range from a person utterly unknown as such (the presumably rare case) through those thought to be such by a few others in the community to a person who is generally thought by many others to be such. If a random sample of a community was a complete enumeration of the adult population, the Latent Leaders should include in their ranks every Manifest Leader. As panels of informants are increased in size, and as the number of nominations as a political leader are reduced to qualify a nominee for inclusion in the Manifest Leader category, the Latent and Manifest Leaders should increasingly overlap, approaching an identity in a complete enumeration.

The sampling rate was highest for Farmdale, where approximately one of every six to seven adult residents was interviewed. Four respondents in that sample were classified as Latent Leaders. Three of those four were also among the fourteen probable Manifest Leaders of that city. This means that if the sampling rate had been even higher, we would have expected the number of Manifest Leaders to have been included, by chance, in that sample to have been higher, until in a complete enumeration of that adult population the Manifest and Latent Leader categories would have approached a complete overlap. If the number of nominators had been increased, and/or a smaller number of nominations had been the standard for inclusion in the potential Manifest Leader category, the fourth Latent Leader would probably have been listed in the Manifest Leader category. He was a part-time city attorney, a very quiet, self-effacing man who was a member of the Conservative poker club but publicly regarded as a skilled legal craftsman without much interest in community decision-making except in his professional capacity. He had been nominated by a few members of the two panels, but not quite to the degree necessary to meet the standard of five nominations by the second set of panelists for nominees to be classified as potential Manifest Leaders. He was in this particular sense a man "behind the scenes."

The slightly different procedure used in Oretown affords an opportunity to observe the effects of slight changes in the operational definition of potential Manifest Leader under the conditions in that community. Because a comparable procedure had not yet been fixed, only eleven of the forty-one nominees who had received one vote from the twenty members of the first panel of nominators were included on the list shown to the second panelists for their nominations. Thirty-two of the potential Manifest Leaders, that is, those receiving five or more votes from the second set of seventeen panelists (as "very high" or "high" in influence on policy formation and in getting things done) had received two or more votes from the first set of panelists. However, six of the eleven people who had received only one vote from the first set of panelists also made the final list of potential Manifest Leaders because they received five or more nominations from the members of the second panel. Thus, if the other thirty people who had received one vote only from the first panel had been included on the list from which the second set of panelists were to choose, additional numbers of potential Manifest Leaders would, in all probability, have been identified. Fortunately, those thirty people had also been interviewed. An analysis of their characteristics and political perspectives reveals that even if they had been included in the list of potential Manifest Leaders the analysis presented of the Manifest Leadership would not have been appreciably changed. On the other hand, it is most important that further work be done in this regard, because in communities unlike Oretown greater differences might have been discovered.[7]

Except for Farmdale, where the three inner-clique Manifest Leaders received a majority of the second panel's nominations, there were no "natural" breaks in the other cities in the frequency distribution of the second panel's nominations of potential Manifest Leaders.[8] If the number of nominees (three) resulting from the natural break in Farmdale had been used in all of our communities, an insufficient number of Manifest Leaders would have been identified for some of the purposes of our analysis. If we had used the same number of most frequently nominated potential Manifest Leaders in each community (exclusive of Oretown, where the data in point are not quite comparable), let us say sixteen—the number turned up by applying our standard of five or more nominations by seventeen members of the second panel in Farmdale—we would have had the following situation: that number in Farmdale accounted for more than three-quarters of the nominations by the second panel; in the Metroville White subcommunity that number would have accounted for 56 per cent of the votes cast by the second panel; and in the Petropolis White subcommunity, the sixteen most frequently nominated potential Manifest Leaders would have accounted for but 36 per cent of the second panel's votes. This finding tended to confirm the impression that the universe of perceived, prominent, White political leaders was larger in Petropolis than in the somewhat larger city of Metroville. Another bit of supporting evidence was that the panel in Petropolis nominated a considerably larger number of people as being influential in decision-making than did the first panel in Metroville, and the number of votes cast by the second set of panelists in Petropolis for a list of nominees that was one-third larger than the list in Metroville was two-thirds again as large as the number of votes cast by the second set of panelists in Metroville.

It was for such reasons that a standard for inclusion of nominees as potential Manifest Leaders was purposefully set to produce a greater number in the Petropolis than in the Metroville White subcommunities. Again, further inquiry is needed to establish the comparability of such methods in cities of different sizes and kinds, as well as to assess the connections, if any, between variations in size of presumably equally prominent political leaderships and variations in size of less renowned, of Latent, and, therefore, of the total leaderships. Further work needs to be done not only on this matter of identifying and estimating the sizes of leaderships, but also on such "technical" matters as the wording of questions designed to collect the list of names of potential Manifest Leaders. As one example, we would suggest that comparative studies be done on the effects of asking questions with and without the phrase "that nearly everyone would accept" which was included in the first question asked to obtain nominations of potential Manifest Leaders from the first set of panelists.

Variable VII: Types of Power Structures

A. Political Leadership's Ideology: convergent or divergent

The group structure at the Manifest Leader level was mapped in the following way. Approximately six relatively knowledgeable informants were selected from the two panels of informants in each city. These informants were asked questions, which varied slightly in wording from community to community, as to whether there "were influential men or groups who differed with each other about the best policies or kinds of local government the community ought to have." Three distinct sets of people were named in response to that question in Oretown, two in Petropolis, two individuals in Farmdale, and one person in Metroville. Any group or individual named by one of the six informants was included.

In response to the next question, "Of these people, which ones would you say were the leaders of the people or groups who felt as they did about the best policies of local government?", a tabulation of the informants' responses in Oretown revealed that the most frequently nominated "leaders" of those named formed two sets of four men each and one set of three men, and in Petropolis, a four- and a five-person set of "leaders." The tabulations revealed that in Farmdale and Metroville those identified as differing from others were not leaders of groups, but simply individuals whom we classified as "dissidents." These sets of people in Oretown and Petropolis were classified as the "inner cliques" of reputedly antagonistic political groups. In Petropolis, some of the six informants indicated that the five-person clique was actually two cliques; but the majority agreed, when asked to "think about them in relation to the other group; do you generally feel that they should be thought of as two groups or one group?", that they should be thought of as one group but with two parts.

In Oretown these respondents named as the leaders of one group three men who had not been named with sufficient frequency to be included as potential Manifest Leaders; otherwise, all of the members of the other two cliques had been so classified. In Petropolis, PECORR was mentioned by one of the six informants as a group of distinctive policy views that had been trying unsuccessfully to become powerful, but he could not identify "leaders" of that group in response to the second question. Individual Negroes were named in response to the first question in Petropolis but not in Metroville; however, no Negro was mentioned as a "leader" of a group in response to the second question.

The potential Manifest Leaders in Farmdale and in the White subcommunity of Metroville were individually asked to select from a list of the potential Manifest Leaders—plus others they might have wanted to add—"which of these people you would consider to be among the ten people who can get a major policy or project adopted in this community." The potential Negro Leaders in Petropolis and in Metroville were asked, "What three people in this community would you say are the most influential in local-government matters? . . . in political-party matters? . . . in school matters?" Since depth interviews had already been conducted with Negro informants, and their overwhelming consensus was that there were no major rival groups of Negro Leaders, the inner cliques of the Negro Leaderships were classified as such in the same manner as were those in Farmdale and in the White subcommunity of Metroville.

The classification of the inner cliques in Farmdale and in the White subcommunity of Metroville was accomplished by including in that category the three most frequently nominated people in response to the question about the ten people who can get a major policy or project adopted, and in the two Negro subcommunities, the three most frequently mentioned persons in response to a single tabulation of the names offered on the three questions.

The following questions, asked of all probable Manifest Leaders, served two purposes: first, they served as validity checks on the classification of members of purportedly rival cliques in Oretown and Petropolis, and of purportedly "dissident" members in all communities; and second, they provided a method for classifying the remaining Manifest Leaders by their political-group positions. These questions were, "Which of the people on this list [of all Manifest Leaders] do you generally or have you worked closely with on community projects or policies? Which ones would you say have views which are most similar to yours about the needs, policies, and future of [this community]?"

In Oretown and Petropolis, no members of an inner clique named a member of another inner clique in response to both questions, although there were instances of this in response to the first question. In both of those communities the "dissidents" were named by one or more members of at least two of the rival cliques. In Farmdale, the dissidents were not named by the members of the inner clique, while in

Metroville the dissident was named by White Manifest Leader clique members as someone with whom they worked closely, but not as a man of similar views. The Negro inner-clique members of Metroville named the dissident as a man of similar views, with two of those three inner-clique members also reporting having worked closely with him.

The rules for classifying the non-inner-clique members among the Manifest Leaders by their political-group affiliations were as follows. In Farmdale and in the White subcommunity of Metroville, any person named by a member of the inner clique in response to both of the above questions was classified as an ally of that inner clique. Any person who named a member of the inner clique as a person of similar views with whom he generally, or had, worked closely on community projects or policies was also classified as a member of that group. However, if the inner-clique member who was named specifically rejected that identification and reported that the individual in question had views with which he generally disagreed, the former individual was classified as a dissident. This was the case with publisher King in Farmdale.

Councilman Cox, the other dissident in Farmdale, was not named by any inner-clique member, nor did he name any inner-clique member, in response to either question. The dissident in the White Manifest Leadership of Metroville named and was named by other Manifest Leaders who were members of the single group there, but he did not name and was not named by inner-clique members. He was, therefore, more of a member of the single political leadership group there, although a fringe member, than was Councilman Cox in Farmdale; but according to the classificatory rules both were designated "dissidents."

In Oretown and Petropolis, if other White Manifest Leaders were named in response to both of these questions by one or more members of one inner clique, and they themselves named one or more members of the same clique in response to the same questions, they were considered members of that group's set. If this kind of reciprocal identification occurred with members of two or more such cliques, these Manifest Leaders were classified as "uncommitted." If they did not report having similar views and working closely with one or more members of an inner clique, and were not so identified by the latter, they were also classified as uncommitted. If Manifest Leaders were identified as having similar views and working closely with inner-clique members by those members but did not themselves report such a relationship, they were classified as members of the group in point, or as uncommitted if so named by members of two or more inner cliques.

If Manifest Leaders were named by members of two or more inner cliques but identified themselves with only one clique, the latter was the classificatory criterion used.

The political ideologies of members of each inner clique in each city were then investigated through interviews. The five defining variables of political ideology were each made the basis for a series of questions intended to ascertain the views and perspectives of each inner clique. These variables were: the conception of their community as consisting of individuals, interest groups, or collectivities of inextricably inter-dependent citizens; their opinions of who the appropriate political leaders were; their sense of cultural class, including a high-low di-mension, and indications of their political values and general policy preferences, particularly in regard to the ideal power structure and regime, and also in regard to sentiments toward actual or potential political-group rivals; their sense of socio-economic class; and their attitudes toward the appropriate principle of allocation of values in the community, especially the appropriate general role of local govern-ment in the local economy and society. The analysts then assigned the inner cliques to one or another of the many possible classificatory cells that were produced by these variables and their subcategories. At this point classificatory labels were assigned to the combination of variables that constituted the particular ideological pattern discovered, such as Orthodox Conservatism or Progressive Conservatism.

With the exception of one member of the classified Community Con-servationist inner clique in Oretown, it appeared that there was a much greater degree of general ideological similarity within inner-clique circles than there was between cliques in the cities with two or more such cliques. The exception in Oretown was a man of mixed Orthodox Conservative and Community Conservationist ideology; he was classified a member of the latter group. In the cities with one clique, Farmdale and Metroville, intraclique ideological orientations seemed to be homogeneous compared to the range of ideologies manifested by members of cliques in all of the cities. This further classification of ideologies of cliques was done only after data had been collected as of Time M in all four communities.

The data used to classify the respondents on each ideological vari-able were collected in the interviews in a much less systematic manner than would have been followed had the importance of the variables been recognized at the outset. Questions were devised for each vari-able; some were asked in a standardized manner, but others were tailored somewhat to fit smoothly into an apparently informal inter-view of the guided, conversational type. In addition, the interviewing protocols, which contained extensive notes on the remarks of the respondents, were analyzed for additional remarks pertinent to the ideological dimension that were made in response to other questions. For example, to try to assess the respondents' conceptions of the character of their communities, they were directly asked whether they saw their cities as consisting primarily of people and families pursuing their own legitimate individual needs or as sets of people whose interests varied—for instance, factory workers and employers or, in the Southern cities, Negroes and Whites; or as sets of citizens whose interests were relatively common and who shared fundamentally identical public interests.

Remarks that contributed to the assessment of the respondents' conceptions of their communities sometimes were volunteered in response to questions about who should rule—that is, whether public policies should be made primarily by industrialists and bankers who were the backbone of the community; by a collection of civic-minded, successful merchants and professional men; by smaller, less well-to-do businessmen whose needs gave them the greatest stake in good government; by representatives of the working man; by the tax-paying property owners; or by public officials, particularly those who were expert administrators in particular policy areas.   For example, a person selecting public officials as the appropriate political leaders might comment that they were the best qualified to decide about the public interest; this would suggest a conception of the community as a collectivity.   Useful information was sometimes obtained from questions about the respondent's sense of cultural class, such as "How much attention should be paid by public officials to the views of industrialists (small businessmen, labor unions, and so forth) if the latters' views generally conflict with those of public officials?"   The choices of answers might have been: "Public officials should pay no attention; public officials should still give as much weight as they can to such views; public officials should give precedence to those views no matter how difficult it is to put their own views aside; public officials should give some weight to the views of industrialists but make their own decisions, since they usually can make better decisions in the public interest."   The obvious danger, which the authors could not altogether avoid, in using volunteered comments to some questions as data for other assessments is that a respondent who did not comment spontaneously might have had the same perspective as one making such a comment and might have indicated this if he had been asked.   Where possible, such spontaneous comments were used as validity checks for responses to questions that were asked specifically.

Because of the apparently high, positive political status given to each set of inner-clique members by other members of the same clique, or, in some instances, because of the high, negative political status given clique members by informants or members of other groups; because the inner cliques evidenced a comparatively articulate, firmly held ideological orientation; and because the basis for classifying other Manifest Leaders as members of particular political groups was in part that of "shared views," each political group was treated as if its members shared the same ideology as did the respective inner clique. Less systematic interviews with a portion of each political group's non-inner-clique membership indicated that this was the case, although the membership's adherence to the ideology of its inner clique was generally, but with striking exceptions, less articulate and less deeply felt. Intragroup discipline, in terms of acting on decisional matters in ways that were consistent with the group's ideology—that is, the inner clique's preferences—was on a number of occasions less than perfect. Sometimes even an inner clique differed within itself, and intragroup factions were not unknown. However, each and every political group did to some extent act politically as if the preservation or strengthening of the ideology propounded by the inner clique was an important goal.

At this point it was possible to classify the political leaderships of Farmdale and Metroville as having had at Time M convergent or consensual ideologies, based on our judgments that there was one political leadership group with a relatively distinctive ideology. The individual dissidents did not appear to constitute aspiring ideological competitors to the single group in either community. In Oretown and Petropolis, assuming that the multiple political-leadership groups had relatively distinctive ideologies, the degree of intergroup ideological divergence or convergence had to be assessed.

This classificatory assessment was based on responses to a series of questions asked of inner-clique members. Our initial expectation that the inner cliques would consist, for the most part, of relatively non-ideological, pragmatic men proved to be wrong. While a different classificatory judgment might have been made if the non-inner-clique members had been asked these questions, the assessment was that in both Oretown and Petropolis a condition of ideologically divergent or competitive political leadership existed as of Time M. The questions that led to this assessment were designed to ascertain the degree to which each clique viewed the political success of the others as something to be resisted. Questions were asked about the consequences to the community if the others—ordinarily referred to as "the people led by X, Y, and Z," the names of each set of inner-clique members —obtained firm control of the city government or were able to get most of their policies adopted. Questions were also asked about how much effort the respondents, that is, the inner-clique members, would put into trying to prevent or undo such a condition. The specific wording of these questions varied, but the objectives remained constant.

The kinds of comments that led the analysts to conclude that there was competition, particularly between the Orthodox Conservatives and Community Conservationists on the one hand and the Liberals on the other in Oretown, and between the Orthodox Conservatives and the Liberal wing of the Community Conservationist-Liberal political group in Petropolis were: "I'd sure consider leaving this town if *they* got control of City Hall"; "I think that would be the end of [this community]"; "I'd just as soon go broke fighting that as I would anyway if they got control of the taxing power"; "That's a worse machine than that Kansas City gang"; "The whole city government would be corrupt, and worse"; "We might as well vote for communism as that group"; "It would be a return to the Middle Ages"; and so forth.

In Oretown responses made by some Orthodox Conservatives about Community Conservationists, and vice versa, typify the kinds of evidence that would have led to a classification of consensual political leaderships if they had been the norm: "It wouldn't matter much; we'd guide them"; "It would be a shame but they wouldn't last long"; "They're misguided; maybe they would learn once they tried to run the city government"; "No, I'd work with them because I think they are at bottom pretty reasonable"; "They are young; they'll settle down and I think work with the other civic leaders here"; "What harm could they really do? They'd learn or they'd get out of civic affairs"; "No, I wouldn't get out of civic affairs; the more people who continue to work for civic improvement the better community we'll have"; "They're behind the times and it would mean that the city's problems would get worse not better before the people woke up to what needed to be done."

Such remarks for the most part were made by non-inner-clique members of both those political groups, but such sentiments were shared in some measure by the clique members of the Orthodox Conservative and Community Conservationist groups in Oretown. However, the groups also commented about one another in more unfavorable terms. If it had not been for the Orthodox Conservative antipathy toward the White and Negro Liberals in Petropolis, whom they believed to be politically associated with Community Conservationists, there might have been even less competition between the Conservatives and Conservationists there.   In any event, the power structure was deemed competitive in both Petropolis and Oretown, particularly because of the mutual hostility of the rival Conservative and Liberal groups.

Comments: The first general comment that needs to be made about this operational definition of one of the defining variables of power structures is that at every point in the process a variety of choices was available to the analysts.   Little is yet known about the consequences of making such different analytic or operational decisions.   Although some literature exists on the wisdom of using one or another general method for identifying political leaders, much of it is without firm empirical foundation.   More carefully designed research needs to be done on the implications and consequences of such procedures as selecting informants or judges; using different cutting points or votes to classify people as within or outside inner cliques; using more or less structured instruments to measure the content and intensity of ideological sentiments; estimating ideological similarities and differences of large and small political-leadership groups; varying the definition of such membership; and so forth.   One dilemma facing analysts is the need to conduct field research on the usefulness and effects of different methods for identifying and classifying political leaders by groups and ideology and at the same time conducting studies that will produce valid knowledge about political dynamics.   It may be that these needs cannot be satisfied simultaneously, since such "methodological" studies may affect the political dynamics of the situation.   On the other hand, bearing in mind that resources frequently are limited, it may be that the latter need cannot be met until more is known about the validity and results of other such methods.

The second general comment is that from our point of view the measurements used herein suffer from having been developed during the course of these comparative studies and are not yet as carefully tested and checked for validity and reliability as they should be. Although they are probably as valid as many comparable measurements made in political field research of a case-study character or in studies of political history, they are not yet as developed as are some of the measurements used in the best studies of voting behavior.   The Survey Research Center at the University of Michigan, for example, has developed a variety of useful measures of such matters as nationally oriented policy perspectives (see Chapter 9).   Certain standardized questions are asked of the respondents to measure, for example, sense of social class. These include not only questions about occupations, incomes, and other indicators of "objective" socio-economic class positions, but also questions about what class the respondents feel they belong to.

In this connection, we agree with the sentiments expressed by David Gold and John R. Schmidhauser, ". . . it can be shown that in most social research operational equivalence furnishes less positive 'validation' of relationships than does lack of operational equivalence accompanied by conceptual equivalence. The generality of scientific propositions does not rest upon narrow operational procedures. No coherent body of knowledge can be built in which each investigator must replicate precisely the operations of another investigator in order to achieve comparability of findings. It *is* necessary that the operations be faithful to the concept. For example, there are many different operations by which the physical concepts of force, mass, and acceleration can be measured; but the relationship found by different operations will always be the same as long as the operations are logically consistent with the given conceptual definition of each variable." [9]

One must beware of what analysts may claim are operational definitions of "conceptual equivalence" when measurements are taken by the use of questions that are variable in their wording, and that are precisely formulated only in the course of an interview. This situation occurred to some degree in the present study. It is particularly dangerous when one is investigating areas of political behavior wherein the researcher's values may be involved, as was also the case in the present instance. Of some fortuitous assistance in making valid assessments about this power-structure variable was the fact that we actually expected that ideology would not prove to be a differentiating variable, that all four communities probably had nonideological political leaderships or, possibly, leaderships with but one general ideology, and, in either event, consensual power structures. Having studied Farmdale first (at Time M), this expectation was reinforced. At the least, therefore, the analytic judgments reported do not represent what the analysts had expected or wanted to find. Future studies should make every effort to develop standardized measures of the component ideological variables and standardized instruments for administration by interviewers to political leaders and others in communities. This effort is currently under way on the part of the authors.

In making judgments about the ideological perspectives of people, it is most important that rapport be established between interviewer and respondent. In most interviews with inner-clique respondents, excellent rapport was established very quickly. On occasion, two or three informal chats were necessary before the respondent would agree to a more formal interview about his private political and personal sentiments. What helped particularly in these cases of initial resistance was being seen with close associates and friends of the particular respondent in a variety of luncheon and other informal settings. In only a very few cases of attempted interviews with political leaders was rapport impossible to establish, leading to a continued refusal to be interviewed or to an interview that was unsatisfactory for making assessments about the content and approximate strength of the respondent's political ideology. What also helped establish good rapport was the interviewer's obvious understanding and sympathetic appreciation of the respondent's perspectives no matter what these were. This interviewer role came quite naturally as the studies proceeded. The interviewer's own political values ceased to intrude as he typically became engrossed in understanding a respondent's outlook on political life. This meant not only careful weeding of interviewers at the outset, but the substitution of interviewers by others on the more senior staff as some interviewers proved to be unsatisfactory for these particular Manifest Leader interviews. It proved to be possible to establish excellent rapport with Negro Leaders, but only with selected Northern graduate students or senior-staff interviewers.

The final comment that will be made here in regard to the operational definition of convergence-divergence of the political leadership's ideology is on the extraordinary difficulties of making such estimates backwards in time, i.e., of making more historical estimates. The theoretical interests dictated such assessments for as far back as a decade or more in some communities, not only for this variable but for others as well. Of great help was the opportunity for each of the three analyst-authors to defend his own analytic judgments when confronted with those of the other two. Yet the fact remains that reliance on a miscellaneous collection of newspaper analyses, documentary materials of various sorts, and, primarily, the reports of people in each community about their own thinking and the thinking of others was far less satisfactory than being able to ask people what they were currently thinking or believing. Although this meant that our typing of power structures, as well as other assessments, for the periods between the end of the Second World War and Time E in each community seemed, on occasion, to be fiction rather than fact, or in the realm where fact and fiction are indistinguishable, we are not sure that our assessments are any more fictional than other political histories that are concerned with equally significant political variables which extend even further back in time. What we are pointing to here is the need for other studies to devote a significant amount of resources to careful historical studies of such variables as the one in point, and, hopefully, for some research that is designed to be long-range in character to make careful observations over time of "current" affairs or recent history to provide a pool of ultimately more "ancient" historical data of at least equal reliability to the data that represent current states of mind. What Professor Allen Nevins of Columbia has started in the way of collecting permanent records of national political events through the words of those who were major participants in them might well be extended to political leaders in selected communities, with special attention to the political ideologies of such people and to other theoretically relevant factors.

B. Distribution of Political Power among Citizens: mass or elite

The second defining variable of a power structure is the extent to which citizens shared in the units of political power analytically accruing to the contributors to the selected political decisions for a given time period. Each one of the selected political decision-making processes for Time E to M was reconstructed through historical analysis that relied on both interview data and documentary materials—that is, records of attendance at meetings, counts of ballots, newspaper accounts, and so forth. This analysis consisted in part of estimating numbers of active participants with varying decisional preferences. These observations were combined with the results of an analysis of the stages of each decisional process in order to assess whether such participation might have permitted the participants to influence the decisional outcome as of Time M. For each decisional process in each community an assessment was made to determine whether the proportion of adult citizens who might have influenced the production of a decisional outcome was, approximately, less than 5 per cent, 5 to 20 per cent, or more than 20 per cent. In Farmdale and Metroville it appeared that there was no political decision during Time E to M wherein more than 2 or 3 per cent of the adult citizens—for the Southern communities "adult citizens" refers to both White and Negro citizens—were likely to have contributed to a decisional outcome, thereby sharing in political power. In both Oretown and Petropolis it appeared that more than 5 per cent of the citizens had possibly contributed to the outcome of a minority of political decisions by Time M, and in an even smaller minority of decisions more than 20 per cent of the citizens might have so contributed. On this basis the power structures of Farmdale and Metroville were classified as elite and those of Oretown and Petropolis as mass for the period E to M.

A second way of making, or to partially validate, the same assessment was to compare the data collected in the four communities on citizen participation during Time E to M, including the individual reports of the extent of discussion, meetings attended, and more active roles in the making of the decisions occurring in that period. The results of the two methods of assessment were similar.

For the time periods prior to Time E, and for those after Time M, the observations were for the most part restricted to three to five political decisions in each community. Informants, documentary evidence, or both, suggested that these were most likely to have had relatively broad citizen participation and "mass" distributions of power. Since sample surveys were not available prior to Time E, nor after Time M—with the exceptions of two post-Time M periods in Oretown—the first method of assessing the distribution of power among the citizens was used. Although there was occasional evidence of such activities as "mass meetings" or large-scale demonstrations, the paucity of such information led to a dependence on the ability of informants to recall how many active participants there had been, and what they and purported political leaders had done in the making of the selected decisions. Although it was assumed that if in the selected decisions a relatively small set of people appeared to have produced the outcomes the power structure was elite for the period in point, a check of newspapers and informants was made to see whether any decisions had been omitted in which a larger number of people might have participated, thereby warranting a classification of mass for this dimension of the power structure.

Comments: The difficulty of making valid assessments about the distribution of political power among citizens for any time period stems from several problems. The first major problem is the need to assume that it is impossible to acquire power without participating; and that in the absence of evidence that the participants do not have access, or for other reasons cannot exercise influence on a decisional outcome, political participants are likely to have such influence, and those among them with the appropriate decisional preferences are likely to have shared in power. To the extent that this assumption, which in various ways also underlies a variety of the operational definitions of such concepts as political leadership, can be made less tenuous, the estimation of this dimension of power structures can be improved.

A second major problem stems from the inadequacy, in the present study, of the systematic comparative data on participation, of information about the interactional settings in which participation took place, the perspectives of the participants, and the location of such acts as inside or outside the chain of events that were cumulatively responsible for particular decisional outcomes. While most severe for earlier time periods, they could have been improved for the period Time E to M, as well as for succeeding periods.

A comparatively minor but perplexing classificatory problem was the finding that, on occasion, a citizen vote on a measure such as a bond election produced a turnout wherein the voters on the winning side constituted something more than an estimated 5 per cent of the adult population in a period which was otherwise elite in its decision-making distributions of power. Special mention was made earlier of the fact that citizens of Metroville had voted during Time E to M to produce the outcomes in three decisions on civic-improvement measures. Although the turnout was very small, and the voters on the winning side constituted a small fraction of the adult citizens, it is not difficult to imagine a case of a well-managed election wherein a relatively small group of people wage a successful campaign to turn out a relatively large number of voters to approve a particular measure. To be sure, other studies than ours have also found a correlation between large voter turnouts in special elections and controversies (competition) over decisional outcomes, but exceptions can and do occur. In the event of a generally elite distribution of power among citizens in most decisions, but a relatively mass distribution in a decision involving a citizen vote on a measure, the analyst might find it appropriate to make a double classification of that power structure on this dimension.

With only four communities, albeit over a series of time periods, single summary classifications were felt to be the most that could usefully be made of this power-structure dimension. This meant submerging similarities between elite and mass power structures in the sense of not specifying the degree to which both had narrow distributions of power among their citizenries on particular decisions in a given time period. Future studies comparing larger numbers of communities, or future comparative studies of intracommunity decision-making, may well find it useful to classify by particular decisions or sets of decisions.

Variable VIII: Types of Regimes

A. Sense of Electoral Potency

Whether or not citizens expected severe illegitimate sanctions to be used effectively against them if they engaged in political action to shift the scope of government was determined in the following way. We assumed that certain categories of citizens were most likely to have a low sense of electoral potency: racial and ethnic minorities, race-relations extremists, organized and unorganized labor, and small businessmen. To these categories were added citizens with extreme attitudes toward a rapidly growing municipal government and toward a rapidly growing community population. Formally and informally organized groups in these categories were then identified through interviews and referrals; then leaders of such groups were interviewed to disclose evidence to assess that assumption. At the same time any other renowned dissidents in community decisions or policies and those who had been the object of sanctions—for example, medium- or relatively large-scale businessmen—were included for assessment. Finally, a few members of each current or aspiring political-leadership group were interviewed to complete the set of citizen categories that served as the subjects of these measurements.

At Time M, questions were directed to the respondents regarding their fears of losing their jobs or housing; being deprived of credit, sales, or other necessary economic resources; being deprived of friendships; or being subject to actual physical intimidation or violence. The questions were related to the following conditions: if they discussed with their friends, neighbors, or other citizens whom they regarded as important things they thought the local government ought to do (policy deliberation); if they actually tried to organize a political group to pressure City Hall for policies (organization of political support); or if they tried to organize an election campaign for candidates of their own choosing (organization of electoral support). The questions were intended to establish how many of these respondents were actually fearful of the consequences of political action and the extent of their fears, rather than the extent to which they were hopeful of immediate or even long-term political success.

For the periods prior to Time M, similar assessments were used. Informants in these same categories were asked about their own past actions and about the actions of others in their categories who were not available for interview.

Comments: In no community at Time M, including Metroville, did it appear that there was more than a small group of citizens who feared illegitimate sanctions. In Metroville, the one community rated as low on the sense of electoral potency at Time M, the observations revealed the following patterns. A small number of White labor-union and Negro informants indicated that they believed they would be subject to severe economic deprivations, including losing their jobs, if they engaged in organized political support of demands to replace officials at City Hall with men of their own choosing. Most members of these categories did not seem to be concerned about such sanctions, but the minority of fearful respondents justified the classification of the sense of electoral potency as *relatively* low at Time *M*.

White Supremacists in Metroville had, prior to Time *M*, organized an interest group to consider ways to reinstitute more complete subordination of Negroes and to maintain such patterns in areas where they still existed. The members of this organization constituted only a small fraction of White citizens with comparable cultural-caste feelings. Some of them seemed to be concerned that illegitimate sanctions would be used against them by White political leaders if they became overtly active in local political affairs. The sense of electoral potency of some nonmembers who had comparably intense White Supremacist sentiments may have been even lower, and this may have mitigated against their membership in the organization. However, most of the organization's members and most of the aforementioned White blue-collar workers and Negro Leaders did not allow their fears of illegitimate sanctions to stop them from discussing or petitioning for preferred shifts in the scope of local government during Time *E* to *M*.

Individuals were classified as having a low sense of electoral potency if they were afraid to take part in organized efforts to replace city officials with more responsive officials of their own choosing, even though they might still be willing to participate in discussions of shifts in the scope of local government. In the historical reconstruction of earlier years it appeared that such fears of sanctions had extended even to peaceful, polite petitioning as well as to various forms of intragroup policy deliberation in both Metroville and Petropolis.

Actually, instances were encountered in Metroville—even though it had the secret ballot—of some Negro respondents' being fearful of voting for candidates of their own choice. It has been noted by commentators that the secret ballot has the consequence of removing the possible risks of punishment for the individual voter since there is no way of knowing how the individual did vote. While this would seem to be the general effect of that device, it may not be sufficient, particularly early in its establishment, or with newly enfranchised groups, or under conditions of a history of successive failures of candidates elected by the secret ballot to take and hold office. It is possible to punish groups of people rather than selected individuals should the results of an election violate the preferences of an entrenched political leadership with such powers of punishment. Moreover, and in point here, groups of people, as some Negroes in Metroville, might well fear this even in the absence of its likelihood, particularly when a group with known characteristics is concentrated in certain vote-casting and vote-counting units such that patterns of bullet or bloc voting are relatively easily perceived.

It was impossible to determine how much political activity or in-activity there might have been if people had not feared the use of illegitimate sanctions. But the assessment of the sense of electoral potency was not an effort to establish a relationship between par-ticipation level or power-structure type and regime type, although it is necessary to investigate that relationship. The hypotheses that a complex state of mind which includes interrelated feelings of electoral impotence and political inefficacy or futility constitutes an inhibition or impediment to political participation, and that this aspect of regimes relates more or less directly to the state of power-structure variables, are both worthy of more intensive research than they have received in this or other studies.

In Petropolis at Time M, interviews with people in the aforemen-tioned categories produced responses of a very different kind than they did in Metroville. This was not to say that all the interviewees felt completely assured that illegitimate sanctions would not be applied to them, but they evidenced a sense of their own potential political influence and a confidence in their own ability to acquire sufficiently satisfactory resources from their friends and acquaintances to thwart illegitimate sanctions. Such sentiments distinguished them clearly from the more fearful of their fellows in Metroville.

An analytic rule was adopted that in those cases—several in Ore-town and two in Farmdale during Time E to M—where a fear of a boycott or other such sanction was expressed, accompanied by evi-dence that the respondent in question had not ceased his political activity, even though its form might have changed (e.g., it might have become more covert), and he reported being unafraid to help nominate or campaign for candidates of his choice, the assessment would be a high sense of electoral potency. Shifting from relatively open, public political activity to more covert, private political activity may well lessen the impacts of such action. And it is true that the opportunity to participate in elections may be ritualistic unless there are also opportunities to participate openly in a full range of delibera-tive and organization-of-political-support activities. However, after much weighing of the pros and cons, we decided that in the few in-stances of such expressed fears of boycotts by merchants in Oretown and Farmdale who also reported no cessation of their political activities, and no inhibitions against working for candidates of their own choice, they would be credited with a relatively high sense of electoral potency. Other researchers might want to adopt the contrary rule.

The analytic problems associated with fears of illegitimate sanctions by business and professional men who feared boycotts, and the analytic conventions adopted to solve them for this study, had such consequences as these. It proved to be analytically "easier" for industrial workers who feared the loss of their jobs to be classified as having a relatively low sense of electoral potency than for merchants, business, and professional people who feared boycotts to be so classified. The reason is that merchants may still have a variety of relatively accessible and effective channels in which to exert political influence covertly; blue-collar workers typically will not. Rather than knocking on someone's door as a political worker, the merchant may use his telephone to escape public visibility and possible boycott on the part of a segment of the political opposition following the revelation of his political position. He may easily leave his place of business for short periods to exert political influence on his fellow businessman. He may contribute a sum of money for a variety of political purposes without having his name attached to the spending of that sum. All of these things are less easily done by less affluent blue-collar workers on assembly-lines, at least under many conditions of community life. A comparable analysis would reveal the political disadvantages under many conditions of such minorities as Negroes vis-a-vis Whites.

One of the major reasons for deciding finally to classify a businessman fearful of boycotts as having a relatively high sense of electoral potency if he continued to participate politically in covert rather than overt ways was to take into account this differential advantage that such a businessman seems to have over the blue-collar worker. On the other hand, it could be argued that it is just for that reason that any such shifts from overt to covert forms of political participation ought to have had the consequence of changing an assessment of the sense of electoral potency from high to low; to recognize to some extent the reduction of the relative advantage that men with a wider range of political actions or with lower costs of political action had over those with a narrower or higher-cost set of such actions. Further research needs to assess the consequences and usefulness of such alternative classificatory rules and conventions and to measure comparatively the ranges and costs of political action available to different sets of citizens.

One other instance of a classificatory problem in this connection might be mentioned. Instances were revealed of an employer telling his employees that he would have to cut his working force severely, or actually close down, if a vote on a particular measure were to go one way rather than another. Was this an instance of fears of an illegitimate sanction wherein the employees who voted to protect their jobs were to be classified as having a low sense of electoral potency?

Let us suppose that an employer in making the threat in point is motivated for the most part, or even entirely, by a desire for political retribution, not only against those who proposed a measure he disliked, but also against his employees for aiding, abetting, or permitting the undesired decisional outcome. In such a case, we would decide to view the threat as an illegitimate sanction for legitimate political behavior. Even if it had its desired impact, votes for a particular outcome, it still might not have caused fears, or a low sense of electoral potency, on the part of employees so affected. Some employees might have been grateful for what they considered useful information about the economic consequences of voting one way or another. Yet it might have caused some employees to become economically fearful and, moreover, to apprehend the political intent of the employer's message. If so, they would then be classified as having a relatively low sense of electoral potency, at least in regard to the decisional matter at issue.

In the particular instances in which such threats were made, there was some evidence that they made an impact on voting behavior, although it is important to develop better research designs than we had to assess such impacts. However, there was evidence that the employees viewed the message not as an act of threatened political vengeance but as a factual statement of, or a prediction about, the future course of economic events should the message be ignored. Finally, there was no evidence that the employees in Oretown (where it most frequently occurred) felt constrained to vote in a particular way because of fears that unfair job deprivations would follow from a politically motivated act of the employers who had warned them in this manner. Here, too, it is important to develop more adequate measures of the sentiments of the recipients of such communications before such assessments rest on a tolerably firm foundation.

B. Permeability of the Power Structure

The following operations were performed to assess at Time M the permeability of the power structure; that is, the probability that nonviolent efforts to shift the scope of local government would be met and stopped by illegitimate sanctions. From responses to questions in the sample surveys, interviews with potential and probable Manifest Leaders and with political leaders of the sectors selected to assess the sense of electoral potency, and from other sources, a list of important decisional preferences and demands was constructed for each community. The list included those involved in the political decisions from which the picture of the power structure was derived, since these all involved actual demands; but it also included decisional preferences that had not become the subject of policy deliberation and demands that had been "arrested," that is, fixed in a policy-deliberation stage.

We then tried to determine whether efforts to block these demands had been made during Time E to M which involved the threat or use of such sanctions as loss of job, denial of occupational advancement, loss of important friendships or associations, unequal application or enforcement of licensing, inspection, and other ordinances of local government, foreclosures on real property, selective withdrawal or withholding of basic municipal services, including schools, welfare payments, and hospital facilities, and physical violence. The latter three categories were of particular relevance in the Southern communities. The primary focus was on the actions of men who had become political leaders by Time M, but any report that a citizen had threatened or used such sanctions against anyone was noted.

Instances also were noted of any effective use of such sanctions to block or stop an individual's political activity, either through a lowering of his sense of electoral potency or through effectively distracting him by forcing him to expend his time and energy in developing substitutes for the resources which were endangered or actually kept from him. Respondents among the political leaders were questioned about such instances, about reports from people who had said that they feared such deprivations would be applied to them if they pursued a potential or actual political demand, and about the list of potential and actual demands referred to above. These ordinarily ranged from general questions about what the respondents would do if those with the demands tried to get them adopted to more specific questions about whether they actually would use any of the kinds of sanctions mentioned above—and if so, how—to defeat those demands.

In the few instances (in Farmdale) of responses that indicated that such sanctions would continue to be used if certain kinds of demands were pushed by their proponents, we assessed their probable effects. Since they had once proved effective, and the conditions of the sanctioned seemed to be similar at Time M to what they had been during Time E to M, we assumed that the sanctions would be equally effective after Time M; hence, the permeability of that power structure at Time M was relatively low.

The pre-Time M periods were approached in a manner comparable to the Time M assessment, but with less complete and comprehensive information and a heavier reliance on the memories of relatively few informants. These informants were chosen from among older people who had themselves remained in the community and who had been relatively active or at least aware of political events since 1946 and, in numerous instances, before and during the Second World War.

For the periods after Time M, the same general procedure was followed. Even though available data on the identities of Manifest Leaders and on the citizenries were neither as systematic nor as complete, since we could not undertake extensive field work and sample surveys, we had an even greater sensitivity to the need for data on this variable.

Comments: We should like to emphasize that the concept of illegitimate sanctions refers not so much to the nature of sanctions as to the use of particular sanctions for purposes deemed more or less illegitimate. Actually, there is one component of the nature of sanctions that is involved in the notion of legitimacy. There is an increasingly widespread opposition to taking human life for any reason, particularly as a punishment for crimes. There is a lesser, but increasingly strong, minority sentiment for the elimination of incarceration in traditional custodial, penal institutions. There is a relatively broad consensus that certain safeguards are essential for an authoritative sanction to be adjudged legitimate, a sense of due process of law. The notion that for sanctions to be regarded as legitimate, they must be applied equally under the same conditions—that is, every citizen of the polity must be potentially subject to them in the same ways—is becoming a tenet not only of Anglo-American and continental systems of jurisprudence, but also of other systems. The fact that differential law enforcement may be used as a means of political duress seems to be leading, however slowly, to a sense that apparently legitimate sanctions should be viewed as illegitimate if they are applied inconsistently according to such factors as wealth, status, race, religion, or political views. Thus, it appears that the basis for distinctions between legitimate and illegitimate sanctions may be shifting.

This study focuses on a relatively broad community consensus on generally legitimate sanctions that become illegitimate under many conditions when used to block legal efforts to shift the scope of local government. No class of sanctions remains legitimate under all conditions when used for such political purposes. However, it is deemed not useful and contradictory to our models of man as well as of that community consensus to classify the withholding or withdrawal of respect or affection by one person from another as an illegitimate sanction, although under some conditions such withdrawals theoretically might be so classified. If, for example, such withdrawals are likely to isolate a person from all satisfying social interaction, they might be classified as illegitimate in the present context. One factor that operates to distinguish relatively legitimate from illegitimate sanctions is the severity or weight of the deprivation, which, however, is sometimes modified by the individual's ability to provide substitute resources.

The procedure for assessing the legitimacy of sanctions when they were used or threatened was, first, to ask ourselves as analysts and as citizens of the United States whether they violated the spirit, or the intention, of the United States Constitution in its concern with maximizing political liberty. Second, we asked potential sanctioners whether they would consider the use of the sanctions in question proper or improper, right or wrong, if used against people like themselves. Although there were interesting variations in the standards of political morality revealed by these two methods, in general the results were congruent, enabling us to specify sets of sanctions regarded by both analysts and informants as generally illegitimate. The probable effectiveness of such sanctions was then estimated on the basis of assumptions that appeared reasonable—but which should be investigated further—as to their impact on the sets of potentially sanctionable people involved, given the various socio-economic and political sources of support available to them.

The status of one kind of sanction was questioned by both the analysts and the potential sanctioners who were asked to assess the legitimacy of the use of sanctions for political ends. This was depriving a person of a job with the municipal government. Employment by, or job advancement in, local-government agencies, just as with contracts between private parties and local government, were excluded from the category of ordinarily illegitimate sanctions when refused or terminated for political purposes. In this case deprivations that seemed severe were not treated as illegitimate because they apparently were not regarded as a general right of citizens and because substitute opportunities in the private economy were perceived to be plentiful. In Metroville, for example, relatively few Negroes were employed by the municipal government, but it is easy to see that in such a community municipal employment might be a major channel for such a potentially sanctionable set of people to earn its living. In such a case the analysts, even if not the White citizens living in that community, might well consider municipal employment sufficiently important that a deprivation therein for political ends should be treated as an illegitimate sanction—and as one of potential effectiveness as a blocking or deactivating tactic.

A few instances were noted, in Oretown in particular, of statements made by employers to employees, particularly in certain large industrial firms, to the effect that if a vote on a special measure had a certain outcome, the firm would have to shut down and relocate in another community. Apparently, such messages did not reduce the sense of electoral potency of workers, although they may have engendered certain fears of economic deprivations in regard to the decisional outcomes in question. Regardless of the ultimate economic objectives or motives of such employers, their actions were classified as political since at least one end in view was impact on a scope of local government. Whether they were instances of the effective use of illegitimate sanctions depends on two additional factors: another aspect of motives and impact.

If the messages about the economic impacts of a particular political decision were thought by the employers to be true, they were regarded not as threats to apply illegitimate sanctions but as legitimate efforts to engage in political education. If the employers thought such messages to be false (an effort to manipulate rather than educate), and if their messages apparently contributed to the decisional outcome, such actions would have been classified as instances of illegitimate sanctions blocking legitimate efforts to shift the scope of local government. Regardless of the intent of the message sender, if such messages did not seem to contribute to a decisional outcome, they were not classified as instances of the effective use of illegitimate sanctions.

In Oretown, and in a post-Time M period in Metroville, the first and last of these possibilities were noted. There were a few instances of such messages thought to be false and not intended by their makers to be pursued in the event of a "wrong" decisional outcome, but in no such instance did those messages seem to make a contribution to the decisional outcome. The most frequently occurring incident of this kind was one wherein the employers were seriously contemplating a cutback in the working force or a move from the community should a vote be other than the one desired, not an example of an illegitimate sanction. It should also be noted in passing that there were instances of fears of plant relocations to other communities on the part of some citizens at times when such relocations were not the subject of messages to that effect on the part of industrial executives (as in Petropolis in regard to annexation of industrial areas). Such instances of political status were not classified as instances of the disposition to use illegitimate sanctions effectively for the assessment of the regime variable in point.

To assess the impact of the messages in point, the following operations were carried out. The first task was to see whether the vote accorded or not with the objective of the messages in question. If it did not, regardless of the possibility that the messages had been influential on the votes of employees, the incident was regarded as an instance of an unsuccessful effort to apply a possibly illegitimate (depending on the motive of the potential sanctioner) sanction. Lacking the resources and time for more carefully designed studies of such messages, in the remaining cases a few interviews were conducted with employees who had (during Time E to M, earlier, or later) received such messages to see whether, in response to open-ended questions as to why they voted as they did, they reported the content of the messages in question as among the reasons for their vote. This is a most inadequate procedure, especially with pre-Time E situations, but the best that was possible with limited resources and the failure to anticipate fully the need for such assessments.

In Metroville at Time M, one member of the White Progressive Conservative inner clique had indicated that the use of force was not out of the question should Negroes press for integration policies of various sorts. A minority of the other White political leaders urged that severe economic sanctions and withdrawals of basic welfare services by municipal government should follow in the event of any attempted Negro take-over of City Hall. Various nonleader members of the new White Supremacy organization advocated all kinds of severe sanctions, including physical violence, for Negroes who engaged in public demonstrations or in other activities supporting decisional preferences disliked intensely by such Supremacists. Yet the probability of such illegitimate sanctions being used effectively to block Negro efforts to shift the scope of local government was assessed as low as of Time M.

The reason for this was not that such illegitimate sanctions, if used by members of the White political leadership, would have been ineffective. To the contrary, they probably would have been most effective in deactivating members of the Negro subcommunity at that time. However, there were a sufficiently large number of White political leaders, including members of the inner clique, who seemed to the interviewers to be so seriously committed to the use of peaceful persuasion that the use of such illegitimate sanctions was judged most unlikely. Given the generally strong group discipline among the White

Progressive Conservatives, and given the evidence of compliance, albeit unenthusiastically, on the part of the advocates of force in the face of the token-desegregation decision reached by their fellow White political leaders, it was deemed improbable that any of the then extant potential political demands of the Negro community would bring about the use of such sanctions on the part of the White leadership.

This assessment at Time M rested also on the assumption that there was a high probability that legitimate sanctions and counteractions would be sufficient to block efforts by Negroes to shift the scope of government in directions most disliked by the most White Supremacists of the White Manifest Leadership. Given the control over the use of the municipality's police power by that White leadership, with the key man in that regard being the most accommodating White leader (Mr. Williston Russell, III), it was expected that a resort to mass political actions or demonstrations by Negroes, as well as illegal acts by lower-status White Supremacists, would be met by the forces of law and order most effectively. It should be noted that this aspect of democracy, a low probability that illegitimate sanctions would be used to block efforts to shift the scope of local government, rests in part on the assessment that legal means would accomplish that end. In a sense, then, this element of democracy may be best secured when political control over the legal machinery is firmly established on the part of a political leadership. This seemingly cynical conclusion needs to be qualified, however, by the following two points. It was impossible to assess adequately, given how little is known of the behavior of men under various conditions of political (and other) stress, but we suspect that should the forces of law and order in Metroville immediately after Time M have proved to be inadequate to block a rising Negro militancy, the White political leadership might well have withdrawn (to the county-government arena, or to another community) rather than resort to illegal sanctions. Given the rise of the White Supremacists-Radical Right after Time M, there was no possibility to test in a natural-experimental setting this particular hypothesis. This may have been the preferred course of action partly because very large profits and national prestige, not simply community political power, were at stake for the industrial executive White political leadership, and partly because Metroville was an open political system within the domain of an increasingly active federal political authority (increasingly responsive to appeals from such illegitimately sanctioned political minorities in local communities as Negroes).

Secondly, the broader study shows that illegitimate sanctions may prove to be ineffective in situations of political competition, so that this aspect of democracy may rest on firmer foundations than simply a monopoly of control by a political leadership of the formally and informally authoritative stages of political decision-making such that illegitimate sanctions are not necessary. This was evident in Petropolis, where a comparably racial bicommunity condition resulted in a similarly "high permeability" assessment for other reasons. The reason was not that there was a low probability that illegitimate sanctions would be used by political leaders, but, rather, that there was a political-group structure diluting the effectiveness of such sanctions. The fact that there were moderating political leaders in Petropolis made it easier to reach that conclusion, since their interests in averting community-disintegrating political conflicts resulted in a disposition both to inhibit the use of such sanctions by protagonists and to lend resources to the potentially sanctionable who were most vulnerable to such sanctions. If that community had been more polarized between a more militant Negro-White labor Liberal group on the one hand and a White Supremacist group on the other, depending on the relative size and strength of the two sides, one or another might have been subject to the effective use of illegitimate sanctions and there might have been a relatively impermeable power-structure condition. Rather than assume that political competition is automatically effective, or that effective political competition might not lead to a condition of Oligarchy as one group gains dominance, we would point to the need to make careful assessments about both the disposition of potential sanctioners to use illegitimate sanctions and the impacts that those sanctions are likely to have on potentially sanctionable people under particular conditions of resource vulnerabilities. More research is in order in both regards to make more valid assessments of this major dimension of regimes.

The foregoing comments illustrate the tortuous route sometimes taken to the task of making analytic decisions about variables and their subcategories when a more straightforward, simple-minded, naively intuitive approach might have produced equally useful results. One of the major reasons for detailing some of the problems encountered and the steps taken to solve, handle, or sidestep them in the course of constructing the conceptual framework and bringing that framework to bear on the tasks of making the relevant observations and assessments is to communicate something of the kinds of operations facing those with a need to be as self-conscious as possible in these kinds of endeavors.

The need to be self-conscious stems in part from finding a host of unexpected analytical problems on matters that were thought to be relatively straightforward. Rather than encountering them in the field during data-collecting operations, or having them crop up after leaving the field and during an analysis, the reader is urged to devote as much time as possible trying to anticipate such problems prior to the point of finalizing concepts and developing operational definitions, at the expense of a possibly superfluous pseudo-sophistication. Such may be the necessary costs of efforts to meld abstract theory and empirical investigations in the pursuit of valid, reliable political knowledge. It is also to be hoped that the paucity of methodological work revealed by the foregoing commentaries will encourage even elementary efforts to improve the tools which so affect the prospects of political-system theory-building. The comments so far have been on the operational definitions of the major variables; the next section will be a simple listing of items in the interview schedules at Time M.

Variable IX: Decisional Preferences, Political Interest, and Perspectives

The respondents in all four communities were asked at Time M, in addition to the political-participation items mentioned above, questions relating to such political variables as whether they were registered to vote, how often they voted (always, nearly always, sometimes, or never were the choices of response for separate questions on voting in local elections, in school elections, and in state and national elections), and with what party they identified themselves. They were also asked about such socio-economic variables as the frequency with which they read what newspapers; their memberships and participation in formal and informal social, kinship, and other kinds of voluntary associations; the extent of their discussion of local-government or community matters with members of their own families; their formal-educational levels; their occupations; the size and sources of their incomes; their length of residence in the community; the size of their families; the type of community in which they were raised; their disposition to move away from the community; and so forth.

The respondents in the four communities also were asked at Time M questions that were designed to obtain information pertaining more specifically to decisional preferences, political interests, and perspectives. The following section lists these questions, starting with Farmdale. If identical questions were asked in more than one community, the question is listed only by number when subsequently mentioned. The data collected by the use of questions not listed here were used in less systematic ways to obtain additional knowledge of these perspectives and preferences and of other aspects of the politics of these communities.

Farmdale: Political participation Items 1a, 1b, and 1c were followed up for those who said either "often" or "once in a while" by:

Item 4:   "What matters have you discussed?"

Follow-up questions were then asked to establish the preferences of the respondent when they were not clear from the answer to those questions.   (See Item 81.)

Political participation Item 2 was followed up by asking those who responded "yes":

Item 5:   "What group held the meeting and what was it about?"

Follow-up questions were asked, if necessary, to establish the perspectives or preferences in regard to the topic or topics discussed by those who had participated in such settings.

Political participation Item 3, the activist-role item, was followed up, for those responding "yes" by questions which were used to classify Latent Leaders in each random sample (see Variable V) and which helped to obtain a picture of the decisional preferences and political perspectives of non-Latent Leaders.   Those questions were:

Item 6:   "What was the nature of the issue?"
Item 7:   "What was the nature of your activity?"

Follow-up questions were asked when necessary to establish what the political perspectives were or, if the matter was a political decision, what the decisional preferences of the reportedly active participant were.

In addition to a battery of questions about the degree of associations with city, county, and state officials, who were to be named by respondents reporting "frequent" associations with such categories of officials, the respondents were all asked:

Items 8–10:   Whom do you regard as the most influential persons as far as having a say or determining what decisions shall be made in regard to local-government matters? community welfare? school matters?

Each respondent was asked not only for the names of such persons, but also:

Item 11:   What do you think is the reason for [his or her] influence?

The following questions were also asked of each respondent (see Variable VI: The Political Leaderships: Manifest Leaders).

Item 12: Of all the people in your community, whom do you regard as the generally most influential? (Names and positions.)

Items 13–15: Whom do you consider the best informed and best qualified to judge whether existing or proposed policies are good or bad in regard to local government? community welfare? school matters?

Items 16–18: Whom could you go to among your personal acquaintances, or persons you feel you could go to, for advice as to what should be done in regard to local-government matters? community welfare? school matters?

Items 19–21: Has anyone come to you within the past year for advice on what can or should be done in regard to local-government matters? community welfare? school matters? (Yes or no.)

If a respondent answered affirmatively on Items 19, 20, or 21, he was asked:

Item 22: [10] Who was this?

Oretown: The questions asked of Oretown respondents at Time M that were identical to the ones asked in Farmdale were Items 5–10 and Items 12–15. Questions asked in the panel study after Time M are listed at the end of this appendix.

In Oretown at Time M the following additional questions were asked. To follow up Item 12, the respondents who named anyone were asked:

Item 23: With regard to the person named [as generally the most influential person in this community], do you feel free to discuss community problems with [him or her]? (Yes or no.)

If the response to Item 12 was "don't know" or its equivalent, the respondent was asked the following question (Item 24):

Item 24: Whom among your acquaintances would know who the most influential person is? (Name)

Item 25: Which of the following statements best describes your relation to the hospital drive? (a) I was not concerned one way or another and have pretty much remained on the sidelines. (b) I have become quite interested and have discussed the subject on many occasions with friends and acquaintances. (c) I have become very much concerned and actually have tried to influence my friends and acquaintances one way or another whenever the subject came up. (d) I have felt the decision was very important and have actively engaged in support of one or the other by helping get signatures, making special calls on the individuals, writing letters, talking to officials, speaking to groups, or some other means of seeking to affect the outcome.

Item 26: (The same as Item 25 except concerning the establishment of a city-owned electric light and power utility.)

Items 27–30: Which of the following statements do you think best applies to city officials? To park and recreation officials? School officials? County officials? (a) They do pretty much what the citizens want. (b) They do what *some* of the more influential people want. (c) They do not pay much attention to what the people want but tend to do what they themselves think best.

In prior analysis this item was used as the measure of political cynicism. Respondents selecting answer (a) were classified as politically trusting; those selecting answer (b) or (c) were classified as politically cynical. Those who "did not know" were classified as politically distant.

Items 31–34: If you were concerned about a local-community problem and contacted the appropriate local officials, how do you think they would react? Which of the following statements best describes the way the officials in each group would respond to you? (a) They would try to understand my problem and do what they could about it. (b) They would listen to me but would try to avoid doing anything—would try to pass the buck. (c) They would ignore me or would dismiss me as soon as they could.

Following Items 31–34 respondents were asked:

Item 35: Have you ever had this kind of experience? (Yes or no.)

If the response to Item 35 was "yes":

Item 36: With which group of officials was this?
Item 37: In general, how do you feel about living in Oretown? (a) An excellent community to live in. (b) A very good community to live in. (c) A good community to live in. (d) Not a very good community to live in. (e) A poor community to live in.
Items 38–42: How would you rate Oretown for each of the factors listed below: Opportunity for economic advancement? Schools? Availability of adequate housing? Community spirit or attitude of people toward the community? Willingness of people to undertake and support action to meet community needs and problems? (a) Excellent. (b) Very good. (c) Not very good. (d) Poor.
Item 43: If you were free to choose from among these factors, which would you rate as the most important and least important for a community where you would prefer to live? Would you indicate your choice among the following by checking the three items most important to you and the three items least important to you? (In addition to the factors listed for Items 38–42 the following were included on the list: climate, opportunities for religious worship, freedom from pressure to do the things you don't care to do, friendliness of people.)

Items 44–46:   How satisfied or dissatisfied are you with each of the following: Electric power and light service? Planning for community development? Street construction and maintenance? (a) Very satisfied. (b) Somewhat satisfied. (c) Somewhat dissatisfied. (d) Very dissatisfied. (e) Undecided.

The following two groups of questions were asked only of Manifest Leaders:

Items 47–49:   Usually people's leadership activity or influence is in relation to some community problem or issue. We want first to find out what have been or are the most important problems or issues in your community today or during the past two years. Would you list, as near to ten as you are able, those problems or issues that you regard as the most important? Would you now indicate for each one listed how active or inactive you are or have been? (a) Very active. (b) Active. (c) Somewhat inactive. (d) Very inactive. Of those listed, which three do you believe are the most important for your community?

Eight decisional processes were listed and for each the respondents were asked:

Items 50–53: [11]   Would you tell us how active you regard yourself on those issues listed below which were not mentioned by you in the preceding question (Item 49)? (a) Very active. (b) Active. (c) Somewhat inactive. (d) Very inactive. Using the same list (Item 50) would you indicate for each one, as far as you are able, those individuals you believe have been or are the most influential in one way or another? We would like to know who people work with. For each problem or issue in which you were "very active" or "somewhat active" (Items 49–51) would you tell us who you worked with most closely?

Petropolis and Metroville. Identical questions were asked of Negro and White respondents in Metroville. However, because of the lack of funds, the Negro interview schedule in Petropolis omitted certain questions which are marked below with an asterisk. When the items were not identical for Petropolis and Metroville, this is also indicated.

The questions asked of Petropolis and Metroville respondents at Time *M* that were identical to those asked in Farmdale, Oretown, or both, are as follows: Items 5–10, 12, 16–21, 23*, 25, and 26. School desegregation, school consolidation, and attracting new industry to the community were substituted for the establishment of the municipal utility and the hospital drive, Items 25 and 26 in Oretown. Other identical items were 27, 29–31, 33, 34, and 37. For the changes in Items 38–42 see Items 54 through 62; for Item 43, only the "most important" aspects of a desirable community were asked for; for the changes in Items 44*–46* see Items 63 through 80 below; for the changes in Items 47–49, which were asked of respondents in the sample surveys as well as of potential Manifest Leaders in the Southern communities, see Item 81 below.[12]

Items 54–62: [13] The factors to be rated were: Opportunity for economic advancement, schools, availability of adequate housing, friendliness of people, race relations, responsiveness of city government to people's wishes, community spirit of the big companies, labor relations, and people's pride in the community.

Items 63*–80*: Would you tell us what you feel about the following things or people, whether you strongly approve, approve, are undecided, disapprove, or strongly disapprove of: Zoning regulations. Consolidation of the city and county schools into one school system. Consolidation of the city and county government into one government. Spending some local tax money to attract new industry to this area. A rapidly growing city. Slum clearance. This city's labor unions. The city council. The county commissioners. The mayor. The city manager. Public housing. Fluoridation of the city water supply. Property reevaluation. Attracting a large number of residents to the community. (Metroville only:) Harmony House. A new regional industrial area like Petropolis' Locus Laboratory. (Petropolis only:) PESNEG. The New Municipal Biracial Race Relations Commission. The Locus Laboratory.

Item 81: [14] What, in your opinion, are the most important issues, problems, or projects facing [the community] at the present time?

The responses in Farmdale concerning what citizens were discussing (Item 4) were interpreted for this comparative analysis as approximately equivalent to the responses on Item 81 for the purpose of assessing political perspectives of citizens. Item 81 seems to have tapped more impersonal, spectator concerns than did the discussion item, but in a pilot study in Farmdale the correlation was so high that the "most important issues, problems, or projects" question was omitted. In 1959 in Oretown, both items were included in order to assess their equivalence. A correlation was found of .717 between matters named in response to both items. Since there were usually more responses to Item 81, those who undertake such studies in the future may want to bear in mind these differences. The high correlation between both number and content of responses to the two questions in Farmdale probably would not be the same for other communities. The problem of interpreting responses to such differently worded questions can be minimized by the greater use of batteries of questions about perspectives on particular policy and decisional matters.

Item 82:   How would you rate this city's downtown business district? (a) Very good. (b) Good. (c) Not very good.

Items 83–89: We are now going to show you sketches of planned redevelopments of downtown business areas in other cities. While no one is proposing these particular developments for this city, do you think that you and the following groups would support such drastic renovations of the city's downtown business district with state or federal funds? You yourself? The downtown merchants? The leading financial institutions? Property owners in the city? The major manufacturing companies? (And in Metroville only:) The civic leaders? The newspaper? (a) Would support. (b) Would oppose.

If the respondent answered that he would personally be in favor of the redevelopment, he was then asked:

Item 90*: Suppose such a rebuilding involved some increase in city taxes? Would you still be in favor of it? (Yes or no.)

Items 91–94: So far as intelligence (responsibility; morality; ambition) is concerned, would you say that, compared to Whites, Negroes are *by nature:* (a) Superior to Whites. (b) The same as Whites. (c) Inferior to Whites.

Item 95*: Some people have suggested that the Supreme Court decision ordering desegregation was wrong and that the states ought to be permitted to decide for themselves on this question. The proposal is to go through the process of getting an amendment to the United States Constitution to take the power away from the Supreme Court. How do you feel about this kind of proposal to try to amend the U. S. Constitution? (a) Strongly approve. (b) Approve. (c) Undecided. (d) Disapprove. (e) Strongly disapprove.

Item 96*: In one state in the South, the governor has threatened to withhold state school funds from any school district which desegregates the schools, that is, which permits Negro children to attend the same schools as White children. How do you feel about withholding any state money from school districts here in Southern State, as any of these districts start letting Negro and White children go to school together? (a) Strongly approve. (b) Approve. (c) Undecided. (d) Disapprove. (e) Strongly disapprove.

Item 97*: Some people have suggested that if need be, the public schools ought to be closed altogether rather than have Negro and White children go to school together. How do you feel about this? (a) Strongly approve. (b) Approve. (c) Undecided. (d) Disapprove. (e) Strongly disapprove.

Item 98*: Once in a while you hear it said that if need be, people ought to get together and resist with force any attempts to mix Negro and White children in the same schools. How do you feel about this? (a) Strongly approve. (b) Approve. (c) Undecided. (d) Disapprove. (e) Strongly disapprove.

Item 99 (Metroville only): Do you favor expansion of the old White mental hospital on its present site; or improvement of the old White mental hospital and a new branch hospital built on another site; or abandonment of the old White mental hospital and construction of a new hospital in a new location; or don't you care?

Items 100–109*: Generally speaking, how important are the following groups in making the key decisions on important policies in [the community]? The mayor and city council? The out-of-town companies? The leading civic organizations? The banks and insurance companies? The businessmen? The voters? The county commissioners? The labor leaders? Negro leaders? (And in Metroville only:) The largest firms? (a) Very important. (b) Not so important. (c) Unimportant.

Item 110*: Generally speaking, which [of those listed in Items 100–109] would you say is the most important group?

Items 111–114*: Would you say that there are any leading citizens who are too much prolabor? Too much antilabor? Too much pro-Negro? Too much anti-Negro? (Yes or no.)

After asking the respondents for the names of any organizations or associations to which they belong, and if they belong, whether they attend regularly, hold an office, held any past offices, serve as a member of a committee, pay dues or made a financial contribution to the organization in the last year, each respondent who reported belonging to at least one organization or association was asked:

Item 115* [15]: Have you personally worked in these organizations on any important community problem, policy matter, or issue? (Yes or no.)

If they answered "yes" to Item 115, they were asked Items 116*– 118*:

Items 116*–118*: What organization was that? What was the problem, policy matter, or issue? What type of work did you do?

Item 119*: Which three civic, fraternal, or social organizations would you say are the most influential in the making of important decisions affecting the whole community?

Item 120*: What, if any, city or county offices—elective or appointive— have you held?

Items 121–131: How frequently, if at all, do you associate with: City officials. County officials. School officials. School teachers. State-government officials. Political-party officials. Labor-union leaders. (And for White respondents:) Negroes. (And for Negro respondents:) Whites. (And, except in the White subcommunity of Petropolis:) Civic leaders. Members of labor unions.

Item 132: Are any of your close friends in any of these categories? (Yes or no.) If yes, in which categories?

Item 133*: It has been said that [the community] is growing much slower than other cities in Southern State and the South. Would you agree or disagree?

If the respondents agreed with Item 133:

Item 134*: Why do you think this is so?

The respondents were then shown the same list of names as the second panels of informants used in defining Manifest Leaders (see Variable IV).

Items 135–139*: We have talked to a number of people in [the community] who have given us a list of people whom they consider to be important in community policy making. We would like you to look at this list and indicate which of these people you would consider to be among the ten most important people who can get a major policy or project adopted in [the community]. Which of these people on this list do you generally or have you worked closely with on community projects or policies? Of the ten most important policy-makers, which ones would you say have views which are *most similar to yours* about the needs, policies, and future of [the community]? Are any of the people on this list related to you? If so, which ones? Would you consider any of these people close personal friends?

Item 140*: As a final question, could you tell us who you voted for in the last election for mayor of [the community]? (a) Specified name. (b) Didn't vote. (c) Don't remember.

Petropolis White respondents were then asked:

Item 141: To what extent do you think the NAACP dominates or controls PESNEG? (a) Very much. (b) Somewhat. (c) Not very much. (d) Don't know.

Petropolis Negro respondents were asked:

Item 142: How can Negroes best get ahead: By getting a better education? By seeking better jobs and higher pay? By getting the city government to help them? By getting the political parties to help them? What is the second best way? What is the third best way?

Petropolis Negro respondents also were asked the three following sets of questions:

Item 143: In 5 years, to what extent do you think Negroes and Whites will be working side by side on the same sorts of jobs in factories and businesses in Petropolis? (a) Much more than now. (b) A little more than now. (c) About the same as now. (d) Less than now.

Item 144: In 5 years how much integration do you think there will be in Petropolis' public schools? (a) Much more than now. (b) A little more than now. (c) About the same as now—that is, none.

Item 145: Which of the following would you say is doing more to help Negroes in Petropolis: businessmen, labor unions, the city government, the political parties, PESNEG, the NAACP. (The respondents were asked to choose one or another of every possible paired combination of these six categories.)

Further Measures of Political Perspectives

In the Southern communities at Time M and in Oretown when it was revisited in Period $+6$, a form was left for each respondent to complete and return by mail. That form contained a series of items regarding the political-perspective variables specified below. Since the rate of return in the Southern samples was relatively low—somewhat more than 20 per cent from the Petropolis Negro random sample to slightly more than one-third of the other three Southern samples— the data obtained in this manner in those cities were used to validate material reported earlier in the book, but not in and by themselves.

In Oretown the response was about 54 per cent. A differential response rate was obtained from those of different socio-economic positions. For example, 50 per cent of those with less than an eighth-grade education filled it out and mailed it back; 54 per cent of those with one to four years of high school returned it filled in; and slightly more than 60 per cent of those who had been to college at least one year completed and returned it, a finding of a response-rate study.[16]

Since the one scale reported in tables in the text (Chapter 13) applies to particular socio-economic categories, there is little or no danger because response was biased by class; therefore, information obtained through this mailback procedure probably presents an accurate picture insofar as the reported relationships are concerned. Moreover, the special study referred to above indicated that the differential response rate within class categories seemed to be more a reflection of individual idiosyncrasies, the situation, or accidental factors than it was of such psychological factors as sociability, authoritarianism, sense of political efficacy, feelings of civic duty, and the like, within socio-economic strata. Comparing the findings for particular socio-economic categories across communities was the procedure ordinarily used in the analysis; this rests in part on the assumption that whatever factors were responsible for a differential response rate were similar from community to community.

The items used to measure the following variables are listed under the descriptive title of each variable.

National Political Ideology: liberalism-conservatism. A set of items formulated by the Survey Research Center of the University of Michigan were put in a "strongly agree" to "strongly disagree" response format to measure attitudes toward the appropriate scope of the federal government.[17]   Four of the items refer to government's role in the economy and in welfare; one item refers to government's role in welfare for a racial minority, or social reorganization; and one item refers to governmental autonomy from business domination.

Item 146:   The government in Washington ought to see to it that everybody who wants to work can find a job. (a) Agree strongly. (b) Agree somewhat. (c) Agree slightly. (d) Disagree slightly. (e) Disagree somewhat. (f) Disagree strongly.

Item 147:   The government ought to help people get doctors and hospital care at low cost. (a) Agree strongly. (b) Agree somewhat. (c) Agree slightly. (d) Disagree slightly. (e) Disagree somewhat. (f) Disagree strongly.

Item 148:   If cities and towns around the country need help to build more schools, the government in Washington ought to give them the money they need. (a) Agree strongly. (b) Agree somewhat. (c) Agree slightly. (d) Disagree slightly. (e) Disagree somewhat. (f) Disagree strongly.

Item 149:   The government should leave things like electric power and housing for private businessmen to handle. (a) Agree strongly. (b) Agree somewhat. (c) Agree slightly. (d) Disagree slightly. (e) Disagree somewhat. (f) Disagree strongly.

Item 150:   If Negroes are not getting fair treatment in jobs and housing, the government in Washington should see to it that they do. (a) Agree strongly. (b) Agree somewhat. (c) Agree slightly. (d) Disagree slightly. (e) Disagree somewhat. (f) Disagree strongly.

Item 151:   The government ought to see to it that big business corporations don't have much to say about how the government is run. (a) Agree strongly. (b) Agree somewhat. (c) Agree slightly. (d) Disagree slightly. (e) Disagree somewhat. (f) Disagree strongly.

Sense of Political Efficacy (Political Potency).   These items were put in the same "strongly agree" to "strongly disagree" format to measure general feelings of political impotence. They also were developed by the Survey Research Center.[18] The scale was not intended to measure the sense of electoral potency, however, but rather to measure a general sense of political potency.

Political Cynicism. This measure was a more general form of the measurement of political cynicism reported earlier in the book (Items 27 through 30).[19]

Political-Behavior Items for Oretown Panel Study

Item A: Would you tell what you feel about urban renewal?   (a) Strongly approve. (b) Approve. (c) Undecided. (d) Disapprove. (e) Strongly disapprove. (f) Don't care.

For the table reported in Chapter 13, (a) and (b) were collapsed into an "Approve" category; (d) and (e) were collapsed into a "Disapprove" category; and (c) and (f) were collapsed into an "Undecided" category.

Item B: Would you tell us what you feel about increasing taxes to provide improved city services? (a) Strongly approve. (b) Approve. (c) Undecided. (d) Disapprove. (e) Strongly disapprove. (f) Don't care.

The same collapsed categories were used for the tables in Chapter 13.

Item C: The people behind urban renewal in Oretown are trying to push people around. (a) Agree strongly. (b) Agree somewhat. (c) Agree slightly. (d) Disagree slightly. (e) Disagree somewhat. (f) Disagree strongly.

Item D: Did you vote in the city election this year? (Yes or no.) (If respondent voted:) Were you in favor of abolishing or keeping the housing code? (a) In favor of abolishing. (b) In favor of keeping. (If respondent did not vote:) If you had voted, do you think that you probably would have voted to abolish or keep the housing code? (a) Abolish. (b) Keep. (c) Undecided. (d) No interest in the matter.

Item E: Did you suggest or urge anyone—your family or friends or others—to be for or against abolishing the housing code before the election? (Yes or no.)

Item F: Do you remember anyone suggesting or urging you to be either for or against abolishing the housing code either in a personal conversation, at an informal social gathering, or at a meeting or any of your organizations? (Yes or no.)

If the respondent voted for or probably would have voted for abolishing the housing code, he was asked:

Item G: Here are some reasons that people have given us for voting to abolish the housing code. Which one of these would you say was the single most important reason for your being in favor of abolishing the housing code? (a) Abolishing the housing code would stop further urban-renewal programs. (b) It's something the politicians and bureaucrats want but not the people. (c) It invades private property rights. (d) It hurts elderly and poor people most.

NOTES

1. An excellent introductory work on sampling, with comprehensive technical references, is Frederick F. Stephan and Philip J. McCarthy's *Sampling Opinions, An Analysis of Survey Procedure* (New York: John Wiley & Sons, Inc., 1958). Another useful volume is Herbert Hyman, *Survey Design and Analysis* (Glencoe, Illinois: The Free Press, 1955).

2. Much work remains to be done on assessing the validity of responses to questions concerning participation. See, for example, Elihu Katz and Paul F. Lazarsfeld, *Personal Influence* (Glencoe, Illinois: The Free Press, 1955), Part III, Chapter II, pp. 149–161; Hugh J. Parry and Helen M. Crossley, "Validity of Responses to Survey Questions," *The Public Opinion Quarterly,* Vol. 14 (April–May 1949), pp. 61–80; and Harold L. Wilensky, "The Labor Vote: A Local Union's Impact on the Political Conduct of Its Members," *Social Forces,* Vol. 35, No. 2 (December 1956), p. 115, footnote 7.

3. The postulated functions and consequences of membership in subsidiary political organizations rest on assumptions that need much more research than has been done by political analysts. A study by S. M. Lipset, M. Trow, and J. Coleman is in point: see their *Union Democracy* (Glencoe, Illinois: The Free Press, 1956), especially Chapter 5, pp. 83–105. They found in one union setting that membership in manifestly nonpolitical clubs resulted in increases in political knowledge, interest and involvement in union politics on the part of some categories of union members during a union-political-campaign period. Although not controlling certain crucial variables, Herbert Maccoby's "The Differential Political Activity of Participants in a Voluntary Association" is also an example of where research might be profitably directed on a comparable point; see *American Sociological Review,* Vol. 23, No. 5 (October 1958), pp. 524–532. His theoretically relevant uncontrolled variables were socio-economic class (of members and nonmembers of the association studied) and memberships in other associations. See also the excellent report on the impact of a politically oriented local union on members by Harold L. Wilensky, "The Labor Vote: A Local Union's Impact on the Political Conduct of Its Members," *loc. cit.,* pp. 111–120.

4. Another example of discrepancies between the political perspectives of those highest in the political influence structure and those highest in the social structure may be usefully offered here. In the White subcommunities of both Petropolis and Metroville, the level of education was positively related to approval of the idea of spending local tax money to help acquire new industry and to support of the Locus Laboratory in the Petropolis area and its counterpart in the Metroville area, although in both instances there was much greater approval in Petropolis than in Metroville. On both items, the highly educated active influentials in Metroville had comparably favorable attitudes to those of equally high educational levels who were lower in the political-influence structure. However, in Petropolis the highly educated among the active influentials were much more favorable than were the highly educated of lower political-influence rank. On the former item, the ratio of approve to disapprove or undecided was 21:1 for the highly educated among the active influentials but only 3½:1 among the highly educated lower in the political-influence structure of Petropolis' White subcommunity. On the latter item, the comparable ratios were 22:0, and 5:1, respectively. If the active influentials were more likely than those of lower political-influence rank to exercise influence in such matters, knowledge of political-influence position would seem to be as essential as knowledge of socio-economic position.

5. These are variations of questions asked by Robert O. Schulze in his study of Cibola. See his "The Bifurcation of Power in a Satellite City," in *Com-*

munity Political Systems, ed. by Morris Janowitz (New York: The Free Press of Glencoe, 1961), Appendix B, p. 74.

6. One aspect of this problem is discussed by James L. Price in his useful analysis of Selznick's discussion of "cooptation," wherein he distinguishes "ersatzism" from informal cooptation. See Price's "Continuity in Social Research: TVA and the Grass Roots," *The Sociological Review,* Vol. 1, No. 2 (Fall 1958), pp. 63–68.

7. The findings of Robert O. Schulze and Leonard U. Blumberg regarding the results of different panels of informants with "power attribution" or "reputational" techniques of identifying Manifest Leaders are provisional until other communities under various conditions are investigated. See their "The Determination of Local Power Elites," *American Journal of Sociology,* Vol. 53 (November 1957), pp. 290–296.

8. Edwin H. Rhyne mentions this as having occurred in three Southern counties. See his "Political Parties and Decision Making in Three Southern Counties," *American Political Science Review,* Vol. LII, No. 4 (December 1958), pp. 1091–1107.

9. Reprinted from David Gold and John R. Schmidhauser, "Urbanization and Party Competition: The Case of Iowa," *Midwest Journal of Political Science,* Vol. IV, No. 1 (February 1960), p. 63, footnote 4. By permission of the Wayne State University Press. Copyright 1960 by the Wayne State University Press.

10. See also Items 121 through 124, which were asked of Farmdale respondents.

11. Items 121–124, *infra,* were also asked of Oretown respondents.

12. Revisions in, or additions to, the foregoing questions asked only of Petropolis Negro respondents were as follows:

(Item 5): Was segregation discussed there?

(Items 6 and 7): Was the matter of segregation involved in the issues? Do you belong to PESNEG? Do you belong to the NAACP? (If yes:) To the local chapter, or just to the national organization? Have you personally worked in either PESNEG or the NAACP on any important community problem, policy matter, or issue? Have you in any other organizations you belong to?

(Items 16–18): If you wanted some advice on local-government matters (school matters, political-party or election matters), whom would you go to? Does this person live near here? In the past have you actually talked over school matters with this person?

(Item 43): If you had to choose one or the other, which would you rather have: better job opportunities, school integration, low taxes, or better city services, such as street repair, fire and police protection? Alternatives: respondents were asked to choose one or another of every possible paired combination of these four things.

13. For the Petropolis Negro subcommunity, only Items 54–56, 58, and "recreational facilities" were asked.

14. The form of the question asked of Petropolis Negroes included the word "three" immediately prior to the words "most important. . . ." An analysis of the first item mentioned revealed substantially the same pattern of items named as revealed by the analysis of all of the responses. Asking for "three" issues, problems, or projects may or may not have produced a larger number of responses than in the samples which did not specify the number to be

given. We doubt that it accounted for the very large difference between the proportions of respondents in the random samples in the two Negro subcommunities being unable to mention a single issue, problem, or project (there was a much larger proportion of such nonresponses in Metroville than in Petropolis). Moreover, the stress on the need to improve the economy in the responses by Petropolis Negroes, in contrast to those in Metroville, was apparent from the analysis of first responses, a procedure which other studies have also shown to give very much the same picture of perceived (or salient) problems produced by an analysis of all reasons in a question eliciting as many problems as respondents can mention.

15. See note 12.
16. Details on a special study of the characteristics of those in that sample who did and did not return the form are being prepared by the authors, as is the information on the procedures used to construct Guttman-type scales for the following measures.
17. These liberalism-conservatism items were devised at the University of Michigan for a national study of voting behavior in 1956. See Angus Campbell *et al., The American Voter* (New York: John Wiley & Sons, Inc., 1960).
18. See Angus Campbell, Gerald Gurin, and Warren Miller, *The Voter Decides* (Evanston, Illinois: Row, Peterson and Company, 1954), pp. 187–194.
19. For the specific items and a technical report on its use in another small metropolis, see Robert E. Agger, Marshall N. Goldstein, and Stanley A. Pearl, "Political Cynicism: Measurement and Meaning," *Journal of Politics,* Vol. 23 (August 1961), pp. 477–506.

APPENDIX B   BIG CITY POLITICAL SYSTEMS:

a speculative extrapolation

We shall conclude this volume by extending our speculations about the political systems of four small- to medium-sized communities to the possible character of the political systems of the giant metropolis. These speculations are questions that should be pursued by political theorists through systematic, comparative investigation in the years ahead.

In extending our speculations we shall be concerned with the big cities of the East and Midwest, rather than the newer large cities of the West. But the extent to which cities like Los Angeles and San Francisco resemble St. Louis, Chicago, Philadelphia, and New York more than they do an Oretown during the late 1940's and early 1950's can only be decided by further research.

The model of the big city's political system is simply a variation on the three models described in the text—as each of those models is a variation on the others. Actually, several political-system models are needed to describe the political systems of big cities. And sufficiently sharp differences in degree on given variables are indications that different models might be more appropriate.

For the purpose of this extrapolation we shall assume that the model of the big city includes a Developed Democratic regime.[1] However, let us introduce another variable into the regime typology that might be called political anomie, apathy, or distance. We might expect that much larger proportions of the residents of big cities than of smaller communities are anomic, apathetic, or distant. At least we might expect that the degree of anomie would be less variable or more stable over time in the large city than in the small city.

If in the two cities the proportions of citizens who did not participate were comparable, we would expect that the nonparticipants in the large city would be more distant politically than their counterparts in the small city. Consequently, it would be more difficult in the large city to activate ordinarily apolitical citizens. If such citizens of a large city could be induced to participate as electors in a particularly interesting campaign, a smaller proportion might be expected to remain active after the issue was settled than in a smaller city. However few subsidiary political organizations might exist in a small city, a greater number of citizens might, under such conditions, participate politically for longer periods of time than in a large city. The model and these inferences therefrom, might be framed as hypotheses to be tested by using a natural experimental design.

We would expect that political cynicism also would be substantially higher in a big city than in a small one. This might be particularly true of middle- and upper-class citizens. For example, the strong inverse relationship between political cynicism and level of education found in Oretown in 1959 might be weaker or absent in the larger city. In other words, the middle and upper classes of a large metropolis might regard the "politician" more negatively than would the same group in a smaller city. However, the lower-class citizens of both might be comparably cynical, as well as distant.[2]

The professional politician, the machine, and the boss or district leader are all associated in the literature with big-city politics. What does this mean in terms of the power structure of the big city? A prototype power structure in such a system might be something like this: a Consensual Elite system in which the political leadership is composed primarily of professional politicians. One variant might be a single political leadership representing, for example, one dominant party in firm control of municipal government. Another variant might be a competitive political-leadership situation in which two parties contend for elective office, assuming the community has partisan local elections. In the latter case, because the competition would be between sets of professional politicians, a single ideology and, hence, a Consensual power structure would exist.

In this prototype power structure, what would be the ideology of the professional politician? A dimension of pragmatism is implicit in the ideological schema presented in Chapter 1 and used throughout this book; but this should be reassessed in the present context. First, the schema applied primarily to pragmatism about policy perspectives and decisional preferences, rather than to the defining component variables of ideology. Second, if introduced as a defining variable into the ideological scheme, the schema would result not only in a redefinition and increased number of ideologies, but it would also result in the reclassification of individuals who were assigned to one or another ideological category—for example, Ben Kelly of the Community Conservationists in Oretown. Some of the uncommitted Manifest Leaders also would be assigned, presumably, to an ideology marked by a relatively pure pragmatism.

The professional politicians among the political leaders—and there were some in the four communities, particularly in Oretown and Petropolis—would be characterized as adhering to a principle of community organization such as the following. The good community results from patterns of governmental and private resource allocations that represent the accommodation at any moment in time between and among individuals or interests who have made political demands. The ruler should be the professional politician, whose twin guidelines for action are the preservation of his political-leadership position and the community's interest. He should see the community as a complex of individuals and interests. His sense of cultural class should be moderate and his central political-cultural perspective a view of his fellow man as a mixture of the venal and the good. He should consider everyone's basic self-interest or selfishness the key to unlocking the door to necessary compromises; the major exception to the latter would probably be the self-righteous citizen of upper cultural class, but of any social class, who cloaked his selfishness and need to dictate to others behind a mask of idealism.[3]

Because of the realities of modern politics, the professional politicians in control of Democratic party organizations in big cities have needed the support of economically and racially underprivileged masses in the central city. Some of the professionals have actually been Liberal in ideology, quite pragmatic, and more recently, Community Conservationist in orientation. Others have allied themselves with distinctly Liberal groups and individuals. In cities where a professional politics has come into being and a traditional Liberal-Conservative split already existed, the competition between professional politicians may become a Liberal-Conservative fight, with an emerging competitive power structure. The return to two-party competition in some big cities has been marked by the counterorganizational efforts of Conservatives to build the organizational base that is so important to the professional politician. The inducement for businessmen to enter politics as precinct workers frequently has been less than the inducement for lower-income, more marginal people to whom patronage, payoffs, and the possibility of a career as a professional politician supplement the feelings of dignity and social satisfaction provided by the professional politician's organizational settings.

Since the Democratic party does not have what has been termed the "natural organization" of the Republican party,[4] that is, the business-, civic-, and community-association network in all cities, the Democratic professional politician has needed to build a grass-roots organization to ensure that organized labor and racial and religious minority groups go to the polls on election day.

One can assume that even in the big cities a certain proportion of the citizens will be active politically, at least in contests for local-government office, and especially when there is actual or threatened two-party competition. Actually, it would seem reasonable to expect that big cities have larger proportions of completely nonparticipant citizens than do smaller cities. However, the proportion of active influentials in the large city might be as high as or even higher than that in the small.

The distribution of political power in the big city is, we think, ordinarily elite, at least in regard to other than regularly scheduled elections and nominations. This would be due partly to the presumed greater nonparticipation of the more distant and cynical citizens, and partly to the development of an extensive, complex administrative politics and the nature of the demand flows in the political system.[5] As in Oretown and Petropolis during Time E to M, control of City Hall would become important in party politics.[6] With professional politicians in control of the administrative process, citizens and interest groups might tend to focus upon the sort of administrative relief that relatively responsive, accommodation-minded professional politicians provide in their guidance of the city's bureaucracy. The active party member might begin to think automatically of petitioning or pressing a demand to the appropriate department head or official instead of the top political leadership of the party, perhaps with the assistance of his fellows one step above him in the party hierarchy. In numerous studies of urban party politics, analysts have portrayed a big-city pattern in which the minor party official monitors his neighborhood for demands that he could either meet himself or pass on to his "superiors" in the next level of the party organization's hierarchy.[7]

To the extent that professionals dominate the political leadership —and the larger the metropolis, the more this is expected to happen— there is a greater likelihood of "personal favors" and administrative-decision-making satisfactions, and less that political demands emanating from citizens low in the structure of political influence will reach the organization-of-political-support stage. At the same time, the professional politicians at the leadership level are pushed to make accommodations rather than draw the masses of people below them in their own organizations, or citizens who are otherwise nonparticipant, into the decision-making process. The pragmatic principle mitigates against what other ideologists are impelled to do in a competitive ideological power structure, that is, to draw into the political battle as many people as they can.

Let us assume for the moment that political leaderships dominated by relatively nonideological professional politicians—which are, consequently, consensual power structures—are more characteristic of the big metropolis than of the smaller city. Why is this more likely to be the case? One might speculate that the answer is related to the relatively greater need in large cities for the occupation of professional politics. The larger the numbers of people making implicit or explicit demands upon government, the more likely it is that there will be specialists to meet those demands. People in sparsely populated areas may need certain economic goods and services, but producers or suppliers may not find it economically worthwhile to operate within those areas until the population and demands increase. When more and more people begin to sell their labor as professional politicians, they may try to market a product most likely to appeal to and be demanded by the largest numbers of people. At times this may mean that the professional politician sells a Liberal program because his potential customers—for example, blue-collar workers, immigrants, and minority groups—might be most likely to buy that product. At other times, or even simultaneously, the professional politician may not want to pass up the opportunity to sell to Conservatives—for example, businessmen—so that he finds it best to market a service that has the widest possible appeal. This is essentially the reasoning used by the pluralist in explaining why politics of interests rather than of ideologies is likely to exist when politicians need to appeal to many sources for electoral support.

With a heavy demand for his services in the big city the politician cannot be the sort of part-time politician that so many political leaders in smaller communities seem to be. Those who would like to be in politics part-time find that others are in politics full-time. Politics in the big city pays, and it is not an unattractive career, particularly for the less affluent person who has little or no reason to expect that he can follow his father in business or that his alumni association or professional school will place him in a good white-collar position. It is not only the industrial executives, the financiers, and the merchants who find that part-time political participation is insufficient to acquire a position as a political leader, but the union official as well. Perhaps the person who finds it relatively easy to combine his career and professional politics is the lawyer, or the insurance man; and frequently even this is not as easy to do as it is in the small town.

The businessman or union official who would like to act politically, partly on the basis of protecting or furthering an ideology, finds greater difficulties in the big city than in the small town. First of all, he may find that his political, occupational, and after-hours, social settings are widely separated. The suburban residences of businessman political leaders in both Oretown and Petropolis permitted them to meet downtown after a ten- or fifteen-minute drive, whereas the difficulties of commuting from suburban residences are frequently much greater in the large metropolitan areas. The social settings such as country clubs which served as milieus for political discussions of community affairs in three of our four research communities may not, in larger cities, serve as well to integrate the social, economic, and local political lives of their members. Since specialization in the economy has developed to a great degree in large cities, the politically integrating and coordinating functions of such groups as the chamber of commerce or the central labor council may not be able to overcome as easily the forces of political disintegration resulting from a multiplicity of business associations and labor unions. This is not to say that such settings are not used at all as community subsidiary political organizations in the metropolis, or even that businessmen and union officials are completely absent from the ranks of professional politicians. But it suggests that there are features of big-city life that facilitate the dominance of the professional politician in the political leadership of the city.

Recent studies have indicated that membership in voluntary associations is lower in the largest cities than in small communities in the United States.[8] Although consumption of the printed mass media tends to be higher among members in such settings than it is for people who are not members, a larger portion of the latter in the big city may be *relatively* more dependent on their newspaper as a source of information in regard to local politics. This lesser degree of community integration creates an opportunity for both newspapers and professional politicians to exercise political influence in the gap that is presumably filled by the voluntary association in the small town. In a sense the newspapers tend to become the rival of the professional politician insofar as they tend to report the seamier side of politics— local political problems, political corruption, and the like—regardless of whether the newspaper is a "scandal sheet" or a self-pronounced independent pillar of civic virtue and a devotee of "objective" reporting. Little is known of the relative political effectiveness of daily newspapers in big cities as compared to dailies or weeklies in small ones. But it is not unlikely that it is in big cities that newspapers contribute to the opportunity of professional politicians, by creating or reinforcing feelings of political cynicism and distance on the part of readers.[9]

It should be noted in this speculative context that most groups with which professional politicians are likely to be allied—businessmen, unions, and racial as well as ethnic minorities—lack one motive for entering politics in a more full-time manner. This is the feeling that ordinarily the politicians understand, and will not threaten, the group's most basic interest. The feeling is frequently confirmed by interactions with the politicians on various boards and commissions and in a variety of other settings. Little is yet known, for example, about the relationships of such politicians as Curley in Boston, Daley in Chicago, or Wagner in New York with their business communities, but various reporters and novelists have noted the reciprocal accommodations, and sometimes mutually active support, between business groups and such politicians.

In discussing New Haven's politics, Robert A. Dahl makes the important point that the "political stratum," that is, the minority of politically participant citizens, adheres to an axiom that "in allocating rewards to individuals and groups, the existing socio-economic structure must be taken as given, except for minor details. . . . Except perhaps for socialists, local reform movements have concentrated on defects in the political system, not the socio-economic structure of the society."[10] In New York City's 1961 election the programs of the local Democratic and Republican organizations were quite similar except for minor differences to be expected between the "ins" and "outs." At least two degrees of ideological conservatism were offered to the voters in the candidates of the Citizens Party and the United Taxpayers Party; and two variants of a very liberal ideology were offered by the Socialist Workers Party and the Socialist Labor Party. The professional politicians in both major parties had little reason to feel that any of these manifestly more ideological parties would constitute a significant electoral threat to their supporters.

Two sets of professional political protagonists, representing different parties or factions within single parties, may become locked in major battle in the big city. They tend to do so only when their more ideology-minded sources of active support press for conflicting decisional outcomes that are difficult or impossible to compromise, reconcile, or give up. That this is frequently a potential development may be inferred from a description of the general political situation in St. Louis:

. . . two broad configurations of interests.   On one side are the locally oriented labor unions, Negroes, neighborhood businessmen, and lower income people generally . . .   Downtown business interests and the middle and upper-middle income residents [constitute the forces on the other side] . . . two fairly distinct groupings have appeared *within* whichever party was dominant in a particular period, one representing the larger business groups, the newspaper, ward areas, and the forces of "Progress" generally, while the other is characterized by the "Politicians" who are spokesmen for a medley of lower income, labor, small business, and minority groups.[11]

Seattle has been described as having "two powerful and effective con-centrations of economic and political power," with business leaders constituting the core of the conservative power center and labor lead-ers the core of the liberal power center.[12]

Why a Consensual Elite power structure, dominated by professional politicians, becomes a relatively Competitive Elite or Mass power structure in large metropolitan areas needs to be studied, as do the conditions under which major metropolitan political controversies occur between, and among, administrators and politicians around City Hall.   These individuals have personal power drives, interests, and ties to various interest groups.   Within a basically consensual political superstructure controversies are contained that elsewhere or under dif-ferent conditions become conflicts in an ideologically competitive leadership.   When metropolitan politics are described as essentially administrative, does this reflect the actual situation or might such descriptions stem from a failure to assess the degree to which political decision-making occurs within and away from City Hall?

The possibility that in the big urban centers which have professional politicians and a highly developed administrative politics, a relatively high proportion of citizens are nonparticipant is, in fact, supported by a comparison of political participation of citizens of New Haven, Connecticut, and that of the citizens of Oretown and Petropolis.   Al-though New Haven is larger than both Petropolis and Oretown, it is not a big city compared to New York, Philadelphia, or Chicago. However, it does have a history of two-party competition and pro-fessionalism in politics similar to that of big-city models rather than the models based on our research communities.

The proportion of completely nonparticipant citizens was higher in New Haven than in Oretown in 1959.   In Oretown participation had dropped substantially from Time M, 1953 (Table B-1).   The propor-

TABLE B-1   Index of Political Participation: Registered Voters among City Residents

| Index Points | New Haven * 1959 | Oretown | | Petropolis 1957 | |
		1953	1959	Negro	White
2 or 3	29%	25%	15%	27%	21%
1	32	62	57	48	57
0	39	12	29	24	22
Totals %	100%	99%	101%	99%	100%
N	525	353	309	160	190

* The data from New Haven were adapted from Robert A. Dahl's *Who Governs?* (New Haven: Yale University Press, 1961), Appendix D, The Index of Noncampaign Participation in Local Affairs, p. 342.

tion of nonparticipants in New Haven was three times that in Oretown when the latter community had a Competitive Mass power structure. And there were proportionately more nonparticipants in New Haven than in Petropolis at Time M (1958). However, at the same time New Haven had a higher proportion of relatively active participants than these other cities. Thus the distribution of political participation, apart from simply voting in local elections, was not a "normal distribution" in the statistical sense in New Haven. It was relatively high at both the lower and upper ends of the participation scale, compared to the predominance of "moderate" participants in the other cities. This curve fits the aforementioned expectations that New Haven as a community with comparatively "big-city" politics had not only a relatively large proportion of apolitical citizens, but also a relatively large number of active participants involved in party or subsidiary political organizations. The moderate participants in Oretown and Petropolis were for the most part people engaged in discussion of political affairs, but that was the extent of their activity in the political organizations of their communities.

Perhaps New Haven is a special case of a generally developing pattern in big-city politics. This pattern seems to be one of increasing conflicts between Community Conservationists and groups of lower cultural class, similar to the trend observed in three of our smaller research communities. The Mayor of New Haven and his lieutenants were in one sense professional politicians and in another politicians of a strong Community Conservationist mixed with a Liberal orientation. Some of these top politicians had risen through the ranks of the local party organization. Like reformers elsewhere, these men became associated with the professional politicians of the regular party organization. At the same time, they built a coalition that included the city's industrialists, bankers, and major businessmen, at least in the outer rings of the group. An important person in the Mayor's group and a chief strategist in building the coalition was a leading organization chief who himself was a successful industrial executive-financier. As Robert Dahl said of one of the important men in the group, "If Golden's policies could be said to coincide substantially with those of the Economic Notables (insofar as the Notables agree among themselves) they could be said to coincide substantially with those of union leaders, school teachers, and factory hands." [13]

The success of Lee's group is attested by the fact that in the elections of 1955, 1957, and 1959, "the correlation between the various socioeconomic characteristics of the wards and the vote for Mayor Lee was, for all practical purposes, zero." [14] This means, in effect, that the Mayor and presumably his program were popular with the affluent as well as the underprivileged, with the Connecticut Yankees, the foreign-born, and the Negro. Dahl remarks that the Mayor's following in New Haven in 1953 was remarkably similar to Eisenhower's in the nation in 1952: "Both men developed followings that bore only slight resemblance to the party coalitions of their predecessors; in both cases, the followings cut across ethnic and socio-economic lines to an unprecedented extent; in both cases, *their policies emphasized shared benefits to citizens in general rather than to specific categories*." [15] Progressive Conservatism at the national level thus was analogous to the Community Conservationism in New Haven at about the same time.

As Dahl's study of New Haven politics points out, the key decision during the late 1950's was to initiate a major program of urban redevelopment. This was done by convincing the heterogeneous segments of the community that the program was in the total community interest; that it could be done at minimal cost to the city with no increase in tax rates; and that if it were not done the consequences might be disastrous. The various segments included the most important men in town: top industrialists, top labor-union leaders, and top university people. Members of that commission described themselves as a selling organization which never modified proposals issued to them by the Mayor and his staff; they felt they were important in presenting the program to the community in such a way as to elicit support or acquiescence, thereby preventing organizational opposition. Potential Conservative opposition, on the grounds that net increases in the scope of local government and federal participation in urban renewal were undesirable, or potential Liberal opposition, on the ground that the benefits were primarily geared to the downtown business community, was effectively forestalled.

The Economic Notables of New Haven were described as opposed to tax increases and against the expansion of public services; however, blue-collar workers also were described as favoring low taxes. In the urban-redevelopment program the massive infusion of federal funds meant that local taxes did not have to increase, and the Community Conservationist political leadership was successful in building and maintaining a broad consensus behind that policy formulation.[16]   The professional politicians in the leadership were successful in building their coalition apparently without a stratified political-cultural class system developing as it has in other big cities.[17]

A business-politician Community Conservationist coalition did not find itself strongly opposed by professional politicians whose political base was the lower cultural class.   Although the Mayor's organization was described as an "executive-centered coalition" that was "no monolith," his one defeat in the area of public education came when he did not exert his influence: "There is little doubt that if he had vigorously insisted on the promotions policy they sought, the Board would have stood its ground; if the Board had remained firm, the Superintendent would have complied." [18]   When the administration was threatened with defeat, it seems that the threats came from factions within the relatively consensual political leadership, and not from ideological opponents.

One of the three major factors Dahl uses to explain the Mayor's ability to avoid costly opposition was his "unusual skill at negotiating agreement and damping down potential disagreements before they flared into opposition." [19]   This needs to be explored further, as do the other two factors that Dahl suggests might have wrecked the attempt to "transform the independent sovereignties into an executive-centered order"; that is, the absence of pre-existing widespread latent support for urban redevelopment and of the "evident" need for intragovernmental collaboration on the part of city agencies.   Although Dahl recognizes that such factors do not "necessarily exist in other cities," it would seem that only further comparative research can clarify why comparable efforts in other cities resulted in a professional-politician–lower-cultural-class coalition which defeated such efforts to build a consensual, Community Conservationist political leadership.

In St. Louis, for example, where efforts to consolidate numerous local governments into a single metropolitanwide government were unsuccessful, the major political forces seemed to represent the sort of leadership divergence that was successfully avoided in New Haven in regard to substantially similar Conservationist proposals. Professional politicians were said to be allied with the locally oriented labor unions, Negroes, neighborhood businessmen, and the lower-income person who generally focuses his "attention primarily on the specific bread-and-butter issues of jobs, stop signs, spot zoning, and the like, and exhibits a sharp antipathy toward any suggestion of increased tax rates." [20] On the other side were the "downtown business interests and the middle- and upper-middle-income residents . . . primarily interested in broader policy questions—economic growth, urban renewal—and their approach to problems of fiscal solvency is more sympathetic to the needs for more tax revenue." [21] To be sure, loss of political power on the part of Negroes in such a governmental consolidation as proposed for St. Louis was not an issue in New Haven; but it was in Petropolis, where it was opposed by Negroes, when the same policy was formulated by that city's Community Conservationists. The Radical Right did not spearhead an opposition to urban redevelopment in New Haven as it did to urban renewal in Oretown, perhaps because of the traditional developed party organizations and the absence of a perceived opportunity to crack the organized political leadership. In any event, the St. Louis pattern of political conflict did not develop in New Haven, but it was in evidence in recent years in such big cities as Philadelphia and New York.

This pattern encompasses efforts by Community Conservationists to become professional politicians and win support for their Community Conservationist policies; their initial success is followed by a rebellion or increasingly successful resistance on the part of professional politicians and their Liberal allies—that is, the unions, minority groups, and the disadvantaged.

In Philadelphia, after years of successful rule by professional politicians of the Republican party, the Democratic party rose to control City Hall, starting with certain key minor posts in 1949. One key professional has been described by James Reichley as a believer in political organization.[22] His "true objective seems always to have been victory for the Democrats rather than municipal reform" but he was convinced that the Democratic party "must present candidates identified in the public mind as 'good-government men' in order to win." His theme was "Good government is good politics." Thus was the modern reform movement brought to Philadelphia politics.

Two "patricians" symbolized and took an active part in hammering out the new Community Conservation ideology. Describing these men, Joseph Clark and Richard Dilworth, of "shared upper-class background and their common interest in reform," Reichley characterizes Dilworth as the more conventional but Senator Clark, quoting a friend, as "the most conservative leader in American public life today." [23] Reichley goes on to say that:

If so, it is the calculated conservatism of Disraeli rather than the visceral conservatism of Burke. The Senator has given ample evidence for his attachment to such non-radical concepts as class, authority, and tradition, but he appears to believe that these concepts can be preserved in the modern world only with the assent of the mass of ordinary human beings. He has thus become the aristocratic leader of the commons against the "oligarchs" who seek to diminish the formal government so that their wills may be informally absolute in their private baronies.[24]

Thus did Community Conservation, in the persons of such men, enter Philadelphia politics in the 1950's. Reichley criticizes their "good-government philosophy" on the grounds not only that it is so oriented toward particular projects that particular policy successes undermine the popular support of the movement, but also that at bottom the philosophy, or ideology, has a fundamentally economic view of man "coupled with a prevailing individualism which insists that government must limit itself to removing the obstacles to fulfillment of the economic needs of the population rather than undertake to fulfill them itself." [25]

The success of professional politicians in outlasting semiprofessional Community Conservationists is traced to a sense of frustration on the part of reformers and voters; this, in turn, seems to be due to the failure to extend "the opportunity for active political participation to the larger number of ordinary citizens." Thus, professional politicians maintain their organization because the Community Conservationists have not been able to instill their Conservationist ideology into the pragmatic professionals—including the notion that in the metropolis the city administrator-planner rather than the professional politician should rule.[26] Neither have they managed to overcome the distrust, cynicism, and negative attitudes of many big-city citizens toward politics and thereby to build their own grass-roots organization that could take over from the regular organization.[27] The hostility and mistrust directed by the lower classes toward the advantaged, and the reciprocal sense of cultural superiority of the latter, works to maintain the cleavages in the body politic of the big city that the Community

Conservationists have not been able to bridge for more than short periods.

In New York City these big-city dynamics seem even clearer. In 1961, the so-called reform movement defeated the regular Democratic party organization, "Tammany Hall," not only by electing a mayor who had lost the regular organization's support, but in removing the man who symbolized the professional politician to the nation at large: Carmine DeSapio. New York City's politics is well known for the cyclical character of reform movements: citizens throw out the bosses and the machine, but they are regularly returned to control or else a new set of professional politicians emerges. The latest reformation has been described by an analyst as not a "death-rattle" but a metamorphosis of sorts in the ordinary control by the professionals of the city's politics.[28] In this city where "minority groups" are in the majority, professional politicians have been identified with Liberal rather than Conservative causes. However, to a greater extent than ever before, a new ideology, that of Community Conservation, seems to be challenging the professional-Liberal political leadership of the city.[29]

Describing the reform movement itself as ambivalent, Blanche Blank describes one wing as against patronage, against compromises on basic policy, and as oriented toward ends or policies rather than means or party organization.[30] The outlook of the other wing was much more like that of the professional politician who controls the party organization, City Hall, and the political leadership in general, but who feels that improvements are needed in the regular organization. The first wing is characterized as including persons who are likely to be "benevolent despots."

The purists in the new politics . . . fail to note that they may be . . . singularly removed from the over-all constituency of the Democratic Party—and even from the enrolled party members in their own districts. The reform movement is almost exclusively a middle-class movement, while the Democratic Party is still primarily the party of the lower classes. *The value systems of the underprivileged are virtually estranged from those of the middle class.* . . . If a club, open to all though it may be, does not in fact truly encompass or represent such a population group, then its efforts at forcing its own will (no matter how democratically demonstrated at the club) upon the party functionary is simply another form of elitism. Indeed, one may reasonably ask whether it is fundamentally possible for those reformers who are merely *for* the people but not *of* them, to maintain any sustained political leadership at the grass-roots level.[31]

Whether or not modern Community Conservationists in our terms can in the big or smaller American city develop and maintain a political organization that extends to the grass roots is a most important question. To the extent that any political leadership becomes dominated by a single ideology such as Conservationism, our models suggest that a mass power structure is unlikely. A process model of big-city politics suggests that when Community Conservationists become an aspiring political-leadership group, they try to take over an existing party or other political organization. Their moves are resisted by dominant professional politicians whose fundamentally pragmatic ideology puts them in a competitive position with the aspirants to power, as far as their different answers to the question of "who should rule" are concerned. Ordinarily the professional politician will try to tap the sense of cultural inferiority of citizens below the middle class and will play on the idea that there is a great gulf between the political-cultural position of those at the bottom and that of those at the top. Such a sense of cultural inferiority may become stronger and more hostile to the upper cultural class as the Community Conservationists are initially successful in local politics. Thus, political success may breed the conditions for political defeat.

Relatively little is yet known of the conditions under which such groups as Community Conservationists, Liberals, or "reformers" attain some of their immediate objectives in a big city like New York. Under what conditions have such forces been able to reach portions of the "grass-roots"? What portions have they reached? How have they managed to maintain support? Who has supported them? For how long? To what extent has the New Haven story been repeated in other cities? What were the conditions? What has actually happened in such situations to the sense of political involvement on the part of culturally disadvantaged groups? Has it been maintained, or increased, by successes of Community Conservationists and professional politicians? What, if any, were the consequences? Under what conditions are Community Conservationists subject to the revival of a Liberal-Conservative cleavage in their own ranks? What are the consequences for the position of professional politicians in the big city?

Blank poses these further questions about the "true" reformer in New York City:

Is he, perhaps, an egoist whose own sense of personal worthiness is undermined by another's rise to prominence? Is he therefore constitutionally unable to work for another man's success unless that man stands at a very great social or political distance from him? Is he allergic to the team spirit of politics? . . . Among the Pure Reformers, the sin of personal venality may have simply given way to that of personal pride. [32]

Is her last suggestion another way of characterizing the modern Community Conservationist as a person with a sense of superior cultural class? If so, to what extent are there, and can there be, variations in the pattern of the ideological variables that seem to define Community Conservationists in our research communities? Is it, perhaps, this very sense of membership in a class or category of men who know the road to the good community that sustains the political interactions of Community Conservationists with their fellows? If it were absent, might the result tend to be an academic, cynical commentary on the problems of the city rather than involvement as an increasingly significant political force in American urban politics? The questions posed by Blank about the "pure" reformer in New York City might well be posed about Radical Rightists, as well as Radical Leftists, who proverbially have not been able to submerge organizational and doctrinal differences in a common, organizationally united, cause. They could, and should, also be posed about political ideologists and categories of all kinds, with carefully designed research undertaken to provide better answers than so far exist in the body of knowledge that is labelled "political science" or "political sociology."

We have already mentioned the question of whether New Haven was a special case of big-city politics, since sharp community conflict between different cultural classes seemed to have been avoided as Community Conservationists became a major political force. In the absence of comparable observations or measurements of such variables as the ideological orientations—including the degree of pragmatism— of identified sets of political leaders in the big cities, it is easy to say that certain cities deviate from a norm. The notion that big-city politics is dominated by the pragmatic politician with a relatively flexible ideology may be to some degree a myth. [33] A recent study of New York City's elected committeemen and committeewomen has presented a different picture of that city's party understructure than held by some analysts. [34] Policy perspectives, if not ideology in the sense defined in the present volume, seemed to be much more relevant than earlier assumed, and the popular picture of the activist in the party organization—particularly the Democratic party organization— as a person of marginal means or marginal status was found to be inaccurate. The extent to which the top political leadership is increasingly Community Conservationist in such cities as New York City is as yet undetermined. [35] The fact that in local elections in big cities, where majorities are vital, it is frequently difficult to distinguish between major parties does not mean that on major decisional questions the party leaderships share similar preferences.[36]

The extent to which widespread political conflict has erupted in the biggest cities over such programs as urban renewal is variable. In some big cities, such as New York, opposition to urban renewal or to public housing seems to be centered in particular parts of the city. Organized Radical Right political activity is not unknown in large cities, although it seems to be a relatively minor force. It is possible that in the future the metropolis will have an increasingly competitive power structure, the major protagonists of which are Liberal White and Negro political groups on the one side, and Community Conservationist and Conservative political groups on the other. With the hardening of racial lines and the political crystallization that this might mean inside and around the central city, the professional politician of an earlier era may find that his chosen occupation demands a commitment that he cannot make. It is difficult to predict what may happen in big city politics when some of the implications of urban redevelopment become more widely appreciated. The same is true of what will happen as the new relationships developing among cities, states, and the federal government in the remaking of life in the metropolis, and the reordering of relationships between central city and suburbs, begin to make a greater impact. As Dahl has said of New Haven, ". . . except for a few men who dreamed and spoke of changing the face of the city, until recently the political stratum has assumed that the physical and economic features of the city are determined by forces beyond their control."[37] It is difficult to predict what will happen as larger numbers of people become aware of the increasing invalidity of such an assumption. The two main reasons for this are that increasing proportions of the population will become highly educated in the years ahead—including those minorities which have hitherto had little access to many of the values of American urban life—and that so little is yet known about the patterns of politics in the largest as well as the smaller cities and communities of the United States.[38] To forecast that there will be a continuation of a relatively Consensual, or Competitive, Elite power structure, no matter how much such consensus characterized the biggest cities of the land, we think would be rash.

NOTES

1. More precise measurements are obviously needed of the degree and extent of fears of illegitimate sanctions in the big cities. These may vary from

city to city and time to time.   There is a very great need for systematic research on the relationships between organized crime and politics that journalists and various government investigating committees have reported in their occasional explorations of the subject.

2. This might be inferred from Murray Levin's study of Boston, *The Alienated Voter* (New York: Holt, Rinehart and Winston, Inc., 1960), but his findings are difficult to evaluate.   A more conclusive finding of the absence of a relationship between SES and political cynicism in selected parts of Boston and in a Boston suburb, a negative relationship between class and political cynicism of the kind found in Oretown during the revisited periods and reported in Chapter 13, is in Edgar Litt, "Political Cynicism and Political Futility," *Journal of Politics*, Vol. 25 (May 1963), pp. 312–323.

3. According to Seymour Freedgood, the professional politician may refer to such advocates of good government as "the Goo-Goos."   See his "New Strength at City Hall," reprinted in *The Exploding Metropolis*, Editors of Fortune (Garden City, N. Y.: Doubleday & Co., 1958), p. 63.

4. Alfred DeGrazia, *The Western Public* (Stanford: Stanford University Press, 1954), p. 185.

5. See Wallace Sayre and Herbert Kaufman, *Governing New York City* (New York: Russell Sage Foundation, 1960).

6. It has been estimated that there are 75,000 to 80,000 municipal patronage jobs available in New York City, plus an unknown number of "positions with associated politico-economic groups in contracting, insurance, real estate, banking, and relocation firms."   Frank J. Munger and Ralph A. Straetz, *New York Politics* (New York: New York University Press, 1960), p. 20.

7. See, for example, William Foote Whyte's description of "Politics and the Social Structure" in Chapter VI in his *Street Corner Society: The Social Structure of an Italian Slum* (Chicago: University of Chicago Press, Enlarged Edition, 1955), pp. 194–252.

8. Much work remains to be done even to obtain valid estimates of such relationships.   See, for example, Murray Hausknecht, *The Joiners* (New York: The Bedminster Press, 1962).

9. Hausknecht, for example, speculates that newspapers contribute to the difficulties of citizens in interpreting political interests as well as in assessing the roles of voluntary associations. *Ibid.*, p. 118.   Norton Long, on the other hand, generalizes that the daily newspapers of the typical metropolitan area are committed to, and agitate in favor of, what we would term Community Conservationist perspectives.   Although able to reward politicians and civic leaders with publicity, and able to "by appropriate news selection determine to a large extent what most people will be thinking are the hot issues," they can rarely carry a "general proposal for governmental change."   See his *The Polity*, edited by Charles Press (Chicago: Rand McNally & Co., 1962), p. 159.

10. Robert A. Dahl, *Who Governs?* (New Haven: Yale University Press, 1961), p. 94.

11. Robert H. Salisbury, "St. Louis Politics: Relationships among Interests, Parties, and Governmental Structure," *Western Political Quarterly*, Vol. XIII (June 1960), pp. 500, 503.

12. William J. Gore and Robert L. Peabody, "The Functions of the Political Campaign: A Case Study," *Western Political Quarterly*, Vol. XI (March 1958), pp. 55–70.

13. Robert A. Dahl, *op. cit.*, p. 75.
14. *Ibid.*, p. 61.
15. *Ibid.* (Italics added.)
16. Dahl suggests that the Mayor, in avoiding a higher tax rate, was concerned over the local newspapers, the voters at large, and businessmen, large and small. *Ibid.*, pp. 81–82.
17. That New Haven has not been without such strains and stresses is suggested by Dahl's comments that the Socialist Party may have served in recent years as the vehicle of middle-class discontent, as in the election of 1947. *Ibid.*, pp. 54–55.
18. *Ibid.*, p. 213.
19. *Ibid.*, p. 310.
20. Robert H. Salisbury, *loc. cit.*, p. 500.
21. *Ibid.*
22. James Reichley, *The Art of Government* (New York: The Fund for the Republic, 1959), p. 12.
23. *Ibid.*, p. 113.
24. *Ibid.*
25. *Ibid.*, pp. 114–115.
26. For a description of the "general-manager plan" see Wallace S. Sayre, "The General-Manager Idea for Large Cities," *Public Administration Review,* XIV (Autumn 1954), pp. 253–258.
27. There are exceptions to this possible general pattern. Seymour Freedgood describes DeLesseps Morrison of New Orleans as such an exception. See his essay "New Strength at City Hall," *op. cit.*, p. 68.
28. Blanche D. Blank, "Reform Politics: A Biopsy," *The Nation,* Vol. 195, No. 9 (September 29, 1962), pp. 174–177.
29. See Frank J. Munger and Ralph A. Straetz, *New York Politics*, p. 22. They describe the New York reform group as being interested in "power to effectuate social changes and social planning on all three levels of government." James Q. Wilson describes New York City reformers quite differently in his *The Amateur Democrat* (Chicago: University of Chicago Press, 1962), especially Chapter 5, "The Goals of the Amateur," pp. 126–163. Wilson's working conception or definition of ideology is narrower than used here, particularly in suggesting that a hallmark of ideology is ordinarily a specification of relatively concrete policy goals in a doctrinaire fashion. See pp. 127–128; 153; and 156–158.
30. Blanche D. Blank, "Reform Politics: A Biopsy," *loc. cit.*
31. *Ibid.*, p. 176. (First italics added.)
32. *Ibid.*
33. Note, for example, the various descriptions and interpretations of Carmine DeSapio by Blank, *ibid.*, p. 177; by Munger and Straetz, *op. cit.*, pp. 23–26; and by Robert Heilbroner, "Carmine DeSapio: The Smile on the Face of the Tiger," *Harper's* (July 1954), pp. 23–33.
34. See Robert S. Hirschfield, Bert E. Swanson, and Blanche D. Blank, "A Profile of Political Activists in Manhattan," *The Western Political Quarterly,* Vol. XV, No. 3 (September 1962), pp. 489–506.
35. It should be noted that the ideology of New Haven's political leadership is our interpretation of what Robert A. Dahl has described and is also subject to errors of both the second- and first-hand interpreters.

36. See Hirschfield, Swanson, and Blank, *op. cit.* They also have relevant un-
reported interview data on the responses of selected sets of precinct committeemen and committeewomen in New York, by party organization, to a
question identical to that used in the present study: "What are the most
important issues, problems, or projects facing New York City at the present
time?" Classifying these respondents as Regular Democrats, Reform Democrats, Republicans, and Liberals (the Liberal party), they found that "slums"
was the most frequently mentioned general item, but the response was mentioned by almost half of the Liberals compared to from 24 to 32 per cent
of the other partisans. Matters relating to the condition or quality or needs
of the public schools were the second most frequently mentioned responses
by the Liberals and Regular Democrats, but by 24 per cent of the former
and only 6 per cent of the latter. Reform Democrats and Republicans
identified crime and delinquency (juvenile and other) as the second most
frequently mentioned items of greatest importance (by 16 and 21 per cent,
respectively) while only 9 per cent of the Liberals and none of the Regular
Democrats mentioned that subject in response to this question. Corrupt
politics was mentioned by 12 and 9 per cent of the Republicans and Reform
Democrats, respectively, by 4 per cent of the Liberals and by only 1 per cent
of the Regular Democrats. Such findings as these contribute to a picture of
different orientations and perspectives of the several sets of party activists
in regard to their community's problems, with Liberals being a group most
focused on slums and schools, Republicans being concerned with slums,
crime and delinquency and corrupt politics, Regular Democrats being most
concerned with slums and few other community problems.
37. Robert A. Dahl, *op. cit.,* p. 94.
38. On February 11, 1963, a suit was filed in Federal District Court in Nashville,
Tennessee, regarding alleged racial discrimination in a motel that was built
on an urban-renewal site developed with Federal funds. With increasing
cognizance of the socio-economic impacts of urban development and redevelopment, whether it has supported the *status quo,* and whether it has been
facilitated by local, state, or federal government policy, the prospects of an
increasingly sharp, competitive class and caste warfare over basic socio-
economic questions would seem to be high. Apart from the unpredictability
of the international situation, the increasing scope of technological unemployment and other such factors make it foolhardy to attempt to make
many such power-structure predictions about big or even smaller cities in
the years immediately ahead until more systematic, comparative research
has been done.

NAME INDEX

SUBJECT INDEX